IN TOUCH

THE LETTERS OF
PAUL BOWLES

IN TOUCH

THE LETTERS OF
PAUL BOWLES

EDITED BY JEFFREY MILLER

FARRAR, STRAUS AND GIROUX
NEW YORK

LIBRARY OF CONGRESS CATALOGING-IN-PUBLICATION DATA
Bowles, Paul.
[Correspondence. Selections]
In touch : the letters of Paul Bowles / Paul Bowles ; edited by
Jeffrey Miller.
p.   cm.
Includes index.
1. Bowles, Paul. —Correspondence.   2. Authors,
American—20th century—Correspondence.   3. Composers—United
States—Correspondence. I. Miller, Jeffrey. II. Title.
PS3552.0874Z48   1993   813'.54—dc20   [B]   92-36994 CIP

The publisher would like to thank the following
translators for their contribution to this work:
Linda Coverdale for her translations from French;
Alfred Mac Adam for his translations from Spanish;
and Vincent Cornell for his translations from Moghrebi Arabic
and for providing a Moghrebi Arabic/English glossary.
Except for this glossary, all translations
appear in footnotes to the letters.

PHOTO CREDITS
1. Courtesy the Bettmann Archive
2–5, 8–11, 13. Courtesy the Paul Bowles Photographic Archive at
the Swiss Foundation of Photography, Kunsthaus, Zurich
6, 7. Courtesy Allen Ginsberg
12. Drawing by Don Bachardy
14–17. Courtesy Cherie Nutting

CONTENTS

Photographs follow page 332.

FOREWORD

Paul Bowles has led an extraordinary life and his letters, spanning more than six decades, are a chronicle of the avant-garde for the better part of the twentieth century. His intelligence and restless energy have put him in touch with many seminal figures in the arts, and his friendships and correspondences have ranged from Gertrude Stein to Allen Ginsberg in literature, and from Aaron Copland to Peggy Glanville-Hicks in music. His gift for friendship and for remaining in touch across so many decades with those effecting revolutions in the arts is singular. When one considers the vast amount of travel he did while young, and that Bowles's expatriation in North Africa has lasted almost a half century, the importance of his correspondence becomes apparent.

Virgil Thomson discusses this talent for friendship in his review of Bowles's autobiography, *Without Stopping*: "His life as told unrolls like a travelogue . . . Paul has always been so delicious in talk, games, laughter, and companionship, so unfailingly gifted for both music and letters, so assiduous in meeting his deadlines with good work, so relentless in his pursuit of authenticity." In short, a man of immense charm, intelligence, and creativity. And a tireless writer of letters—a correspondent—commencing with his childhood.

The earliest extant letter written by Paul Bowles is dated January 4, 1915: "Dear Miss Anna, Thank you for the erector. I have been making letters with it. Monday the 3rd I was playing with a little yellow spider but he was so tiny that I lost it. Do you notice my other little Santa Claus? Love from Paul."

This was written a few days after his fourth birthday. It's interesting that Bowles has deployed his Erector set for a purpose entirely other than intended, and one of his own devising. Rather than constructing a bridge, crane, or castle, he creates letters from the small metal bars perforated with holes allowing them to be fastened one to another with tiny nuts and bolts.

Bowles's childhood friend Mary Crouch Oliver offers another example of Bowles's precocity in a letter she wrote in 1939, reminiscing about an evening in their childhood: "Do you remember the night that you first played your composition . . . 'The Valley Storm' and then we went outside and roasted marshmallows?

". . . I can still see you now, walking up the hill in pink shrimp rompers

vii

quarreling with some imaginary companion, 'Get away you worm! you dog, get away!' " Letter writing, construction of letters from a child's toy, musical composition, and invective rhetoric all began at a tender age.

In his adolescence, letter writing offered a way of disguising his youth in his first attempts to enter the world of literature and adults. His first foray was an amusing combination of artifice and automatic writing. Bowles tells us in his autobiography that he wrote his first poems for submission to a literary magazine in his last year of high school "without conscious intervention," and then informs us, "These 'poems' I sent out to *transition*, 40, rue Fabert, Paris, certain that nothing in the presentation of my manuscripts betrayed the shameful fact that I was a high school student. The material itself, being beyond my control, also escaped my judgment, but this did not matter; the important thing as far as I was concerned was that no one seeing it would guess that I was only sixteen."

André Gide's *The Vatican Swindle* and *The Counterfeiters* made lasting impressions on young Paul Bowles. "And one spring evening I bought my first Gide: Knopf's edition of *The Vatican Swindle* . . . Like my fifteen-year-old counterparts all over the world, I was seduced by Lafcadio's *acte gratuit*." In fact, Bowles chose to review *The Counterfeiters* for his high school magazine, *The Oracle*: "A boy of sixteen leaves his home clandestinely to wander the streets of Paris. After six weeks he returns home as unexpectedly as he left, but he has changed his entire viewpoint, and the reader has had a glimpse of a great series of lives; in other words, a glimpse of life . . . it will please everyone who reads . . . for intellectual enlightenment."

There are connections between Bowles's close reading of these two works and the artifice he employed while writing his letter to the editors of *transition*, disguising his youth from them. Bowles's notion of the artist's role was formed, in part, by his New England puritan relatives and ancestors: "My own conviction was that the artist, being the enemy of society, for his own good must remain as invisible as possible and certainly should be indistinguishable from the rest of the crowd. Somewhere in the back of my mind there was the assumption that art and crime were indissolubly linked; the greater the art, the more drastic the punishment for it." *The Counterfeiters* is a rich portrait of the moral collapse of the Parisian bourgeoisie. It chronicles the adventures of two precocious adolescents, Bernard Profitendieu and Olivier Molinier, children of this class, as they find their way into the world of literature through various stratagems and *actes gratuits*. Less than two years after reviewing Gide's novel, Bowles would enact what he had found so arresting in *The Counterfeiters*; he left America, in secret, to wander the streets of Paris and get "a glimpse of life." Fifty years after the event, Bowles recollects with precision a single book which he took with him on his voyage to Paris: Gide's *Journal des Faux-Monnayeurs*.

Sometime after submitting his poems to *transition*, "I arrived home one afternoon to find that a small packet had arrived for me from Paris. I tore it open. It was a copy of *transition* 12, with my name among those on the cover. I had imagined the moment so many times that the reality was almost like a *déjà vu*. I jumped into the air and let out a shout of triumph . . . My joy and excitement were such that I remember little else about the spring of 1928."

One wonders what made him more excited: the triumph of his strategy, or the publication of the poem in an important literary magazine?

As a freshman at the University of Virginia, Bowles made the acquaintance of Bruce Morrissette, a student at the University of Richmond, and a few years his senior. Morrissette edited his university's literary magazine, *The Messenger*, and invited Bowles to guest-edit an issue: "I jumped at the opportunity and immediately sent off a dozen or so letters to writers, none of whom I had ever met or corresponded with . . . I got back material from William Carlos Williams, Gertrude Stein and Nancy Cunard, among others. I continued to write Gertrude Stein and sent her a copy of the magazine when it was printed." This invitation allowed Bowles to enter the adult world and community of letters in another and perhaps more important way than had the publication of a poem in *transition*. *The Messenger* gave him a legitimate reason for contacting those writers whom he considered important; many responded with contributions, and friendships were begun. Bowles began the process of self-definition by the expression of his literary tastes.

While in Paris for the first time, "I went all the way to the rue Fabert, where *transition* had its offices, climbed upstairs, and stood outside the door for a while. Then I decided that it would be absurd for me to go in and announce myself. No one could be in the least interested." Bowles was just eighteen and presumably still uncomfortable with the guise of maturity he had assumed in his first letter to the editors of *transition*.

He was back in Paris two years later. In the interim he had corresponded with Gertrude Stein, and had become a pupil and protégé of Aaron Copland, so he presented himself at 27, rue de Fleurus, where he received a most humorous welcome: " 'What is it? Who are you?' she said. I told her and heard for the first time her wonderfully hearty laugh. She opened the door so I could go in. Then Alice Toklas came downstairs, and we sat in the big studio hung with Picassos. 'I was sure from your letters that you were an elderly gentleman, at least seventy-five,' Gertrude Stein told me. 'A highly eccentric gentleman,' added

Alice Toklas. 'We were certain of it.' They asked me to dinner for the following night . . ."

Whereas Gide's character had wandered in the streets of Paris for six weeks, young Bowles managed to wander for six months before unexpectedly returning home. During this second visit to Paris, Bowles got a most privileged "glimpse of life." In addition to having met Stein and Toklas he was quickly introduced to Bernard Faÿ, Ezra Pound, Richard Thoma, Jean Cocteau, Samuel Putnam, Virgil Thomson, Pavel Tchelitchew, and others. Many of these introductions resulted from Gertrude Stein's initial amusement, the discrepancy between her impressions of the letter writer, "an elderly gentleman, at least seventy-five," and the appearance at her doorstep of a handsome and charming young man of twenty. Stein, in a fit of mirth, announced, "This is the season for *lancering* Freddy. We're going to *lancer* Freddy." (Stein thought Bowles's middle name, Frederic, was somehow more appropriate, and teased him by addressing him as "Freddy".) When Aaron Copland and Bowles visited Gertrude Stein at Bilignin, Stein continued this banter, asking Bowles's teacher if his pupil had talent and worked at his music. "Aaron said he could imagine someone who spent more time at it than I. 'That's what I thought,' she said. 'He's started his life of crime too young.' Aaron snickered and told her never to pay attention to what I said —only to what I did." The tone and humor of such banter between Copland and Stein could only have been prompted by the youth, guile, and evident talent of their young protégé.

Bowles had also solicited work from Edouard Roditi for *The Messenger*, and this initiated another correspondence. The contact proved to be useful; Roditi wrote letters of introduction for Bowles to Christopher Isherwood and Stephen Spender. Bowles made their acquaintance shortly after arriving in Berlin. Indeed, many of the literary friendships Bowles began in his youth were to be lifelong, and many had resulted from simply having written "a dozen or so letters to writers."

Bowles's early letters are, in large part, addressed to his first mentor, Daniel Burns; his friend Bruce Morrissette; the poet Edouard Roditi; his teacher Aaron Copland; and his second mentor, Gertrude Stein. These letters reveal the struggles, conducted ruthlessly, of a young man trying to transform himself into a painter, a composer of music, a poet, and a writer of prose. At times the emotions of conflict and turmoil, doubts and difficulties seem almost overwhelming. Taken as a whole, they constitute a portrait of the young man in the act of becoming an artist: a portrait of an artist's *formation*.

But the character of most of Bowles's correspondence was to change quite dramatically, and it seems to have stemmed from a single unfortunate incident. In early 1931, after lunching with Ezra Pound in the afternoon and drinking considerable amounts of champagne with dinner, he wrote a letter that evening to express his chagrin with the editorial policy of *The Left: A Quarterly Review of Radical and Experimental Art*. It appeared in their second issue, and reads: "The Editors: I have read the first number of *The Left*, and since that time I have understood quite well why the few things I sent several weeks ago are quite unsuitable for it. And for it all I see no excuse. As a staunch enemy of all things proletarian, I deny that your enterprise has any value whatever. I approve of fever, but not when it is directed toward social ends, not when it arises from a realization of one's innate inferiority, or the futility of expressing it. And I have the impression from *The Left* that your contributors are quite aware of this futility. Inasmuch as there is no danger of the proletariat's ever attaining its ends, what slight inflammation *The Left* can arouse in the vague minds of those who read it, can have no effect, otherwise I should be interested in it as a dangerous protagonist in the contemporary literary field. I daresay you have several brilliant contributors in the first number; I know some of them myself—and I can merely express my sorrow that they should have found it necessary to turn aside through a snobbism and bow to the masses. *The Left* . . . a fashionable gesture, a charity ball given in honor of 15,000,000 defectives. No thank you. I prefer to spit upon you from a Fokker, and I believe sincerely that all workers are born to be crushed, and that it is a form of snobbery, and a virulent form at that, to think otherwise.

"And I thank you most frightfully and hope you send me two dozen Tunisian orchids. Paul Frederic Bowles, 9 rue Vavin, Paris 6e."

Bowles wrote this letter under the influence of alcohol and was perhaps swayed by conversation with Ezra Pound. When asked, decades later, why he'd written such a letter, he replied, "I was twenty-one years old, living in Paris, I was in love with life, and I was drunk and exalted the night I wrote that letter. I never imagined they'd print it, it was so deliberately insulting; it was more a joke than anything else."

Publication of this letter was to have unpleasant consequences for the young Bowles. The difficulties which ensued taught Bowles never again to write with indiscretion.

Part of the motivation for this letter came from his annoyance with an error, intentional or otherwise, which had appeared in the pages of *Front*, published in the Netherlands. (*The Left* came from Davenport, Iowa.) In a letter of September 18, 1931, to Gertrude Stein he wrote, "*Front*, a magazine published in

Holland, sent me a copy of their no. 4 recently. They have been growing more and more populiste of late, and in this number they committed a supreme atrocity. In a beautiful romantic poem of mine all about waking up in the morning in the desert they substituted for the word: 'waker' the word 'worker.' Poets of the world, unite!" He also wrote his friend Bruce Morrissette about this error and his chagrin in a letter of September 21, 1931: "*Front* of Amsterdam prints my Mist, mist who in the morning, and for 'waker' substitute 'worker.' Le comble! In a notice they say: henceforth we will only concern ourselves with literature as art when it arms the worker against the bourgeois. Bon!"

It may be taken as a given that Bowles had neither a commanding mastery of politics nor of history at age twenty-one; for that reason it is fruitless to look for theoretical or ideological causes in attempting to understand why he wrote such a letter. His letter to *The Left* may, I think, be seen as analogous in function to the letter he had written to the editors of *transition* and those written on behalf of *The Messenger*: the assumption of a mask, a way of entering but also distancing himself from interacting with the adult world. But this mask has two faces: Bowles avoids confronting the alleged source of his displeasure in public as well as in private correspondence. Moreover, the tone he assumes is that of the literary dandy, and its tone echoes Baudelaire's original formulation: "Can you imagine a Dandy speaking to the people, except to insult them?" In both the earlier instances (*transition* and *The Messenger*) he had reaped immense benefits: friendships were made and the world of letters had opened generously to him. *The Left* had rejected poems he'd submitted for their pages; *Front* magazine had, in his opinion, deliberately subverted his art to politics.

Ironically, Bowles also considered himself politically to the left. In fact, in high school (only a few years earlier) he had been made to feel uncomfortable about his interest in leftist politics: "Once I brought out a copy of *New Masses* and passed it around while the teacher was explaining a theorem. After class a boy named Goldberg came over to me and said, glowering at me: 'What are *you* doing with *New Masses?*' I countered by saying: 'Why, what's the matter with it?' 'It's not for you,' he told me and walked away. This left me speechless; for months my mind replayed the scene. Why did Goldberg think I was unfit to be reading *New Masses?*"

Whereas his letters to *transition* and for *The Messenger* had invited participation and had led to friendships, his letter to *The Left* sought closure: Bowles had not been welcomed by the political left in the way he had been by the community of writers, and he retaliated with sharp invective rhetoric.

This letter to *The Left* took on a life of its own and its publication would haunt him. In the late 1930s it became difficult for him to rehearse theater orchestras because most of the musicians were members of the Communist Party, or leaning to the left; having heard about his letter, they considered Bowles a fascist. But Bowles continued to equate the experimental in art with the radical in politics. In late 1938 he joined the Communist Party (and two years later asked to be "expelled" when informed he couldn't simply quit). Although he took the threat of fascism seriously he nonetheless quickly became disenchanted with organized politics and the extreme tendencies on the left.

Kenneth Rexroth, who had a prodigious, if selective memory, remembered this letter's publication after almost a half century and would tell his slightly mythologized version with great delight. In this version Bowles deliberately and publicly thumbed his nose at the orthodoxies and sophistries of the left, thereby demonstrating, according to Rexroth, that Bowles was a fellow anarchist. "Of course Bowles had to disappear as a writer for ten years or more," Rexroth claimed, "he had to go to Africa, he was finished." Then Rexroth burst into infectious laughter before continuing with another of his tales of the intellectual and political life of the 1930s and 1940s.

Bowles's epistolary activity subsequently became more guarded, lapidary. Though there are still intimate and honest letters, they are never again so direct in expressing his innermost thoughts and feelings. One might say this letter marked the end of Bowles's youth.

The body of slightly more than four hundred letters and communiqués here are mostly from the far reaches of Bowles's explorations—geographical, intellectual, artistic, aesthetic, fictional, musical, chemical, and imaginary. Many might be taken as models of correct social intercourse, whereas others are truly dispatches from the edge of the abyss. Fitted together like the tesserae of a mosaic they complete a portrait of the mature man and his singular life, describing as they do his manifold interests and activities: the works, writers, and composers he admired and was influenced by; the music, ethnology, fiction, geography, and languages which engaged his attention; the landscape which arrested his observant eye, and distant lands which invited his interest. This portrait shows him in his many relations: as son; as protégé of Daniel Burns and Gertrude Stein; as student of Aaron Copland and Virgil Thomson; as husband to Jane Bowles; as colleague and friend of innovative writers and composers. Moreover, they describe his travels to remote and isolate lands—Mexico, Guatemala, Colombia, Spain, Algeria, the Sahara, Ceylon, India, Thailand, and, of course, Morocco, his outpost and home for almost a half century. This volume also includes many of his letters from native shores—New York, Massachusetts, Virginia, California, and other American locales—as well as London, Paris, and Berlin. Correspondences with editors, publishers, scholars, critics, librarians, students, protégés, and admirers complete the portrait.

Bowles is America's most resolute expatriate writer since Henry James, and Bowles is, along with James, one of the country's few great prose stylists. Many of the virtues found in Bowles's fictions are to be found in his letters. But Bowles's expatriation is diametrically opposed to James's; whereas James sought the epicenter of civilization, Bowles has consistently searched its outermost fringes, the other side of the mirror. Bowles has chosen to live and work in Arabe al-Maghreb; Muslim in religion and Arabic speaking, it's a part of the world of which comparatively little is known outside its boundaries. Significantly, Bowles titled his collection of travel essays *Their Heads Are Green and Their Hands Are Blue, Scenes from the Non-Christian World.* He traveled to the very extremities of the civilized world, where it intersected with the unknown and beyond, and mapped states of being only possible at such remove from civilization's stationary, central loci. His youthful travels into the Sahara were conducted in regions so recently "pacified" by the French Army that travel was via military transport, from fortified point to fortified point.

North Africa in the twentieth century has hardly impinged upon the consciousness of America. There have been a spate of Hollywood films with North Africa providing exotica: *Morocco* (Gary Cooper and Marlene Dietrich kissing in the desert sands); *Algiers*, a frame-for-frame remake of the remarkable *Pépé le Moko* (with Jean Gabin suffering *le cafard* in the Medina); and, of course, *Casablanca* (Everyone Meets at Rick's). There was also *Beau Geste* (again with Gary Cooper) and lesser movies of the genre, variants on the "Western" with the *Légion Étrangère* standing in for the cavalry and Berber tribesmen for the Indians. Recently there has been Bernardo Bertolucci's *The Sheltering Sky*, based on Bowles's novel (with a cameo appearance by the author), and David Cronenberg's *Naked Lunch*, set in William Burroughs's fevered and hallucinated version of Tangier, "Interzone." In literature, Albert Camus's *The Plague* was set in Oran and *The Stranger* in Algiers. Algiers and the Sahara are the backdrop for *The Sheltering Sky*; Tangier and Ceuta for *Let It Come Down*; Fez for *The Spider's House*; various North African locales figure prominently in the brilliant collections of short stories, *The Delicate Prey, The Time of Friendship, A Hundred Camels in the Courtyard,* and *Midnight Mass.* Several of Gide's early novels have North African settings and there is Wyndham Lewis's *Travels into Barbary*.

But Paul Bowles is the only American to have rooted his life in North Africa and to have mined the terrain, transforming his knowledge and experience into important literature. Bowles has done this through both a love of and mastery of peoples and place, and his writing is informed by an extraordinary and rare empathy. Gore Vidal has put the matter nicely: "Whenever I think of the authentic I think of the meticulous Paul Bowles creating his own landscape and peopling it with characters never before seen in our literature. His short stories are among the best ever written by an American." What is background and usually incidental in almost all the other literature and cinema touching on North Africa, is foreground in Bowles's fictions: he has entered into and discovered the wellsprings of a culture alien to American and English literature. It is this quality which distinguishes his writing from the mainstream of American literature, and his sensibility might best be compared with that of Graham Greene, or V. S. Naipaul. Like Bowles, their works are predicated on alienation from the familiar, based on sources far from home.

Yet, through all the decades of travel—and while creating a large corpus of art, both literature and music—Bowles has remained an inveterate letter writer and correspondent. Some of the raw material for his travel essays, and for his fictions, is to be found in his letters. His letters to Peggy Glanville-Hicks are filled with lyrical descriptions of Moroccan landscape, beauty, and people, the stuff of which his travel essays are compounded. He has, however, been characteristically modest about this immense output of letters.

The letters contained in this volume have been selected from among almost seven thousand pages of correspondence; presumably thousands of pages more have either been discarded by their recipients, lost, or have not as yet become available.

Bowles's own autobiography, *Without Stopping* (humorously referred to as "Without Telling" by William Burroughs), and other works about him never manage to illuminate either his person or work in the way his letters do. His autobiography was written under inauspicious circumstances: everything contained in it was recollected and written without benefit of or reference to any documents whatsoever. Bowles had counted on having access to his letters to his mother and father to use for both chronology and detail but unfortunately the institutional library holding this correspondence was moving their collections when Bowles needed them. Bowles has been forthright in saying he accepted a

large advance to write his autobiography in order to meet the medical expenses
incurred from his wife's extended illness. But he was neither anxious to write
his autobiography nor does he see the genre as one of acute interest. In con-
tradistinction to the autobiography and works written about him, his letters
weren't written with an eye to publication. Their tone is singular and personal,
the events described contemporary.

Aside from the work itself—the short stories, novels, translations, essays, and
musical compositions—his letters are the best record we have of a major figure
in our literature and perhaps also a major figure in our music. They have a
primacy and authenticity shared by neither his autobiography nor by accounts
written by others.

The importance of Bowles's letters may perhaps be gauged by remarks made
about journals in a letter to James Leo Herlihy of April 8, 1966: "Your mention
of a journal echoes what Bill Burroughs has been telling me for years. 'Keep a
journal,' he says. 'It's the most useful thing you can do.' . . . Who is one writing
for in a journal? If it's oneself, it's obviously a farce. If it's for publication, then
it's immediately censored, while one is writing it, and is no longer strictly speaking
a journal. Is there another way of looking at it? A letter, I suppose." This doesn't
preclude the possibility that a letter can be used for other purposes, as a mask,
for instance, or as a communication whose meaning resides between the lines,
relying more on inference than information, more on absence than presence.
While in Paris for the first time he wrote a one-line note to his friend Bruce
Morrissette: "Please save the letters as they're the only record I have of what I
have done here."

Although I have closely reviewed with Paul Bowles all of the letters in this
volume, there are several letters he would not have chosen himself. Nevertheless,
he has graciously consented to their inclusion, since in many instances a single
passage could be valuable in creating a more rounded portrait. Of the letters
that were chosen, almost all of them appear in their entirety. A few deletions
within letters have been made for editorial reasons and these are indicated with
asterisks. In general, the text of each letter has been reproduced verbatim.
Bowles's early correspondence in particular simply wouldn't be the same without
his deliberate orthographic and typographic variations and his other linguistic
experiments. Where any corrections have been made for clarity or consistency,
Bowles has approved the changes.

Rather than attempting to characterize further diverse correspondences conducted over more than sixty years and with a large number of correspondents,

I would like to end with a passage from one of Bowles's letters to James Leo Herlihy, which speaks to the mystery of the self and fiction: "Whatever words one puts down under whatever circumstances are meant for other eyes and minds. Your mention of 'witnesses' is a good way of illustrating the existential dilemma of consciousness (the impossibility of being the thing in itself for itself) . . . Too much importance is given the writer and not enough to his work. What difference does it make who he is and what he feels, since he's merely a machine for transmission of ideas? In reality he doesn't exist—he's a cipher, a blank. A spy sent into life by the forces of death. His main objective is to get the information across the border, back into death. Then he can be given a mythical personality: 'He spent time among us, betrayed us, and took the material across the border.' I don't think a writer ever participates in anything; his pretences at it are mimetic. All he can do is to keep the machine functioning and learn to manage it with decreasing (we hope) clumsiness. A spy *is* devious and, as much as is possible, anonymous. His personal convictions and emotions are automatically 'masked.' "

The letters included in this volume are the clues left along the way, the best glimpses we are going to get into the machinery of one of our country's few fiction writers of genius.

—JEFFREY MILLER

CHRONOLOGY

1910 Born December 30, an only child, to Rena and Claude Bowles in New York City. Grows up in NYC and Jamaica, Long Island, with summers in western Massachusetts and upper New York State. Public schools.

1928 Begins to publish poems in *transition* magazine and other literary reviews.

1929 After one semester at the University of Virginia, goes on his own to Paris; travels in Alps and on French Riviera. Back in NYC, studies composition with Aaron Copland before returning to Virginia for a second semester.

1931 Meets Gertrude Stein and other leading figures in the arts in Paris, then to Berlin. In late summer, with Aaron Copland to Tangier. Travels in Morocco, then returns to Paris. First public performance of one of his compositions, *Sonata for Oboe and Clarinet*, London.

1932–33 Travels in Europe, Algerian Sahara, and Tunisia. Returns to U.S. in May 1933. Composes music for voice and keyboard, a symphonic piece, a film score.

1934–35 Travels in Spain, Morocco, Central America, then to U.S. Henry Cowell publishes Bowles's pieces in *New Music*. *Scènes d'Anabase* performed. Composes more film music and a ballet.

1936–46 Divides time between NYC and Mexico, with excursions to Central America. Marries Jane Auer, 1938. Composes ballets, film scores, and incidental theater music, including plays by William Saroyan and Tennessee Williams. Music reviewer for the New York *Herald Tribune*, 1942–45. *Two Serious Ladies*, a novel by Jane Bowles, published in 1943.

1947–48 Bowles's short story, "A Distant Episode," appears in *Partisan Review*. Returns to North Africa. Travels in the Algerian Sahara and throughout Morocco. Begins writing novel, *The Sheltering Sky*. Also at work on an opera, *Yerma*, and on theater music.

1949   *The Sheltering Sky* published. Recital of *Concerto for Two Pianos and Orchestra* at Salle Pleyel, Paris. Travels in England and Ceylon (Sri Lanka).

1952   *Let It Come Down*, a novel.

1955   *The Spider's House*, a novel.

1959   Travels throughout Morocco, recording indigenous music.

1959–63 Association with William Burroughs, Allen Ginsberg, Peter Orlovsky, Gregory Corso, Jack Kerouac, et al. *A Hundred Camels in the Courtyard*, short stories, 1962. *Their Heads Are Green and Their Hands Are Blue*, travel essays, 1963. Incidental music for Tennessee Williams's *Sweet Bird of Youth* and *The Milk Train Doesn't Stop Here Anymore*.

1964   With *A Life Full of Holes* by Driss ben Hamed Charhadi (Larbi Layachi), begins to publish translations of the stories told by his Moroccan friends that he records. More than fifteen volumes will follow between 1967 and 1986, eleven of them tales by Mohammed Mrabet.

1966   *Up above the World*, a novel. Bowles's parents die. Travels to Bangkok for book assignment, abandoning book and returning to Tangier after Jane suffers second stroke.

1967   *The Time of Friendship*, short stories.

1968   Teaches one semester at San Fernando Valley State College, Northridge, California.

1970   *Antaeus*, a literary review founded by Bowles and Daniel Halpern, begins publication.

1972   *Without Stopping*, an autobiography.

1973   Jane Bowles dies, May 4.

1979   *Collected Stories, 1939–1976.*

1981   *Next to Nothing: Collected Poems 1926–1977.*

1982   *Points in Time*, historical tales.

1990   Travels to Paris for premiere of Bernardo Bertolucci's film version of *The Sheltering Sky*.

1991   *Days, Tangier Journal: 1987–1989.*

1993   *Too Far from Home*, selected writings. Continues to live in Tangier.

EARLY
LETTERS

———————————•———————————

Summer 1928
Jamaica, New York

O sugar babe! O girl of my dreams! Oyez! Oyez! How is hell o sugar babe o beloved since I met your sweet lips o blue eyes o red lips! How much is gas? O girl of my Sigma Chi the damned things won't work o sugar babe! O Monticello! O dream river! O thick meals of grease lucky strike a coca cola why goddamn it o beloved thutty ayut mahls o beloved o red lips before me o camels o chesterfields o Virginia! O god o hell o damn o Virginia! O beloved beloved beloved beloved beloved. Contempt always changes to pity, when understanding opens the door. That is an adage of mine own. Intéressant? As I grow older, all the things I formerly scoffed at become things to grieve over. Think what a soft old heart I shall have by the time I am fifty! You'll be able to push your finger through it like a creampuff.

My not imaginary illness having long ago passed over, I now feel able to write as unintelligibly as I want to. Unfortunately, I find it slightly less easy to be thus than I used to. Perhaps that is because I have not *thoroughly* recovered. N'est-ce pas correct? You never seemed to be able to understand that pure inspiration is bound to be unintelligible, and that until it is refined into something legible or intelligible it is worth understanding, but afterward it is as nothing. The great majority of persons insist upon their brainfood's being refined, and go so far as to claim that the pure inspiration is worth nothing until refined—that thoughts must be chained, and trained into the narrow passages which society has chosen to "understand." You can understand anything if you leave your mind free. From this it is clear that a geologist cannot go on a picnic without stuffed eggs. Nor can Buddha go into the mountains without his barometer.

Jesus lives, and Greenwich Village is most fascinating in August. Suffer the little kids to come unto me and I went avant-hier to the Fifth Avenue Playhouse to see *The City without Jews*. M. Royé seems to be acquainted with you, of which I may add $3.49 at a bargain. Brass is more sufficient que Elinor Wylie. Of which Jennifer Lorn is exquisite, but of what avail to utter faint praise. All of her romances are exquisite. Mr. Hodge and Mr. Hazard. The Orphan Angel. As to this *The Gateway to Life* by Frank Thiess, *The Magic Mountain* and *Fools* by Thomas Mann are some Germanic literature I have read recently.

Attempt, while you are in London, to purchase *transition* 13, which so far is unattainable here.

May I retract some? It is when one is sleepy that unintelligibility arrives. I had never realized it before. Drowsiness is exactly the same in my head as Fever, Delirium and Tipsiness. The last mentioned I have experienced but once, and do not need to go through it again, as I can attain the same effect by staying up until one o'clock. And I am positive I should write the same in both cases. Only when mine soul is weighted with physical illnesses do I become pensive and conventional.

As far as I can see, I haven't said anything, and so I may as well lay this aside. Or perhaps you enjoy this pathological ramble? I always fancied you had a morbid side. If my whim was correct, you must certainly be interested in watching me stagger along like this. And so I shall prod myself a bit farther for your benefit.

Tell me all about England, for I am extraordinarily excited about it. I feel as though the United States were only a temporary exile and England my true home. Which in a way is idiocy and in a way is the truth.

The same two discouraging ladies who in 1927 informed me that I am less than an amoeba, this year decided that I am at the end of a civilization, that I epitomize a decayed civilization, in its last feeble flares to resurrect itself in the eyes of the other civilizations. They maintained that all my paintings and music merely strengthened the case for them, and were representative of imminent death: the final false energy of the moribund. Their absurdities are really the only absurdities of other people I can bear, and probably I can bear those only because they pertain to me. (They have been reading Spengler.)

Mary Crouch, the fascinating person I told you about, is in Vienna exploding all over town. She's fought with Dr. Adler and Countess Obalowski or some such etymological freak, and rooms at the French Embassy. My eyes are too rebellious for me to see clearly.

TO BRUCE MORRISSETTE
———————◆———————
November 16, 1928
Charlottesville, Virginia

At five minutes after ten I darkened the room. I had read my mail, among which was your card of instructions. I laid myself into a pile of cushions on my bed, covered my head tight with a quilt, and uncorked the bottle of ether. It was a few minutes before my extremities began to freeze. Gradual climbing of numbness up and down toward a center. Heart beating furiously. Deliberate long breathing. Abstraction of thought. Suddenly the odor became more pungent. Hot flames of ice poured down my throat and the blankets were soaked with ether. I can remember all the tunes in Petrouchka. The organ grinder tune, the flutist's piece, the gypsy dance, the pursuit and finale. It's coming. Whining while I breathed. Today is Wednesday. ABCDEFGH oh God. Shifting a little in position of foot which no longer exists. Something is singing. Several tones. They're going to stop one by one until only one tone is there and then there is the sea. Columbia the gem of the ocean oh God oh God ABCDEFGHIJK12345— I can remember all the tunes in Petrouchka and the sin of $180°-A = \sin A$. La mer bleue. An esker, a kame, a terminal moraine. Glaciation. I can remember all my subjects. I'm all right. 1234567 Paul Frederic Bowles. Wednesday. Long breathing. Now—if you can get out of this you shall be saved. Out! Save yourself from eternal damnation! Pushing back of quilt. Gasping on pillow. Corner of mouth all down and jelly and blue. Oh sick! Oh mottle mouth! Oh face of tragic muse! The room is grey and winks. I can still feel stucco of wall. Material of blanket. Gasp slowly. Do you love me? Down! Down! Don't, Paul! Don't fall! The fall of Lucifer! Come, darling. I'm getting all right. Snuggle quilt over head. Breathe again into fumble bottle. ABABAB Wednesday. je suis tu es il est elle est nous kimono Columbia the God! Oh God! Only three tones now. Being born. Hospital. Fuzzy slow aaaaah! aaaaaaah! I remember being born. I was blue and soft at the corners of my mouth. Oh sad face! Oh sick lips! I can remember. This is the base. Here! I can still realize that this is the base. I'm going back home. Two worlds. One is daylight and touch. I'm going away to Death's Black Arms. Oh God! Idiot! Don't quiver your feet. Lie still. This is the base. Below all our life. How fast is my heart? Move far away. Sink. I've spilled mall of the eathe. All eithe all ove. Clearsh. Silly laughing wakes somewhat. The negro maid will hear. Door locked—strange how I remember how one thinks even now. Down! But this is the base below all our life is death. Underground water. A long period of slow involuntary wrenching of lungs. No thoughts. Only tones. One will end. Two will be gone. Only one. It's a sea of one thick thin tone lasting long.

And then the absurd pushing away of quilt again and raising head. Whole room making fun of me. Sit up. Oh gone daffy down dilly where have you been? Get up onto knees. Look into mirror. Get away. I'm heterosexual. Oh my face! Only one hope. Oh God over and over. Knock over picture of tree in corner. (Still on floor, now) Hang onto black curtain on closet door. Assume crucifix posture, gasping. Remember Mother. Gasps. Think of her now that you're going away. Fall back into bed. Repetition of all that went before. Hear nothing. No Petrouchka. Where is the base? Oh—God! What comes below? But I can't!

But what comes below? There's got to be a base! Run! There's nothing. Theyvebee theyvebeendeceiving. There's nothing. Not only noteven on on on no no no

And at half past two this afternoon I arose. No nausea. Only my heart is still crashing at five o'clock. Take me away. Go away. I want to be dead. I taste swollen and sick and delft blue. Anemone. Don't ever come back again. The whole bottle of ether is empty and was on floor. I threw it sometime. I threw the cork too, but I can't find that. Augusta ich liebe dich. Dietrich Ostrich. Ich. Sick. Sticky. Go away and never come back. Nothing can ever be beautiful any more. Everything spoiled.

But really no more ether. I have bought a lot more but I don't want it. Anyone can have it. I won't bring it to you.

Give us away. Crazy!

Elegy in a Country Churchyard. $\cos(180°-A) = \cos A$. feuilles d'automne. Jesus saves. Never again. You've *got* to comfort me.

TO DANIEL BURNS

November 1928
Charlottesville, Virginia

Your letter was slightly depressing, I thought. Don't tell me you think you're getting old! And it seems as though *I* never should be old. Still *seventeen*, although the happy part of it is that down here everyone believes I'm nineteen. Not that I've told anyone such a lie, or even pretended to admit it when anyone remarks about it. In fact, I deny it vigorously, look extraordinarily (more than usual) innocent and say incredulously: but do I LOOK nineteen? I have painted four things since I came. The first was called Sacrifice, and was done in black and white. I sold it to a student. The second was a portrait of Virgin Mary which shocked everyone. The third was Nausea and the fourth The Poet. You will undoubtedly be amazed at my new style, which is almost monochromatic and extremely heavy.

I have composed and written one piece, called Monotonal, and it bores almost everyone. I have made literally dozens of friends and most of them are intelligent and sympathetic. He's really a good St. Bernard. Watches after children, never shows the slightest sign of temper, obeys— — — $95—bargain.

And I am doing all manner of strange things, one of which is to inhale ether until I am quite drunk. It's a fad here among some circles.

Last night I saw Dracula. The Count was William Tilden the tennis player, if you can believe it. He behaved most hammily, I thought, although the mob cheered him as though he'd rescued Jesus from the cross.

One sees very little here. Concerts are infrequent. Maier and Pattison came and I heard *them*. The Barrère Little Symphony came and I heard *it*. And that's all. However, this weekend I am going down to Richmond and the Chicago Opera Company will be there for two nights. Don't you enjoy all these little provincialities?

As I told you, I am making a collection of records, and add to it daily. Think of Bach, Haydn and Palestrina figuring prominently in it, not to mention Gluck and Wagner! I am having a headache and I think it would be wise to rest a bit. I've been staying up all night too many nights in succession, and it will indubitably ruin me unless I stop it.

I haven't written to M. Royer since I've been here, and for the love of God please forgive me for writing you such a bromidic and unnecessarily dull letter.

TO BRUCE MORRISSETTE

Spring 1929
Paris

The very possibility of your coming over here helps my morale tremendously. Since I returned from my trip I've been depressed—so much so that I haven't hunted up anyone, or scarcely anyone. It's the most contemptible of weaknesses: to allow oneself to become depressed, but quoi faire? E adesso io studio italiano, e la lingua è molto incantevole, ma, felicemente, abbastanza facile.* (If you can get the sense of what I'm trying to bleat!) It's a lot of fun. Gotta do something to get my mind off my inconceivably stupid dejection.

---

* And now I'm studying Italian, and the language is most enchanting but, fortunately, easy enough to learn.

But, old top, I'm serious. Can't you really come over? And I'm just as serious when I say, your arrival might prevent an untimely suicide. You see — all I'm doing is borrowing money right and left, and it's discouraging. Not that your advent would stop the borrowing, but it would put an end to the discouragement. I have abso no-one to go anywhere with. All my acquaintances are the appointment kind. Between appointments I lie exhausted on my bed—not physically exhausted, but morally so. And besides, two together can live so extremely less expensively. For example, it's possible then to cut one's room expense precisely in half, one's taxi-fare precisely in half, etc., and—how much happier one is with a companion in Paris! It's not a city where you feel comfortable alone. Unless you have someone to talk to, the continual effervescence seems futile— the gaiety unnecessary, and one becomes involuntarily embittered.

You want information? You need a passport—for that one must have a photostat copy of his birth-certificate, ten dollars, some photos of his mug, and a witness. Then afterward you need a visa—ten $ more, at the French Consul, French Line Pier, west end of 14 or 15 St. Your boatfare—if you are willing to dispense with lace and incense, you can come over on one of the ships of the Atlantic Transport Co.—Minnesota, Minnewaska, Minnehahah, and several other Minne's. About $85, in season, I believe. I came Tourist 3rd on Holland-America Line, off-season—$112 complete. In season about $125. You wouldn't want a pension—God! no! not in Paris. In Nice, it's very convenient. I lived at one there a week and got out of it très bon marché, but in Paris they're expensive and hellish, and there's no chance of eating out at restaurants. As to your health, bosh! Of course it's important, but I'm just as delicate, if not moreso than you, and I'm as healthy now as ever before. The food is excellent and almost given away, if you go to the right restaurants. Taxi-fares begin at 1 fr. and go up by 25 centimes. That is: four cents for the first ½ kil., and one cent for every ¼ kil. thereafter. Cheap as hell!

You can live comfortably here, including entertainments and everyth. for at most $1.50 a day. That as I say includes room, breakfast brought up to you in bed, tips, meals, taxis and concerts. I bought my ticket an hour ago for the Stravinsky Festival Friday. 6 fr. counting tax—that is: 24¢. And I shall hear Le Sacre! plus L'Oiseau and Petrouchka! The concerts here are marvels, and there are dozens of them.

If you could only come before July, you'd be here in time to see the Salon des Artistes Décorateurs, which is the most wonderful exhibit I've ever seen.

I was surprised to hear that my records are on sale. I don't know who's selling them, or who's receiving the money they bring. Strange things occur, indeed!

Further — I should enjoy knowing the various theories as to the reason of my leaving Virginia. I've no doubt that everyone attached some very sinister or at least disgusting import to my sudden exodus. It doesn't bother me, but it interests me. Tell me. And tell me, I implore you, if you are coming over. I mean, cable me immediately if you decide to, and then I shall stay here and meet you at the port for the boat-train. Otherwise I am likely to go to England and live at a friend's home.

If we went to live down in the Alps, from where I just returned, expenses would be considerably reduced further, and it is — — I can't quite say — it's too beautiful to try to put into words; it's the only place I've ever seen where I could walk alone for twelve hours and think of nothing but external objects. One day of solitude in the Alps refreshes your mind as aspirin does to a wilted rose. You mayn't believe it, as C. L. Dodgson says, but I'm not exaggerating. We could stay here in Paris until the tourists became too insufferable, and then we could clear out to any one of fifty little villages I have explored during the past three weeks. If you want my itinerary, voici: — Annecy, La Roche-sur-Foron, Chamonix-Mont-Blanc, Les Praz, Les Tines, L'Argentière, Col des Montets, Vallorcine, Le Châtelard (Switz.), Tête Noire, Trient, Col de la Forclaz, Sovernier, Sembrancher, Orsières (where I spent Ascension Day, and wrote a piece which I called Ascension Day at Orsières!), Martigny, Territet, Vevey, Lausanne, Geneva, Annemasse, Aix-les-Bains, Chambéry, Grenoble, Aspres-sur-Buëch (God's own countree), Veynes, Peyruis, where vermillion poppies grow wild by billions, Digne, Puget, Nice, Monte Carlo, Cannes, Antibes, Hyères, Toulon, Marseille, Lyon, Bourg, Paris.

I'd have stayed in Switzerland in aeternum unless I'd bought an aller et retour ticket that couldn't be prolonged more than twice; a ticket that forced me to come back to Paris because I didn't want to have it become void and worthless.

My drawings—I have no idea. My books my mother took home with her (I hope) in the car. She drove down shortly after I left. My records, God save whoever's selling them. I wrote for them to be sent here.

Yah! I'm going to the Comtesse de Lavillatte's for tea! Ain't I gettin' swell? And I have four poems in the new "This Quarter."

But you've got to come. For you, as for me, it will mean so much more than "a trip to Europe." I had suspected it would. I who discovered that when "people" said "honeysuckle smells sweet" they were expressing in words what was utterly inexpressible verbally to me, also have discovered that I cannot tell what I have found here because it means so much more than I can translate into thoughts, and so much more than even yet I realize. It means, as I said, dying and beginning another life. It would mean the same for you. For Pollard, it meant becoming what he hoped to be, "more sophisticated." It meant nil.

Get together what you have and viens. I shall share with thee that which I have. Your mother objects—it cannot be otherwise. Mine wrote at first that she would die and acted Verdiesque, but I notice now that she's bridging, faisant des emplettes, picnicking, etc. comme ordinaire. And I am a fils unique. Yes, you may say, but mine is older, would be sadder, more deeply stricken — — but, mon vieux, the offspring does not live for the old stock. The old stock has fulfilled its purpose. The offspring is ten times more important. It must get away. The old stock becomes reconciled much more quickly than you think. And it means so much to you. And it means (I can't deny it) so damned much to me. Write. Arrivederla!

TO DANIEL BURNS

Autumn 1929
Manhattan

I was pleased to get your letter. I'm working as you know at Dutton's and it keeps me so occupé that I have no opportunity to do much else, like correcting papers, much as the cash would aid. Yes—aid, especially now, since I'm no longer living at home, but alone in Greenwich Village. I find it more interesting, if less comfortable, than going to Jamaica each evening. I live at 122, Bank Street, and get home about 6:30 in the evening. Épaté to hear you will give me your *transition* nos 16 & 17 because they're all I need to complete my set. I received a copy of *Tambour*, that little brown French-English review you liked so much, and it had two of my poems. Then I received *Blues* no 7, with four of mine, and the *Morada* with one. I love to see them in print. You understand the complex, if it is one. It's prevalent, anyway.

Whether you meant this Friday to meet you or not I couldn't tell. You said "I go to Columbia on Friday evening. Couldn't you join me either for dinner before or a movie afterward?" My phone here is Plaza 7400 and ask for me. Oh! I saw Martha Marsh Sunday and am to see her again tonight. She wants to see you only she fears you don't want to see her. Why, I don't know.

TO BRUCE MORRISSETTE

◆

October 23, 1929
New York City

My latest literary misdemeanor is a four part fugue on sex. The characters are an I, a woman, a curé and a Lesbienne. Someday I shall type and mail it. But this weekend I intend to post you a copy of Tambour no. 4, which arrived last week from Salemson. One exemplaire numérotée, which I keep. I also shall send This Quarter no. 4 which I have discovered was kept out of this patrie curious as it may seem. 1, 2 and 3 are still procurable at advanced prices, and then the first issue of the new series published by Titus and popularized horribly. But no no. 4. My mss. aussi, and a little book of verse in french interesting because the translations from the chinese might as well be in English by Arthur Waley, so much the same impression do the words convey. I like the binding, too, and perhaps you will after a while. You will keep it, at any rate. Two books I read last week are good: The Future of Futurism by John Rodker, rather a scholarly bit of writing (He has contributed to The Exile; and unless my memory tromps me, to transition.) and Lars Porsena, by Robert Graves (!!) an amusing treatise of 75 pages on profanity and obscenity. Really, even he! I am into "Jeune Fille" by Gerard d'Houville now. Ordinaire comme caporal. Pas d'étui riche!*

The only girl I have ever lost weight lying awake nights for is back in New York. and I had not seen her for 18 months. Reunion. Bonheur éternel! BAISERS INFINIS! Glory! Gorgeous! Préoccupation quotidien. Téléphoner. Cinq heures et demie. The only, the only, the only. 'Ve given her about three dozen of my favoured discs to play to herself in her room. 'Ve lent her books, money, everything. Because she really *is* only, only, only! (Strangely, her ma is Lesb. and her pa an awful rake, from his looks.) 'S been expelled from every school she's ever attended, here and en Angleterre. She and I shared our enthusiasm for Stravinsky back in winter 1927–1928 and we heard together "L'Histoire du Soldat" at its Amer. Première. We saw Eva le G's Three Sisters together. 'Twas she who used to injure old Italian crones on Ninth Avenue by tossing empty bottles down from the elevated cars onto their pates. 'Twas she who used to Charleston on the edge of the parapet of the roof on Central Park South. 'Tis she who is intimate with drunks and subway guards, who masques as a boy and

* As common as cheap cigarettes. No fancy wrapping!

frequents men's toilets to read the inscriptions. O merveilleuse! Only! Only! Only!

Honegger—o-neg-guerre. Au moins, à Paris. S'il était français, ça serait—o-neg-jé. Étant suisse, on dit celui-là. Pourquoi, je n'ai pas d'idée, parce qu'il n'y a pas de langue suisse. (Aux Grisons, il y a des dialectes, presque des langues, mais composées d'un mélange d'allemand et de l'italien, autant que je sache.*) Called up Carl Van V. tonight and he says he has a "nasty cold"!! Visited his quarters last week. Quite gorgeous. De Luxe, Greenwich Village, Harlem, Park Avenue effect. Chinese mainly, with brilliantly colored walls and ceilings. He was garbed also dans la façon chinoise: salmon pink silk shirt open at the gullet, black satin mandarin coat, glowpurple leather slippers, white socks, silver bracelet with large turquoise. He sat for most of the time at a low table of onyx, serving Martinis which were frightfully strong and with which he was admirably generous. His collection of books is breathtaking. And he is fascination himself. His eyes envelop you. He seems to be given to gazing at you for long stretches of time, during which you feel yourself passing in and out of him.

My photographiccomposition is one of a dozen or more which I took about two years ago here in N.Y. It is merely a little statue I made, photographed against one of my machinery motifs. She's mine, all mine. The statue is the only try at sculpture I ever made. I think that year I stabbed into everything: linoleum cuts, woodcarving, primitive design in the three primary colors, making boxes, furniture, photographs, automatic writing, becoming a connoisseur at odors (I did manage that better than anything, although not to any great degree. I collected incense and perfume. Had 28 kinds of incense and knew them all blindfolded, raw or burning. Then I mixed them and got some interesting results. The perfumes I sometimes sprayed into the powder. Ravishing). No, stabbed is not the correct word: pricked!

I object to your aversion to de Falla. He may be cheap, but not any more so than Respighi. The El Amor Brujo is quite magnifique, and El Retablo de Maese Pedro is at least amusing, and Nights in the Gardens of Spain is beautiful. The 3 cornered hat is rather rotten, but so I think is La Fille aux Cheveux de Lin and Beau Soir; also parts of Respighi's Trittico Botticelliano. Even of El Sombrero de 3 picos or whatever it is I like the Danse du Meunier. (Also de Falla did La Vida Breve. Terrible, I think. Albéniz and Bizet putting together

---

* Honegger—o-neg-guerre. In Paris, at least. If he were French, it would be o-neg-jé. As he is Swiss, it is pronounced the first way. Why, I have no idea, because there is no Swiss language. (In Grisons, there are dialects, almost languages, but they are mixtures of German and Italian, as far as I know.)

their worst efforts.) Milhaud has a propensity for mixing his major and minor and that's his most distinctive feature. Van Vechten pronounced Poulenc correctly and he's the only person I've heard who has. (Save Lehman, I must confess, but sh-h!) I like Dukas more, daily. I don't know La Péri, do you? Mon bien cher (hell!) you most emphatically did call Hilton a blonde I insist, and it's possible that I still have the letter. You did ! You did! A personable blonde, tall etc. . . . . God damn that Farquhar or however the son of a bitch spells his name! He cast aspersions on my taste when he heard I was collecting Arab music. Perhaps he would be forgivable if he didn't collect Brahms so assiduously. That is, if he were a purist he'd have some grounds for his violent objections to a sociological interest in music. But he is merely 19th siècle. He depressed me intolerably. I never set foot in his nest but once, and had the feeling I was a victim. Perhaps of a defective cinnamon bear. Extraordinary Women and Vestal Fire. Have you read "Lady Chatterton's Lover," Lawrence's excrement? I skimmed through it one night in Paris, but was unmoved. Sleeveless Errand raised a hubbub in London, but remains unmolested here. In Paris it was on sale in street bookstalls with "The Wild Party," "Ulysses," "The Crimes of Love" by good old de Sade, and Frank Harris's autobiography. However, here raids are taking place in the better bibliothèques. Mr. Marks, who keeps a store in W. 47, told me Sat. that a neighbor of his had been indicted for selling Chansons de Bilitis of Louÿs. Imagines-toi! Mr. Marks sells the books of the Black Sun Press of Paris. Nice Joyce, but $30 for a pamphlet is too much.

You must come to N.Y. I want to see you. Assez de raison! All I can clearly remember of you is your eyes, too clear, and reminiscent of marshes by the sea. But I can always see your eyes looking straight at me, which aids, at any rate. Naïf to the stranger, and frightening critical to the acquaintance.

I have a feeling that my recordlibrary lacks nineteenth century music. That is, *true* 19th cent. music, like Beeth., Schumann, Chop., Schub, Rossini, etc. (Not 19th Cents. like Wagner, Franck, Moussorgsky, etc.) I think that's exactly what it does lack. Too much Bach and Bax. Carl v V has Les Biches of Poulenc.

Bon soir — parce que je suis fatigué.

TO BRUCE MORRISSETTE

November 18, 1929
122 Bank Street
New York City

Just heard the Rare Book Manager reading a list of Machen bookprices. First Edition of Anatomy of Tobacco $95.00. Already! Surprising, Amazing. A run on William Blake not so surprising. A new edition of the Urizen at $8.00. But I go on forever. Montague Summers has an unexpected popularity, also. His two tomes on Vampires sell quite well. All this is strange amid tornadoes of demands for Milne's new book, for Ex-Husband, Farewell to Arms . . . *En Route* of Huysmans I want to read. Just now I'm eating Berlioz's Autobiography. Rather nice. Easy going. Less musical than romantic. My letter to *Blues* elicited a reply asking if it might be run in the January issue. The ed. called it relevant. Vox Bowlensis. I hope you enjoy the Flute de Jade. I merely skimmed it. But my dictionary gives Névritique, not Néritique as you typed. And you say yours says Neurotique. I prefer that, if possible. When was your lexicon published? It is probably a matter of epochs. Mine is Mid-Vic. Yours is sans doute more recent. The newest includes *lyncher*, a form of execution, etc. rather to put to death by means of, etc. . . .

Why are you astounded to find a difference between our outlooks? We are most decidedly antitheses. And as you say I am a paradox in the shell of another in the shell of another in the shell of another and on up into infinity. Inconsistency. But you too have a few incongruities: being able to stand Prokofiev, an unbalanced interest in eroticism, your hair, une couronne raide, your eyes, the windows of a luxurious asylum. I suppose, however, your "outlook" is more sustained, more intensive and specialized than mine. And I think you have a credo. You have the right to one, even if not. Whereas I, a victim of arrested development, I who have never yet had an adolescence, and have no conception of anything as it is, I have no right to anything save perhaps discipline.

New York is dark. I will be famous. The elevateds blow past at the end of the street making a sound like the winter wind unobstructed in the forest. White grins and snow. Chagall.

All the people in my Bank St. abode know each other. The landlord is the ' liquorprovider. I shall kill him. He cleaned my room in company with his paramour Saturday and broke the jade off my matchbox (threw it away moreover), knocked down le matin dans la mer, took a large segment out of the second record of the fountains of rome, and filched a box of pall mall (corktipt). The entire house is packed with quarterbaked aesthetes who display their pitifulness more satisfactorily when ivre. Horrible monsters who know no Debussy save la Fille aux Cheveux and L'Après-Midi, who rave inordinately over things like Metropolis, a miscarriage by Grofé which appeared last year, and who "do" batik in the bathtubs during moments of sobriety. Girls with bushy hair who lock their doors and play Chopin ferociously. Guys who can say nothing but guts and god damn this country. I'm going to clear out. Worse. Worse. Each one I have seen seems to look on me as a "discovery" and has threescore acquaintances he or she insists that I meet because he or it is positive his or its friends would "be interested in me." Never a word about whether I'd be interested in them, in any of them. They all assemble and cook indigestible suppers over kerosene stoves and fireplaces with faulty flues. Oh! Rather garlic, dandelion wine in Little Italy beyond MacDougal St.

Are you coming up Christmas? I advise it. Really do. See the Roerich Musée and Van Cortlandt Park at snowy dawn. Go to Coney on a raining afternoon and smell the ocean, lying on your back at the end of the breakwater. No one will be in sight in any direction. And we must hunt up the new Chinese Theatre, the Thalia having burned. I believe nothing is lost. Do you want the *Morada* and *Blues*? If, I'll post them. The chimes of St. Thomas across the ave. are ringing. Charming. Yes, the no. 4 *This Quarter* is stagnant. Fresh water that has run into blind channels and backed up. Mine solely a hoax, I admit. But hush. Not Here I am, at least. Write as always, a delicious letter.

TO BRUCE MORRISSETTE

November 29, 1929
New York City

It is such a vilely inclement weather today and the postoffice is such a long walk and I feel so ambitionless with my useless arm that probably the mailing of your parcel will necessarily be remiss until monday. (I enjoy tucking things and things into a parcel, and I enjoy receiving a package into which the sender has stuffed several crops of afterthoughts. I love the shock of finding, besides everything I had expected to be in the bundle, some surprise. Of course I am positive you prefer to ascertain beforehand exactly what is to be mailed you, and so I always divulge the contents to you during a period of several weeks before

I finally get to the point of tying it up and going on the gênant pilgrimage to
the postoffice with it.)

Wat of Osbert, Edith and Sacheverell?

Please describe me the Sacre. You know I have heard it only once, and I
have forgotten (Stupid word for Sacre because there is no remembering or
forgetting there. One visits it as one does a garden, walks along the bordered
paths and admires the masses of flowers. Each time he may walk along some
different route until he has as he believes exhausted them. (He never thinks of
making his own paths in any direction he wants, straight across the beds of
flowers, into the clumps of shrubs and sitting down behind a hedge to look
about. Ceci va sans dire.) And I suppose then he tires of the garden and says it
no longer holds any interest for him. It is too late to approach it from any other
entrance, and so he visits it only very rarely, to show it to a friend, or to experiment
with its colors at unusual times, such as to see the sundial by moonlight, or to
see the hollyhocks at sunset on an autumn day. He cannot either remember it
or forget it. All he can do is recognize it when he sees it, visiting it.) it almost
completely; we will say completely. All I retain is an overmastering rhythm and
some low notes somewhere in the interior. Describe it for me in time order.

The only difference I can see between the Romanticist and the Neo-Romanticist is that besides not having had the Realistic school from which to learn
lessons (nor the Dadaists nor Surrealists) the Romantic having faith and hoping,
wrote as though he had lost it, while the Neo-Romanticist having lost all hope
and faith of the kind the Romantic had, makes his faith in his creations. But
Jolas says the neo-romantic attitude toward life and art is doomed from the outset
because its aim is irrationalism. Be that or be it not, I should never be capable
of holding any other than a romantic outlook. In the beginning, romanticism
was understood to have originated from a decision that nature in all its manifestations is something which corresponds most nearly with the ideal which man
has formed of "beauty," no? Before that, generally nature was taken more or
less for granted; was seen only in the light of its relation to human activities.
The romantic sees all human activities only in the light of their relation to the
abstract idea he has formed of beauty. (It is only when romanticism is bound
up with morality or religion or convention that it becomes tedious or might one
say nauseating.) I am a romantic perhaps pathologically. It is a mania, obsession,
psychosis, idée fixe, complex, fixation, whatever you like. Non capivro, but I
do know that the romantic conception of nature is so inextricably messed up in
my subconscious that I have in some cases absolutely no control over the effects
certain phenomena produce on me. e.g.: — I may be reading, completely

engrossed by the book. The wind may blow in through the window without my noticing it. In a few moments I am distracted by an oppression. I realize my heart-action has been accelerated considerably. I am forced to reason back through the few preceding instants to discover the cause. I know it is nothing in the book. But if I reread the page, I will find that at a certain passage the heart jumps. At the same time now I am conscious of the breeze which entered and struck my cheek relatively long long ago. I realize that the three things are inseparable: the subconscious registers the breeze and rejoices. At the same time the impression conveyed by the book I am reading reaches the sub. The reflex bangs the heart, forces the blood to my head, causing me enough discomfort to make me cease reading. The second time I can reconstruct the drama; after that there is no reaction. I suppose it is the same principle (the reconstruction) (the reenaction) as the retina-tricks one can do. But the fact that feeling the wind causes any kind of stimulation, especially through subconscious channels, proves to me that an essentially romantic system of behavior has been set up in me by environment sometime during my childhood. I deplore this, not only because romanticism is sadly déclassé, but because I realize romantics are necessarily weak mentally, from the pedantic-materialistic point of view anyway.

TO BRUCE MORRISSETTE

December 13, 1929
New York City

. . . writing with the new *transition*, out today, in my cap. It is [*word missing*] the most important revue published. It does no good to revile it or to ridicule it; it is like the Mercury was a few years ago: it pops up and goes right on like a wartank. Only now it has become an institution. People are using the word "transitionish" when referring to ultimae thules of any modernism in art. But after all, why not? It deserves its popularity. One recalls the modest "natal number," sage green cover, looking like a thin "roman à 10 fr." now an elephantine thing. 295 pages, red and yellow cover by Schwitters (the man of Hannover about whom I told you, he who gives vocal sonatas at home), with the inscription: *transition* no. 18. from instinct to new composition, word lore, totality, magic, synthesism. Its table of contents is divided into six parts: the Synthesist Universe (or Dreams and the Chthonian Mind), Little Anthology, Explorations, Revolution of the Words, Work in Progress (J. Joyce) and Narrative. The Synthesist Universe uses at least six score words that nobody ever heard of, but which can all be found in the unabridged. The Anthology seems excellent, with such as Kay Boyle, Hart Crane, Bravig Imbs (still my minion) and Edgar Calmer. Explorations devotes itself in the main to cutting Joyce up into millions of little pieces and tagging them: Asyndeton, Hypotyposis, Chiasmus, Auxis, Paregmenon, and on and on. The Revolution of the Word is engrossing, consisting as it does of lengthy articles and poems in la nouvelle française, cette langue amusante; also of a tale in what Jolas names palaeologisms. The Work in Progress as usual is obscene and guffawing and Narratives are quite good.

I am tired of modern décor. The time's up. It must go on. Rather it shows unmistakable signs of crystallization and rot. It will linger on commercially, but aesthetically, adieu as far as I am concerned.

C'est tout fini entre la Seule et moi. Je l'ai présentée au garçon qui habite la chambre directement au-dessus de la mienne, et maintenant chaque soir elle vient *le* voir, sans me regarder. Plus d'évènements dramatiques!! Et rigolamment, lui, il est amoureux de trois filles et cinq garçons. *

I have been devoting all my time to travelresearch. I am charting a journey from Casablanca to Bergen. It will be stupendous. If you weren't coming up I should do it alone, starting in March. But if you are coming (in June?) we will go ensemble. Right? Then of course the complete itinerary will be reversed: from Bergen to Casablanca. Bergen, down to Oslo will be épatant, and I have roadmaps with distances. Then on down to Göteborg, Hälsingborg, Kjöbenhavn (scarcely recognizable as Copenhagen to me), Schleswig, Kiel, Hamburg, Bremen, Oldenburg, Apeldoorn, Grave, Gheel, Liège, where we can visit Georges Linze and the Belgian avantgarde, Mersch, Luxemburg, Thionville, Metz, Nancy, which has a townhall I did not see when I was there, Charm . . . [*letters missing*] Épinal, where I bought some green apricots (a charming, yes, town), Remiremont, Vesoul (a dull place—even its name), Besançon, which I must see, Champagnole, Gex, Bellegarde, Rumilly, a gorgeous, gorgeous town (only the ones I comment on are the ones I happened to stumble on, on different trips. I've never been to the others). Aix-les-B, Chambéry and Montélimar, to all of which I paid short visits. And we shall go through the château at Chambéry

---

* All is over between The Only and me. I introduced her to the boy who lives in the room directly above mine, so now she comes every evening to see *him*, without even a glance for me. No more dramatic events! And funnily enough, he is in love with three girls and five boys.

together. I didn't. It was closed. Across to Aosta and on to Lugano, then to Menaggio and Gravedona, Chiavenna and Davos, where two dévoués of Mann are staying. You, they and I have much in common. From Davos to Zernez, Santa Maria (I am doing this at lunch in a restaurant. Don't think I'm looking at a map. It would hurt my vanity), Merano, to Venézia, Trieste, Fiume, Ragusa (Dubrovnik, in Slavic) and across to Bari from which we can make a sidetrip (much as I detest sidetrips) to the Castle of Otranto, south of Bari, back to Auletta . . . [letters missing] and down to Messina, Cefalù and Palermo. Palermo to Tunis (another sidetrip up to Carthage) and then 2122 km. across through Oran to Casablanca. One may ask — yes — a dead end — where to then? But from Casablanca we can go anywhere necessary by ship for practically nil: that is, Paris for $16 or so (remember, the trip is on foot and takes about a year) (no, about 40 weeks). Starting in June is rather late. But 3 mo. across from C. to Tunis makes it the end of Sept. which is very bad all around. We must start from Bergen and end up in Maroc or wherever we'll be in March or something. It will make it fall, through Rumilly region. What more celestial, and the cold days will be saved by the Italian sun in December.

You will get a passport and I shall get extra visas for mine. You must write and modify my plans because I shall return home to save money for the journey. In the interim I shall continue adding mileages and days. (You will notice I have kept as much as possible in the countries which have a low currency value, avoiding Germany & Switzerland.)

Écris et pardonnes ce furor.

Tu peux, je le sais. *

TO BRUCE MORRISSETTE

December 30, 1929
Hotel McAlpin, New York

You write too seldom. I suppose you're being dragged as you put it from person's house to person's house. The holidays are uneasy unpleasant days. It is so much more peaceful and encouraging when everyone has shipt back off to college and left the city behind. However these days are the same as all other

---

* Write and forgive this furor. You can, I know.

days to me and I am glad of it. It is one the morning of my birthday. A nineteenth one. So old and so little to show for it. Discouraging. But I suspect one feels so much worse one's twentieth. I wonder if I shall see my 20th? Probably.

A good play is *Death Takes a Holiday*. Philip Merivale. Banal in material but delightful in treatment. I am going to Tudor City New Year's Eve. Hush!

Tonight I had dinner with the three of N.Y.'s best artists, and don't tell me you haven't heard of them: Glenn Coleman, Stuart Davis and Maurice Becker. Coleman does village scenes and urban compositions, Davis does abstract designs and landscapes and in the very modern genre (It is he whose *Egg Beater no 4* was hung upside down for quite a while before it was discovered) and perhaps you've seen his stuff in *transition*, while Becker does Indian women and subway scenes. After dinner Davis and his wife and Becker and I went to a movie and enjoyed ourselves later eating hotdogs. I had been amusing Becker's wife who is ill in bed, this afternoon by reading aloud to her from *Blues* and *Tambour*. (She occasionally interrupted me with "God damn good!" or "Son of a bitch!" depending on whether she approved or not.)

The name of Romany Marie has been hanging over my head and about my ears for a long time and I think the occasion of our meeting will be soon. I have a feeling that I am coming closer to the time when I shall be introduced to her. I want quite a bit to meet her, because she is one person about whom I have never heard anyone say anything derogatory. Extraordinary condition of affairs.

I am tired. Europe, Europe. America, America. Africa, Africa. Eighth Avenue, The Battery, Place Masséna, Quai des États-Unis, Kurhausplatz. Have you heard any of Edgar Varèse's music? I haven't. Miche Danilov's aunt, who got me the introduction to Prokofiev, told him she would never forgive me. I am an ass, an ass.

THE 1930S

January 2, 1930
Jamaica, New York

Victor has some Fushiwara records, but unfortunately they are occidentally piano accompanied. Darius Milhaud has three small operas recorded. The voices sound like not much more than an impromptu if clever parody of Italian opera. The orchestral acc. is often interesting, however. Daphnis et Chloe seems up to the Ravel precedent. Sterns Bros. have a studio where one can go and play the piano into a disc which is successful and which costs only $2.50. If I were flush I should make a few of my pieces for friends. Maybe I shall be able to, later, in which case you will be the first recipient. The novel is growing slowly. I quote from Chapter IV, afin que tu puisses get the style. "A white goat's shadow. They were walking down the shale steps during the next reincarnation and he was ahead of them so that they dared to discuss him. The lake was blue and the woods shrieked with locusts. In the field the dust itself quivered with heat and all the grass was dead but on the east verandah it was cool with the venetian blinds let down all round. They were sitting in deckchairs sipping bacardis. As he entered they frowned slightly and continued sipping. This will never do. Blast them. Bloody rebound with a blash take me back to my other life . . . Slowly the dusk fell to a serenade of taxihorns. It is the supreme test to be alone the first evening surtout after an April rain when the twilight is scented with adolescence. Pang, pang says the night as it falls quietly layer on layer. I am so tired. The world is just coming out of ether. A passive spirit. Twenty francs a day is too much because at that rate I shall have that makes oh my god what shall I do? I do not eat, neither do I sleep."

Of course you will disapprove, perhaps even of the idea of writing a novel, but I want to write it. You say I have maybe a persecution obsession. Yes; I think it is more likely than that I am a "moralist at heart." Although it is quite possible I am the latter, and that the latter entails the former. Remember please that *all* my ancestors, including my parents, are New England Puritans of the first rank. Black velvet chokers and Unitarianism. What is nice and what is improper. The parlour and the shed. Can you expect me to discard completely my heritage?

I had lunch hier with Anne Carroll Moore whom I allowed to persuade me to return to Virginia in March. And so it is probable that I shall see you after

all, reasonably soon. Tell me: is it betraying myself to go back to college? I think
it is, but I am willing to do it for convenience's sake. Et maintenant, mon vieux,
riez si vous le voulez. Vous, qui ne pouvez pas sentir aucune émotion, ou qui,
au moins, prétendez d'être incapable de toute émotion.*

There is a suburb of Oran called Eckmühl-Noiseux. Someday I shall live
there for an afternoon. Will you be with me? Probably not. But nothing forms
so close a connection between me and someone else as to have in common
many geographical experiences. Oh dear, oh dear, ô dear me now, I trow, I
vow. Ma foi, marry, that I will. ô dear. ô dear. ô dear.

You force me to the admission that the theft of the books was accomplished,
then justified, as in fact is nearly everything everyone does. The important thing
in such a case is to remember when the justification took place, and this is what
few can do. Before long they believe quite thoroughly that the motive which
arrived really as a liqueur was brought in as an apéritif. Unhappily, my apéritifs
are simply my savage desires, and whatever thought there is involved in an act
appears only long afterward as a liqueur.

Please, when you know I allow others to read your letters! Please spell every
word right. My God! You misspelled in this most recent letter Qu'importe and
ghastly. In another hypocrisy appears as "hypocracy." This must not go on.
Unintentional orthographical fauxpas are always slovenly. My God, you *must*
be more careful.

But what gorgeous letters you write. Because you know I have the quasi-
physical weakness which makes me thrill before anything stupendous, you shower
tons of erudite words at my feet and I murmur with pleasure, quite vanquished.
It's the same. If a singer screams loud enough, my heart goes out to her. If the
stage is large enough, and enough people gather on it in brilliant enough costumes, if three organ-consoles rise simultaneously from the pit, if my opponent
roars at me in leonine accents, shivers of ecstasy ripple behind my vertebrae.
What can I do? At a movie I am even brought to the point of tears if the
American flag is shown and people cheer. The sight of soldiers marching turns
my inside out. A parade, even military music, makes a sticky sweat come on
my temples. I avoid all these things because I hope to lose this susceptibility
(not in a physiological sense) which in my case, besides being completely ex-
tracerebral, is pathological.

New Year's Eve is gone. A good time high up in an apartment in Tudor City,

---

* And now, you old man, laugh if you like. You, who cannot feel any emotion, or who
claim, at least, to be incapable of the slightest emotion.

looking out on the new group of skyscrapers in the Grand Central District. At seven this morning I walked home. Lyric? Ah! But not as much as Paris. To walk down from Montmartre to Montparnasse at daybreak is the most celestial experience for one's senses! The broad empty streets, the complete silence, the air, the air full of occult odors, the Seine which lies black under the low bridges, the trees along the bank—all always managed to bring larmes à mes yeux, and a spotless, immaculate feeling to my chest, inside me an emotional douche. (I was nineteen three days ago.)

McAlmon is in New York.

If only I might live as many centuries as I shall years
My pleasure would be choking me
I should stand in the fleeting wind on a high hill
And watch the stars swim over me for years
At each rainstorm I should feel the rough earth draining away
Beneath my fingers like sand at the outgoing tide
I could afford to take years at each hill at each garden
I could lie at the oceanshore for the time of two lives
And watch the waves roll in and creep out
I should find myself in northern castles nights where long since
All is dead and the cobwebs waver in the midnight chill
I should crawl down stony glens at the edge a crystal sphere this large
Could not kill my thirst
I should hunt out a planted slope high over the city at evening
And watch the lights and watch the shadows and ships and the black
Islands and I should find a deep hot valley bursting with shadows
Of leaves creeping with life and let beetles and ants crawl at noon
To see if I were dead I should spread my fingers fanwise in the near sun
And challenge it to shrink me or drain my fiery blood
At dusk I should listen for footfalls in the thicket of vines near
I should hold my breath

PAUL BOWLES
there is a youthful effusion showing
my attitude four years ago

TO BRUCE MORRISSETTE

January 7, 1930
Jamaica, New York

Where is your report on Rimbaud? I have tried to find his books places for sale (I mean his book, and the various letters and biographies) but he is even inconnu, which breaks my heart. Perhaps some day I can stir up a reinterest in Rimbaud. It would be interesting. Une Saison en Enfer, have you ever seen it? It seems to me his attitude is completely justified, and would be even moreso were he contemporary.

There are some lovely tales about him. Before he became precocious enough to run away from his mother the first time, he one day asked her to buy him a bull's eye in the public square at Charleville. Upon her refusal, he picked up a chair, and threatening her with it, screamed: "Bitch!" As a result of what a meek Britannica historian terms his "extravagant relations" with Verlaine, that worthless man shot him on two different occasions. It seems unnecessary to end an affair that way, but doubtless Verlaine had his excuses.

He passes through three stages:

1 Revolt against Art: (I came to prefer ridiculous paintings) Employment of poetry as an incantation potent to destroy the accepted order of things.

2 Accustoming himself to pure hallucination.

3 Saying vale to the world and entering into Hell. At this time he's eighteen or so. He disappears, never writes another word of poetry.

New Year's Eve I was complimented highly by the son of Madame Danilova (who was so swell to me in Paris). He said while I was playing: He is more Russian than the Russians. My satisfaction had an abstract root. I was pleased not to be called Russian, but to have a very nationalistic die-for-*old*-Russia, Russian say it. And also, I suppose, because the Russians are a glorious people and I always get along with them perfectly. Unfortunately, I know only too well that I don't look Russian (except in boots and a coat buttoned tight about the neck. In that garb I was frequently mistaken in France for a Russian, the most marked error being that made by a Russian lady in a pension at Nice. I had walked up the first evening from the gare into the Quartier St. Maurice, where I whimsically turned into a street romantically named (I forget what). I saw a sign hung over a honeysuckled covered gate, Pension des Ananas, and went in. The front door was locked, so I went in a sort of service entry. I heard voices in the kitchen, and coughed. A charming person came out, her face illumined itself and she greeted me effusively in her mother tongue. When she had done, I smiled guiltily, and said: je ne parle pas russe, j'en suis désolé!).*

L'entrée dans Nice était une chose que je ne pourrai jamais oublier. La vallée du Var, après avoir été platte et grande pendant quelques heures de l'allonger semblait devenir plus fondue entre les montagnes, mais le train restait à une hauteur assez amusante au-dessus de la rivière. On arrivait à un faubourg—La Madeleine. Le foliage était enfin tout-à-fait des tropiques, et derrière les petites maisons sur la seule grande rue qui divisait le village en deux minces parties on voyait des forêts miniatures de bambou. C'était là que j'ai vu mes premiers palmiers vivants. Tout à coup on tourna brusquement à gauche et entra dans une tunelle assez longue. On pouvait senser qu'il descendait au même temps. On rentra dans la grande air encore une fois et fit une semicercle serpentine en descendant rapidement. La végétation était de plus en plus riche et soudain à droite, voilà Nice avec ses toits rouges et la baie—hélas, grise!—dans le soir qui arrivait. La gare était juste au fond de la colline. Je suis descendu gaiement sans baggage, et je me mis à marcher dans une direction opposé à celle qui menait à la plage. La ville était somnolent et paresseuse, et entre les branches des hauts arbres qui lignaient la rue large, la lumière grise-et-mauve du soir de printemps filtrait dans une manière étrange, inconnue. Il faisait chaud, mais pas trop chaud. Les odeurs, les odeurs glorieuses!!!

Ne me décourages pas trop, ou je cesserai d'écrire mon roman. Tu vois, je suis si facilement empressé par des autres, et par toi—bien sur!† But never mind, I have no idea of having Oeuvre published because I should never find a firm who would consider it. In spite of what you say regarding the unreadaloudability

---

* I am so sorry, I do not speak Russian!

† The approach to Nice was something I will never forget. We had been traveling along the broad, flat valley of the Var for several hours, when the terrain seemed to begin melting away into the mountains, but the train stayed at a rather entertaining height above the river. We came to an outlying district—La Madeleine. At last the foliage was completely tropical, and behind the little houses on the one large street that divided the village into two thin sections one could see miniature forests of bamboo. That was where I saw my first live palm trees. Turning abruptly to the left, we plunged into a rather long tunnel. We could feel the train going downhill at the same time. We came back out into the open and made a rapid descent in a serpentine semicircle. The vegetation grew more and more lush and suddenly, on the right, there was Nice with its red roofs and the bay—gray, alas!—in the gathering dusk. The station was right at the bottom of the hill. I stepped gaily off the train without any luggage, and set out on foot, heading away from the beach. The town was sleepy, indolent, and the gray-and-mauve light of that spring evening filtered in a strange and unfamiliar way through the branches of the tall trees lining the wide street. It was hot, but not too hot. The smells, the glorious smells!!!

Do not discourage me too much, or I will stop writing my novel. You see, I am so easily influenced by other people, and by you—of course!

of my letters, I think I could perform the leggere successfully. I have always done it satisfactorily with my least intelligible things. When writing, the part of my gullet near the uvula contracts and expands as I pronounce the words. I hear them said by my mouth as I write them, all of which is congruent with your lyric diagnosis, isn't it?

(You may use either address which pleases you.)

(I still prefer some of Tzara's and Desnos's jeux.)

And now, exactly why do you think my proposed return in spring is silly? Tell me if you can, quite seriously, because perhaps you can put forward some arguments which will make me reconsider. Please again don't neglect to mention the subject in your coming letter.

I don't understand your explanation of the state of and reference to your virginity. Mechanical integrity means nothing to me. Perhaps you will essay an elucidation if the subject is distasteful enough to you. And your " . . . and speaking always hetero-ly, of course" seems strange. You seem to imply that a homosexual could live to be an octogenarian and die a virgin. It seems to me that as soon as an infant masturbates it is no longer a virgin. At least it's a surer basis for understanding.

A holder keeps your fingers pink; keeps them from assuming the worldly brown.

What do you mean by "better" "to have Bach's self-discipline—than to be an elementalist—"?; do you mean more agreeable or more advantageous for development of character!? Or do you mean that one can accomplish more for the world (humanitarian, moi) or what? I should say that no matter what you meant, you should have believed what you merely professed to believe. (To-morrow I may think differently.) But damnit, the disks cost $2.50 apiece, and I am broke. In a later I shall tell you as much as I shall be able to discover about the process.

Arabic music continues to absorb me. During hours I play it; it will some day be revealed to me. It is so obviously more complicated than European music. The tiny variations in tone and rhythm are all indicative of a highly developed system of composition. And the effects of musical environment: constant association with the genre of harmonic formation will accustom me to it as much as heredity is supposed to. Strange to listen to, it makes other music sound vapid afterward, and more wonderful still, after listening to it solidly for two three hours, I find my mental state altered; —the visual and especially auditory impressions are slightly unusual—so that vague shocks accompany each. No — don't smile indulgently and say: "Imagination." I know what I say is true.

If I could only "get into" Chinese music the same as I can into Arabic, I should be happy. And I suppose it is possible, only it requires more submission. Perhaps afterward it will require less—less than now.

Saturday night I met Romany Marie. I was tight and introduced myself. She said "out of a clear sky": you compose music. You will be able to compose very good music if you continue. We talked on, and then she said that Varèse is the only man with whom I can study. I am inclined to think that is an exaggeration, although Lloyd, the uncivil person to whose room I took you in Charlottesville, said always the same thing. And he knows his music as well as anyone I have met. The nontechnical—the appreciation side, the feeling for what is good, what il faut faire.

Today I went to see the Roerich. I met him once again and told him of how I had served him at the Banker's Trust. Rather charming person. He made me play for the head of the musical dep't of the institution, who I found is a formfiend. He noticed nothing unless it was so obvious that a child of three could make the same distinction. In Wheels, where the first melody gives way to a second, which is supplanted by the first, he murmured about how one must have form. But in the Nocturne Névritique he applauded heartily, what I found to my chagrin was the fact that the melody had the form of A.B.A. My god! Oh, my god! And in Wheels the A.B.A. is almost as obvious, the only variation being that the notes are played horizontally first and vertically second. But the harmony is identical for sixteen measures.

O dieu, gardez moi de devenir trop gênant. Je cesse d'écrire.*
Adieu.

TO BRUCE MORRISSETTE

January 14, 1930
Jamaica, New York

I was born in the Mary Immaculate Hospital at New York on Dec. 30, 1910 at 3 p.m. An hour later several sisters of the institution appeared at my mother's bedside insisting that I be christened into the Roman faith immediately. Upon my mother's refusal, I was bodily wrenched from her by an overambitious nun.

---

* O god, keep me from becoming too bothersome. I will stop writing.

The screams resulting brought about my abandonment on the bed and a hurried departure. A year later I was christened by my uncle in Exeter, New Hampshire, into the Unitarian Church.

At birth I was an exceptionally ugly infant. My head had been pulled badly out of shape and my eye had been nearly put out. In a few days the head was gradually forced back into place, and as the cartilages became harder it assumed a shape to all appearances similar to other heads. The scar over my eye today is a reminiscence of the natal difficulties. Besides those deformities, my hair was a brilliant fire-red, and because of the refusal of the liver to function, my skin was everywhere a vivid orange hue, mottled artistically with yellow here and there. I think my ugliness caused the dislike which my father immediately formed for me. During the first winter he used often to steal into my room and wheeling the crib over under the window, open the window directly onto me. My mother could not stop these displays of viciousness, but she became more vigilant.

From the first I was an abnormal child. I talked volubly before I made any effort to creep. I startled my parents by reading words on household objects at the age of twenty-three months and wrote a story two pages long when I was three. I was considered a prodigy by friends of the family and some of my earliest recollections are of a circle of adults about the room with me in the center answering orthographical questions put to me by astonished visitors, while my parents sat by uneasily.

I spent half of each year in the "Country." Three months in Massachusetts and three on Lake Seneca. I was an agreeable child and always did exactly as I was told. Early, however, I exhibited sadistic tendencies. Undoubtedly my projects were carried out in the light of sound scientific investigation, but they were not regarded as such by my distracted parents. When I was six, I read the five volumes we had of E. A. Poe. I reread them the same year. And then I was sent to school. Up to that day I had never been in contact with another child. The troubles began. I developed a superiority complex the first day. I could read, write, spell, and add better than anyone in the class. Taking it as a matter of course, I conceived the opinion that all the other pupils were horribly stupid and so I refused to participate in any group activities. This was attributed to "shyness," and the teacher had patience. But when I told her brazenly that I had no intention of doing anything she asked me to, I was a given a D in deportment every month. This pleased me immensely. I had this sort of wrangling all the way through primary school and I developed a dangerous (to myself) temper. I would stand still and have rather epileptic spells grinding my teeth and turning blue and black in the face. The parents wisely overlooked these.

When I was eight I wrote an opera. We had no piano, but we had two or three pieces of sheet-music which I studied and I had a zither which I tuned in various scales and modes.

My first sexual thrills were obtained from reading newspaper accounts of electrocutions. At the time I was quite unconscious of the facts, except that I had the New England guilt about it.

I wrote, and wrote all through childhood and I have preserved practically all my Juvenilia. They number over three hundred stories and about two dozen poems. (Up to 12.) I have them filed in the attic. My imagination was horribly active, and for weeks at a time I had no glimpse of reality. I transformed every-thing, everything, into a machine to fit my psychical needs. In the summer up in Massachusetts on the 165 acre farm I lost some of this harmful psychosis because there things were interesting enough to permit me to look at them as they were. You must remember that in both places I was always alone. I made no friends; rather I discouraged them by making slighting remarks about them to others just within earshot of the maligned ones. This usually resulted in a physical reprisal for me, which was what I wanted without realizing it. I always took punishment stoically and ecstatically, never on any occasion wept, and when in a few moments the fury of the opponent abated and he got off of me, I rose, dusted my clothing and if I still felt the desire to be hurt, levelled some more abuse right to his face. Never did I raise a finger of objection when anyone attacked me. * * *

In school I wrote actually offensive tracts and circulated them about the class. I was usually discovered, and enjoyed an unfavorable reputation among the teachers.

Twice a week from the time I was eight I went to my orthodontist's to have new appliances fitted, x-rays taken, bands scraped off, plaster impressions made, arches tightened (a most excruciating form of torture), and then it was found when I was twelve that all the enamel-contributing properties in my system were going toward the formation of a large tumor in my jaw. This was removed while I watched amid much blood and ammonia and hacking. There was much talk as to whether the growth was malignant or not, and it was decided to wait and see. I don't think it was. This orthodontical work continued until June 1928, and I still wear a band.

I have always been a great snob. I still am to a large extent. My enthusiasm for Joyce is a snobbery. Nearly all my enthusiasms at first were snobberies. In fact, I fear I shall never get out of the mental rut into which I fell when I was seven or so, which makes me assume that I am superior to everything around me. Of course by now it is buried under a fairly well spread pile of inhibitions, but corners of it are found to be protruding at uncomfortable intervals.

The vow to cut short the flow of my letters would have been rather a relief to you, but it would have been a source of annoyance to me. And the paper is swell as far's I can see. Gorgeous colors.

How would you expect me to write anything but naïveté in French, when my vocabulary is so limited that I am obliged to transcribe the thoughts into bromidic words?

I feel bad. Nervous. Something is extremely difficult, but I don't know what it is. I think perhaps it may be the house in which I stay.

But taking it for granted that the world is mundane everywhere as I should think you would, you separate yourself from everything. You have no connection with any mode of life, institution (socially sp.) or individual except through its/ his relationship to its/his environment. And knowing full well that life in Cagnes or Eze or Juan-les-Pins will be exactly as "mundane" as it is at Clearwater, Florida or Bar Harbor, Maine, still you start out looking for loveliness at Cagnes or Eze or Juan-les-Pins, and you find it everywhere, at every turn. But you find it directly next to yourself, and the mode of life and the people and all the rest you cannot touch because of this veil between you and them. And yet always you feel as though you understood perfectly the people and why they do every-thing as they do. Still you are absolutely severed from them. You walk about in the streets and feel as though you were a participant in the life there while you are as detached as it is possible to be. The way to enter a town is to walk into it. The way to go from one side of it to the other is to walk there. The length of time to spend at one hotel is one night. Unless a town is large enough to have distinct "quarters," no matter how lovely it is, the length of time to stay there is one day. If it has quarters, stay in a different quarter each night. I was not disappointed in anything. Everything was so much more wonderful than I had expected it to be that I spent my time sighing with desire to remain in each place, to explore it carefully, but instinctively I felt that there lay the danger of disillusionment and boredom.

I always walked fast, even in a brand new town. I set out and walked in long strides confidently as though I knew where I was going. If I became lost I kept walking, always fast, seeing new vistas down each street, but never looking at them more than once.

And I know that every place of your desire would prove as lovely as you had thought it couldn't be if only you explored it in some such seemingly ridiculous fashion.

Le Lavandou, Collobrières, Vollèges, L'Escarène, Draguignan, la Petite Afrique(!).

I shall soon send you a packet containing the Nocturne and some sketches I did two years ago. Be an art-critic and tell me exactly how you like them.

You must use the fibre-needles or the ones I shall enclose.

I had not planned to affect any attitude in Charlottesville. I think I shall live away from the section where all those I know live. I shall try to be genial. And I shall continue my exploration of the mountains. To be frank, were they not so near to Ch. I should not return.

TO BRUCE MORRISSETTE

◆

February 5, 1930
Jamaica, New York

Not at all. I am not practising my hysteria. And you must write more, or else more often, and on arc-en-ciel paper.

I am happy that one likes the Nocturne, and I can well see why one prefers it, since in the playing of it I forgot to hold myself to the supposedly essential even volume. In the following disks I shall better the tone, I hope. How do you think some Stravinsky would suit? Le Violon and La Valse would be two nice pieces for a record of larger size. And I can make a larger sized one for $1.25. I shall be interested (very) to see your Morceau. When will you send it? I have done another Nocturne, but you would eschew it, and Un Altro Esercizio which perhaps you would like. In it I balance groups of three against groups of four, alternating the hands, and with more involved variations. Fugue form, but fairly loosely.

What does Shantih mean, Sire?

And yes I am assuredly nineteen and shall put on a different face when I arrive in Virginia. I shall grease my hair and part it on the right side, and I shall wear black glasses and a grey flannel shirt with ventilation perforations beneath the arms. (I think it will be a relief from the curly naïveté of last year. This naïveté will be more stupid, perhaps more insane.) And I shall live in the Hebrew section of the University, far away from all the people I know. In that way my room will not be a kind of public salon. Everyone will hate and avoid me, but I shall be friendly with the professors, and I shall continue my expeditions into the hills. And there we have a program for Spring, 1930.

Your paternal feeling is no doubt due to your superior intellect, a thing which manifests itself more forcefully on paper than in the ether. Perhaps (and I hope) you will lose some of the sensation when we remeet. Otherwise I shall be testy, because I detest people with paternal voices.

I think the Saint-Simon note is too lovely to part with, and so, will you?

I am still in Du Côté de Chez Swann, Le Livre de Mon Ami, Les Fleurs du Mal, and I am going to commence Sous le Manteau de Fourvière of Rivère (Inconnu).

Dined Saturday evening with the editor of *Blues*, and with Parker Tyler, whose name you will hear mentioned again by someone. Ford (ed.) gave me the beautiful envelope of Stein's which I send. Her most recent manuscript arrived in it.

Have hit recently a pastoral vein which I know is one of my only hopes. It is a drunken Blunden genre, but I shall ameliorate it with patience. Je peux citer?*

An Poem

When stripèd snakes shall creep upon us
And the nervous scream of birds
Make silent all the fountains and the orchards and when these
Have caught upon the wing each wing
That flutters from the sky
Then shall I and then shall I
Rip out the smiles from garden walks
Transform the minnows into hawks
Tarantulas and bees
Then shall I and then shall I
Unmake each whining thing.

Slow Song

There will be a time not too remotely moonward
nor yet as reminiscent of the moon's disgrace
as the bright pastures in the moonlight of your singing
or the moon's inverted canticle upon your face
when daylight over meadows and the strokes on bells

---

* May I quote?

sent outward into sunlight to the banks of streams
shall rout no more the songless owl in moonward dreams.

Send comp. Niets.

Yes. Yes. Yes. Life is sad only because I am unaware of life. I am hiding
from awareness of skies and garages, town halls and tarvia.

TO BRUCE MORRISSETTE

February 18, 1930
Jamaica, New York

And here is Esercizio Terzo, a piece in which every note is rational. It is
principally in thirds as you see. These must be played legatissimo. And the effect
rests with certain intervals which must be accented. Without the necessary
emphasis on these intervals all remains senseless. E is the predominant tone, a
fact which may not be evident. In the center a modulation into E threatens,
then suggests one into A, then strengthened by that tentative turn toward A it
goes back to threatening E which seems almost positive now. The two hold ad
libitum notes are important to establish a relationship (a false one, but necessary)
between the threatening E and the original form of the theme. Toward the close,
E reenters in the bass brought forward by the phrase used at first, but transposed,
and even though the end is D minor, E must be stressed. Vite, comme ordinaire.

I think it would be good to measure these esercizi as to time, and when I
shall have done six or so, to make a twofaced disk of all of them. Do you approve?
They are not as interesting to people as my pieces, but I want to prove to those
who accuse them of unintelligibility and lack of balance that they are logical,
restrained and fairly carefully planned.

Daniel Burns, who has had two of my cahiers for several months, and who
plays several of the pieces quite well, claims that I exhibit, rather than radical
tendencies, a New England conscience and obedience to laws in my stuff; that
in order to keep a progression of intervals equally spaced I sacrifice sound every
time. I see what he means and it is true as far as it goes, but the point is that
keeping tones as mathematically exactly apart from each other as possible creates
the only possible "correct" sound. Pleasing effects, which would be so easily
gained by altering one note only a half step, are obviously to be shunned, since
the fact that a compromise is essential to obtain them shows that their pleasing

quality is a result of habit; a perverted taste. I admit I often weaken and bring about the alteration, but then I feel absolutely duty-bound to atone for the existence of the aborted tone by incorporating the change in the design somewhere shortly afterward. And so I discover I am not a pioneer in any sense of the word, but merely an unlearned amateur who will develop into an academician with the proper amount of study. Is it possible? Never to be able to do more than tolerate the communists, the anarchists of music? I, who adore the prospect of shocking everyone? Ah, ah, Georgette Camille, how true you spoke when you wrote "The Accursed."

Yet, perhaps, O Jehovah, there is a way.

Perhaps by adhering blindly to arithmetical form and writing with earmuffs I shall evolve a species of music the like of which I dream often along towards morning. Perhaps I shall present tonal equations, arrive at a kind of musical ratio and proportion; an utterly objective music which will be taken subjectively, which will engender the emotions felt by the subconscious mind when the conscious is occupied with an algebraic solution. (Because I say there *is* an emotional quality to the logic of numbers.)

Perhaps, O Jehovah, this will come to pass. Twoscore and seven years from now.

Daniel tells me Crowley lives in Paris and is a disgusting creature. Le Diaboliques ou les Sataniques or the new Demonology or some such thing. What on earth can it be about? How can such a society exist now unless its interest in the subject is historical? Speak of it to me.

The snow is deep outside and people say it is cold. But I can feel, as easily as if I were burrowing in the earth, as easily as if I were wallowing with my snout in the dirt, that things are beginning to change for Spring. As I have said before, the fact is brought to me by my heart which I find beating untowardly when I get out. Merely thinking of it at the moment, brings a shiver to my spine.

TO BRUCE MORRISSETTE

◆

February 20, 1930
Jamaica, New York

My fashion drawings are strange enough. Today being Sunday I went and completed the door. It is satisfying. Next comes the bathroom. To be done in turquoise, delft and gold, with silver woodwork. It will be lightly depressing. In a few days I shall send you a parcel containing several things, such as *Bifur* no. 1, etc. When I return to Virginia I shall carry with me the Hindemith; nothing else in the line of disks. I wrote to Prokofiev last night. Ford of *blues* insists that I take him to see Van Vechten. I hesitate. My esercize are progressing. Esercizio Quinto is in session. It will be difficult to execute, and I shall defy any amateur to play it correctly. (I am totally unable to play it myself at the moment.) I began writing it on the elevated in Brooklyn. I have Esercizio Quarto all written, but I have made a great many additions in the way of grace notes, and several alterations in the way of changing successions of intervals. It will be a sentimental exercise, and perhaps for that reason it will find more favor chez the de Falla fiends. (I use de Falla merely because there are so many people who rave over him who have no understanding of contemporary music, and who scream at Stravinsky.)

Still with me the Fugue in the Hindemith Quartet remains the most beautiful music I have ever heard. I have a feeling your dream of Hindemith's music would find a reality more congruous with it in the Fugue than in any other part. But then of course there is the Trio, which might be the echo.

We are drawing to the close of this period in our correspondence. I suppose all this winter might be called the climax. Later our letters will be sparse, desultory. There will be weeks between them. Then months and years. Slowly will arrive the end. Tripoli, Heligoland, Southampton, Biarritz, Rapallo, Istamboul, Moscow, Jerusalem, Versailles, Bar Harbor, Waikiki, Asheville. January, Tuesday, rainy, depressed, noon, vale. Seulement, quand je serai dans les montagnes de Chine, parmi les nuages, je t'écrirai. Je t'écrirai toujours de mes voyages, car ces voyages seront les choses les plus personnelles de ma vie; peut-être les seules choses que je vais comprendre. Et il y a encore tant que je ne t'ai pas encore raconté, et que j'en veux. Je voudrais te dire de l'après-midi sur le lac Léman, du midi brûlant dans les faubourgs de Genève, de l'usine aux parfums, de la cimetière d'où on peut voir le Mont Blanc, de mon matin à Grenoble, de la crépuscule sur la colline derrière Nice, de l'aube sur la plage et des palmiers qui ne frissonnaient guère. Je voudrais décrire le concert à Monte Carlo, le soir triste à Marseille, la nuit mystérieuse à Bourg, des prés entre Chartres et Rennes sous l'orage, la lune au-dessus de l'océan au Mont St. Michel, le soleil couchant sur les vagues rouges et les rochers à Dinard, mon cœur morne à la vue de l'Atlantique qu'il me faudrait retraverser, ma nuit à Bad-Petersthal, la route entre Neuf- et Alt-Breisach à minuit. Ce sont des choses que je sens, mieux que je ne sens le présent. Tu comprends. Et dis-moi, est-ce que tu crois

que quelque jour nous pourrons tous deux visiter d'autres endroits aussi en-
chantants, que nous pourrons regarder autour de nous sans pousser un mot; tout
ça, ensemble?*

Did I tell you about my new poems? They are derivative from the best *blues*
tradition, but in them I go on ahead in a manner like Sonata in *blues* 7.

I have done a Waltz, Tango, Fox-Trot and Ballade. The waltz is circular,
the foxtrot triangular, the tango serpentine and the ballade sentimental as becomes one. They are on their way to Paris to Titus. Naturally he won't take
them. I shall send the plates in the parcel I mentioned. As to my faith in scales
and intervals: no, I don't call it naïf any more than I should call my faith in
photography that; it is all we have at the present. With all its limitations, it is
the best there is to work with. Quarter-tones mean nothing, certainly, more than
multiplying everything by two; they are no aid to discovering true tone. Naïf, I
object. At least, without it I should be totally dulled, I should never play the
piano again, nor turn my hand to writing any kind of music.

How about Mr. Powell himself? Is he awfully important or not? A Propos, I
have an invitation from Henry Cowell to visit him Wednesday, which I shall
accept. I think both the Fountains and the Pines are quite bad. "Going back
on your old friends, ech? Not good enough for you any more?" No, not good
enough. Or not not good enough. But not satisfying any longer. Perhaps I have
played them to death. Yet Hindemith and Petrouchka have never played to
death, nor yet Franck.

Crosby? Harry Crosby, an associate editor of *transition*, who with Caresse his
wife publishes the books of the Black Sun Press in Paris (Joyce, Jolas, Boyle,
Crosby, Brown, Alastair & others) comes to N.Y. takes a girl to his room, shoots
her and him. 2 dead. One holds a lily and the other a hyacinth or a black

---

* However, when I am in the mountains of China, amid the clouds, I will write to you.
I will always write to you about my travels, because these voyages will be the most personal
things in my life; perhaps the only things I will understand. And there is still so much
that I have not told you, and that I want to talk about. I would like to tell you about the
afternoon on Lac Leman, the burning midday sun in the suburbs of Geneva, the perfume
factory, the cemetery from which one can see Mont Blanc, my morning in Grenoble,
twilight on the hill behind Nice, dawn on the beach and the stillness of the palm trees.
I would like to describe the concert at Monte Carlo, the dreary evening in Marseille,
the mysterious night in Bourg, the fields between Chartres and Rennes in a storm, the
moon over the ocean at Mont St. Michel, the sun setting over the red waves and the
crags at Dinard, my dejected heart at the sight of the Atlantic I would have to recross,
my night in Bad-Petersthal, the road between Neuf- and Alt-Breisach at midnight. These
are things that I feel, more strongly than I do the present. You understand. And tell me,
do you think that one day the two of us might visit other places just as enchanting, that
we might look all around us without uttering a word; all that, together?

narcissus. Caresse is alone in Paris. End. All papers; Poet Slays Self and Girl etc. Society Scion Shoots in Love Plot etc. He came from a good Boston family and worked a while on the Paris Herald. His complex was the sun. Each poem concerned the sun. Etc. etc. Doped, drank, shocked à Paris. Mon cher, I never read the Bookman, nor yet anything scientific nor Eliot. It is all too much travail.

Yes, thanks for the music. Tales of Shem and Shaun or whatever it is, is as is Anna Livia, a part of Work in Progress, from which may I add I received little enjoyment and quite a large pain. This is because as Elliot Paul said only he who has much can bring away much from Joyce. I have little, surprisingly little. I am not a doctor nor a philologist. I don't know Norwegian nor Middle-Celtic, and voilà la fin.

Why does it seem necessary for me to make disks to bring down with me to Charlottesville? I was going to send all I made to you. Why do I want them? While I can play, the disks are an abominable substitute. When I shall be disfigured in the hands I shall beg them all from you. I insist, I don't want a collection of my pieces on records. I want someone else to have it. Certes, I should not play it to me, and I should be an ass to play it to my friends, so?

Hilton will probably be a success in his music. I of course will not. I am too perverse. If I find I am doing a pleasing thing and that people like it, I switch; it must be bad what I was doing. I've got to displease them. Adolescence? Anger. Perhaps you will say it is a part of "panemotionalism." Hooray! If it is, I can still be normal (by that I mean either hetero or homo) but if not, then I must wander down life seeking something to fall definitely in love with, and it is quite likely it will be animals. That will be too bad, because there we have a vice more vicious than ordinary indulgence with humans. But I was long ago aware that whatever I put my hand to is made into some sort of a vice. There can never be any love, any affection, even any satisfaction "in my life." Whatever is to please me must be a vice. True, really. Being beaten, for instance. A Vice. But how enjoyable. Burning woods. How exquisite. Biting myself for the pain. All more enjoyable than misbehaving with some girl or man. Well, Dieu soit loué, at least I am abnormal in a "different" way. But it makes of Life a series of steps down into regions unspeakably foul and deep. There is no other conception of my existence I can form. Each day makes me meat-one-day-rottener. Nothing physical. The glow is in my cheeks, but oh, ah, ah, dans mon cœur, la flèche est fixée. * Talking to you about it interests me. It is like telling a friend about a gruesome accident one has seen and cannot forget. The recounting

* The arrow is embedded in my heart.

brings up the scene more brightly for the moment, it is true, but then it allows one to relax and forget all about it until some night when in dreams he shall see it reenacted.

February 22, 1930
Jamaica, New York

Charles-Henri Ford says he met le Clercy. Quote: He's gorgeous; has big blue eyes. Had lunch with him. He's gorgeous!

A Propos, he says he lacks new contributors for *Blues*. In the next no. he has Stein, Boyle, Imbs, W. C. Williams and others, but he needs new names. Contributions arrive in droves, but none suit. Do you mind if I show him *Nocturne for a Goldfish* and *Etude in Gethsemane*? He will probably complain that the style is archaeological or some such thing, but perhaps it would be of use to him. You won't mind having your name in it, will you? Because it undoubtedly would never reach the hands of anyone of your acquaintances. It would be like sending a notice to a Hankow paper.

I saw Gusta Hartman (Bertram Hartman's wife) who says she bumped into Henry Cowell the other day and spoke to him of me. He agreed to see me sometime and there, perhaps, is a master for me next year. Certainly there is no one here in America I would rather learn from, just as there is no one in America (U.S.) whose music I think more of. (In Mexico there is Chavez, in Brazil Villa-Lobos.) It will be interesting and I shall keep you posted.

This spring weather today! The odors kept me clenching and unclenching my fists all day long as I walked in the Village. The ground gave off myriads of tiny spores of smell, so subtly mixed and so pleasingly proportioned that the entire day was a mild ecstasy. I have the feeling that the odors are composed of infinitesimal discs spinning in the air as they rise from the earth; and that the mucous membranes in my throat catch them and absorb them through some digestive-osmosis process; and in digesting them, inflate the locality, tickle the nerves, bring all my consciousness to focus upon the process. You undoubtedly feel much the same. Smell and sound!!! How one lives to please those two senses. Some day I shall rent a gallery and have an exhibition of odors. There will be cases displayed and labelled with the name of each concoction. The visitor will stoop, pull back a slide in the top which will uncover a hole nose-shaped. There will be tiny pots of salves and ointments for the visitor to sniff. As a feature I shall have a separate chamber wherein each hour I shall appear and deliver an illustrated lecture on the development of the sense which will furnish so much of the enjoyment to be felt in the future. The schema is quite practicable, and rich in prospects.

L'Ersatz d'Amour has an interesting preface.

"Le docteur Havelock Ellis, assez indulgent pour ne pas nous en tenir rigeur, a raison de signaler que, sur le terrain de l'inversion sexuelle, nos compatriotes (les Français) se laissent distancer, de loin, par les nordiques: Anglais admirateurs des sonnets de Shakespeare et de l'*Edouard II* de Marlowe, Américains férus du patriarche Walt Whitman qu'enchantaient les garçons des prairies aux visages hâles, Allemands, Allemands surtout . . . Impossible de lutter avec les misogynes dont regorge le pays d'Eulenbourg!

"Ces cas anormaux qui 'sont des amours aussi tendres et furieuses' opinait Verlaine subjugé par son néfaste Rimbaud, 'dieu parmi les dieux,' ces exceptions . . . nous les jugeons mal."*

But if Daniel Burns likes it, I suppose it must be fairly good. Our tastes do not coincide, but I always find something worthwhile in what he recommends if I take the trouble to look into it, which is very seldom. He claims *South Wind* is the best book written in the last generation. I have never looked at it.

Saw Heywood Broun daybeforeyesterday. Covarrubias's caricature of him is lousy. I can't see any resemblance. He speaks English rather like an Anglomaniac.

At last I can write to you on Arc-en-ciel paper. It is not nearly as good as yours, but at least it is fairly varié. The colors will, and do already, please my eye. All I want is eight or ten fountain pens (Sheaffers, like this one) and a different hued ink in each. Then the combinaisons would be marvels. Of course, people (the stupid ones) would accuse me of rifling the idea from Peter Whiffle; but anyone can see that it is something any person would evolve for himself. O dear me now. I vow. I trow. O dear. O dear. Ma foi, Mein Schatz!

---

* "Dr. Havelock Ellis, who is kind enough not to hold this against us, is correct in pointing out that in the area of sexual inversion, our compatriots (the French) lag far behind the Nordics: the English admirers of Shakespeare's sonnets and Marlowe's *Edward II*, Americans enamored of the patriarch Walt Whitman, who was enchanted by prairie lads with sunburned faces, Germans, Germans above all . . . The land of Eulenburg is simply swarming with misogynists!

"These abnormal cases that 'are loves just as tender and tumultuous,' in the words of Verlaine, captivated by his ill-starred Rimbaud, 'a god among gods,' these exceptions . . . we judge them harshly."

I am halfway through L'Ersatz d'Amour. I find it extremely engrossing. You
might not. As literature you probably would find a dozen faults. I can find two
or three myself. But as a homosexual document I enjoy it. Willy does not treat
his material like Gide does. Gide makes his inverts and exverts vicious. Willy
makes them "tendres," oh oui, si doux, si aimables, si adorables, l'on ne peut
que les aimer. * You would probably find them vapid and sentimental. But can
a person who is totally heterosexual be indulgent towards the amiable perversions?
Can such a one as you be anything but indifferent towards these petty (as
Somebody Vassos depicts them) loves and lovers? and so on? And so on? I think
not. It is only the individus who find every vice amusing enough to indulge in
it who can be truly sympathetic with the others. These "great souls" through
the ages who have forgiven their fellow-citizens every weakness are found to
have possessed the same vices. Bah and Blah! The yellow sheet disturbs me.
But homosexuality is a thrilling subject to me, just as sanguinary killings are
and rapes, and tales of drug addicts. They are exciting because they are melodramatic. Struggle! And who really would not give several years of his life could
he but strangle someone with impunity? Moi, I should like to know intimately
all forms of pleasure, knowing yes, Ja, si, da, oui, yeah beforehand that to all
I should remain equally indifferent. As of course under vices I list either heterosexual or otherwise indulgence. Any form—a vice. We must have it thus. I
have a feeling that bestiality or whatever one calls it would be more idyllic than
human intercourse. (At any rate I shall go on my way alone, searching a pleasure
which can stir me as much as music or the odors of the countryside.) But animals
are so infinitely more lovable than persons. That is the secret. There has never
been a person, même my mother, for whom I have felt the affection I feel for
almost any cat. It is a nostalgia, a tristesse, a soft and at the same time, savage
uncontrollable sensation I experience. (And it is quite lovely. Several times when
I have been caressing female cats, they have suddenly looked at me with an
utterly indescribable expression and spit ferociously, clawing me at the same
time. You say any cat does that to anyone. Perhaps, but I recognize the look
behind the eyes. I have never seen it directed to anyone but myself. It says
something to me no human could put into words. I know they feel my desire
for them.)

      You are always lenient concerning my rambles (assez hypochondriacal, I
know), and I suppose you are willing to listen to hours of such confidences

---

* Willy makes them "tender," ah yes, so sweet, so likable, so adorable, you can't help
but love them.

because they amuse you objectively. This occasion, as always, you will overlook my rudeness in discussing myself (a thing which you never do) and that will be all.

An amusing item. Today I saw the grande dame for whom I am working open L'Ersatz d'Amour, browse about a bit for effect, and after closing it, look lingeringly at the cover. She said: What does Ersatz mean? I told her. "Oh yes," she mused, pointing to the word ROMAN in red letters under the title: "Substitute for Love. I guess old Roman was always a great one for writing that sort of stuff!" (She pronounced Roman quite impeccably, too, which made it better.) I replied "I guess he was" in a tone which implied that she had just imparted a bit of news to me of which I had been unaware up to the moment, but which I was eager to show that I believed. After which she declared: "Yes sir! What those French don't think up nobody will!" I find she has lived in Paris six months. Can one believe such obtuse souls exist?

I am tired; I have been responding all day to the superb weather. Chills of volupté scurried along my spine each time the breeze moved the curtain.

Pourquoi Dieu a-t-il fait un monde si ravissant, si beau?*

TO BRUCE MORRISSETTE
———————◆———————

February 28, 1930
Jamaica, New York

Because in your letter you indicate that you have no desire to read L'Ersatz d'Amour, I shall not include it in the parcel. Splendid that you have Gertie's original ms. Keep it as an investment. I too like Au Jardin better than the others, and I gave it as well to Ford. No, he probably will be unimpressed by them, although it is quite likely that he will say of them as he has said of certain of mine: nice, but not for *blues*. He considers *blues* pure propaganda, you see.

You would like Daniel Burns after you had known him at least three years. His pompous seriousness would repel you all the first part of the time.

All right, maestro mio, list me the things I must never know (although I feel more or less certain that I shall intuitively avoid them). Cabell, I suppose for one; Congreve, Thomas Love Peacock and Petronius, I daresay!?

Vice seems to me a necessary word. Destruction is synonymous. (My intro

---

* Why did God make such a ravishing, beautiful world?

letter from Cowell to Copland just came. I shall take it in sometime today.)
According to Burns, I am a reactionary all 'round. He claims he feels no necessity
to be either positive or negative as to immortality, and quotes Montaigne at
length. Que sais-je? (He studied eight years for the priesthood, by the way, and
then went to live in Valence for a year and a half. He never became a priest!)
My "indictment of desire" is a heritage from three centuries of the tightest-laced
New England Puritanism (on both sides of my family). It skipped a generation
in my parents, but here it is on my shoulders with redoubled weight. But I insist
that I am not "revolted by the sight" of "fornication." I consider it a necessary
evil and au même temps a delightful background for existence. Tolstoi: Debauch
begins only where sentiment ends. Thus I feel happy to think that there is always
a diversion and a harmless one, to be had when others have lost their savor.
The diversion will be love, not vice. I have a conception of vice. I tried several
forms in Paris, but it depressed me. Love will not. We will say Mlle. Seule was
my first love, but how pure it was, after all! No farther than the lips. How about
Esercizio Terzo? Yes, I write to your letters, having forgotten you entirely. All
I can recall is a white face, featureless save for Svengalish grey eyes, and a
couronne raide of black, black, black hair. But have no fear as to the unpleasantness of my adjustment. Impossible. It will not affect me at all; even if I find
you lacking in every characteristic I hope to see I shall be unmoved.

It will be nice to have a poem in your magazine. I want Lucidity. Now I find
I have no copy of it — yes I have:

Lucidity

Always turning
sufficiently the stupidities
Sugared. I have sugared the steel bird
I have crushed him. Ah yes, I know!
He barked like a cow
but I took his skin off
He wanted to hide in the drawer
but I found him in the mists
He bit me. That is
why I open my eyes
Look to the back of my brain
Have no fear. What do you see there?
Sugared. I have sugared the steel bird

The bitter American bird no. 15
I have thrown him against the ceiling
There he stays
who turns
turning

Please don't insist that I let you put something else au lieu in. *Lucidity* is one of my favorites, and no one has taken it. And if there shall be any note on me, again, je t'en supplie, put it thus: "xxx has published in this country in *blues*, *The Morada* and the *Virginia Spectator*, in France in *transition* and *Tambour*, in Belgium in *Anthologie*, and in Monaco in *This Quarter*." That will give me a satisfaction I have needed for longtemps. *Tambour* no. 6 arrived last night. I shall send you a copy which you may have. I had a letter yesterday from Hilton. It was on tiny shellpink paper in Italian. Is he an It. student all'università? God, I shall be driven to study Turkish yet. I have Le Jeu de l'Amour et de la Mort, of Romain Roulant, as someone calls him, and Daniel has given me Le Génie Latin of France, or, if you prefer, of Anatole Panse, as the same person says. That makes Gide (André), Roulant, et Panse the three outstanding literary géants of yesterday. Awfully important.

The bathroom is quite gorgeous. I shall try to take photos of all my int. dec. jobs to show you, because I think you would be amused.

Your letter has an air of finality about it. You are not putting a stop to the correspondence, are you? I need the continuation. These days are dull. I always had a feeling that traistly meant staunchly or steadfastly, and so I never asked. Now I do, in case I have erred all these days.

Did I say I want to stop off at Wash. en route to hear at Lib. of Cong. Schoenberg disks? They are hearable nowhere else. Does your mater still consider me a pest? Will she continue to refuse to put me up overnight?

TO BRUCE MORRISSETTE

August 3, 1930
Watkins Glen, New York

Not at all—and I'm grateful for the information. I could not make it out. I have no idea why the Verlag sends me news of Lissitzky, because I wrote asking them about the magazine Sidney Hunt said they published. The Schweizfranken you misread. Not kranken. I think brosch must correspond to buck (i.e. that the mark being the unit of exchange, they have pet names for it, as no doubt Mike Gold would. e.g. "New Masses'll cost you a buck and a half per annum" I can see him writing). Because dasselbe kostet Schw. 7 & 5.85 brosch. Schw. is worth $20 and brosch is worth $24. It would seem to be that way. I send another enigmatic reply from Munich which perhaps you'll be generous enow to do too. The other helped a lot.

I've discovered a beatific beerjoint on the lake about a mile from the house. I wish you were here. The beer is swell and costs only 25¢ for two large *bottles*. I couldn't believe it d'abord. And look at the rejection slip from *Hound & Horn*! My tiara, please, Suzette. Why do you spell lousy lousey? No slip with you; premeditated. My grandpère is presenting me with various Spanish dicts. and grams. He has been finishing them. Surprise! The other day he admitted that Dumas was a waste of time. I shall not hear Aaron the ninth. Larmes. Sang-lots.

Aaron writes that he most possibly will be at Yaddo with me during September and October. I hope sincerely that he will, because I doubt that anyone else there would prove as stimulating. (Did you see that Lola Rudge's "Firehead" was dedicated to Yaddo?) Mrs. Ames pulled A. aside the other day and let loose her private fears concerning me. My "connection" with *transition* it seems had upset her, and she had become afeared lest I be a surréaliste or a dadaiste or on and on. Pauvre!

I have discovered that the aesthetic quality of your missives, due to the typography perhaps more than all else, prevents me from wanting to discard them as I do others. And then too they match the other gross I have already collected. You know my weakness for collections. However I am often strong enough to throw them out, because I should never be able to carry them all with me. Only the best. (An amusing variation of "désormais" which I created yesterday is "déjàmais"!) I am at the moment starting on a motor trip. Later . . .

Being here now in some woods by Cayuga I can continue. I received yesterday more information from Germany regarding art, literature and viewpoints. I was better able to decipher this dispatch than the others, as it was much more detailed and better arranged. The famous Anna Blume of Kurt Schwitters was there for sale for one mark. I think I shall send for a book of reproductions of Paul Klee. I'm especially fond of Klee's work. And one can get an aquarelle (lithographed) I believe for 1 mark 50. Ever since I saw Klee's lovely little fool in trance last December and his *Suicide on the Bridge* shortly afterward I have been waiting to see some original Klees. At the Modern Art Museum at Heckscher Bldg. there are two gorgeous ones: *The Goat* and *Slavery*. Have you yet been to the exhibition? Be sure to look up the Klees. They are in the little room to the left as you enter the deskroom. I think my favorites at the show are the Chirico in the big salon and the Klees. There are a great many Picassos of all periods, and some of the latest ones are amusing. Aaron said of one of the smaller ones that it was the first Picasso of which he could say he was definitely fond. There are a few Dufys; not very happy choices, some Matisses I didn't like, some Gauguins that are nice; one in particular was a piece of glass he had painted on, and which for some reason I had the feeling had been done in Tahiti, or on the boat that carried him there. There are some Derains that look antiquated for some reason again, and some swell Cézannes. Some Van Goghs that I liked fairly well, except for his oily technique, rather like Epstein's sculptural style, in one small way, if you know what I mean. There are some lousy Seurats. They look like ads for Hartford Fire Insurance Co.: "Scene on the Estate of George Frances Smith at Glen Cove, Long Island," or on and on. There are two very good things by Jean Lurçat which take a long time to get past: one is a marine called "North Sea" in which the colors are quite awful, but whose composition neutralizes the somewhat dubious chromatic arrangement. Perhaps the colors are perfectly well chosen—indispensable for bringing out the design. At any rate, I liked it tremendously. The other was a smaller one, rather Picassolike, with the same "tic" of composition, you will notice (if you haven't already), but with very lovely colors. There was a Kuniyoshi I couldn't bear, two Burchfields I liked, because of their feeling for place, and a Utrillo that was good. The others were rather mediocre: Gromaire, Léger, Pop Hart, Kuhn and many others—oh yes!

A *lousy* Demuth and a terrible imitation of Léger's immense composition in the anteroom by someone whose name I can't recall at the moment. But ah! The Chirico is superlative! Fortunately there is a bench directly in front of it, and one can regard it by the minute in comfort. For some reason they have put a strident "Figure" by Picasso next to it, and it somewhat detracts from the color. Chirico is one of the "few." Picasso belongs to the older rank, I think, along with Dufy, Matisse and all the others. But the "new" good ones are surely a very decided "few." Miró, Roux, Klee, Picabia (?), Tanguy, Chirico, Lurçat, Stuart Davis, and not many others. (The Picabia questionmark was meant to say: Is he to be considered "new"?)

Perhaps you'll enjoy the typical *Blues* note! Don't return. But *do* please the Rays. I forgot to mention.

TO BRUCE MORRISSETTE

October 29, 1930
Jamaica, New York

i write this from home where again i have found a place to be quiet, where again perhaps i may become sentimental, if indeed i have ever succeeded in being anything else at any other place, and where i shall start on le cote de guermantes. i spent the afternoon in the gramophone shop listening to beautiful music and by that i mean glorious. they have a collection there of javanese music. perhaps you heard it; if you did you couldn't have been much impressed by it or surely you would have mentioned it, because really it is at times beyond description. it is more beautiful even than chinese music or annamite; that perhaps because it is a bit less classical and a bit more languorous. it seems to be midway between spain, china and the hawaiian islands. i shall probably write more of it because i may buy it. the set costs $10.50 which is a bit cher. however, what i should get out of it! tomorrow afternoon aaron and i are driving to philadelphia. vladimir sevitzky, koussevitzky's brother, is directing the strings of the philadelphia symphony as the philadelphia chamber orchestra and two of aaron's pieces are to be given. there is a reception afterwards which he warns me will be "as dull as ditchwater." hearing the javanese music brought back much of a nostalgia that has been latent in recent times. I want to set myself to work looking again at maps and planning a getaway. but as one says hell one must learn something. i thought you might like to see the announcement of the Golls' book now published in a reasonably priced edition. i saw one three years ago at weyhe's gallery for $25 and i believe it was without the chagall illust. me, what i have seen of chagall leaves me quite cold, but then, he is so famous that he must be good. ah, the suburbs of Alger: le Hamma, Belcourt, l'Agha, Isly, Bab-el-Oued, and then Eckmühl-Noiseux of Oran; it is too much. In Tunis there is a part of the city called: Quartier Sans-Souci, and just outside the wall of Cairo there is the Colline.

[The story that follows was enclosed with Paul Bowles's letter
of October 29, 1930, to Bruce Morrissette.]

◆

11/23/29

Paul Bowles

122 Bank St. N.Y.

An Short Story

my GOD but youre late why didnt you give me a ring if you were coming so late
well you must have known soon enough to let me know oh hell its all right
perfectly HELL why do you have to say that you make me feel as though i was
the guilty one all right lets forget it did you get the gin swell its the same stuff
WHAT what the HELL why didnt you get the same stuff we always get whats the
idea come here sit down and lets christen it its not as good as we usually get oh
hell its not your fault i wish you wouldnt always keep trying to efface yourself
the backward bow the bashful beau come on have a swig and tell me if you love
me any more no sit HERE and well sample it together to hell with the gingerale
this is good enough for me i was not i never said it wasnt good stuff i only said
it wasnt quite as good as usual the way you get things mixed up is pitiful oh im
sorry i didnt mean anything oh GOD oh GOD why cant we ever come to an
understanding i mean why do we always mind what we say to each other i mean
why cant we pass it off and laugh you know i never mean what i say oh GOD
you must anyway lets have some what do you mean ive had some just a drop
to try the stuff all right you have some i can always understand you better anyway
when youre tight you wont you wont get tight dont make me snigger did you
ever drink anything and not get tight i know you dont you never have to get
tight YOU dont because you begin long before trying to psychologize yourself
into thinking youre tight oh HELL i had the lousiest day today give me a swig
and lets put on a record shut the window so the el wont make so goddamned
much noise when it goes by lets have some franck the sonata its soothing and
it seems to understand why WHY do we all think were miserable ALWAYS why
are we always miserable why are we always groaning OH FOR THE LOVE OF GOD
I DONT MEAN YOU im the one whos doing it right now but you do too we all do
everybody is always groaning and i want to know why gimme a little more im
getting warm inside at least even if i dont feel it yet yes what i want to know is
WHY are we all miserable all the time its a cloud that hangs over our heads and
none of us can get out from under it oh god i thought that when i went to
europe id come back happy because id understand whats wrong with us all here

but its only worse all i want is to get back there now all i can think of is chardon-lagache pantin grenelle maubourg oh god oh GOD i want to get out of this dump oh HELL im not crying dont im not crying no im not and im not tight either shut up oh im sorry oh hell i wont apologize this time im tired out you can think what you like i want to listen to the record isnt it swell you know im sick of stravinsky and honegger this is just what i want this and you really i love you really only you wont give me a chance to prove it you you oh i you dont know anything about it put on the other side i love it old césar knew what he was doing all right once i was walking on the boulevard saint michel and all of a sudden the air from his third chorale came to me i hadnt thought of it for ages and at the same minute i glanced up and there was a tablet saying it was in this house that césar franck died and stranger still the third chorale was the last piece he wrote oh dear oh hell this stuff is ROTTEN no kick at all my god and my stomach my GUTS feel like pepper oh hell i heard a story about a sadist the other day i know dear life is hopeless and no nobody knows why we keep on i love you dear doesnt that sound trite doesnt it sound like an emetic i love you blawwww kiss me that sounds a bit better ahhhhh oh god im miserable when youre not here theres nobody else in the world i can stand having around but you i know it i do wish it too KISS ME that was swell listen that goddamned girl upstairs is beginning to play the piano the piano the pianoforte let me turn it off its no use trying to play that thing any more when SHES making that noise CHRIST if i couldnt play any better than that my god oh my god when i get up whoooo WHOOOO said the owl im all alone in the forest whish said the bat im all alone in the ruined castilio the ghosts are coming flap flap GOD let go of me you lie down again dont tell me lie down. LIE DOWN fido thats a darling what the hell well let it run down it wont scratch long it wont be long oh my god OH GOD my GUTS as one would say its all gone the whole bottle there aint no more thats all there is already listen dear you stay right there were going to lie here and listen to that lousy piano upstairs just to be little stoics poor kid you had too much whoopee i feel as though i were in the aquarium the beautiful aquarium at napoli oh why are we so oh come all ye faithful come unto me suffer the little bastards to come unto me for we and ye died for me for theee for all bless thee little lamb of god. GOD GOD GOD my intestines my god dont just lie there ouf OW im going to be sick its better to tell and YOU had more than i did oh god i never WAS any good just rotten oh oh oh oh oh OH OOOH OOOOOH god oooooOOOOOOH   god   OOOOOoooooh
never mind
       im all right

its all right im not going to be its just pains
OH thank godthankgod OH wheres your ear i want to whisper to you

TO GERTRUDE STEIN

[*December 1930*]
150-10, 86th Avenue
Jamaica, N.Y.C.
U.S.A.

Dear Miss Stein:

I wonder if you could be persuaded to donate one or two things to a small revue published in Richmond, Virginia, called "The Messenger"? I am not the editor, but I have been selecting European material for my friend Mr. Morrissette, who is the editor. I cannot overemphasize the fact that I should like your pieces solely because of their literary value which I feel to be immense, and not to exhibit as curios (which I have discovered, alas, to be the motive underlying the printing of your work in one or two, at least, of our American "avant-garde" mags to whose editors I have talked. They are still unable to understand that anyone who writes English today with any degree of mastery owes you an inestimable debt).

I sincerely hope you will have something to spare for us.

P. F. Bowles

TO BRUCE MORRISSETTE

January 2, 1931
Jamaica, New York

The Capriccio is still lovely. I shall always feel he does not mean it as much as the Sacre and for that reason it is not as good, even though it may be, and probably is, much better "musically." The beginning is effective, with especially the strings playing the duet and the woodwinds resolving into a dominant seventh with the tonic, and then the reverse, with the lovely manner in which the strings seem to grab hold of the chord—do you know what I mean? and then the marvelous feeling of starting, getting under way gracefully. Flow, flow all the way through. The Sacre comes out in numerous places, thank God, shortly after the beginning of the second side, and then as I recall at the beginning of the fourth side particularly. There are spots I dislike: one is where the Brahms section of the sixths on the second side comes to a close and the coda begins— the long drawn out clarinet and bassoon or whatever it is, chord, and the nasty note that comes after it announcing the coda. It seems like a hole in the evenness. I still think L'Histoire has a sorcery the Capriccio hasn't.

I now have plenty of *Messengers*. Aaron has a nice volume of Hölderlin in the original. Last night (the Eve) among other things I went to Harlem to a gudge place called the Clambake or some such, and heard swell swell music and songs. A woman called Gladys Brenton I think sang a long repertoire of songs my mother never taught me. Afterward we tried to get into another place where Van Vec. had told us to be at five o'clock, and he was there and went in but we were not admitted. How about asking Ford for a poem? Would you want it? or a shortshortstory? I have started another song on words in *tambour*: SO EARLY IN LIFE. I NEVER SAW ANYTHING LIKE IT, etc. I don't know Aaron's reaction. He wants me to play my suite: the Aria, Chorale & Canonic Rondo, at the Concert, but I will not. I assure you it would ruin me at the outset. Mes nerfs. I should pull a Hilton and rush out frothing at the lips. Maybe I can get Marc Blitzstein or someone to do them, and with the songs I would be well represented. Koussevitzky plays the Capriccio here next week. I must go and hear it. The rest of the program is good, too: Bach, Ravel's orch. of a new Moussorgsky and Beet's 7th I believe. The League Concert Sunday will have "Aspects of Modern Music" by Eugene Goossens; *Quartet*: Lebhaft und sehr energisch; Sehr langsam äusserst ruhige viertel; usserst lebhaft, played by the Budapest Quartet, and all by Hindemith, *Piano Variations* (1930), Aaron Copland; Kodaly's Qu: Allegro, Andante quasi recitativo. I think it will be the best League concert (that is, regular) of the season. Of course the big show at the Met. will be the most exciting. Schaeffner says of Stravinsky: It (the Capriccio) is *Le Baiser de la Fée* without Tchaikowski, *Mavra* after a few year's reflection. Mastery of form, mastery of orchestration. Whether we listen to that ever mobile orchestration, although always full, even in its least sonorous parts, or to that effect of variety produced by the repetition of one tonality in the finale, we think of what Schubert said of Beethoven towards the close of the latter's life: 'Art has already become for him a science: he knows what he *can do*, and his imagination obeys his inexhaustible power of thought.' Since Apollon, Stravinsky has entered into that extremely mysterious period which certain geniuses reach only when they are old men, and others at about forty-five years of age. His possibilities have extended in a new direction, just as, when we look through a lens we see stars in the sky which up to then had been invisible. Henceforward Str. will depend much more upon himself, upon his own power of thought than upon external objects. He will not so much try to limit his means, as to increase his efforts. He now knows that he can get much more out of himself and that the essential point is to find within himself his own power of meditation.

I don't approve of calling it *Mavra*, etc., but otherwise all right. John Powell I see will be here soon. I suppose he will have some of Hilton's pieces to play?

A note in *Le Canard Enchaîné*: Mme. Charlotte Rabette et M. Fernand Divoire viennent de faire paraître, en collaboration, *La Bourgeoise Empoisonnée*. Le livre porte en sous-titre: roman javanais. Hélas! c'est bien ce que nous pensions. Mais pourquoi Mme. C. R. et M. F. D. n'ont-ils pas essayé de l'écrire plutôt en français?* To Divoire's list of attainments in case you ever use his *Conjurations* which I feel you will dislike, can be added the book's title. I have a little grammar containing Danish and Swedish, and Aaron would teach me German. If we could get enough German covered by the time we take our trip so that I could understand the simpler things, I could learn a great amount during the week or so in the auto when there would be nothing to do but talk. *Ondt* I find means "that" (pronoun) in Norwegian-Danish. Stuart Gilbert never mentioned it, but said it denoted the business-man type of personality: "on-to-it" in contrast to the Gracehoper who knew nothing but what he had heard tell of a thing. But what the Norvège may have to do with it I can't see. Perhaps you, with your Anglo-Saxon, could find a more sensible connection.

I have another friend who lives in an even nicer Park Avenue penthouse, as those things go. (It has terraces with high oldfashioned "faggot" fences like one sees in New England, rather than railings, and looks generally country-homish.) Tomorrow night I am to be initiated into a game there I have never played: Murder. It sounds fun, especially if everyone is tight, and one can use the roof and terraces. All lights are extinguished and a false murder is committed and then etc.

The text of the *Ondt & the Gracehoper* is very much changed from what it was when it came out first in *transition*.

When you come to here you must go with me to the Harlem place and see the woman, who becomes more and more wonderful as I remember her. A sort

---

* A note in *Le Canard Enchaîné*: Mme. Charlotte Rabette and M. Fernand Divoire are the co-authors of the recently published *La Bourgeoise Empoisonnée*. The book bears the subtitle: A Dutch novel. Alas! We thought it was written in double Dutch. But why didn't Mme. C. R. and M. F. D. try to write it in French instead?

of colored Jane Heap, if you can imagine her. But quel rhythme! quelle angoisse voluptueuse! quels yeux, quels gestes des doigts, quelle voix séduisante!*

TO BRUCE MORRISSETTE

January 22, 1931
Jamaica, New York

a dozen thanks for the story. i have made another copy of it now and sent it to the handh. i hope you received the parcel i sent daybeforeyesterday. i think the possibilities for a good march *messenger* are good. william carlos williams sent a short poem for it yesterday, in company with a note which read: yessir, wow. but you m-u-s-t keep out everything else mon dieu because as i say it is i who shall receive the damns if it isn't a modishlooking mag. i shall send the addresses of the various contributors, if there are any more, as they come, so you will be able to post them copies, gertie's is 27, rue de Fleurus, but i think you have that. williams's is 9, Ridge Road, Rutherford, N.J. berlin plans go on daily: we are going to have an apartment with a piano in it and that will be aaron's piano. i shall take an extra room outside to work in, with another piano. aaron plans to entertain quite a bit and insists i take a course in german before we go so i shall be able to be a bit civil to his guests. i think i shall get a l'allemand par vous-même idea in some secondhand bookshop and get him to give me the accents as his is reputedly exact. cowell was in yesterday before i had my lesson and he and aaron had a most enlightening argument on music. tickets should have been sold. cowell turns out to be surprisingly rational, and late 19th century to my mind. he dislikes the capriccio intensely, calling it cheap and dull. he maintains that if a piece is made up out of banal material it is bound to be a banal piece! screaming: what else is there besides the material? what else is going to give you an idea of what the artist is saying? there is nothing but the material! and like the pigeon in alice: if you say there's anything beyond the material a piece is made of, then you're metaphysical, and not musical! aaron all the while believes that only what is unable to be resolved or analyzed is great, that that is what greatness consists of . . . what lies behind the material and can't be expressed . . . &.&. cowell went away in disgust when he had put the question: can the

---

* But what rhythm! What voluptuous anguish! What eyes, what movements of the fingers, what a seductive voice!

note c mean anything but the same thing to everybody if it conceivably could be an entire musical composition? and aaron had answered: of course, the letter c means something different to everybody who hears it. he said: that's way over my head and went off in sulks, perhaps little realizing what a true confession he had made. after he had left aaron said: he's awfully nice but he gets a lot of people all mixed up. ruggles is staying at the place where he lives and was sickabed, otherwise we should have had some jesuses and bastards to punctuate the seance. just had a phonecall from brewer who last week took a plane to u. va. where he says things are very quiet. everyone it seems is on a pledge. ridiculous things. decadence, last wailings of an old morality. of course one says it is easy for the eunuch to condemn the desires of the other people, but my morality is an individual one. if i seem like "a child having come across fornication" and being repelled by it, it is nothing that will "wear off." i get lovely ads from harlem dancehalls from time to time. i try to leave my name on the mailinglists as much as possible. a poem just came from barber to whom i wrote asking for the particular poem. it is good, i think. tell me if you like it. he says macleod is in new york here working for *new masses*. i shall have to look him up. i think it is swell the manner in which every one to whom i've written so far has sent immediately a mss. salemson wrote me the other day hoping aaron and i would visit him at mescalero new mexico and i wish we could. it is near the mexican border. oh god oh god. to wait weeks to go to berlin. angoisse. and even then berlin is not the riviera. it will probably rain forever, mais qu'est-ce que ça fait, enfin? i have five modulations using diminished sevenths to do in solfège, and i must get to work doing them. it hurts my sensibilities to leave all this paper blank. (leftover from childhood, when paper was the most precious thing that existed for me. what do you want for christmas? pencils and paper. no toy. blocks of paper all clean and without wrinkles, and it still persists.)

i envy you your arcenciel as i've said.

TO BRUCE MORRISSETTE

February 21, 1931
Jamaica, New York

The charming names of places to the southeast of Paris are fresh and contain nothing exotic about them—rather suggest open countryside and limpid evenings with the pastoral unsullied by even railroads (which, although they can be very beautiful in certain parts, seem to have no place here). Names: Fère-Champenoise; Arcis-sur-Aube; Les Crocs-Larrons; La Cense de Blacy; Pringy; all lovely and represent a tiny part of the country I should love to visit. It is a singularly open section, towns are few and far between, and in the middle of forests even small farms are recorded on the map, with names such as "la Belle Idée Ferme!" and "Bonne Voisine Ferme" and one dangerously named: "Ferme de Morte"! One would think the main idea there among the provincials would be to eschew such a badly-named place, but a mile or so down the road is "Les Cerisiers Ferme." The section seems to be hilly, wooded and swampy, and lies about 150 km. away from Paris, nearest to Troyes. I should be happiest if Aaron would buy a small auto so we could go about and pry into places. Maybe he will. We are going to Munich in May to a Music Festival, to Paris in June to visit, and to Oxford later, as you know. Is there any chance of your making the trip to Oxford? If Bloomberg and all the others go? It would be swell. We could go later to Brittany and explore the islands offshore which people say are merveilleux. And all the Druid remains to ponder over. I have an invitation from some people in La Rochelle who have a gudge summerplace on the Ile de Ré, de Maupassant's story-place, to visit there during the season. I should love to. Also I should like to go back to the Lavillatte's château which I loved and see them. I wonder how it will "work out." O dee o dee, what I shall do for cash is depressing. No money at all. My freighter bids fair to be fun, though. Linze invites me to passer quelques jours à Liége the first of April. I hope I can. He says *La Revue Mosane* has just published a poem of mine. I wonder which one. Nancy Cunard sent a lot of material about "L'Age d'Or" of Bunuel & Dalí, on which account all that happened to Noailles, you know. She thought we might like to put some of it, notably the scenario (in French) in the *Messenger*. A propos, I hope the "vote" was propitious, although I have the blackest fears as to its outcome. I did write to Mr. Hutcheson, and dared him to call me "a certain New Yorker." Damn his soul. Thoma sent a rather good poem. You see, we should have had a swell number. Never compromise. The issue of sop will never cease to kill me. Aaron's publicity ought to draw a good house. The theatre seats 1200. He is advertising everywhere. The editor of *Modern Music* is having me translate two articles for a coming number; one by de Schloezer and the other by someone else. I hope it is typed and not in longhand. Milhaud's calligraphy, for example, is utterly illegible, and strangely enow resembles Aaron's to a marked degree. I have been doing designs again recently, and find they are quite pleasing. I made a small book of my sketches, using tinsel, cellophane and photographic negatives as décor. Quite brittle and fun-looking.

Cowell's concert of Theremin was enlightening in spots—percussion effects, a quartet of electric instruments playing Palestrina, keyboard instruments, relation entre tone & rhythm, etc. Also some Arabic music illustrating third tones. I went the next night to a lousy concert save for a charming Hindemith duet for two flutes unaccompanied: Canonic Sonata. I expect to hear from you tomorrow or so. I have been translating my recent poems into French, and wrote a scenario which I should like to see given. At least, something like it.

Yes, do send the arcenciel. I shall be happy with it. Nothing could be nicer. I send some relics I found in various drawers—map of Marseille which I found in the Gare St. Charles—in English; with the passport snap of the girl who, as far as my Switzerland trip no 1, and my Riviera trip, etc, were concerned, "made it all possible." Miss H. Monroe returns my poems now and then (and still I have never enclosed postage; a triumph), saying most recently that it "does not seem like poetry" to her. They say she is a pathetic old lady. I wonder what she thinks of Zukofsky's number of her mag!! I hope you rec'd. *De l'Étoile au J. des P.* Brewer may pub'sh. Thoma's novel. I hope so. Thoma seems always able to get himself into scraps with everyone. He has fought consecutively with every member of the *transition* crowd. "I suppose" he is "too tender and beautiful." It is one way out. I ran crash into Gerhard Wednesday who insisted on my going with his party to a speakeasy, but since I was on the way to one myself with people I had to decline. He said "Hunter Stagg is one of my very best friends. I am trying to get him to come up & stay with me." He begins to look like Crispin, the lovely hero of *Portrait of a Man with Red Hair*. I am going to write I think to André Breton about the Surréalistes. Also I insist upon meeting Tzara and perhaps it can be done through Breton. Not that I want esp. to see Tzara, but I should like to get the friendship because of Miss C who loves Marrakech. To be a friend of Tzara's is in her estim. the supreme manifestation of one's worth. He will not allow her to take friends to the house. His wife is in Stockholm now, which makes it all worse, as she is friendly.

I suppose I shan't hear from you tomorrow, as it's a holiday. How I detest holidays! I prefer U.S.S.R. with only five a year or however few they have.

I never get a chance to study German.

soprasottosopra

TO DANIEL BURNS

◆

April 1931
Aboard the S.S. McKeesport

I am writing this from the ship, where time goes along more or less slowly, but still more or less pleasantly, for the sea air pleases me a great deal. Unfortunately we shall be very late arriving at Le Havre, inasmuch as we lost a lot of time the first two days of the voyage owing to the unusually rough weather we encountered. It was really quite almost unprecedented, according to the various officers and sailors about the boat. I thought perhaps at first I might be going to be seasick, but everything went beautifully. Still, we don't expect to land before April eighth, which probably means you will receive this sometime in late April. The eleven day boat turns out to be a fifteen day boat.

I want to thank you for the kind and useful gesture you indulged in just before my departure. Nothing could have pleased me better, as I daresay you knew (and as I have not smoked a cigarette for a month at least, I am very glad you didn't send a carton of cigarettes). It was thoughtful and generous of you.

So I told you, I intend to stay a day in Rouen and there I think I shall take a boat up the Seine to Paris. The first thing that attracted me to Rouen was of course Jeanne d'Arc, but since I have discovered all sorts of personages who are buried there, who figured in its history: Corneille, Richard-Cœur de Lion, Flaubert, etc. (I suppose in almost every French city one discovers literary & historical connections which one had not suspected existed.)

I have a desire to set some of Poe's poems to music. Some like:

> "In the spring of youth it was my lot
> To haunt of the wide world a spot
> The which I could not love the less
> So lovely was the loneliness . . . "

etc.

and

> "Mountains toppling evermore
> Into seas without a shore
> Seas that restlessly aspire
> Surging, unto skies of fire
> Lakes that endlessly outspread

Their lone waters, lone & dead
Their still waters, still & chilly
With the snows of the lolling lily."

(I don't guarantee the quotations, as I have no volume with me.) Then there is a lovely one about "The breeze, the breath of God . . . hangs upon the trees," and one that goes "Dim vales & shadowy floods . . . whose forms we can't discover, for the dews that drip all over." It is Poe's earlier poems that I should like to use. His others, *because* of their Poësque quality, have "lost something" by becoming well-known. I like "Ulalume" for instance, as well as any, but it would seem silly to set it to music. By setting to music I mean "make songs of."

Did I ever confess to you my passion for Donne? For Blake? For Coleridge? Probably not! I think it is better that way! I should be thought of by you as a person springing from contemporaneity, uninterested in even the Mauve Decade. (I have discovered some likeness between the poems of James Macpherson, a contemp. of Johnson's (Dr.) and my long "What tentacles of clematis?")

TO BRUCE MORRISSETTE

April 1931
Paris

Your letter arrived and it had been awaited a long time. I am sorry about no April. Of course I find it difficult to understand why exactly you are "forced" to wait. But I suppose you are. But again, June seems impossibly distant. Probably my mother will be here by then. We shall be forced to live where it is cheapest. Mallorca, Ibiza, Bayern, Lombardia, Salzkammergut. Probably probably not France because it is more expensive here. Spain is about the best bet at present.

And Spain is too beautiful.

The music of Hilton's you sent is even worse than I had dimly imagined his present output would be. Oh! Oh!

Really I wish you were coming sooner. I had counted on April. For several weeks I have felt the urge to go away where it is warm, but thinking of you, I decided to wait a few weeks more and go with you. At news of June I shall now undoubtedly go running off to Aveyron or somewhere or Guipúzcoa or whatever. Alone and with my customary vegetable nostalgia. Not a great deal goes on here. Met Jolas endlich and we talked persons nicely and otherwise. The concerts have been sometimes good, and others dull. Reheard La Symphonie des Psaumes and for first time Pulcinella entièrement, and it is well. Milhaud gets worse. Prokofiev is hopelessly meaningless. Perhaps the Berlin Symphony will bring Das Unaufhörliche with it. I rather like Cossio, a new painter. Miró in Monte Carlo, Rous in Abyssinia. I am reading Lautréamont. So much of it is so wonderful, and tiny parts are like Atget's photos of couronnes mortuaires or archaic butchershops. Fancy brass gas jets and potted palms. *The* nocturne!!! Have worked very much and have done a two movement concerto for flute & piano. Shall be doing symphonic morceau under Rieti.

Saw Ch.-H. Ford yesterday. He lives in a sort of lace valentine Viennese ballroom with Djuna Barnes. We went to tea at Samuel Putnam's, who spoke of having lunch daily with Pirandello who lives also here. We did not enjoy ourselves, as Putnam served us no tea and we had made a rather long trip to Fontenay where he lives. I saw the new *transition* which from point of view superficial is a disappointment. Begins to look like Front or other arty tri-lingual mags even though it has between 300 & 400 pages. Gertrude thinks Ford's novel best since *This Side of Paradise*. Oh! Oh! *Transition* now semi-annual. Although I am not living in my room, but at Suarès's yachtlike penthouse, I am going to keep it as sure headquarters; so use that address. Try May, try April, try, try again. Paris starts to be lovely.

Je suis navré, désolé, abimé, tout-ce-qui est triste. J'avais compté te voir beaucoup plus tôt. Rien à faire. Il n'y a pas moyen? Écris plus souvent.

Je ne connais pas ta destinée cachée; tout ce qui te concerne m'intéresse. *

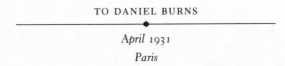

TO DANIEL BURNS

April 1931
Paris

The sky is incredibly black at the moment of writing and it is depressing. One never knows when it will pour and so it is wiser to stay in the house all day I think. When I arrived at Le Havre I decided to stay all night and see the town and I thought it a charming place and even nicer than Rouen where I stopped on the way to Paris the next day. One of the first things I did here was meet

---

* I am distressed, heartbroken, destroyed, everything-that-is-sad. I had counted on seeing you much sooner. Too bad. Quite impossible? Write more often. I do not know your secret fate; all that concerns you interests me.

Jean Cocteau, and to go the following day to his house for tea. He rushed about the room with great speed for two hours and never sat down once. Now he pretended he was an orangoutang, next an usher at the Paramount Theatre, and finally he held a dialogue between an aged grandfather and his young grandson which was sidesplitting. I think never have I seen anyone like him in my life. He still smokes opium every day and claims it does him a great deal of good. I daresay it does. By definition, the fact that it is considered harmful for most mortals would convince me of its efficaciousness for him . . . I am going to a dinner given in his honor tomorrow night. His house is quite fantastic, giving one the feeling that outside are the tropics, and that these beige and taupe hangings and mattings are put about for coolness's sake. One room is devoted to a titanic Picasso which extends from one end to the other, and on an adjacent wall is Marie Laurencin's portrait of him. Another afternoon I called on Gertrude Stein and found her charming chumming and completely sans eccentricities, which is to say I suppose without shams. She is having me invite Aaron to dinner the night he arrives, and is also having Bernard Faÿ whom she wants us to meet. I think it will be a great deal of fun as I like her extremely. The room she received in was huge, and had at least fifteen Picassos in it, as well as some Juan Gris pictures that I had liked for several years in reproductions. Yesterday afternoon I had tea with Ezra Pound and Michel Arnaud, who directed Cocteau's cinema: *Le Sang d'un Poète*. Arnaud also writes, and did the long poem "Onan" for *Tambour* last year. He has an immense collection of records that I am going up to hear tomorrow. Arab music and such stuff that I love. Pound talked with me about an hour and a half about sound movies and the various methods of recording the soundwaves and I found I knew nothing about it whatever. I also found I knew nothing about opera when I mentioned that topic. At least I found that he did know about it, and he went on to show to what degree. He said if he were a young musician he would aim straight at the talking picture without giving a thought to stage music. It is about the same idea that Hindemith has, I suppose, but somehow it seems rather sad and not nearly romantic enough for me. I am a reactionary in such respect. I have been enjoying myself extremely, but I am eager to start working again. In fact I feel slightly empty without an all day purpose in mind, and the absence of it makes me a bit ill. There is a good new bar in Montparnasse called Le Bar de la Marine, with Surrealist decorations and an affectation of 1899 in what it calls its "Fancy Bar." I am reading Cocteau's "Opium" and like what I have read. A completely insane book is *La Femme 100 Têtes* by the Surrealist painter Max Ernst. It is a novel in almost 200 engravings that send the shivers down one's spine. André Breton did the titles. You must see it when you come over this summer. I bought a copy so I could study it as it is quite unusual, quite magical. Alastair has disappeared, saying that when he returns in two years he will have green hair and albino eyes, and everyone believes it. Care American Express, Berlin . . .

TO EDOUARD RODITI
———————————————◆———————————————

[Spring] 1931
Paris

Somewhere there is a furious vermillion hiding for you at the top of a flight of stairs. In Crimea on docks at dawn it stoops sighing for you. When languid afternoons slide octaves along the pianos of deserted conservatories it waits breathless outside the hot window. And this time, this time, between the clouds as the chimes cry, there is no longing for it. Only the idea of life in tiny, far up above the highest stratum, laughing like a kite that has escaped in a hurricane. Only the long line of years looking from ahead up to you, with capes embroidered in alleys and ports. Only the disappearing sound of sobs like stones. And the determinations, the slammed doors, the hair in the hands, it all knows each afternoon as it goes past. The untrue friends at cafés, laughing as the thunderstorm grows in the east behind the trees, the bottles of perfume on the table blown over by the wind at night, the hinges of the door when it opens, all the tramways that hurry in all directions, they remain only there outside the skin, unapproachable, while within pant the blood and the music.

In a dark cellar the vermillion has found some mushrooms growing. Above there is no sound, no light. But in the dark parlor a black goat sits at the piano, grinning malevolently, while a lone beggar slinks past in the street outside, glancing over his shoulder at the moon which will be covered by clouds. The air in every room of the house wishes the goat were gone, but no wall dares to suggest its departure. Later in the night a clock strikes outside.

Perhaps then you will see me drinking cocoa.

TO EDOUARD RODITI

April or May 1931
Ave. de la Bourdonnais
Paris

I was sorry to hear of Mary [Crouch]'s indisposition. If you see her soon tell her I shall write her again in a few days. I am greatly encouraged by the idea of a possible concert. It probably would be more amusing if pieces by other people were given. Perhaps we could make it a two-man concert: Festival Thomson-Bowles, or Copland or somebody! I daresay I wouldn't have quite enough stuff to make it all mine, much as I should like to.

Much as I should like to make love too much as you claim you do, I see no way even of beginning. Aaron would say: There's nothing to worry about. When you really want to, you will. I don't think I agree with him. I went to Versailles yesterday and the aeroplanes were as thick in the sky as ever, as crows. There were many people in the park wheeling baby-carriages. I wished for summer, but a summer without pain. I am always ill—now it is my eyes which must be attended to, as well as rheumatism in my arm which is maddening pain all time. I have nothing in *transition*. But I received my poems, thanks, and had not waited to send a sheaf to *Modern Editions*, without *no village*, because I was in such a hurry. I think it doesn't matter because they can't be such idiots as to use any of them anyway. I can't be a poet because I am so sure my stuff is unimportant. I must be a musician because although I am not believing my music is important, I am not convinced it would always necessarily remain unimportant. I might be a painter some day. So now let us sit in the sun and wish for clearer air and use not the royal we.

Write and say what you think when you have time. I look forward to seeing you. Are you voyaging for Pfingsten?

TO EDOUARD RODITI

April or May 1931
Paris

Je t'assure que je ne sais pas me débrouiller.* One must have money wherever one goes. She shall have music wherever she goes. Rings on her fingers and bells on her toes. Ride a cock horse to Banbury X. But it is quite unfortunately true. I have no kind friends in London who might conceivably have me to dinner every day, & as days go on, money slowly even with care slowly disappears until there is no more of it. My circumstances are quite unhappy and not unusual. And and. But don't you see how one must work and when Summer i-cums go to the cheapest little hamlet to spend it? Must not rush off to London? Shan't won't you be in Paris at any time ever? Enough of plans. Who I say knows about next Tuesday indeed? There is no method of telling it. Mornings slip past, curtains fly up, grass grows, one says why why what several times and then it is the next season and everything is changed. Perhaps an uncle comes from Leningrad inviting one to go to Cardiff to see the circus. Maybe one misty morning a telegram arrives saying: "What are you doing here in Europe? Go back home to America where the haystacks are even sweeter." Or perhaps the chapel falls on one, burying him with a great many unsatisfied ants who were all on their way across the road where there is a grove of pines. One never knows no. And so it is possible a day I shall arrive in your abode grinning having ceased to hope you will know how to stand me. Always it is like to being a miracle when someone accepts one as easily as the key turns in the door. So that at the finishing of forty-five minutes both are suddenly a bit chagrint at remembering that neither has known the other long enough to know the important unnecessary things as hot showers, strawberry shortcake, two pillows on the bed at night or what color was your mother's hair and do you look like her? To know. Both are chagrint and then pleasantly pacified to recall the existence of other people, other cities and kinds of trees and taxis, more hours, varieties of nights and the great long wide life around in all directions. &&&&& then when necessity for consolation is gone, all the further sparkle in the new person who has provided one with this means of having newness, with himself which when put with one makes the mysterious chemical formula. &&

But here it is heartbreakingly beautiful and I should like life to be the one

---

* I can tell you I don't know how to get out of this mess.

long cry it is now. The one long green sound of trees, water, birds and animals and curtains making noises on the windowsills.

And so. And so. And so. You will write if you find a fine wealthy friend who will give me gold to come to London? Good. And I shall write again from Berlin where the sun is not quite so bright.

Not quite

TO DANIEL BURNS

June 1931
Berlin

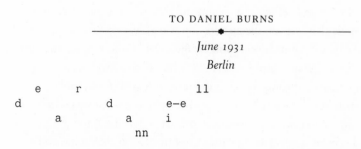

.i found holland épatant and krishnamurti extraordinary P.hilosophy par excellence. arrived back here after two BU.sy weeks in münchen, salzburg, salzkammergut, heidelberg, OMM.en and trains. the castle where krishnamurti lives is A LO.vely early eighteenth century place standing in the MIDDL.e of a standing moat green with water green from STANDI.ng years on years about the castle. one lone swan SWAM SU.lkily about hoping for crumbs which were often FORTHCOM.ing when various extheosophists decided to feed THE NOISY. pigeons that complained throatily all day. and THEN AT NI.ght the peacocks would begin to scream insanely SO THAT ONE.wondered how the owls in the forest could conTINUE THEIR.silly noises the way they did. oh yes, birds a PLENTY THERE.back in berlin it was hot until the spell BROKE.YOUR LET.ters were very much fun, and carlo suarès COMPLETELY APPR.eciated the variations on a theme by me. WHY HE THOUGHT I.n the cupola cubical nightcaps was the BEST I COULD NOT.imagine as there were others i preferred. IT IS PROBABLY THE.french spirit:cupola cubical.la boule ROUGE BOUGE ETC.THE.beautiful nash poem i wept over, but STILL I CANNOT REMEM.ber committing the atrocities ascribed THEREIN TO ME.WHAT DI.d you mean by it all?oh dee oh dee it IS PROBABLY MERELY BEI.ng in a new place that did it.news FROM BRUCE TELLS ME ROS.ser reeves was in an autodrunk acCIDENT WITH IRWIN.DO YOU.recall glenn irwin?the latter was KILLED AND ROSSER'S SKULL.was fractured but he will live.

OH VIRGINIA OH VIRGINIA!AS.to other news:harry dunham will LIVE
THIS SUMMER IN DRESDEN.hasket derby will be in tours. edouard roditi
insists i come to london and live with him.richard thoma has a good time in
paris.bernard faÿ writes from budapest telling how good wine and women are
there,and how bad bach and coffee are.gertrude stein writes saying come and
visit.michel arnaud is very busy in paris translating alice, and sylvie and
bruno.mrs.crouch is in paris.my plans are not definite.i shall probably visit
gertrude stain! my new name for her, in the latter part of july while copland
goes to london, and then he will pick me up there and we shall go to cannes,and
that will be the end of all.can you come to berlin before the end of july?
tu,vois,mon,argent,ça,disparaît,beaucoup,trop,vite,et,je,ne,peux,pas,penser,à,
accompagner,copland,jusqu'à,londres,ni,même,à,paris,* so if you could manage to come here first we could amuse ourselves during days,although paris
would be funner.aaron is going day after tommorroe to paris for several days.that
is too say,he will bee their untill probabuly the fifteenthe of juine.perhaps you
can get one more letter off to me before you leave america.tell me your inten-
tions.copland says he recalls having had mr.swann as a french teacher and even
greeting him at one of his concerts years ago.a thundershower cuts short my too
short note since i am writing on the balcony.blintz.

TO EDOUARD RODITI
———————————◆———————————

June 9, 1931
Berlin

I have arrived back from Hannover where I have been with Kurt Schwitters,
setting, or rather translating, his vocal sonata into piano music. It was rather
fascinating work, the little I did. I had time only to do one scherzo. Have you
read much of his stuff? Its importance is rather past, but I still think it has some
merits that are at least fun. He as a person is quite mad, but one wonders
occasionally if correctly so.

It is amusing, and mysterious to go about hearing of you from first one person,
then from another. I have the feeling you are primarily two people, one of which
should be killed. Only the Suarès version of you should be left living. Not that

---

* you, see, my, money, it, disappears, much, too, fast, and, i, can, not, think, of, accompanying, copland, to, london, or, even, to, paris,

the others do not give what they consider highly complimentary accounts of you; they do, but for me, only what Suarès tells me of you interests me. You see, the others, Jean Ross, Isherwood, von Braun, even Thoma, all speak of you as clever and witty and amusing, and in the back of it all there is the heavy shadow of nothingness, indecision, unhappiness. Suarès says less brilliant things, but there seems in what he says a comprehension which quite outweighs everything the others say. I goad everyone on into talking about you for hours. (All Renée Sintenis said was that your skin was dark and that she was of the opinion that you really hailed from South America.) And they all seem willing to do the talking, on and on. von Braun insists you are mad. He, by the way, seems extremely hard of understanding. No matter what I say, he says: I don't understand you. It begins to be a sort of song. However, he is pleasant, and seems to enjoy being flabbergasted, so it is all right. Only I had always had the idea that I spoke as simply as anyone going. With him, the mind works cautiously like an animal at bay, and we disagree on whatever he does think he understands. Mais ça va. Jean Ross is of a sort of motherly attitude toward you which is nice.

Aaron Copland is hoping to see you when he goes to London next month. I hope you will be there. He is a great person. Me, I am stuck here in Berlin while he is in Paris enjoying himself. Ah me, ah me.

Music is so difficult. One follows on the heels ten years behind of Antheil, Copland, Blitzstein, twenty behind Hindemith, thirty behind Stravinsky. Stravinsky, who said: Les autres, ils sont encore romantiques. Moi, je suis déjà romantique.* Is that right to say or not? I have not decided.

Goodbye. It is too late for me to say all the things I should like to say, and anyway I have forgotten what they were. It is May, no June 9th and it is not raining.

TO DANIEL BURNS

June 1931
Berlin

i have come to the decision that berlin is the least amusing place i have ever seen. it is the synonym for stupidity. i should be quite happy if i never saw the city again after today. of course at this moment i am prejudiced as copland is in

---

* The others, they are still romanticists. Me, I am already a romanticist.

paris and i am all alone and it is raining and it looks as though it would never clear again.i have been to bad pyrmont and it rained there and then i went to hannover and it rained there.i see now why europe is so green.it ought to be.in hannover i stayed at schwitters's house.he is amusing and pleasant.he and his wife kept insisting that i stay a little longer so that though i went to stay two hours I stayed nearly fortyeight.heard his vocal sonata and then he asked me to translate it into pianomusic.so most of the time was spent working at that.we took a walk about the dumping grounds to hunt for materials for his statues he has in his studio,and found half a tin spoon,a piece of mosquitonetting and part of a thermosbottle.he was very thankful.and he went along picking up small pieces of glass and china that could be broken into still smaller pieces,and dashing them with zest against stones,then turning grinning toward me.once he found a whole vase,and was very thankful.it made quite a crash.we were bitten severely by mosquitoes who he claimed were angry with me because i had not been to norway and spitzbergen like he had.he kept asking me to run out and buy him chocolates,two at a time for 2 and a half pfennigs apiece.they were frightful little things and after the first two i refused to eat any more and let him eat them all alone.he has six salamanders,seven guineapigs and five turtles,oh yes,and two lizards that run about on the floor when one is not looking.at night the guineapigs squealed sulkily on the balcony so i could not sleep.he had never heard of gertrude stein.before that.before that.the bauausstellung here has a few amusing things in it,but it is much too large to see all in one day,and too tiring to visit more than once.the egyptian girl [Jean Ross] had jaundice before i left for pyrmont.i wonder how she is now.i have met dozens of people here,but i long for paris and the narrow streets.tomorrow i have a date with gabo,the man who did the sets and costumes for diaghilev's production of la chatte.if you saw it,you will remember the shining glass and aluminum,and eisenglass.die million is here.i sent your poems to bruce.i wonder if he is still alive.the mountains about pyrmont i found gorgeous to walk in.but berlin!the duc writes asking me to the chateau again.where are you going?i have no money.no money to go running about.perhaps i shall not even go to cannes.but berlin is too horrible to stay in.i have written not a poem since march.nor any music.nor drawn a picture. nor learned anything,but what of it?

good bye

TO BRUCE MORRISSETTE

June 13, 1931
Berlin

schwitters was swell. exactly as he should have been. his studio was quite incredible. there is nothing like it anywhere in the world, i am sure. only in the brains of madmen. he has spent years building it, with plaster and cement and glue, and it would take about as long to see it all. two days i stayed there, and we went walking on the dumpheaps to find things for his studio. the bowl of a tin spoon. part of a thermosbottle. a square of wire screening. his vocal sonatas are much better than i had expected, and one can sit easily without fear of exploding into laughter. the true reason of my remaining was to translate the scherzo of a sonata into piano music. gieseking lives in hannover too, and they go around, so he wants him to play it, but i know goddamnedwell he won't; i should ask him not to, for i have got rather a snotty idea about my music now, which is in part that it must have its debut under the right auspices, and i think dadaism would stamp it schnell wrongly with everyone. besides it is lousy, je t'assure. i mentioned gertrude stein to schw. and he looked vague, and finally admitted he had not heard the name! on sidestreets he would pick up milkbottles furtively and after a moment's hesitation, dash them to the ground, turn grinning with satisfaction and proceed. at night the guineapigs on the balcony used to squeal longly, and it was all fantastic. besides, he had a huge jar of worms on the mantelpiece, as well as two salamanders, four lizards and many turtles. he wonders why he is so famous in america. is he? in berlin i looked up gabo, the man who does constructions in glass. he did sets for diaghilev. one i saw in paris two years ago, and admired it, but the things in his studio now are disappointing. to be sure, they are nightmarish and startling, but some are quite godawful. renée sintenis is too lovely to live. she has a horse she rides in the tiergarten each morning, and she loves it so much she can scarcely talk about it without weeping for joy. she does sculpture, in fact, is the best known german plastic, man or woman, but everything is very small, and of young things, usually animals just born and looking too unused to it to go on any longer, but sometimes gangly adolescents, standing about very seriously. but everything is young all over the place. rené crevel has just done a new book about her in german. i took her a sheaf of my sketches and she had interesting things to say, not always complimentary. the lurçat show at flechtheim is excellent. he is a difficult one to decide about. terribly difficult. there is a swell exhibit of photos given to flechtheim by everyone from vlaminck to max schmeling to hemingway to gide. max ernst is quite enough to cause cauchemar. his eyes would drive anyone mad in two minutes. i think he must be mad. certainly the farther he goes, the farther from land he seems to get. have you followed him at all? ten years ago his things were understandable. now they are the maddest maddest one can find anywhere anywhere. klee is fascinating. his eyes look as though they were made of velvet. rené crevel was coming to dinner one night at gertrude stein's but bernard faÿ came without him as he was very ill. he is always rushing to switzerland for his consumption. pauvre. the card in enclose was written a week ago and never mailed. sorry. i spent this afternoon at lerski's, he is without a doubt the best portrait photographer whose stuff i've ever looked at. there is no describing it. quite marvelous. he is going next week to palestine, and then to africa, russia and spain to finish doing a beautiful series of jewish pictures that he began here among the unemployed. he takes them all with an immense lens, so that they are larger than natural size without any enlargement. every pore is huge, and all being magnified and extremely clear looks somehow magic. he thinks he may next year give a show in new york, and i tried to sell him stieglitz's, which he took to strongly. stieglitz's is a good place for such stuff, and besides he knows him. jane heap and margaret anderson arranged gabo's show in n.y. years ago, and gabo as well wondered why it was liked, for, he said, i thought all the people in america were as stupid as cows. schwitters has a passion for cold countries, and has spent summers in spitzbergen. now he goes each year to norway to paint. aaron writes from paris that antheil's article in the new review is "really *too* childish"! bob brown writes from cagnes he is using my readies in his book which is probably out by now. a readie anthology by everybody from kay boyle to marinetti, can you figure how frightful it could be? and probably will be? i am going to visit gottfried benn soon and see how it works. a man with his brain can't be stupid. if we don't get along it won't be his fault. i am reading suarès's book "la fin du grand mythe" and it is good. i shall do up a packet some day of stuff to send you to read, and then some later day you can send it on to jamaica for me. yeh? please. suarès is a friend of boulanger's, so he and aaron and she can all get together and understand each other for two hours. what fun. thoma might too but he is an imperialist, and that is too snobbish after all for suarès. notice the beautiful nota bene i send in pink and what do they want, hey? and why will you not write, hey? and shall i ever see you, mon vieux?

[*Postcard enclosure*] The music played was nearly all characterless stuff. To hear hour on hour of mediocre idea-less atonal music is frightfully depressing, je t'assure. A. will do articles for *Melos* (which I suppose one might say corresponds to *Modern Music*), but I shall really write them and get the money. Hooray! It is a rainy day in the hills and the train moves as slowly as oxen. This morning I was taking a walk and ran into a store whose proprietress was called Gertrude Stein. It was too fascinating to see the name painted in immense letters over the show window. At the moment I am faring nach Hannover to visit Schwitters, who said: "Ça me ferait beaucoup de plaisir de vous voir. Vous connaissez Arp?"* Ah, ah, primitü ta. Merz. Anna Blossom!

TO EDOUARD RODITI

June or July 1931
Berlin

bon sol et terrain rapporte. † life is at a loss. to be well fastened to the crust. my dreams are like ostrich feathers. i have never dreamed of you, to be sure, and that is a blessing. the fewer people one has to dream about, the less complex his life is. and then after i have met you, i shall have you to worry about as well as all the others. last night i was standing on some high step above the joachimsthalerstrasse and there were many people passing in a great hurry through the street but i did not watch them because my eyes were noticing a black shoe which everyone had to step across. but no one looked at it. at last, at the end of my patience, i went down the steps to the sidewalk and at an instant when there were not so many legs and feet moving to and fro, snatched the shoe and carried it back up the steps slowly, scrutinizing it with curiosity. it was a high black shoe, and had a grey heavy silk spat when i had unbuttoned it there was a grey silk sock that hung limply out, and whose toe went down inside the shoe. with a certain amount of distaste i pulled back the sock on all sides to look down into the shoe, as i could tell by the weight of it that there was something inside it. when i had pulled the sock back all around i looked and there was a splintered pink bone that stuck up just to the top of the shoe. giving a long sick cry i hurled the shoe down into the people who were hurrying past. an elegantly dressed gentleman with a monocle saw it fall, and picked it up. the sock was pulled back and he knew immediately what was inside. as he hurled it away he gave the same sick cry, and i stood on the steps feeling myself

---

* "I would be very pleased to see you. Do you know Arp?"
† fine soil and good yield.

turn into long shreds of flesh, feeling the space around resolve into an enclosed area. it was nearly dark, and i was in an L shaped room with ragged tapestries sagging from the tops of the walls all around. there were seven beds, all in various states of extreme disorder, and some of them had high black canopies above them. i realized that it was absolutely essential that i get into one of the beds, but i was afraid that there was someone else in the room. finally after pain i slept all night in the bed near the center of the room so that i could see down both dark corridors of the room. it remained peaceful all night, and the quiet was broken by nothing save the sound of stone being chiselled in the courtyard outside. but the next night my fear was augmented by the wind that blew about from behind the dirty cloths that hung on the walls, and rustled the canopies. i moved the bed out from the debris by the wall and looked carefully at the three largest beds. a head was looking out of a door between them at me. i was frightened, but knowing there was no means of egress from the room, i jumped powerfully to the floor and rushed across the floor to the door which opened quietly and let out a man with black hair who argued with me for several minutes on unimportant subjects. then we talked a mixed french and german, and then he said he intended to break a chair over my head. laughing scornfully i jumped onto my bed and was immediately back on the stone steps of the joachimstha-lerstrasse, only there were few people walking and i felt it must be near the end of the century. a man with very blond hair was standing beside me repeating the words: You're god damned right! you're god damned right! and i turned and knocked him all the way down the steps and went home.

if only the world were stronger! if only there were more dimensions! if only we thought in terms of perfumes! if only there were a third world where we could hide from the other two. then the other one would not be always grinning in feeling so perfectly well that we could do nothing when it intended to enter. there would be two of them there, and the two would be easier to fight than the one. but now it is always either one or the other, and neither one stays away long enough. in full noon sleep falls upon one for one tiny second without measurement and one knows there is no escape.

i am in good health, but today is one of the rare ones when it is difficult to get away from the heavy arm that hangs above like a threatening pressure. berlin is not a beautiful city.

copland intends to look you up. von braun will discuss you, but thinks nothing complimentary of your poems, which subject i feel it is useless for us to argue upon, and so i say i haven't read them. oh, really, they're utter rot, he will tell me, and he writes them in trances which is even more ridiculous, &&&&&.

sintenis and i were going to the races yesterday, but i forgot to, and stayed all day at the wellenbad. from what the baronin said when i arrived home, she was not pleased, and i am heartily sorry and hope she is not really angry.

had lunch with jean ross few days ago, and as usual we talked on about you. and on. she is better.

have you seen jolas's article in *transition* in the june *american mercury*? he is incredibly naïf, and thank god, or we should have had no *transition* at all.

if you write ten letters a day, you can easily send me one even more occasionally, no? i write not so often now, as i am working on mozart, and am trying to finish my sonata. which i have been doing since last autumn, and of which i have completed but one movement . . .

ah well

TO EDOUARD RODITI

June or July 1931
Berlin

As long as you don't propose to be angry with me you can do what you like with fate. One never knows. What's the use in saying? Now I plan to be with Gertrude Stain while Copland goes to London, and then he plans to pick me up enroute to Cannes, where we do plan to be the summer where the Palm Beach is. The essential thing for us is to be able to have two pianos wherever we go, and such a thing would hardly be possible at Bagnères de Luchon, for example. So we must be near Genève or Cannes or Munich or always some large city. And then Copland bores himself without crowds of people which I consider an immense weakness but what to do about it? But as I have been saying one never knows. What's the use in saying? It may be we'll see us ere that. I felt that I had an unfair advantage over you having seen the snap of you that Isherwood had, so I enclose one of me that I had automatically done yesterday for you and I daresay it is scarcely better than your passport one. Pictures are such liars. I should say for instance that this of me makes me look gentle, and I am not gentle, makes me look soulful, and I am not, makes me look companionable, and of all things I am not. So it is lousy.

Be sure to let me know about September.

Suarès is a swell person I think, don't you? Krishnamurti I had no long conversations with, but I am convinced of the limpidity of his mind. That means

I believe that I would rather have his mind than anyone else's. With it I could be happy and *know why*, a thing I had never considered necessary before. Now I can be happy, but as to knowing why, I can only see why I am unhappy. The happiness finds no answer. On se demande. C'est essentez? Scherze. C'est obligatoit?

I think you had better attend to fate. It seems to be unrelenting about the orthography of your surname. Rodiki, rodoti, rodito, radiki, rodoki, rodoko, rokoko,,,,,soon it will be rakosi, which would be frightful, as I dislike his work. But here is the thing from the NewYorkHeraldTribune, fiendishly cut, so that my literary style seems just too awful, &&&& but never mind. You of course will pardon all the crap, but I had to say something interesting for New York. Ah well.

Richard Thoma writes Ch.-Henri Ford is to be in Paris. No for him. No for his whole crowd. They don't know a circumflex from a dactyl. They haven't the manners of goldfish being fed. They have no sense of values, of proportion. They are snobs without the slightest excuse. All they have is good taste, good business sense and immense egos. Hum.

Bernard Faÿ writes from Budapest where he says tea is bad and Bach is bad, but coffee is good and chocolate too and swimming and wine and women. Do you know him? I like him. I should like to meet Cassou and Camille. I have read some things of hers in Bifur etc . . . Must close. It has not one redeeming feature. Well yes, the fresh air. I forgot.

TO BRUCE MORRISSETTE
———————————◆———————————
July 1931
Creuse

i fear i am merely lazy. nothing can induce me to start on the chorales i must do before august first. you write so seldom and at such brevity that i feel slighted which is rather good. call me up someday at the manor if you are in town. you remember the number. remember september? think of the provinces there are yet to be visited. and one gets about so well these days what with gasolinewagons and railroad conveyances. corrèze, cantal, ardèche, drôme, gers, tarn, ariège, landes, lozère, aveyron, lot. think how new such territory is. think how many explorations can be made into these wildernesses. think of the largest cities in each place being respectively tulle, aurillac, privas, valence, auch, albi, foix, mont-de-marsan, mende, rodez, and cahors. think. i think especially of gers,which has cities named samatan, saramon, condom, mogar, le houga, gondrin. i feel life would be four dimensional there and thick and unheard of. shall go unearthing some day down in tarn, shall collect ferns in gers, quartz in corrèze, shall try to discover new kinds of mustard in drôme, sample the waters in parts of cantal, sleep in landes, weep in lozère, wander across aveyron looking at the sky, and eat a great deal in ardèche. as for ariège and lot, they can go to hell. (i feel that in ain one ought to pick daffodils, but you know how hard it is to find them in july.) creuse is lovely, rocky, farviewy. aaron writes from berlin of riots and banks all being stopped up. he says it is frightful. but he is always sociallyminded and there's no helping it. you scoundrel. p u i d m t . a l h n e i h. there is a swell sort of enigma for you, rapscallion. roses are still in bloom, but the rain is assommant. and the child comes in saying alos, voualle à la meth? th'est l'habitude. there is none. no cave of jade.

TO JOHN WIDDICOMBE

July 1931
Bilignin

I was surprised by the rapid delivery of your letter. it seemed as though I had just written to you. but now that summer is here, and so well here by now, time goes past quickly and the weeks melt into each other. I spent the holidays in paris with thoma and charles-henri ford and the fireworks were worth it and the colonial exhibition was crowded. at the chateau in the creuse I did a lot of solo tramping about the rolly countryside, deciding important issues as always. my thoughts become more and quite like strata of rock. there are only two or three actual varieties and they repeat themselves in alternation when they please. it is a suffering. the country here is quite the most lovely in france, and all of gertrude's books have been on it: an acquaintance with description, the george hugnet one, lucy church amiably, and now an entire suite of plays, the first one of which is called: madame récamier, an opera. 50 typewritten pages. it is very beautiful and we take rides all about each day. she has a new ford and the same dog. her friend is embroidering a tapestry that picasso drew for her when he was here last weekend, and it is pretty. when aaron comes next week he will stay a day or so and then we shall go to the côte d'azur and see some really frightful people like kay boyle, robert mc almon, laurence vail, antheil, and

some perhaps amusing ones like bob brown who does the readies and his mother.
no, doesn't do his mother. maybe cocteau at toulon, stravinsky at nice, picasso
at antibes, probably not. dear john: . . . are you in the center of life? because
i am not yet. are the days long or short? what are dreams? is correspondence
facile? at tea this afternoon there were guests and gs read to us from her poems
and then talked splendidly about just where she came in in literature. and what
a help. what a help. her things become realer than chairs when she reads them.
lyric, thoughtful. take care of the sense and the words will take care of themselves,
said carroll, and she says there is nothing in her work but sense and she cares
not a whit for the words or sounds as sounds.

speaking of georgianna king, she said she had written her that you were to
visit her but that you never arrived or such a thing.

showing her sense, she repeated time and again for the two women who had
come from chicago to see her and shaw in europe "do orange mushrooms grow
in thickets and were they mother and daughter or only neighbors." "do you see
the sense? do you see that it is perfectly sensible? do you or not?" "do orange
mushrooms grow in thickets and were they mother and daughter or only neighbors?" "do you see? . . . . . ."

dear john: . . .

what does life do for you?
how far is the edge?
what is throbbing worth?
is it better empty?
in the morning what is it like?

,dear john.

TO BRUCE MORRISSETTE

July 1931
Bilignin

I usually write long letters because the waste of stamps seems a frightful thing.
But shall we let this be short? I have been here eight days and shall probably

be staying on five or six more. It is more than exquisite, the house and land. And Gertrude always remains fresh, and she has hundreds of beautiful tales to tell about everyone, but she doesn't know what Fuller Brushes are. Of me she says I have a rational intelligence, which is more common among Jews, and not so common among my little Christian brothers. Of Ezra Pound she has lovely things to say: the village informer, but thank god he believes the news he gives out at any rate. Of Nancy Cunard: she looks like a third grade school teacher; she has that delicate uplift they have, and of course she is hopeful. Of Kay Boyle: Horrible woman, bitter, commonplace, and her mother is a cook. Of George Antheil: an apprentice. Of Laura Riding: unfortunate. Robert Graves: sweet. Caresse Crosby: very good business woman. She made $25,000 in sanitary napkins. Bob Brown: good soul. Tzara: dead. Cocteau: soft spot in my heart. Hemingway: weakness for him. Harry Crosby: he finally learned to read, but his wife never did. Jolas: nobody will claim him. The French say he's German. The Germans say he's French. The Americans say he's European. Too bad. Brancusi: a real peasant. Of Aaron: he is probably a good teacher. Virgil Thomson: Yes, his music has something of Emerson. Hugnet: Before the flowers of friendship faded! Charles-Henri Ford: I should like to meet him. His magazine has always been so innocent, so foolish. Picasso: He has very few friends. But of course his wife is enough. Either bitter and clever or kind and clever. Of herself: I never could stand people who yell at me. Of Hunter Stagg: beautiful and frail. Of Firbank: He did it, and nobody else can. Van Vechten: He's always been sweet.

Night before last we went to the Fratellini Circus at Belley and it was all swell. Really too lovely. The most beautiful humor I have ever seen.

We take drives to distant places with celestial views. And Mont Blanc looks always like a heavily frosted cake above the mountains. The Lac du Bourget is even bluer than some of the Mediterranean, and Aix-les-Bains is quite nice with English ladies from 1900 parading about saying: "Yes." "They look like pansies," said Gertrude naïvely. There are various ruins on far hills to which one can walk alone, if one hurries. Beautiful, beautiful, beautiful, is all one can say.

En train de lire: *La Vie de Chatterton*, by Bravig Imbs. It has been translated into French because no one was interested in it in America, and it is really good.

And of course much of Gertrude herself. *Dix Portraits, Lucy Church Amiably*, which is a description of a certain view of the Marais du Rhône, 240 pages long, and Madame Récamier, a play of the countryside around here. All her recent books have been attempts at putting into words the subtlety of the paysage here, a task anyone else would have given up long ago. Really the landscapes are difficult.

Is the godmother to Hemingway's first child, and calls him Goddy, much to H.'s dismay, as he is a rabid Catholic, having been converted. (Oh so rabid.)

And oh the war! G. drove the supply wagon everywhere. I enclose picture, but do return it. The dismal lady by the door is Miss Tucker, who is here also. No one else but the maids. And the dog, the white caniche, to whom one can become attached, in spite of vows d'abord.

And oh the war! Such beautiful tales of it all, in Spain, in the Midi, by the Marne. And oh the war.

Daniel Burns yes nice enough. I never said he was épatant. The quotation is Lamartine, not Musset or Hugo. Really, will you be coming? How about a ménage together in Paris. So cheap compared to separate establishments. My money, oh! But I shall have enough some way. Yes, there is something about America, and particularly New England, that nothing can imitate. It will always be my nostalgia. You seem particularly satisfied where you are.

Widdicombe is in Virginia not studying enough. Where is I shall go home. Yes, NOW!?

The drawing not too much like you. But I have the photo. Caresse invited Hugnet out to her chateau last winter, and they went skating. She was not so hot at it, and he was good. He did 8's. She tried, fell; he laughed and laughed, skated away. She saw that he left on the next train.

Tours in near nothing.

Burns is seasiding in Denmark. August will be spent bicycling in Alsace. G. says the Alsacians are just like the Irish. They have a deep secret conviction that they're simply wonderful and that everybody hates them. Born persecutees.

Next week Aaron comes and we take bus for two days thru Basses Alpes, through Aspres, of the ants that will never descend into the valley, toooooo Nice. Guten tag.

    you will come?

July 1931
Bilignin

Having had only too much to do with the mails through the American Embassy Company, it is with a certain number of doubts that I entrust this letter to that organization. Faith, a cardinal virtue?

You are abandoning the idea of going to Biarritz, are you? It *is* rather a long distance from Alsace, and I suppose the latter will quite well fill your time. The only parts of that place I know are Saverne to Marmoutier via the Haut Barr, and from Neuf Brisach through the Vosges to Gerardmer, which is épatant. Strasbourg I merely took a tramcar through out to the Rhine, and it struck me as being frightfully strange, since it was the first city with a German feeling that my eyes had ever lighted upon.

This section I love. Ten days I have been here, and each day Miss Stein has taken me on splendid drives through the mountains, to Aix-les-Bains, to Chambéry, to St. Génix, to Vieux, where there are lovely Roman remains, and to even tinier spots on remote hills in desolate valleys, each lovelier than the last. She has shown me Lamartine's weeping place on the Lac du Bourget, Madame Récamier's dwelling, Brillat-Savarin's summer residence, and the chapel of Lucey, the heroine of her novel: Lucy Church Amiably. Incidentally, her own house here at Bilignin is as charming a place as one could ask for. High on a hillside overlooking a lovely valley, built the middle of the seventeenth century, wall, parapets, gardens, summer houses, all.

Tomorrow evening Aaron arrives from Paris at Culoz, and we are driving up to get him. He and I will probably leave next Monday from Aix-les-Bains by autobus P.L.M. for Grenoble, where we shall spend the night, having visited the Grande Chartreuse en route. Tuesday night we shall arrive at Nice, our Mecca. Our Minervana. There our address will be care of the slightly more trustworthy Nice American Express, at first, anyway, until we find our house. I expect to finish my sonata, and work on several other things I have begun recently: a piano piece, some songs for soprano, and some other stuff. Quite stuff.

I am reading an excellent biography: La Vie de Chatterton, by Bravig Imbs, one of my pet poets. I think his prose is even better, if one can judge by the translation which Miss Stein claims is first-rate. I am also getting a light on Miss Stein's own works, which become constantly more difficult. All my theories on her I discover to have been utterly vagrant. She has set me right, by much labor on her part, and now the fact emerges that there is nothing in her works save the sense. The sound, the sight, the soporific repetitions to which I had attached such great importance, are accidental, she insists, and the one aim of her writing is the superlative *sense*. "What is the use of writing," she will shout, "unless every word makes the utmost sense?" Naturally all that renders her 'opera' far more difficult, and after many hours of patient reading, I discover that she is telling the truth, and that she is wholly correct about the entire matter. And what is even more painful is that all my poems are worth a large zero. That is the end of that. And unless I undergo a great metamorphosis, there will never be any more poems.

Good-bye, and write.

TO RENA BOWLES
◆

August 4, 1931
Aboard S.S. Iméréthie II

I dropped you a postcard this morning from Marseille, but that was before the hectic time I experienced immediately afterward. It was one of those things that come (one hopes) only once in a lifetime. The ship we intended to take was to sail at eleven o'clock, and nothing opened, that is, information offices, travel bureaux, until nine. So, promptly at nine we walked into Cook's on the Canebière to find out all about it. They were not particularly helpful, and told us to hurry down to the office of the Paquet Line for information. We got into a taxi, and . . . arrived at a sumptuous place with a Moroccan doorman clad in a purple robe and a red fez, who ushered us into the luxurious office where we were to take out tickets. We waited a while and were informed that there were places still to be had, but that we would have to buy the tickets at the dock, as it was too late otherwise. At that moment, Aaron remembered that he had no money, and so we rushed out to a bank where he presented his letter of credit to no avail . . . the branch where that sort of thing was handled was up at the other end of town. We grabbed a taxi, and after being held up several times by the mobs which were gathering to see the Pacha of Marrakech arrive in the port, got to the designated bank, where he had to go upstairs and be shown into an office. There we waited and waited, and finally a gentleman came in, and taking the letter of credit, asked Aaron for his passport, which, unfortunately, he had left in his valise, still, with everything else, in the baggage at the Saint-Charles railroad station. There was consternation on the part of the French gentleman, who went out and did not return for such a long time that we decided I should go to the station for the bags and meet Aaron at the docks. I ran out and took a cab pell-mell across the crowded city to the station. As I got out, I realized to my horror that Aaron had the baggage tickets. Besides the four pieces of baggage there was my typewriter which I had checked at the *consigne*. In my (more or less) agony I lost the ticket for that somewhere as I rushed around the station among the Chinese and Arab soldiers. By that time it was about 10:30. I finally took a taxi and told the chauffeur to go to the . . . bank, whose name I had forgotten, but whose address by some miracle I remembered. Suddenly I decided Aaron would be just about gone by the time I could get back, so I changed directions and went to the docks. When we arrived I was sent to the end of the pier, where they advised me to go on board the ship if I wanted to buy a ticket. On board Aaron was not, and had not been, so I waited around nearly ten minutes, which needless to say seemed like ten hours, for him to arrive. He came in all smiles, having realized that he had the baggage tickets, and having been already to the station and gotten everything save my poor typewriter. When he heard that story he nearly collapsed. I had an idea that perhaps the boat would be late in getting off, so I asked the purser about it, and he referred me to a director of the company who was just coming down to see the ship off. I explained my plight to him, and he went up to see the captain. When he came down, he said the boat would sail at 11:30 sharp. That was great news, so I ran back out to the taxi, which was still waiting on the dock, and told him to rush to the station, as it was then just eleven. Just as we got to the foot of the hill that leads up to the station, he stopped, and groaned: Je suis crevé! which meant merely a flat tire, and when I got out and looked, I saw that the rim was right on the pavement. I ran on to the station, and as I was entering the checkroom, a porter ran up to me asking if I had lost my ticket. I sighed yes, and he gleefully explained that he was the lucky finder. We went in to the counter, and got the typewriter without difficulty. I had been planning to try to get it by showing the key to it which was in my pocket, and telling of the maps which I had inside the case. But that was unnecessary. Back to the dock, where Aaron was all worried again, as he could not buy the tickets because the purser had left, and they would not allow us on the boat without a ticket apiece! It was then 11:30 and no purser was visible. I have no idea how long it was before he came, and when he heard where we were headed for he looked surprised, and informed us that the boat did not stop at Tangier. That was nearly

the last straw, but we persisted, and discovered that it did stop at Ceuta, in
Spanish Morocco, and that we could take an autobus from there to Tangier.
So we bought the tickets for Ceuta, and had our baggage put in our cabin . . .
(not the cabin we had reserved at the Paquet office: that order had gone completely
astray) and installed ourselves. The trip takes about 90 hours or perhaps a little
more. The sun is boiling over the sea, which is calm as Seneca. We stop at
Oran en route, and I hope it is during the day, as I should love to see the port.
Supper is ready, and I shall continue later.

POSTCARD TO JOHN WIDDICOMBE
_____◆_____

August 12, 1931
Tangier

here I shall live until the eucalyptus leaves all fall and it starts to rain across
the strait. It is unbelievably lovely here and the sea is peacock feather blue. The
rest is whiter than Jesus's soul, so white the eye's pupils are pained to grow tiny
enough. Little lizards, and spiders three inches. c/o American Legation. Tangier,
Morocco.

TO BRUCE MORRISSETTE
_____◆_____

August 13, 1931
El Minza Palace Hotel
Tangier

nearly a week we have been here. i should not mind a year. perfect place to
live, save for the paludisme, a fever which is said to get one after so long. think
of the island off the croatian coast called krk, another called pag, others named
vis, brac, hvar, mljet! for some strange reason the letters l and j were not made
to follow each other in that fashion. even on the typewriter they don't fall correctly
one after the other: mljet.

we landed at ceuta, which is plain spain. bright blue and pink and green and
white and palmgarlands and flowers and waves rolling in from the blue sea. it
is quite a new place and everyone is very proud of it. the hôtel de ville was built

only four years ago and looks like the paramount lobby with its urn and marble staircases.

after innumerable difficulties which it only pains me to recall, we have managed to get a villa far on the mountain, with a treehidden garden and even a lodge by the gate to the road. the furniture is being carted out today, the furniture which we have been compelled to buy rather than rent and which we shall sell at auction when we leave. the piano is not as bad as i had feared. the house is swell, with palms and olives waving in the secondstory windows, and a view toward the mountains far away south. there is a cliff out across the road which falls into the strait of gibraltar, as peacockcolored as any mediterranean, and it is a long way down, so the waves one can see crawling in make no sound at all. there is the strange side to staying there, what with the utterly immense spiders we discovered in corners before the three moorish women went out to clean the place out. never will one see such large arachnidae again, i daresay, save perhaps the tarantulas in the berlin zoo. the plantlife is no less amazing, with cacti growing as weeds all about, and as many varieties as there are of weeds, it seems. we have an arab to keep house, and god knows what else he will keep before we realize it.

the town is too beautiful for words. like no dream one could have of a place where streets are absolutely indistinguishable from hallways. it is often necessary to walk into a house to tell whether the street is the hallway or the hallway a street. the sky disappears for long stretches at a time, and the walls are of tile. overhead are immense beams for the ceiling. it will take weeks to learn all of it.

when do we finish? we have the villa until october 15. have you any possible way of coming over to live free? if you could come early enough, it would make it worth while. there are ten rooms, bath, kitchen, pantry, all one needs. and i should be too épaté to hear it was possible. there are always ships sailing for gibraltar and always ships from there to here. if there is any possible way of getting over, come quickly, and collect your thoughts here. fare on a freighter would be from $70 to $90, I should say.

the postal is from java, and is like the music.

but try, try

TO DANIEL BURNS

August 1931

Tangier

Your letter arrived today, and by sense Gertrude Stein means just that. Signification. The same sort of sense one expects to find in Carlyle, or Thackeray. Of course, as she points out, it is very subtle: the sense of the motion between the sense made by various seemingly unrelated sentences.

The heat here is like that of a Turkish bath. It is utterly delightful, and it is permanent. There is never any objectionable let-up that makes one so conscious of it all when it returns. Steady, hot, dry weather, with a sun that burns a white hole in the ultramarine sky, with a moon that is like the sun when it is full.

Sometimes there is music being sung from a distant part of the mountain, and often there are complicated drum rhythms that continue hours at a stretch. We live at the top of the cliffs over the Strait of Gibraltar, and Spain is always clearly visible for a stretch of 100 km. along its sandy bluffs, across the blue expanse. The countryside is blotched with cacti of all varieties, and the roads are narrow and fenced in by waving walls of a sort of bamboo that grows fifteen feet or so in height. Our villa is big enough for 10 people, with spacious gardens where palms, figs, flowers, grapes, huge eucalyptus trees and dozens of other things rush about madly in the wind. And the view down south to the Riffian Mountains is épatant.

TO GERTRUDE STEIN

August 1931

Tangier

The pictures arrived the other day, and I was extremely pleased to have them. Some of them were very good. I was a bit surprised to see how indistinct the enlargement remained, but I sent it on to Mother, who will undoubtedly find no fault with it. She wrote me last week, saying she had mailed you the recipes, and I shall be disappointed if they all do not "turn out" well. Although of course it was not I who suggested that she send them. I shall be good, I shall be good. I am still gluttonous, only here it is on the good grapes and melons. There is not much else to covet.

We live up on the mountain, about three kilometers out of Tangier. Going into town is an event. Our estate is so secluded that it is rather easy to forget one is in Morocco, and to take the roosters' crowings and the donkeys' brayings as normal sounds. But when we are landed down at the Grand Socco, we are always pleasantly shocked. Our piano is still a great problem. We have had the tuner twice, and it is all out of tune. There is not another tuner nearer than Casablanca, and that is a discouraging thought. Occasionally Aaron vociferates: "Well, you'll be able to go exploring again soon, because I'm not going to stay here much longer." He is unable to work, and it upsets him. But if he goes away, I shall stay, because I like it here. And it is cheap as to living expenses. Thus, I may stay until December.

I enclose the story I mentioned to you.

We have an Arab servant who looks sad all the time. It takes him a minute and a half to go upstairs. He always sees to it that he gets his little rake-off when we send him to market for vegetables. When we question him and discover that he has paid a little more for everything than we had last week, we look surprised, and he hastens to add, always with his sad look: there were others at three francs, but they were no good. After lunch, at about two o'clock, when he has done the dishes, he comes out on the terrace and stands on one foot scratching his leg with the other, looking intently at his arms. When either of us is unable to endure it any longer, whichever one it is says: are you all finished? And he looks *terribly* sad, and shrugs his shoulders very higher, and goes on inspecting his arms. Then we send him home. He is supposed to stay until six.

Up here on the mountain there are drums that beat a lot. That worries Aaron, as he cannot get it out of his head that the Arabs are grieved about something, and are all set to go on the warpath.

When I think about Belley, it seems as though I had lived there with you for several months. Aaron is a little crazy. I asked him whether I should send a card to Mme. Simon de l'opera, and he said: certainly not! Yet when I told her I could send her a card only if I remembered it, he thought I was quite impolite. The trouble is now that I remember it only too well, only I have no desire to send it.

This letter is to both of you. Love,

Frederic

TO EDOUARD RODITI

August 1931
Tangier

i had planned to write you before the sun went down. before it went under for darkness and came back out for light. but here it is back out and there is no word from you again. Here. here it is that time of month when the year seems exceptionally short to come, and stays seeming short until another month is broken into, like another thousand franc note changed. here is the moon, rising farther behind the bay each night, having been full and now waning, and all the mountain is alone, and drums beat as i walk alone in the crying white shine between long strips of walls. dogs bark far away and i walk alone. and the road is alone. when the moon returns (for it will soon be gone), the leaves will all be gone from the figtrees, and it will be colder. especially nights. tourists will wear their tweed coats, and say it is cool tonight. i think of when we shall see each other for the first time. you will laugh, you know. i more perhaps. i always laugh. it makes me more at ease. the arabs think my laughing is ridiculous, since they never laugh without a definite reason. the drums beat all night, in rhythms that keep one awake, make one think of the heat of the sun in its pitiless beating on the hot hills. i was out for hours today under the sun, walking, and whenever i sat me down under mimosas to rest, the waves along the ground made everything dance in wriggling arabesques. even the mountains, far to the south, moved tinily and continually as i watched. the cicadas screamed all through the noontime. a boat slowly entered the strait, making towards Tarifa. but the sun has come again, and one can smile. the crisis is over, as poe would say, as i love to say, thank heaven! can one learn to discard thinking of one's self? it makes happiness sprout from under the armpits of trees, it makes scorpions dance for joy, and cliffs shudder in ecstasy. can one learn to discard one's self? the drums beat all the time. blood knocking at the door, the voice of eros, under the palms, behind the walls, by the fires at night, woven with the singing, mixed in with the pipes that shrill tunes we cannot understand, even as we climb the hill. mixed with the insects that drone. mixed with the rising crisis of our cheeks that lose their scrofulous aspect and become smooth as the plage once more, mixed with the blood beating all night in the hot room. with the fever hovering at the blinds, the ferns scraping, about which we have said so much years ago. will you ever learn the secret? shall i? do you intend to try? do i advise you to? is the world strenuous? in the café sit the stupid people, while the beggars crawl about in the gutter whining their old songs. the stars still show in the sky, and outside the town the donkeys bray and hope that god will come cantering over the sand to deliver them. i love the sun, as you say you do, and that is why i love it here. it is frightful that there is no way you can come here, rather than go to Sainte Maxime. there are cacti here just the same. and geraniums. i owe an inestimable debt to you for all your friends who have been generous to me. and for suarès's fin du grand mythe, which shines like a jewel, although you are not to tell him such a thing. i send a picture gertrude Stein snapped of me at her house last month. she also has been good to me. and when the world is good to one, what can one do but thank it and work for it? everyone is good, and i am not worthy of it. when they are all no longer good i shall think i am worthy of better treatment. write care of american legation, tangier, morocco. and tell me about the poems you sent away.

TO GERTRUDE STEIN
◆

September 18, 1931
Tangier

I was glad to hear you liked the story, and thanks for returning it to me. It's the one Mr. Titus saw no excuse for a grown man's having written. *Front*, a magazine published in Holland, sent me a copy of their no. 4 recently. They have been growing more and more populiste of late, and in this number they committed a supreme atrocity. In a beautiful romantic poem of mine all about waking up in the morning in the desert they substituted for the word: "waker" the word "worker." Poets of the world, unite!

I have been thinking of the view of the marais from the hill as we saw it on the drive past the bathing lake. It insists peacefully upon being remembered.

The piano has not been such a complete calamity. I have managed to finish my sonata and after a few more weeks of copying its parts and the instrumental score for Miss Boulanger to read I can begin to pray nights to have it played.

Mother has very kind thoughts of you, which she expresses in nearly every letter. She was pleased to receive a note from you about the recipes, and all that lacks to make her wholly happy is my return to Europe. She was thrilled to think that you liked Whittier.

Tonny is here with Anita Thompson. They are keeping house for about six dollars a month and have a maid without any nose. Their house and ours are separated by the valley of the Oued-el-Youd, and we see them only about once a week. Anita is always asleep, and Tonny is quite bored. They intend to go to the Congo next spring. It seems they gave an extremely successful cocktail party in Paris last winter. I suppose they are resting on their laurels.

Copland and I are going to Fez in October and then he returns to Berlin. I shall have so little money by then it won't matter where I go. He will lend me some until January.

The sun is always wonderful. And it always shines all day.

TO AARON COPLAND
◆

October or November 1931
Hôtel du Béarn
Marrakech

Here enfin in M! It is not such a shock after Fez as Fez was after Tanger, but it is different enough to warrant the trip. Marvellous pink-rose-salmon-red walls and houses, and high date-palms in clusters everywhere, with the large mountains always visible in the background. The Djemaa-el-Fna is like the Makina at Fez the afternoon I lost my wallet, only every day, and much larger. The Ville Nouvelle is charming, full of eucalyptus and palm trees which make the long wide streets reminiscent of Nice, only the buildings are all in shades of rose to brown, so there is never the glare. The souks are like those in Fez, only more primitive, with matted branches overhead rather than the sort of bamboo-cane in Fez. The streets are a bit muddy and the skins much darker. Harry [Dunham] wants to adopt the chamber boy at the hotel and take him with him wherever he goes. He wants to know my opinion. I reserve it. We are going with the owner of the hotel 250 miles through the Atlas to a military post overlooking the beginning of the Sahara. Thrill! Oooh! I found a piano to play (and a good one), in a photographer's studio, and I go at 9:30 each a.m. and work 'till lunch. Casablanca is god-awful, but *lousy*! Rabat seemed fairly decent. Meknès lovely. Harry got some sort of poison food there and has been fasting ever since. How he keeps going sans nourriture is an enigma. He thinks one should eat once a day at most. Our boy brings us pomegranates for breakfast as an hors d'œuvre.

Our last few days at Fez consisted of a continual round of appointments with various Arabs—for lunch, tea, marriage, bathing, hunting (actually) and about everything. The bathing took place in an oasis where there were hot springs. It was all charming. Pools, some indoors, others out, connecting, where always the water was just up to one's chin. Everyone walked leisurely about, naked, with his head sticking out!

Harry's money disappears visibly, daily. I wonder how long it will hold out, inasmuch as I am living entirely on it. It is a ticklish business, living with him in such a manner. He is a bit of a wild-man, and has fits of temper which are quite irrational, but which he enjoys, quite obviously; so I never interrupt them. He is now hoping for a revolution in Germany this winter, so he can fight in it. (He hasn't decided with whom to fight.) But he is really quite mad at times. At Sefrou he went climbing about the gorge quite naked, in spite of my entreaties. At Moulay Idriss he insisted on getting out of the taxi four km. below the town, and kept the driver and me waiting an hour while he climbed up to join us. Here he beat some brats about the legs with his belt for following us in the medina. They nearly died of fright! Yesterday he bought a pair of boots to climb glaciers with. They are waterproof, hobnailed and lovely. Abdallah made him a present of a huge drum in Fez, and he carried it under his arm when he came to Marrakech. The Arabs everywhere took pains to enlighten him as to its use, saying: c'est un tambour, ça, tu sais. We had a really chic Arab meal in Fez at an actor's house. Some sort of native dramatic company which is presenting Haroun-al-Raschid at Fez and soon at Tanger. Several large courses, of which Málaga's meal was but a shadow.

We have a fairly big room with two beds, for 20 fr. for both a day. It is a bit noisy, but it has a terrace like the Ariana, and oh the moon and the incredibly high mountains. Really high I mean, and like a wall behind the town.

Harry is yelling from the court.

Write to Tanger.

All my love.

TO AARON COPLAND

November 1931
Marrakech

Harry has run off and here I am left alone again in Maroc, only this time with Cadour the Arab boy, who is more bother than help.

And worse, Mesdag, the Hollandais, actually spied me out the other day, and

I have found no effective way of escaping his visits quotidiennes, although to date he has succeeded in extracting exactly one franc "for potatoes." Fortunately a friend of Cadour's, whose identity I have never been able to trace farther than the knowledge that he is the "fils du Caïd," is driving us both out to his farm in the bled tomorrow, so I shall be spared the pain until Monday.

But is Harry fou? Not all I had counted on when I wrote you will materialize, financially speaking, mainly because of Cadour, who will be expensive to transplant from here to Paris. But Harry left ample for that. Simply, not for me. But, but, that is all right. He is so utterly scatterbrained, and so insisted that this boy was the one essential thing in life, that his life here was ruined (as I daresay it was, after Harry threatened the former employer with the revolver), that I allowed him to convince me that a slight duty of mine was to stay. Although this time, mon cher, I am not eager for Maroc, and wish bloodily and heartily for Paris, and would give a lot to be there at the moment. All at once Maroc fell like a Grand Guignol curtain, or a bride's first sponge cake.

How does it happen you haven't written since Oct. 11th? Have I written myself too rarely? I suppose. But do you know how busy we two have been? Do you know how we went across the Atlas to the Sahara and were ordered back by the commanding colonel, how on the way back (I shudder still) the Tichka Pass (2100 m.) was thick mud, puddles, old bus, no treads, slipped to the *edge* of a precipice that will forever chill me to the marrow at thought of it, how I jumped out and remained on the running-board for hours, how Harry went more & always more crazy, packing up to leave, the second day at Fez, going naked at Sefrou, scattering money, returning to Marseille 4 days on deck with rien but dates & nuts? But write Tanger. Concert? Ah, mon cher, la vie elle-même est folle!

TO BRUCE MORRISSETTE

♦

November 1931
Marrakech

Your letter was lovely — I sent it on to Gertrude because she asked of news from you in a letter which came the other day. "and what is the news of the french young gentleman whose letter I liked . . ."

I have not written because in the last month life has become like the end of Anna Livia Plurabelle. But when I get back to Tanger and my typewriter I shall.

Fez I shall make my home some day! Marrakech too is a sort of sunset with Cannon-shot city. Pink walls, red walls, palms, magnificence, ostriches, mountains with snow, cobras, camels, drums and murders. And I went across the Atlas on a produce-truck into the war zone and down and down to the Sahara. The next a.m. the Colonel happened to be making a tour of inspection, spied my unfamiliar sort of face, thought I was a German spy, sent me away on the first vehicle into the Atlas again, where it had poured, was cold. The treads of the "vehicle" were all worn smooth, the roads muddy, the valleys eight and nine thousand feet below, my heart in my throat. The thing skidded, I jumped out. To the edge. Arabs (no whites) went to get weeds for friction under the wheels. Four times to the edge. I on running board! Fifteen hours to Marrakech. Beautiful to remember.

Here the odors in the dark souks are gorgeous. Another life. I have bought eight packages of things to burn later: sandalwood in large knots to be splintered, tib, nid, myrrh, hasalaba, and others I don't remember. Also the oil of flowers in glass tubes at 2 fr. & 3. You shall smell them all. I use them in tiny but efficacious bits on ends of cigarettes. I have babouches, oui, & three silver rings, one from the Soudan, shoes of goatskin in white and buff, even cushions I could not resist. Tout ça pour Paris. Enfin, un Arabe discovered by Dunham who will accompany me to Paris to keep me comfortable, to carry things, to cook. Who will believe I am penniless. On that score, comment je dirige ça? Fate keeps on happening. One never knows. No liaisons, rest assured. Besides, there are no milliners in Maroc. From Tonny's I shall write. In Paris I begin by stopping with Bernard Faÿ, who is *swell*. To hell with this letter.

TO AARON COPLAND
———————————◆———————————
November 28, 1931
Café des 2 Magots
Paris

Your letter arrived, ported by the Arab, who is pretending to stay with the Countess. I am at Faÿ's for a while. I suppose by now you have Virgil's letter and are furious with me. But and so on. I am quite ready to go to Boulanger. Only he presented such good reasons why I should go also to Dukas and tell at the end of a certain time which I preferred. A few day's waiting.

Harry comes après-demain. Why I don't know. The Arab has gotten in with

André Gide, and visits him at his home tomorrow! I met him hier at the Galeries Vignon, and he seemed kindly-disposed, but Bernard says that belies his true character. I shall tell you about the Arab's finding Gide. It is extremely rigolo. Met Imbs, Julien Green, Sir Francis Rose, Mme. Picabia, etc. Gertrude is fachée because I stayed with Tonny, whom she detests at the moment. I daresay he doesn't know it. We are going to see André Maurois demain. Also Gertrude, who sent me a card today saying she hoped I was still with her, whatever that may have meant.

Yes, I was all upset about the parts not having arrived, so I cabled to find out. I hope there are no more drawbacks.

Are you going to London the 10th? I want to go when you go. Suarès is going at about that time, & asked me to go with him. Virgil also, but Suarès has priority.

Write. Love.

TO DANIEL BURNS

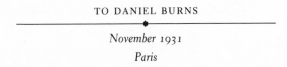

November 1931
Paris

My mother had written me of Miss Anna [Hoagland]'s death. I was extremely sorry. As a matter of fact, I find it very difficult to believe. Only when I get back and have visited the house and seen it without her will I be able thoroughly to believe it. And I daresay even then I shall feel she is merely out for a walk. Do you know that feeling?

Much happens here in Paris. I see Gertrude Stein often. Her teas are often amusing. I even visit Virgil Thomson with whom she is furious. And at a vernissage the other day I met André Gide, Julien Green and Bravig Imbs. There is worse about Gide, however. My poor Arab, whom I soignéed all the way from Marrakech through Spain to here, met the scoundrel the other day in the street, and was invited to his house, where he was given silken robes, djellabas etc. Fortunately the naïf child forgot the gifts when he left. But the scandal is rampant! I shall tell all some day!

My sonata will be performed 16 Dec. in London or did I tell you. I am going over a week early to rehearse it. Harry Dunham arrived tonight from Dresden. Write chez Lavillatte. I am not staying there!!

December 10, 1931
London

I have crossed the little water that is mightier in its human gap than an ocean, and fallen again into the great pit of London. The chalk cliffs at Newhaven were all greyer through the dawn rain than any human eyes could be, and white gulls fluttered out of the black wind into the vague lights of the boat, and seemed to cry when their flight crossed the boat, but to be silent when they went back into the darkness again. There is little change, save that Piccadilly grows more and more like a sprawling Times Square, running down Haymarket and Coventry and Regent, all garish and burning with neon. It doesn't fit. In New York, the great planes of the lifting buildings can carry it off, in London it stays right there, on the ground, on your mind, on your hands, and you can't lift it. I am sad for this.

Paris left me empty. I look only, everywhere, all hours, for that new way of looking at the human thing, the heart, I suppose, of the world, and I found it not there. I was childish to look for it. Only the echo of the beat, not the strong pulse.

At any rate, it was good of you to lead me about by my nose, and to let me meet so many people. As you know, I like to meet everyone in the world at least once.

What do you feel you are taking back to America with you, from Europe? Is there something, like a pocket piece or a lucky coin, that you feel you have your hands on? I hope you find something back in America. I think there's something to be found, rolling down the gutter on Second avenue at six in the morning, before the sweepers get it. I hope you'll do something with the mss. novel, too. Or write another that will have clarity, the cleverness not of life but of eyes.

I drag off to Oxford in a couple of hours, having found that it began yesterday, and will settle down to live the life of almost a gentleman for a while. I sweat and toil inwardly to make a unity out of the phases of the earth there, but it is equally complicated by a vacuum of thinking and a lack of plumbing! I despise too much—the literary and art talk, the clever quips, the intellectual hatreds. Literature has never lived on literary talk, and literary acquaintances. I want to take every poet and shove him down into the dung-heap, kick all his literary friends in the ass, and try to make him see that writing is not word-bandying, like Stein, and the thousand legions of her followers, but an emotion seen through the mind, or an intellectual concept emotionalized, and shaping its own expression. You can't write from a literary vacuum, and all of Paris, I felt, was trying to. They get all tangled up in trying to write cleverly and as no one else has, and get lost in the timber hills of their effort. I can't help thinking Shakespeare never worried about writing a new kind of blank verse, just went ahead instinctively and did it.

But hold, enough.

Write me, from New York, and even from Paris if you have time, as to where the wind of yourself is blowing, up what dark streets. Again, with much thanks and thought of you.

TO BRUCE MORRISSETTE
◆

January 1932
Albergo Club Alpino
Clavières, Italy

These empty days. How do you spend them? Not writing letters to me. You write less often than anyone. What are your plans? The argent amasses? Croatia or Corsica or Basses Pyrénées? Or Perpignan, by which Gertrude swears. The eternally rediscoverable, mysterious countryside. Below sealevel, hot, artichokes, owls and peacocks. Yes, Freddy, go and explore that part. It's a strange part and there's no other quite like it. Of course not for your health. But for a while. And thereabouts: Rivesaltes, Vingrau, Estagel, Thuir, Elne, Sournia, le Barcarès, Velmanya, Céret and Banyuls. January makes an apocalyptic limbo. My Corona is broken, having uttered a heartrending shriek one damp horrible afternoon in Tanger. The catgut in back broke. In Paris André Gide smacked his lips, invited the Marrakech voyou I had imported via Madrid to his house "pour déguster de bons gâteaux, mon p'tit." And each Sunday thereafter: "M'sieu Boule, le vieux m'a invité chez lui. On va rigoler bien. Il est très gentil, la pauvre."* Julien Green arched his eyebrows. Gertrude sighed with contentment at the lovely idea. Sir Francis Rose giggled. In London Roditi chuckled, and I was drunk at eighty different naice cocktail-parties. Virgil Thomson arrived. Aaron from Berlin. Lady Cunard declined, likewise Lady Colfax. Edith Sitwell left for

---

* "to taste some excellent pastries, m'dear." And each Sunday thereafter: "M'sieur Boule, the old guy invited me to his place. We'll have lots of fun. He's very nice, poor thing."

the country. Middleton Murry, George Moore and T. S. E. communed with Jesus near Oxford. Mary Crouch gave vicious and resplendent evenings. The concert had a limited success with its limited audience. George Cattaui of the Egyptian Legation knowing reporters introduced me: scandalous articles! Even a reporter! My picture taken in Tanger for the Evening Standard. All about the Bible, pagan strains with an oboe. Others: ya gotta have more skill to put that stuff over on us! Aaron's piece: meaningless and painfully discordant! Virgil's made a great stir: headline: Queerest Stein Song! Subhead: Runaway Composer who never saw a Bible. That means so much to England. It seems I left home at age of six and went to Paris, following a scene with my cruel father who was jealous of my immense talent and who ordered my piano removed from the house. Not until I was twenty did I see a Bible, whereupon I stated I was thrilled by it. Reporter telephoned asking for interview, came, fired questions: Has your father always been cruel to you? Just how did the Bible affect you the first time . . .

[Later]

Les Rois Mages

Mont Genèvre, France

Alors, en France après Londres, en France pour Noël, Miró exhibit, met him at Gertrude's, swell & naïf, unconscious, like a realestate agent or necktie salesman. He drew me a map of Spain that looked like any one of his abstract designs. Harry Dunham visited Gertrude and she took him on as dogwasher, once a week. Advised him to go to Man Ray, which he did. M. R. charged him 10,000 francs to study until March with him; so now he is installed with M. R. & Lee Miller, the erstwhile mistress, heroine of Cocteau's film "Le Sang d'un Poète." He took a large studio for him, his sister and me on the Quai Voltaire, bought two immensest of Miró's new creations. Now apartment waits for me, with good concert grand, but I am ill. Markevich bashful, too mondain, too redolent of the last rose of Diaghilev, his music a bit Hindemith, also Sacre. Had lunch with Rieti, of "Le Bal" done with Chirico. He knows his orchestra, sure thing. Visited Cocteau, who had a nervous crisis, sent a Chinaman to the door. The floor was littered with valises and knives in leather scabbards. Bravig Imbs is like cake. Jolas back on transition, which ought to be out now. Djuna Barnes & Ch. Henri Ford stalked into Gertrude's one day. Bernard Faÿ vomited at sight of them, was elected to the Collège de France: Franco-American History. At a cocktail party chez Roditi amid halls of mirrors and room of zebra met Léon-Paul Fargue & Robert Desnos, also Allanah Harper, ed. of Échanges. She seemed dull. Desnos nice. Max Jacob, who looks horrible. Tchelitchew impossible. There are few enough to know in Paris, je t'assure. Milhaud is as fat as several Whitemans, grins. Desormières gave Satie's "Parade" a month ago. I missed it. Thoma is ill in Nice. Gertrude is still impressed by your letter. "How's his French? He knows how to write English. Oh, yes, he knows the language all right." And each day I go. "How's the friend in Virginia. When's he coming over?" And what can be said but: "in June"? After Christmas I became mad and ran away with Anne Manheim, with her to Italy, but got ill. Am still ill. Here the snow is deep as hell, and the air is quiet. Rocks line the border between France & Italy. We come over to France for cigarettes, and to post letters. I work on a string trio, what the hell. Before I left Paris Virgil played & sang all the opera: Five Saints in Four Acts. Swell, swell, really. Capital Capitals almost as good. Dunham sent the Arab, Abdelkader, back to Casablanca last week. I wager he got no farther than Tanger, inasmuch as he has a soft spot in his heart for Anita, Tonny's galfriend. Certainly he would stop there. "C'est une jolie putain, Anita, mons ami." Rather a slump in art at the moment. What's exciting? After I brought the little idiot all the way from Marrakech. He was enamored of Sevilla and the oranges one could pick above one's head as one walked all along the main streets. He called it Lillia, which seems to mean something nice in Arabic. There never was such a difference between two villages 2 km apart as there is between Clavières and Mont Genèvre. At C every peasant speaks Italian, no French. Here, contrariwise. They have never been allowed to cross the border. Besides, it is a natural boundary, a col.

Write at 17, Quai Voltaire, Paris 6e

Pigeons on the grass alas. —Gertie

TO AARON COPLAND

January 1932

Paris

Your letter came about two days ago and there is no need to say I was extremely glad to have it, as it provided a part of the muchneeded discussion I felt I wanted to have about it all. It is rather difficult to be among a great many people and to feel rotten and not be able to tell anyone so, and why. For the T.B. myth Harry's prattlings I daresay finished long ago. He and his sister are at least threefourths mad as hatters. A way of being mad is to contradict one's self, a practice they both seem to have . . . etc. . . .

There was even more. I had to have an operation in Turin, and then I stayed in the mountains two weeks. The same day I came back to Paris, I went to bed with acute tonsillitis. The doctor said it would be impossible to remove the tonsils for two months. And every day I have a swollen neck and can't go out, and gargle, and can scarcely walk certain days after *piqûres*, and yes I am miserable. For one thing, it is difficult to work here. In the middle of the afternoon the concierge came up and asked me to stop playing the piano as people had complained. It is as bad as Berlin. Where can one go where one can play? And then I have exactly two hundred francs left, and the Dunhams have made it quite clear they will give not another penny. The sister has gone to London for two weeks and Harry has a lot of American friends and never comes home for meals, so I am obliged to get dressed and go out to eat. It is arranged that way more or less exprès so that I will have to buy my own meals. And when in hell my money is coming I have no idea. I don't hear from home at all. I have a slight suspicion the concierge hasn't my name straight, or something like that. She probably slips up occasionally.

I received a bill the other day from Boulanger for the two times I went to see her when she discussed prices with me and looked at my sonata. The letter said: to settle up accounts. But she is crazy. We never came to an agreement on any price and she knows it. I haven't seen her since the one time just after I got back from London, and her last words were: I haven't time now to talk about that. Ah well, but I hope she doesn't expect me to send her $30 for those two talks.

Virgil says I ought to go and live in Rome and see Casella, rather than write him. Rome merely because the weather here keeps me eternally sick. But I am afraid it would be just as damp there. Good God, but what a waste of time I am perpetrating and what can I do? My fury at being ill has abated, and I accept it as one of the conditions under which I must live, but when I put all the conditions together, the fury returns sometimes. I feel as though I were already entered into an impasse, and the $800 will only take me to the blind ending. Beyond that there will be nothing. That is a feeling, but I admit I am unable to believe it most of the time.

Much of the time, too, I spend wondering how in hell I got sick, how long I've been that way, &&. And how long it will be that way, and why it hurts, and several dozen other wonderings.

I wrote the fifth group of songs during the last four days. It is about a maiden walking in the platinum forest, while slow white tones rise from her throat. I am going to make ink copies of the group and ship them to you, hoping you will give them to Mrs. Reis with a nod of approval. I think they mark the close of a "period" in me. Even the new ones are a hangover of an enfantin spirit, you know? to go with the words.

I have no idea whether Lederman ever received my translation of Petit's article or not. And à propos, I never saw a copy of the M.M.[*Modern Music*] wherein was our gorgeous article about Oxford. Does it look convincing?

Harry has gone to Gertrude's enough times during my six weeks of seclusion to make her think I am an idiot, and so I don't go to see her any more. He has also made a great friend of Bravig Imbs, who also looks at me now very askance. I can't imagine exactly what he says to the various people.

This is a difficult winter and I see very little use in anything, but it is probably because I am ill, and so there is nothing to do but to get well. Hell. I have been to one concert, and heard La Création du Monde, which was faultless, I thought. But no, I don't want to see anybody. I don't know. I don't know.

TO AARON COPLAND

———————————————————◆———————————————————

March 1932
Algiers

Your letter was a great success, particularly coming as it did when I was absolument sans le sou, during the time the banks were closed and I had no way of getting any money and was living on three-franc meals picked up here and there, and buying them with 100 fr. the patronne lent me with suspicious frowns. At least, I felt, when this is over New York won't be as bad a poison. And so I do hope you will find some sort of lodging. It sounds hopeful; is it? And then I am épaté one will give the flute sonata, only I want to hear it myself some day. I can see that in the end I shall be forced to acknowledge U.S.A. as my home if only to know what sort of music I write. Can't go on forever this way. Who is going to play the flute part? As to my return, it ought to be before June. In the Summer where can one go? Does the MacDowell Colony accept paying guests, or does one have to be invited, or elected, or what? What are you doing this saison estivale? I am leaving here immediately and going probably to Menorca, if not there, why then to the Canaries, of course.

Life here is nice. I sit in dark cafés smoking kif and haschich, and drinking tea and goatsmilk, and we take walks with the lambs, to put them to graze on the sides of hills. The flute here is very lovely, terribly pan, and played with expertise. Sometimes we have teaparties, with several guitars and drums going. Alger is not all ville nouvelle, as you said, by any means, only one has to stay a month to find that out. But the Kasbah is even more, much more, native than that of Tanger, and it is swell. Recently I stayed in Constantine several days with Ramani, an Arab boy who invited me to his home to live and it was all nice. Not like Morocco at all, because I met his mother and sisters, unveiled, and we all made merry together, with dancing and music. (I can count to a million in Arabic now! Isn't that nice?) I can only write long letters when I am in the sun. Then it makes no difference how long it takes to finish. Except that at the moment I am beginning to get hot. I have a wonderful oil, made by Molinard at Grasse, which when applied browns one just like roast chicken.

Well, I went to Biskra, and was disappointed like hell, so I left for farther south, to Touggourt, where it is worthwhile. Negroes, and piles of red grasshoppers to eat and not much else, but long streets completely dark always, where one bumps into every manner of frightful creature. Many mad people, and leprous things like spiders which crawl about eating the grasshoppers others toss them. You know how it is, like Tanger, only really serious. The streets burrow about inside the houses, and the light never gets there, but at least it is not hot under there. And then I took a nice camel trip across the desert, sleeping in bordjes nights, arriving at El Oued, a glorious town in the center of the region of great dunes. And then a bit over a week in Tunisia, which is all right, but less exciting than Algeria and Morocco.

Bernard Faÿ wrote me an amusing letter from London saying he would always be my friend. He is extremely nice to me, always. Böske Antheil wrote me an amusing letter saying America was sympathetic at the moment . . . Amelia Dunham writes many amusing letters, but what she says in them is more than I am able to tell. Sometimes she sends checks, but I receive only half of them, because she gets the addresses mixed up. And then her father wrote me and seemed quite put out that both Harry and Amelia should be turning over their money to me, and he asked me please to put my demands to him personally. That would be very dull, naturally.

Another amusing letter is from my servant in Ghardaïa, the rascal, who never sent a sou. I enclose it. His franchise: devant mes amis, is too wonderful.

Also a card: Les avant-coureurs de l'Orage au Désert à Laghouat! All the damned furs for nothing, if you read the card well. A great sack of stinking jackal-skins to lug about with me . . .

I have an Arab friend, Ali, who has a canary in a cage which he takes with him everywhere. Even out into the country so that it may get the fresh air. Tu entends? Comme il chante bien. Toi, tu n'y comprends rien. Moi non plus; mais lui, il comprend bien ce qu'il chante là . . . La putain sa mère, écoute comme il chante bien, tu sais bien qu'il m'a coûté cent francs. C'est cher, mais qu'est-ce que tu veux, et puis il ne mange pas grand'chose. Li zoiseau. Li zoiseau.*

You never mention Tiger Tiger.

And Good God I hope you can, will, find some sort of place for me to live when I return. Say the end of May. Write. Tell Theo to. Write. Love.

TO AARON COPLAND

—◆—

May 1932
Café de la Bidassoa
Tangier

This is going to be what I shall call an unsatisfactory letter, but I suppose nearly any letter would be that way after the long period of time which has gone by since the most recent letter from me to you. As a matter of fact, I have no idea when the last one was. I know I waited for a reply and did not receive it until last week, when two letters arrived at once, forwarded by Suarès. But of course such things are the unessentials in correspondence, and so I can let them drop. And it must be admitted I could have written even not having received a letter, but pride —

So you rec'd my songs and my flute thank God, and you do think the flute needs a 3rd part, as did I, but Virgil said it was not necessary. At any rate, I have ideas for a 3rd. I am a bit surprised, very pleasantly so of course, to learn you like the 1st. As to middle part of the 2nd, I wonder whether the piano part should not be marked pp, as the flute must be 3 times as strong. Not the piano part, but the right hand, might be marked soft, as the bass & flute should be well-heard. Really, I like the part all right, only I am dissatisfied with the

---

* You hear? How well he sings. You, you don't understand any of it. Me neither; but him, he knows exactly what he's singing . . . Son of a bitch, just listen to how well he sings, you know he cost me a hundred francs. That's a lot, but what can you do, and anyway, he's not a big eater. Ah, the birds . . . the birds.

transition from theme one to it, particularly the little island of 2 notes in the flute: a fifth, halfway through the bridge.

The next thing I send you ought to be done by July. I have been working on it since March. I realize now that my "Problem" will never be solved by steady work, as you insisted. It consists of a few other things besides scholastic paresse. It is rather unfortunately larger, a non-musical, non-literary preoccupation, of which music is the tangible manifestation. But still it remains as vague as can be. But less disturbing.

I have now spent a year, as you see, without a lesson. It seems to me a bit silly, but I have never been so mentally upset, so ready to die, so ready to live.

Mother sent me the invitation to Yaddo's fest, but I noticed my name was not there. Did they (you) give the songs? Were they too difficult?

I object heartily to Paris and have no desire to go on living there. The entire group of inmates is extremely annoying. I visited the Marquise de Casa Fuerte with Virgil and swore to myself never to go again. I think it is the life, the schedule of life of Paris that upsets me. I still insist I do not want to live in any city, but as far as possible from all of them.

de Falla is pleasant, at any rate. I went to see him in Granada six weeks or so ago. And Claude McKay, despite the propaganda sent out by Anita & Tonny, is charming. Tanger is the same. Mrs. Ironsides triumphantly greeted me with the news that our house on the mountain is rented for ten years, so that if I wanted it I should have to wait a long time to get it. The old Jew in the Petit Socco is gone, but the same awful shoeblacks are there. Ricardo turns his head always when he sees me coming. But I have many Arab friends there, in Fez, everywhere now, so I am assured of places to stay if I ever return! Tonny is in Rotterdam, Anita has a nice house all alone by the cliffs on the Marshan. Mr. Bonich still rides alone in his Buick. The Antheil who we decided must have been under the impression he was beautiful and who used to follow us up to the taxis at night, has disappeared. The little child who came with colored skullcaps to the music-café the first night, always approaches me seriously, shakes hands and then asks for a penny.

There are undoubtedly many things I have omitted, but I am tired, and I send all my love. Write at Suarès's always.

TO RENA BOWLES
—————————◆—————————

June 1932
The American Hospital of Paris
Neuilly

I am up in the ward now. At first it was difficult to sleep, but they brought
me some wax affairs to put in my ears, which worked wonders. Dayaftertomorrow
I leave. Bruce is coming out to help me with my baggage, which is all here,
including my trunk. He may go to Grenoble University for July, in which case
I shall accompany him, as Grenoble is a place I like, right in the Alps, not far
from Briançon. I wrote to Gertrude Stein to see what she thought of me, and
it seems we are still on excellent terms. It was Amelia who did her best to break
off, or up, our friendship. So if we go, we may stop off a day there on the way.
Grenoble is only a four-hour drive, or so, from Belley. Suarès wrote me the
climate at Annecy was perfect: cold, rainy, and damp; just what he needed. But
I replied that it was not quite what I was looking for. And the prices are not
very low. All the same, write me there, as it is quicker than as if you address
me care of him in Paris, as it only is forwarded to Annecy, and then to me.
The address is Aux soins de Carlo Suarès, Abbaye, Talloires, Haute-Savoie,
France. Later I may go on down to Monte Carlo, where it will cost me very
little to live, and where I shall have a grand piano at my disposal, and the sea
right under the window. The invitation finally came. Only that more or less
depends on whether you find you can get a ship on the Italian Line to Villefranche. Virgil Thomson tells me they are more expensive. If they are frightfully
much more, I suppose there will be nothing to do save land at a northern port,
and I shall come up and get you. It is a trip, however, of over a thousand km.
You ought soon to be letting me know where you will land, that is to say: you
ought soon to be having your ticket. Virgil says the Hamburg-America Line is
the cheapest. I imagine they are all more or less alike. I know you will have a
wonderful trip, and all I hope is that it is sunny and calm. Miss Cowen writes
she will be here in Paris the fifth of July, so I ought to see her. The Duc de
Saint-Simon writes he will be highly honored to receive you in his house and
to make your estimable acquaintance. Mary Crouch was planning on my coming
to London during July, as I had expressed a desire earlier in the season to return
for a while. Her cousin, a girl from Boston, is staying with them, or will be.
Roditi has gone to Berlin for the summer, so I shan't be going to London, as
Mary hasn't invited me to stay there. It's rather ridiculous, as the house has

about twenty bedrooms, and plenty of servants. I think her husband has always been suspicious of me, as if I might persuade Mary to elope, or something like that. He doubtless wonders why she gave me so much money three years ago, why she had me to lunch every day when I was in London, why she gave me the use of her car and chauffeur. Indeed, I even stayed the night there at Pembroke Lodge once when she invited me to a murder-party. Jock is one of these silent Scotchmen whose thoughts one can never divine, But I think he thought I was a menace to his household. Perhaps because Mary and I would talk at length about Glenora, where he had never been, and because she wanted to read me her novel, which took hours, and which I never heard the end of. It was not bad, considering her minimum education. She had picked up a style used by Joyce twenty years ago, but which is still effective. I suppose she is still in Corsica. I enclose some pictures of a building in Calvi, Corsica. There are seven private studios within, and it is on the Mediterranean. It must be rather a nice place to live. Strange to say, I have finished the two volumes I had of Proust. I found them excellent. Most of it takes place at Balbec, on the ocean-front, only this time he is without his grandmother, and the description of his recurrent sadness, at thought of her being dead, all the way through is beautifully done. I became ambitious the other day, and wrote an article for *Modern Music*. They used to pay $20. What it is now, I don't know. Probably the same. The editor, as you know, has asked me two or three times to do some articles, and I have always shunned the task. It's an easy enough job if one has something to say, I discovered. Virgil Thomson came out yesterday and told me about my new piece. He thinks it is excellent, but as I feared, it will take complete revision, and alteration, to arrange it for a diatonic harp, which is the most common kind. For a chromatic harp it would be possible, but they are still a scarcity. So it will have to be either for harpsichord or piano. Abdelkader came out again the other day and brought with him Anne Manheim's mother-in-law. She is a rather pitiful old creature with a very good heart and not much money. She has been drifting about Europe for four or five years all alone. Her two sons are angry with her and won't write. Her older son made some sort of investments for her and then told her there was nothing left. She racks her brains trying to imagine where the money went to, but inasmuch as he did the same thing to his younger brother, Anne's husband, there is not much doubt as to where it went. I believe the father left things in the elder son's hands when he died.

I am still going on the money I received in February. Thanks to Suarès and Amelia, it has lasted. But still, I have had a lot of expenses, such as my piano and my apartment, which together cost me about 800 fr. a month, and my travelling in Morocco, hotel bills, extra railroad expenses through Spain. If I go to Monte Carlo, and come up to get you, it will make about 1000 fr extra. Although I fear the difference between the Italian Line and the others may be even greater. Whatever you do, I shall be so glad to see you, it won't make any difference. I may not work so much during July. It will depend on how I feel. Since I have been walking around I have lost the meat I was putting on in bed by dint of highpressure feeding. Now I am on a general diet, with moderation. No alcohol or sauces with pepper, etc. I shall be glad to be out. Shall go to Bruce's hotel in the Latin Quarter. I went up today to the roofgarden. It is very pleasant, with flowers all about, awnings flapping in the wind, orange wicker chaise longues and tables. It was strange to see the Eiffel Tower and Montmartre suddenly, after having been in a little America for a month.

I ought to have a letter in a day or so. Much love.

TO AARON COPLAND

◆

[November or December] 1932
Monte Carlo

Your first letter from Mexico I read night before last on returning from Paris. You must be right that Europe is a convention, and what a dismal one! I am so completely "fed up" with it that I should love to leave, but the prospect of living chez moi is always a bit worse than anything that has presented itself so far, so I go on living precariously here. I also went to London, from where I believe I wrote you, although it is always possible that I didn't. Did I tell you I met Peter Arno there? I don't think so. Yes I did, and Cyril Scott and a jillion other nonentities, just like him. Yes, Europe is such a lousy convention, like a barber's convention. Bal de Coiffeurs à la Gare d'Orsay. Je t'en prie, amène-moi, mon chéri; je n'ai jamais été à un grand bal, pas même de plombiers, alors tu vois comme je m'amuserais, n'est-ce pas? Ah, mon chéri, je t'en prie, je t'en supplie, sois adorable . . . Comme tu es malin! Je te demande s'il n'y a pas un truc à faire avec quelqu'un pour moi, et tu n'y réponds pas! Tu sais très bien que j'ai à peu près deux cents dollars au monde, mais tu n'en parles pas! Tu dois savoir que c'est mon idée fixe, mon obsession, comment trouver un peu d'argent pour vivre, pour ne pas être forcé à y penser, mais tu ne dis rien. Rends-toi compte qu'en deux ou trois mois je serai vraiment sans le sou, et ça pas comme autrefois, avec assistance au fond, mais sans le sou, pour la première fois. Alors, qu'est-ce que tu crois que je ferai? Demander à quelqu'un d'autre? Ça ne marche pas. Il n'y a personne qui s'intéresse à moi dans le sens qu'il n'y a personne au monde qui réussit tellement bien à me comprendre que toi. Alors, si tu y vois une chose qui vaut la peine d'être sauvée, est-ce que tu ne feras pas quelque chose pour la sauver? Mais, non, je parle sérieusement. Je dis sauver, et c'est cela que je veux dire. Je ne sais pas si tu crois que j'ai changé depuis l'année passée, que je ne suis plus capable de me débrouiller, même moins sérieux, peut-être. Mais ce n'est pas vrai, c'est une délusion. Je n'ai jamais travaillé tellement. (Et ici je dois dire que je ressentis une manque quelconque de force, de moyens techniques, c'est sans la moindre doute le contrepoint qu'il me faut. Après, je crois, avec le même effort, je ferai trois fois plus de travail. C'est ça. Ce n'est pas l'effort qui manque; c'est la technique. Du reste, tu sais tout cela avant que je te le dise.) Bon, je travaille. A quoi bon? J'ai le sentiment que la fin de mes jours va arriver bientôt, parce que je ne vois pas où sortir. Mon type me met à la porte au mois de janvier, même avant, je ne sais pas. Maintenant il me donne *un repas* par jour, l'autre il prend ailleurs; moi, je me fais du pain grillé et du thé parce que je n'ai pas de quoi me payer un dîner au restaurant. C'est tout ce qu'il y a à la maison le soir, mais à midi ce n'est qu'un déjeuner. Et "tous mes amis" à la Riviera? Ils n'existent point. D'ailleurs ici en Europe tout le monde vous donne des cocktails, personne la soupe. Je ne te parle plus; je veux seulement que tu te rendes compte qui je suis dans la purée.* Good

---

* A Hairdressers' Ball at the Gare d'Orsay. Please, dear, take me there; I have never been to a ball, not even one for plumbers, so you see how much fun I would have, don't you? Oh my dear, please, I beg you, be sweet . . . Aren't you mean! I ask you if some deal might be made with someone for me, and you don't reply! You know perfectly well I have about two hundred dollars to my name, but you never mention it! You must know that it is my idée fixe, my obsession, how to find some money to live on, so I would not have to think about it, but you don't say a word. You realize that in two or three months I will be truly broke, and not like before, with something to fall back on, but penniless, for the first time. So what do you think I will do? Ask someone else? That does not work. No one is interested in me in the sense that there is no one in the world who manages to understand me as well as you do. So, if you see something worth saving, wouldn't you do something to save it? No, really, I am speaking seriously. I said save, and that is what I mean. I do not know if you think that I have changed since last year, that I am no longer able to manage, that I've become even less serious, perhaps. But it isn't true, it's a delusion. I have never worked so much. (And here I should say that I feel a certain lack of strength, of technical means, that it is without any doubt counterpoint that I need. Later, I think, with the same effort, I will do three times as much work. That's it. It is not effort that is lacking; it is technique. Anyway, you know all this without my telling you.) Fine, I am working. What for? I feel as though it will soon be all over for me, because I cannot see my way clear out of this situation. I will be turned out into the street in January, or even sooner, I don't know. At present the fellow is giving me *one meal* a day, and he goes out to eat the rest of the time; me, I cannot afford to go to

and proper. I have no passion for any piece. As a matter of fact I don't give a damn about music at the moment. I haven't heard a concert since last February. I think Duke Ellington is really the best source of inspiration. And La Niña de los Peines with Niño Richard. In Barcelona [rest of letter missing]

TO RENA BOWLES

———————————————◆———————————————

December 29, 1932
Hotel Transatlantique
Laghouat, Algeria

Tomorrow is my birthday, and next it will be New Year's. More holidays to pass alone! Not that I am bored by that, but I think particularly the holidays of Winter are the ones indicated to pass with one's family. However, there will be more of them soon enough. Much too soon to suit me. I am continually haunted by the idea that time goes by without my accomplishing anything, even when within a given period of time my output could not possibly have been more. I suppose everyone feels more or less the same way: a powerlessness in the face of the fourth dimension. Ah well, my cold is gradually passing off, but none too quickly. It is a difficult sort of climate to lose a cold in, what with hot days and cold nights.

I have never eaten so splendidly for so long a period of time. Each meal is a chef d'œuvre. I shall surely put on a great deal of weight, which will suit me, as I never yet have had too much of it.

Well, I wrote an airmail letter to Mrs. MacDowell at Peterborough, inquiring conditions of admission to the Colony, but I daresay it will be several weeks before I have a reply. One has to count nearly twice as long as from Paris.

The other noon at luncheon there was a table of strange-looking people, from the bled somewhere around, with several Arab notables accompanying them. About halfway through the meal, at a given signal, they rose, and all gathered about a high spit, which I had not seen, where was roasted an entire fullsized sheep, head and all, with the eyes glaring out of their sockets across the room!

———

a restaurant for dinner, so I make myself some toast and tea. That is all there is in the house in the evening, but the midday meal is only lunch. And "all my friends" on the Riviera? They do not exist. Anyway, here in Europe everyone offers you cocktails, no one invites you to dinner. I will drop this subject; I just want you to know that I am really in the soup.

It was most peculiar, particularly as they ate the eyes as well. The dish is called "mechoui," and is the greatest delicacy of the Southern Territories. I had heard about it, but had never actually seen it; the last place I expected to see it was in the diningroom of the hotel, as the normal place for mechoui is outside a tent in the desert. The same evening we had a gala after-dinner entertainment consisting of ten magnificently-attired Ouled Naïl girls and their musicians. They danced for two hours in the salon of the hotel. I had never seen such costumes, and such jewelry. It was really very gorgeous, a sort of de luxe version of what one sees in the native cafés of the region. The dances were identical: first the dance of the hands, and its variations, then the stomach dance with its own many variations, and last the cane dance, much of which is done with the shoulders, and the rest with the abdominal muscles. Then we were given a very amusing novelty: two extremely tall men, a Soudanese and an Arab, were bound up, feet against feet, with burnouses and ropes, in such a way that they looked like a long caterpillar, which proceeded to wriggle and execute various vermicular contortions to lovely music of the same feeling. Cobra, tape-worm, I mean the little green measuring-worms we have in America: inch worm, and the hookah-caterpillar of Alice. I think it resembled the last more than anything. At intervals, the girls all screamed bloodcurdlingly, when it would raise one of its heads towards them.

The girls were absolutely covered with ornaments of solid gold which made a beautiful clinking and clanking when they did certain steps. They wore very dashing turbans of silver and gold cloth, and long earrings. Each had a silver tray in front of her (they were seated in one long row on the floor, and no more than two danced at one time) where the servants put tea, coffee, sirops, and packages of cigarettes. The air was soon blue with smoke. An old, old man played a ballade on a reed flute, and a girl sang with him. The instruments for dance were a sharpsounding oboe, and drums.

I enclose cards showing the architecture of Laghouat in contrast to that of Ghardaïa. You can see how negroid Ghardaïa is. I also send one of the Gorfas of Tripolitania. They are group-homes, and they look rather like the houses I used to draw at the age of three.

I discovered that it would be impossible to have a piano here in Laghouat, and so I went to the Pères Blancs, missionaries, no more nor less, and asked permission to use the harmonium in the church. It was granted, and so my work is being done in the church in that fashion. Half a loaf is better than no bread.

I am still reading Proust. It seems to get more and more complicated, and the sentences go off at tangents, so that one page is quite likely to take me five minutes to get through. Sometimes the sense escapes me even then. The volume I am reading takes place only in his head, and so far absolutely nothing has happened, or even started to happen. Have you finished Cities of the Plain?

I was invited to tea day before yesterday to the house of an officer, with Mme. Delaunay, of Paris, who spends half her time down in the Sahara with her husband shooting. They have been as far as Tombouctou, on the Niger. M. Delaunay runs the Auto Services Delaunay between Ghardaïa and El Golea, and seems to have much money. The service runs once a week, but the prices are so high that it is worthwhile for him. The Sahara is the most expensive part of the world to tour. The average cost of life per month for the tourist who crosses it is 25,000 fr., and if he is alone, the cost is quadrupled. I saw a tour advertised by the Compagnie Transsaharienne for one person for three months at the small price of 161,000 fr. Of course the tour doesn't exist unless one orders it, and one has guards, guides, etc. But 161,000 fr means about $6500, and one has one's tips, one's wine and all one's incidentals to pay on top of that. I must close. All my love.

TO AARON COPLAND

January 1933
Hotel Transatlantique
Laghouat, Algeria

Another stab in the dark; are you there? You gave me Tlálpan until Christmas, beyond that I am forced to recall the stipulated date of return given in a letter which reached me at Agadir Irir last May. I remember the evening; the pink sky, the Atlantic calmer than one could believe, the cactuscovered mountains turning red for an instant. There was a photograph by Carlo V. V. using as background a Navajo blanket, or was it a patchwork quilt? They resemble one another so much anyway. I read your letter walking along the road, already full of typhoid germs, but fortunately unconscious of the fact, beautifully baked by the sun, awaiting the moment when Abdelmjid would be finished with his work and we would climb up to Talborj together for dinner. You spoke about the flute sonata and the kasbah glistened whiter than ever, an alabaster eagle's nest perched up in the sky. Already Mejico was elected. And I suppose now its term is over. I do hope. Otherwise how shall I ever get word through to you, and the most important word there is for me. It circles about my head in the sun on the desert, gets between me and the sun, and at night it gets between me and oblivion. The day of reckoning has come, and I can't run backwards. The latter fact I don't think I fully appreciate even yet. I have always had a secret satisfaction in believing that my life was just a trial tube, and that when I had finished it, I could order a fullsized one. But now I begin to have sudden lucid moments when I feel I am well into the only one. Of course being I, my first impulse is to bash my head against the wall, or to run as fast as I can down the road and get away from "it." But perhaps my weekends in Islam have helped. Now I light a cigarette and go on reading Proust. (Still at it. It seems never to be dull an instant, and what is lovelier, it is better at 22 than it was at 17. Perhaps it's because Scott Moncrieff's rendition was not really as good as I used to think, since I do it in French now, but I doubt that as a reason.) At any rate, I am reasonably convinced that I am on my way somewhere and can't turn back. It is a nasty feeling at first, worse than when one takes one's first airplane trip and the plane rushes along the ground and suddenly rises. Cocteau did say: La vie est une chute horizontale, but I have always felt that the chute was a chute de rêve and that one woke up just before landing.* It's growing pains, and how much worse than back of the knees at eleven. As I said, the day of reckoning is here. I have no more money, and I want to work again with you. But Aaron, isn't it possible? Isn't it possible for me to live in Manhattan, and not in Jamaica? Can't you make it possible? Is there no one in New York who can assure me food and lodging while I work? Is there no one who can spare the price of a piano per month? I ask actively, not believing I am owed anything, but what can one do besides ask? It is so important that I *land* in New York. Once landed in Jamaica, there is a greater task than before. The parents, now, are quite resigned to the fact that they will never have me again as a permanent resident; they ask only that I be in America! I have used up, with my money, what one might call my spiritual fuel. I must hear a bit of music, see someone, talk to someone, have a purpose other than making this thousand francs go another week by getting myself invited to some frightful person's house from Friday to Tuesday. Next year it would be from Saturday to Monday, and the year after Sunday dinner . . . (I become discouraged when writing to you, because I depend unfortunately completely upon you, and you are so apt not to write at all. I suppose it is like addressing one's self to a deity of whose existence one is not

---

* Cocteau did say: Life is a horizontal free fall, but I have always felt that the fall was in a dream and that one woke up just before landing.

quite convinced. But one addresses one's self anyway. But Good God, I am desperate! Do you know who I am? Do you recall ever having seen me? I am skinny, with green eyes! I grin a great deal! I like sahnenbaisers, and not cream cheese! I must have jam in the morning! I go to pieces if I am tired! I find people to give me Spanish lessons, used to buckle my belt on the side, drink cocoa, worry if I didn't sleep, love to argue, have fits of anger, write for *transition*, put my feet on the chairs at the Romanisches Café, let young whippersnappers order champagne a mon compte at the Kleist Casino, find a virtue in unintelligibility, admire Hindemith, get ecstatic about the weather, about Arab music, about Gertrude Stein, used to sun bathe, used to profess virtue I didn't possess, used to go without washing my face, even that.)

Now I find a pleasure in wishing away time. To do it I write music. Where it was two it will suddenly be six. It is more fun than sleeping. I have all sorts of things ready to send you: Anabase, Piano Sonatina, Andante for five instruments, Cantata which will be shortly. Of that I have done a first part, adagio, for soprano, male quartet and harmonium, second, presto for reader and harm. (that is, declamation with music background), third allegro for soprano and h., fourth interlude for harmonium all alone, poor thing, and I still have the long last part for quartet with sop. to do. Pour revenir à nos moutons, je t'en supplie, expédie-moi de bonnes nouvelles. Je ne *peux pas* continuer à me trainer ici sans rien, sans rien, sans rien. Dis-moi que tu me laisseras descendre chez toi pour huit jours, afin de me débrouiller un peu au commencement. Je sais que tu peux m'aider, si seulement tu es là, mon Dieu, si seulement tu n'as pas décidé à passer toute l'année en Mexique.* I count altogether on you. Antheil disappeared two months ago, and never a word since. I want to see you. It will cease to be life and death, once I hear from you that there is some way I can return and live. I still have with what to pay my boatfare, in Jamaica. Please, please send word, avion Paris–Alger. Love.

---

* To come back to the point, send me some good news, I implore you. I *cannot* continue dragging around here with nothing, with nothing, with nothing. Tell me you will let me stay with you for a week, just to help me out a bit at the start. I know you can help me, if only you are there, my God, if only you haven't decided to spend the entire year in Mexico.

TO AARON COPLAND

February 1933
Afric-Hôtel
Algiers

You seldom write, you know, and when you do, you say nothing of importance. Sometimes I find an old letter of yours in a trunk, and upon reading it over, manage to imagine that it was written recently and is still valid.

I sent you a roll of music the other day from here containing Anabase, and the Piano Sonatina. I do hope you receive it. And I hope you like it. That's about all.

The weather is mad. Snow, hail, rain, lightning, tempest-wind for a week without cease. Suarès says Geneva's weather is frightful. He is looking for a new Noah's Ark in which to escape the apocalypse of 1934. I hope I shall be somewhere distant from the war. Or perhaps it will be less awful than the last decade. At any rate, *some* guilty people will be killed.

Sirens blow in the harbor. I suppose there is a fog as well. It is all too damned much trouble. Why don't you ever write and tell me what I could do if I returned to America? Of whom I could take counterpoint lessons, what would happen to me, and so on. Can't you possibly do the caring I ought to know how to do? Certainly no one else ever will.

Never mind. I am tired of here, that's all. Tired of being perpetually cold, of being alone, of not working, of having nothing to do, of trying to eat for five francs, of having no idea of what I shall do in any part of the future, of finding nothing but newspaper in the cabinet de toilette, of having nightmares about being at home, and of the general feeling of hiding and procrastination I find like an aura about my head. We shall see if I have the energy to return to America. I leave it all to myself and not to me, so I never know how it will come out. (Did you tell me *to*, or *not* to sleep with someone different each night? I have forgotten.)

Something is wrong, and who can find out what it is? It does not produce a deep normal unhappiness which could be constructive. Simply a mal-de-mer and inertia with chills. Don't write here. No address. Love.

February 1933
Hotel Beau-Séjour
Bou Saada, Algeria

At the moment I am in pain, having just been thrown off the back of a crazy mare into a dry river bed. Which makes various parts hurt very much. I have had enough of riding beasts in the Sahara, but still I should like to see the Aurès Mts, so I am leaving this p.m. for Biskra. On the whole, camels are more fun.

In a little while I suppose I shall be going to America. It is time to show Copland my output. I am sure he will be pleased. In case I pass by Paris, I do hope you will be there so I can see you once or twice. (If I am still able to walk about by that time. I mean, I *am* all strained up in the tendons.) I don't know what ailed the mare. She ambled beautifully in the oasis, but the moment she saw the open desert ahead of her, as we came out from between the walls, she was suddenly falling fast horizontally, and the saddle was coming to pieces. My beret flew off and I wondered how long it could go on. Above the dry river she stopped, but I kept going. After that I let her wander here and there, but she remained extremely sulky, and seemed to take no pleasure in anything I did for her. The camels are really nicer, and they can't run more than twenty meters at a time.

I think I shall go to France in a few days. I never have any money, and when one is that way it's best to make one's journeys radiate from the Riviera.

The harmonium worked wonders. I have a lovely cantata from it. Love, Freddy.

March 1933
Algiers

your letter i got last week thursday, although it may have been here in alger days before that. Too bad you won't have the Canaries. I am sure they are lovely, and I think I should like to go there even in May. Next Monday I am going up to Palma and from there to Mahón on Menorca, where there won't be anybody. If I had the cash sufficient, I should go to Casa and from there to Las Palmas, and from there to La Orotava, which I insist on seeing. Of course the Arabs are ten times more wonderful than the Spanish, but it costs too much to stay with them. The prices are just about twice as much. I have just spent des sommes folles taking a trip down into the Sahara for a month. And now I really have no money, and less prospect of getting some, as I have exploited all productive mines. Anyway, the trip was wonderful, and quite worth whatever consequences it might entail. To Constantine, Batna, Biskra, Touggourt, by camel to El Oued, by desert car to Tozeur, then to Kairouan, the holy city of Tunisia, and up to Tunis. Back through Constantine. There I stayed at the house of an Arab boy whom I met on the train, and who had a frightfully amusing family. Somehow I was allowed right into the circle, with the women unveiled and so on. Evenings the entertainments were swell. Here too I have plenty of Arab friends, but not of a very high caste. The principal pastime here is to sit in a dark café in the casbah smoking kif and playing dominoes. Haschich also, but it costs three francs a pipe, and knocks you out out out as well. Some days I am invited on promenades into the country to put the lamb to graze, as everyone has at least one whose throat he intends to cut shortly. I imagine the festival will be nice in Tanger. I just missed it by two days last year there, being in Málaga, of all places. There is one drawback to Arabs, and that is their insupportable jealousy. Don't you find it true? But once I shall be away from them I shall immediately regret it, and am sure I shall return and spend all my life somewhere among them. In Tunis they are intelligent, moreso than here, but they are also a bit rundown. In Morocco, inland, I think they are at their best.

Please do send the novel. Please do. I have nothing to read save Proust, Stein and Lautréamont, and all that is a bit rarefied I think. Read a good book in Tunis: *Malaisie*. Have you read it? You can get it in the collection Le Livre Modern for 3.50f. I like it very much . . .

I take back the assertion that Morocco is really the only place in North Africa, after seeing Touggourt, El Oued and Kairouan, which are so good and so different from anything in Morocco. El Oued is like a city one has dreamt about sometime just before waking, and whose sweetness is prolonged into waking. The mountains of grasshoppers in the market at Touggourt are appalling. Their red wings are thick in all the streets, like leaves. Can they be digestible?

You ask for a naked place. Why not Agadir? You can go naked there for twenty miles along the beach, and what a beach! But of course it is not an island. There are no islands, unless you want to take a chance on Fernando Po, in which case write me. Or on Cabo Verde Is., which are certainly naked. One goes from Cádiz I think.

TO AARON COPLAND

May 1933
Aboard Juan Elcano

Are you in New York? I do hope so, for I am on my way there, and I want to see you terribly. Perhaps I wrote you after receiving your letter, telling you that I really thought the manuscripts were corrected. But as naturally I must admit that I didn't go over every note, you are quite right in calling me an idiot. The true cause of it all is that one practically can't do decent work on the Riviera and in Africa. The landscape is all against meticulousness. One is convinced one is working carefully, and then one finds one isn't. Then one says, but it's careful enough. Because one is always so many thousand times more careful than anyone within a thousand kilometres. In America I think I ought to be better. Either that or worse. Well, I have had a long and excellent vacation, at least.

On the boat I have been writing a book. In a month if I work, I ought to finish it. Claude McKay's idea. He wanted me to stay on in Tanger and live with him. He is charming, but I discovered the last day that his inner self is ten years old. That's why he is so happy there, year in and year out with the Arabs. Perhaps if I hadn't made the unexpected discovery I should still be there, but as it was, I packed that afternoon and left the following morning. Djuna and Charles-Henri Ford were living in my house, and they didn't appreciate it. I am slightly angry with both of them, and shall never mention either.

Will it be possible for me to live in the city? Have you seen the businessman, or has it fallen through? Is there hope of a happy life or not? These things you will tell me when you see me, but the questions are asked in case there is still an opportunity to accomplish something between the time you receive this and the time you see me.

The Canary Islands are lovely. The sea here is covered with masses of red seaweed, so that one feels it can't be very deep. Still, it is.

Mon cher, si tu savais combien je tiens à te voir! Et toi?*
postscript: I should say not later than May 15 N.Y.

TO AARON COPLAND

◆

Summer 1933
Westhampton, Massachusetts

I suppose by now you will have been already to Yaddo; I hope the Aperitif
goes through. Moonlight nights like tonight distract me terribly. I feel like the
walking death, and I stalk through fields sighing, holding my fingertips up to
the wind. Or return to read Maldoror, the Übermensch. I should like to make
some music that is heard in les Chants. It is just for me. Maldoror Music!
Perhaps a piece for the sublime lampe au bec d'argent, the hermaphrodite, or
the mad dogs that run through the countryside. It would have to be très dix-
neuvième siècle, in the manner of Dalí. Or Berman. Unrelieved calm with
synthetic climaxes, if any. I often need a literary skeleton to think around, even
if it is all covered up in the end. That is, it makes it all easier.

Did I tell you I saw Sessions? His classic approach is annihilating! Music is
a language, he insists. I insist it is an art. He thinks he can hear it just as well
by reading it from the page: it is all there. But how about the sound? At any
rate, he is nice to me, and can't object too much to me, as he offered to teach
me once a week next winter: Harmony! Counterpoint! Will this go on
indefinitely?

The Mrs. Norman who has been being nice to me is the one you know. I
haven't ever seen her, but Anne Manheim has been begging for me down at
Wood's Hole. She has a piano found for me, on which I have merely to pay
cartage if it suits, and drag it away to wherever I live. But I want to keep Mr.
Becker in mind, because with Harry [Dunham] and me there will be two others,
which may easily complicate playing when I like. In fact, it may complicate
everything. Harry seems to be going to announce, write plays, God knows what,
but it is definite work. According to him, the whole apartment will be a sort of
steaming mass of artistic production!

Salon Mexico? ¿Qué es? May I send you the Symphony as I do it? Or do you

* My dear, if you knew how I long to see you! And you?

prefer to wait? Still, it would help me if I might ship it piece by piece for approval. But if you are too busy to do that sort of thing, tell me. Remember, you are still my godfather.

Of course I hope to get to Yaddo. But it costs cher. Fortunately it's fairly far away, the end of September.

I think I shall be going across to the Finger Lakes in two weeks or so, or a bit more.

Theodore has written twice. He is sad, but Sunday his vacation begins, and he fears too much some misplaced birdcall may ruin it for him. "I can't risk spoiling it . . ."

Thank Victor for his love.

As to love, I am waiting to find some. So far it has really been buying and selling. I suppose love is one of the recompenses of old age, when one averts one's eyes from the mirror. I imagine love is a fine emotion for those with fine perceptions. Perhaps fancying it excels possessing it. My buying and selling has been fun, anyway. I have tried to gyp wherever I could. In selling, by not giving full weight, or by getting the contract signed in advance; in buying, by not paying and taking the article. But that market is in Europe (and Africa). What the Hell good is America? If I remain here Virgil's prophecy will [*end of letter missing*]

TO AARON COPLAND

Summer 1933
Westhampton, Massachusetts

It is quite insulting for you to say my letters amuse you! Like a monkey doing peculiar things in his cage, I daresay. Certainly not like Mme. de Foutredieu or M. Coupandouille. I shall have to grow used to life actually being nerveracking and terrible, I can see. When it gets that way, as it does once or twice each week, I want to rush off into some place where it will all be different, and often I do and it is. But only for a few days more. You mean I must bear its horrors and not be impatient? If only there were round trip tickets into death, I should spend half my time there. Sleep is no good. Cocteau is crazy to advocate it. In sleep the horrors grow into worse things. I dread sleeping. In Europe, I dreaded it because I dreamed of being in America, which reminded me somehow that I had escaped from prison and the guards were on my trail. Back in prison I dream I am right here, or I dream I am dreaming I am here, which is even worse, because I see myself lying there asleep dreaming of being right in the room where I am. It is like the pictures on boxes of cereals, where one sees a picture of the box with that picture painted on it, and another inside, until they disappear. And each day drags on, with nothing but a night between it and the next. The days drag because I have too much energy and I have no idea what to do with it except to take walks, which make me furious! I walk along and kick the poor stones, repeating little thoughts that soon have no meaning at all, like words one says over and over . . . Even to go raving mad I think would be fun, but I'm too healthy!

I never do mean to generalize, mon cher, but certainly it seems permissible in regard to America. You exaggerate when you claim sex is here, for instance. Where in this country can I have 35 or 40 different people a week, and never risk seeing any of them again? Yet, in Algeria, it actually was the mean rate. Or do you think that really is not what I want? I think it's what I want, so it must be!

People in America we can let go. They're just about as impossible everywhere, I admit.

Art in America we also let go, because I don't know the first thing about art, and amn't interested in it at all. I hate America because I feel attached to it, and I don't want to feel that way. In Africa for instance, I can sit and feel unlocated; I can look at the landscape and turn the page and look at another, and it means nothing. But here I look at the landscape, and it looks back at me, and I am frightened of it, and want to get out as fast as possible, and that's about the whole story. But as I said, even in Africa I would wake up wet with sweat from dreaming I was back in its clutches again. I think every place in America is haunted.

It would be nice if the whole symphony were to be called Apéritif music, with Albumblatt, and Reverie, and Consolation and so on inside. But apart from that, you discourage me, because the theme you find first rate dates from two years ago in Tanger. Whereas the one you dislike is brand new. And just about all my new ideas are along that order. And really, I don't like them either, but absolutely nothing occurs to me, and I sit at the piano all day itching to be anywhere but there, itching to be bending over pulling weeds even, anything but the torture of sitting sighing, kicking the piano pedals, trying to have an idea. I just have none, et voilà. The hell with America! You know!

I dreamed last night I was busy pulling all my hair out in little tufts, just as one plucks a chicken. It was unpleasant.

TO BRUCE MORRISSETTE

Summer 1933
Westhampton, Massachusetts

I like this paper. It is like the skin of an egg. You are wrong to envy me my summer. It is a lovely one, but I am spending it discovering my deficiencies in music. Never have had such difficulties working. I can see that the direct reason is being in America, but still the deficiency is mine. I am trying to write the asked for symphony for next winter. I want it to be very sweet. Poison chocolates for the young bombthrowers. They gave three concerts last winter which were great successes, which means just as it would in Paris that everybody was there and looked at everybody else. I have tried to persuade Aaron to resume his concerts, and he seems willing to give in. But he is now on the League, which will probably keep him from doing it. The only trouble is that the League concerts are not exciting enough. I hope my reader whispering sets the example in the hall next winter.

I am copying the Cantata for future needs. Do you mind being depositary if occasionally it involves posting a copy of whatever, and receiving it later, after performance? Or what the case may be? As to Cantata, I finished it, and it seems fairly satisfactory.

[John] Kirkpatrick wrote asking for *Tamanar*, and after copying it returned it saying he did not like it as a piece, mais "y'a certainement des qualités." He will probably be pianomss. dept. He has made some arrangements of various new orchestral works, such as Aaron's Jazz Concerto, which Cos Cob Press has recently put out.

Did I tell you how wonderful is Aaron's Short Symphony? It comes next to Stravinsky's best. The dialectic . . . "Stravinsky m'a joué sa Sérénade. Ce qui frappe c'est la dialectique de l'ouvrage. Un notaire expose une affaire d'argent très compliquée. Impossible de se baigner de place en place dans cette suite. Perdre une maille c'est perdre le fil, c'est écouter par pure politesse."* The Sérénade as it happens had more influence than anything since the Sacre. Antheil and Markevich went in for it hammer and tongs, as well as Virgil!

Incredible amiability of Miss Mizner (sp?). Do thank her for me, or if necessary

---

* Stravinsky played me his Serenade. What is striking is the work's dialectic. A notary explains a very complicated financial affair. Dipping in and out of this progression is impossible. Dropping one stitch means losing the whole thread, listening out of sheer politeness.

give her address to me, and I shall. Too visual? Is it bad? I was eager to read it after praise of Roussel sung for me two years ago by Michel Arnaud (of *Onan*). Not only that, or rather more particularly *Locus Solus*. But when I wrote you asking for it I intended to write my book on the Sahara. The Sahara is not what anyone imagines it is. It is Picasso's later abstractions come to life or Miró's landscapes, together with Ernst? And the Sahara has its own "dialectic," as hard as nails, and fifty times more sharp and beautiful than anything else. Who the Hell said: Le Sahara attend son peintre? Have you read Eugène Fromentin? He spent two years or so in Laghouat back in the middle of the last siècle. Enfin, with all this greenery and detail here to stop and look at, and all the little sad noises of crickets, roosters faraway, birds, cattle lowing in meadowside waiting to be noticed, is it any wonder work is difficult? When there time was bare clay to work, and the air bore imprint of each idea that came to one?

The Tokalon did not come. It will be too much if it is lost now. Just too much.

Will you go with me to the Antilles in the Winter? I have enough money left for one, if you can manage to have $150 or so. A few months of wanderings could be had. Or do you prefer to have $300 and make it Mexico?

I have been wanting to see a drama in the cinema turned backwards. Film begins with immense closeup kiss, then the two protagonists walk slowly away from each other, arms outstretched, back through two doorways. Trains rush backwards, shooting from great proximity with the screen into distant pinpoints on the horizon. Man lies alone on floor in heap. Second man backs cautiously into room holding dagger, pulls handkerchief out of pocket and rubs dagger's point, which becomes dark. Replaces handkerchief with great rapidity, and sidles up to man on floor, crouching over him. Slowly inserts dagger in man's chest. Backs quickly to doorway and peers wildly about room, disappearing through doorway. Closeup of clock, four thirty. Closeup of clock, quarter of four. Man with dagger floats clumsily onto his feet, grimacing horribly. Dagger suddenly leaves his chest and flies out window handle first . . . The sound effects in the same way would often be lovely, but the chief gain would be in dramatic purpose. Ballet of motions with purposes . . .

Is it impossible for you to bus up to N.Y. again and go with us to Glenora? Really the swellest place in America so far, and a month to go, boats, etc. Solitude. In case you don't go to Chicago or New Orleans. Around the sixth of August to tenth. That is, you and I would not live in the same house as my mother and father. If only you could.

Gide has some good conversation in *Journal des Faux-Monnayeurs*. Do you know it? The ménage on the train outside Paris? Also, the "ne jamais profiter de l'élan acquis."* Which means I shall have to reread the damned Faux M. after six years.

And Jean Cocktail insists: "A toutes les extases je préfère le sacrifice"!†

He lets himself go anent the Loeb-Leopold Case. Chef d'œuvre, leur attitude . . . est impeccable. Léopold charmait les oiseaux!**

In the woods here are wildcats, deer, rattlesnakes, copperheads, lovely mushrooms and birdcalls. Much like Maine, only warmer . . .

I have been thinking I might write and ask to be taken into Yaddo again if you were unable to be in Glenora. But they would probably refuse me. I was a comet and a sunbeam for only a few weeks.

The Mozart piano sonatas are still the nicest.

Write more details.

Gertrude's *Atlantic* articles are good, but she told me everything in them when I was there. Really, just about everything, and twice as much again during those two weeks at Bilignin. My Aunt Jen, at whose house in New Hampshire I finally read them the other day, said: "Well, it's more sensible than I had supposed she could write."

More details, hasta luego.

TO AARON COPLAND

———————————◆———————————

Summer 1933
Westhampton, Massachusetts

You see, I shouldn't be so wretched if there were only some way I could be sure that some day, be it fifty years hence, I shall be able to justify to myself the fact I'm alive, but now I see no way, not even a vista of what might become a hope. It is not a help for me to repeat that life is its own excuse. I say: my life is no excuse. I have a horror not of anyone else's failing to find merit in my existence, but only in my own. And in order for me myself to find me worthwhile, I have got to be pretty brilliant, and understand everything. What I await most

* "never take advantage of acquired momentum."
† "To all ecstasies I prefer sacrifice."
** A masterpiece, their attitude . . . is impeccable. Leopold was a bird-charmer.

of all is a revelation. Then I shall find life explained for me! As to being sure, why do I want to be sure? Naturally, if I were sure, I should not even be interested, but that might at least make me calm. Mon cher, it is simply that I am perpetually discouraged. The heart of that is music. When I have the illusion that I am working well, on my way toward something, everything is bright, but all the rest of the time it is too terrible . . .

And here is life nearly over, and how far have I got?

Little ideas.

How long will you be where you are? In September? Perhaps I could come by some day then, before or after Labor Day. My uncle and aunt are driving me over from here to Glenora in one day, so it is impossible when I had expected it. I am glad you invited me quand même, because perhaps it will hold over until the trip returning . . .

Not an idea since Laghouat. Still I shall be expecting one some day soon. It may never come.

Would it be a good idea to stop writing for this year, and spend my time doing counterpoint etc., with Sessions? I do feel utterly sterile, and it's agony to try to do something with the poor things that do come to me.

What do you think?

ps. Next Monday leaving. Write so I get it before, if you can. If not, Glenora, Yates County, New York.

TO VIRGIL THOMSON
———————————◆———————————
Summer 1933
Westhampton, Massachusetts

I am so very glad you are coming in October! Be sure to! I look forward to a gloomy Winter without you. Was entertained a while ago at the MacLeishes with Sessions, and that sort of thing, wrote my objections to Aaron, and sighed for you, Paris, Côte d'Azur. He replied that my impatience was charming and had got me far, "But don't let it send you rushing back to the arms of Virgil or Abs-dabs-salaam!"

But anyway, he tried to get them to give my Apéritif Music at Yaddo and they screamed that they wouldn't consider it. Cheap, wrong, Brahms . . . what

else. And now not your Quartet either even? What is wrong with him? I should
not have minded if the objection had been that I had no métier, or that it was
badly arranged, but to argue that it was cheap really is too much. Aaron soothed:
"I believe that when you perfect your technique so that you achieve a really free
and complete expression of what you have to say . . . it will impose itself . . ."
But I don't believe myself more than 50% of that.

I wish you were coming to Yaddo anyway. I'm going to try to get there, but
of course I have no money here in this country, and not even an idea of how
to get it. My father is hurt that I don't accept his invitation to live at home! I
cordially *invite* you! And even then you won't! Very well, it's quite all right.
Still, I may have to.

What will Antheil be like in New York? I have trouble imagining him. And
Sidèry playing in Peter Pan. Are you fixing it all up with Gertrude or what? I
hear she considers me a fruit, and that I must be had in season. So they say she
says in her Toklas autobiography.

I have been back for ten days with aunts and relatives, back in the accustomed
mist of Besant, Leadbetter, Krishnamurti, Prince Mozumdar, Nirvana, Life,
Omniscience, the Oneness, the partless Brahm, Blavatsky, Karessa, clouds and
darkness and Karma, the Master and Truth, Truth, Truth. Everyone agreed I
had had a spiritual awakening, and so did I and brought out the Koran to prove
it. Later I was asked to give a little speech telling just how the revelation could
come to one so young, with details of life at Eerde.

I am so completely alone here that sometimes I am at a loss to know what to
do. And that for the first time in my life. I really do want to see people once
in a while. Instead, I have to follow brooks to their sources and plan new four-
hour walks. Utter silence, utter country. And chastity, moreover! Since Morocco,
without one break. It gets on one's nerves, there's no doubt about that. And gets
into one's music, but America is America.

I never told you about Porquerolles. How finally I managed to get one of the
two who held out for fifty francs. Not *the* voyou, but one of two who came up
to us on the quai. The next day he came to my house there and went away
satisfied with a handshake. Le jour même j'ai pris un coup de soleil. C'était
fini!* I was encouraged by those tactics and used them perfectly everywhere
later: Marseille and points south.

On leur donne la main . . .

"Ti po'm trouver n'importe quelle nuit ici sur la place." "J'y conny un p'tit

---

* That very day I had a touch too much sun. All over!

hotel chinois." "On est camarade, hein?" "Si ti vo, j'y travaille pour toi . . . ,
je fais le maquereau et je te fais le manger." Je t'attends.*

TO AARON COPLAND

September 2, 1933
Westhampton, Massachusetts

I think I could come by train to Albany. How far is it from there? Or to
somewhere nearer than that. But do be specific as to time, day period, week.
Toward the end means how many days to the end? At any rate, you know I
should love to come, and shall wait to have your next more definite word. Is
my name Frederic now? Charles Ford writes me she says of me, of Freddy:
Sensible and delightful in Summer; in Winter neither sensible nor delightful.
What a Grimalkin! His book is out: *The Young and Evil.* He sends advertising
cards. Thoma's book is also out: *The Promised Land.* He sends a copy, illustrated
by Mayo, who did Maldoror, *Bar de la Marine, La Croix du Sud,* undsoweiter.
Ford says he and his friend Pierre de Massot went through all the movie magazines, marked with an asterisk the pederasts, and sent them all announcement
slips. It was a good idea if it works. He worships Tchelitchew who spoke of
Markevich and me in the same breath, figure-toi: we are both whores according
to him! Paris does think in that direction. Miss Toklas tells everyone she is
frightened of me; quelle vache! She knows on the contrary that everyone is most
scared when she is around. She is the danger in that family. My comrade
Abdeslam sends me registered letters now and then. All he says is lovely: "Après
tous mes meilleures et sincères salutations que je vous envoie dans cette présente
lettre, je vous fais écrire ces quelques lignes premièrement pour vous dire que
j'ai reçu votre dernière lettre que vous m'avez envoyée datée le vingt-neuf juillet,
1933, qui m'a fait une très grande joie dans mon cœur de me voir recevoir tes
nouvelles, cher ami, et comme santé, grâce à Dieu je suis parfaitement bien,
seulement j'espère beaucoup et toujours que vous soyez vous aussi le même et
aussi que votre appréciable famille. Je ne sais pas comment je peux vous expliquer
la gloire qui j'ai eu pendant que j'ai reçu votre charmante lettre, combien j'étais

---

* You shake hands with them . . .
  "Any night you finding me here on the square." "I am knowing of a lil' Chinese
hotel." "We friends, eh?" "You like, I working for you . . ." "I playing the pimp and
buying your food." I am waiting for you.

heureux d'une manière très extraordinaire, mais j'espère beaucoup, cher ami, de te voir pendant une autre fois, car moi, je vous considère d'une amitié très rare pareille au monde, mon cher."*

(Which is the first paragraph.)

Likewise Bruce writes charming letters about incest in Ohio and graham crackers in outoftown quarries. I was confronted by the girl of three years ago, who went on to say when would we be married. She clung just like an octopus, and I discovered that I no longer desired to amuse myself with her in any manner. It was an ordeal. Long kisses for an hour, and finally it was over. Comme il serait dangereux d'aimer les jeunes filles, comme on aime les garçons: plusieurs par jour! On serait déjà en prison quelque part!† Virgil writes saying you asked him to Yaddo, but were silent on the quartet, so what the Hell! I suppose by what the Hell he means he won't come, inasmuch as he says elsewhere I shall be in New York sometime in October. I don't think Sessions sets much store by you as a teacher! But of course he is wrong. You have been for me. I shall write soon, and do you. Love, platitudes.

TO KATHERINE COWEN
—————————◆—————————
September 1933
Westhampton, Massachusetts

I am so pleased to find you are in this country. Are you leaving it soon, or will you be in New York all through the Winter? As I see what seems to be Mektoub, that will be my lot. A year spent working won't hurt, I daresay. I am eager to see you, did not receive your card, or else did and answered it. That I can't remember. What have I been doing? Everything, of course. I could be a chronology, an itinerary, a crime chart, a case history, even a fever graph, but

---

* "After all my best and sincerest greetings that I send you in this present letter, I am having these few lines written to you firstly to tell you that I received your last letter you sent me dated the twenty-ninth of July, 1933, which gave me very great joy in my heart to have news of you, dear friend, and as to health, thank God I am perfectly well, except I hope always and very much that you too should be as well and also your most estimable family. I do not know how to explain to you the pride I felt during the reception of your charming letter, how happy I was in a most extraordinary way, but I hope very much, dear friend, to see you during another time, because myself, I consider you with a most rare friendship as big as the whole world, my dear."

† How dangerous it would be to love girls, the way one loves boys: several a day! We would already be off in prison somewhere!

what is it but a year and a half. I remember Piège de Méduse with you one evening and taxis past the Neon lights of Boulevard des Italiens, I remember testing your olfactory pleasures on djaoui, hasaluban, eheud, m'ska in my room, and having a difficult time walking, but are there no more recent recollections? Are there no letters sent back from places sometimes telling plans, accidents, hopes? You knew I went down to Agadir and caught typhoid, I am sure, and after that my mother appeared and we went about together on the Riviera and eventually to Mallorca, but not to Dubrovnik. We found one of the more peculiar watering places of Europe in Santuario de Nuria, in the Catalan Pyrenees. My headquarters remained Monte Carlo, and I lived in Paris, London, Auvergne, Cannes, Villefranche and places like the Iles d'Hyères, where I got a terrific sunstroke and was cured by a witch who lived there, whom of course I never managed to see. But she lived there. There was a nudist colony on the island but the adherents were all very pudiques. They would hide behind the pines along the beach. I used to pretend I hadn't seen them, and sit down by the water where they had been, so they had to stay in hiding back in the woods until I went away. I visited Gertrude Stein up in the Alps again, and she forgave all and was very sweet. I visited de Falla at his little house in Granada and of course he had grapes in a flat dish. Antheil was my preceptor all the Autumn; he was always pleasant and helpful. Soon I had to return to Africa: it was the third time, so I made it a big closing scene to act I. I went to the M'Zab, and it *is* wonderful, I explored the cities of their heptapolis, got laid up with carbon monoxide poisoning from the charcoal burners Azous put in my dining-room, was taken to the Lieutenant d'Armagnac's to recuperate, went to Laghouat and asked the missionaries for use of their harmonium to write my cantata, whose words I had written in Paris during several mornings after champagne. In a month I had finished it. I went back down to my house in Ghardaïa to rest and had the most lovely weather. I bought boa skins, jackal skins (16), fox skins, beautiful rugs and wearing apparel, and went to Alger where I made many friends in the Kasbah, and played dominoes after noon. Soon I took a trip down to Bou Saada for a few days, where I took the wrong mare to ride and got thrown into a oued. Alas! my new Van Cleef & Arpels wooden watch was smashed, as well as my finger. The inevitable Biskra came a few weeks later, and Touggourt, where I got fitted up: Chambaa trousers and all, for a camel trip across some sand. Ali called the camel Ida, sometimes hot Ida, which I thought very curious. Ali was toothless, and a villain, but he came out all right when the trip was over at El Oued. He was ecstatic over 5 francs tip for three days walking. Then the desert autos, which made me really nearly seasick. Finally Kairouan in Tunisia, dinners with M. Mohammed Redjil in his very gilt house with a goat complaining by the table. And then Tunis whose souks I did like, and Sidi bou Saïd where I visited the Baron d'Erlanger's house, but he had just died. His secretary was incredibly wise, and we talked for hours about Arab music. At Carthage the cows ate grass. I went back to Constantine, where I stayed at the country house of my friend Hassan Ramani, near the top of the gorge. The water roared all the time and it was very misty. We used to have musical reunions in a hammam, where the ouds tummed until morning, and various people would get up and dance with turkish towels twined behind their necks. The tile floor was always wet, the steam came out in clouds from the hot chamber, and the music went on and on and on, hands clapped . . . Back in Alger I played more dominoes, and went across to Fez, but Abdallah was in the country. To Tanger, took a house for a month, went horsebackriding, bathing, visited the Negro Claude McKay for dinners two or three times a week, gave Djuna Barnes my house after a while, and lived in a hotel. Learned to smoke opium and hasheesh and kif. The lights on the Strait at night would blink, and inside the café the people sat on the matting playing lotto calling out the numbers: arbao achrine, tleta, hamstach, ouahad settine. Abdeslam and I used to go donkey riding out to Tandja Balia and pick orange blossoms and mint for tea. The pomegranate flowers were red. La Fête des Agneaux, Ahmed Ghazi is married, he invites me to the ceremony and the old negress screams with her drum, I drink twenty glasses of tea and quiver, the orchestra plays from three to ten thirty, they shave Ghazi's head, the procession. The dollar falls, I go to Cádiz and take a boat to the Canaries, to the Antilles. My ticket is for Panama, but I get off at Puerto Rico and go up into the hills to Barranquitas where I meet a crazy man who can barely speak German but insists we speak it all the time. I get horribly sick and return to New York post-haste. And now I am better. But I have lovely things to tell you about the Sous, and Mogador, and Tamanar. Of course you must not object to my great lengthy letter. It comes perhaps from Proust, or else it is that I am really being laconic, but trying to squeeze in a great deal too much. I shall save the rest until we see each other. Music it goes without saying never slept exactly: I found that doing things pleased me more than doing music, and I am satisfied. I hope the League of Composers will give my missionary cantata for harmonium. And a symphony is scheduled, but I am still in the middle of it now. In a few days I am going to visit Aaron Copland at Lake George and see what he thinks about it. The movement I have just done uses Berber ideas, and I am eager to hear it. I set Saint Jean Perse's *Anabase* last year, parts of it. Have you read it? The most amusing event of the Season will be Virgil Thomson's opera: *Five Saints in Four Acts*, the libretto by Gertrude Stein, with negroes singing. At least, that was the idea the last I knew. (In New York I went around with Countee Cullen; and discovered the most inouï group of Haïtiens in the negro quarter of Brooklyn. Le Prof. Auguste, at whose house I was entertained. He served vanilla ice-cream, strawberry "pop" in highball glasses, and said: "Voici un petit morceau qui m'a toujours plu: c'est le numéro quarante-six de Czerny." And he proceeded to play it. Everyone was solemn, and several applauded saying: "Ouiiii, c'est *trés* joli, *trés* joli.")* I shall be right in the city thank God. But you will have to call my mother to get my telephone number, as I haven't any idea where I shall be located. And do it. Ou mieux, écrivez, bientôt chez Orville Flint, R.F.D.#1, Northampton.

Un détail: j'insiste si on va parler français ensemble, qu'on se tutoie. Vous est assommant.† Have you seen Gertrude's new book? Alice B. Toklas? I'm eager to see it. It's about everybody.

I'm reading El Korán in Spanish, the nearest I could get to Arabic! hasta luego . . . I enclose a bit of djaoui for a cigarette.

TO GERTRUDE STEIN

◆

September 1933
Westhampton, Massachusetts

I think I am writing because I am leaving tomorrow for Lake George to stay a few days with Aaron Copland. I always feel much improved just before leaving where I am. I have been here all Summer long working, and now I am going down to New York shortly and work, living as usual with Harry Dunham. We imagine that we shall be together all the Winter, but his sister will not be there, and so there is no reason that I can see why everything won't be bearable.

I found a very bad review of the autobiography in the *Springfield Republican* not long ago, and that was the first news I had that the book was out. I managed to get the reviews in the *New York Times* and *Herald Tribune* later, and thought the last one was the only good one. I hope the book is very thick, very long.

A little play was given here last month, and I send its program for the children's names. Then there are some ladies' faces and names that came in a patent-

* "This is a little piece I've always liked. It is the Number Forty-Six of Czerny's" . . . "Yes, that is very pretty, very pretty."
† A detail: I insist that if we speak French together, we say "tu." "Vous" is deadly.

medicine leaflet. I like Leafy Buffington. Also Morrissette's latest and saddest letters from Richmond, where I hope he won't stay long.

Bernard Faÿ thought he might stop here going to Paris. I waited and waited to hear from him, but I never did again. Charles Ford wrote that he was to visit you sometime in September. That Faÿ was, I mean. Tell him to stop next year when he comes through.

America seems satisfactory. Perhaps a little more solid than Europe. I don't know why, unless it is that I feel better. Daniel Burns was here, and asked me what Bruce thought of your "work." I said: "Oh, he loves it." "I know," said Daniel, "we all love it, but what does he think of it?"

Of course I am not looking forward to the Winter with much besides apprehension because the cold shrivels me up so that all I want to do is stay in bed. I hate to have to put on overcoats, and rubbers, and hate it so much I prefer to be sick in bed to do away with those things. Once you're sick it's not so bad, except nights with a fever, which is about on a par with walking outdoors in the snow.

I wonder if *The Young and Evil* is really our generation! I found all the people in it far too serious about being evil. Or are all the young people serious? I can't keep up with them any more, and I think I shall just forget about them and stick to the old ones, as I always have when my good judgement prevailed. Young people always resent my pretending to be living instead of living, and older ones don't notice it. (Is this too vague or does it mean anything?)

I am trying to wander about the room and pack while I do this. It is useless, and besides, I should prefer to send you clippings altogether, to writing a letter. It upsets me more than it does to write to anyone else. I fidget. Best, Freddie.

TO GERTRUDE STEIN

◆

February 1934
Jamaica, New York

Here is the stub of my ticket for the opening night of *Four Saints*. I have collected some of the notices about it. At first, at any rate, I cut them out. Later there were so many references to it I stopped. But since I don't know whether you have them all or not, I am sending those I have, in another large envelope.

One day there was a larger snowstorm than we usually have here. Everything was covered. In the front page of an evening paper was an account of the city's thoughtfulness towards the birds who could find nothing to eat. The pigeons around the Public Library were quoted as begging crumbs and saying "Alas." Then they referred to themselves as pigeons and said "Alas."

The opera's success is very pleasant until one returns these days, now that the suburbs are there, when one finds the theatre full of people who laugh when they should not, and vice versa, and particularly who refuse to applaud afterwards. At least the theatre is full.

The smart thing among the younger artists is to be violently against it. Stieglitz decides also to side with them. Most of the defense must be taken for Virgil, against whom they allow themselves to rage for having had the audacity to give Gertrude Stein in modern dress. That is all I make of their fury, anyway. People walking on Broadway and sitting in Automats talk of "the Saints Play" and usually sound doubtful as to whether it would be worthwhile trying to get tickets for it.

People were regretful because there was no word from Miss Stein the opening night. Henry McBride suggested: "She's a great bourgeoise after all, and is too busy." But Virgil said: "No, nonono. She's just being royal."

I should love to know how much fan-mail you get each morning. It must be a great deal.

I am living in the city and doing music, which is not as much fun as doing it in the country. I have made songs out of two short things from Useful Knowledge, but no one has seen them yet, because I want to do more. I am glad to know that they are as different from Virgil's settings as anything could be. But I should like some more short romantic poems to make a group out of. What I want is to write several lieder on your words, but I can't find the right words to use. Would you at any time be interested in writing four or five lieder? Perhaps you would prefer hearing my music first. Still, I should like to have them all written when I return to Paris, and show them to you. I think you would like them very much.

Harry (Dunham) is married and has taken his fifteen-year-old bride to Trinidad. It is very strange, because she was not precocious, and collected stuffed birds. Three years ago when I was staying with her family she ate before the grown-ups and went upstairs to bed. Her father is a colonel who makes photographs of ectoplasm, and her mother is a lady from Louisiana. Harry met her long ago in Princeton and immediately vowed to educate her. He used to borrow French books from me to lend her: Gide and Proust. He must have felt her education was getting out of hand. But he writes he is happier than Byron.

My Sonatina was played a while ago by the League of Composers, and got

the best reviews of the evening. That made the Winter less harsh. And I think
the Spring will be sweetened by a Symphonic piece about Berber tunes and
Flamenco songs.

I send my best wishes to you and Miss Toklas.

TO BRUCE MORRISSETTE
◆

March 1934
Jamaica, New York

The symphony has still a movement to go. I had given Balanchine the Apéritif
which is to be 2nd mvt., and I just got it back from him. After Antheil's opera
I went around to see him. (He was upset by the adverse notices he got in the
papers, but appeased by the fact that a good lady doubled his allowance just on
that account.) At his house was a conductor—Balaban, a motheaten person who
listened to George sell me to him and then evinced an interest in being shown
the piece. I cut the e from your name in addressing you a scroll the other day
because I had lost the number on Grafton Avenue, and still haven't it. I shall
try 420. Do you have any times away at Easter? Do you object to describing
what you do there? Life in this country would be dull no matter what happened
to one, I am convinced. Sometimes I wonder whether it is confined to the nation
or is spread about the hemisphere. Puerto Rico was not very happy. Perhaps
Mexico will be better. And Guatemala sounds better. Everyone is going to
Mexico next summer, and probably prices will rise on that account. They observe
Quatorze Juillet in Guatemala, and in the large and detailed Atlas we have the
district north of Guatemala City is marked as unexplored. "Very little is known
about the course of such & such river . . ." I bought a book (Popul Buj) the
other day which corresponds to the Koran, in Quiché, one of the Mayan dialects.
It was printed at Guatemala City and has a facing translation into Spanish. The
language of the original is startlingly like the trade names American firms have
been inventing for the last fifteen years. Like Golflex, Kodak, Electrolux, Kotex,
Cutex, Kwikstick, and so on. As Brentano's were having a sale, I bought a good
many other books: *J'adore* of Desbordes, *Les Tragédiens* of Desbordes, *Recon-
naissance à Rilke, Les Cahiers de Malte Laurids Brigge* of Rilke, *Dernières
Histoires Extraordinaires* of Poe trad. de Baudelaire in a nice numbered edition,
Los Tortos (sp?) of Conrad, for practise, and some nice obscene Spanish books,
greatly reduced. There is not much doing in New York. The opera excitement

has died down. *Four Saints* stops its New York run at the end of the this week. I saw it four times and found it grew more enjoyable each time. But I hated to have to write the review of it for Paris. I doubt if Koschnitzky publishes it. I have had to translate some more Italian and they pay less each time. The money situation is always annoying. Dunham is in Trinidad (Libertad, Unidad) pretending to be making a movie. My Samoan film opens this Saturday at the Cameo. They have changed the name from *Siva* to *Bride of Samoa*! Shortly I shall do the music to a new one all about Morocco. That will net me some money, which I intend to put away for the Summer if possible. Must fly somewhere to breathe deeply for three or four months. Will you say aught about it?

I saw Caminadés's name in *Minotaur* the other day. He had written, together with scores of others, his greatest experience. Dalí is illustrating *Maldoror* for us. But the cheapest copies sell at $90 and the others at $125, ce qui est idiot. I have been making a series of records for a doting lady whom I met in Monte Carlo two years ago. But each time, she has me make one for myself. If you have a phono there you might be amused to have them.

No, it would be difficult to write about inner states now. The inner state is too foliated or ramified or diverse or complex or too something to be put into words. Besides, would you be interested in trying to do it if it were possible? I keep remembering an afternoon in Touggourt when I sat in a garden with my back against a wall, and was served tea by an Arab who tried to convince me that life would be quite enough for me if I would be content to settle down there, take a little house, and buy some date-groves. His point was that I could always sell the dates for more than it would cost me to grow them, and that thus I should be well-off. Even Touggourt would be sad. Even Laghouat. There always comes the afternoon when all the countryside explorable on foot even at a near-run, in five hours, is exhausted. One walks slowly out and down the road, looking at cracks in the walls along the way, at each camel carefully, watches merchants at the market haggling, wanders into the public park built in a square, full of eucalyptus trees and low figuiers, where no one ever walks, and where there is no one now but the boy who always works there, pulling weeds. He has a wheelbarrow and is almost too busy to talk. But he looks up and one of his first curiosities is to know why you are living there in the desert all alone. And that suddenly reminds one that it would be just as nice to live somewhere else. The room later in the day has the sadness of a room at home because one no longer lives there in spirit. Then it is so difficult to find a new town.

I am doing a new Piano Sonatina, but it sounds *fade* and unnecessary to me.

Aaron had only 3 words to say: "Perfectly good Bowles." But there is no trouble really. It is only New York. When the pressure gets too high, I shall be elsewhere and everything will be otherwise. I want terribly to see Suarès. But he's staying in Geneva indefinitely. I enjoyed noticing how you put "10e edition" after Breton's *Manifeste du Surréalisme* and *only after* that. It seems Stephen Spender is really the great poet of the day! And I shouldn't doubt it, considering what I recall of him.

TO BRUCE MORRISSETTE

March 1934
Jamaica, New York

You must by all means count on me. Too bad it must be so late. End of June, but I suppose the later it is the more money. I of course have only boat fare at the moment. If Dunham feels inclined to when he returns from Trinidad, he will give me some more. My sojourn however must be longer than one month and a half, and because of that I am afraid I shouldn't be able to move about much once I got to the place I liked. I want to take a house or apartment and stay a while to work. Still, with sufficient flouss, naturally I could bear wandering a bit first or afterward. (Is your passport still good?) Probably must be renewed by June, no? Although I believe you need no passport for Mejico at all. Only a tourist's card for 48 cents. I have a friend who thinks he wants to go to Haiti in August, late, and early September. Living there is cheap too. Do you think we could make Port au Prince so as to coincide with that? Do write to Cooper, and convince him his pounds will be millions now in Mexico, etc., which is perfectly true. Also that probably never again will he have the opportunity to be with two people exactly like us, at once. That is really the hauptsache. A while ago I made a list of what seemed to be the best places there: Campeche, Necaxa, Toluca, the baja part of Baja California, Mazatlán, Patzcuaro, perhaps Lago Chapala, Morelia, which look to be lovely, Tepatzlán, Cholula, Amecameca and Xochimilco. Aaron says Acapulco was nice, on the Pacific beside Mexico City, but I imagine it if any would be a touristy spot. I still want to see Quetzaltenango and Chichicastenango in Guatemala, but if Mexico sounds better to you than Guatemala I really don't care.

My movie producer called me up the other day and sent up a Chief Monte Azul from Peru with his "original compositions." Such a mess of lousy stuff I have never never seen. He brought with him an aging rebel poetess who had her scrapbook with her and was eager to tell how she knew Norman Macleod and Parker Tyler! Next she began on me to do music for one of the eight Indian pageants she has dashed off. I went out to lunch and left them to wrangle.

Tonight I am having dinner at the Swanns', where there will be new news of Daniel. To Elmira and Glenora until Tuesday, taking Victor who was in Mexico with Aaron. (I shall want to see Chavez and Revueltas there.)

[Later] There was no news of Daniel. Seems still to be in Arizona.

Kirstein told me this afternoon that Balanchine had found my music not danceable. Antheil is going to learn some of them, and have Bal. up one night to his house, when he and I will play to him. George is doing a ballet for Balanchine called Dreams, with sets by Derain. The music is facile and Lisztlike, with pages of Weill thrown in, and of all things, the 3rd movement of my Sonata included practically verbatim as to the first theme! He is really unbelievable. I noticed it, he blushed and stammered about, and said he had forgotten my piece; which incidentally he was very fond of at the time in Cagnes, and played over and over. He keeps saying now that there are only three of us who are "on the right track": Virgil, him & mich, but Virgil unwittingly made a list to me recently which included himself and me, and not George! How they are difficult and how they love cliques, even if the cliques are imaginary. I thank them both for inviting me, though. The Allegro, is that the piece you learned at Clermont? Have you it or should I have it somewhere?

The Dalí illustrations for Maldoror are not very satisfactory. Mrs. Julien Levy (née Loy (of Mina)) showed me them, and I got her to agree that they showed no real understanding of the book. I doubt if Dalí has even read it all. No one seems to have. I have it nearly all synopsized so that I can turn to practically any page I want without having to hunt for it. On exhibition were some Sir Francis Rose, rather frowsy things and too pretentious, some Bérard, about whom I can't make up my mind, particularly after the large new canvas which I hadn't seen, and which represented an immense Lesbian in a greasy blue wrapper lying on a flat beach, with some misty mountains across the bay, and a second head with the same curious inquiring expression and the same shaven pate emerging from just behind her abdomen. The other people were Tchelitchew, whose sepia drawings are always nice (and never yet has he drawn a female face or figure) (a supercilious sort of wretch to have anything to do with) & Berman, who really can paint like an angel and whose lovely landscapes are on their way from Dalí, and easy to like right off. (He is a nervous and humble little person.) So write.

TO BRUCE MORRISSETTE

Summer 1934
Hotel Victoria
Ronda, Spain

not a word from you for two months. What are you doing by now? All I fear
is that you lie reeking with fever in Mérida. You will write soon, please, if you
are able, and soothe, won't you? Me I have been having swell times here and
there all summer, not doing any one thing, just vacationing, asking extra hazards.
First the excellent trip over on the Savoia, then buying in Tangier and Fez,
then Cádiz, and Sevilla with amusing night-life until all hours: Eritaña, Rosales
and Plaza de Toros, where I saw the most amusing bull-fight, considered "comic"
because the bulls are young and are killed in amazing fashions, by an orchestra,
etc., but I believe I wrote you about that long ago. Then Granada, with Niño
del Pueblo among others singing Cantes Flamencos in the Antigua Plaza de
Toros until 2 in the morning, and the Alhambra, which I liked just as well as
and no more than before, except that this time I saw the Hammam which was
one thing I had missed before. At Sevilla however the Alcázar is quite lovely,
and the thermes mysterious and lime-green-white underground stretching with
arches reflected in the pool away into utter darkness. The Arab Palace also is
more grandiose than the Alhambra, but classical and not romantic. And Gibraltar
is amusing for a few days, with a thundering rocky beach belonging to the hotel
where there was never a soul in sight. The waves breaking do it so strenuously
against the cliffs that on certain days there is a constant large cloud that forms
at the rock's top, and obscures the sun, floating landward like a tremendous
feather when one sees it from the coast. They have talkies in the public gardens,
with the sound greatly amplified. People stand on the hillsides all evening
watching Lupe Velez. Tangier again, and then up into Xauen after spending a
whole day getting permission. Lovely and high in the Rif Mountains, with
running water everywhere and storks crackling and ratcheting from the ramparts.
There in a grotto as I probably told you, I came one day on the only other
foreigner who had set foot in the place, during my stay, and he said he was
waiting for John Widdicombe, so we went back to Tangier and waited together,
I having a fight with my friend Abdeslam because I had left him in prison in
Fez a few weeks before when the N.Y. gent and I took him along to be kind.
The feud has grown to larger proportions since then, and Abdeslam has knocked
Hamed down, and Rhazi objects to it all, and Abdallah thinks Abdeslam is an

idiot . . . I send Abdeslam's letter to me in Granada. So John W., Fletcher and I set out for Marrakech, get stopped in Casablanca, go to the Quartier Réservé, where John is mobbed by naked belly-dancers, and my hair is pulled out, and oh! oh! on to Marrakech where we go British in sun-helmets and shorts and drive around all day in tinkle-bell victorias to ostrich-farms and tombs and oases. John makes the acquaintance of several halfwits who amuse us all greatly. It is lovely. We then get a taxi a few days afterward to take us across the Atlas Mts. Night's stay at Asni. They keep stopping the chauffeur, who has brought along a Chleuh boy to translate from Chleuh into Arabic for him to take movies and stills. The chauffeur worries but says nothing. At Asni the trees are full of large peacocks that scream murder. The road swarms with children who hand us amethysts until we have nowhere to put them. We come away with some peacock tail feathers eating chocolate and drinking rum early the next morning. The mountains are wonderful, and after the crossing when we go down into the Sous valley it is hotter than I have ever felt anything. One keeps waiting for one's hair to blaze up. Taroudant is strange and silent, with high mud battlements everywhere, and very little inside but mud huts and streets covered over with grape vines. And especially banana plants, which abound everywhere. And the wind blows hard down off the peaks to the north where one sees thick layers of snow, and the banana leaves flop about and sound like raincoats on a clothes-line. The heat is quite oppressive after all, so we stay inside the hotel which is so dark one can see nothing, and play the phono I bought in Casablanca, John insisting on doing the rumba with no clothes on every day in each patio. The hotel is completely empty save for the servants. The road to Taroudant has been open only 3 months. Suddenly I leave for Agadir, where I look up Abdelmjid Temsamany, and go bathing on the beautiful beach. A few days later they appear with Paul Valéry's nephew who has a car and has driven them down to Igherm, a foreign legion post where no civilians have ever been before and where the officers have sent them right away again before they could ask for food. In a few days their temper is improved. P. V.'s neph. leaves, they stay. We all have legionnaire outfits made for us, with long bags to the heel, and goatskin sandals. We go about Agadir all dressed up and are very much pleased. I leave for Mogador, buy more Chleuh music, leave next day for the north. After too much traveling, here to Ronda, quite a fantastic town up in the mountains, whose hotel is really swell; whose gorge is better than I had been told it was, which means pretty good, the best gorge in the country.

Do you want to live in Constantine, speaking of Gorges? An old photographer there writes asking me to help him with his business. He is sure I am vigorous and enterprising. But I reply I am sewed up with the burros in Fez. And then there are the massacres now in Constantine. Even my mother writes imploring me to stay away from Constantine!

Reading Spanish poésie, to be set to music soon. It is pleasant, something like this:

> De tanto como han llorado
> mis ojos se van hundiendo;
> y es que forman sepultura
> para enterrar mis recuerdos.*

And there are Flamenco ones in dialect that will make pretty songs:

> Yo he bisto a un hombre biví
> con más e cien puñalás,
> y aluego le bi morí
> con una sola mirá.†

And the Spanish language altogether I like so much more than the Italian. Easier and more fun to speak as well. I get on beautifully in it, anyway, and Italian goes against the grain in me, with its stress, and dancing rhythm.

Virgil wrote says Porquerolles would be nice and to write and come, but I got the letter 3 weeks later . . . Do you want Stein songs? Write c/o Fondouk Américain, Route de Taza, Fez, Morocco.

TO JOHN WIDDICOMBE

◆

September 1934
Continental Hotel
Tangier

We have moved to a much better hotel, and I am too lazy to go downstairs and get some proper stationery. How are you? Your letter was a bit sad. Do be

---

* From having wept so much / my eyes sink deeper and deeper / and they are turning into a grave / where I can bury my memories.
† I have seen a man live / with more than a hundred stab wounds, / and then I've seen one die / after a single glance.

well to enjoy Spain, and buy some Saetas. Except that when you get this that country will be finished for you. But perhaps you can get some in Portugal, and some records by Marchena.

Fez goes on being lovely, and I have discovered corners as usual I had heretofore ignored. You should have gone with me on some of my recent hunts: the results magnificent. The Senegalese village, where we dared not go that day when we looked and saw the guard at the gate, turned out to be quite allowed, and I explored all the parts. There were huts of mud, with gorgeous tall black ladies standing by the entrances. There was splendid music, and great laughter. The whole quarter was very friendly and took particular interest in my white flannel trousers. "Mon vieux, c'est bon," in soft tones, from pink lips in ebony faces. Then there was a gate we didn't bother with, where every day there are two complete circles of Chleuh boys dancing, exactly as at Marrakech. I have had good opportunity to study the dancing, and I agree, and insist that it is the most exciting yet. They played some of one of your records.

The garçon d'hôtel or someone here stole 100 francs from me last week, and I have been rather bitter with the world since, but it is wearing off. Except when I see something native and de luxe that I must refrain from buying: ". . . but with that 100 . . . !" I have had most beguiling experiences since you left, of course. And lovely walks discovered, in the country, and a ruined subterranean palace, where one takes one's friends, pour épater la bourgeoisie, and they always want to repose themselves a while down in there. Cool.

Dark.

Abdallah I have avoided since he asked me just who intended to pay for his djellaba, and just who would régler the babouches . . . I hear he is well.

Then last night it was strange. At Merinides Café on the hill dusk came down as usual. The dog walked outside the paling of bamboo, sniffing downward, howling. A corpse had been there many days, stank to high heaven, lavender with wine splotches in the twilight. The Arabs put it onto a stretcher, naked, with handkerchiefs around their faces, which they raised occasionally to spit fiercely from underneath. They carried it around and up to the road. It had fallen from the high cliff beside the café, lay there too bloated to be limp, the pubic hairs still angry and black in the middle of the soft plasterlike flesh. And after dinner I met in the grand rue du Mellah someone I didn't know, and we went to drink, and I had no money and he paid, and we drank, and we drank, and we stopped to see friends of his, and drank dozens of bottles of beer, and one of them was pleasanter than he, but, but, and in Moulay Abdallah where the lights flicker and the sidestreets are dark after midnight, the first pulled me aside into an alley, and said hurry, and around a corner we stopped, and he pulled from his pocket a very large knife and stood waiting for the second who was following. I said you wouldn't do anything bad in front of me would you, and he nearly wept, and handed me the knife, and said no no no no you keep it, but he put it back into his pocket, and the other had been warned by God I think, because he did not appear, and we joined him in a minute in the lighted street, and later we went into a house, and were served tea in a private room all cushions, mountains of them, by a girl jangling with jewelry, with brickred feet from henna, and I got angry and smashed a bottle of beer on the floor and ran out, and was pursued, and jumped into a taxi, and was followed by the first, who screamed to the driver—Arrah! Arrah! But the second ran out sobbing and jumped onto the running board, and the first knocked him off, and we went to the Ville Nouvelle squirming around. At his house I had a fight immediately, and tore around, and ran out practically naked, stumbling over animals in the pitchdark. He tried to receive me in someone's kitchen, where a burnous was spread out on the tiles near the sink.

Tonight I met our pleasant friend who was sent home the night of the party. We have a rendezvous for tomorrow, as Mr. Williams is off to Casablanca for two days!! And Sunday to his house for dinner. Je t'assure qu'il est même plus amusant que nous avons pensé.*

There are plenty of other things to say, but I think this is keeping Mr. Williams awake. He received the money and asked me to write you a letter for him. Will you say I did if the subject ever arises????? Write me. Thanks medersa tickets. Love.

TO DANIEL BURNS

———————————◆———————————

November 2, 1934

At sea

ITINTRIGUESMETOKNOWINWHATWAYOURHANDWRITINGBRUCESANDMINEHAS
CHANGEDANDSINCEWHENAFTERALLWEAREOLDERANDNOLONGERWRITETHESAME
THINGSEITHERBUTTELLMEIFYOUCANINJUSTWHATWAYTHEALTERATIONHAS
MANIFESTEDITSELFOFCOURSEYOUKNOWYOURSHASCHANGEDGREATLYTOO

---

* I promise you that he's even more fun than we thought.

But not before I was already planning to leave! It's in ill worm that has no turning, and one wallow does not make a slummer. What a plight to be in Spain now that's state of war. Police here and more there, and government and army papers to carry about without so much as a qué guapo, but to be sure the propina has not been completely forgot, and that's a comfort to some.

Your letter said very little I could not have guessed in the direction of, had it occurred to me, but I was a bit startled to know that Strachey makes one sheepish. I have thus always been right not to read him. Everyone seems to be studying harmony this year. A zeitscheiss, or is it scheissgeist, which would do well to overtake me, but I doubt if it arrives at it. But I imagine it will be like the Société des Nations. The more harmony they study the more atonal they become. I suppose one must know a thing thoroughly before one can discard it.

John's malaria left him at some small station between Málaga and Granada. Sneaked out while John was in the Retrete, and took his trenchcoat and an orange. I enclose a subsequent letter from the bereaved, after he had arrived at Oxford, and saw his journey in perspective.

I am pleased you enjoy the songs. Margret ought to be able to sing them, as they are not high. And you to play them! But you play better than I anyway. I did not get around to send Helen Ormond a copy, but I shall. And if you do not get have not got around to send the francs it is just as well, as they would do me no good now. At any rate, I am intending to post this at Puerto Rico en escale. Escale: Santo Domingo, 1, Venezuela, 2, Curaçao, and then Puerto Colombia, where I hope you will write me Lista de Correos. I wish you were having your Sabbatical now and were to meet me there.

I sent you a mess of poems resulting from a trip to the Tafilelt three weeks ago. It is magnificent country. Still murderous. The night I arrived bandits set fire to a busload of Arabs, and killed 37 of them.

I have some lovely records: from Fez, choral works of ancient origin, accompanied by strings and drum; from the Atlas (Sous), Chleuh songs and dances, from the desert, songs with flute and chalumeau accompaniment, from Andalusia, saetas, with drum and trumpets, songs by Marchena, with guitar, and solos by Montoya, Sabicas and Maravilla. And some extra, from Algeria and Egypt.

Also a collection of chromos beautiful to behold. All these things cost me days of searching through the Medina and Fez-Djedid, miles of walking from shop through tunnel to shop, searching the least expensive. All must be bargained for . . . Even a bus ticket is haggled over a half hour. And en route! Whizzing along. White-robed figure appears from behind rock ahead. Holds up staff, like Moses, beard blowing in the wind. Bus slows down, stops a hundred feet beyond. Slowly ambling up the road after the bus stops, toward it. Asks chauffeur: where to? Chauffeur says: where do you want to go? Says: Midelt. Chauffeur says: other way, behind. Starts up. Arab screams. Waves staff and pulls at beard. Bus stops. Arab saying: Ksar-es-Souk. Chauffeur says: we go there. Arab says: two duros. Chauffeur says: five. Arab says: three. Chauffeur starts up. Screaming behind. Chauffeur stops. Arab breathless says: four. Chauffeur without replying starts up. We go a hundred feet. People in the bus cry out, beat on the glass. Chauffeur stops. Arab runs after bus. Panting, says: four fifty. Chauffeur says: five. Arab hands him five duros, and runs back down road to get furniture, wives, sheep, fruit. Then bargaining begins for tariff to be asked for these luxuries.

Écris bientôt. Je vis toujours. p*axUxıx e*nzr@o*uxtXe

TO BRUCE MORRISSETTE

———————————————◆———————————————

November 7, 1934
Mid-Caribbean

creo que es el último día sin vista de tierra. Mañana por la mañana llegamos a La Guaira. Pues que en este país hay el dictador Gómez, y que él no quiere que los extranjeros vean su capital, Caracas, creo que no podré subirme a este lugar. Pero se puede siempre que sí . . .* The sky is strange, with solid pillars of cumulus that begin at the clear horizon and tower to the center of the sky. Here and there in the circle, they are topheavy stalagmites. And yesterday all day we skirted the île d'Haïti. In the afternoon the odor of the land was fraught with green. We waited three hours in the harbor of Santo Domingo, and from the low cliffs nearby, negroes draped in white stood sheltered by the chaotic trees and watched. (I stayed at the prow and sniffed.) There was a thundershower up above, but all of it that came to the harbor was the lightning. The weather was like certain days in America farther north, at the crux of Summer, when

---

* I think it's the last day we'll be out of sight of land. Tomorrow morning we reach La Guaira. Well, in this country, there is the dictator Gómez, and since he doesn't want foreigners to see his capital, Caracas, I don't think I'll be able to go up to that place. But if I can I will . . .

the sky and the earth are overheated and still, and one awaits the dénouement. I cannot help feeling now that Summer has finally come. The dry heat of Africa could never seem like Summer to us. Il nous faut cette moiteur, ces nuits haletantes pour nous faire croire que c'est l'été.* Tortured and dusty in Morocco, with heat that one only believes when one sees the thermometer. It was Summer coming into San Juan . . . a thunderstorm, a soft wind, silent green firecrackers of phosphorus exploding under the foam at the prow . . . I finishing Le Temps Retrouvé. One really does need a journey or a convalescence or a villégiature to read him, particularly after the great excitement is over. The excitement is the sort of precipitation of elements within one which had been in suspension. Once they are there, and plain to be seen, and the reading is no longer completely subjective, one reads along much as one would any other book, and comes upon passages, which would have brought tears of recognition before, with a certain ennui. (Probably because there is said the same thing that was said a thousand pages back, and because it has already brought the tears once.) But now that the state of seeing has been translated to paper, one waits for someone to create out of it, to carry it on. Critics seem to regard Proust as a sort of culmination of a certain kind of intelligence; it is really no more than the definition, stating of principles. I still do dread the day when I shall have read the last sentence. For that reason I read sparingly, and reread rather than go ahead. Gertrude says everyone during his youth finds one great book which influences more than any other; hers was Anna Karenina! The mountains of Haiti were high and distant. I wanted to disembark there and go up high and stay. Enough water. Two weeks tomorrow morning, and nearly another to go. I posted you a parcel of three books at San Juan: 1900, a French Hemingway vaguely, and Les Cahiers du Sud. Whether you have time to read at all or not, I don't know. Do you think you will be in N.Y. at Christmastime? Has Daniel invited you? Somehow it seems natural that he should. I may be back then, and if, we must see each other. I have the idea of publishing music mensuellement, simply things by Virgil, Citkowitz, Moross perhaps and others, and getting a subscription first which will just permit printing. Later, wider. The stress to be on lack of chichi, simplicity. Cos Cob and New Music are the monopolists in the line, and they both are too hopelessly fond of complexities. Which means that the market is limited perforce to the inner circle. The two organizations do nothing to discourage the specialist-performer; the contrary. But I should want to print what "anyone" could play or sing, and it is that which will rescue music, if it is to

* We need this humidity, these panting nights to make us believe it is summer.

be rescued, from the radio, the phono, the Carnegie audience, and the critics. Death to Sessions who thinks music is philosophy, death to Cowell who thinks it's a science. You know, your daily bread, 100 standard songs which should be in every home, father 'round the melodeon . . . . . . mais c'est vrai. Poco meno mosso. Temp primo.* In San Juan I discovered the Italian sculptor with whom I came across last year. He is covering the island with his godawful façades, statues, and "ornamental stone-work." He beamed at seeing me, and took me around to see his wife, who spoke a bit of English: "Oh, that's awal roight . . ." she said apropos of anything, and smoothed her long white kid gloves. (She was just going out.) To find him I had gone to the boarding-house where I stayed last year. The negress nearly fainted with joy, thinking I had returned to eat there: "¡Dios, ah, Dios! ¡El señor de Nueva York! ¡Que estoy contenta!!" Over her head hung an elaborate sign, the words suffocated by venomous purple roses: DIOS BENDIGA NUESTRO HOGAR. "¿Quiere algo? ¡Toma algo! ¿Chinas?"† (The same word the Arabs in Algeria use for oranges. But I never have heard it in Spain.) I had to drink a large glass of violently iced orange-juice, in horror lest the same pain should find me this time that found me last. I walked out along the beach to a suburb called Punta de Tierra, where I went into the Public Library and asked for some maps of the Antilles. The librarian was stern. She said: "We have not any maps. You would have to see the Carnegie Library." I suggested an atlas. She stared at me, and finally replied: "You evidently do not know we just begin." Then she had a change of heart, and said "We have some beautiful enceeclopaedias, however." She got up, and led me to a shelf where there was the promised set. "Some pages miss, but you will find something." So many pages missed, that I was unable even after half an hour to find WEST INDIES. So I gave it up. As I went out, she looked up, and said: "Is that all?" When I said it was, she pushed forward a notebook and a pen, and said: "Would you sign please, because some day we hope to be bigger." The library incidentally was in the same building as a printing office, and a political party rendezvous. And as usual in Puerto Rico, they all had the same ceiling, with nothing but partitions perhaps eight feet high between. So one could hear everything that went on in the room on each side. In hotels it is more annoying. But I think the natives never sleep at night; only at noon.

As I have suspected, de Falla is for the Spanish no Debussy . . . rather a

---

* . . . but it's true. A little less animated. Back to the old days [A play on *tempo primo*, back to the time of the first movement].

† "God, ah, God! The gentleman from New York. How happy I am!!" . . . GOD BLESS OUR HOME. "Want something? Have something! Oranges?"

Gershwin or Stephen Foster. Any sailor on the boat will ask if I have no records of "Falla." Any waiter will speak of Noches en los Jardines de España . . . muy bonito . . . They know Amor Brujo and Sombrero de Tres Picos as well as an American sailor knows Old Black Joe. The clerks in the hotels in Spain speak of Marchena, "Falla," and Segovia in the same breath. All that is completely admirable. Who else in the world can be presented with premières auditions chez Polignac, à la Sérénade, League of Composers, International Music Festivals, and still be the best known to everyone in his country. It is incredible, the extent to which he is known in Spain. Known, really, to the porter who carries your trunk from the station, to the taxi-driver, to the grocer-woman, to everyone. And the Spanish are surprising in a certain strange indifference they exhibit: In Granada one day this Summer I was talking in a lane with my friend Valdomero. De Falla walked past at the end of the lane a few metres distant. "That was de Falla, wasn't it?" I said. He assented, without any surprise that I should have recognized him. So, pursuing: "He is very well-known here?" "Yes, very famous here and everywhere." Which ended that subject. Conocido yo famoso, aquí y en todas partes, but with no change of expression on face, inflection in voice. Sometimes it is as though one were talking with madmen. I am used to it because of having been with Arabs, but with them it seems expected. One exchanges banalities: It is warm, the war will come next year, I like mint tea. (The more educated ones this time I discovered to have turned in "formidable" and "épouvantable" for "lamentable" and "catastrophique.") But with the Spanish it comes about naturally that one should be talking as one would with the French, and suddenly one finds one's self leaning against the air.

I am copying the group of piano pieces. Then I shall send you copies of them, of Danger de Mort, and of the Cantata, none of which you have. I am rather vague as to what you have and what you haven't, of the preceding things. Can you remember?

Before leaving Fez, I was tempted to write to M. Bompain in Constantine and ask him if he still wanted me to help him in his studio (I told you of the letter he sent me?), but remembering the sad February weather there, and the nearly as sad March rains, I shivered. And there is also something threatening about the town, perched there above the roaring in the gorge, with its hollownesses in the rocks opposite, like Dalí's bones, and its blue houses and slippery streets, and trembling footbridges and vultures and vistas off over the open countryside far below. Tu comprendras dès le moment que tu le verras, et tu n'oublieras jamais.

Je sais que tu as toujours le temps de lire tout ce que je t'écris, autrement
j'écrirais beaucoup moins. Sachant que tu le liras, je pourrais écrire indéfini-
ment, si ça ne me fatiguait pas.*
Écris American Consul, Barranquilla, Colombia.

TO BRUCE MORRISSETTE

November 29, 1934
Hotel Atlántico
Puerto Colombia

here it is a nest of germans, coming from inland to spend the holidays which
begin now. bathing. i leave tomorrow for panama. ¿usted no es alemán? ach!
pero la cara parece. ach, so.† lovely jungle and streams behind. i suppose no
more like that for a good while. certainly not in the united states. but the last
boat-trip was too horrible. millions mosquitoes. black water. river bank. stagnant
stink. boat bumping into the banks each ten minutes, backing up, scraping tree-
boughs against the sides. mosquitoes screaming about, biting. boat shivering
always as it went ahead, blowing its ungodly whistle at every turn of the narrow
passage. i tried to ease the bother with beer. no good. had no marijuanas with
me. they would have done the trick. after one of them i hear my african records
anew, find them more wonderful than ever. but had none. so forewent the
magangué trip. the country aches to be explored. here one person is said to have
been, here no one has ever been. here on the maps is marked unexplored. one
is told tales at each turn, of buried treasure, is shown ancient square coins, gold
noserings. bought a pair of birds of paradise the other day. bought a set of seven
little silver rings all to be worn on the same finger. bought a record. my spiders
decayed of course. now i have naught but a tarantula-leg, which i am growing
rather fond of. it has a good deal of character, with its black hair, and its knee-
joint. signs in the street: LAXOL . . . EL PURGANTE DE LA GENTE DISTINGUIDA.**
And one to the effect: be careful which worm-medicine you give your child.

* You will understand the moment you see it, and you will never forget.
  I know you still have the time to read everything I write to you, otherwise I would
write much less. Knowing that you will read it, I could write on indefinitely, if it did
not tire me out.
† You aren't German? Ach! But the dear boy looks German. Ach, so.
** THE LAXATIVE USED BY DISTINGUISHED PEOPLE

there is only one: SAINT TERESA. there is a boat in barranquilla called: the abundance of bananas. of course no mail came for me. i suppose no one wrote. there was certainly enough time for it to arrive. if there is any, some day i shall get it and somewhere. in santa marta an acquaintance of the hotel invited me to meet his mother. con mucho gusto. gracias, muy contento, señora. no, acabo de llegar a colombia. no, pero vengo ahora de africa.* she would scream ay, ay, ay, ay after each sentence as i finished it. finally she called her daughter, who punctuated my phrases with "¡Caramba, caramba!" so i told them all about the girl in ghardaïa who killed her child and how the dogs found it and ate it, and how i found the newborn baby with its throat cut. i must have talked half an hour. when finally i decided to go, the mother, who up to that moment had been propriety itself, shriveled herself up in face and body, held out her hand, and said in a hideous whine: ¿y puede regalarme veinte centavos para comprar el pan?† i gave them to her and fled. never quite so befuddled. aquí no sé lo que hay, pero me molesta bastante . . . tengo siempre un poco de fiebre; a cualquier hora del día está siempre más que normal. ¡Algunos creen que tiene un origen palúdico, otros dicen que sin duda he bebido agua mala y que eso me ha dado un cólico! Pero así tuve miedo de irme muy lejos de la costa, donde hay algunos americanos. y por eso no he visto el interior del país; lástima, lástima, dice todo el mundo. la próxima vez, talvez (es curioso, pero aquí no se dice quizás se dice siempre talvez, y dios sabe lo que quiere decir). también aquí se dice horita para ahora mismo, un momentico para un momentito, y bonitos, y me gustan.** DANIEL WRITES THAT YOUR HANDWRITING HAS CHANGED SO MUCH . . . AND IN THE SELFSAME WAY THAT MINE HAS. what does such a statement mean? i have tried to get an answer from him, but he ignores my queries. (en este momento los mosquitos me comen vivo.) (mañana por la mañana escribiré otras paginas.)‡ (the animals here are covered with a coalblack

---

* I'd be delighted. thank you, happy to meet you, madam. no, I've just come to colombia. no, but I've just now come from africa.
† And could you give me twenty centavos to buy bread?
** I don't know what's going on around here, but it's bothering me quite a bit . . . I've always got a slight fever; at any hour of the day, it's always above normal. Some people think it's malarial in origin, others say that no doubt I've drunk bad water and that it's given me a stomach problem! But for that reason I was afraid to go too far away from the coast, where there are some Americans. and that's why I haven't seen the interior of the country; what a shame, what a shame, everyone says. the next time, perhaps (it's strange, but here no one says *quizás* for perhaps, only *talvez*, and God knows what that means). They also say *horita* for right now, *un momentico* for just a moment, and they're charming, and I like them.
‡ (right at this moment the mosquitoes are eating me alive.) (tomorrow morning I'll write some more pages.)

powder, and hold their hindlegs coyly behind them in the air when they alight. and how i hate them, and how i hate them. misery of an otherwise highly amusing place.)

[*Later*] adages i contrived to learn in sleep last night (having sent my mother with two strange women to wander in the kasbah of tanger, having entered an enormous department store where they sold nothing but dominoes by the pair in little boxes. Ivory, and all double blank. all the clerks having asked me if i wanted to buy a pair of cufflinks for my girl . . . the dominoes it seems being cufflinks . . . i objecting, they finally showing me white kid gloves and gaudy neckties which i was starting to buy for myself . . . then i discovered the adages pressing in from above, with voices):

Never put a dollar in a pound cent envelope, and you'll have one less under your snow.

Walking gives us the right to be danish.

He who gives a garden to a tea-glass friend laments and lakes afresh.

and by the time the third adage had got through and i had devoted enough attention to it to learn it, i was looking at colored postcards of which i disapproved, and of which i said to myself: "it's only alger, after all." then having found subconsciously the adages amusing i woke myself up before i should forget them.

in santa marta the hotel manager boiled the water his family consumed, but not that which he gave to his clients. mosquiteros over the beds are important because of the scorpions that fall off the ceiling during the night, but they did not supply them unless one asked for them. coming back to barranquilla i went to the hotel magdalena. there the maid immediately asked me if i had my own sheets, and seemed a bit scornful to find i had not. and there they put bananas into the soup, which seemed to me the last word in chic. je t'envoie un instantané . . . moi déguisé en légionnaire à erfoud le mois passé . . . est-ce possible? vers le dix octobre . . . mais je dirais il y a six mois! tu auras une carte ici et là, et tu écriras?*

---

* i send you a snapshot . . . me disguised as a foreign legionnaire in erfoud last month . . . is it possible? around october tenth . . . but it seems like six months to me! you will have a postcard here and there, and you will write?

TO JOHN WIDDICOMBE

December 4, 1934
San José de Guatemala

The sun shines on the sharks. The Chinamen lean over the deck-railings catching fish: Oh ee yo mow high ow! I think I sent a card from Santa Marta. Colombia was quite insane, and a longer sojourn there would have made me the same. First of all, the food was mad. Everything came onto the table at once: soup, full of bananas, rice, beans, meat, salad, fish, fried bananas, papayas, dulce de leche, coffee. In the hotels the servants came into the room asking: I suppose you carry your own sheets with you? Upon hearing I did not, they were always quite unfavorably impressed, and went off in a sulky mood. Then when the bed was made up, with one sheet, never more, they would inform me that inasmuch as scorpions usually fell off the ceiling onto the beds at night, and as there were a good many mosquitoes (which unfortunately I knew without being told), it would really be better if I had a mosquito-netting over the bed. But, of course, they added, it cost a certain amount more. And the water was full of brown mud that took a half hour to settle. Even then it gave me colic, cramps, fever, and every sort of unpleasantness. I gently inquired of the waiter if everyone drank the water there. He assured me that no one ever did, unless it was boiled and filtered first, as it came from the nearby river where lived many alligators, and was not exactly pure. Then I was a bit indignant, and asked him why he had served me with it every day. "You asked for water, and said nothing about boiled water, you know," he reminded me, "and the proprietor only boils enough each day for his own private use, unless the clients want extra water boiled, in which case they must pay extra, of course." I was bathing on the beach, and wanted to get across the mouth of the river. A boy said he would enjoy carrying me across. I scoffed at the idea, so he accompanied me along the riverbank to a part of the village where he lived. Negresses crouched about under the tremendous trees, wearing nothing but a cache-sexe; screaming at the children who peeked down the great crab-holes in the mud, waiting for the huge claws to appear. Parrots vied with them from above. The boy wanted to know if I would like to meet his mother and sister. Con mucho gusto, and so on, I said. So when we arrived at a bamboo hut with sugarcane roof, he bade me wait, and soon appeared his mother, Indian and Negroid slightly. The sister hovered in the middle distance while I told stories of Africa, she murmuring ¡Caramba! at the end of each phrase. The mother screamed outright at the statement of each fact, and rocked back and forth. When twilight had come, I begged leave to go. The mother smiled, and suggested I give her twenty centavos to buy some bread with. We are very poor, she sighed. And you are a pleasant gentleman. "How much did you ask him for?" said the daughter. "Twenty," said the mother. "¡Caramba! He'll never want to understand," replied the daughter. So she counted up to twenty for me, fearing that I might pretend to have heard only fifteen. Then after I had given the coins, she whispered to me: "Why don't you take my son to the movies tonight? He loves it. Then afterward you two could take a walk on the beach!" Which is just what we did. About Barranquilla are signs advertising Saint Teresa Worm Medicine. In smaller type beneath it warns: Give your son only the best worm medicine, not any old kind. And there is a product called Laxol, which they strive to sell by calling it El Purgante de la Gente Distinguida. On the Magdalena there was a ship called: The Abundance of Bananas. I went off into the most beautiful jungle imaginable with a horse, which the next day turned into a mule for cliff-work higher up. With a machete to hack away what extra vines might bar the way. Too lovely. Go some day, and tell me when, as I should like to go back, and not stay in hotels the way I did this time. I doubt if there is one mediocre hotel in the republic. They are all lousy. A gentleman shares my cabin with me. His given name on the luggage is Ike, which seems exaggerated. But there it is. He has recently been despoiled of all his teeth. "I got noo ones made," he informed me, "but I keep dem locked up. Dem Chinamen schteals everyting." There are two aesthetes who came aboard at Panama. They eat only fruit and raw vegetables. The gentleman is fascinated by them, and inquires at each meal what they are eating, as they eat in their cabin. "Do dey eat fish?" he says. "No," I say. "Why for dey dun't fish? Fish is gut." And the same formula has been used for every kind of food and drink he has been able to think of. He awakes at midnight, and walks about, talking of the good times "when Hoofer vas." And when various passengers were late back last night from San Salvador, "Dem louses, dey make us vait vile dey rob the public in Mexico." "This is not Mexico," I insisted. He was far from daunted. "All publics iss alike," he proclaimed.

Next week I shall be in Los Angeles. What then I have no idea. Did you get my letter from Tenerife? Write to Jamaica, and it will reach me. I wonder whether you will go to Morocco for Christmas. And whether Mary Oliver will go. I shall try to get to England next year sometime, as I think I should like living there. My entire trip from Canaries to West Indies was spent in the

Infirmary with tonsillitis! My Chleuh discs saved the day. Now I have swell Cuban and Mexican ones.

entonces, no puedo escribir mas ahora. hasta luego. *

TO DOROTHY NORMAN

◆

December 1934
Quetzlcoatl and others, S.A.

To be heard to the tune of an electric fan. Along brighter lines. Only too well. S.A. (Société, Anonyme), Gibraltar's Main Street to which you refused to write, dark, nearly all the Hindus having gone home. But buslines still function. Reina Cristina, with the Reina crossed out. Tanger as always, annexed Abdeslam against my advice. Fez brought about arrest and tears. Moi je m'en foutais. Le légionnaire dit: C'est un Arabe, enfin. † So we left him in prison, and sped off. Garments in Arabic. Kaftan. Cádiz with the cathedral smile. In streets too shining, squares too screaming: el diario, el diario. Las mujeres son bonitas, yo te lo digo** . . . Sevilla and blood, searches along the empty boulevards at midnight, taxi rushing. Summer air and the Alcázar. Oleanders along the paths. Snails dried to the thistle-stalks. Who cried out? Taste this Tio Pépé 1847, free to all. Gonzalez and Byass. And the bulls dropped slowly. ¡El aficionado está en la cárcel! ¡Olé!‡ And why live longer? And the village below the Alhambra. Sunlight heats Cuevas de los Gitanos. But here, señor, you will find it cool. Have some water, never mind the moss. Beyond cry the hills, drying brown, drying hot. The talking films in Gibraltar again. Kill me soon, I merit only that. We are pinkly aware, my dear. Into the Rif. Grottoes and excrement, flowers, cedars on the heights. ¿Qué busca aquí?§ And the distant evening. And the serpents knew the dance, and did it. And the drums knew the music, and played it. And the water fell always beneath the weeds, gurgling. Marrakech camels laughed at nudity in the streets. They were installing a sewer system in the city. Beneath the mud houses. And the garbage alleys. Menara once again, frogs singing at the far end. Aguedal once again, olives not yet ripe. New road across

---

* well, I can't write any more now. good-bye.
† Me, I didn't give a damn. The foreign legionnaire said, "He's an Arab."
** paper, get your paper now! These women are sweet—and how!
‡ The *aficionado* is in the pen! Olé!
§ What are you looking for here?

the Atlas, my God! Yes, peacocks and amethysts, all offered free of charge. Only
for to be shown the Kasbah. Mud, sun, south, goodbye. And a naked week by
the Atlantic. And a windy day on the roof. My red na'als, my white serouals,
my return to Spain, my return from Spain cursing, to Fez. My fight. My own
with Abdeslam. My Fez. And the journey to Sahara, when they all killed thirty-
seven of them. I lay in bed listening. Like that. It was very quiet. Pinkly aware.
All too well. Date harvest. Killing them all in the palmeraie. Next malaria,
fever-worry. Centigrade and quinine. Alsacian doctor. Military low in Spain.
Forbidden this, y prohibido eso. No move from here. Canaries and too god
damned hot. Infirmary to Antilles. Rumba once again beneath the papaya tree,
for me, all for me! Santo Domingo or bust. Did. Venezuela or exclaim. Nearly
did. Gómez is an idiot, old thing. Curaçao and marijuana. Quelle faim que ça
donne, mon dieu! Si j'avais su, si j'avais su, j'aurais attendu jusqu'à demain.
El estómago vácio. Papiamento. Colombia por fin.* A trip up the mosquito,
does it attract you? This touristless territory. Pinkly aware, my dear. The Goajira
will be the death of you yet, with its heat and its Indians. Never miss with their
arrows, señor. Never. We boil the water only if you ask to have it boiled. But
of course it will give you diseases unless you ask. Tarantulas jumping. Scorpions
falling stupidly from the ceiling. Nearer, so easier, so duller. With one machete,
one mule, try the selva virgen. Smell the ferns, touch the orchids. Diagnosis of
a maniacal civilization. So far from the music. ¡El purgante de la Gente Distinguida! Vermifugo Santa Teresa. El Mejor para su Hijo. Finca de Café.† And
the quiet lady from Bogotá caught the tremendous arachnids in her hat. Mosquitoes for sale, basement bargain. Cristóbal at eveningtime. Gatún Lake over-
flowed. Panama City pretty wet, fellow. By wet, wet. Salvador lad who wanted
a bathing-suit, and badly. Thinking again, said the Red Queen. Atitlán, sugarcane gables, all too well. Serais-tu prêt à faire une longue fuite?‡ That's what
he said. All too well. And Mexico with socavones, tristes, highlands, frijoles.
Oh, he knew well, pinkly aware. No more cirrus to beware. No more mornings
to seduce . . . è ben trovato . . . . . . è ben trovato, anche vero. All too
true** . . .

---

* How hungry it makes you, my god! If I had known, if I had known, I would have
waited until tomorrow. An empty stomach. Pidgin Spanish. Colombia finally.
† The laxative used by Distinguished People! Vermifuse Santa Teresa. The Best for your
Child. Coffee Plantation.
‡ Are you ready to take a long jaunt?
** And Mexico with washed-out roads, sad, highlands, beans. No more cirrus to beware.
No more mornings to seduce . . . well put, and true. All too true . . .

TO DANIEL BURNS

December 1934
At sea, between Mazatlán und San Pedro, California

I am tempted to begin: why have you not written? Because it seems always that you should have. I have had no mail in practically two months. Comble d'ennui. So saying, I enclose you a poem, proof of impending boredom. When the exterior life palls, the interior starts working. If I moved always to new places, I should never work at all: no music, no nothing. If I were enclosed ill in a room, I should work prodigiously, be happy in a way at the antipodes. And it is immaterial to me which befalls me. Only not deprived of sight. Comble d'ennui. So saying, I left Colombia. A pleasant couple had a brother, wanted me to wait. Fonseca was their village, in the jungle. Plantation. And they asked me to accompany the brother tomorrow all about the interior, on horses, in autos, in boat. And they asked me to stay with them at their plantation for the winter. But the intervening fifteen days with nothing to do disgusted me. And so I used them to journey to California in. Now I should like to wake up tomorrow morning at Santa Marta. But it will be Los Angeles. Disappearing hasaluban. In a wave of negligence I managed not to bring anything with me from Morocco this time, when there were dozens of things I meant to bring. Particularly incenses. Instead I carried what I had from New York there, burned it, and came away empty-handed. Curaçao was an amusing place. There I began marijuana, which I have since decided is not quite healthy to use. Thus I have sold all I had, and profited thereby pleasantly (inasmuch as all I had was given me by a frightened person who was carrying pounds!). The only souvenir is the very strong odor in my luggage, which will probably intrigue customs officials who sniff it out. I shall say it is a variety of South American civet, one of them having discovered my luggage one evening in a prowl onto the verandah of the finca in the selva. I have not devoted so much attention to the care of my fingernails since typhoid in Auteuil. Apart from that, there has been sun, usually much too hot to sit or lie in, the sad fin of Le Temps Retrouvé, Grammaire Historique, El Genio del Séptimo Arte, Les Variations du Corps Humain (il-lustré), a thoughtful gift from John S. Widdicombe, who bought it in Meknès on coming out of a disappointing hammam, copying of a group of piano pieces, attempts to continue the creation of a violin sonata begun in the Grand Hotel of Fez, my consoling little phonograph which plays for me all my Fassi, Chleuh, Oranais, Flamenco, Cuban and Mexican records, an idiotic little old Jew who inhabits my cabin, and is forever using the word "fanatic" ("Yeh, here on the ship they givityuh fanatic"), the Filipino and Chinese waiters to argue with, the crew to watch catch barracudas, the agreeable passage through the Canal, with a day at each end to shop, and the escales at San Salvador and Guatemala. (At Mazatlán it was too rough for anyone to go ashore. The vendedores tied their rowboats alongside and vended and vended all the day long.) I have an address in New York which I shall strive to make popular, if it is amusing. 79 James Street. Nick's. Toward a colder clime. Now the Pacific looks quite like the Atlantic. I should like to continue up to Alaska, now that I've left behind comfortable weather. If you want news, you will have to ask Bruce for letters. I can't say the same things in two different letters. Even be there twenty, one will get the news, the others bits of refuse, certainly no less flattering, je t'assure, perhaps even less langweilich. I suppose New York is fun. I should like to be there. But I have to travel to do, you know. As long as it doesn't get me into a rut. (Or into rut. Or this or that.) Write me at my home, as always. I shall not be there, as usual. They will forward, as required. I shall receive, as expected . . .

My fingers are paralyzed with yawning.

TO BRUCE MORRISSETTE
———————◆———————

December 1934
Creston Drive
Hollywood

The wire just arrived. Merci. I don't know just when it will be. There seems no hurry to reach New York. The climate here is now seductive, sunbaths, birdsong, roses' Junish odor, Indian Summer haze spread thick across the valleys, ocean with more than Mediterranean calm, more than Carib calm even some days. And nights when I lie in bed and my earstops loosen, I hear one coyote barking across the arroyo. It all has a charm, all save the town which one avoids as much as one can, and which is really no more than the midway of a mediocre exposition which has been held over longer than it deserved. Men wear blue shoes, women wear bangles about their legs unless they have on trousers. They all still believe the directors seek talent on the boulevards and it is too dégueulasse. Aaron writes he doesn't think New York is particularly active. I shall go up to San Francisco in January, where Cowell will be master of ceremonies. There is a Mexican Greenwich Village here, quite the artiest spot in existence, but where one can engage in good long Spanish conversations with the natives; which brings one back to reason. It is all gone now in America our country. One sees it better each time. The entire life is like a jeu whose rules are purely arbitrary and mean next to nothing. And speaking to most of our countrymen requires the same finesse as speaking to obsessed old people. Out here it is worse: idiocy in the sunlight, madness beneath the palms. But I remain alone on hikes to swell views, magnificent valleys, colored mountainranges, complete quiet. It is still easy to escape out here. Riding I came to a town one day called Tarzana, honoring the great author Burroughs, whose estate was somewhere nearby. But to see it all on large U.S. Highway signs was too cockeyed. And on the benches along Hollywood Boulevard there are bronze plaques: Lawrence Tibbett! Thoma has some lovely stills Cocteau gave him, of how they made Le Sang d'un Poète. Salemson is too awful. He was giving a lecture at the John Reed Club night-beforelast to which we promised to be, but we failed to go. He has Marxism to such an extent that his mind is quite paralysed. But Thoma and I lit into him for several solid hours, and annoyed him. Mme. Thoma brings out her autograph books each time, and it is quite fun. Everyone has left a picture, a sentence, a page, a letter, a line of music. In the composers' section she has letters from Puccini, Godard, d'Indy, Saint-Saëns, Massenet, Honegger, Ravel, who wrote some Bolero for her, Stravinsky, who wrote some Sacre, Antheil and on and on. And letters from the Queen of Madagascar and the Queen of Roumania and the Queen of Belgium, all that being in the queens' section. She looks mad, wears her hair shaved, and horrible black suits with a white shirt and a black "tux" tie. Rather like a sad old waiter. Her tales of Rachilde and Alastair are fun. I went down the other day to make you a copy of your portrait. The place turned out to be the local broadcasting station, and the prices were about ten times what I had expected to pay, so I came away recordless. One has to make an appointment, and chicy and chichi . . . I have a copy of the Cantata for you, as well as the group of piano pieces, and Danger de Mort. My friend Turner writes from Chicago insisting I visit there en route. Aaron has just returned from there where he turned out the ballet ordered of him, and he says it is very lively and he likes it. T. tells me Gertrude was a total flop and has cancelled all her lecture tour. But Four Saints went to Chicago. It was suggested there for the audience that they try listening to it with "blank minds." A. says Virgil is in N.Y. Woollcott says Gertrude is in N.Y. . . . So it can't be too horrible. "Victor Hugo était un fou qui se croyait Victor Hugo." Il y a des choses très bien dans L'Essai de Critique Indirecte. L'as-tu lu? Il y parle enfin du

Zauberberg, de Dalí, de Baudelaire, et de Smara, dont je t'ai parlé à Fez. Michel
Vieuchange qui est allé chercher Smara au milieu du Río de Oro. Il y a cinq
cents Espagnols dans toute la colonie: ils ont une peur bleue des indigènes, qui
ne leur font pas même attention. Que ce doit être désagréable, la frousse d'être
dans leur pays: la même frousse qu'aurait un cambrioleur surpris dans une maison
dont le propriétaire vient de rentrer. Il parle du visage de Vieuchange au retour
de Smara. C'est un livre que je dois acheter. J'en ferai son pareil peut-être un
jour. "Un regard qui nous regarde et qui voit la ville!"

Je suis fainéant, lent.*

Dis bonjour à Hilton, Hunter, others you see.

I am pleased with Gertrude's fiasco. Greatest success.

TO BRUCE MORRISSETTE
———————————◆———————————

January 27, 1935
San Francisco

I have been busy with music this way and that. My "Scenes from the Door"
I took to National Broadcasting, did I tell? and they wired to N.Y. for permission
to use the words. Next day word came from Harcourt Brace, so they scheduled
them for last Tuesday. They were well sung, and the publicity over the mike
was three times as long as the two songs. Quotes from Toklas, about me, the
Ford, and the War. It was enjoyable. I see Columbia has recorded Varèse's
"Ionisation." I heard it played twice in succession last winter. All right, for that.

Cowell took me down to the campus of Stanford to listen to him lecture on
rhythm. The class consisted of twenty or so students who sat about and banged
on every sort of percussion instrument, following the exercises he wrote out on
the blackboard for them. I had to play the claves, the click, click, click, clickclick

---

* "Victor Hugo was a madman who thought he was Victor Hugo." There are some very
nice things in L'Essai de Critique Indirecte. Have you read it? There he finally discusses
the Zauberberg, Dalí, Baudelaire, and Smara, about which I wrote to you from Fez.
Michel Vieuchange, who went off looking for Smara in the middle of the Río de Oro.
There are five hundred Spaniards in the entire colony: they are scared stiff of the natives,
who pay absolutely no attention to them. It must be unpleasant, that fear at being in
their territory: the same fear a burglar would have, surprised in someone else's house by
the owner's return. He speaks of Vieuchange's face when he came back from Smara. It
is a book I must buy. Perhaps I will write one like it some day. "A gaze that looks at us
and sees the city!"
I am slothful, slow.

of the rumba. Then we extemporized, and he waved his arms, and said: Yes, it's quite jolly.

And one evening he made copies of several of the discs. The Chleuhs captivated. In return for the favor he gave me some Central African ones, from the Yoruba tribe, and from the Ashanti, and from Eastern Sudan.

Ensuite he borrowed my mss., and decided to publish some in April. We saw the engraver today. Using a song from Anabase, two from Danger de Mort, and a piano piece, and perhaps a letter of Gertrude's which I set last week, and which tickled him. The things will be coupled with Espiral, for Violin and Piano, of Chavez. Thank God.

Set one of Cocteau's this week.: Les statues dorment l'étrange sommeil animal, etc . . .* The help from God seems all to come through an unexpected medium. C. has also arranged an evening, day after tomorrow in Berkeley, when they will have a pianist, a singer, a fiddler, an oboist (for Anabase), and a flutist, so I can hear all the things. It's a swell idea of course, and is what I have wondered for, for years.

The happiest part of the sudden late acquaintance is C's promise to provide me some sort of recording equipment to take with me to Middle Africa. The best one belongs to the International Society for Comparative Music, which hearts in Yale. They have just let him have it for an expedition to Ecuador, which will be back this Spring. The whether depends upon the condition in which it is returned. Otherwise a less good apparatus. The Yale one cost $3800, so it must be quite swell. Cowell agrees with me that the territory to explore is the Niger valley, Tchad, Mauritania, etc.

John is at Oxford, trying to be severe.

What will you do with the thèse?

The Ballet Russe is here, doing the worst it has. Went to a tea for Adolph Weiss, of it, yesterday. Dukelsky has been following Massine all over the continent this Winter, trying to get him to take a ballet. M. finally gave in. Carl Ruggles, whom I visited in Vermont a few years ago, has been being supported for years by a kind lady who has never heard a note of his music. This Winter Slonimsky was to play something new of his, and Ruggles was coming to rehearse. The last minute R. sent a wire cancelling the performance. It seems the lady had decided to journey down from Boston and hear it. R. was in a sweat. She imagines it sounds like Brahms of course. He lives in constant terror for fear she will drop in as a surprise and ask him to play for her.

---

* The statues sleep their strange animal sleep, etc.

It is pure Spring here now.

Daniel writes a ridiculous letter telling me of the beauties of San Francisco, of his charming friends, all of whom I have met and none of whom I hope ever to see again if I can help it. "You will surely come to love it as much as I do. You will think you're in Amsterdam or Copenhagen. There are breathtaking views from every hilltop. Wait till you have seen the Seal Rock and the Palace of Arts (quelle horreur!) and the Court at the Legion of Honor and the Park. Sometimes you will think you're in England, at other times in Vienna or Paris or a provincial town of France. You will eat excellent food and hear good music and meet interesting people."

I can only believe that Daniel ought to do the sop for the Chamber of Commerce. There is nothing like all that. It looks like an uprooted Brooklyn.

And he sends me a crisp dollar bill in the letter with the instructions: "Please use the enclosed for a little "do" with Brad. Take her somewhere and treat her to a cup of tea or something—sans faute."

c'est trop

Mary Oliver asks me to go to Spain and boat with her this Summer. How? j'attends la tienne.

TO GERTRUDE STEIN

February 1935
San Francisco

I am on my way back again to New York from Africa (I know you don't call it Africa), and this has been such a nice place I have stayed on. But now I am going to leave for Chicago. I have made a song out of one of your best letters and "New Music" wants to print it. What I should like is your permission written or printed on paper, which I can send on or show to the publisher, otherwise the editor, Henry Cowell, is frightened that you may be angry about it. If you are to be in New York in a few weeks, and prefer to wait until you see it, it can be done that way, but it would be easier if you could send word to me c/o Turner, 1915 Colfax St., Evanston, Ill. as soon as it is convenient. I hope very much you will be somewhere in the East when I arrive there, but you will probably be out here. Best, Freddy.

TO BRUCE MORRISSETTE
❖

April 12, 1935
Jamaica, New York

First the Vipères would publish Virgil, then me, then Virgil, etc. V's five piano pieces will be out soon. Heard his Second Quartet last night and it was lovely. Wednesday heard his Mass at Town Hall which was amusing. Only he said it should have been sung by nuns, not American virgins. I wrote it up for *Modern Music* next number. Piano Fantasia is new, and I shall hear it in a fortnight at any rate. Whether it will be given to the public or not I don't know. Just composed and haven't written yet a composite portrait of Virgil, smiling sweetly, Aaron remembering the World, Roger looking careful and honest, George Antheil in a hurry to go, and Israel Citkowitz being as pleasant as he can. It passes from one to the other. There is to be another concert up at Hartford next month, and something will be done about it. Week ago last Saturday went to the Boston Symphony or did I tell you about it with Lillian Gish and Stravinsky? Or Cecil Beaton party? It was completely mad at any rate. Tchelitchew did the costumes and Charles Ford gave him a black eye. Marlene Dietrich sent over a pile of records which they smashed every one. Princess Paley sat on a couch with Nabokov looking coldly about, and soon she decided to go. Nicholas was overjoyed, and danced a jig with Hoyningen-Huene about it. Then they broke everything and threw pots of geraniums at the dancers, pulled the gold sequin butterflies off the piano, had a prolonged battle with madonna lilies. Beaton was dressed as Mephisto, and lay on the floor packed in ice! Drank large bottles of Chanel no. 23 or whatever. One bathroom was Bérard and one was Beaton, whose drawings I never liked too much; but he had some wonderful photos, really wonderful.

Someone threw a stack of Max Ernst engravings at me and I pursued him and hit him until I broke his glasses, and then I went home just before dawn.

It would be splendid of course if something were played down there, but would it be?

I am worried about the doctor's bill. No, don't you pay it, whatever you do. But I think you could write the doctor and have him send it to Margaretta. I wrote her thanking her for having paid it. Long ago. But I haven't three dollars at the moment, and if I ever got it, it would mean as much as fifteen meant ever before as I never have been so fauché.

Perhaps if you do come, we can devise a way. And do, when you can. Bus is cheap, no? Daniel is free at Easter of course too, and he does often pay. At least for me. Reminiscent Piano Pieces include Café Sin Nombre, Guayanilla, 8 Impasse de Tombouctou, the little Prelude about Maldoror, and La Femme de Dakar, dite Cornichon.

How amusing was New York then? I don't know just when you mean, but take it the days after returning from Europe. It's always amusing if you see the right people. Carl V. V. is about again (not one of the right people, but) and he said to me the other night: You don't change at all, but in an impudent sort of way. The Berman show is nice. Berman himself is nice. The African show lovely. Come while they're on, if you can. That is, now.

¿¿¿toz sen vait???

TO WILLIAM TREAT UPTON

◆

[Spring 1935]
Jamaica, New York

The briefness of what is to follow is due partly to the fact that I feel that this letter may easily not reach you in time to be of any use to you even though it contains some points which you have not considered (which I doubt); and partly to the effect upon me of my own approach to all music, which is preeminently an instinctive one and one which thus all but precludes any consciousness of method.

Art-music will get what it needs not from new subjects to sing about (i.e. the proletariat or a hundred other literary ideas), nor from technical devices (quarter tones and careful rhythms, etc. as such), but from new ways to sing, which means that it will be increasingly conscious of folk-musics of all corners of the globe, particularly the now unfamiliar corners. The Italian idea will be but one among scores of others. Singers will have to master the cante Flamenco, the difficult Chleuh songs, the Annamite lyrics, the Mexican, Cuban, and other Latin-Indian tricks, as well as the Central African declamation and the myriads of Arabic innuendos (to mention a few of the more important styles), in order to sing what should be written in the near future if the solo art-song is to be expected to remain in existence. (I say all this not because I have written such music, but I have begun to write such music because I have lived exclusively in the places where the musics mentioned above are sung, which is a little different.)

When one considers the potentialities of endless variety lying latent in the human throat, and hears the miserable and pitiful sounds which issue from a concert hall during a famous singer's recital, one commences to realize the size of the task that lies ahead of the composer and the truly creative interpreter to keep this form of music alive beyond the time of the present dying generation. Because the next generation won't take it.

(For myself, I have used Arabic declamation more than the others because it comes more readily to my subconscious. In *Memnon* I have also used hand-clappings, which are executed by the singer between strophes.)

With apologies for being unable to send you music.

TO KATHERINE COWEN

August 21, 1935
Watkins Glen, New York

Il y a longtemps déjà que je te dois une lettre. Tu me pardonneras?* Yes, a little change in the Portrait, little in notes, big in effect (audible only to me and Copland). If you like I'll send the revision. I'd like some day to publish a volume of portraits. There are scarcely enough now. No, no longer ill. But chilled at the prospect of receding summer which I should like to detain by clutching hold of crickets, green leaves. It was no fun in Wood's Hole. I met two nice girls who invited me back later, but at the last moment I gave it up. The town doesn't please me. This one however does, and I shall always love it. I enclose old reference to the letter from Norman. You see? When will you be going down to the city next? I expect to be back there in a fortnight, after seeing an aunt in New Hampshire en route. Now I have a book I feel you must read if you haven't. And it's not to do with literature exactly. *Fascism and Social Revolution* by R. Palme Dutt. Your suggesting that I might be, and subsequent declaring that in all probability I was, a Fascist, upset me to the point of needing to find out. But you were not right, of course! Since then I have read at least fifteen works on the subject, subscribed to the *Daily Worker* (which arrives each noon here in the large galvanized-iron mail-box on the dusty road), and thought each day

* I have owed you a letter for a long time now. Forgive me?

and dreamed each night of naught but the subject. But the book I say you should
read by all means if you can get hold of it. International Publishers, 381 4th
Ave., N.Y.

Yes, Satie is always good.

No, Bill [Saroyan] never looked me up.

Of course not.

You know quite well I shan't get fat. Am having poems in the next numbers
of *Le Dernier Carré* (Poitiers) and *Alentour* (U.S.A.). If they send me copies I
shall forward them to you.

Quand la guerre arrivera, viendras-tu à New York aider tes camarades dans
leur travail?

Glenora via Dundee, New York

mes amitiés à ta mère.*

TO GERTRUDE STEIN
——————————◆——————————

Spring 1936
Jamaica, New York

I am really a very good correspondent, but I have to have something to write
about. I might almost say, a favor to ask or something to disagree about. I have
been intending to write to you for well over a year, but I had no favor I could
ask you, and I should not be writing this certainly unless I had just read the
Money piece in the *Saturday Evening Post*, about which of course I disagree.
We are all voting for Roosevelt in November, and we believe he will be elected
again. We certainly hope so, not because he is any good himself, but because
his staying in will keep a Republican out. And they must be kept out by every
possible means. As far as the spending goes, it doesn't worry us a bit.

Harry Dunham returned today from a long stay in the vicinity of Mount
Washington, where he has been making a ski-film. Virgil had lunch with us,
and the two of them discussed the movie, which was a good thing, as I imagine
Harry hasn't thought of it for a few weeks. There is a certain amount of argument
about where the film is to be made: Harry wants to do it in Cincinnati where

---

* When war breaks out, will you come to New York to help your comrades in their
work?
  Glenora via Dundee, New York
  My regards to your mother.

he can use his home and his friends' gardens, but Virgil wants it to be done here in New York because he is tied here himself by the W.P.A. Theatre Project. I don't give a damn where they do it, because if they go to Ohio I can't be with them because the Dunhams are after my head, and if they do it here in New York I shan't be here anyway. Virgil is taking Cocteau to see his play tonight. It is really of course not Virgil's, but he arranged some music for it. Negro Macbeth. Did I tell you I saw Miss Etta Cone frequently this Winter in Baltimore? I often enjoyed her stories of the early days, if not her Matisses, which have seemed to get bigger and bigger as the years progress. The most recent one is I should say about six feet by ten.

I am getting tired of New York again, but I haven't a very good idea of where to go. I suggested Morocco to my family a while ago, but my father said with an air of suspicion: He just wants the trip. Aaron Copland is going to Mexico tomorrow, and Genia Berman thinks he'll go in six weeks, but he has such a fear of being as he says embêté, that it's all he can talk about. My friend Morrissette who motorcycled me to Bilignin is going down shortly, to study at the newly established Workers' School. None of it sounds very good to me; I'd like to go to Ecuador.

Sometimes I have seen Donald Sutherland, who acts as though you had abandoned him. He is a very moody person, and consequently is often a bother. But I think he is only twenty or maybe twenty one. He probably writes you his changes of mind every so often. We are going to get Maurice Grosser up from Alabama when production starts on the film. It's all his idea, and he is very definite about it. I am still to do the music, which I think will be grisly, because the film will need it that way. Have you any preferences in music? I should love to be able to see you and Miss Toklas at Bilignin, and when are you coming back here?

What I mean about the spending is that it seems silly to talk about being far-sighted in a time when far-sightedness is a useless quality. We can lose only what we have, and after that somebody else loses, and we see to it that he does lose it, and doesn't try to put us in debt for it instead. Well, anyway, I'll bet Roosevelt gets in!

I hope you have a very pleasant summer. Best from Freddy Bowles.

TO DOROTHY NORMAN
·
April 1938
Hotel Aurora
Antigua

I didn't mean to leave you without a word as to the article I was expected to write for you. I thought I would get married so I did, and we started off for various parts of the world, as you might expect. We have been living in Costa Rica until last week, when we arrived in Guatemala on a Hamburg-America liner (and they were voting there on the occupation of Austria: 178 ja und 1 nein. Actually. I think we had the dissenter for lunch the next day). So excuse my disappearance. How could I have done it anyway? Will you use the diaries of Bluey in a number? And will you send a copy of the first issue when it appears? When we finish with Guatemala we shall go back to Costa Rica and thence to Panama, and thence to France unless Daladier makes so much trouble there that no one can get in, which I suppose wouldn't be surprising. But it is so difficult to get news here. Yesterday we had a panic in the hotel during luncheon. There was a sharp earthquake, and the rush to the patio would have pleased Orson Welles. The screams were not lacking in interest either. We own a beautiful parrot which I suppose we shall have to leave behind somewhere along the way, but I shan't care very much, as it is omnivorous, and has eaten its way through toothpaste, a pair of glasses, a copy of "I LOVE," a copper cage meant to keep it in, and a large mahogany armoire. We are quite used to animals now, having lived a while in Guanacaste with every known variety, and we scarcely ever revert to speech except for finer shades of meaning. And of course for correspondence. I was here in Antigua last May, and it is as beautiful as before. Good-bye.

TO CHARLES-HENRI FORD
·
January 1939
New York City

the letter came bringing no good news, considering pattison or however it goes. do you know it? it was the thing that censored our venus and adonis film back three years ago at the composers' forum concert. anyway i suppose it could be gotten around one way or another. but i should think you could help too in that. a smile properly placed. a wring of a hand at the warm moment, even two. all i can do is look correct and grin obscenely, assent and be dull to it, and maybe it asked more. it doesn't matter much. i'm sick in bed these days anyway, and don't get out. tac asked all about the opera, disappeared. i didn't mind. then *new masses* got wind of it one day, had me up to their new theatre on site of old club mirador at five two and broadway. had to play and sing and they approved so much and were sunk to know that it wasn't nearly finished. tony's was all right. it gave the protagonists a chance to make a few dollars for singing, me a chance to show my teeth above a white tie and hang my head before applause. we had a fire here in our house last night, and our room is pure barcelona tonight. we have to camp in other rooms until things are done for us. piles of rotten wood and bricks form barricades before the bathroom. the rats injure themselves en route from the west wall to the icebox. as soon as i am well i have to march in grand protest from washington square to city hall to cry injustice. it seems genia is back, hanging his head. i wanted to ask you questions about life in general but i have forgotten which ones. there is a small book by herbert aptheker called *the negro in the civil war* which i meant to send you but being ill in bed i gave it to juanita hall (where janie is tonight eating pancakes) but there is one thing i want so badly in vesey and that is someone somewhere to suggest the assistance of some willing whites, then denmark to refuse furiously. i think it would be truer, more beautiful, pointed, effective. the place for such an insert i can't indicate. you can. i'll send you the little book anyway, as soon as i can be up and out. touche is still more than annoyed that we should be collaborating, has threatened often to get himself a librettist, or is my subconscious showing through—and do i mean composer—and sure enough, i do, and he has. jerry moross who joined the party at the age of seventeen and let people know it and went to berlin with antheil and to cagnes with antheil, and to hollywood with antheil. other stops enroute. you guess which. no let me. is pavlik [Tchelitchew] misanthropic? thank you for your letter which contained no good news really.

(harry [dunham]'s address is in *Dilatory Domiciles* for any year, or don't you use it up there? 10 Patchin Place, but I am suspicious of you.)

August 1939
Staten Island, New York

Part one is written before I read the pages of Denmark that just arrived. Then I shall get them and write part two. It all goes with thanks for promptitude after such delay. This is my literary day. August is so hot and sad. I can never stand anything when it comes to the middle of it, and summer is that way. I love summer more than any other season, but I love to feel that it is on its way . . . never that it has actually arrived. There seems to be no way of experiencing it. In spring I always imagine I shall. In the autumn there is a slight relief because I no longer care, since everything is over, and I never believe another summer will come. So here we are in the middle of immense summer, with locusts and trees getting heavy with pears. It is sad. Crucify me. Why do you send encouragement to Tokyo, that city of little misguided monsters? I do agree that Dalí is a snot, but perhaps it's only because I haven't seen the Fair's Dream of Venus. We are so far from it all. Yes, Mrs. Reis now has Denmark, which she is studying. Jane made an extra copy to send her. Karson does the sets each week at Radio City Music Hall, also the Hot Mikado and other things I can't remember. DuBose Heyward is doing an opera on Denmark Vesey called Don't You Want To Be Free? I believe. I was afeared Karson had been assigned the sets and costumes and had been asked to get a look at our business so he could spy, but I don't think that is the case. However I shan't give the script to any more people-about-Bway. Peter Lind was here for a weekend ten days ago, and he told us a good deal of gossip from over there. I think Bruce Morrissette who is with Virgil in Italy will have more inclusive and detailed information if we can only hook him on his return. How the pedagogues do turn soft. I don't mean Virgil. America is hissing like a nest of ants, all about Father Coughlin. The stabbings on the streets are becoming more frequent. Disorders take place each day at Times and Union Squares. Lines of Coughlinites harass Jews and sell *Social Justice*. Non-Coughlinites hawk *Equality*, the new magazine to promote tolerance. Cops leer, but when they disappear people somehow get stabbed and are found lying on the sidewalk bleeding and accusing Coughlin. There is an increasing number of Jewish intellectuals who are taking lessons in marksmanship. Say they: At least I'll get a few before they get me. They fear a new war will unleash widespread fascist activity in the States. The Party I am sure frowns on these ridiculous people who now have double bolts on all their doors. The

Party says we must have no fear. Prospects look very black. The coming season sad. Irene Sharaff says there are no shows opening in the fall. No good ones, she means. Paramount is making a series of fascist movies, incredibly raw and stupid. I tried to get *Foyers d'Incendie* last year in Paris, but it wasn't published yet. Tried again here in the Autumn. Not yet. Get me a copy, and I'll buy it from you. Whom is Kirstein marrying? His monstrous sister? I have been setting folk music for months. Assez. There was a little boat and it sailed out on the sea, and the name of that boat was the Mary Golden Tree, and it sailed along the low land, lonesome, as it sailed on the lonesome sea. Have such things any basis in fact? Or don't you have them in Mississippi? I've now read Scene Five, which will do swell. But how will you fit white aid offers in at the beginning of the sheets you sent me? Two groups in succession, visiting Peter Owl, the first surreptitiously suggesting collaboration with certain sympathetic white forces, the second threatening and cajoling? It seemed the wrong place for that tome when I read it. Then since I thought the offer should come in Scene Four I reread that, searching for a place where it would be logical to the poetry. Found none. I think your idea is better. I shouldn't think it would have to be long. As I remember from the book in which I found the mention of white involvement (*The Negro in the Civil War*, by Herbert Aptheker I think) there were four white men arrested for being implicated in abetting or giving information, aid or encouragement to the conspirators. But obviously mere offer of aid or moral comfort given verbally would suffice here. Save that it must be strongly presented by the whites and refused bitterly by the blacks. Wouldn't you say so? It would make the problem, a still unsolved one, more closely related to the attempts to solve it today. Which after all is one of the reasons you wrote the play, I suppose. Find a way. I am disgusted with the weather. And when I say attempts to solve it today I don't mean the Communist Party; rather the questionable Southern Tenant Farmers' Union, for example, and the C.I.O., and the NMU etc. The flies are biting. It must be going to rain.

send me extra text please.

TO KATHERINE COWEN

September 1939
Staten Island, New York

I can't seem to find your most recent letter, although I know it's somewhere right here among the papers on my desk. I still do have the one giving the recipe for huîtres a la poulette. ah, here is the other. Thanks for the Portrait of G. B. Did you see the notice somewhere in the correspondence section of Tac, from W. B. Cowen about theatre audiences? I've forgotten what he said. I certainly don't think there's any hope whatever of reviving Federal Theatre. As I remember, the Daily Worker thought Roosevelt was ill-advised to give in to the "Tories" to the extent he did. That's about all. I think they expected just about what happened, and for that reason they made very little to-do about what everyone was indignant over. They have not been satisfactory either about the recent pact that reversed the democratic front strategy. They seem reluctant to admit the new tactic, which is absurd on their part, since it's a perfectly straightforward revolutionary tactic. Trying to work with and through the democracies wasn't fruitful and quick enough, so Stalin abandoned them, as far as I can see. The only regret I have is that I live in one of the abandoned democracies. Anyway, I should be more pleased with the Worker if it would say what it means instead of clinging to the idea of democracy on page two, and making it evident it isn't interested on page three, and praising Roosevelt on page one, and saying he is worthless on page five, and practically blaming the Soviet Union's present policy on page six, and stating that it will save peace and bring war faster on page four. We have telephoned various friend-members of ours, and they seem to think the Party should divorce itself from Moscow. I think that would be the most asinine procedure they could follow. As far as I can see, most of the members have actually believed what they have been preaching about democracy's being the hauptsache. Those people should be expelled, and the party reduced to those members who understand what it's all about, and who are ready to follow the lead of the Soviet Union. I think it would really strengthen the Party myself, if all the liberal, hesitating members would leave. You probably don't agree, but I don't see what else you can believe. Were *you* ever taken in for a minute by the Democratic Front? That is, did you believe it was sincere? I hope not. I believed in it implicitly as a tactic, yes, but I think it's a dead one now, and consequently can't support Roosevelt any longer as long as he stays on his present tack. I'll be interested to see what the Party here does. The trouble is that they have so far received no instructions from the Comintern, and consequently are all up in the air. And they may not get any very soon, because I think Stalin is pretty much uninterested in the various affiliates about the world, and feels they aren't doing much to help the Soviet Union. Chamberlain could have avoided Stalin's vengeance by showing a little eagerness and solicitude, but there's nothing to do now, but for us to abandon France and England and hope for the best.

Be sure and try to come down. We'll be here all through September and October as well. I enclose a strange letter from Mary Crouch Oliver which I think you'll enjoy. Let me know what you think about it!

Jane has read the letter, and thinks you'll disagree violently. Let me know if you do! It's usually that way.

TO KATHERINE COWEN
◆

September 1939
New York City

This goes on in the office of the Music Project, where through some bu-reaucratic mishap I suddenly find myself forced to remain seated for an hour and a half without permission to leave the building. Of course I haven't your letter with me so I can't do any answering of questions, which is too bad because it seems now that your missive consisted principally of question-marks "???" Anyway, I was surprised myself to hear that you didn't disagree with my proposed refusal to assist the democracies in retaining their present prestige. I expected you to join the shrill choir of defenders of dear England & France. So I'm delighted. After all, if England & France come out victors in any war, it only means that still another must be fought in all probability, and so on and so forth until capitalism in its present stage disappears.

Unfortunately, I can't conceive of the USA's remaining aloof while Eng & France are vanquished by Germany, or even if they seem to be being fatigued by protracted warfare. So for the moment I at last feel the pleasure of being pro-Communist and anti-war! What fun! (By anti-war I mean anti-imperialist war.) I'll be watching for various realignments here in the U.S. Kuhn has formally repudiated the Russo-German pact! We laugh a good deal as we sit glued to the radio evenings. One of the clearest, in fact, the clearest of the commentators is Johannes Steel on WMCA. Can you get it? He's on each night save Mon. & Tues. at 10:45 p.m., and recently, now and then to report extraordinary developments. Did I tell you we have a Siamese Kitten? And that Colin McPhee gave it to us? And that he has been down for two weekends?

Jane wrote a wonderful letter to Mary Oliver, but I wouldn't let her send it, for fear of riling her. So I wrote a very careful one asking her to come, and describing in detail the frugal way in which we live. She hasn't even replied to date, and she's had nearly a week. I'll have to write you again when I can have your letter in front of me, and then I'll enclose Jane's reply to Mary.

We're delighted you're coming, and we hope you'll stay weeks. Too many times Jane has sat pouting and saying: "Oh, I *wish* Kay were here."

I enclose funny item Latouche discovered in the Post yesterday. Will you return it? I never understand Broadway gossip—that is, how those columnists get their stories. As far as I remember, I never told anyone but Jane about the conversation that night, because it was so typical of Saroyan that it didn't seem humorous. But on paper it looks [*words missing*]. Saroyan will probably boycott me.

THE 1940S

January 3, 1940
Columbia Heights
Brooklyn, New York

thanks for your card. i never send any to anyone, and so i always have at least a score of notes to write after each christmas. still i refuse to send them. yours made sense because it was really a message, but others . . . as to getting *horse eats hat* for you, i have no copy. i think virgil has one in paris. but i'm not sure. orson probably has one, and so has denby doubtless, but orson is in hollywood, and denby's whereabouts are unknown. when last heard from he was in wyoming. i haven't even the score. my only suggestion is that you write augusta weissberg, c/o the mercury theatre, empire theatre building, broadway at 40 street, n.y., and maybe she will have a script. i prefer not to do that myself because i have bothered her so many times.

have you read virgil's book? I loved it. jane gave me kafka's *the trial* for my birthday which i enjoy very much. also enjoyed isherwood's *goodbye to berlin*. auden lives up the street from me and i see him occasionally. he's pretty eccentric, and does strange things like picking his nose and eating what he finds, like a small child. however he's very bright and fun to talk to. i thought you might come to town for the holidays. perhaps at easter? jane, mary oliver and i all live now at separate addresses. it works better that way. jane and i get more work done. mary entertains the mdvanis and the hapsburgs and the princess of ka-purthala and they're depressing anyway. à bientôt, i hope.

February 1942
Sanatorio Würzburger
Cuernavaca

While I was down in Tehuantepec it seems Jane wrote you asking for the Saroyan manuscript. She had gone and lost the one Bill sent me last Autumn.

No, I have been bored with Mexico for the last ten months, but it is somehow a difficult place to get out of. One feels one will have to make such an effort to live correctly if one gets back to civilization. An effort to be pleasant to one's friends, to discuss God knows what with them, to wear a tie, to keep appointments, to know what day of the week it is, and a thousand other things. There is the advantage, of course, of feeling well (possibly) back there, a thing practically inconceivable here. But when I think of that, I say: Feel well, for what? and come and stay at the Sanatorium where one isn't expected to feel well anyway, and no one does. Even my nurse is a paralytic. I have been ill off and on for the past year. Probably amoebic dysentery, but including derrames biliares, ictericia, colitis, and lots of funny and original pains. I'm fed up with this act. Thanks again very much.

TO AARON COPLAND

Summer 1942
Watkins Glen, New York

Your letter came what is probably two weeks or so ago. One's sense of time is deformed either by Mexico or by Summer. I don't know which. We should have loved to make you a weekend visit, although I suppose it's rather far, and by indifferently connecting railroads. Let me know if you would like to see us and if your cook has returned. Antonio is working very hard still, trying to get an exhibit ready for the Autumn. I think a vacation from work would do him good. Life here must be very difficult for him, as he doesn't dare look at a cat for fear of being deported. As it is, we have both been arrested three times here in Watkins Glen, as well as having undergone innumerable questionings and unpleasantnesses. Everyone thinks he's a Japanese and thus I'm a German. The national mentality has sunk a few more inches already since the beginning of the war. Can you come here? There's lots of room. Or let me know your plans. We could go there.

TO ROSS LEE FINNEY,
SMITH COLLEGE, NORTHAMPTON, MASS.

February 21, 1943
New York City

I have your letter and questionnaire regarding my compositional activities during the year of 1942. I think it can be pretty easily answered. Most of the year was taken up for me by illness; however, I did write a one-act opera, whose libretto I translated (and arranged) from the Spanish, using as text a play by Federico García Lorca. This is being given its premiere the 16th of March at the Museum of Modern Art. I also wrote a few songs, and a piano piece. First performances during the year were, as far as I know, absolutely nil. At present I am writing a group of songs. For your last question, I hope I won't meet with your disapproval if I answer that I feel that the composer's war-time function, unless he feels himself particularly qualified to carry on some specialized sort of war work, is to keep right on composing whatever he thinks should be composed. I think the majority of composers are not very versatile, and probably function most fully for the community when they are busy writing music. If music is needed for the war effort, and a composer feels he can provide it, I should naturally expect him to try. But I should not expect him to stop exercising his profession in order to learn to do something else—at least not at this point in the war.

TO GEORGE ANTHEIL

August 3, 1946
Southampton, L.I., N.Y.

Now it is my turn to apologize for tardiness in answering letters. Only my excuse is non-existent. I have merely been having a vacation, and haven't felt like writing letters. Your wire also came, and I got it when I went into the city. I have been here at the beach since early June. I think I had been working too hard all winter in town. I did a two-piano sonata and five scores for the theatre, as well as a lot of songs, so I felt justified in taking a rest.

Your letter was very kind and I am glad you think you can do something about *Esquire*. But I'm not "going in" for writing instead of music at all. On the contrary, I resigned this past winter from the *Herald Tribune* staff where I'd been working three years and a half, precisely because I wanted to write music instead of having to write about it. But in between scores I have felt like writing short stories, and so I have done it, and fortunately I have disposed of all those I have sent in. But I have two more that I haven't tried on editors, and the ego being what it is, I should like also to have them published. If it can be by a paying magazine, so much the better, of course. *The Partisan Review* is fine for prestige, but it is nice to get a good check as well, I think. *Harper's Bazaar* is printing one in the September issue, I think. I thought of you in connection with *Esquire*, and resolved to ask you about it, and if you believe they might be more inclined to read a manuscript if it were heralded by a note from you, I naturally should like to have that note. But I don't want to be a nuisance. Anyway, that is the situation; —they're not commercial writing; they're just straight short stories.

I bought your book the other day at Brentano's and had it mailed out here. It arrived yesterday afternooon and I have read only three chapters. Could life have been so insane only twenty-five years ago? I suppose it could. I certainly used to hope so, at that time. I don't quite know what the atmosphere of the present postwar era is going to be, but I'm sure it has very little to do with the other one. I suppose it will bear the same relation to the attitude toward the war just past, as the jazz age did to the doughboy-trench war. It will be far less dewy-eyed, less hopeful, less disorganized—perhaps less fun. The Existentialists are symptomatic of the whole period to come, I think, don't you? Let me know what happens.

TO PEGGY GLANVILLE-HICKS

July 8, 1947
S.S. Ferncape, off Graciosa, Azores

I can't believe you find a similarity between my letters and a seed catalogue. Still, why not? Or a telephone directory. Shipboard ordinarily is a good place to write letters, but this ship has distracting elements. There are two mad women aboard, taken on as waitresses, who have a tendency to hang out in the staterooms telling strange jokes, and they seem to have very little work to do, so that they are free nearly all day to run about the ship. The only place where one can escape them is the tiny deck at the very top. There, if the weather is fine, one can sunbathe, and it is forbidden to them to climb up there. Otherwise one has to plead illness and lock oneself into one's cabin. I secured this passage about ten days before the ship was to sail. Gordon Sager intended to go on the *Ernie Pyle*, but when he found he had to share his cabin with 120 people he cancelled his reservation. Then he tried this line, having heard I was leaving on the first of July. Of course there were no vacancies, since they carry only three passengers. The strike settled everything: one of the booked men had to remain in Philadelphia, and Gordon, being clever, was on the phone regularly twice a day, hoping for a cancellation. Of course he got it. So he is on the boat too, and it is much pleasanter than being alone. I should recommend the line to anyone, considering the year. I have a large stateroom with a wide bed, a private bath, a huge desk at which I orchestrate, portholes to two sides of the cabin and a double door onto the deck. All for $200, which you must admit isn't bad. This is the first letter I have written since leaving New York, and I am not in form. More seed catalogues. Why I am here? The advance came through, and I felt I had to leave New York. The only ship I could get at the late date was this, and it went to Morocco, which, although I wasn't as eager to get to it as to various other parts of the globe, is already known to me, and is near Spain and Portugal in case it is too uncomfortable. I have a nice phonograph with me, and lots of records, and I am busy writing a new story, not wishing to start the novel until I am fairly well settled somewhere. I don't know whether Gordon will strike out on his own on arriving in Morocco, but I imagine not. However, he too is writing a novel, having got an advance on his first from Simon and Schuster. When the story stops in its tracks, I work on the orchestration of the new two-piano concerto. Bobby and Arthur persuaded me to do it up for full orchestra. They seem certain of a few performances. I only hope they are right. I was out to visit them shortly before I left; they are in the Matta house again. In a way I envy them. It is peaceful and a perfect place to work. Jane also is safely ensconced at Libby Holman's for the summer, unless she suddenly makes a mad decision to hunt me up, which is one chance in a hundred. I think she'll be all right there. It's quiet and she is working hard on her book. We all seem to be working this summer. And on books. Now Touche claims he is writing one. Can it be? Do you think you will receive this before you leave for New York? Mary Phillips called me the day I was leaving and said she had just received a letter from you in which you said I was going to die in 1989, or have I the date wrong? She was down a night or so before, and I gave her a copy of the two-piano sonata . . . the record album, I mean. The records of *The Glass Menagerie* have been issued, on vinylite discs. But my name is nowhere to be seen. Do you think I should be indignant? I do. When I arrive in Morocco I expect to go directly to Fez, but that is really only tentative as an idea, because I haven't been there for thirteen years and I don't know to what extent it has changed. Probably very much. And if for the worse I don't even want to be there at all. And not only do I not know where I shall be, but I don't know for how long, although I promised everyone I'd be back in New York in time for the rehearsals and performance of the Concerto on October 31st. Still, boats are difficult to get, you know. I think it's a wonderful idea, the orchestrating of the Hawkins Indian number. You ask if I was pleased about the Hess-Hargail album. Of course I am, very much so. It's a real success. Soon I'll write again, if you are still there. And how shall I know.

TO CHARLES-HENRI FORD

October 24, 1947
Tangier

You'd never recognize Tangier; it's completely changed—the boom town of the Eastern Hemisphere. Night shifts keep the buildings going up fast. Everywhere the countryside is being cut into squares by the endless prolongations of the streets. And there is no room for all the people trying to get space to live. I think all Europe's black-market profiteers are here, still profiting away, since the whole International Zone is one huge black market. In any case, it's a very pleasant place to be these days. I have found a house at least, and Oliver [Smith] and I have bought it together. That may mean he'll be coming over, or again it may not. I have no idea how busy he is this year.

Tangier is now so civilized that the latest number of *Horizon* hangs from each newsstand, Sartre, Beauvoir, Camus and Lorca decorate the bookshop windows, and the American Legation hangs a copy of the Random House *Selected Writings of Gertrude Stein* in a glass case outside the entrance so the mules can brush against it as they pass. Reading matter is snapped up in the first half hour after it arrives in the Zone. So send *View*. It will be absorbed like the rain. Or have you discontinued publication, as you had planned?

Ghazi has several times asked for your address, but I have never happened to have it with me when I have been in town. The feast of Aid-el-Kebir is tomorrow and the town is excited. I hope no one comes with a sheep's head on a platter as they did to my shack on the Marshan in the Spring of 1933, when Miss

Djuna Barnes was sleeping in it. I don't remember whether she ate any of that sheepshead or not, but I remember her disgust when she lifted the lid and saw the eyes. I have been completely alone here since July, but time passes more quickly these days than it used to, and there is no question of being bored or stimulated. You might write a letter of gossip, or even one of news. People don't seem to like to spend the postage for airmail from the U.S., and at the same time they are ashamed to send things by ordinary post, so that the result is I get very little mail. Pieyre de Mandiargues seems to sell here in the bookshops. Give my best to Those At View.

TO PEGGY GLANVILLE-HICKS

———————————•———————————

November 8, 1947
Tangier

The reason I've been so long in answering your letter (the second) is that I've been searching for a place to live, because I was tired of living down low beside the sea. Now I'm by the sea still, but on the edge of a cliff high above it, with a small two room cottage surrounded by parasol pines and windblown cedars, through which I can see the Pillars of Hercules rising above the Mediterranean, bluer than ever. The incessant wind does more than its share in cooling the place, and the poor parrot has to be moved constantly from one sunny spot to the next, all day, for it shivers otherwise. I think it augurs ill for its future health.

I have found a new candy: hashish almond bar. I shall bring you some . . . it's absolutely unbelievable in its effects, but you have to eat it carefully, like Alice nibbling the mushroom, otherwise . . . ! The transportation is rather sudden, like gusts of golden wind along the vertebrae, and an upward sweep into the clouds. Strangely enough it leaves no ill effect that I can find. The obtaining of it is almost as much fun as the eating . . . down through the rat holes of the Mellah, tunnels of the rue Ibn Batuta. The results do go on for a very long time, however, and one can't rely on its wearing off in time for dinner. And the hotel is purely British and correct.

Jane writes that Oliver has lost the story you hope to borrow. Perhaps he had merely lent it to you and didn't dare to tell her so. Someone wrote me Higg was married. Is that false? The full score of the piano concerto is right here, and not finished by any means. But I want to finish the first part of the novel before I embark on that sort of work. How wonderful you are at last on the

Tribune. I suggested it years ago. Remember? The parrot is bright green, of course, since he is from South America. You never told me your friends' reactions to Stan Kenton. I'm sure the jazz addicts hated it, and those who hated jazz hated it even worse. The mind loves orthodoxy . . . I'm thinking particularly of the jazz lovers. The music here is wonderful, of course. I keep thinking I wrote it myself, and that they are the plagiarists! I enclose picture taken by Smail Abdelkader, just as you asked . . . taken at the Grotto of Hercules. Thank you for the address of Delkas. An Arab is putting in a new pane of glass the wind blew out, the phono is going, the parrot is cleaning his feathers, so the atmosphere is scarcely conducive to the writing of a true letter. But how many times a week is it? I was glad to hear "Call at Corazón" had been published. Of course I have not seen it. I hope you do send it. The only disadvantage of being on the other side of the earth is that one fails to lose completely interest in what goes on back there. Otherwise it would be perfect. I used to sever all connections. Now I don't feel like it . . . old age, obviously. So what? How I love to get long letters . . . endless ones with all the details of life in New York, since only with details can one construct an impression of reality. If I bring this to a close, it can be posted today, and in that way you'll get it sooner than if I were to make it longer. Besides, it is a failure, and a small failure is better than a big one to send someone. No? I send my love,

                                                                        Bupple

Some P.S.'s:

I was told the other day my name was Cornish. Is that true? I was amused by the tale of the Atonalists in Copenhagen who sought the way out, and your wondering if one wasn't really seeking the way in. I never received The Age of Reason which you said you had sent me. I suppose it is waiting for me in Tenth Street, which I hear is being lived in by a great many people at once. I wonder—. And did you read the book? I've been trying to get it here in French ever since I arrived, but it is unobtainable. The wind gets worse. It sounds like bombings, people screaming, animals crying, a shipwreck, Niagara Falls and a downpour all at once. And everything rattles and bangs, and one would say that the tin roof would rip itself off and go skimming through the air over the cypresses and goats and cliffs, and land on a freighter plodding past through the Strait. Why has Touche never answered my letter? I enclose a document for your admiration, in red ink.

TO CHARLES-HENRI FORD

November 19, 1947
Tangier

Thank you for your letter. It arrived opportunely, as I am sickabed with grippe, up on the mountain where I enjoy living more than in town. So I have time to answer it immediately, although there really is no reason why I shouldn't have time to do the same if I were well, except that when I'm well I work and walk more, and that seems to take up all the time.

I can't say that your description of New York made me want to be there, because I have never known it to be anything but unbearable no matter who gave dinner parties. (Perhaps I got invited to the wrong ones always, but my suspicion is that I was the wrong person instead.) As you know perfectly well, I've never yet felt a part of any place I've been, and I never expect to. But naturally, the fewer people there are in a place, and the less there is happening, the less conscious I am of missing what is going on under my nose. Which is why I like the most difficult places . . . in fact, if there is no one at all, I can say that the reason I am ill at ease is that the place is such that no one could live in it, therefore it can't be surprising that I too should be unable to stay there. In other words, it's a question of finding uncomfortable situations and putting up with them as long as possible before escaping; the desire for escape then can be called perfectly natural. Anyone would want to leave Aïn Témouchent or Hássi Inifel or Puerto Cabello. And so on.

You ask about Tangier's sex-life. I have a feeling it is now completely changed. I never knew it very well, even when I was young. My feeling is now that the American cinema has taken over, and everyone wants to go dancing swing at the Emsalah Gardens. There are several dance joints with hotjazz. I haven't been to any, and know nothing about it. Of course the people I knew when I was here before are middle-aged and fathers of families, and I'm inclined to avoid them. I haven't met any new friends in the few months I've been here. The reason is that I have a hovering feeling of not being really in Tangier at all. It is terribly changed, and I can't bear to try to imagine what it used to be like. Part of what it used to be like was of course what I used to be like, and since that too is gone, it seems that it would be needless torture to search for a past which has left no vestige. I've found I'm always happiest in a place I've never been before and about which I know nothing. There is absolutely no way to be again in a place. Whether or not it has changed, it's never the same. Isn't

that true? And by never being the same one means of course: not being alive
any more. Every place one revisits seems to have lost the life that made it exist
the first time one knew it. Certainly I never meant to stay in Tangier again, but
for no reason at all I have remained on and on, perhaps because one can get
everything one wants here and the life is cheap as dirt, and travel is so damned
difficult . . . visas for Spanish Morocco and currency restrictions for French
Morocco, and suspicious men in the trains . . . and mainly the great fact that
I haven't the energy to pack up and go anywhere else. Which is a surprising
thing when I think of it. If I haven't the energy to do what I used to like best,
what in God's name have I the energy to do? And where does energy go? Perhaps
I need vitamins. My parrot is terrified of children. Otherwise he seems happy.
You ask about exchange. The dollar is around 350 francs, or 40 pesetas, and is
expected to improve this week. Pension complete at my hotel, with a two-room
cottage overlooking the sea, is 75 pesetas, or under $2 a day. French Morocco
is cheaper, but less comfortable because certain things are scarce and rationed.
Here of course one can get anything made on the planet. I hear Italy is terribly
cheap. But it's Europe, and that would never do. Anyway, I want to go southward
if I do move. Working on the novel, yes. I'll never show it to you, naturally.
And I've spent all my advance! Have you sent Joe Massey his mss.? He keeps
writing me aggrieved letters. The house is in Amrah, two doors from Barbara
Hutton's. She bought the old Blake place, you know, in Calle Sidi Hosni, for
$75,000, and fixed it up just swell. Our house is tiny, but it has a beautiful
view. As to *View*, you have abandoned it? Why? How ridiculous! Or maybe a
temporary rest. Well, Good bye. I must shave. That will be my major effort for
the day.

TO PEGGY GLANVILLE-HICKS
◆

December 1947
Palais Jamai
Fez

Your letter came yesterday, forwarded from Tangier to Fez-Batha. I have been
here a little more than a week, and am still trying to get the various permissions
to go to Oujda, and thence to Colomb-Béchar. Since the war it has all become
extremely difficult. There are no more tourists. Not one. It's become an extinct
species for the moment . . . perhaps for all time, but I can scarcely believe that,

what with a new crop burgeoning back in the U.S.A. I'm sitting up in bed in the streaming sun, all windows open, birds screeching outside, the parrot's cage in the window (he always looks at me silently, suspiciously, whenever I type), the city of Fez lies below, very slowly disengaging itself from the morning mist and smoke, while a million cocks crow at once, constantly. There is also the faint sound of the water in the fountains of the palace gardens. I have been especially lucky this year in pursuing my avoidance of noise; I've actually been able to escape it . . . in Ronda, in Tangier, both on the beach and on the mountain, and here in Fez as well. As you know, I'm a great lover of natural sounds, and they have been present to fill the spaces which otherwise would have been only silence. Wind, water, birds and animals, and (here) human voices, make a fine auditory backdrop. The human voices make the most beautiful sound of all, when the muezzin calls during the night, especially the one for dawn, which begins about five fifteen and finishes a little before six. They preface the actual *mouddin* with religious remarks, sung in freely embroidered florid style, each man inventing his own key, mode, appoggiature and expressive devices. And when you have a hundred or more of those incredibly high, piercing, birdlike voices doing flamenco-like runs in different keys, from different minarets, against a background of cocks crowing, you have a very special and strange sound. (At the moment I am having tea trouble. They brought me both lemon *and* milk, and I took the milk for water and poured it into the cup: horreur! Now people are telephoning madly and running up and downstairs with pitchers of hot water and teapots and cups and saucers. Someone finally came and took away my entire tray, so that my breakfast was truncated neatly in the middle. Shortly they will bring it all back . . . Yes, now it's all finished; another breakfast. I only hope it's not on the bill.) Fez is still the most beautiful city of all. I always feel at home. Everything looks like my apartment: —the mountains, the walls of the city, the streets, and the houses themselves. I went to tea yesterday in the Derb el Heurra, to the house of an elderly gentleman named Moulay Ali Ktiri. The court was magnificent, with an arbor of grapevines twisted over the central fountain in which water really splashed. The main salon had a door at least ten feet by fifteen, with a huge curtain nonchalantly looped up at one side. Doves kept fluttering up and looking in at the tea tables. He spoke wistfully of the time of his father, when they had kept gazelles in the rooms. His wife returns from a pilgrimage to Mecca today . . . I hope not with cholera. He brought out a little book of notated melodies and made me play them at the piano in open octaves. Soon the slaves were crowding around the grill, murmuring: Mezziane. Then he said that I was the only person he had shown them to who could get them right. The others had played the right notes, but it didn't sound like the pieces. I was delighted to hear that, and said that it was because I really liked the music. "Ah, the heart is everything in getting the emphasis," he said. They have a passion for falling back on the "heart" in explaining a thing. "El qulb," they whisper, nodding their heads. I passed a blacksmith's shop the other evening in which someone had decorated the walls with painting that would set Oliver croaking with joy. Mingled with the Klee-like pictures were small patriotic remarks in Arabic and Roman script. One read: THE MAROCCO IS ONE. I stepped inside and called the smith's attention to the fact that there were two errors in the sentence. His answer was: "But it's the heart that counts, isn't it?" The British Consul and his wife here have turned out to be charming people, and are taking good care of me, telephoning from one end of Morocco to the other trying to get me special permission to go to the Sahara. It's not finished yet, of course. We have been twice to the police and he has phoned to the Algerian border, and still he must talk with Rabat today. They had me to tea yesterday and cocktails afterward at the Legation. I never knew that British Consuls considered themselves responsible for Americans, but they seem to take it as a matter of fact that in the absence of any American representative, it is incumbent upon them to take over, all of which is remarkably kind of them, and fully appreciated by me, naturally. I sent a pile of snaps yesterday to Oliver. You must ask him to show them to you, especially the one of the leopard and the views of Moulay Idriss, which is a magnificent town but not of any use to a non-Moslem, since it's forbidden for an unbeliever to eat, drink or sleep within its walls. So that's that. I don't know about chewing gum within the walls, or smoking, but I shouldn't be surprised if there were a *dahir* prohibiting even those simple substitutes for partaking of sustenance. This is my last sheet of paper, and must do to complete the letter, so I am single-spacing at this point. I had a letter from Charles-Henri Ford in which he said that Lincoln Kirstein would like to produce *Denmark Vesey* next season, and would probably commission its completion. Unfortunately Romolo has the only existing copy of the damn thing and I don't know his address. If you should ever see him, please get it away from him. It's utter madness that he should have the one copy, anyway, but he's had it since August 1946, to be exact, when we made the DISC album of songs. If it should really go through, the plan, I suppose it would change my plans considerably, because I should have to work like mad on it, and I really doubt that I could get it done for next season's presentation. Or maybe yes. It's bugle time of the morning; the fanfares are resounding back and forth between the forts of the hills. I'm completely surprised that you liked "Cold Point" so much. Of course it would be the one story of mine I am displeased with . . . perhaps because *Partisan Review* didn't like it. When they sent it back, I cut it down with a knife, having decided it was too long and discursive. I don't know now. I've written another since, and sent it directly to Jane. It's called "How Many Midnights." The novel seems to be taking a short rest. It has 152 pages done. I read it the other day, and found it too depressing, but it goes without saying that I'll complete it anyway. It probably won't depress other people the way it does me. It probably won't even interest them the way it does me, for that matter! I had meant to kill the "hero" off halfway through, but I can't seem to let him go. He lingers on in agony instead of dying. But I'll get rid of him yet, I assure you. Once he's gone there'll be only the heroine left to keep things going, and that won't be easy. Still, it's got to be that way; there's no other possible design for it. You ask me about a hypothetical son? I should hope for an unfrustrated life for him, naturally, and if he should turn out to be frustrated anyway, I should certainly not be "flattered," as you put it. Good God, no! Nor should I try to change him, either. I should say: "It is written, There's nothing to do about it, except to hope that he can make an adjustment that will keep his life from having been lived wholly in vain." Because I don't really attach much importance to sexual directions. One way or the other, the importance lies more in constructing some sort of inner whole that gives existence its validity. I know you agree, so I don't have to elaborate. I don't agree with you, however, that the heterosexual is more likely to find his life satisfactory when the moment of stock-taking arrives. I think it's pretty much outside such considerations. Naturally, a complete fulfillment of emotional functions may make the attainment of satisfaction easier. And again it may completely prevent any kind of self-knowledge. I'm speaking always of men; I'm sure it's quite otherwise with women, but I shouldn't venture to say what they're about anyway! Baby Guinle? What can she have to say about me? Not very much, I should think. I think I went twice to tea last year, and we discussed the few people we know in common. One day there was a thunderstorm. That's about all. I expect (hope) to go from here to Oujda, thence to Colomb-Béchar, and from there to Taghit, Igli, Beni-Abbès, Timimoun. With the parrot, who hates traveling, but will get used to it in time. My health is all right now. It was grippe, in Tangier.

A French mother went into the bathroom while a native fathma was bathing her baby, because the baby was crying, and said, "Mais, pourquoi il pleure? Peut-être l'eau n'est pas de la bonne température." "Non, non, Bébé est bien," said the fathma, "tu ne vois pas qu'il a blanc?" "Évidemment il est blanc," said

the mother. "Alors, moi sais qu'il y a bien, et l'eau bien aussi, parce que quand
Bébé il tout bleu moi sais que l'eau il y a trop froid, et quand Bébé il tout rouge
moi sais que l'eau il y a trop chaud, et maintenant Bébé il blanc."* That's the
kind of stories the French tell here over their apéritifs. Love.

TO PEGGY GLANVILLE-HICKS
—————————————◆—————————————

January 16, 1948
Hôtel des Territoires du Sud
Timimoun, Sahara

It's impossible for me to give you an idea of what it was like to receive my
mail this evening. I've been housed for four days by a sandstorm that howls
outside like a blizzard, only the snow is a pinkish dust that enters every crack
in the ceiling and walls. My room is small, but fortunately very high, so the air
doesn't get vitiated too soon; I keep it shut day and night, never opening the
window, naturally, and opening and shutting the door into the hall only when
I must go out. I had read my books, and was reduced to writing intensively on
the novel, but so intensively that I was getting depressed. Last Sunday I had had
a telegram from the director of the Compagnie Générale Transsaharienne saying
he had sent my mail via Mardouch on Saturday. So when Tuesday came I
expected it. But I had forgotten that Tuesday was the thirteenth. Of course it
was nowhere to be found. I spent Wednesday going to the agency where several
apathetic Negroes knitted and ran a sewing machine, telling me that maybe my
mail had blown out of the truck en route. I sent a telegram up to Colomb-
Béchar informing Monsieur Cassu that the mail had not arrived, and to everyone
I spoke of nothing but my mail, like a maniac. Why I am so eager to hold onto
the lines that connect me with the rest of the world, I don't quite know: a
weakness, of course, but one that I admit willingly. Today I had another wire
saying that the mail had been sent four days later than the sender had previously
thought. Bahli kept telling me that nothing could arrive before next Tuesday.
And the wind howling, and the six gazelles outside my window scampered about
in an ecstasy. God knows why. The sand, dust, grit, earth in the air is so thick

---

* "But why's he crying? Maybe the water's not the right temperature." "No, no, baby
fine," said the fathma, "don't you see he white?" "Obviously he's white," said the mother.
"So, for me I know he fine and water fine too, because if baby all blue, I know water
too cold, and if baby all red, I know water too hot, and now baby white."

one can't see across the *place*. The old man had come and built me a fire in the stove, and I was reading Berber poems and making notes, when Bahli arrived with a small grin on his face and handed me about thirty letters, plus all your wonderful magazines and the Sartre book from London, and my story "By the Water" translated into German from Berlin, as "Am Wasser." The electricity has just gone out . . . it is supplied by Captain Leprieur at the Poste de Garde for two hours an evening, and my oil lamp isn't very good, having been sent up from the Soudan, where such things come from in this part of the world. When I finish this sheet I shall wait until tomorrow before going on. I must answer all your letters, one by one, if not chronologically, and that ought to make up for any lacunae in recounting my daily life. I can't imagine what you want in the way of details in that quarter. Minus the purely superficial matter of decor, my life generally consists of exactly what I tell you it consists of. Here for instance I wake up, take my Drenol, lie back down on my right side for twenty minutes while the parrot clamors to have the wool djellaba taken off its cage, rise, take off said djellaba, call for a monstrous black pygmy child to bring me my breakfast, which he does. It consists of mint tea, native bread, black, grilled to make it blacker, and jam. The sun is up by then. I put the parrot in the window, feed him four biscuits soaked in tea, smoke one Bastos Bleue because if I smoked more I should be ill, and lie there in bed gathering my thoughts. I assemble the papers around me, generally have a mild fight with the pygmy, who comes to fetch the tray and finds some excuse for not getting out of the room immediately, and start to write. I continue writing until a little before twelve, when I go into the kitchen, shake hands with the proprietress, and ask that some hot water be brought me. Then I struggle with shaving and washing for a half hour. By the time I have finished (my razor keeps falling to pieces because it is broken, so that I cut myself repeatedly), the pygmy is knocking at the door yelling in Zenati (the local gibberish) that lunch is ready. If Touche were a jet black Negro and about four feet high, were imitating a frog, he would look awfully like this number. Lunch is long and complicated. I am the only partaker of it. Two strange dogs, native to the Gourara I'm told, keep coming in and looking at me. Then they go out. Then they come in. The pygmy waits on me, slamming the plates down as if he hated my guts (which obviously is the case) and telling me what the dish would be called in Zenati if the people who speak the tongue had ever heard of it. Luncheon over, I come back into the room, give the parrot a dry biscuit, one of several hundred I bought in Adrar, watch it eat it, and (until the sandstorm began) take it onto the terrace and leave it partially in the sun and partially out of the sun, so that when it gets too hot it can walk to the other end of its perch and freeze in the shade, since there is a difference of about fifty degrees between the two. The temperature here goes to 125 in the shade, 167 in the sun. Also it goes down to 20 before daylight, so that water left outside freezes solid. I've held the pieces of ice in my hands, but I haven't experienced the 125 shade because I haven't been here in July. So this is the cold season, you may have gathered. The parrot on the terrace, I come below and sit down to type what I wrote before lunch. Unfortunately I work slowly, so in spite of all my application, very little progress shows. But I have nearly two hundred pages typed . . . probably shall have by the time you receive this. And I have no idea whether it's laughably bad or pleasingly original or pretentiously romantic or startling or childish or unreadable or engrossing . . . It's absurd not to know. The middle of the afternoon is an empty spot in the day. I smoke several Bastos Bleues because I have been fortified against them by lunch, and read or work some more. One day captain Leprieur sent me a glass of huge white termites to try my DDT on. His house has been destroyed by them, is in ruins. A new salon has been built by the Negro workmen, and is full of leopard skins and leather objects from Tombouctou and Gao. But the rest of the house looks as though a bomb had caught it unawares. I think that was the only unexpected diversion, the arrival of the termites. Today a garrison of meharistes came in a hundred strong, all done up in white veils, but the wind was so extreme in its violence, and the sand so thick that I caught only a glimpse. Toward sundown my day is over, but there remains my walk in the oasis. It is a series of great gardens arranged in steps down the side of a long hill, the oasis, and it's one of the loveliest. At that hour there's never a soul, and I can wander where I like, following any of the hundreds of streams of water that form its complicated irrigation system. The palms wave in the breeze, the birds chatter, the butterflies hover, and it is all a rather puritanical Eden . . . puritanical because one feels that it is not meant for a minute to be beautiful. I usually go as far as the *sebkha*, a vast dried marsh that separates the oasis from the *ereg*, which the French call Le Grand Erg Occidental. (It is large, and contains the highest dunes in the Sahara, and it begins at Timimoun and goes north all the way up to the southern slopes of the Algerian Atlas. I spent Christmas *in* it, up at Taghit. New Year's Day I spent at Adrar, 180 kilometers south of here, and decided against going on to Tombouctou, which was only three days further by truck. Everyone said the mosquitoes were awful right now along the Niger, and *everyone* has a virulent form of malaria here. I think I was wise to renounce all that, at least for this time.) I turn around at the sebkha, always planning my novel, believe it or not, and climb back up through the oasis to the town, which is a mysterious-looking place with streets like gorges in the red rock, and very black Negroes who give me the military salute when I pass (probably because I wear the seroual, na'als and burnous of the French army here). I come back to my room, make tea on an alcohol burner, and wait for the electricity to be turned on at six sharp. Then I work some more. Sometimes at that hour there are drums, and I go in search of them. One night I discovered a magnificent dance going on in a huge ruined courtyard . . . a circle of men and women singing together . . . music reminiscent of the Pygmy music of the Congo. In the center was an old woman moving about as though in trance, making a wonderful dissonant embroidery on the basic syncopated refrain of the circle. And everyone was in long white robes, the jet black faces nothing but holes of darkness above. But so far that was the only distraction I have discovered in Timimoun. Fez will make up for all this when I get back! I haven't managed to seize the essence of Timimoun yet. It's a very strange town. You will love the photos I've taken of it. The camels are everywhere, even craning their necks in the window while I eat lunch. Two goats ran into my room the other morning and made themselves quite at home. The camels and the gazelles, incidentally, are the two main sources of meat here. This is quite enough Baedekering for one time, I think. I shall read over your letters now.

I see that in my seed cataloguing of the day I have left out the fetching of the parrot and the taking of him to the kitchen to place him near the stove so he will be warm enough. His arrival is always accompanied by cries of pleasure from the proprietress and the servants. "Coco!" she screams. She feeds him oranges and petit-beurre. Of course it's a seed catalogue, but how otherwise, save by long integrating thought, can one arrive at giving an idea of one's life to someone far away? Of course you can easily say that I don't in any way give you an idea of my life, but if you do, then it's because you place undue importance on the inner life as an ingredient of my present whole. If I weren't working, perhaps you'd be right. When (and if) you read the book, the great part of what goes on in my head will be there before you in words. Occasionally I feel that I'm myself as I walk down through the gardens and see the ocean of sand in the distance.

There are no English pensions sprinkled through the Sahara. I have not met even one tourist, either, since I left Fez. Life is pretty uncomfortable here until one makes one's nest, and then one is disinclined to budge, quite naturally. Romolo never returned the score of *Denmark Vesey* to me. He went South the day after we made the recordings, and since then I have been waiting for him to find it, as well as the Sleep Walk, of which he also has the only copy.

Naturally the latter is relatively unimportant, but I mention it to lend reality to my story. No! If you should ever get the opera in your hands, please only hang onto it. I dislike to say what I think has become of it. New York sounds pleasant, if one had the means to pass through for a fortnight, and continue to distant parts. The snaps of Tangier I sent to Oliver were numerous, so that the one of the walls and sea to which you refer is already lost in my memory. In any case, unless you wandered out to the region of Oued el Ihud, you wouldn't have seen the landscapes I photographed in that series. Unless in a vagrant dream. Did "At Paso Rojo" appear in the January *Mademoiselle*? Thanks once again for sending me the tear-sheets of "Call at Corazón," along with the Hollywood picture of me on the Editor's page. Hint: "At Paso Rojo," treated in like manner, would make me very happy. You have been marvelous in sending me reading material; the difference it makes to existence here is much too great, I confess, but still, one is what one is . . . that is, until one changes. And I haven't arrived at any spiritual self-sufficiency. Not yet. I still want to read and write. Thank you for shipping "Cold Point" to Palinurus. Of course I have had no word from him. Even worse, I sent a new story to my agent in November, and she has never acknowledged its arrival. I'm fearful lest it has been lost. Jane has the other copy in Vermont. She has written me lengthily about it. Called "How Many Midnights." It's a better story than "Cold Point," but you might not like it so well. Mary Phillips wrote me suggesting that I was both father and son in "Cold Point," an idea which hadn't occurred to me. I confess I don't get it at all. Father, yes. Son, no. And for her Fat Brother C. is civilization. That seems somehow nearer the truth, although I had never thought of it. But often people discover truths for themselves in one's work, and make one conscious of them for the first time. How lucky you are to have all your music played, recorded. I am always discouraged about my music. To write it at all seems to me to be looking in two different directions at once. The writing of music is of course a communion with the unknown, nothing more. But then one feels the necessity of making other people hear it, which is an absurdity. And everything after that, once one has admitted the second step, is an absurdity too. Whereas writing words is a candid challenge to the other minds, writing music is a purely personal experience, mystical and hermetic. Not for that less valuable to the one who writes it . . . I don't mean that for a minute, but hardly a life's work, unless one is free from all economic necessity. And I don't mean that writing words is more likely to pay. I mean that the writing of words seems to me a purer act if one considers creation of art a form of communication. The writing of music can't possibly be communication; it happens, and after that one pretends one meant it to be communicative . . . thus the inherent lie in the act. Enfin, it all sounds complicated when typed out. Orally it would be short and simple. I've always enjoyed Colin's Balinese music, but I've heard so little of it, and I've never quite known what was transcription and what was paraphrase. I suppose it doesn't really matter: in the case of so divorced an idiom every Western approximation of it is a personal expression. I suppose it's all McPhee, from whatever viewpoint he approached any given piece. I scarcely slept last night for having read all that mail. And I have a headache this morning from my late lamplight hours. Good working light is unknown in the Sahara. Unknown, unfindable. The rooms are dungeons to keep out the light, which is synonymous with the heat. And at night it is dark. Period. What *is* this preoccupation of yours with the term "psychologically impressive"? To whom? *Life* magazine? I realize you use it quasi-ironically, but I'm not sure of your real meaning. I have come upon your complaint of the seed-catalogue. I wonder why you can't believe that by dint of trying very hard I can reduce my life to exactly the things "everybody does." The self-imposed order, the inflexible regime is an exotic thing to me, and I flourish under it for short periods . . . flourishing being understood to mean finding conditions conducive to work. I have not read *The Unquiet Grave*. There is no current Arab, nor current anything. The Sahara is hostile to miscegenation of such varieties. The Sahara is not Algeria, is not Morocco, is not Senegal . . . it's a great stretch of earth where climate reigns supreme, and every gesture man makes is in conscious defense from, or pro-pitiation of, the climatic conditions. Man is hated in the Sahara . . . one feels it in the sky, in the stones, in the air. It might as well be written in the stars: God Hates Man Pinky is a Rat. But of course that can be exciting. Where life is prohibited, it becomes a delectable forbidden fruit, and that is the feeling one gets here: each instant is begrudged one by an implacable tyrant.

The walls of the rooms here are covered with fantastic designs carved in the red mud by the Negroes. They are all symmetrical, teeming with symbols of all sorts and stylized objects. The resultant richness is a joy to the eye and the mind. Outside the architecture is of barbaric austerity, but imposing in its fashion. The perpendicular is almost unknown. Everything is a truncated pyramid, and the millions of pats given by the human hand to the surfaces lend a redeeming softness to the texture. Domes are crude, with palm trunks sticking out in all directions. The protruding branch is an important motif. Color decoration is supplied by lime green wash being dashed against the uniform tomato bisque walls and allowed to run down at its will. The vegetation is the tall palm and the low, feathery tamarisk which drops its grey-green needles over the red earth.

All colors are dusty, refined. All, that is, but the incredibly green grass that grows as a carpet throughout the oasis under the trees. It is coarse grass, and looks like the stuff they put in Woolworth's windows on the floor of the display cases at Easter time, when they want to sell their chocolate rabbits and baskets of sugar eggs. I have made myself a prisoner here. Naturally I want to leave and go somewhere else, but the trips are so unpleasant when one makes them . . . And I can work perfectly well here, so why not? I'm a good many days from Tangier. It's a day to Adrar, a day from there to Kerzaz, another to Beni Abbès, another to Colomb-Béchar, another three days from there to Fez. And a final twelve hours by train to Tangier. So that if one does it all with any degree of leisure, the trip takes two weeks, since here the trucks are few and far between, and one has to wait for the next if one stops off to sleep. Two or three weeks, really. If I go in the other direction, I can make El Goléa in fourteen or sixteen hours, but then I am even further from Morocco, of course. Besides, I have already spent a winter in that section of the Sahara, while here, although it's wilder and really less interesting to stay in, it's at least different from what I've known. In Adrar the White Fathers made pleasant companions. When I left after my five days' sojourn, they said to me: "Don't forget that we are the intellectuals of the Sahara." Which is true. They had all read Sartre and Simone de Beauvoir and Camus, and discussed them with a naturalness that would put most American intellectuals to shame. After all, the subject matter is within their own terrain. Nothing strange about the terms of Existentialism to them! Naturally they prefer their own doctrine, but that is their privilege. I should prefer to prefer theirs, too. But I'm I. I see the Ballet Society Year Book still has me born in Brooklyn in 1909. I thought I had scotched that, but someone's malice is powerful! Why not the Bronx in 1906? And woe to the day that Gina Hohensee enticed me into sitting before her camera. Oy weh! I have at least twenty-five letters to write. This is the first. Why hasn't Oliver written me in two months and a half? Not even a postcard. Is he coming? You have my eternal thanks for your letters and literary envois. The pygmy just arrived bearing a cable from Jane saying she will arrive with a friend at Gibraltar on the 31 of January. I can't believe it. Now I must leave. You see? Someone always saves you from your masochism. How carefully life is arranged. I approve of it completely. Love,

bup

TO CHARLES-HENRI FORD

January 25, 1948
En route Algiers–Fez

The script of *Denmark* arrived in my room in the Soudan about ten days ago. Of course it's a wonderful scenario, but what good does it do me, when my score appears to have been completely lost by De Spirito? I can't imagine how the hell he could have lost it so easily, or why he didn't phone me to ask me to come and get it if he was going to move . . . Anyway, I am depressed about it, because it represents two years' work, and naturally I shall never start it again. It's my own fault and I'm crazy to be so careless. But of course I always act as though I had twenty more lives to live. Not only that, but as if all twenty were to be exactly alike . . . the same one over and over. It's a definite impression I have, that at any moment I shall begin over again and go through the whole business again in detail. So I never take anything very seriously, not even when I should. Except food, naturally. Food is the one thing I'm not so sure of being able to have again. So of course there's a certain anxiety there. I was going to stay all winter down south with the Negroes, but a cable from Jane changed my plans suddenly, and I began coming northward immediately, mostly by plane. Even so, it's been an endless trip. I land in Fez tonight sometime after midnight, stay over a day or so to get my visas to proceed to Tangier, and go from there over to Gib where she disembarks. And I've already been traveling six days since receiving the cable. Edwin Denby also arrives this week. Perhaps Tangier will become pleasant after all—at least, for me. I want to build an house in Timimoun now. The Captain there is going to choose an oasis for me. It's my favorite spot. When I arrived in Algiers I discovered a ridiculous, libelous article about me in the *Echo d'Alger*, describing me as distant, chilly, and eccentric, and even worse, describing my parrot as skinny and featherless, which is certainly not the case. So that the staff of the Hôtel Saint Georges seemed frightened to let me loose in the lobby, because as soon as I signed my *fiche* they all knew I was the crazy American from the desert. Of course I was really delighted. No one can ever heap enough insults upon me to suit my taste. I think we all really thrive on hostility, because it's the most intense kind of massage the ego can undergo. Other people's indifference is the only horror. This trip is endless; I am trying to write a great many letters to make the time pass, but the roadbed is uneven, and it's difficult to type. And the light is awful. I'd already be in Fez by now if the customs at Oujda this morning hadn't demanded a health certificate for the parrot and thereby caused me to miss the Micheline and spend the day searching for a veterinary. Of course it was Sunday, and not one was to be found. At the last moment, that is, after I'd walked miles and had a terrible lunch in the Hôtel Terminus, the customs inspector found me and told me not to bother, and to take the five o'clock train with the parrot, certificate or no certificate. So of course the five o'clock train is a horror of slowness, has no diner, selling nothing to eat, and gets me into Fez at some outlandish hour after midnight. It's the war, surely! The Sahara is fine, however, and I don't like any place nearly so much. The new spots (for me) turned out to be quite wonderful: Taghit and Timimoun especially. Further south it was a little nightmarish, a little too distant and lost in feeling. We just arrived in Taza. I got down to see if there might be something to eat or something to drink, but came back disappointed if not surprised: unmentionable coffee with liquid saccharin and "sandwiches" of pork paste. How does anyone live here, I wonder? Anyone, that is, save the people who stay at the two or three luxury hotels where the food is good. Tennessee thinks he will come down: Laughlin wrote me from Switzerland asking for living details. I suppose he would be disappointed in Morocco; he wanted to know if he could swim here now. I told him I couldn't even swim in the summer. Jane arrives the 31st at Gib, and I hope to get there in time to meet her boat. It's problematical because at the moment I'm dead from fatigue and I must stay in Fez in any case to get my visas for the Spanish Zone and for Gib. You can't go to Tangier any more without permission from the Spanish. Fortunately the Spanish are favorably inclined toward our nation at the moment, so they make

as few difficulties as possible, which isn't to say none, but still, considering
. . . Jane thinks it would be ignoble of her to set foot in Spanish territory. It
seems a lot of people feel that way, even now. I don't quite see why, but if that's
the way she feels I shan't try to persuade her. I find Spain pleasant enough, and
certainly the people there don't live in any greater misery than the people here
or in France at the moment . . . probably less. Libby [Holman] thinks she will
possibly come later in the spring. Oliver and Marian Dunham say they'll come
in May. All we'll need is Djuna, you and Claude McKay. And Tonny, I forgot.
British Post Office.

TO JAMES LAUGHLIN,
NEW DIRECTIONS, NEW YORK

January 25, 1948
En route Algiers–Fez

Please make allowances for the bumpy roadbed and the lack of springs in the
train. I received your letter as I got off the plane at Colomb-Béchar after a six
weeks' trip through the Sahara. Too bad about the mislaying of "Pages from
Cold Point." Perhaps by now you've found it.

I'm still here, with a vengeance—that is, I've bought a house in Tangier and
expect to be repairing it this Spring. At the moment I'm on my way to Gibraltar
to meet my wife who is arriving from New York. A cable arrived unexpectedly
in Timimoun; otherwise I should have been spending the whole winter down
there. There's no place like it. But it's too far to return to this year.

Your questions should all be answered properly, but if I did that, I should
have to wait until I had other conditions for writing, and that would put off the
operation for a while. Distances are great and transportation is subnormal, to
put it mildly. In any case, Tangier belongs to nobody. It is internationally
governed, there are three postal systems: French, Spanish and English, and every
kind of money goes. The rates are the highest to be had anywhere I know; I
mean the rates for the dollar. The entire city is one large black market. I shouldn't
say it was warm enough to swim, although there are always a few Britishers who
can be seen wandering on the beach in bathing trunks, even at this time of year.
I won't even go in, in the summer, because I'm used to the real tropics, where
the water is ninety degrees Fahrenheit or over. If you go on down to Agadir
(French Morocco), you can swim all year around, and there's an excellent hotel

there—the Marhaba, right on one of the best beaches in the world. At least, in 1934, which is the last time I was in Agadir, it was a magnificent beach, wide, flat, empty, white, immaculate, and stretching on to the south along the Atlantic as far as one could see. We may be going down there later. Tangier is useful principally as a base where one stocks up on things like butter, Scotch, English cigarettes, and so on, as well as francs at the rate of 325–350 per dollar, which makes full pension in French Morocco at the best hotels cost about $3 a day. (In the Sahara I lived beautifully for a little over a dollar a day.) If you want to swim I recommend Agadir, which has the best climate in Morocco, as well as the only really good beach, and one of the three or four good hotels in the country. (It's considered this year to rank with the Mamounia of Marrakech.) You ask, too, what the place is like. It's hard to answer that offhand. It's full of Arabs. It's full of Berbers. And some French, who run the hotels (fortunately for one's stomach), and the banks and the larger shops. The cities I find very beautiful indeed: one feels removed in time rather than in space. Europe before the Middle Ages must have been very much like most of Morocco. Fez dates from the eighth century; you're sometimes invited to lunch in a house built in the tenth or eleventh century by the forebears of your host. And basically very little has changed since then. The landscape is grandiose and barren mostly . . . something like the Pyrenees enlarged. There is skiing in the Atlas, which has peaks 12,000 and one 13,000 feet high. South of there you have the valleys of the Sahara, strewn with oases. It's an inexhaustible country if you like moving about and observing barbaric customs. I've traveled for five years in it . . . at least 30,000 km., and there are still a good many places I haven't been: Kasba Tadla, Oued Zem, Beni Mellal, Ksabi, Boujad, Debdou, Tiznit, the Assif Melloul, and Khouribga, to name a few I still want to see. The country is rather forbidding once you leave the cities, wild life is abundant, and although the lion has been virtually exterminated, there are still huge snow leopards, monkeys, panthers, cobras and all the exotic fauna one would expect to find in such a place.

The joggling of the train is increasing and I'll have to stop. I expect to be in Tangier in another three days. British Post Office. Tell Tennessee that Edwin Denby arrives in Tangier this week, as well as Jane (my wife). Perhaps we shall see you, too.

TO TENNESSEE WILLIAMS

April 27, 1948
Hotel Belvedere
Fez

No word from you for two months or so. I don't know whether you are still there in Rome or not, but I'll hope you are. If so, you are probably disinclined to leave the place. I had a letter last week from Audrey telling me about the plans for *Summer and Smoke*, and asking me if I wanted to do it. I answered saying yes, and to let me know the latest date when I could return to New York, adding that it would be fine if I could see you beforehand, or at least get hold of the script, so as to feel what the thing is about before I actually began work on it. She will probably communicate that to you. Have you given up the idea of coming down here?

Oliver Smith has been writing me recently about an opera he wishes we might do together, for two years hence. From what he said, he already has written you about it, but has had no answer. You could do a wonderful libretto, and naturally I should want to be the composer. So don't go and do an opera with David Diamond or William Schuman or Leonard Bernstein. Oliver will be in Italy sometime this summer; perhaps you will see him so he can talk with you about it. Or are you leaving, or have you left?

By now you may have seen Edwin Denby, who has yet to write us and let us know whether he has arrived safely in Rome. He left Morocco long ago. Jane and I are alone here in Fez with the parrot. I'm trying to finish my book during the coming month so that when Oliver arrives I shall be free to wander about the country with him. Whatever happened to Laughlin? I had a letter from him when I was in Colomb-Béchar, answered it, and that was that. I read Mary McCarthy's excited attack on *Streetcar* in *Partisan*. Could she really have been so very much upset?

Let me know about everything. The above address will remain valid.

TELEGRAM TO TENNESSEE WILLIAMS

April 27, 1948
Fez

RECEIVED FORWARDED WIRE TODAY IMPOSSIBLE SECURE BOTH RIFFIAN ITALIAN
VISAS WITHIN WEEK THANKS GENEROUS OFFER BUT TERRIFIED FLYING WILL TRY
BOAT GENOA IF YOUR TIME PERMITS OR COULD YOU STOP TANGIER GOING NEW YORK
WIRE ANSWER LOVE SEE YOU BOTH SOMEWHERE POSTE RESTANTE FEZ BATHA -
PAUL

TO PEGGY GLANVILLE-HICKS

May 10, 1948
Hotel Belvedere
Fez

Jane is dressing to go out to lunch to the American Fondouk with me, and
I shall try to get this off while such things are happening. I am also heating
some water on the alcohol burner to make some Viandox to stay my starvation,
since the way to the Fondouk is long, and breakfasts here are execrable. Oy
weh! All letters go first to Tangier, which explains their taking four to five days
longer to reach me here in Fez. I was wandering in the Ville Nouvelle last week
and came on a book I thought you'd like: *La Musique Chinoise* by Louis Laloy.
So I bought it and shall send it as soon as I can get some paper to do it up in,
which may not be for ages. God knows. It is a day's job to do *anything* at all
here. There is nothing to do with. You can imagine . . . very simple to get silk
robes, jewels, soft sandals and every sort of Oriental luxury, very simple to call
a carriage with sleighbells on the horses' saddles and fringes hanging from the
canopy over the seats, but impossible to get a piece of wrapping paper or a bit
of twine. Il n'y en a pas, they say, if they've ever even heard of such a thing.

I suppose Oliver will be leaving soon on his blessed Mary. Why does he want
us to go to Europe, I wonder? We have no intention of doing so, in any case.
It would cost a fortune. Is Maggie Dunham coming with him, or later on another
boat? We have no plans whatever, ours being quite dependent on the plans of
those who come to Morocco to visit us. If no one comes, no one will come. I
have finished my novel at last, and have a certain amount of correlating to do,

a certain number of pages to retype because they have been corrected too often and I want the copy to be as neat as I can make it. But it will all be sent off within the week. I don't quite know what I'll do next—perhaps some stories I have had on my mind for a while. But my agent doesn't seem to be selling any, so what's the use of writing them? She sends them all to *Cosmopolitan* and *Esquire* and *Good Housekeeping* and *Today's Woman*. "Under the Sky" had been to seventeen other magazines before she would consider sending it to *Partisan Review*. Then she did and they took it. It's strange that she should think my things are possible for such publications, but I suppose there is method in what she does, since she is not interested in prestige publication at all, and hopes I'll become commercial after a few years. How does one do that? Probably the magazines and the book you've sent will arrive sometime in June or July. I hope so, as I'd like to read them. I was so delighted to get the shipment that came to Timimoun; it was wonderful. I took no more walks in the oasis after their arrival.

I think the Viandox is hot by now. My novel is just a novel like any other: a triangle laid in the Sahara. Jane is busy farding her eyes with kohl at the moment. She bought the stuff from a crazy woman in the Grand Socco. She has almost decided to be tattooed like a friend of hers, the daughter of the patron saint of Tangier. Her friend has blue designs on her chin and on the end of her nose. Yesterday at Sidi Abdeslam Ben Moulay Ali Ktiri's house we sat through the most ridiculous tea I've ever witnessed. One member crawled in on all fours, with a tablecloth over her head. She looked and sounded just like Touche when he does Lester O'Toole or Queen Victoria on her deathbed. We were choking back the laughter and it was painful. There was a madwoman who looked like Ethel Barrymore in a new part; she came in done up in bustles and hoods, and leaned on a very thick clublike cane. They all kept wanting to know why Jane wasn't with child, and they repeatedly pressed their abdomens and breasts and smiled at her. Then they all try to feed her up because they think she's terribly thin; of course she weighs more than she ever has before. But after all, if a lady can walk by herself in the street she's still too thin. It's elegant only when she needs a slave on each side to hold her up. Jane's conversation with the daughter ran: "How do you do?" Reply from daughter: "Merci." A cat walked through the patio. Jane: "Do you like cats?" Daughter: "Not very much. There are many cats." I am being paged for lunch, so good bye. Libby wires she is coming to Fez next month. Isn't that fine. Love,

Bupple

TO PEGGY GLANVILLE-HICKS
———————◆———————

Spring 1948
Hotel Belvedere
Fez

At last the weather has come off crystalline, and naturally the sky and the air grow hotter each day. Everything is thereby changed. One seeks the shade and the cooler currents of air, one's thoughts turn to drinks colored green: Menthe Verte à l'Oulmès. The young storks can fly fairly well by now, the figtrees smell strong all the time. And I can sit up here on the terrace of the hotel leaning against the loud scratchy sound of the café phonograph that plays Abd el Wahab, Louisa Tounsia, Oum Khalsoum, and Salim Hillali. These would be ideal days to explore the regions round about, but it's impossible because Jane has a horror of buses, horses and trains, so that there's really no way of getting out of Fez save on foot. We are thinking in spite of everything of going to Marrakech before it grows too hot for her to be comfortable there. This summer if Oliver comes we shall doubtless go there, but it may well be that then Jane will stay in Tangier where she feels more at home and where the climate will permit her to work; she finds it impossible to work in the heat. Of course I have sent my novel off to New York and for the moment have nothing to do but lie about and read and revel in the magnificent weather. That proves to be highly disturbing to her, as she needs to have me in the next room working in order to be able to work. She has just completed a long story and wants to get back to the novel she started years ago and never got well into.

Thank you for the magazines; they arrived at the right moment, just when I needed something to read. And it had been so long since I'd read English, save for a clipping now and then. We have a great variety of books here in Fez— the table in Jane's room is piled with scores of them, of every sort, but they're all in French, and sometimes that's not of much help. There are times when one definitely wants to read English. I'm enjoying the Palinurus book. I find myself agreeing with so much that he says, and yet the tone of the book is somehow alien. Perhaps it's his sentimentality and querulousness; he gives the impression of a very old, peevish and whining gentleman. And I know he isn't. Perhaps if one is an intellectual one automatically becomes that way . . . (I mean a 100% British one . . . or a 100% one and British to boot.) His difficulty in living in the present seems strange in one so young as he. But perhaps it's because he's condemned to live in London. Condemned by his own tastes.

When I'm in New York my misery is boundless, and if I stayed there forever I should very shortly grow to be like him—without his cleverness, it goes without saying.

I'm casting about for something to write about, but obviously I'm not ready so soon after finishing the other. What I ought to be doing is writing music, but I left the Concerto in Tangier, not thinking *The Sheltering Sky* would be done so soon. They are playing a fascinating record at the moment . . . the first I've ever heard of the sort. True Flamenco: a typical guitar background, but the singing, which is *almost* indistinguishable from Spanish style, happens to be in Arabic. A Fandango in Moghrebi. I've been waiting for modern inter-reaction.

That was yesterday. Last night we made a fantastic walk by full moon, through the Guerniz quarter and along the river in the heart of the city, from El Qantara Ben Guezzam to El Zantara en Recif. Exactly like photos of Lhasa, the way the huge buildings are piled one atop the other, up the hills and down, in vast terraces. Also tried a very peculiar drug called Oisiset, Copravasanda, from the Senegal. I still feel strange from it, but I can't recall the exact effect it had, save that it seems to me I was wrapped in boiling rags and blankets and put away in an oven for the whole night, and it was pleasant, but nothing like hashish. Especially there was a feeling of being completely protected from all possible harm or trouble.

Forgive the amorphous letter.

I enclose one of a series of drawings by Ahmed ben Driss el Yacoubi. There are some incredible ones, but Jane has fallen in love with them and insists on keeping them. One of the parrot is the most extraordinary thing I've seen in a long time. Hilarious and very sad, all at once. He names each one. I have one called "Three Men Running Past a Mosque in Aït Baza, Three Hundred and Eighty Kilometers from Fez"!

January 10, 1949
Palais Jamai
Fez

Thanks for your letter; it arrived while Tennessee was still here. Soon afterward he left for Italy, having attempted unsuccessfully to persuade me to go along. I am perfectly content here, and there is no reason why I should leave. He on the other hand was violently perturbed by the Moslem scene, and couldn't leave fast enough to suit him. And he has never written since. He's a strange one. I suppose he thinks I'm mad to like it here, although he pretends not to. His line was I'm not strong enough now to take it. I want to come back some day when I'm less nervous. Perhaps that was sincere. He surely was nervous—practically hysterical all the time.

Naturally I was disturbed by Warburg's decree regarding my book. I fully expect Lehmann to refuse it also. However, I should like, if possible, to send him the few major rewrites I have done. Or don't you think it necessary? The only fully corrected copy is here with me. You might send me his address, and I should be deeply grateful if you would also send me that of *Horizon*. I remember Lansdowne Terrace, but that's all, and perhaps even that isn't correct. Cyril Connolly has the only copy of a story of mine, and I should like to get it back.

A greatly cut version of a story of mine called "Pastor Dowe at Tacaté" is coming out in the February *Mademoiselle*. I'm curious to know what you think of it, in case you happen to get hold of it. They made me remove seven pages to fit their advertising commitments.

Thanks also for sending me the little book of French Short Stories. It arrived today. I have a feeling it was sent a very long time ago. Reading matter is exaggeratedly welcome here in Fez, especially in English. It's the sort of place where when one has a newspaper one reads every single article on every page and finds it all curiously interesting.

Yes, some day you should drop around this way and see the Sahara and the Moroccan river valleys: the Drâa, the Ziz, the Dadès and the Todrha. I shall be joining Jane in Marrakech in another week or so, but my address will remain British Post Office, Tangier, Morocco. I hope to hear from you in the near future. Perhaps by now you are back from Utah. I send my best.

TO JAMES LAUGHLIN,
NEW DIRECTIONS, NEW YORK

April 7, 1949
Poste de Taghit, Sahara

Your letter of March twenty-first came today, having been forwarded from Tangier, Fez, and Beni Abbès. Not bad as to time.

You should have come here for sand skiing. The dunes are five and six hundred feet high here behind the hotel, and below Kerzaz they are a thousand. I should think that would suit you. Besides, it is quite the most astonishingly beautiful place I have ever seen. The hotel is a part of the fort, and is run by the army. Completely primitive, but with good food (much of it game) and not a soul here besides Jane and me. The weather is absolutely perfect.

I'm sorry about my agent—both for your sake and mine. She still says (I heard again from her today) that I must repay the thousand bucks to Doubleday. I suppose there's nothing to do about it. But I hope that her recalcitrance about recognizing your usefulness in getting the French and Italian contacts will not get in the way of the book's being done in those countries. I should have known better than to sign up with Eddie Cantor's and Jack Benny's agent. Except that I was ignorant at the time of the entire species, as well as of the fact that William Morris specialized in such luminaries as those two.

Lehmann says he would like me to go to London at the end of this month, but that seems extremely soon to me. I should be pleased to go later in the Spring, since I shall be in Paris in June in any case. I should think whatever needs to be done this month could be done by mail. I shall write him and suggest that I see him in London sometime in June or July. I hope that won't postpone the publication of the book. But I don't see quite how I can get up there so early, when I am still en route toward the south, and have no intention of going north as yet.

This is a great place. The silence is absolute, for once. The isolation is enormous, the beauty constantly breathtaking. Why there is no one here is a mystery, unless one admits that humanity doesn't want those things. The longer one stays, the less one wants to leave and return to the "world." You must come, and you will understand immediately what I mean.

Thank you for the little poem, which far from being "offensive," is, as you quite well know, flattering. However, it is nice to be flattered when one is so far from everything.

I am trying to write this by a dying carbide lamp, and it isn't easy. I hope to hear some more about contracts soon. Miss Strauss (forgive me for mentioning her again) says that the Doubleday money will come "only out of your royalties on the New Directions publication." Literally that would mean that it would not come out of those on the Lehmann publication. Do you think that is the case?

TO JAMES LAUGHLIN,

NEW DIRECTIONS, NEW YORK

◆

April 30, 1949

Palais Jamai

Fez

Your letter was sent to Tangier, then to Fez, then to the Hôtel de la Compagnie Transsaharienne in Beni Abbès, Sahara, then back here to Fez, and although it was written a month ago today and was sent by airmail, it came this noon. Thus I am answering it immediately. The contracts reached me to sign while I was in Beni Abbès, and being able to buy no envelopes to send them back to William Morris, in, I kept them until I returned to Colomb-Béchar and mailed them from there. I suppose Miss Strauss has them by now. I shall be fascinated to read the novel called *The Hyenas*. When I returned here, I found the page proofs of *The Sheltering Sky* waiting for me. They are corrected and en route back to London via airmail now. The English have done a rather thorough job on the text, with their corrections of Americanisms (*curb* is spelled *kerb; tire* comes out as *tyre; date-pits* appears as *date-pips; damned* is *dam*; when someone says: "Is there a hotel?" he is made to say: "Is there an hotel?" and so on). I mentioned some of these to Lehmann, explaining that if the same plates were to be used for the American edition, critics might easily get the impression that I had approved, or even written, such things (out of Anglophilism and snobbism), but at the same time I could scarcely object too much, since he was the publisher in England, and, after all, those terms were correct there. Perhaps it all has no importance whatever. I haven't run into John Russell; where is he? How come you have never used me to translate anything? I have been translating for decades, from French, Spanish, and even Italian. It's true that one can't do a good job unless one really admires the material. But I should like to do a book of Jorge Luis Borges into English sometime: *El Jardin de Senderos que se Bifurcan* it's called. That and another by Adolfo Bioy-Casares, *La Invención de Morel* would please a good many readers I think. Have you run across these two? They are both Argentines. And they are both good, albeit a bit hermetic. It's wonderful, but not surprising that *One Arm* has sold out. The edition was beautiful and the stories were fine. How is the volume of Sartre stories doing? And *La Nausée*? Has it appeared, and if so, is it selling? It's certainly his best work. I have been lending my copy out since 1942, and it's in a sad state now, but without any pages missing. What is the *New Directions Series* of which you spoke when you mentioned doing my stories? Did Capote publish a volume of stories this year as he said he was going to, and if so, were they good and how were they received? You see, I get absolutely no literary news from anywhere. Have you read the two most recent Cocteau books, *La Difficulté d'Etre* and *Lettre aux Américains*? He has certainly mellowed considerably since before the war. I expect to return shortly to Tangier for a while, and after that I'm not sure where I'll be going. We had a magnificent trip into the desert in spite of the sandstorms. I'm sorry the agent business has been so harassing for you; each time I sign up again it is from over here, and I do need some sort of link with New York, naturally. Incidentally, I think the novel will look very well—the type is good and the whole thing seems to have been done with care. There were very few corrections to be made. Do you intend to publish it simultaneously with Lehmann? He writes he is to be in America in June, which was when I was thinking of visiting London. However, I shall put off my trip there until he has returned—perhaps in the late summer. He wrote to ask me if I had any ideas for the jacket, and I suggested that an Arab whom I know here in Fez, and who does very amusing and very strange drawings, do the design. I hope to hear from you soon in reply to the various questions put to you in this disjointed missive.

TO GORE VIDAL

August 26, 1949

Tangier

I started this (the heading) this afternoon while sunbathing on the highest terrace of the house, which you would never recognize now. Then it got too hot and I got too lazy. And some old turbaned Arab arrived to gab with the masons who were building the stairway below and I was trying to listen to what they were saying, but I couldn't understand. Now Jane and Truman and Jack are out at Cecil Beaton's, where they seem to go every day at one time or another, but where I haven't been as yet. Although Truman gave a mad party on Monday night at the Caves of Hercules, with a large Arab orchestra, much champagne and hurricane lamps fainting in the gale. Themistocles passed out on hashish, after drinking several bottles of champagne. Cecil said, "How heavenly!" The Arab orchestra, plus porters and pussycats (Vidalese) had cases of Coca Cola. The sand sifted in and Truman found a huge centipede at his feet, nearly dying of horror; everything went wrong. But I shan't tell about it for nothing. I could get good cash for a synopsis of that evening. At one point the place was in absolute darkness and bats wheeled about, just missing people's heads. Anyway, Tangier isn't the same now that Cecil is here, and, to make it still more interesting, Mary Oliver has returned from Paris. But you don't know her. Ask Touche about her, though. But he knew her years ago while she could still move. My Saharan novel came out today in London. Do you really want to go there? I shall be here I daresay. And we could take our time on the great trek. But we mustn't stay in Tangier at all—the weather is too unreliable. Tennessee is already in New York, isn't he? Or, I mean Hollywood, whither he and Frank [Merlo] went the other day. Let me know more about your Sahara plans. I may go to London next month for a week or so, although I don't quite see the point, do you? The novel was chosen by the *Evening Standard* as its September Book of the Month. But Lehmann says that means nothing. Shall I hear from you one day soon. Luap sdnes tseb.

TO TENNESSEE WILLIAMS
————————◆————————

August 30, 1949
Tangier

I am writing from the top terrace of our house, which is now enormously high and has the best view in Tangier. There is a madman in pajamas a few roofs away, who is looking through an endlessly long brass telescope—at another house! Not out to sea at all. The sea is magnificent, incidentally, from this terrace. I could never tire of sitting up here sunbathing. The masons and other workmen are still busy, however, so we can't live in the house yet. Truman and Jack are fine; they see Cecil Beaton just about every day. I was most surprised to hear you were leaving for Hollywood. I hope the film turns out to be somewhat better than you seem to think it will. I also hope they use my music (for purely personal reasons)! But I suppose that now they've heard it they won't. I wish they had been willing to let me do the whole film score for it. Or perhaps they would be. I'll send your song to you care Liebling-Wood. And I hope you'll have time one day to send a note.

TO GORE VIDAL

October 14, 1949
Tangier

Weather unbelievably beautiful these weeks; we are living in a rather fancy modern house called Villa Mektoub, where Cecil Beaton stayed when he was here. Jane hates it, and has retaliated by having measles for the past ten days or more. Now she is over the reddish phase, but can't see. If and when she is well we are driving up into the Rif for a few days' proper convalescence. In ten days we'll leave on the *Djenné* for Marseille. If only the weather holds! So far I've seen only two rave reviews of my book: one the one you mentioned and the other from *The Observer* (Sunday). Most of the others seemed respectful but puzzled. And one reviewed Prokosch's *Storm and Echo* along with mine, because they were both about trips in Africa. I must say that there I came out a bit better than he did, although neither book called forth ecstatic noises from the reviewer. Our own house is about finished, or so we think. Allah doubtless knows otherwise and has already imparted His knowledge to Mohammed Ouezzani, our contractor, who, each time he goes to the place now, unmakes it a bit more, so that soon it will be back where it was in August. It's comforting to know that everyone is living in the Chelsea even in these troubled days. We lived there, on and off, for years beginning in 1936, and going on into 1943, although since October of that year I haven't spent a night within its precinct. I'm going to write Tenn this morning. By the first of December I ought to be en route back in this direction UNLESS I take a boat to Ceylon and stay there three weeks or so, and then return here. I still have a mad desire to see that part of the world, even briefly. And how long will one be able to? Not long. So then. While one can one should. Tangier always amusing. As long as there's no rain. Rain here ghastly. I leave for Sahara at first drop. So would you, I think. But I'm not sure. Pussy conditions here really enticing, really. Perhaps not for you in Sahara. So. Love.

TO CYRIL CONNOLLY

November 24, 1949
Wilton House
Salisbury, England

Our evening broke into several strands when you left. I agreed with you about the horror of the music, but I had the impression you wanted to go home to bed at that point. We sat on, each feeling his own reactions to the puissance du chanvre,* Sonia with her head in her hands and the other lady wearing an increasing look of anguish. (She finally became ill, it seems, which is the first time I ever heard of *that*.) I began to feel most strange, and suddenly realized I had had too much and that it was going to have a terrific effect. Somehow at the last moment the cab the ladies had called turned out to be for me, even though it hadn't been intended so originally. They walked off up the street to Sonia's house, I suppose, and I rode away, my feeling of terror mounting by the second, into the most sinister experience I can remember ever having undergone. Outside my own head absolutely nothing happened, of course.

I wanted to thank you for having been my host all that evening. I felt somehow we should all have left together, but I suppose nothing was really amiss, unless the other lady, whose name I have forgotten, turned out to have been sicker than I knew.

I shall call you when I get to London, and I hope we can meet again. I think I have passage to Ceylon [*word illegible*] or the first week in December.

---

* power of the cannabis

THE 1950S

January 12, 1950
Homagama, Ceylon

Your first direct letter to Ceylon arrived today. Thanks. I was amazed to learn that Sky had touched the best-seller list. That is certainly good work on someone's part. I hope you saved a clipping of the list, as I should love to see it, just for the satisfaction the sight would give me. I'll await the envelope of reviews eagerly. I imagine I have received all your letters by now; perhaps not. They are forwarded by boat from England, and the quickest trip is three weeks or over.

I expect to be spending some time on a tea and rubber plantation. There I can ride elephants, so if you want me in sarong, loincloth or trance with my typewriter sitting on an elephant, instead of a water-buffalo, I'll ask my hypothetical host to snap me! Incidentally, I've wondered why you chose the photo you did for the publicity pictures. Wasn't there a better one among those I sent? This one wasn't so bad in the original, but it seems to me it reproduces awfully poorly. Of course, now it's too late to change, since there will be no more need for photos, I imagine. I was disappointed to see it in print, however, and I suppose you were, too.

On my way to have my second bicuspid extracted this morning I ran into an elephant eating branches under a tree beside the river; I was crossing the bridge from Slave Island onto the mainland. I must say it looked very large and rather mauve in color—in general ridiculous and touching. Not at all nasty-tempered, like camels. While I was bathing this noon a colony of several scores of thousands of ants appeared on the floor out of nowhere, in a minute. It looked like a dark puddle gathering there in the doorway while I watched. I bent down and blew lightly into their midst. Then the strangest noise began as they seethed over each other in all directions at once, furiously. It sounded like a bolt of very soft cloth being ripped . . . very faint, but quite perceptible. Or perhaps like extremely fine rain falling on a still pond when one is in a row-boat and it is very quiet. In the afternoon I went riding in an open car with a Cinghalese lady in a magenta saree, out to some ganga where we sat in the twilight on the bank and watched long covered boats with bonfires on them floating slowly past. There was a tremendous tree above us with a small altar built into its trunk on one side. They keep a lamp flickering there always, to frighten the spirits that live in the tree so that they won't leave it and wander about. A night bird came and began to bark like a dog on one of its branches, and that worried the servants very much. It seems it was all extremely evil and sinister, the fact that that particular bird should have lighted in that tree. So they came with huge American flash-lights to drive it away. It finally left, after staring down somewhat insolently for a few minutes. Afterward we drove for miles through the forests to return here to Homagama. This rest-house is haunted, or so everyone claims. I've seen nothing, but a professor whom I saw this morning said with great seriousness: "I have some rather disturbing news to tell you about your rest-house . . ." and proceeded to go into the details about howls and lamentings and so on. Otherwise he is a most rational person—a Communist, to boot. (Stalinist, I mean.) The Trotskyists are stronger than the Stalinists here, which is most peculiar. The Fourth International has huge signs up all over the place.

I had to interrupt this to write a recommendation for an assistant rest-house keeper. The poor man insists that with my letter he can get a better job, so all I could do was to type out my praise.

Let me hear everything you know about the book. I'm very happy it's going along the way it is.

TO JAMES LAUGHLIN,
NEW DIRECTIONS, NEW YORK

January 25, 1950
Maldeniya Estate
Dehiowita, Ceylon

Thanks for your letter of the 17th. I telephoned to Colombo and asked the bank to send what mail there was for me in a registered envelope up here to Dehiowita, so I got yours, even way up in the hills, exactly a week after you had written it. It's a strange place here—a rubber and tea plantation that spreads over steep humplike hills and into deep valleys where coconut and bamboo-bordered rivers run. There are enormous black boulders balanced here and there on the hillsides; they look rather like elephants until one gets closer to them and sees how large they are. The bungalow is open enough for snakes to get in and lie coiled on tables, which is exactly what happened yesterday morning, to the consternation of the servants, who refused to go near it. It was not a cobra, however, nor a tic polonga nor a green adder, so I take it no one would have been dead even if it had decided to attack. Those three varieties are the only common venomous ones in the region. The tea-pickers are the ones who usually get bitten—not the planters and their wives. Since I was in Lunawa I have been around a bit, from rest-house to rest-house because none of them was satisfactory, although all were worth seeing and staying in. From there I went to Kesbewa, opposite one of the large "tanks" (artificial lakes where the temples often are, and the people and bulls bathe). That was most uncomfortable, and I went on to Homagama, from where I probably wrote you about the wailing woman in the next cell to mine. Then I took a zebu-cart through the forest three days later to Kaduwela on the bank of the river. There I spent a week very pleasantly, until I was invited here. I am writing a Ceylon notebook just to have everything down for future reference. Everything is fine except the weather, which is supremely dog-day—a sort of excessive reductio ad absurdum of our worst August weather in America. Muggy, heavy, lazy, threatening, with occasionally a small breeze as hot as the breath of a man with fever. And the birds in the shadeless trees around the bungalow don't sing: they cough, choke, gurgle, grunt, hammer, sputter, croak and yell, a welter of ridiculous noises that have no right to come out of the throats of birds. There's one at the moment which sounds exactly like a telegraph in a country station buzzing out its Morse code. The night sounds, made by reptiles, birds and insects, are more pleasant, until about three, when a kind of electric drill begins, sometimes right in the bedroom, which is already lit up for the occasion by fireflies almost as bright as pocket flashlights, which crawl slowly up the walls and then flop downwards to begin again. The planter is lending me his car this afternoon for two days. I shall go down to Colombo and take care of my mail, returning day after tomorrow.

The short stories. I should like them to be in a volume the same size as *Sky* . . . same format if possible, and approximately same number of pages. It seems to me a thicker volume of stories has more impact (or will in this case) than a thin one. Perhaps it is a question of momentum, since the tales are enough alike to acquire a certain impetus as the reader progresses. I also think a larger volume would get more critical attention. Of course not all the stories can be included, as they would make too many pages. But about fifteen could be used, saving a few in the hope of selling their serial rights! I sent the list to Helen Strauss. However, I can repeat it here for you: "The Scorpion," "The Echo," "A Distant Episode," "By The Water," "You Are Not I," "Call at Corazón," "At Paso Rojo," "Pastor Dowe at Tacaté," "Under the Sky," "The Delicate Prey," "The Fourth Day Out from Santa Cruz," "Pages from Cold Point," "The Circular Valley," and "Señor Ong and Señor Ha." I don't suppose you have read them all, but I think Miss Strauss has copies of all of them and will submit them to you if you ask her for them. The only one about which there is some question legally is "Señor Ong and Señor Ha," which was bought some time ago by *Mademoiselle* and has not yet appeared in its pages. But I have already written to their fiction editor asking her plan thereon. Probably the story will be printed sometime during the year. I wish the jacket could be in greens, reminiscent of a jungle. (My personal fantasy!) If there is a title among them which seems better to you than *The Delicate Prey*, tell me. The story, incidentally, was printed in No. 2 of *Zero*, a little magazine I'm sure you know.

The Gallimard advance may as well stay in Paris, as even if there should be further devaluation the sum is stipulated in dollars, and I certainly expect to be in Paris sometime this year, and usually stay just across the street from their offices, so that it is easy for me to run in there as often as I like. I may even be going to Paris during the Spring. Jane is there, and Oliver Smith writes that he expects to be going to discuss plans for the production of her play with her.

I hope to have an envelope of reviews of *Sky* from you . . . and ads and whatever printed material is relevant to it. Jane sent me the *Herald Tribune* and *Times* clippings yesterday. I was astonished at Prescott's favorable reaction, not surprised however at Gannett's unpleasant remarks. Of course I'm delighted it's selling; Miss Strauss writes that *Life* wants to run a blurb of some sort, and is looking for a picture of me. Why don't you give them the seated profile I sent you along with the one you finally used? It reproduces very well, that I know. Such an article would surely boost sales noticeably, perhaps would keep it a while longer on the Best-seller bulletin, if it hasn't already tumbled off.

It's so hot that even typing makes the sweat trickle down all around. Fortunately the available space is about exhausted, since I seem determined to get my money's worth out of this air-letter. I think I've said everything necessary. I always am eager to hear from you about the book's vicissitudes. It's doubtless the only time I'll ever have a best-seller, so I take it very seriously and hope to remain on the list as long as possible. I hear Gore Vidal is coming to Ceylon in February. I send my best.

TO GORE VIDAL
◆
February 22, 1950
Galle, Ceylon

What nonsense! Missed the boat, indeed! How was I to know that? I was literally expecting you from one day to the next, put off trips in order to make them with you when you came. I wrote you in Rome. Perhaps you've received the letter by now, if the American Embassy knows enough to forward it to New Orleans. Yes, it's perfectly true that I refrained from going to Dambulla, Sigiriya, Anuradhapura and Polonaruwa, which are the island's sights, in order to be able to do it all with you. Now, unfortunately, I haven't time to see them. Nor, to tell the truth, does the prospect of touring in that way alone interest me very much. So I'm not unhappy about it all. However, I did keep all plans static, waiting from one day to the next to hear when you would be arriving, so I could go down to Colombo and meet the boat. Why the hell didn't you write long ago and let me know at least that you had not taken the boat? Never thought of it, I suppose. Getting ships out of here is practically impossible. Not that I want to leave, but I'm afraid of getting stuck completely, in which case I should have to remain until June or July. The great exodus toward Europe begins this month. I must say that the opportunities for happy living are greater in Ceylon than anywhere I've been so far. You never would have done any work if you'd come, so perhaps it's just as well. * * *

I was walking down the street here in Galle last night when a man hailed me from inside a house. I paid no attention, so he came out and followed me down the street, all the way to the sea-wall. In the end it turned out he was a gem merchant and hoped I'd buy jewels. At his insistence I accompanied him to his house, where he brought out masses of rubies, sapphires and emeralds. When I smoked and asked for an ashtray he said: "Please put the ashes on the floor. It makes the servant more attractive." I couldn't figure that out, so I asked him what he meant, exactly. He said: "My servant, he likes to be lazy. I had ashtrays at one time, but that was a bad experiment. My servant, then he only cleaned floor once daily. If I put ashes on floor all time he cleans more industrious. Then more attractive." So Professor Bowles said: "Do you mean more attractive or more active?" His answer was Sinhalese 100%: "Yes, better that way." A few minutes later he noticed that his bracelets and rings weren't making headway in the winning of my favor, so he stood up dramatically, raised his arms Allah-ward, and cried with inspiration: "Scorpions! That is what your people require!" He hurried out and came back with two gold scorpion brooches set with rubies and all the rest. "You see?" he said triumphantly. "Exactly as I say. We know these by the name fancy scorpion." Then he took me into his dining room when an elderly lady on the floor made it quite clear in Tamil that she wished to hell he would get the filthy Christian out of the house, and said, showing me one of the most wretched rooms I've ever been in: "Kindly note decoration. Not framed pictures. No. Nothing more than mirrors, so one can see on forever.

And from my office I can see entire house." Which was quite true. He had eight enormous mirrors arranged to reflect the main entrance of the house from every possible angle. He said: "This is to be of use and beautiful at once." My paraphrase: "Practical as well as ornamental," brought from him his prize, his crowning remark of the interview: "A writer's statement, sir." So I bought nothing, and he nearly wept when I left, making me promise to write a postcard from Tangier. End of paper. Never heard from Tenn. Hope to hear from you.

TO GORE VIDAL

———————————◆———————————

March 18, 1950
Cape Comorin, Travancore, India

Over in India, where you ought to be, too. The letter explaining the missing of the boat never arrived, I can tell you. I managed to get my return passage put off until April 25th, so I had the time to come. The Cape is a wonderful spot to work and bathe. Not much else, of course, as it is unfrequented and the village consists of fishermen's huts and three or four shops and a very large Hindu temple with bathing ghats, all directly on the sea. The sun is vicious, and I got dreadfully burned by it. With such a strong, cool wind one doesn't realize how strong it is itself, and of course the latitude is such that the damned orb is directly overhead in the middle of the day. That is my news. That and the fact that I finally visited Madura temple, which was worth the god-awful trip I had to make to get there. Also that Laughlin cabled he was suing me. He is in Switzerland skiing. Suing my agent, to be exact. I have written him various times saying that I don't understand why. Either one has done something illegal or not. I imagine I shall hear soon from the agent, saying to worry or not to worry. Yes, Touche said you had fallen in love, which was why you hadn't left America. You say no. I think it would be very fine if it were true, but I'm more inclined to believe you when you say it isn't. You ask me my plans. I shall go to London because I can't help myself. Then to Paris and down to Tangier I suppose. Then probably to Spain, if Libby [Holman] comes over. Then probably to New York, if Oliver Smith comes over and decides to do Jane's play next season. Perhaps to New York anyway, I don't know. Today I feel headachy from my sunburn and fever, and it irks me to think ahead more than one minute. Or more than one minute ahead. I'm trying to write a book, and finding it a bore. Perhaps it's the heat. I'd rather do anything than try to think of those damned characters, who are automatically boring because I'm writing about them. Probably, too, they're boring people anyway, or I shouldn't be writing about them. I really have no interest in writing books if all one can get out of one which has been on the best-seller lists as long as Sky has, is $337.50. I thought I could make two or three thousand dollars, but it just isn't so. There's absolutely no money in it. Fortunately I'm not starving, as I brought some checks with me, but I had imagined it would be possible to send for a thousand dollars, let us say, after three months or so. Not only is it not possible, but it never will be, unless I am being unduly pessimistic. There is, however, another possibility on the horizon, but I never believe anything until I see it accomplished. Why do you suppose my book hasn't made any more money than it has? Laughlin says that no books are selling—even those at the top of the list. No one is buying. 1950's little enigma. I think I should go to New York and find out what it's all about. There's obviously a mistake somewhere. I think the trouble is the friction between Laughlin and my agent. How is Gordon Sager's book, I wonder? Is it the one about Jane? Did you see Truman as Cupid in *Vogue*? Themistocles swears you gave Rolo the information for his article on Tangier in *Flair*. I haven't seen it, so I have nothing to say beyond: did you? Sorry about this letter; it's an awful effort.

TO DAVID MCDOWELL,
RANDOM HOUSE, NEW YORK

❖

April 17, 1950
Haputale-Diyatalawa, Ceylon

I am sitting under a tree on the side of a mountain conversing with a crow. There is one that comes around and mimics human speech beautifully, without, however, using words of any known language, unless "Pang-go-strauchhhh!" turns out to mean something, this being his usual ultimatum as he flies away. I wish I were going directly to New York from here; I could take some mynahs with me. The very finest talkers cost less than a dollar up here. (The hill mynahs with yellow neck-feathers.) The ordinary black ones, which are also expert linguists, one can get for about a quarter. But of course they speak only Sinhalese and Tamil. Your letter of the seventh came this morning an hour ago, and I suppose it is the last I shall have from you while I'm here, inasmuch as I sail a week from tomorrow for London.

I want to tell you that it was not sheer stinginess which prevented me from cabling you in answer to your cable. The principal reason was that I received it nine days after I had posted the contracts from Galle, and I figured that Helen Strauss surely had the contracts by then and would notify you. I hope she did. Also there was the fact that I received it in the impossible settlement of Hambantota, from which I had a terrific time even trying to send a letter to the U.S., which they thought was a part of India. And I had no faith in a cable's ever reaching its destination if sent through that post-office. So I allowed those two good reasons to persuade me that it was unnecessary and hopeless to reply to the cable, and I daresay I was right on both counts. Moving around, I can't send for my mail so often, since I don't know where I shall be. When I strike a place which seems bearable for a few days I put through a telephone call to Colombo—it often takes several hours to do—and ask them to forward what is on hand for me. Sometimes, however, eight or ten days elapse between mails, which is what happened in the case of your cable; it had been waiting in Colombo for me practically since my last mail had gone out (to Galle). Hambantota was a rather wonderful place, at the edge of the Yala Game Reserve, which is real old Kipling jungle. But it was also on the Indian Ocean, which provided fine bathing. The fishermen there are Malays, brought over about 150 years ago, so they say. The sarongs were different, the language and facial structure different, the eyes slanted. The heat however was the same, only moreso—I nearly gave up and took to bed, my energy seemed so far away from me. And then Sinhalese New Year came banging in with fireworks twenty-four hours of the day. New Year's here is not a day but a season, and the accompanying festivities are by no means confined to a well-defined period. Which is all very well, except that public services fall off, some of them ceasing altogether, although not officially, which makes it worse because one gets all varieties of information and has no idea which of it will turn out to be true. Certainly the bus service stopped for a few days, so that I had to hire a car which had literally been rebuilt with pine boards and strips of rubber, to bring me up here. And amazingly enough it did get me here, through fifty miles of jungle and up another thirty of Alpine grades, up to 6,000 feet finally. The stops were innumerable, the motor did strange things and sometimes would go only twenty feet at a time, but we did get here, and all in one day. And I saw villages where bands of large capucine monkeys were living in harmony with the inhabitants, neither paying any attention to the other—the people on the ground and the monkeys (just about half the size of the people) busy living in the trees upstairs. Their fur was the color of wet cement and their posteriors looked like sunset on a grocer's calendar.

It was very kind of you to get and send the information on the printings of Sky. Also I'm glad Helen Strauss has them. I'm curious to know just what will happen on the threatened suit. Strauss finally admitted to me that she had been scared, which was why she held up sending me the contracts for such a long time—so I was correct. I take it, however, that she wouldn't have sent them on unless she had been pretty sure that not too much trouble would be made. I hope to hell Laughlin doesn't bring suit; I was once sued by a landlord who had been tracking me down for seven years, after I had broken a lease (justifiably, I might add, although that did me no good), and the affair kept me from working for months, just because the average citizen like me is terrified when confronted with the Law. (I always foresee jail and the third degree—not intellectually, but emotionally, which is worse!) I'll be glad to know that the advance has been deposited to my account, at least.

As to the order of the stories, it might be well to start with "At Paso Rojo" instead of "Pastor Dowe at Tacaté," since the latter will have been in both the O. Henry and the Martha Foley Collections (or do you think that has absolutely no importance?). Also "At Paso Rojo" has a simple, direct beginning. I must absolutely get to New York to see that the right versions of these stories reach you. Some of the versions Helen Strauss has are very askew. I know, for instance, that the only correct version of "The Delicate Prey" is that which appeared in the little mag Zero last summer, because I corrected the proofs myself, and made changes at the last moment. There's no point in having earlier versions set up, is there? "You Are Not I" was mangled by Mademoiselle, and Miss Strauss has no copy of the original, nor have I, of course, so I shall have to get the only one of whose existence I know, from Lehmann in London. By now I suppose you will have read them all: I'd love to know from you if there are any which you intend leaving out. Can you write me c/o Lehmann, London? And thanks again for the information on Sky's figures.

TO GORE VIDAL

April 24, 1950
Slave Island, Ceylon

My wonderful holiday is over; I sail tomorrow from Colombo for London. But I must come back; the longer I stayed the more I liked the place. I've found a house on its own small island off the coast at Weligama, which I'll rent, not having the money to buy it (even though it's cheap). Failing that, I have some others in mind up-country. I found one the other day for sale for $2,000, including four acres of jungle, and the house was delightful, with its own power plant, and two bathrooms with real plumbing, and garage. If I'd only looked sooner, I might easily have got a place with five or six rooms and garage very cheaply. I've about come to the conclusion that it's the best country to settle in, from all points of view. For one thing, I've never felt so well as I have these four months . . . no digestive troubles at all, no liver attacks as I have in Morocco. And then, the climate is fine and the company is even better, and the countryside suits me beautifully. And the way one is taken care of by the servants appeals to me . . . there is no such thing as service in Europe or America after one has been attended to by Sinhalese. So the nightmare is about to begin again, I suppose. One can't stay in Paradise forever. I'll stay a few days in London and go on to Paris to see Jane, see if she wants to go to Tangier, or what. Oliver is coming over shortly, and expects us to return with him to New York in the summer. I was glad to find you hysterical in your letter. Good for the spirit. I hope you do blow up Washington, but I very much doubt it. You'll have forgotten all you said by now, and will be wondering what I'm talking about. Still, you did admit that you "look forward to the day when my protest is perverted to acceptance," which means you must be conscious of friction, so perhaps you do remember.

No, there will be no payment from New Directions on *Sky* until March 1951, according to contract. Why said document stipulates such a thing I don't understand, nor do I understand why my agent allowed such a clause to be included, but she says it's there and I have to take her word for it. Whether or not there was an option on a story book I don't know, but certain agreements had been made between Jay and the agent, and it was orally understood that the volume was to be done by ND, until I got a cable from her saying that she had a far better offer from Random House and strongly advised me to take it. They were making up my income tax report and obviously I need some money to send the government. The other offer was thus accepted and all is finished. I haven't heard from Jay Laughlin since, so I don't know how he is reacting. But it's scarcely criminal to want to make as much money as possible. Perhaps Themistocles was furious because his name was misspelled. (I refer to *Flair*.) I wish you had come to Ceylon; you would have loved it. I land in London May 15th. Bombay on Thursday at midnight. Abrazos.

TO DAVID MCDOWELL,
RANDOM HOUSE, NEW YORK

July 10, 1950
Tangier

I have just returned from a sojourn in Fez; it was hot as two hells. Now I am disturbed by the rumor, brought here day before yesterday from New York by an American, that the State Department is relieving Americans returning from abroad of their passports on arrival in port; I wonder if it is true. Naturally if it is I shouldn't want to return since it will be for only a month or so, and I already have my passage back on the Italian Line. I suppose there is no way to find out. I am leaving Friday for Spain to be with Libby Holman a fortnight there before taking the *Vulcania* on the 30th. The dedication should be "For my mother, through whom I first became acquainted with Poe." As a small child I used to be read to by her, and the first short stories with which I came in contact that way were Poe's *Tales of Mystery and Imagination*. They also made the greatest impression; and she told me the story of his life, so that I resolved then to go to the University of Virginia, which I did, solely because he had attended it. I have the page proofs of the English edition, including the original version of "You Are Not I." You can write me at the B.P.O. here, and the letter will be forwarded. Let me know about possibilities of being stuck in U.S.A.

TO CHARLES-HENRI FORD

August 18, 1950
Tangier

Libby Holman has left and I am alone with Brion Gysin here in the lighthouse. The weather is, as usual, quite the most wonderful in the world. I suppose the rain will be coming along for two or three days next month, then October will be perfect again. The big rains don't come here until November and December. Then January and February can be either rainy or clear, with more rain in March. But in Fez it rains any old day after the end of October, until May. One never knows. Marrakech is lower but drier, with more sun, of course. The studios of the Beaux Arts are free in the sense of gratis—not always in the sense of unoccupied, which is why one must write ahead of time. However, I'm sure

Pavlik [Tchelitchew] could easily get one, since most of the artists who go and use them are the sort who do pretty water-colors of minarets and trellis-covered souks, of whom no one has ever heard or ever will hear. It might be possible, considering his fame, to get one for the whole winter in one place, instead of having to change towns after a month or two, which is the usual procedure. (Most painters want to "do" the whole country—a month here and a month there, of course, which accounts for the short terms of occupancy generally granted. But it would be well worth a few letters to find out.) Didn't you and Djuna have the Wiley house one spring? (1933?) A California couple now live in it; she says "Aloha" instead of "good-bye." She also has a $10,000 car which she designed. Everything is changed; the place is very European. Barbara Hutton arrived this week, but she is staying indoors because she is ill. The town is full of American marines who sit and drink in a chichiteux bar decorated with fake zebra-skins, to look like the La El Morocco. They all get rolled by the same two or three Arab bathing-boys, who are making a fortune this season. Everyone is high on hashish ALL THE TIME, including the two little Ruspoli princesses, who carry it around with them in silver boxes. Étienne de Beaumont was here last week, wandering on the Avenida de España at three a.m. You can see what our old town has become. It looks like pictures of Tel Aviv. Irra Belline's shop has just closed; I don't know why.

TO DAVID MCDOWELL,

RANDOM HOUSE, NEW YORK

November 3, 1950
Palais Jamai
Fez

Jane left for Tangier day before yesterday taking with her the galleys. She promised to post them to you as soon as she was able, and I hope that by now they are off. I had them all in a large envelope I had bought in the Ville Nouvelle, addressed, marked and so forth, but the envelope came to pieces in my hands as I gave it to her. Naturally, it was made of some sort of French garbage; they're incredible. So she will have had to find another envelope somewhere in Tangier, and it won't have been easy, I assure you. Things like that, like stoppers for a sink, zippers, screwdrivers, teaspoons, are practically impossible to buy anywhere. Because there's no big money in them; that's the only reason.

You can get the latest model Frigidaire or wire-recording set with perfect ease, but I'd never advise it, for if anything is amiss, you might as well throw the whole thing out: no one can repair it, and even if they could, they'd have no parts. Which is all a way of saying that she may not have yet found an envelope, and thus may not yet have sent the proofs.

Perhaps we had better cut all dedication. I suggested the Gertrude Stein idea to Jane, and she immediately insisted I must dedicate the book to Toklas as well. But that would entail asking her permission, and I don't want to get all tied up in that. Jane thinks she would object to having the dedication (from me, that is) read: to Gertrude Stein, without including her. The only reason I thought of Stein was, as perhaps I told you, that it was she who first suggested I come to Tangier, and took me to the train and saw me off. (When I was staying with her at Bilignin.) So that without her suggestion I should probably never have come down here. However, many people might assume a literary reason for the hypothetical dedication, and that would embroil (or do I mean *embrouiller?*) everything, and it doesn't seem worth while. It can sneak through dedicationless, don't you think? I'm dashing this off so you can have the news about the dedication before you include it. Let me know when you get the proofs.

TO DAVID MCDOWELL,
RANDOM HOUSE, NEW YORK

◆

November 6, 1950
Tangier

I arrived back in Tangier tonight after a hellish trip which began yesterday morning at five o'clock. Somehow the French had arranged to have the trains just miss connections, so that after having to change in Casablanca one has to spend the night in Rabat; both places are devoid of decent hotels and as noisy as factories, all of which would have been acceptable if I hadn't been sick as a dog for the past ten days, first with a terrific head and chest cold and sinus complications, and then with a liver attack which won't leave. The liver attacks come from amoebic dysentery, which I caught in South America in 1934 and have never been able to shake off completely. They are hell, because they extend to the gall bladder and the stomach, and it is impossible to eat anything. Thus one gets weaker and weaker, and can finally just about drag around. To add to my difficulties I have had crops of various families of intestinal worms, some of which got in while I was in South India and others of which are natives of Morocco. Being of differing religions, they get on badly with each other, and not at all with me; sometimes I feel that I'm merely a symbol of today's world: the Christian who is bound to be got the better of by Moslems and Hindus. He may hold out for a while, but in the end he goes under! However, I don't expect to be vanquished by my Moslems and Hindus this winter; a good doctor, if there were such a thing in these parts, could probably send them all packing.

I am not even staying at my house now, having put Count Esterhazy into it when I went to Marrakech. (He does me the favor of living in it when I go away, so that it won't remain uninhabited—a dangerous state for a house to be in here; and I forgot to wire him that I was returning.) So I am in a mosquito-infested hotel. Fortunately we have DDT bombs here.

I had three letters from you, as well as the finished cover of *The Delicate Prey* waiting for me. Thank you for a voluminous correspondence. There are several points you raise which need answers, and I shall try to give them now. I still have a first-class ticket for the *Vulcania* or the *Saturnia* to New York, but I am afraid to use it. I have an absurd but unhappy premonition that some sort of objections would be raised to my departure, and you don't seem to be able to furnish me with any sort of consoling information on that score. It would be idiotic to risk being trapped in a place I so dislike, just to be present at publication. Perhaps I overestimate the importance the State Department attaches to Communist affiliations of prospective voyagers, but there can't be much doubt that they are aware of my adherence and (slight though they may have been) activities, since I joined under my own name, not thinking it necessary to use a party name (though that wouldn't have done much good, anyway). If it had been only front organizations it would be different, as one can always plead vagueness, liberal inclinations, innocence, more or less. But it wasn't, nor did I break with the Party when the Ribbentrop–Molotov pact was signed! What do you think about all that? Do you think I am being hysterical?

The title Let It Come Down is tentative. What's your reaction? (*Banquo*: It will be rain tonight. *First Murderer*: Let it come down. *Stabs him.*) It would be extremely bad to mention the title in any releases if there were any chances of its being changed.

I know that Libby Holman doesn't want the opera mentioned to anyone, and so, while it wouldn't bother me at all, it's best not to speak about it.

Would you mind asking Harry Sions at *Holiday* whether they mind mention of the Sahara article? I don't know, myself, but it would seem only proper procedure to inquire of them. In case he objected, I might easily find myself without the assignment, which would be a stupid blunder on my part. Nothing as yet signed on that score, because I haven't sent in the outline which is a prerequisite.

As to the music, the only thing I have been doing recently is the García Lorca opera for Libby Holman. However, Columbia just issued a recording of my Concerto for Two Pianos, Winds and Percussion, which got some good reviews in the American press. That might make good copy. I believe the work is being given in New York on December 12th; at least, that was my last information. They would know at Town Hall. I have a contract from Columbia which came today, too, for the recording of a piece called *Night Waltz*, for two pianos. But that is a short work. (Also a wire from Goddard Lieberson, of Columbia, asking for the music I did a few seasons ago for *Cyrano de Bergerac*, which he thinks they are going to record with José Ferrer.) I mention these things only because they are current, and represent about all there is to be said about my present musical activities.

I want to call your attention to a couple of misrepresentations on the jacket of *The Delicate Prey*. Don't think I am carping; it is too late for that! But what does the following sentence mean?: "Of the seventeen stories in this volume, all but one are set in Arab North Africa, the Far East or Latin America." Actually, two are set in the United States, one in the Canaries, and not a single one in the Far East, for the simple reason that I have never written anything about the Far East. How did such a salient error escape your notice? And then the final sentence, about violence—"particularly that violence arising out of the clash of the Westerner with the alien world of the East." There is only one possible story which could answer such a description: "A Distant Episode." The other sixteen, in no manner. I am completely mystified by these statements, which appear on the back of the jacket as well as on the flap. They are untrue and misleading, as you will readily agree if you give the matter a thought. While I'm in no way annoyed, I am curious to know how such things got by your eagle eye. The blame for that can't fall on me; it can only fall on the publisher. The only explanation I can invent is that some ethnologist wrote the copy, and was trying to put across his theory that American Indians are essentially Mongols, thus represent the East; that being accepted, naturally South and Central America would be the Very Far East, and their indigenous cultures, being certainly "alien" to ours, could rightly be called "the alien world of the 'East.'" I think my observations are important, because that Far Eastern tack should certainly be abandoned immediately in all publicity and advertising. And it will be really annoying if reviewers make cracks about looking in vain for one story about the

Far East; it's just the sort of easy thing that they like to waste space on and sharpen their tempers on—and of course one can't blame anyone too much if he has been led to expect something he looks for in vain. So, the "clash of the Westerner with the alien world of the East" is false, as is any mention whatever of the Far East. I hope you will find it possible to keep those references out of copy that goes out from your offices. For everybody's sake.

I rented a house in Marrakech for the winter, but after that God-awful trip back, I don't know whether I can go back down there or not. A while here in Tangier will tell. At the moment I feel lousy, and not at all inclined to try and buck the rigorous climate and general filth there. (It's only bearable if one lives at the Mamounia, which has good food, central heating and Winston Churchill during the winter.) I may go to the Canaries, or Zanzibar. When shall I have a copy of *The Delicate Prey*? I'm eager to see the finished product. The cover is exceedingly handsome. Let me hear from you, please.

TO PEGGY GLANVILLE-HICKS

November 27, 1950
Tangier

I enjoyed your long, varied letter. It contained a good deal of news, in spite of your conviction that nothing could be news to me now because I have been away too long. However, it would seem from the things you said either that your own separation from the city has prevented you from keeping up with events, or else that actually there are few events these days among the little friends. Perhaps there are no more little friends—who knows? One of the pleasures of being away has always been that I could have news of all their scrabblings and at the same time be preserved from taking part in the scrimmage. So now I am just away. No one writes at all. A Spanish acquaintance here tells me that he has read in the papers that Oliver is in Paris. I wonder if it could be that Jane is, too. Probably not.

A friend in New York, Catherine Jacobs, whom I have known since 1925, has written saying "congratulations on this best of good publicity" referring to your article in Vogue, except that she didn't say that it was about music or that it was by you, or anything at all. I shall be eager to see what you have said, what monstrous photo they have used (for it must be monstrous, or it couldn't be chic, and you said it was chic).

Suppose I answer your disparate questions, one after the other. No, you never did send a copy of your Concertino da Camera. I have not read any Moravia. (The only new Italian book I have read is *Mariam*, by Flaianni, which I thought excellent.) The reason I thought the Concerto for Two Pianos, Wind and Percussion was being played this winter is that Bobby wrote me recently that they were going to play it at their Town Hall concert on December twelfth. Perhaps their plans have since been modified; I don't know. The new book is about Tangier. I thought of going to the Canaries simply because they are nearby, and it is extremely difficult to get passage anywhere just by going into the agency and trying to pick up a ship on the spur of the moment. I believe the islands are warmer than Morocco in the winter. I have called twice at Tenerife, but once it was in October and once it was in April, so I know nothing about the winter climate.

I want absolutely to finish the new book before returning to New York. And as a matter of fact, I don't want to return to New York at all unless I can get some sort of assurance (somehow) that my passport won't be confiscated so that I am a prisoner in the U.S., which seems to be the fate of a good many people these days—people who are "suspected" of having leftist sympathies. Of course, the days in which I had political leanings of any sort whatever are long since past, but as you know, that is extremely difficult to make clear, and the other thing is there in black and white, dated 1938.

I have been "reading" the Danish version of my novel, and find the language beautifully pure in feeling. Perhaps I told you that. Several translations are en route: Swedish, Norwegian, German, French and Italian. I should like to get it into Spanish, but that is more difficult. The Danes cut it badly, evidently finding passages they thought unfit for Danish eyes to see. I also have my new Random House volume: The Delicate Prey, which they have done very prettily, if a bit on the Bauhaus side. What I am eager to see now is the pocket edition of Sky: I love pocket books and the idea that they're sold in the subway.

It was nice to have news of Virgil. He never writes, naturally, although there is no reason why he should, since I never write him, and he is the busy one. I never understood his calling my Concerto a "whorehouse." It seems to me that one's musical messages can go much further astray than one's verbal ones. Certainly no one could have said of my novel that it was an interesting study of the housing problem in Chile, for instance. (I've seen some good reviews of the recording of the Concerto, incidentally.) *Who* is Sidney? I'm delighted to hear that Mary Phillips is married. I daresay everyone is delighted to hear that Hawkes has dropped dead.

I am living in a good English hotel in the Marshan. Wonderful hot running water—very unusual here. Meals in bed if I like, and well served. A garden for sun-bathing, and the sun is very hot these weeks. Another pleasant feature is that I am the only person in the hotel, and have been for over two weeks. Baby Guinle writes occasionally from Rabat, inviting me to visit her.

In Marrakech, as I may have told you, I had a liver attack. I have slowly been recovering, and now feel very well. The doctor here treated me for gall bladder, rather than liver, and it seems to be working wonders. I had always called it liver because I didn't know what it was. I probably also told you that I rented a house there, to which I may possibly return during the winter. It's near Bab Doukkala, so that one can get outside the walls in one minute, and bicycle out there among the palms and pink cliffs to one's heart's content, the ice of the mountains shining above like white enamel. I heard a lot of magnificent Berber music this time; really it has nothing in common with what we think of as "Arab" music, nor yet with Negro, save superficially.

TO DAVID MCDOWELL,
RANDOM HOUSE, NEW YORK

December 15, 1950
Tangier

I returned last night from a twelve-day sojourn in the French Zone, to find, among the items of my mail, the first reviews of *Prey*. Shocked, scandalized and disapproving. And all wrong. I think some of the critics didn't bother to read all the stories about which they spoke so glibly. How could Charles Jackson make such a boner as to say that "How Many Midnights" was "a story about a suicide" if he had read it? There's not the suggestion of a suicide anywhere in the book, for the very good reason that the idea of suicide doesn't enter into my personal conception of the patterns of life and destiny. However, one would scarcely expect him to guess that. But neither would one expect him to guess at the outcome of the story instead of reading it, if he intends to single it out and make remarks about it. Another lovely error he made was the one in which he mentioned "the small town where" I "was brought up." Born, raised and educated in New York City, and never lived anywhere else until I went to Virginia for a bit of college. Of course, all these things are unimportant; I am just letting myself go in correspondence to you because I have no one to talk to about my reactions to the reviews. What does interest me is the fact that a while ago you mentioned to me the possibility of there being a second edition to the book, for which I might fashion some jacket notes. I certainly don't want to write the actual text, but I should like to furnish a clue as what I consider the stories to be and as to how they can be read in order to be understood—if that is necessary, and it would seem that it is. No one seems to have realized that practically all the tales are a variety of detective story. Not the usual variety, I admit, but still, detective stories in which the reader is the detective; the mystery is the motivation for the characters' behavior, and the clues are given in the form of reactions on the part of the characters to details of situation and sur-roundings. If Chalia moves her bed out from the wall each night before she goes to bed, there is a reason for it. If Van says: "Gee, I was burned up last Friday," if Bouchta's eyes in Mokhtar's dream remind him of the eyes in the head of a roasted sheep at Aid el Kebir, if the employee on the river boat has a "somewhat simian" face and the husband walks toward him offering to pay the supplementary fare to him and then "remembers" that his wife has his wallet, there is a reason, and it is usually the reason for the entire story. Often the action of a story is predicated on a bit of unmentioned, subconscious knowledge on the part of a protagonist, but the suggestion is always made and placed in an emotional frame which serves as a clue to anyone who really read the story. If you could form a sentence or two for the jacket of that hypothetical second edition, which would embody these ideas, I should be delighted.

It is interesting to see the enormous disparity between the English reviews and the American ones. There is no indication of the English critics' having been morally outraged, no use of such words as "decay," "putrescent," "re-volting," "loathsome," "sensationalism," "horror," "disintegration," "evil." On the contrary, they speak of strength, directness, clean writing, being left breath-less. Which I must say is a damned sight more pleasant to my eyes.

But what can one do? Hope to see more reviews.

TO JAMES LAUGHLIN,
NEW DIRECTIONS, NEW YORK

December 22, 1950
Tangier

Thanks for your letter of December twelfth. I think it is rather a long time since you had written. I have been here in Morocco all the time, and since nothing ever happens here there are no landmarks to use for keeping time straight in one's mind; one has to invent the landmarks. Mine are usually trips, but this year I have been unusually stationary. My liver, gall bladder, spleen, or whatever it is, went on such a rampage while I was in Marrakech that I came crawling back here promising to be good, and have been lying low ever since. I did get up to Asni, the amethyst village in the Grand Atlas, but no further, this time.

I do intend, however, to go down to the Senegal and on to Liberia this winter. The weather here is hysterical, with gales, thunder, downpours, brilliant sun, duststorms and hail. (Even clods of red mud pelted the town two weeks ago; the walls of the houses are still spattered and stained with it.)

I've seen a few reviews of my book of stories. The critics seem less ready to accept them than they were the novel, and I have no idea why. The stories are no more "decadent" than the novel. If they are "decadent" at all, they are so unconsciously, whereas the novel was so consciously. Which makes the stories truer, which is probably the reason for the critics' disapproval. So perhaps I have just explained it all to myself as I typed!

As to the "New School of Decadence," the concept of which Tennessee thinks could be combatted by means of a manifesto, it seems to me that unless it included statements by at least as many people free of the suspicion of belonging to the group as it did by those involved, it would risk defeating its own purpose. Otherwise, there would be the group, united under one cover, proving it was indeed a "school." At the same time, it could never be proved that the ideas propounded in the works by the members of the "school" were not decadent, since that word is open to interpretation. Personally I have no great objection to being called decadent, if the word is used in such a way that it is clear the user considers my work to be a reflection of the period in which it was written, a period which by every possible cultural standard is assuredly a decadent one. There would be no particular virtue in escaping one's age, even if it were possible to do that. Obviously, if the word is used to imply that decadence is in any way at variance with the times, which by implication would then be held up as something normal and desirable, I naturally object, and violently. Likewise, if the argument is used that in decadent times the writer's duty is to avoid adding to the general disintegration by ignoring the process of decay around him and devoting himself to "constructive" thinking, again I should object. Perhaps all this isn't what you and Tennessee mean, at all. I don't know. In any case, the idea of lumping together such disparate writers as Gore, Truman and Tennessee (not to mention me) is manifestly ridiculous.

Is the new N.D. annual published yet? And when it is will it be sent to me here? I hope so. I take it you used "Doña Faustina"; you wrote me earlier in the season that you intended to. One more "decadent" work, certainly! The thing happened (the facts on which the story is based) while I was in Mexico ten years ago. It fascinated me because it was obviously a case of personal psychosis based on racial memory, a vestigial tribal obsession cropping up several centuries after the religious meaning has been lost. But I have noticed that the Mexicans of the Aztec region are particularly sensitive to the idea of eating any kind of heart. The heart is a very special organ there, and one can understand why just by going into certain churches in small towns, where the fount that contains holy water is actually the same stone basin used in Aztec days to hold the hearts and the blood, and the bas-relief cut into the stone is a design of human hearts strung together. I have seen that myself, and I have had Mexicans become squeamish when heart was served at the table at my house. (I remember one who turned pale and left the table until the heart was removed.)

Back in September or thereabouts I wrote asking you if you were interested in bringing out Jane's *Two Serious Ladies* in the New American Classics. It seems to me you replied that you had had no luck in getting hold of a copy. Am I right?

It is midnight of Mouloud, which is the biggest holiday of the year in Tangier. They make it into a carnival here, where everything is allowed for three days, even ecstatic dancing by cults which are forbidden. The town is strung with thousands of colored electric lights, so that the whole Siaghines is like a vast Christmas-tree.

I can't follow the ins and outs of the war scare here. People are all mad, as far as I can see. Some say: if there is war we are lost. Others say: if only there is war we are made. I'm perfectly serious: plenty of men go around here saying that a war in Europe would improve business.

TO PEGGY GLANVILLE-HICKS

◆

February 25, 1951
Tangier

On receiving your next-to-the-last letter I wired Libby in Paris, asking her about the possibility of getting into the closet to get hold of the necessary scores. Her reply came last night, and is as follows: CONTACT JACK CLAREMAN ELEVEN WEST FORTY SECOND STREET NEW YORK CITY FOR MUSIC. I hope that may lead to something feasible, although I have no idea who he is or what his connection with the closet may be. Nor do I know how likely he is to let you in without some proof of Libby's approval. She said nothing about getting in touch with him, but it's possible she will notify him that I am sending someone to remove something from the closet. If you do manage to open Sesame successfully, it would be magnificent if you were able to take out at the same time the score (if it is there) for *Cyrano de Bergerac*, as José Ferrer wired me the other day that he had been trying for months to get hold of it, in order to record the play for Columbia with my music, and not having so far been able to get hold of it, had been postponing the recording, as he did not want to go ahead without the music. My remembrance is that his lawyer kept both score and parts when the show closed, but it is possible that the score was returned during some hectic moment of my life, and that I put it in among others and completely forgot about it, not expecting it ever to be required again. If by any vague chance you do see it, it would be a great favor to me if you could grab it, and let either me or Goddard Lieberson know about it, as he has been writing me about it since last November. I hope you do manage to get in, and find everything in good order; it would reassure me considerably to know that everything is there as I left it so long ago. The American Legation here has ordered ten sets of the Concerto—I don't know what for—but it has to do with culture. They lent me the set they had as a sample, and I have at last heard it, the set Columbia claims to have sent me months ago never having arrived at all. I do hope you can get hold of the Cantata. Unfortunately I wrote the harmonium part for an enormous instrument left over from sometime in the last century, that had found its way to Laghouat to the White Fathers' church there. And it had a great variety of stops, which I in my innocence took to be more or less standard equipment, so I scored it for those particular stops, which of course mean absolutely nothing except on that instrument in Laghouat. Thus the registrations can't possibly be indicated. Some day I shall either orchestrate it or redo the registrations in some way that will mean something. At present it is wide open to anybody's interpretation; I can't imagine what can be done with it, unless it is played on a tiny Salvation Army harmonium, in which case, how will it sound? Terribly unvaried, I'm afraid. On the Laghouat organ in 1932–33 it sounded full of invention (sonorously). You may have to abandon the project, but perhaps not. It will certainly be accused of being chichiteux; one can count on that, I'm afraid—if only for its French text and its reader. For God's sake, stress the date, if you give it; let people realize I was twenty-one when I started it and twenty-two when I finished it. It's practically a museum piece by now. Somehow I have a feeling you won't present it, at all, but I hope you will find it possible.

So you sail in April, earlier than I expected. I know you have asked me several times where I shall be in the summer, and I have been able to give no concrete replies, because I have absolutely no plans—no more now than I have ever had. However, I can tell you what I *think* I may be doing. I expect to go south with Brion soon, return here toward the first of April, go across to Spain and slowly up through that country to France, by which time Libby will presumably get a good deal done on *Yerma*, before returning here to Tangier, where, since summer is the best season, I shall probably spend the summer. Many things may come between the statement of the plans and their realization, of course. One is the production of Jane's play on Broadway. If that materializes I may have to go across and do the score for it. I have always promised I would. It's about the only thing, short of some other job, that would draw me there. I naturally want to earn some money to help pay my taxes, and to go on living, and whatever definite and acceptable thing that presents itself has to be seized upon without too much hesitation. Apart from wishing Jane's play could be produced, I ask nothing better than to remain here indefinitely—or at least until I finish my novel. There is nothing I want to do in either America or Europe. And there is a great deal I want to do in Africa.

To answer your questions: The article on the Sahara is indeed for *Holiday*, although *The American Mercury* has also asked me to do one, which I haven't yet begun. The opera is still the García Lorca one, of course. It is just begun, really. I have met George Sebastian once, in New York, at least fifteen years ago. But I have heard about him from a great many people, both before and since the meeting. As to news of myself—how can one send news of himself if nothing happens to him? I have breakfast brought in each morning at nine. Here I can't live the way I used to in New York—staying in bed until one. The weather is generally rainy, so I stay in and write letters, or brave the rain and walk into Tangier, arriving dripping at the Boulevard to inquire for my mail. I have to be back up here by two for lunch. At three thirty I usually meet Brion at his house in the Casbah, and we go somewhere, or sit and talk. Tea we have these days at a place called the Normandie. I come back out here—always at least a half hour walk—and have dinner. Then I work, read or go to bed. That is the outside of my life. Inside I am waiting to escape to somewhere else. I don't quite know where. Naturally one always wants to escape if one has no reason for being anywhere. And I have no reason for being anywhere, that is certain. If I work, I don't think of that, and feel the escape urge less, so that the work is largely therapeutic. But when one feels that the only reason for working is in order to be able to forget one's life, and that the only reason for living is in order to work, one is sometimes tempted to consider the work slightly absurd, like the pills one takes to make one's digestion easier. There should be something else in between, but what it is, is anyone's guess. Some will say one thing, others something else. I suppose the trouble is that one thinks one's life instead of living it. Occasionally one enters into contact for a split second, when the wind blows across one's face, or when the moon comes out from behind a cloud, or a wave breaks against the rocks in some particular way which it would be impossible to recognize or define. Then one catches oneself being conscious of the contact, and it is lost. Thus, a great desire to lose consciousness. Yet in sleep nothing is different; there is always the same cage around. One is conscious that one is dreaming, and that the same forces operate there as elsewhere. Actually the pleasantest solution is a rather regimented day, with a certain number of hours of work, and the whole thing arranged as if one were in a sanatorium. "I am here on earth for my health"—you know!

Your last question . . . supposing there is a war, where would I go? That's really impossible to answer. I am inclined to take it for granted that somehow I should manage to die immediately. But obviously that's absurd; I might survive quite a while. I don't know where I'd go. Not America, unless I were sent there at the point of a gun, or figuratively that way. But what could I do here save eventually starve to death along with everyone else? The war would be everyone's death-knell; it would merely be a question of the length of time between the announcement and the event for each individual. I never think about it, never read the papers, know nothing about what is going on. There seems no point in knowing any of it. When it comes, it will be here. Then one won't have to bother to think about it. One can act. Menuhin was here a fortnight ago, playing at the Mauretania. So was Orson, or did I tell you.

Love, and let me know about the closet.

TO PEGGY GLANVILLE-HICKS

———————————◆———————————

July 22, 1951
Xauen
Protectorado Español, Morocco

Avant-propos: there is only one "r" in Morocco. That is because you are writing a piece using the word, and you may misspell it in the title. Lao-Tze says there is no greater crime than the exciting of envy, and so I feel I should refrain from describing Xauen to you, for in doing so, I should certainly be conscious of trying to do exactly that. But I feel he meant envy of material things. Besides, there is nothing to prevent you from coming to investigate my reports another year. And perhaps all I should be wanting to do would be to awaken your curiosity. I wonder if Poe in his most extravagant hallucinations evoked any landscape more to his liking than this one I see from my window on nights of full moon. It is the very essence of Romantic fancy, savage and vast. And the ensemble then is so beautiful that one must turn away and look at something concrete and precise like the design made by the tiles on the floor, because there is nothing one can do with such a scene. Unfortunately, too, one can't wander out to it, because of the cobras which come down from the rocks to the spring to drink after dark, and which are all too real, however phantasmal the decor may be. No one ever ventures out toward Ras-el-Ma at night, but I didn't know it. I merely thought no one happened to be there, which is how *I* happened to be there and came on one of the silent black beings sliding along on its way back to the cliffs after having drunk. In the moonlight it moved almost like water itself, making much wider undulations than I have ever seen any other serpent make. And how fast it was able to move, in spite of the great lateral motions! I was fascinated, satisfied, too, that Ras-el-Ma was to be visited by day only. The rest of the town, however, is perfect for moonlight exploration. It is like a minute Granada, and indeed, was called New Granada when the founders built it after being ejected from their city across the Strait. The houses are tiny, many with outside staircases of stone, they have steep gables and overhanging eaves, tile roofs as in the mother city, and most of them are built into the rocks of the steep mountain. The streets and walls look as if someone had poured tons of white cake-icing over them—resplendently white, and some-times light blue, but by moonlight it all looks brilliantly, blindingly white. The town is built like one side of a forum, so that wherever one is, one can always see it spread out above and below and to the sides. There are a great many tiny mills in the streets, the clear, icy spring water that comes out of the mountain's side keeping the wheels turning, and the cold, vaporous air rushes out like smoke into the warm air of the street. The Moors, especially those from Andalucia, have always loved fountains, and they are everywhere in Xauen, presided over by flowering trees and vines. The main street is merely a long tunnel of green, being completely covered by ancient grapevines whose thick trunks twist up the walls of the little white buildings like great snakes before they become the vault of foliage and fruit that hides the sky. In the ruined Casbah there are palms, oranges and roses, storks and peacocks, and, of course, the inevitable fountains. And the town is drenched in the musky smell of fig trees in summer, and slightly spiced with jasmin. By day the cicadas scream, and at night it is treetoads and insects that sound like dry leaves. Then there is the spring which, by the time it reaches the valley below my window, has become a river which rushes over the rocks and reverberates between the cliffs. All of these things would be little enough if it were not for the music in Xauen, which, because the customs have remained intact longer here than elsewhere, is still more or less untouched. And there are both kinds: Andalucian and pure Berber. Two weeks ago I heard the most incredible Berber music I had yet heard—a full evening of it, accompanied by dances of self-immolation and a good deal of blood-letting. Weddings are Andalucian; there was a fine concert last night which I listened to for two hours sitting in a garden. Even the Koranic schools are inexhaustible wells of music. This afternoon in the breathless sun I stood and absorbed part of a "lesson." You would have been overjoyed at the incredible part-singing that came out. That is, you would have been, if you like Andalucian music. It is extremely dignified, never primitive—merely ancient in feeling, and not even particularly Oriental. The childhood of melody, Berber is of course utterly primitive, music from caves, much more shadowy and basic I think than Negro music. And to think that it is here, complete, and has never been recorded! Perhaps it is fated merely to disappear, leaving no trace, for it will disappear, and very soon. I must answer your questions before my paper is gone. There is no particular reason to think that I shall be coming to America this Autumn. Of course if Jane's play does go on and Oliver actually sends me a contract to write the score for it, I shall make the trip. Jane is in Tangier awaiting news of various sorts. I am here working on the novel. Music for a Farce . . . I can't understand where the parts are. You say they weren't at Libby's. Then they must be at Tenth Street with the other music there. If you were to send a score, I should naturally correct it and return it, in order to have the work recorded. But wouldn't that be a nuisance for you? As for my sending Weintraub something, of course I have nothing here. But Schirmer's, who gave me contracts for Three Songs from the Sierra six years ago with the written stipulation that if they had not published them within the year the contract was void, ought to be willing to give them up. I suggest those three because I think they might please Weintraub more than the García Lorca songs. They too are in Spanish, but they are singable separately as well as together, and they are certainly more immediately seizable by the average audience. (El Carbonero, Mes de Mayo, and Que Te Pasa? You know them; at least, you've heard them.) Libby never came this way at all; she went from Italy directly to New York, after renting a house in Tangier. I shall have to wait to work on the opera until I can catch her somewhere sometime. I work very hard on the new book, and am doing what I can to complete it next month. But it goes very slowly, just as the other did . . . more slowly, even. Thank God for Xauen. I have been here three weeks now, and am the only "foreigner." Tourists occasionally come, but have lunch and leave. One must stay on and on.

TO RENA BOWLES

July 26, 1951
Xauen
Spanish Protectorate

I wrote Daddy on Sunday and intended to write you the following day, but managed to postpone it until today, which is Thursday. Nothing at all happens here, no mail comes because Jane is collecting it in Tangier to give me when she comes. Perhaps it is just as well not to be expecting and receiving mail every day, as contact with the outside, at least, incoming news, is likely to take one's mind off one's work, and with a novel the work is a good deal more than just consecrating so many hours of the day to sitting at a desk writing words—it is living in the midst of the artificial world one is creating, and letting no detail of everyday life enter sufficiently into one's mind to become more real than or take precedence over what one is inventing. That is, living in the atmosphere of the novel has to become and stay more real than living in one's own life. Which is why it is almost impossible to work in a city, or with people around. At least, for me. Under the latter conditions I write mere words, staying outside what I am doing, and anyone knows that is not the way to write a novel—at least, not a novel that people are going to become engrossed in. Anyway, this time you can blame me for the lapse in correspondence, as I have really neglected writing. As I may have told you, I am trying hard to finish the new book by the end of August, so that I can relax for a week or so and then start on the translation of the French novel. If I happen to hear from Random House that the December publication can't possibly be made now, I shall let up a bit, but not completely, as even so they will want to publish in mid-winter, and they have to have the manuscript several months beforehand. There really is no legal hurry, as I am not bound to deliver the book until the first of February. But now I am like a horse that knows his stable is ahead; he wants to keep going until he gets there! Jane went back to Tangier last Friday, and I haven't heard from her since. I had gone back two weeks ago in order to be present at the feast of Sidi Kacem, and was very much disappointed to find that it had been postponed a week, which meant that I would miss it, as it took place last week-end instead. Brion Gysin telephoned me the other day from Tetuan, about to take a plane for Sevilla, and said he had gone and that it was wonderful. He had come all the way from Spain just to see it. But I couldn't waste another week-end for it. I expect to hear from Jane one of these days saying she is coming back here. She has some friends coming down from Paris about now whom she feels she must show around Tangier, so probably that is what she is doing. I didn't tell you that the French version of *The Sheltering Sky* had been chosen a book-of-the-month in France, which ought to help it sell once it appears in October. There will be two separate editions, one of the Club's and the regular one by Gallimard. I imagine you are somewhere in New England, looking around for a house. And I also imagine that once you have found one and moved into it you will be very happy, although I should think it would be a good deal more work than where you have been the past few years. I was very sorry to hear that you wouldn't be coming over this summer. I had grown almost to believe that you were coming at last, from the way you wrote of the idea in your most recent letters. But I can see that with such a drastic change in view you wouldn't have enjoyed it much even if you had come, with the thought of what was ahead of you always in your mind. But if and when you get settled somewhere in the country or in a small town, perhaps you will then have the leisure to make it possible for you to think again about it, consider it seriously, I mean. This summer has been entirely different from the way I had imagined it would be. Another difference is that Libby never appeared. She sent a wire to Mrs. Dunlop, from whom she had rented the house, saying that for business reasons she was having to go immediately to New York. Jane and I imagine it had to do with her son's inheritance. In any case, Mrs. Dunlop was not upset, because although she had refused several offers for her house as she was saving it (at my request) for Libby, Libby and Scotty sent her a check for the entire sum, so that Mrs. Dunlop was free to rent it again, if she could. The term was not to begin until August first, anyway. I was worried at first that I had prevented the house from being rented, which would have been serious, as the Dunlops were counting on the rental to pay for their vacation. He is a doctor in Tangier.

Jane's play is being rehearsed now for an opening shortly at Hedgerow Theatre, near Philadelphia. I think sometimes she wishes she were going to be there for rehearsals and for the opening, but when she left, it was probably not so certain, and she had just been terribly disappointed by the thing's not having gone through for Broadway. Now of course there are rumors about another production by

Oliver, although I have heard nothing definite. Someone sent me a clipping from *The New York Times* announcing a production, but that has been done various times before and nothing has come of it, so I am not unduly excited by the "news."

This place is high in the mountains, one of the most beautiful in all Morocco, and with magnificent icy spring water which gushes out of the side of the mountain at the end of town. Strangely enough, it is hotter than Tangier, because it is drier. So while Tangier is refreshed by cool sea breezes night and day, Xauen bakes in the sun, and then becomes chilly at night, far colder than Tangier. But the climate is healthier precisely because of that, while Tangier, with its constant dampness and its temperature always more or less the same, tells on one after a while. The town is amazingly pure in aspect, and the customs have remained more or less what they were centuries ago. The people grind their own flour, spin their own wool from their own sheep, make their own clothing as well as very fine blankets and thick rugs, and live largely on their own produce, each family having an orchard at the edge of town. I am astonished at the beauty of the town, and can't understand why it isn't full of tourists and vacationists. I suppose that will come soon enough, and when it does, *I* shan't come any longer, but will have to seek out some more isolated spot. The hotel, incidentally, is very comfortable, extremely attractive, spotless, with delicious food, and the cost is 85 cents a day, all included. It sounds like our hotel outside Palma, doesn't it? But it's infinitely superior to that place. I think the secret of why no one comes here is that there's absolutely "nothing to do," so that the only people who would want to be here would be those who were working or studying or merely resting and reading, of whom there seem to be fewer and fewer all the time. So perhaps Xauen will be spared for a few years, until they put in a swimming pool or a gambling house or a roadhouse or a race track! Let me hear from you.

TO DAVID MCDOWELL,
RANDOM HOUSE, NEW YORK

September 16, 1951
Tangier

First of all thanks so much for sending the books. I am delighted to have them. I hadn't expected the William Carlos Williams, and am now reading the

Autobiography, having already read and enjoyed very much the short stories. His writing is extremely clean, full of ozone. And incredibly American in the very best sense, in that it shows a passion for scrupulous honesty and an innate respect for human life. I find it does me good to read it, which is a purely personal reaction and of no importance. Still, I tell you because I don't know him, and I suppose you do.

I had wondered when you would be getting back from your vacation, and whether you had ever finished reading the new novel. Even now you don't say, but I take it for granted that you have. The last I knew you had read only the first part. If you think February is better for the book, naturally I am in accordance.

The copy of the mss. I sent Lehmann is pretty lousy; full of additions and blots and cuts and messes. I do think he could do better with galleys, and if it won't be too much trouble I'd appreciate it and I know he would. He wanted to see the mss. immediately, so I sent it to him . . . (I now have nothing.) But I don't know whether he can actually use the copy I was able to give him. I haven't heard from him about it—his reaction, I mean.

Whenever the galleys arrive I shall return them immediately, of course. Thanks for sending *Delicate Prey* corrections to New American Library.

I'm glad you agree about the cuts.

TO JOHN LEHMANN,
JOHN LEHMANN LIMITED, LONDON

Rosh Hashanah, October 1, 1951
Tangier

I was glad to get your letter, because I had begun to wonder if it would ever come. I had wondered, too, if you wouldn't have reservations about the book. I'm unable, of course, to offer a defence regarding the writing. I'm not an old enough hand at construction to be able to see where the interest lags in the first part. (I could, I suppose, find innumerable passages which could be deleted, but then what would be left? Not very much!) I'm sure you're quite correct about the jerkiness and random quality of the first chapters. If you would like them pared down I can do it. The Americans, I'm sure, are not aware that there is a "metaphysical theme," and so the story seems all of a piece—a straight adventure story with particularly sordid trimmings, which is perfectly all right with me.

I was pleased—perversely so, possibly—with your pointing out that you could find no "sense of moral choice" in the book, because that is a lack I meant it to have (as you well know). Of course it's extremely difficult to convince anyone that moral choice is nonexistent save as a social attitude, because everyone "knows" it just isn't so. However, it's a private fallacy of mine, and I think it strikes a sympathetic chord in the younger generation of Americans. Perhaps only because they're young, but perhaps also because they're Americans. I'm not suggesting that the young people emulate Dyar; I'm only suggesting that it would make no difference if they did, since all that keeps them from such behavior is the lack of opportunity and fear of the possible consequences. There are tens of thousands who would ask nothing better than the chance to live the part of Dyar's life described in the book, particularly as he is left at the end unpunished and with a considerable sum of money in his possession. In that sense it's definitely slanted toward an American public, and not an English one.

Personally I must admit that my sympathy remains with Dyar throughout the book, despite the murder, since nothing he does makes any particular difference to the texture of his life. He could have committed it before he ever left New York, save that it hadn't occurred to him. (Perhaps I ought to use the word "pity" instead of sympathy, but the two are confused in my mind. There are two types of people in the world: pitiful and hateful, and I don't know which I dislike more. So perhaps "sympathy" is not really a word for me to bandy about so glibly!)

In any case, while I defend the argument of the book, I am quite ready to make an effort to improve the technique, if you think it would make my point clearer. Only I should need concrete suggestions, I'm afraid, which would be putting rather a burden on you, since they won't be forthcoming from anyone else. There would be no particular objection to certain disparities between the texts of the American and the English editions, would there?

I did receive your telegram, and thank you for it. I hadn't replied earlier because the wire said: "writing very soon," and I thought our letters might cross.

Your prognostic for London's winter is dire; it makes me think twice before going ahead with any project of settling there. I suppose there are a good many pleasanter places to spend those weeks. I shall have to reflect and discuss and weigh, all those things I dislike so much.

The germ is gone. Now Mrs. Bowles, the maid and the Siamese kitten all have them. They (not the kitten) are having daily shots of Penicillin and Strep-tomycin. The kitten is given soporifics; it has become gaga.

Do you prefer *Fresh Meat and Roses* to *Let It Come Down* as a title? Brion

Gysin has been insisting for so many months that a change should be made that I no longer have so strong a faith in my judgment. I have also asked Random House, but only recently, so that there has not been time for an answer.

I am working on the translation of a very bad novel in French, and I regret ever having taken on the work. However, now that the thing is begun, it must be finished. My plans depend somewhat on *Holiday* magazine. I have sent them several suggestions for articles, to write some of which would involve displacing myself, and I am waiting to hear their decision. Also I shall be waiting for yours, regarding the book. McDowell of Random House wrote me the other day that he will send you galleys if you want them. I should think it would be a good idea to ask for them even if you want me to make changes, just to have a more exact and compact copy of the original text than the one you have at present. They ought to be ready soon. He said that McKnight Kauffer had done a fine jacket. I hope he's right.

David Herbert is back here, living out at Vasco da Gama. He makes Tangier seem just like Wilton. Everyone exists in order to be entertaining.

TO JOHN LEHMANN,
JOHN LEHMANN LIMITED, LONDON

October 6, 1951
Tangier

Your second letter on *Let It Come Down* reached me last night. By now you will probably have received my reply to the first, so that you will be able to see that I am not at all averse to making minor changes—if the places in need of them can be indicated for me. I have a feeling that Chapter Three is the weakest section, but not having any copy or even draft of it at hand, it is a little difficult for me to be more precise. I meant the opening chapters to be leisurely and faintly digressive, but I feel that that particular chapter perhaps outdoes itself in inclusion of irrelevant material. I had hoped that each tributary could in itself be of sufficient interest to compel the reader's attention until they began joining to create true impetus. But I can see that it could have been done with far more skill, and should have been, to keep the tributaries from being disparate. As far as form is concerned, to me it's synonymous with readability, so that I worry when you speak of "burden" put upon the reader, and the book's being difficult to get into. Thus, it would be a great service to me if you could tell me—in some detail if you have the time—just where you feel a reader is conscious of strain. (I'm not referring to the credibility of Dyar's behavior; that's too basic, it seems to me, to try to render more believable, and as I say, Americans will find it less far-fetched, in general.) I'm talking about the first few chapters, the antechambers of the book.

I see Truman is getting rave reviews on *The Grass Harp*. How fortunate for him! If anyone was ever being lain in wait for by critics eager to prove he was finished, it was Truman.

TO PEGGY GLANVILLE-HICKS

November 5, 1951
Palais Jamai
Fez

It seems to me that now with my novel out of the way I have less time than ever. But time is always a mystery: it seems, more than anything else in existence, to be subjective. I have nothing to take up my hours but the translating work I have been doing now for two months. It is painfully boring and vain work. However, it's got to be finished, and I should like to finish it before the new novel is published, so I can get into another one; a novel is a good place to hide one's head if one is worried about reviews.

There have been massacres here in Morocco this week; grumblings and strangeness resound below my window in the Medina. I daresay you've read all about it in the news, in any case. There's not much to write about it in a letter; I never know what will get through and what will be kept behind. If the U.S. votes to let France keep Morocco, we Americans will be as popular here as cobras; if, on the other hand, the U.S. stands up for Moroccan Independence, the French will make it next to impossible for us to get in here or stay here. If the U.S. abstains from voting on the question, I suppose both French and Moroccans will hate us. But then we can give money to both sides, and the trouble can drag on. There will be bloodshed on several occasions, in any case. Tomorrow I shall stay out of the Medina, wander in the cemetery; they expect riots during the day because it's the opening of the U.N.O. conference. The whole thing is a mess, but everyone always knew it had to come to this, and go much further than this, before it was finished. Ahmed came up from his house in the Medina three mornings ago to tell me that everyone down there was *maferhanche bzef,** because the police were knocking at doors and searching houses and taking people away. It's too bad the Arabs couldn't have had their revenge by themselves without Moscow's directing the whole thing. They might have enjoyed it a little more. Now all they do is picket and distribute circulars and put themselves into the position of indignant martyrs, and it doesn't become them at all. They'd have been better off with horses and sabers and good old German rifles.

I thought you were brilliant to have asked for a receipt at the Ferrer office. I sent the positive copy to my agent as proof that the score exists, which is quite the opposite of what the Ferrer people say. According to them, all traces of it disappeared several years ago, and they have never been able to locate it. They'd better fish up something to explain the little receipt; at least an old lead-sheet of *Kiss Me Again*. Thank you very much for going to the trouble of having the photostat made. And above all thank you for saving the receipt! I've had no answer from my agent. As usual she is probably the closest friend of Capitol Record Corporation's lawyer, so I can expect to be stalled indefinitely.

You never told me whether you had received the final large envelope of pictures—the one which contained the announcement of the Arab concert. Probably you did; what with all your activities and turmoil you doubtless forgot to mention it. The turmoil sounds particularly ghastly at the Tribune office. Jerry Bohm's behavior must have been exceptionally unwise to be punished so severely. I'm extremely sorry. Who is left at the office? Not Arthur, is he? I heard he had gone over to the *Times*.

The Bowles are not going to New York as far as I know, although Jane may always light out at any moment. She is in Tangier or Gibraltar at present, having taken the car back for repairs. Our chauffeur was attacked by a djinn while driving in the Oued Zitoun. The djinn seized the steering-wheel and jerked it out of his hand while he was shifting gears. He had announced the day before that a djinn was hovering around and wanted him to have an accident, but no one paid any attention. The car went full-speed into a stone bridge. Naturally it has to be rebuilt. I hope the next time the djinn will make him drive off a cliff—always on condition we are not in the car. One night an evil invisible woman appeared to him as we were going over the Col du Zegotta. The car skidded and spun abruptly around, so that it was facing the opposite way. He cursed her and she left. Jane was so upset that she was ill for two days. Whatever happens, of course it was already written. The police say so, and the onlookers,

* not happy at all

so it would be rash to suggest that the driver ought to have some control himself on such occasion. "*Mektoub,*" they say, smiling, shrugging their shoulders. "*B'es-sahh,*"* you say, trying to look as unconcerned as they.

I am back in the same old room as always, here at the Jamai. It's under new management, which doesn't mean a thing, as far as I can see, except that the food is better—so rich, in fact, that I am constantly on the edge of ill. But I can't go all the way to the Ville Nouvelle for my meals. I am now eating only once a day, having consommé in bed at night. Everything seems cooked with goose livers and bits of bacon and quantities of butter and mushrooms. The worst possible food for my indisposed liver. The French seem to think that if food is expensive to prepare, it is beyond criticism. But then, I daresay all gourmets feel that way. I can only feel well eating at home or in a cheap, good restaurant. And the latter is hard to find. There is one here in Fez, none in Tangier. Ceylon and India were very fine. The great amounts of rice and fruit were just what I needed. And the substitution of fish for meat was good. I think I should go back there.

Two hit tunes this year—one Berber, which goes:

The last fermata is to be held, very softly, as long as the breath holds out. Sometimes it can go on a full minute, or more, depending on the singer's lungs. The effect is quite beautiful, especially in the dead of night, which is when it is usually sung.

The other is Egyptian, based on a Chleuh idea. Abd el Wahab has been stealing from the Chleuh recently.

The latter quotation is by no means complete; it's just the important part of the melody. The tritone keeps appearing throughout. The first song is complete,

---

* "It is written," they say, smiling, shrugging their shoulders. "True," you say, trying to look as unconcerned as they.

believe it or not! With the lengthy holds and endless repetition, it makes quite a number.

I should love to hear more news, if in that tourbillon you ever find the time to send them.

TO PEGGY GLANVILLE-HICKS

———————————◆———————————

December 15, 1951
Tangier

Your handwriting has grown almost undecipherable recently; I don't understand why, but I find it extremely difficult to make out parts of your letter of November tenth. However, I shall go back over it and see if there's anything that requires replying to. No, you hadn't replied to the envelope of views of Xauen and other things; I had never known whether or not you'd received them. The previous communication from you had come from Alma, California, and that was a long time ago. (I retract that; there had been the letter enclosing the photostat of the *Cyrano* receipt, but you hadn't mentioned the photos in that.) Perhaps you never got my Fez letter, in which I answered yours telling about Jerry Bohm, and so on. Something must have gone astray. But anyway, it has been a good while that I have owed you a letter, since your last one was written on November 17th. I have been back from Fez exactly four weeks today, and the weather has been foul all the time. It wouldn't be so objectionable if it didn't make one feel foul, too, but it does.

The corrected score of *Farce* has been ready for three months, and now remains only to be hunted up and sent off—not as easy as it sounds. The procuring of an envelope is a major task, often proving impossible, as the post office won't allow one to scratch out the former address and ink in the new one. "Where am I going to get a new envelope like this?" you say piteously. "There are none in Tangier." "Of course not," they say. "But where, then?" you repeat. "Where did that one come from?" they demand. "From America," you say hopefully, thinking that when they hear that they may somehow relent. "Send to America for another like it," they advise, and occupy themselves with the next in line. It has happened to me again and again. However, I should be able to devise a way of getting the score across to you without an envelope. The *Cyrano* business, as I expected, has got so involved that everyone concerned seems to be wandering in a vast labyrinth.

I've written Laughlin about you and your desire to write a book. The letter was posted two days ago, so if and when you call him it ought to be fresh in his mind. Needless to say, I said very complimentary things about your musical writings. I hope he'll be interested, if you still are. If you still want an actual letter of introduction I'll send one, but I thought it would be easiest the way I have done it.

Those English texts for foreign-language songs are always no end embarrassing. Personally I don't think anyone on earth could do a good translation once the pattern is frozen by music. (I'm referring to the García Lorca songs, and Weintraub's suggestion that I do an English version.) It's next to impossible to do, to retain the meaning and texture, when you have all the liberty in the world with regard to syllables and stress; but when your prosody is there like a steel mold for you to fit the words of the new language into, the problem seems insurmountable. Or perhaps surmountable with genius, once in a million times. I can't imagine that they'd sound well in English, anyway, even if the translation were by Shakespeare!

If you send a dubbing of the Cantata, keep a record of the cost, and let me know how much it is. I also want to pay you for the Music for a Farce. There's no reason why you should be saddled with expenses like that on my behalf. In fact, it's unthinkable. I have no phonograph, so I suppose any kind of record of the Cantata would do, as long as it were unbreakable. I can always find someone who has a machine to play it on.

The saga of Ahmed ben Driss el Yacoubi becomes more amusing daily. He came up from Fez with a large portfolio of paintings, met Smail Abdelkader, who introduced him to Mme. Gerofi, who runs the Gallimard agency here. She was delighted with his work and arranged a show for him. The show has been on for almost three weeks, and crowds still gather along the boulevard to gape. But what is better is that he has sold twenty-eight paintings, which is unheard of, considering that they are all utterly unintelligible to the people of Tangier. I think the real reason is that the principal connoisseur of Tangier, who has a house full of Modiglianis and Soutines, bought thirteen all at once, and that impressed the follow-suiters. Anyway, Ahmed takes it quite as a matter of course, says it is Allah who really does the paintings in any case, so that they would *have* to sell. To him it merely means that Allah wants him to have some money, and he goes out evenings in the moonlight alone and intones long prayers of gratitude to his friend Allah for being so good to him. The rest of his behavior is very strange, too. He seems to think there is some sort of danger in letting anyone see that he is being blessed at present, so he tells everyone that

everything is very bad, that nothing sells, that he has lost all his money, that
he is ill and must leave—anything that occurs to him. Also, in spite of the fact
that he has been having the finest sort of suits and shirts made to order, he locks
them all away and never wears them, for fear people will know he is successful.
He says Moslems have black hearts, but he also is afraid that Allah will think
him presumptuous once he gets into his elegant clothing, and that would be
extremely dangerous. The best thing, he thinks, is to keep everything locked up,
and admire it daily, for such a long time that when the day finally comes that
he actually puts the clothing on, he won't feel that it's new, and there will be
no danger of his thinking himself superior to anyone else. It all has a certain
kind of moral logic which doesn't seem to go at all with the mad pictures he
turns out. I asked him to do a little drawing for you to put in this letter yesterday,
and he did, and I enclose it for you. He says it's a present for the Festival of
the Nazarenes, which he knows is coming up shortly.

There's no particular news. Brion is here, in the throes of getting a house for
himself, but that ought to be over shortly. I don't know whether you know John
Goodwin, who is arriving Tuesday from Rome . . . David Hare's brother. I just
corrected the 450-page typescript of the French version of *The Sheltering Sky*,
which I now have to send off to Paris, and whose mailing presents the same
awful problems as the *Farce*. I'd rather correct a thousand pages than spend a
day looking from store to store for some sort of envelope . . . with almost the
perfect assurance that no such thing exists nearer than Paris. It's fortunate I don't
know German, or I'd be busy sticking my nose into that version, which is called
Himmel über das Wüstens, or something equally inappropriate.

If there are any reviews of my piece this time after three years, I'd be most
interested to see if, and in what way, they differ from those written about the
first performance. I'm talking about the Concerto Bobby and Arthur are playing
on the 19th.

The weather is warm, sultry, clinging; the palm and banana leaves sound like
wet sheets flapping in the wind. Narcissus are blooming all over the countryside,
and the mountain smells of narcissus and wet pines. People's gardens are red
with poinsettia. But the sun appears about once a week, if then. I wish I could
be there to hear the Gold-Fizdale concert.

P.S. I hope you still have the note-book of Ahmed's drawings from 1947–48.
They'll be of great interest in a short while.

TO DAVID MCDOWELL,

RANDOM HOUSE, NEW YORK

April 5, 1952
Willingdon Island, Cochin Harbor

Thanks for having someone send me the clippings. Helen Strauss sent me one which pleased me no end, and that was the Times Best Seller List of three weeks ago. Obviously the article and the interview bore fruit. I only hope the book is still there on the list.

I believe I wrote you a short time back telling you that I had written Kurt Enoch a note at Calcutta, suggesting that we meet at the Mount Lavinia in Ceylon. The two Signet editions you said you had sent me turned out to be one when they arrived: *The Delicate Prey* and no *Sky* with it as you had announced. Was one pinched en route, I wonder? And to whom am I supposed to inscribe it? I'll wait and see. Perhaps the copy was meant only to be one copy, and the other two will come eventually, together with orders as to how to treat them.

I'm extremely eager to know about the Vincent Sheean book, because the announcement and description of it make it sound vaguely like something I have been planning and working on here, and I want to be positive what's what before I work too much on a thing which may be accused of similarity with *Rage of the Soul*. If you've read it, please let me know what it's about, or my whole working structure will go to pieces out of sheer doubt.

This part of the Malabar Coast has magnificent boats, rather like enormous gondolas, with carved teak and brass prows, the central part of the vessel covered with arched thatching. If there is a breeze, they put up a great square sail, otherwise, they keep close to shore and pole their way along. The men's hats are huge discs that look like halos above their heads, and the effect is more Chinese than anything else. And as a matter of fact, even the architecture looks Chinese from a distance, with its very high red-tiled gables that curve outward toward the eaves and its predilection for the pagoda principle when it is a question of upper storeys. The hotel is excellent—a complete establishment with post office, bank, travel office and salt-water swimming pool, on an island in the middle of the harbor, so that you have all manner of crafts, from dug-outs to ocean liners, moving past your bedroom window. I am planning to take a boat through the inland lagoons as far as Aleppy, where there is a Dak Bungalow, and from there I can continue to Trivandrum, which is the ivory center. Incidentally, there are a good many thousand Jews here across the bay in Ernakulam, and they came here during the reign of King Solomon, formed a colony to supply him with certain produce he required, and have been here ever since. Some are black and some are white; the black are said to be very poor and the white very rich. That's what one is told, in any case.

Of course I don't remember which corrections I gave you for *Let It*. But I know I sent some and have since found others. One is on page 80, line next from the bottom: ". . . sat next to him on the bench" not "in the bench." Another is on page 81, line 17: ". . . *Wunderschön muss dein' Liebe sein.*" The final "e" in what is now "*deine*" should be supplanted by an apostrophe. Another is on page 66, chapter vi, line six of the chapter: "beside his table" should read "beside the table." I wish you would add those to the list of things to be corrected in the event of another printing.

I hope to be in Colombo by the middle of the month, or thereabouts. You have my address there, I think: Chartered Bank of India, etc. Colombo, Ceylon, same as two years ago.

I'll be waiting impatiently to hear something about the Sheean book, because reading about it in Random House's little announcement brochure has completely stopped my work. I must find out what his book is before continuing. I would be too stupid if the thesis were more or less the same, and I should obviously have to abandon what I'm now working at and think up something else. The mere fact that his book is about an American woman who comes to India seeking spiritual salvation wouldn't necessarily mean that mine couldn't treat the same subject (which it does), but what she discovers here is the important thing for me to know, because it may be the same thing. And that of course would mean that mine would have to be abandoned. So please, if you know the book, tell me what you know, and if you don't, find out if possible, so I needn't waste too much time in waiting. What a mess, what a mess!

TO JOHN WIDDICOMBE

May 29, 1952
Colombo, Ceylon

When was it—a year ago that you wrote me to Tangier, asking where I was? Or did you write to New York, and was the letter forwarded? Anyway, this time you wrote to Tangier, and it got sent on to Bombay, and then later it was re-forwarded to Colombo, which is where I got it. But only last week, although I see it was written about three months ago. M'enfin . . . perhaps this will reach you before you start out for Europe. Myself, I'm starting out for there tomorrow, if the monsoon allows the *Tai Yang* to get in and leave again. I can see out over the entrance to the harbor from my window, and the sea has been being very nasty these last few days.

I was touched to see the stationery from the Hôtel Bellevue. It was a long time ago, and it seems even longer than it was. The place exists, but it no longer functions as a hotel. It was requisitioned during the war and never returned to the Compagnie Générale Transatlantique. Now a ghastly French family lives in it, but fortunately one never sees them. Down the road a bit further there is a new hotel, far more suited to the needs of the day, and it is called the Belvedere. The same water runs through the canebrake beneath the windows, and the same storks (or their descendents) live in the poplar trees below. But it is all very different now, just as Paris is different. Or perhaps it's only I who am different. Anyway, I can hardly believe it's the same town, at all. At the same time, Fez is still the most beautiful city I've seen, anywhere. And it's worth going back to and staying in, a thing I do every year, religiously.

The short quotation from Stein you had typed on the notepaper, however, awoke no memories. It couldn't have been Harry [Dunham], because she and Toklas knew him very well already in 1931, and the party to which she refers couldn't have happened before 1934, since that was the year she first went to the United States, and she states clearly that she had no idea who the young man was. It sounds to me more like Julian Sawyer (Sauerwein to the initiates). He learned all of *Four Saints* by heart and used to give private performances of it, singing all the parts, in costumes made of shawls and lampshades.

I'll go first to Italy. Address: c/o Rothschild, La Bagnera, Orta San Giulio, Provincia di Novaro. Write me there if this reaches you before the first of July or so. I shall probably be there until about the fifteenth. After that I don't know where. But Tangier always reaches me eventually. However, if you are careful of the time element, we might conceivably meet somewhere in Europe, or even Tangier, which now has troops patrolling its streets since the riots in March. I'm afraid all the Moslem countries are going to get more and more difficult for unbelievers to live in. Which is why I have come out here—to cover the joint and see what can be had in the way of a cheap Eden. I spent half of 1950 in these parts, too, so that I was able to get a good idea of where one would be likely to find such a thing. I see paper is finished. The ship is supposed to sail tomorrow, but who knows? Janie is in Hollywood.

TO MR. HOLLYMAN

◆

May 2, 1953
In the Atlantic

Your letter was forwarded to me from Tangier and I received it day before
yesterday, which was the thirtieth of April. Thus it took twenty days exactly to
reach me, which is rather a long time.

I note you are in France now. Perhaps the weather there will be better than
it has been in New York, and better than it is here in this part of the sea, where
the waves are large and the sky uniformly grey.

I am en route to Tangier, Ahmed having wanted to stay on in America. He
may return to Morocco later, and he may not. I was unable to get any definite
intention out of him. He claimed that only Allah knew what he would be doing,
and as yet Allah had not imparted his knowledge to him. He has an exhibit
coming up day after tomorrow at the Weyhe Gallery in New York, and naturally
he wanted to remain for it. Earlier we had gone to Cleveland for a large exhibit
(79 pictures) of his, which was most successful. The New York one will be only
about half that large. He has taken to America like a duck to water, and obviously
doesn't want to be brought out of it. It remains to be seen whether his visa can
be extended or not. Personally, I hope it can't, because the place has ruined
him partially, even in this short time. The School for Corruption, it should be
called. To tell the truth, he departed from my care about two weeks after arriving
in New York, and never returned. We see each other often, but only as casual
acquaintances, and he supported seeing me simply because he needed me for
linguistic and artistic purposes, to introduce him to the proper people, make
publicity for him, and arrange his shows. Otherwise he was invisible, being most
occupied with Café Society, Cartier's, The Stork Club, The Blue Angel, West-
chester, Abercrombie and Fitch, Connecticut, and Radio City Music Hall,
which he seemed to tolerate because it was so big. Walter Winchell and Danton
Walker talked about him in their columns, because he was so often at first-
nights, always in bedeyia, djellaba, belrah, and rezza or tarbouche.* He insulted
Gloria Vanderbilt by telling her he thought her paintings were "very dead."
Fortunately Stokowski didn't hear, and continued to treat him with utmost
cordiality throughout the evening. He met everyone, did everything, got invited
everywhere (including Florida by Tennessee Williams, Guatemala by an uni-

---

* vest, traditional Moroccan burnous, leather slippers, and turban or tasselled hat.

dentified gentleman from Israel, Jamaica by Peggy Glanville-Hicks, and God knows where-all by whom-all). But he stayed in New York and vicinity, and is now living in sin with Libby Holman in Greenwich. Hans Richter made a movie, which he called a "symbolic" story of Ahmed's life, and Ahmed dances, undresses, jumps, climbs trees, swims, plays the flute and smiles throughout, looking rather like a tough Sabu. Fortunately it won't be released for at least another year, by which time I hope to heaven Ahmed will be safely in Morocco. Otherwise, I can see it in my crystal ball, Hollywood would be twinkling with a new starlet. Such dynamic ego-flashing I've never before seen, except for Orson Welles and Bill Saroyan, back in the old days. The awful thing is that all kinds of people fell for it—not only "intellectuals." Hank Greenberg, the baseball-player, had him to dinner and thought he was wonderful, especially when Ahmed, saying good-bye, remarked he hoped to see a game of ping-pong shortly, in order to say he had seen the national sport. It was on the radio the next noon, through a disc-jockey, and the following night, wherever Ahmed went in Cleve-land (in costume, of course), people kidded him about seeing his game of ping-pong. Caresse Crosby had a long conversation with him, although he couldn't have understood what she was saying, but he did it by looking very wise, and repeating parrot-like the final phrase of her monologue each time she ceased speaking to breathe. Fleur Cowles invited him to dinner to meet some Hindu she claimed is the power behind Nehru. If I weren't so annoyed with the whole farce I'd get a certain pleasure out of recognizing its definitely comic aspects. He has collected quite a bit of gold and platinum along the way, I must add, and now has two bank accounts—not large ones at this date, I imagine—but still, he has them, and he sets out for the Corn Exchange Bank (Park Avenue Branch) in a cab, with all the aplomb of Aly Khan, makes out his own checks, that is, signs them and asks the teller to fill them in for him, without anyone's having to accompany him. I could extend my description of his conquest of New York, indefinitely, but it would be repetitious in the long run, like a wall-paper with a very small design. He now bosses a staff of nine servants, I might add. However, I thought you would like to hear how things went in America. How they will go from now on is anyone's guess. I got him passage on May 28th for Gibraltar, but I have my doubts as to his using it. Nothing I can do about it, however. You ask if he worked. He did, and the work was entirely different from what he had previously done. Far more violent and almost non-objective, but still with great flair. The new things have sold quite as well as the old. He also took up oils, and did three big canvases.

If there is still question of the Philadelphia exhibit, I think you should write

him soon, just in case he does sail for Morocco, so that arrangements can be
made while he and the work are still in the States. His address: Ahmed ben
Driss el Yacoubi, c/o Reynolds, Treetops, Merriebrooke Lane, Stamford, Connecticut. It would be difficult to send the stuff from Tangier because of the
customs.

I expect to be in and around Tangier all summer. I hope you'll appear at
some juncture. Best,

Moul Tanja

TO VIRGIL THOMSON
[Published in Virgil Thomson's column, "Music and Musicians,"
in the *New York Herald Tribune*, January 10, 1954]

January 3, 1954
Tangier

I was disturbed to read your review of my incidental score for "In the Summer
House," primarily because it appears to have impressed you as not a proper
musical setting for the play. The cues, you claimed, are so conceived that "they
do not tell us what the character they accompany is thinking about or avoiding
to think about." To me this is a grave accusation, since in writing the score I
sacrificed everything, but absolutely everything, to precisely that consideration.
Each one of the eighteen cues, with the exception of the three realistically
motivated numbers which you cited, was composed and instrumentated with
the specific purpose in mind of explaining as exactly as possible either the
emotional state of the character speaking over it, or the emotional undertone of
the scene being enacted during it, or the emotional key to the dramatic progress
of the play in the time lapses between scenes. That my efforts should be counted
as having failed I can explain to myself only by assuming *sonorously* the music
did not suit your taste. This fact you made clear when you referred to its tone
as "tawdry." And I think your well known and justifiable aversion to the use of
electronic instruments, above all if they *sound like* such caused you, when you
heard an over-all tone which you found displeasing, to jump to the conclusion
that the nebulous, equivocal sounds being made by my musicians were due to
the presence in the ensemble of some sort of electronic instrument; "a Novachord
or Hammond organ is ever present," you remarked.

However, the fact is that the score is written for oboe doubling on English horn, trumpet, harp and percussion. No electronic instrument has been near it. (There is a vibraphone, which sometimes has its vibrators turned on and sometimes has them turned off: but of course this has nothing to do with electronics. Another thing which may have misled you is the presence of a marimba, the mellow notes of whose lower register are not always easily identifiable as such.)

I'm afraid the "cheap radio" effect you deplored is due simply to a basic incompatibility between your auditory nerves and the natural acoustics of the Playhouse Theater. Every effort was made to assure as intimate and suave a general sonority as possible, the musicians having been placed in the fly-wings, their playing space masked by a rectangle of flats, in order to prevent unnecessary reverberation. This also precluded having to use a P-A system, which was a blessing, since to my ears live sounds are infinitely preferable to the best mechanical reproduction one can get.

I have always believed that background music in the theater should be felt and not heard. The great problem is to make it at the same time as soft and as piercing, as inaudible and as physically trenchant, as one can. Perhaps a dog-whistle would be the ideal instrument. But that will be for another play. "In the Summer House" has no supersonics, and no electronics.

TO TENNESSEE WILLIAMS

March 28, 1954
Tangier

I am writing a note to accompany these two epistles from Ahmed and Temsamany. Each one wanted to write you, and to judge from their letters you would think they had a very important tale to tell about Mr. Alberga, when in reality yesterday was a day like any other. It is of interest psychologically (if one is interested in comparative psychology) however, to see how Ahmed's letter differs from Temsamany's, both in style of presentation and stressed detail, because Ahmed is merely trying to tell you what happened, whereas Temsamany is criticizing Ahmed's behavior at the same time, or at least he thinks he is, without being too obvious. The denouement came last night when Mr. Alberga arrived with the suit, and made Ahmed try it on. (It turned out to be a complete suit in Capri corduroy, couleur beige.) Ahmed had no sooner taken it off than he began to make grimaces behind Mr. Alberga's back, indicating that the suit either had crabs in it, or that it had some highly infectious skin disease that had communicated itself to Ahmed's groin. I was in bed, so I didn't need to participate in the comedy, which seems to have been considerable, according to the two accounts I had this morning, with Mr. Alberga cavorting around to make himself attractive to Temsamany, and Temsamany pretending to be asleep, and signalling to Ahmed when Alberga's back was turned, and Ahmed scratching himself and hopping up and down and catching Mr. Alberga watching him in the mirror, and Mr. Alberga thinking that Ahmed had caught him parading suggestively before Temsamany, and giggling inanely. Anyway, I missed it all. Mr. Alberga had arranged to take Temsamany home in a cab when he left, but Temsamany decided to sleep here, so Mr. Alberga had to go home alone. Then Ahmed rushed to the bathtub, where he stayed soaking for a full hour, after having thrown the suit out onto the balcony. Now he claims he is diseased, as a result of having tried on the suit. He doesn't want the suit at all, but he won't give it to Temsamany, who does want it. Instead he is trying to sell it to me. Thus pass the days in Morocco. Janie has gone off to Marrakech with her friends, and El Berred is here being cared for by us. I am still in bed, with some sort of intestinal fever. Ahmed and Temsamany have gone off in the car presumably to look for kidneys to feed Berred, and so I have a few moments of peace. We are all looking forward to your arrival here later in the season. Sometimes John Lehmann wonders why you haven't sent him anything for his new magazine. He wrote me asking for your address. The mag is quite good, but I daresay you have seen it by now yourself. Ahmed is delighted with the cards you are sending him, and of course collects them scrupulously. He now has pelicans, flamingoes and macaws, and speculates on what will come next. I finished my Cantata finally and it was played Tuesday at Town Hall—that is, played and sung. I haven't yet seen any reviews. Not that they will be bright enough to matter, I fear.

I think I shall try and get up and sit in the sun on the terrace, and see if it makes my fever go up.

P.S. It was an Italian restaurant where Mr. Alberga ate old chicken; not a French restaurant. But Ahmed thought that French would make better politics, so he changed it.

TO WILLIAM WRIGHT

July 23, 1954
Tangier

Dear Moul Dar el Beida:

El brea dialek jats rhir el youm; hada bhja ihoul yimkin jats qbel, bel hak ana menarf* because I have been up in Xauen to escape possible difficulties here, and returned only Saturday night, having Temsamany bring me the mail this morning. Up there the food was so badly cooked, in pig's grease, that my liver became ill, and a fever came on, so that I have been bedded ever since my return with a most unpleasant feeling everywhere in my abdomen. I think I'm getting better now because I commence to feel hungry, which is always a good sign.

It was nice to hear from you after such a very long interim. Naturally I understand your not writing, and I hope you'll find a way to return here or to some other country you like before too long.

I'm living, and have been living for the past three months, in the house that Ralph Heard took a year or so ago, on the edge of the cliff at Sidi Bouknadel. I put a good deal of work into it before I moved in, back in May, and it looks charming. Ahmed has the downstairs room and I have the upstairs room, and we work and eat and look at the sea and lie in the hammock on the terrace and so on. Friends come and drink tea and smoke kif. I don't know that I work enough, but living in a house takes so much more of one's time than living in a hotel, as you know, and I haven't yet successfully solved the problem to suit me. I think it's really a question of having enough servants, and well trained ones. But that in turn takes an endless amount of time, so I'm not sure it isn't really more profitable to live in a hotel after all. The trouble with that is that it gets to be a deadly bore. But perhaps boredom is what one needs if one is going to work well. I've usually found it the case. One must have the boredom in order to want badly enough to escape. Then when one really wants to escape, one fashions one's own imaginary escape by creating a fictitious cosmos, and that provides the way out. If one doesn't want to get out, and is perfectly satisfied where one is, then there is very little incentive to make anything. The possibility of being content is the greatest danger, because there it is, in front of one, and

---

* Your letter has reached me just today; it must be said, however, that it might have arrived earlier. Truthfully, I don't know

one has only to reach out and seize it. But if one does, one has only that, and not one's work. Oy weh! And if one *doesn't* have the possibility, then there is no choice but to work.

Ahmed is on a hunger strike, one which is imposed by his emotions and not by his intellect, although apart from the fact that it can't possibly do anyone any good and will simply make him sick, I must say that I can't blame him at all. Temsamany won't eat, either. Obviously they do nibble things now and then, but the rest of the time they moon about without sitting down to a meal. It is a kind of mourning for the mass murders of their compatriots in the French Zone. I should have said for the *victims* of the mass murders, but my head is turned by all this talk and argument, and there is nothing but that. Sometimes one wishes one might see a mob and hear shots. But I don't really wish that. It was bad enough when the town was teeming with French soldiers and Berber goumiers, and radio cars and command cars and tanks went parading up and down the Boulevard Pasteur, because everyone was full of hatred, and all the shops were shut and barred, and you couldn't buy any food, and there were hundreds of French refugees in town, up from Dar el Beida and Rabat, because of course things have become pretty untenable down there. I think we can do without riots in Tangier. But *they* of course want to see blood flow, in retaliation; I think they all do. When you think of what has happened to Fez, you can understand why. I suppose the American papers carry accounts of the war here, but I don't really know. I do know I was cursed in Xauen, and clenched fists were shaken at me from the souks, and when I tried to explain that I was not French but American, the shopkeepers laughed unpleasantly and said that the Americans were the masters of the French, and incha'Allah the Russians would come in soon and deliver the Moslems from both of those pestilences. So you see how things are going here. Not at all well. I think Ceylon will be better, and I'm sorry to have seen the last of Morocco, for I don't ever expect to be able to return to Fez or Marrakech or any part of the French Zone. And why would one want to, with everything burned and smashed, and troops in every street? If you read carefully the piece in August 23rd *Time*, you get a faint picture of one small ratissage. When you then consider that the same tactic was carried out in Fez, Meknès, Khemisset and Settat, not to speak of places like Ougjda, Beni Mellal, Kasba Tadla and the more distant places, you begin to understand the magnitude of the suffering. Best,

Moul Tanja

TO RENA BOWLES

October 11, 1954
Tangier

A very belated birthday letter; I thought of your birthday many times on the first and again on the day itself, and I wondered what you were doing. Then, of course, it was too late to write you (obviously) in time for you to receive it by *the day*. So now it is a good while afterward, but the wish for many happy returns is just as strong, even so! I'm glad you have stayed on in Maine. I know you like the country, just as I do, far better than the city. We have moved out of the Sidi Bouknadel house to another very comfortable little place in the Casbah overlooking the ramparts, with a magnificent view of the whole ocean directly below on the north, and the city and the mountains and shore on the south. It has a real bathroom, a rarity here in the Casbah, with a tub and electrically heated hot water. Not that I care about such things too much, but it goes without saying that life is just a little easier with them. Also the house is better built to withstand the rainy season with the strong winds which will be coming along shortly, I fear. However, we often can spend the day on the beach even in November, lying on the sand and soaking in sunshine. The weather is always irregular here, one year having a January and February which are nearly as hot and sunny as July, another year being really hellish in those months, with driving rain and unrelenting wind week after week. Everyone expects an early and cold winter this year, however. I haven't decided about Belgium. This week I intend to have the car partially repainted (to have the gouges and scribbling made by innumerable brats on the paint remedied), while the driver works on our own little house, to make it damp-proof if possible. During that time I hope to go to Gibraltar, to get as complete a body of information as I can about ships to Ceylon and details on the Jaguar motor in sub-freezing weather. I wrote you that Mr. Trimmer had died, and Mrs. Trimmer had gone to Colombo to live. I think that I must go to see about my island there and see how conditions are in the house, which is still being cleaned regularly and kept in readiness for my arrival by the two servants whose wages I have to pay every month . . . that is, Mrs. Trimmer has arranged with her lawyer to see that they are paid the first of each month. I wish I could entice you both there, because I feel sure you'd love it. There is no more beautiful place to relax and enjoy the days as they pass. Can't you consider it? Actually it wouldn't be any more difficult than coming here, except that you'd be longer on the water. But I know you'd spend an unforgettable winter with me there. I could take the car, so we would have it to use there. I think you'd agree that Ceylon is unsurpassable in scenery. You see, my only reason for a hypothetical trip to America would be to see you both, and I'd much rather, since I must go to Ceylon sooner or later in any case to see to the house and either sell it or make the improvements that should be made (electricity and water), put the money that it would cost me to make the trip to New York and back toward your passages out there so that we could have a really wonderful vacation together, instead of subway trips and short dinners from time to time in Jamaica. Don't you think that makes sense? I've had too many years of pleasant living in foreign places ever to be satisfied to live in the United States again. (I may *have* to live there, naturally, if there is a war, but until then I prefer to use that precious time in places I love.) But it would make me very happy if you could join me here and go to Ceylon with me. And perhaps you would like it so much you'd want to stay—who knows? In that case, I'd also stay, and leave the little house here to Jane, who doesn't want to sell it, and refuses to go to Ceylon, in any case. I sometimes wonder if you ever consider my suggestions that you join me abroad really seriously! It wouldn't be so difficult, once you were on the ship, you know. Then you could relax completely and get a real rest. With Dramamine no one has to be seasick any more. You could come direct to Gibraltar where I'd meet you, and then we could change to the other ship and continue. If you'd consider it seriously, I'll bet you'd find your way to doing it. Don't you think it's worth trying, at least? When you write, don't merely say that you think you haven't the energy to make the decision. Discuss it as though it were a possibility.

I'm sorry to hear you all have colds, and so early in the season, too. We've been well all summer, and still are. My work progresses well, and I'm hoping to have the novel completed before the end of the year. I budget my time and try to make a certain figure (that is, number of pages) by the end of each week. But the work has to be the primary consideration, and everything else is subjected to that. I get up early and work all morning without interruption, first having coffee and then an hour or two later, oatmeal. Then I have a picnic lunch on the beach, sometimes with Jane, sometimes without. Back at teatime, and some more work until eight thirty or nine, when we go out to dinner or make something simple here. Jane is working on a new play. Give my love to everybody, and do discuss the project of coming to see me!

TO DAVID MCDOWELL,

RANDOM HOUSE, NEW YORK

March 1, 1955
Taprobane, Weligama, Ceylon

Thanks for your letter. I'm glad the title meets with no resistance at your end; that saves me a headache trying to find something else equally apposite. The work comprises three "books," each one of which has its own subtitle, as usual. They are, respectively, "Sins Are Finished," "The Hour of the Swallows," and "The Ascending Stairways." But since "The Spider's House" is acceptable, we don't need to worry about the sub-titles. I am now on page 422, and my guess is that there will be around 450 pages. If I budget my time for the month of March, I am certain, barring accidents, that I can ship it off to you by the first of April. I have a good deal of retyping to do, and a little actual reworking, and the carbon copy to correlate. But now I see that you want the script by the first of April, which would mean that I should have to send it fairly long before that: I don't know what the average airmail letter takes from here to New York. But then again you word it: "If we get it much later than the first of April, it would have to go over till the spring of 1956." Which I presume gives me a certain margin beyond the first—at least the time necessary to send the manuscript from Ceylon to New York. But it will be ready.

Finally the weather has been beautiful for a while, which doesn't mean that we don't have very noisy thunderstorms whenever they feel like coming. The house is self-sufficient in eggs, orchids, lobsters and crabs, and that's all. Everything else has to be bought on the mainland. Think how much we should have to spend for our daily supply of orchids if they didn't grow here! There is such a variety of unfamiliar and outlandish-looking plants, vines, trees and flowers on the island that I have given up trying to identify them. There is, I think, an interesting study to be made of the strange psychological effect this powerful world of vegetable life can have on the person who opens himself to consciousness of it. If one stays alone, completely surrounded by it for a length of time, slowly one begins to be aware of its presence, but in a most peculiar fashion, as if, perhaps, one were becoming conscious of its consciousness of one, if you see what I mean. In any case, it's a rather unpleasant sensation on the whole, to feel very strongly that plants are not inert and not insentient. And here, of course, they grow so fast that one imagines one can almost see them moving, and when

you watch their movements from day to day you see how diabolically ingenious
they are in getting the better of one another. Very good and good-bye.

TO JANE BOWLES
———————◆———————

April 25, 1955
Kobe, Japan

A hurried note before the ship docks. We left Yokohama yesterday after three
days in Tokyo. What a shame we (you and I) went no further than Ceylon,
because I know for certain you would love Hong Kong and Japan; they both
have everything you are always searching for. However, you are satisfied with
Tangier, so there's no point in trying to get you to wander elsewhere. I am
annoyed because I wanted to write my parents at least once on this trip, and I
don't seem to have their address with me. They keep moving around from place
to place, and I haven't ever memorized either of their most recent addresses.
Ahmed is scandalized, and says it is a hachouma beyond compare not to know
one's parents' address, and I suppose it is. But if they would stay in one place,
or if they would only live in some place with a simple address like 106 Elm
Street, I could remember, but with addresses like 134-85 147th Street, how can
anyone keep them all in mind? They have had four different such addresses in
the past few years. Anyway, the voyage has been wonderful: Penang, and Singapore, and Hong Kong, where Ahmed left twenty pictures, and even hung
them in a gallery, and then Japan. He'll pick them up when we return to Hong
Kong, and that will have given him an exhibit of eleven days there. Japan is
much more original that I had imagined. Every detail has been done with the
maximum of exquisite taste, down to the lowest café with three seats, in the
poorest quarter. And I have never been in a country where everyone without
exception seemed so civilized. The Chinese are more robust and nearer Europeans, but the Japanese are something quite apart. What a pity we didn't go in
1938! Not that it's ruined, but it's so far that you'll never want to go. We are
going to Kyoto and, I hope, Nara, both of them the old culture-cradles of the
country. Fortunately, certain savants interceded during the war and begged that
they be spared bombing, and the pleas were granted, so that they are intact,
which is more than one can say for the rest of the land. Strangely enough, the
landscape really looks like the familiar pictures one has always seen of it; it's
hard to believe, but there it is. And about half the women still wear what they

wear in the prints, and the other half are partially or completely Europeanized. Ninety percent of the men seem to have gone American, but that doesn't count, for it's the women one sees in any case, everywhere. Anyway, I have been finding it all delightful, and only wish you were here, too, to see it with. Of course I have had no mail since leaving Weligama, so I don't know anything about that film deal or anything else. I hope all is well, with you and the house and Tangier. Hasta luego and much love,

Bupple

Ahmed sends many salutations.

TO PEGGY GLANVILLE-HICKS

July 23, 1955
Tangier

It is hot here in Tangier, for Tangier, and the cicadas are singing wherever the real-estate developers have left any open land and trees. However, the heat never lasts more than two or three days, and it is never as hot as it gets in Europe this time of year. I have a two-room cabin on the mountain where I have installed a piano and go to work each day, although lately the Jaguar has been out of commission and I have had to go by bus, which is a bore, as I must walk the last mile, and it is precisely that mile which is steep and difficult. Anyway, I get a few hours in, and am trying to finish that accursed opera, simply to get it off my agenda. In any case, it isn't an opera. I don't know why anyone ever called it an opera; it's a zarzuela. Most of it is spoken.

The Transposed Heads arrived, and we play it often. It makes a magnificent noise on my machine, with gongs coming out one side and bells coming out the other. The singing is of excellent quality, but I wish it were all instrumental. I get nervous when they start being so Western, don't you? I'm afraid I have it in for bel canto, and I wish it were never necessary to write anything for European voices. It's inhuman to fill the diaphragm with so much air and then let it out, in so much sound . . . a musical counterpart of our penchant for materializing everything. Any second-rate Indian movie-star can make a prettier sound without trying. All this, as you well know, is not directed against your opera, which is delightful and very impressive. And I am very happy that you remembered to have it sent me. Incidentally, the recording is the best yet. Don't you think they make enormous technical progress each year? I'm curious now to hear my Cantata; I wonder when it will be released.

Your postcard of Giglio came the other day. You ask whether I can go to Gibraltar to see you when you go through on your ship. Most of the ships call there for an hour, anchoring in the harbor, and usually it is not allowed for anyone to use the company lighter and board the ships unless he is embarking or disembarking. We have discovered that to our sorrow, over the years. If, however, you are staying six hours or so, and are allowed ashore during the escale, that is another matter, although even then one must spend the night there at the awful Rock Hotel, reserving one's room well in advance, and battle the British Consul here for a twenty-four hour visa. They do their best to discourage anyone from Tangier about going to Gibraltar. We have an unsavory reputation hereabouts. Smugglers, dope-sellers, spies, pimps, plain forgers and criminals—they all live here and get on beautifully as long as they remain in the International Zone where the police can keep an eye on them, but when they cross a border sometimes they cause difficulties, for other governments and police-systems. At the moment of course there is a war on, and all movements are carefully controlled. Tangier is full to bursting with agitators and terrorists and counter-terrorists and ordinary refugees expecting to be assassinated, but nothing happens beyond having all the shops close (or else) so that one can't buy any food. Fortunately we are more or less on the inside of that business, and can generally know beforehand if things are going to be padlocked, so we lay in supplies in time. There is a faint rumor now that in spite of the three-day protest which ended this morning, everything is going to be shut again for two weeks, until the Day of Sacrifice (the Aid el Kebir), in which case we shall all go mad, for the city is like a cemetery with everything closed and no one in the streets. So far we have had no violence here. One after the other, the cities of Morocco have been hit, but Tangier has been as calm as a pond. They are saving the city up for some big occasion, when it will make worldwide headlines. All the battles are carefully planned.

I suppose you can't get a stopover at Gib and take the next ship out? That would be worthwhile doing, if it were possible. I don't know what line the Queen Fredericka belongs to, so the schedules are beyond me, but usually there is another ship a week or ten days later—at least, on the Italian and American Export Lines. Or haven't you the time to visit us? I hope you'll at least try.

Since I returned from the East I have written some texts for a book on Africa, and repaired my novel somewhat—the one which will presumably appear in New York in November. I took on the African book because I thought it would be quickly done, but it needed research and was difficult. Of course! My paper is done, so I stop, and send love. Do write.

TO DAVID MCDOWELL,
RANDOM HOUSE, NEW YORK

November 19, 1955
Tangier

Thanks for your letter of the eleventh, and please thank Miss Ennis if it was she who sent me the batch of reviews. Even when they are bad, I enjoy seeing them, because they help give me the key to the way American literary critics move their minds. It isn't exactly a graceful thing to watch, but that of course isn't the point. *Time* particularly fascinates me, with its surrealist policy of sacrificing sense to sound, in order to bring off its questionable puns and double-entendres. I thought the Mary McCarthy review a milestone along the road to utter destruction of literary reporting. It could easily have been a piece on Audrey Hepburn's newest film, for all it had to do with the business of writing.

I'm sorry you were annoyed by the call from Helen Strauss regarding the galleys. What happened was, I suppose, the sort of thing which is inevitable if one is to do the whole business between two points on opposite sides of the Atlantic.

Here we are in the agonies of becoming democratic. It is done with millions of red banners bearing the green five-pointed star, decorations of palms, chrysanthemums and streamers, and groups of teen-agers marching through the streets shouting slogans in rhythm to drumbeats.

In the country, where I was yesterday, it was done by leading a flower-bedecked bull through the village street and cutting its throat before the tomb of the local saint. "Now we are democratic!" they shouted ecstatically, each man shaking his own hand above his head, in the gesture of a victorious boxer at the end of a bout.

I'll appreciate any further reviews or news you may have.

March 23, 1956
Tangier

Your letter came early this week, and I have been busy all during the week doing nothing but writing an article for *Holiday*, which I finally completed late this afternoon and took into town to mail so it would go off immediately. Now I am free, for a while at least. The opera for Libby is finished and was taken to her by Jane when she sailed, save for seven pages which still had to be composed and orchestrated, and which I managed to do afterward, sending Libby microfilm negatives of them. (It saves a great deal of postage money, although it costs the recipient more, naturally, since he has to have enlargements made of them.) At the moment my mind is going around so fast that I feel I should have something to be working on, just to be working. But I have no project at present. I had a letter this week from the woman who wrote the play which was supposed to be going to need music, and she discovers she must rewrite it a *third* time, or her agent won't take it on. And so on, and so on. It doesn't matter to me too much, since as I told you, I thought it was very feeble anyway. So of course there is no contract as yet.

Tomorrow is Daddy's birthday, and I hope you will wish him many happy returns and give him all my best greetings, even though they will be a little after the fact. Is there any chance of your coming over this spring? The *Constitution* and *Independence* land at Algeciras now, which makes it even easier for meeting them from Tangier. Why don't you come, and we can go direct in the car to Cádiz and take a boat to the Canaries? It would even give me a nice holiday, which would be most welcome. Is it hopeless for me to keep on this tack, or do you think that some day you will really decide to come?

There has been a certain let-up in the political difficulties here. Trouble has been promised several times, but fortunately has failed to materialize. Janie left just before the independence papers were given Morocco, so she missed the big celebrations, but it didn't matter much, because they were something of an anticlimax after the spontaneous outbursts of joy back in November; these last celebrations were carefully organized and purely political, so they lacked interest. The center of trouble is of course Algeria at present, and it bids fair to get worse if France insists on waging war against the country instead of giving it independence. I should say she was cutting off her nose to spite her face, since the important thing for her to retain there is her economic relations, and those she could have retained by keeping on friendly terms with the people, even after severing official governmental ties. But now, after a protracted war, she can scarcely hope to win back their goodwill, whether she has a military victory or not. And even assuming she wins, holding on to a country where you are outnumbered eight to one by hostile Moslems is a full time occupation. What she is doing by waging this war is merely driving not only Algeria, but also Morocco and Tunisia, straight into the Arab League, which is notoriously anti-Western. Which is why Europeans here are very pessimistic.

Speaking of Morocco, I am wondering if you have read my book. In your last letter, received a good while ago, you mentioned having finally received it, but I've never known whether you got around to reading it, and if so, whether you enjoyed it.

A friend here in Tangier, Michael Fordyce, decided back in December to leave his wife and two children here, and make a trip through Africa. So he started out, made a complete circuit through Ethiopia, Kenya, Uganda and the Congo, and got back last week, bringing me an African grey parrot. They are known as the best talkers, but this one is young and says absolutely nothing. Anyway, now I have two! I enclose a picture of the green one and the cat, also two views (not very clear, unfortunately) from two different terraces here in the apartment. One whole roll of film, thirty-six pictures, somehow got lost, so all the ones I thought I'd have, several months ago, and intended to send, never materialized. However, I shall take some more shortly, I hope, and mail them to you.

Let me hear from you about the coming over project! And sooner than you wrote before!

TO JANE BOWLES
◆

March 25, 1956
Tangier

We are back to the same old raw, wintry weather we were having two months ago, with no difference except that the wind is stronger. The Spanish rub their hands and say: "¡Ay, que invierno!" It's hard to believe that it can go on so long. Although there was a short spell of beautiful weather just after you left. It has rained harder the past week than at any time during the winter. Allal el Fassi's big rally in the Stadium last Sunday took place during a veritable hurricane and cloudburst. Of course all the Istiqlal soldiers and official boy-scouts had to be there or else, and they stood in shirtsleeves and shorts throughout, in military formation, but few others could stand it. He has been here in the Calle Holanda, just off the Boulevard, at Doctor Benjelloun's house, all week. (The house is lighted up like a huge altar, with colored bulbs, and protected by uniformed guard twenty-four hours a day.) Each day he has given addresses, parties, concerts at the Cervantes (at 50 pesetas per head a throw) and newspaper interviews. The leaders of the Rif War all came to confer with him although no one else ever saw them, and the authorities claim they have no idea how they got either in or out of the Zone. Today Ouezzani is coming, and a line of trucks decorated with his portraits has been filing by the apartment-house on its way to the airport. There has been no trouble at all, as far as I know. Even the Rif business has stopped for the present, although reports that they were surrendering their arms to the Sultan proved to be false. What they want to do is hold up as large a contingent of French troops as possible, to prevent their being sent against the Algerians, and perhaps send across flying squadrons to attack the French near the border from time to time, but in Algeria, not in Morocco. The suspicious details are several: Allal el Fassi is going back to Cairo from Tangier, without visiting Rabat; he is apparently in complete accord with Franco, who still denounces French policy in Morocco; the Sultan is planning to meet Franco in Sevilla in ten days. I guess that's about all. I haven't seen Cherifa once since you left, nor have I been to the house again. The light bill Temsamany took care of, and I assume the current is still on, because it was Cherifa who asked him to go and pay the bill, and she has not mentioned it again to him. I have been staying in almost entirely during the past few weeks. The weather has militated against going out, and I have been working hard, first finishing the opera, and then writing the article for *Holiday*, which I sent off day before yesterday. For once it went very quickly, which doesn't mean anything until they say they like it, since if they don't I shall have to amend it. It hasn't much form, but then, they don't want it as a regular piece—only as a subsidiary article to stick in the front part of the magazine. And having read a fair number of such pieces, I think mine is just as well-formed as the others. Besides, they pay less for those minor essays. This is all in the way of hoping that they won't want changes. I had had no letter from either you or Libby in the past weeks since you sailed, until last evening when I was brought one from each of you by Ahmed. A week ago yesterday, however, I did have a brief wire from Libby saying JANE OPERA NEGATIVES HERE FOLLOWS LOVE, which was the first assurance I had had that any of you had arrived in America. Let me look over your letter.

Of course I saw Mrs. Southworth, and went with her to the greffier. Later she sent me a copy of the document by registered mail, and also a copy to you, to whatever address you gave her the day we went to her house on the Marshan. I had a letter yesterday morning from Themistocles telling me all about your New York passage en route to Chicago, so there isn't much I could write him about it. Evidently he sees Lilla v-S every day or so. He says he has the rights to *Two Serious Ladies* and all he requires is your signature. If I were you I'd give him permission, but put a time limit on his rights, such as: if the book has not appeared before, say, April first 1957, you will be free to do what you please with it, otherwise it might string out interminably. For God's sake, be businesslike about it, even though there is no immediate money involved. My saying that may sound silly, but one can usually advise others better than one can take care of one's own interests, no? Keep at Tennessee about getting money from the Author's League, for he makes those generous suggestions and then sometimes forgets having made them. I told you Tennessee and Frank want to go to Ceylon—perhaps—later this year. If you see them, ask about it. The house is still there. Ernie Bultjens wrote me recently about a man who wants to rent it on a lease for six years but I am absolutely against any kind of rental. When I go out I want to sell it and get the cash. Maybe we should all go to Ceylon for a Kandy Perahara. Do you like elephant processions? Ahmed says to belarhliks-lem bzef,* and Cherifa is not in the hanout ever. The day you sailed he went to buy slippers for Libby, arrived running, waving them as the gangplank was pulled back. You stayed at the bar. Fordyce brought me an African grey parrot like David's—a beauty who now has a huge cage. Cotorrito hates it with poison in his heart, but that may change. I must write Libby. Much love,

Bupple

TO PEGGY GLANVILLE-HICKS

July 22, 1956
Tangier

Of course you are working like mad, and I wonder you can find time to answer letters at length as you did my last. I have not been working, and still I have

* Ahmed sends his greetings

found it very difficult to keep up my correspondence with my parents here, but that was because I had to be literally with them every minute of the waking hours of the day and night. They left last week after a nine weeks' stay, and since Ahmed is in Fez for the time surrounding the Aid el Kebir, the house is quite empty and restful at the moment. This is giving me the time necessary to answer letters which have been accumulating for the past two months or so. I'm wondering if you are still in the place to which I shall have to send this letter. I suppose if you aren't, whoever is in charge of such things will see that you get it eventually. In any case, I hope so, for otherwise how can we make the plans according to which you will stop by Tangier later in the season? Brion [Gysin] has asked me several times to get a definite time from you about your arrival here, so that he can see to it he is here then. I think he has some more or less vague plans about going somewhere, since he still claims he is definitely closing his establishment on the thirtieth of this month. Of course I have told him that you could not give any such assurances so early. However, by now you may know more about your plans, and you can tell me. It will really be very sad if his place is closed by the time you arrive, and the last opportunity for hearing the music is gone. It *is* the only place where one can still hear the real thing. Musicians are being clapped in the concentration camps now, with severe admonitions to seek other kinds of work when they come out; the same applies to dancers. The true purpose of such nonsense is to outlaw at some later date all "invented" or traditional music, so that the only kind left is that which is being read from the printed page, as in Egypt. But what ghastly sounds result from the reading! One can already hear them on the radio from Rabat . . . very inept imitations of the worst sort of Egyptian commercial and cinema songs. As if the Scotch were suddenly to decree that the mambo was the national music of Scotland, and to insist that the bagpipes play nothing but mambos henceforth. By that time it would be a relief to hear even the worst Cuban band play one. But anyway, can I still hope to see you sometime this summer, when you have finished with Mallorca and Zurich? (Those are the two places you mentioned in your letter, although I feel sure there will be twenty others before you are through.) I shall be simply here, whatever happens, so you need not plan in any direction as far as that is concerned. There is at least one fixed element in that landscape. This summer is completely peaceful compared to last, and actually there have not even been many parades and holidays, which two things are the only interruptions to the normal flow of the days.

A month ago I lent my tape-recorder to Brion for a while, and taught him how to run it, so that between us we have got a good deal of beautiful material preserved on tape. Your assurances as to the possibilities of getting it into more permanent form, on records, are very encouraging. What I should really like is to make a last-minute (and dramatic, very likely) attempt to get more myself in more distant spots where perhaps the Army of Liberation has not yet begun its campaign—if any still exist—and for that it would be essential to have outside financial assistance. Not a great deal, but enough to pay for gasoline, food, shelter and tape, as well as the inevitable and necessary emoluments one has to give here when one hasn't the time required to do everything on a very slow personal friendship basis. To do anything with dispatch here costs more, naturally, simply because as long as one is in a hurry one is an outsider and can't accept the endless invitations and spend the long periods of time which are a prerequisite of friendship, and friendship is the only alternative of commerce. Thus, some sort of grant would be essential, even if it were a small one. Had you not mentioned it I shouldn't have thought of it, but I must say it seems a perfectly valid idea, and I hope we can discuss it (if and) when you arrive. Like any fanatic I'm persuaded of the importance of getting down this music immediately, before it is destroyed by the furiously determined deculturizing bureau of the now so-called Revolution. I think one could even do it with the assistance of the new forces, once someone high-up were persuaded that we Nazarenes realized the music was already a museum piece. However it may be, there is still a frantic hope of saving a certain amount of it for non-Moroccan posterity. Let me hear from you.

TO PEGGY GLANVILLE-HICKS

◆

August 13, 1956
Tangier

A note in answer to your card; I am about to go out to dinner, and shall post it then, so you'll get it as soon as possible.

I suppose you have had the news about Touche. It was a great shock to Jane and me; I could hardly believe it. But then, one always finds it difficult to believe. It was Audrey Wood who sent me the obituary from the *Times*. There is practically no one in New York whom I shall miss more. Whenever we saw each other, I realized that my years of absence had made absolutely no difference; we had not drifted apart at all. And with so many other friends I discover that a time-crack appeared, and I know it will grow wider with each absence.

I must give you the telephone number. The phone is in Jane's apartment (I have none here because as you know I hate having one), and its number is 14353. The address, which is more important, is: Apartment Number 33, Edificio San Francisco, 2, Plaza de Navarra, Tanger. An assisting direction to give the cab-driver is to add: "Frente al Consulado Español." They always know that.

As to shopping in Tangier—I don't know what sort of thing you think of buying. Most things are cheaper here than elsewhere, but that obviously doesn't apply to anything you could get in Spain. The sort of objects which are sold at comparatively low prices are: watches, cameras, fountain pens and so on, French perfumes, tourist souvenirs from India on sale in Hindu shops, souvenirs made in Hong Kong, and above all, Moroccan goods of leather, silver, copper, brass and wool. Other things which are cheap are whiskey and gin and the allied substances. But by the time you arrive there may possibly have been a tax put on everything, because the Sultan needs money, and plans to lay on enormous taxes, up to 300% of the existing ones. Probably, however, that won't happen until October, when the status of Tangier will be decided. If Tangier lasts that long, and we don't have War Number Three before that. There will be difficulties in various places day after tomorrow, since all Moslems must go on strike and engage in manifestations against England, France and America, in answer to the call from Nasser (or do I mean Khrushchev?) for support of his "policy" on the Suez Canal. For once the Europeans feel a little strongly about the barbarian encroachment, but I doubt very much that they will feel strongly enough to risk trouble by expressing their discontent. It looks very much as though the so-called "West" were *really* foutu, and I think most people feel it without knowing what they feel. And if they knew, they wouldn't be willing to formulate it in words, or express it. It's a little too much to admit coldbloodedly that your world's time has come.

And what can we do but sit in the middle of Rome and tell each other how amusing and attractive the barbarians really are, after all, and how it will be possible, if we are clever, to let them have everything and still go on living, perhaps less comfortably, of course, but still, one can get used to almost anything . . . Oh, well! I'll go out to dinner. But I hope to hear from you soon.

April 6, 1957
Nairobi

Your letter did reach me, yesterday afternoon, and we are leaving this afternoon for Mombasa. I left some money at the American Consulate to pay for sending airmail any letters that might arrive afterward, and they will forward them to Cape Town. But I imagine that is the only letter you will have written me here. The address in Cape Town is as follows: P. Bowles, Passenger on the "Kenya Castle," calling Cape Town April 19th, Union Castle Line, Adelaide Street, Cape Town, South Africa. The worst about all this is that there is no Spanish consul this side of Cape Town, and we shall be in Cape Town on Viernes Santo, so obviously it will be impossible to get Ahmed a Spanish visa, so as a result of that we've got to go all the way to London—just what I didn't want. But there's no remedy for it. The Fordyces sent a wire saying they were going to get on the same ship at Zanzibar, so I suppose the haraj will noud* all over again between Ahmed and them. I can't write really a decent letter now because Ahmed and the servant are having a long argument right behind me. I've told him he must go and thank Monsieur David [Herbert] when he gets to Tangier, and he seems happy to hear his flouss is safe. Here in Nairobi they sell wonderful little animals called bush-babies, which are lemurs with tiny hands and enormous eyes and extremely soft fur . . . rather like slightly larger marmosets, but much more appealing, and very friendly. Of course Ahmed wanted to buy one for you, but I did manage to dissuade him. I think we have enough luggage without adding lemurs. The *Isipingo* took eight days to get from Colombo to Mombasa. We arrived a week ago day before yesterday. I haven't started a new book, but at least I sold both the pieces I wrote on the trip out—the *Holiday* piece on Tangier and the short story, which *Harper's Bazaar* took. So I don't feel quite so useless as I did. The trip from Mombasa to London takes about five weeks, I believe. They didn't give me the exact dates, but as soon as I know them I'll send them to you, of course. I think you should conquer your embarrassment if you really want Seth to say: "I am Seth." Or you could go in for something more recondite like: "My name is Seth." Which sounds like an autobiographical novel's title—something awful by Robert Graves on Biblical times. Or: "Ana

* the fuss will start up

smiti Seth."* Ahmed sends salaams and thankyous for taking care of his money and Hamdou'llah Seth can say his name. He says it would be awful if you had *three* illiterates in the house: Cherifa, Ahmed and Seth. He says you must teach him to be your secretary. Seth, that is. I send much love and hope to see you in another six weeks.

TO VIRGIL THOMSON

August 31, 1957
Tangier

   I returned day before yesterday from London, where I had had to take Jane for preliminary neurological tests, and found your letter of August third, together with its enclosure, for which endless thanks. After a short period of indecision, lasting only twenty-four hours, I decided to accept and use the check, because I need it and it will make possible the settling of a lot of bills, mostly local doctors, which otherwise would have had to drag on. Libby sent Jane a total of $900 for the London excursion, and that was an enormous help, even if it did not cover all aspects of the thing; but I can't and won't ask her to send money. The simple fact of the matter now is that Jane has lost her nerve and is at the brink of a mental breakdown. When things get to that point there is no end visible; a sort of spastic stubbornness puts her into direct opposition to any therapy a doctor can offer. She is convinced no one can diagnose her illness and that suicide is the only solution. Her main obsession at the moment is to return to London immediately and see either the neurologist who just released her or some other, but besides the fact that such a step is illogical and expensive, one wonders just what good it would do at this point.

   Since writing the above, I have had a wire from the neurologist in London; it was telephoned by a Spaniard reading English, and I couldn't get most of it, except that I got "strongly advise hospitalization Saint Mary's" out of the 53 words he said made it up. They are sending a copy here shortly. So it looks as though she would be going back, and quite soon. This time they must take into account the psychic side of the question; if they had done that two weeks ago when she was still in the hospital all this wouldn't have been necessary, it seems to me. During the ten days she was in St. Mary's she had all the essential tests:

---

* "My name is Seth."

X-rays of brain and heart, various blood tests, electroencephalogram and arteriogram, and the possibility of brain tumor was removed, as well as the necessity (that is, the feasibility) of surgery. But the facet of her emotional reactions to the illness was left untouched, and that is at least fifty percent of her present trouble; that much should be apparent even to a neurologist. At the moment she has a general practitioner and a psychiatrist working on her every day, and that plus massive sedation is keeping her going—I mean conscious and able to talk coherently.

A break-down of the case: in April she had what has variously been described as a "syndrome confusionelle," a "spasme cérébrale," a "small bleed," a "microlesion," and a "gros accident cérébral." Whatever it was, it resulted in temporary amnesia and a permanent loss of one half the visual field. The latter has naturally been a terrible shock . . . it is "hémianopsie homonyme" of the right side. On July 21st she suffered two epileptiform attacks which further impeded her ability to see; at that point she lost what was left of her morale, and became quasi-hysterical, which she has been more or less constantly since then. I took her to Radcliffe Infirmary in Oxford, to the Neurological Clinic, and she begged to be taken out after twenty-four hours. Finally I was able to get her into Saint Mary's in London, under Dr. Harold Edwards's care, and moved her from Radcliffe less than two days after she had arrived. In Saint Mary's she had the complete tests, which she considers unsatisfactory, but which can scarcely be considered that by anyone else. At the end of the tests she was dismissed, I got passage back here after six days, and we boarded ship. The first day out of the hospital she began to have a new symptom—strong palpitations of the heart which came on in the street. There was then the question of her being readmitted to the hospital, which she finally refused to accept, and we left. On the ship the palpitations became alarming, and led to a further epileptiform seizure, with resulting mental confusion, amnesia and complete hysteria. I tried to get her into the hospital in Gibraltar, which she resisted violently after accepting and refusing it several times, and we came here. That is how things stand now, but I think she will have to go back to London as soon as possible. Anyway, having the check you sent lifts a large immediate burden for me, and I am everlastingly grateful for your having thought of it.

P.S.: This letter is truncated for lack of space, but I'll write again in a few days, giving up-to-date news about Jane, and general news as well. Taking care of her is a totally absorbing chore, night and day, and gives no leisure for letter-writing or even for living, one might say.

TO VIRGIL THOMSON
━━━━━━━━━━━━━━━━━◆━━━━━━━━━━━━━━━━━

September 10, 1957
Tangier

Your letter just arrived; I'll take your suggestion about sending short notes, and dash one off immediately.

It's about ten days since I wrote my reply to your first letter. During that time a good deal has happened. Jane's Tangier doctor came to see her immediately upon her arrival, and got hold of a psychiatrist named Pidoux who had written some monographs on black magic in the Haute Volta and such subjects. He talked each day to Jane for an hour, and seemed to calm her; his sedative properties, however, were most ephemeral, and within two or three hours after he had left she was back in the same awful state. Each succeeding day she appeared to retreat further into an inaccessible region of being. To communicate at all with her one was obliged to discuss her return to London; she could not hear anything else, literally. Her burning desire was to go back to Dr. Edwards of London. So I wired him that, and he wired back that he advised immediate rehospitalization. When I relayed the news to her, however, she made an abrupt shift and decided she preferred Radcliffe Infirmary at Oxford. I wired there and they accepted her. When she heard this news, once again she rejected the prospect, claiming that they would torture her there. At the same time she was increasing her intake of drugs at an alarming rate, and in spite of a daily absorption of a quantity and variety of calmants that would have put a horse out, failed to sleep or relax at all. There was also an undercurrent of violence in her behavior which worried me terribly, directed principally inward, but taking the form of unreasoned hostility to others at times, so that she was impelled to take hold of heavy objects with the idea of hurling them across the room. It seemed time to take action, and fortunately a friend, the ex-wife of the son of old Otto Harbach, offered to accompany Jane to London. I think she had things to do there, and was glad of a free round-trip air passage. I was completely worn out by this time, having had to be available constantly since I returned from Ceylon in May. (It was a nightmare I hope never to have to repeat.) I bought a round-trip and a one-way ticket Air-France, gave the friend $500 in sterling express checks made out in her name, so she could pay for whatever had to be paid for, and prepared for the departure, trying to make myself as impervious as possible to Jane's piteous pleas to be allowed to remain right here in Tangier. The last forty-eight hours were pretty awful for everyone; as the time drew near Jane became much worse.

She was convinced she was being sent to be tortured, that she would never come back again, and her ability to describe and discuss her own state lucidly, at the same time being imprisoned by it, was perhaps the worst part. Anyway, Saturday I had a wire from Anne Harbach saying that she hoped to be able to send me another shortly to the effect that Jane had been transferred to a psychiatric sanatorium, as she put it. Since then I have had no further word, and have no address to which to wire or write, so I must sit and wait for news.

The check you sent was incredibly well timed. It made it possible for me to act quickly in getting Jane out of Tangier; without it, the departure would have been delayed by two or three days, and she might easily have had to be taken on a stretcher if we had let it go on that much longer. Thinking of it was a stroke of genius on your part, and I hope if you see the people who agreed to send it you will tell them how much it meant to me. Incidentally, ought I to write and thank someone else for it? I mean Douglas Moore. (I think you said it was he and Otto Luening, but I'm not positive.) If you think it would be *de rigueur*, I'd appreciate their addresses. Otherwise, I'll wait until I see them if ever.

The television shows sound tempting. How soon must I let you know definitely? Naturally at the moment of writing it's impossible to say anything. I am going myself to London at the end of September, because by that time there will be surely something definite known about Jane's state, and one ought to have at least some idea as to whether it will be a question of weeks or months that she will have to remain in the hospital. Ahmed is having a show from October 1st to November 1st at the Hanover Gallery, and I shall be able to see that and help him with anything in which he needs help.

The records of old jazz do present a problem. There are hundreds of them, and they are all locked into a closet on the top floor of Libby's town house. Who has a key? I don't know. Actually, there are not hundreds of *jazz* records, strictly speaking. Most of them are blues, but I have a certain amount of stuff by Benny Moten, Tiny Parham, the Mound City Blue Blowers, McKinney's Cotton Pickers, and so forth—things I have left over from freshman days in college. I can hardly believe there's anything you'd want. In the blues, perhaps. But hasn't most of all that been done on LP recently? From Ma Rainey through Ida Cox and Blind Lemon Jefferson and Rube Lacy and Teddy Darby on up to Lonnie Johnson? It seems to me I remember seeing that a good amount of it was now available. In any case, you have my permission to ask Peggy to do what she can. Naturally I'd prefer that only those you were going to use left the 61st Street house. You remember the tragedy that befell the records you and Marc used for *The Spanish Earth!* And I do care about my old records, probably to an unreasonable degree. I'm wondering how anyone is going to get into that closet.

This is scarcely a brief note, but there were several things to say. However, now I am going to stop.

TO VIRGIL THOMSON

October 2, 1957
London

Your pre-Berlin letter was brought me from Tangier by Hans Wild, with whom I am staying here in England. We exchanged abodes for a few days; now he is back. I had news of you in Berlin from a Mr. Lester, who I think is musical director for Martha Graham. They were in London last week for a day or two. You are returning to New York today, I think.

I am on my way to London from Northampton, where I've been seeing Janie. She seems a little better than she did last week; in fact, for long periods she appeared to be her own usual self. It was only at moments of emotional stress that one could sense that anything at all was the matter with her. Principally, she seems profoundly unhappy and depressed. They want to try electroplexy, as I undoubtedly told you in my last letter, but since she herself must sign the release permitting them to administer the treatment, and since she is apprehensive about its efficacy, she is receiving no treatment at all for the moment. Which isn't of much use, of course. But I think the security afforded by the place itself, as well as the routine it imposes, has done her some good. Eventually I hope she will come around to asking for the treatment, so I can see with my own eyes just what its result will be, before I return to Tangier. Naturally she wants very much to go back with me, but that is quite out of the question. She is under heavy and regular sedation, which rules out being on her own for the time being. I feel that if she would only make up her mind to take a minimum of four treatments, we would know better where we stand. All the doctors concerned, both neurologists and psychiatrists, insist that in her case, which is akin to the wartime cases of blitz-shock, electroplexy is more than likely to produce a beneficial result in the shortest possible time. She sees its effect on the other patients around her, and rejects it, without understanding that the others are manic-depressives, schizophrenics and alcoholics on whom it is often tried without much hope of its being successful. Sometimes it doesn't seem wise to have her in such an atmosphere—certainly not for any longer than is necessary. The doctors, however, ridicule the idea that the surroundings could have a bad effect on her. The first day I went out, I found her playing ping-pong; she also does weaving as an occupational therapy. But naturally all of that bores her to distraction, as do the other patients, and her only expressed wish is to leave. The most painful moment comes each time when I say good-bye to return to London; she is convinced that I'll never go back to see her.

So in any case I'll have to stay on here until something definite has been decided. I don't think it would make much sense to take her to America at present; besides, it would be extremely difficult to manage. She must be hospitalized. The doctors are adamant about that.

I'd like to hear from you if you have time to write. Thanks for sending me the address of the Am. Institute of Arts, etc. And much love.

TO BOBBY
[Draft of letter from notebook. To Bobby Saltzer?]
•

[October 1957]
[London]

Since I wrote you—last Friday, to be exact—Jane made the decision everyone had been hoping she would make, namely, to start her treatment. I visited her today, and although it is too soon, of course, to draw any definite conclusions, I had the distinct impression that she was less depressed than she had been last Wednesday. She will have further treatments tomorrow and again on Friday and I shall see her again on Saturday. My feeling is that after three applications I should be able to see an even more pronounced beneficial effect. I don't expect her ever to admit, or even be aware, that the treatments are helping her, because she disapproves of them on the grounds of their being dangerous; also, she wants to be in London where she can have more visitors, as is only natural. Her desire is to be in London under the care of the neurologist who was treating her in August, as I may have told you. He has agreed to take her back if after a few treatments she still wants to return to him, an eventuality which seems more than likely, since she hates being so far out in the country. Her doctors in Northampton are loath to let her go until she has completed a course of treatment consisting of a dozen applications of electroplexy, by which time they think all signs of depression will be gone. She does not go along with this theory, because she sees other patients in the hospital some of whom are suffering, naturally, from far more serious troubles than she is, having the treatment and not getting appreciably better as a result of it. But, as her doctor explained to me, if there is any ailment for which electroplexy is virtually a specific, it is simple depression; as they discovered here during the last war with regard to depression due to blitz-shock. These cases responded most quickly and definitively to electroplexy, and there is no reason for thinking that Jane won't do likewise. I firmly believe that, barring unforeseen accidents, she will. My present task is to try to persuade her to continue until she has had enough treatments to enable me to know definitely whether or not they are helping her. This is difficult, of course, because I can't expect her to be conscious of any change in herself, and I have to draw my conclusions by myself, in spite of her inevitable lengthy list of objections. However, notwithstanding the difficulties which lie in the way to her recovery (not the least of which is her impaired vision and her consequent inability at the moment to relieve the boredom of the long days by reading and writing), I think we are making headway; and that Jane has begun an upward climb. I'll keep you informed of any changes.

TO PEGGY GLANVILLE-HICKS
——————◆——————

February 17, 1958
Banking Department
Blandy Bros & Co., Ida.
Funchal, Madeira

The above address is all right for writing me, but God knows how long a letter takes to get from here to New York, or from New York to here. Quite a while, I should think, as there is no airplane service from Funchal which is at all regular. When we asked in Lisbon about it, they told us that no plane had left Lisbon in fifteen days because of bad weather, the bad weather being here, not in Lisbon. So mail must go by ship from here and pick up its plane in Portugal.

Perhaps some sort of explanation is due you as to why I wrote you from Tangier asking you not to write me there. At the moment I knew I'd be leaving as soon as I could, but I didn't know where I was going. The Moroccans had been getting very threatening in their behavior towards me, without however telling me why. It's safe to assume, however, that they are still furious about the last book, which of course is an indictment of their one political party, the one, unfortunately, which won out in the government, and which now has the country completely paralyzed with fear. The first thing they did was to throw Ahmed into jail without trial, the day he returned from London, in late November. Naturally everyone thought that would be cleared up in a few days, but after two months it began to look much worse. They had no law under which they could punish him, but they announced that they were soon going to pass one which would make it possible to convict him retroactively. Then they called me in to question me—the police, I mean. After I had finished there I went to a lawyer to try and find out what was up. He told me he was afraid they were going to charge me with *attentat à la sécurité internale*, which is tantamount to being accused of espionage. When he informed me that it could carry a heavy jail sentence, I thought it was time to leave, even if, as everyone insisted, he was being an alarmist. * * * In any case, the lawyer thought that once Ahmed's case was closed there would be less probability of their getting after me, unless, as they may conceivably do, they decide I am *persona non grata* in the country, in which case they would simply refuse to let me back in. All that wouldn't bother me too much if it weren't for the fact that Jane was just recuperating from her illness when the trouble struck, and she has got consistently worse as a result. I felt I couldn't go off and leave her there, especially since the lawyer thought it likely that she too would be interrogated. That simply wouldn't have done at all. So she is here, and isn't well. She can do nothing but sit silently all day and stare into space. As you see, it's a difficult situation, and there seems nothing to do about it. I've thought that if the recording thing goes through I can apply for the time it would take to accomplish the work, and they would probably make no difficulties because I should be armed with official documents. All this may be a result of the lawyer's fevered imagination, but you can understand why I didn't want to take any chances. I'm simply waiting to hear from him before attempting to go back. What a mess! There's no doubt at all that at the root of it is a desire for vengeance on the part of some high official, but who it is no one seems to know. The Arab League I do know has been agitating to have me kept out of all Moslem countries because of my espousal of the Berbers as opposed to the Arabs in Morocco. But whether they have enough power to get into the police of Tangier is another question. The F.L.N. of Algeria of course could be the liaison, since they are very thick with the police in Tangier, and also are friendly to the Arab League. We've exhausted all the hypotheses without coming to any sort of conclusion. Anyway, I do hope to hear from you soon. And let me know whether you received the piece on *The Transposed Heads*. I was writing it in the middle of all the horror.

TO PEGGY GLANVILLE-HICKS

March 29, 1958
Lisbon

I have heard from Maurice Grosser, probably as a result of your having given my present address to Virgil. Whether I'll still be here by the time he arrives I have no idea. I'm trying to get Jane to go to New York, because she can't continue with the life she is leading here staying in bed all day unconscious, and doping herself at night. She will end up by being totally paralyzed, which she says she wants, in any case. Her morale is worse than ever, but there is nothing really the matter otherwise. She simply isn't interested in anything, short of going back to Tangier, which is out of the question since she is wanted by the police there. Of course her compulsion is to go back, "kill the judge," as she says quite seriously, and enter prison. My job is to prevent her from doing that if I can. I've never had a problem like this, and it occupies every moment of the day after twelve, and of the night until one or two. Nothing else can be touched on in conversation, even for ten seconds. We're getting nowhere, I can't work at anything, and she becomes more embedded in her obsession each day. However, she doesn't want to budge unless she goes to Tangier. But I know it would have the most terrible results. The doctor here found her blood-pressure "fantastically high," and changed her medication, and since she went into her compulsion with him, he also told her she risked a further stroke if she underwent any great nervous strain. She welcomed the idea, thinking another stroke would mean death, but he disillusioned her, saying it might mean only complete paralysis, and that one couldn't choose which areas of the brain to affect. That sobered her a little, I must say, but two days later she was off again. If I can, I'll get her to go to New York. I feel certain that any outside change would be for the better, would stop the wheel of compulsive thoughts from turning. If I could only get her out into the street for a quarter-hour walk it would help, but she refuses everything. * * *

There was something important I wanted to say, and now I've forgotten what it was. You've never told me whether the records containing your *Letters from*

Morocco and *The Wind Remains* have been issued. I sent the proofs of the García Lorca songs off to Ray Green earlier this week. Sylvia Marlowe has asked me to write a piece for her, which is very nice of her, and I have agreed. I don't know where I shall get the chance, but I'll find a piano somewhere between now and next year.

I do rather like Portugal, if only because the people are pleasant. I'm fed up with being surrounded by hostility, which is the rule rather than the exception in the countries where I've been living: Morocco and Ceylon. Even complete apathy is preferable for a change. I know the south of Portugal—the province of Algarve—and it's pretty. But I'm not looking for prettiness.

You ask where Ponte Delgada is: it's in Mid-Atlantic, in the Azores! I've never landed there. I have been wondering if the project to record Moroccan music could be shifted to a project to record the music of some other part of Africa; I don't think there is going to be a possibility of my getting either into or around Morocco. * * * What a shame they didn't get around to my project last year! *The Spider's House* is on the press in Barcelona at the moment, will be given big publicity in Spain because of the territory disputes between Spain and Morocco. That will finish me off in Morocco. But if the Rockefeller Foundation were still willing to give the grant, I could do a good job on Angola. There isn't much else left, since French colonies are impossible. I hope you find time to write before sailing.

TO JANE BOWLES

April 18, 1958
Caparica, Portugal

This is coming from Caparica, where I am in a small pension on the beach. The weather is practically Saharan: absolutely clear sky and strong sun, but a cold wind, and an Arctic night. The place is run by a family of real *peuple*, and they are charming, and the food is perfect, which I know you'll scarcely believe. I think the reason is that the mother of the household has liver trouble, and understands very well how to prepare things in a healthy fashion. So what can be grilled is grilled, and she makes excellent, enormous salads for me every meal. The sort of woman who insists on showing me each thing in the kitchen in its pristine state, and asking exactly how I want it prepared, and then actually doing it that way. So naturally I am pleased. The place wouldn't really have been possible earlier, however, because it requires good weather. One has to go outside to get to the dining room.

The morning after you left I went for mail, and received an enormous batch, including another shipment of forwarded things from Tangier, with as usual a note from Temsamany stuck in. If only that had come one day earlier you could have gone off much easier in your mind, for he had just seen Cherifa twice before writing, and she wanted to remind you that the Aid el Kebir was almost there . . . hinting, of course, that a sheep was in order. No trouble mentioned. I think I'd better quote you his letter, that part of it, so you can see for yourself just what he said. "Pues diga usted a la señora que yo he visto a Cherifa anteanoche y hoy sobre las 1:30 y me dijo de decir a la señora que todo anda mal y que no estamos contentos y que ya faltan 7 dias para el Aid el Kebir. Recuerdos de Berred a la señora y grandes abrazos de Seth."* Evidently jail was furthest from her thoughts. "Todo anda mal" and "no estamos contentos" certainly don't imply police persecution, but rather boredom and lack of money. Anyway, I hope this news changes your mind somewhat. I also heard from the bank, and they had received my check for the rent. The reason they hadn't answered before was that they hadn't bothered to go and get the registered letter from the post-office, leaving it there three weeks. Just Tangier. Temsamany says now that he told Christopher [Wanklyn] to tell me not to write "very much" because of the "asunto de la policía aquí. Todo eso pasó."† How it can have passed I don't know. He didn't mention Ahmed at all, so I don't know whether there has been a trial or not. He obviously assumes I know all about it. Do write and tell me about your trip and how you are. João is supposed to come here to Caparica this afternoon. I imagine he will: he's pretty precise. I spend my time writing letters and walking around the beach, and will write you again shortly. Please give my best to Katharine and Natasha, and Tennessee and Frank if you see them, and anyone else. And let me hear very soon.

---

* "Well, tell the lady that I saw Cherifa the night before last and today at about 1:30 and she told me to tell the lady that everything's going badly and that we aren't happy and that there are only 7 days left until the Aid el Kebir. Berred asks to be remembered to the lady and a big hug from Seth."
† "police business here. That's all over now."

TO KATHARINE HAMILL
AND NATASHA VON HOERSHELMAN

April 26, 1958
Caparica, Portugal

Dear Katharine: *This is not to be read to Jane.*

I received your letter this afternoon and am answering immediately; I think yours arrived only today because it was mailed day-before-yesterday. (I have been out of Lisbon for the past five days.)

What you say about Jane is extremely upsetting. Does the doctor think her present state is a temporary exhaustion due to the trip, or a return of the same trouble she had last summer? You use the word "confusion," which makes it sound more like the latter. Confusion implies the adjective "mental," which is something I had hoped was all finished by the shock treatment. (Please read this to yourself and not to Jane.) During the entire time since she left the hospital in Northampton she has been completely normal from that point of view. Emotionally no, because she had never been emotionally *normal*, and since her illness she has been even more inclined than usual to worry. But still, I should say she has been herself, but moreso. I just had to argue her out of her worrying afresh each day and get her to admit that there were other things to discuss besides the one or two topics that obsessed her. Since leaving the hospital she has not once been capable of admitting the absurdity of her worry. (It was her inability to step out of line and see herself that made the shock treatment necessary, according to the doctors in England.) But I don't know. Your letter makes it sound as though she had taken a very definite turn for the worse, both physically and otherwise. In the first place, since she started taking Epanutin she has had no convulsions. The last convulsion took place in early February en route to Madeira. For a month after that she took Epanutin regularly, two a day, until she came to Lisbon, where the doctor here suggested that she stop and pay attention to getting the blood pressure down. For that he gave her Hepadesicol and Serpasil. She responded extremely well, and the last time she visited him, a week before leaving, the blood pressure had fallen in what he said was a spectacular fashion. I think I wrote you what it had been and what it was the last time he took it, and I can't remember the exact figures now, but it was in the neighborhood of 150 over 80, I think, having gone down from something like 220 over 150. Of course, like all the other doctors, he gave us nothing written, so there are no records. One of the great troubles is that Jane never takes the medicine regularly unless one keeps at her constantly, which I did. However, I can't see how, even if she neglected to take *any* Serpasil for a day or two, the pressure could have risen so dramatically in so short a time unless something else is very wrong.

I'm trying to convince myself that it wasn't the fact that I let her go alone on the plane which has made her worse. She insisted that she didn't dread the trip, and I'm convinced that she didn't, at least consciously, because I should certainly have known it if she had been dreading it. What she said she dreaded was seeing her mother, which I understand, since she has kept up the pretence of being well ever since her stroke, and it has involved such a tremendous structure of lies that she automatically overestimates the adverse reaction her mother would have when the whole edifice collapsed. I can see that, and even at the beginning I was not a partisan of keeping everything from her mother: however, I had to play along in spite of myself, since Jane's mother is not my mother.

The immediate situation worries me terribly. Obviously you can't be a nurse to Jane, and if as you say she really needs a nurse, then I don't know what to do. I can go back to New York, but what will I do with her when I get there? I suppose that's my problem; it's one I can't see any solution for, at least from here. John Goodwin wrote me saying he thought I should be there, and I can see that he's right. But there seems to be an element of immediacy in it all that throws me. What matters seems to be this very week, not next month. All my possessions are in Tangier and I want very much to get them out before leaving this part of the world. I want to empty the apartment and get out of the lease on it and pack up my clothing and personal effects (and Jane's), and shut the door on that, because in spite of all that Jane says, I don't believe we are going to be able to live there again—at least, not peacefully or for an indefinite period—even if all goes well there politically this year, and there are no definite signs of the dawn of a better political day at the moment. I think I should take a chance and go back and try to salvage everything myself, if I am going to America. It would be better than leaving it in the present mess, with my having to pay the rent every month. Does Jane feel she can't leave New York at all for the present? I wish she'd write me and give me an idea of what she is thinking about. Did she get my letter telling her Cherifa was not and had not been in jail at all? If so, it must have been after you wrote me, which seems a long time, since I wrote her over a week ago. But there seems to be no way of knowing how long letters are going to take.

I'm sorry that Jane's arrival in New York should have made all this trouble for you; I didn't foresee that a twelve-hour plane trip could make such a difference. Do you have Oliver Smith's address, so that I could write him about the possibility of staying at his house? Please write when you can, and ask Jane to write, unless she is too ill even to do that. And please give her my love and sound her out about what she herself would like me to do.

TO JANE BOWLES

May 2, 1958
Caparica, Portugal

No news from you, which is rather worrying to me. I wish you'd write, if even a few lines, to let me know how you are. I've had two letters about you, of course—one from Katharine, and one from John Goodwin, both of whom told me that you weren't very well. But I should like to have one from you, yourself, if you can type a short one, just to let me know in your own words how you feel.

I am wondering, too, whether you want me to try to write your mother, or whether you will be sending signed notes like the one you sent last week for me to post here and send on to Saltzer's address. I'm perfectly willing to try and compose some Jane-like notes, only I don't think I could counterfeit your signature very well. But let me know what you want me to do, and as soon as you can, so that not too much time will go by without your mother's having a letter.

Did you manage to hang on to your money, traveler's checks, and the Libby check? That is another thing I must hear about—whether you have money and whether you need any; and if you do need some, be sure and say so, because I still have some, as you know, and will send it. But don't say you don't need it if you do, please, because it will just make everything more complicated later. I've been hoping to hear from you for the past ten days. Both Katharine and John told me you had had a convulsion shortly after arriving. That must mean you neglected to take your Epanutin, because you surely wouldn't have had it had you taken it. Have you got the various papers I gave you the night before you left? I mean the ones listing your medicines, the treatment you had in England and where each treatment was given? They were all with the letters from Bensadon and the compte rendu of the Tangier case. I know you said you'd probably lose them, but you couldn't very well have lost them, since they were in the small grip along with the medicines themselves.

I have been continuing with my dental work, staying out here in Caparica most of the time, and going into Lisbon only when I had an appointment with Dr. Alcoforado. My time for staying in Portugal has run out again and I went Tuesday to the International Police and applied for a prolongation of the permission. They have my passport at the moment, so I don't know how much extra time they've granted or whether they will grant any. I intend to go today and find out. At the same time I'll go to the Embassy and see what mail there is. I hope you got my letter telling you that Cherifa had not been in jail and was not in jail, and hoped for some money for the Aid. The Aid is of course long past now. I've heard nothing since that letter of Temsamany's which came over two weeks ago, but everything was obviously all right at that time, and there's no reason to think it would have changed since. Have you written Temsamany? In my reply to him I didn't tell him you had gone to New York. I'm wondering, too, if there's been any word about your passport. Do let me know about all these things, and do take whatever medicine you're supposed to take, regularly, at the appointed times. I'm hoping there may be a word from you waiting for me at the Embassy. I'll close and write again soon. Much love.

TO JANE BOWLES

———————————◆———————————

May 14, 1958
Caparica, Portugal

Thank heavens! After one month I finally heard from you. I suppose it demanded a terrific effort, but I must say I was delighted to know you could and would write. It was perfectly intelligible, and better, I think, than the few notes you typed during the winter in Madeira and Lisbon.

Everyone has written me, of course, telling me how ill you have been. Even Themistocles Hoetis, who I'm sure hasn't even seen you. But you are better now, according to these same people and according to you yourself. Is it really worse than it was here? It seems hard to believe. This worse applies to existence, not health. Health goes up and down mercurially; I don't suppose the feeling about existence does. It was very sweet of you to put forth the energy to write.

I'm right here, with no intentions of going to Japan. I haven't heard from Libby, although perhaps I shall fairly soon, since I wrote her last week begging her to answer. Obviously I have no inkling of her plans. Maurice has not yet arrived, but according to a note I had from him, posted in Paris, he does expect to arrive this week unless he is held up en route by blizzards, which seem to have been taking place all over this part of Europe. I expect him within the next three or four days. I'm very eager to see him. Caparica is extremely empty, which of course suits me perfectly. But it will be more fun if he is here. I'm not sure he'll want to be here, but I imagine he will. It's only forty minutes from the center of Lisbon, and very cheap, and the food, as I think I wrote you, is excellent. I'm working on the harpsichord piece for Sylvia Marlowe. In a "dancing" here I found quite a decent piano where I can go and work. The place functions only in summer.

There is no particular news from Tangier, so that even if I wanted to write you about it I couldn't. Temsamany writes that the police have taken his passport away from him and he despairs of ever getting it back. A. has had no trial, and none has been set. Things according to T. are terrible in Tangier; he seems very discouraged, and warns us against coming back, as the police are more vengeful than ever and are determined to pop us into jail if we so much as show our faces.

I shall pay the last two installments in London when they come due—I mean to Dr. Tennant, of course. I have sent the letter for your mother, and written another more recently, although I shuddered to sign your name, which to me looks like a very clumsy forgery. I hope to God she doesn't suspect anything. The new medicine must be good if it can stop a fit in the middle. Forgive the shortness of this, but I am on my way into Lisbon and want to get it off today. I was very happy to hear from you, and I'm glad you will be with Dione. I assume she's better these days. Give her my best.

TO JAMES MICHIE,
WILLIAM HEINEMANN, LONDON

September 18, 1958
New York City

Your letter was read over the 'phone to me this morning by Miss Strauss, and I hasten to reply.

The matter of the photograph is not immediately soluble, inasmuch as all my papers and documents are in Tangier, whence I was chased, back in February, by the local authorities, who appeared to be intent upon clapping both me and Mrs. Bowles into a concentration camp. Accordingly, it has since seemed the better part of valor to remain outside of Morocco. I have specific plans, however, for recovering whatever of my property is transportable, without returning there. But this isn't of much interest as far as getting hold of a photograph is concerned. It may be that William Morris has some photos somewhere, or Random House. I'll get on the wire and try to discover one somewhere in this city.

The two hundred words of biography. I was born in New York City and brought up here during the age of Prohibition. When I had completed secondary school at sixteen, I enrolled in an art school. At the end of the first term painting seemed silly, so I went to the University of Virginia because Poe had gone there. When the first year was half finished, I went off to Paris, where I'd already published in various so-called avant-garde magazines, including *transition* and *This Quarter*. Paris also palled, so I started walking around Western Europe. Eventually I returned to the United States and the University, only to escape again, this time to Berlin (where I first met Isherwood and Spender). Then Gertrude Stein suggested I go to Morocco, so I did, immediately deciding to remain in North Africa. I wandered about Morocco, Algeria, the Sahara and Tunisia for four years, then went to the West Indies. After that, South America and Central America. Then Mexico for four and a half years. In between I came back here to write scores for Broadway shows, of which I have done about two dozen, including among others the first William Saroyan play and the first Tennessee Williams play. When the war finished I went back to Morocco where I bought a small house, in order to feel settled. Then I went down to the Sahara and wrote *The Sheltering Sky*. After that I went to India, where I began *Let It Come Down*, then to Ceylon, where I saw a little island I liked, off the south coast. It wasn't for sale. I went back to Morocco, returning the next year to Ceylon, where the island was still not on the market. However, I laid the groundwork for an eventual purchase, and heard in Madrid the following autumn that I could at last buy it, which I did that very day. Again I went out to Ceylon, lived in it and wrote *The Spider's House*. Then I went to Japan. Back to Morocco eventually, where I put together the book called *Yallah* (no edition in England: only a German one published in Zurich and the American one which McDowell & Obolensky brought out last year). Then I went to South Africa and back to Ceylon, from where I arranged a Rockefeller Grant to record indigenous music in Morocco. Then I went to visit Tom Mboya in Nairobi. I'm almost up to the present. Back to Tangier, where my political past caught up with me. The trouble ensued, I settled in Portugal for a few months, was in Albufeira of Algarve when a telephone call came from New York asking me to return here immediately to aid in staging a play I had adapted from the Spanish and written an extensive score for (García Lorca's *Yerma*). I didn't want to come, but I came, and here

I am, still working on that production. I'm also doing a score for the new
Tennessee Williams opus, *Sweet Bird of Youth*, which Kazan schedules for
shortly after New Year's. I still intend to record the music of Morocco. That's
about all, I should say.

TO VIRGIL THOMSON

December 27, 1958
Tangier

I'm sorry I didn't manage to get in touch with you during the last week of
New York. I wasn't my own master from the moment I got Janie from the
hospital. The great worry was about whether she would be able to make it to
the ship before deciding against going at all. I could see the signs of that calamity
approaching, and I didn't want to give her a moment to sit and begin to brood
about it. The ship sailed with us on it, and the trip across was difficult. Jane
was beset with every sort of symptom at all hours of the day and night. Her
heart beat too fast. She felt her blood pressure in her temples. Her head ached.
She was nauseated. She was jittery. She had no appetite, save at four in the
morning, when she ordered in sixteen sliced chicken sandwiches without mustard. (This was routine throughout the voyage.) I was trying to write an article
for *Holiday* in record time—the length of the trip—seven days, and needed
complete solitude, or at least quiet for a few hours during each twenty-four. All
passed. We got to Algeciras, where Jane decided the police would very likely
arrest us. They didn't. She refused to come to Tangier until I had sent a telegram
to the police asking them if we might return. This I did. Suddenly it became
the worst thing we could have done. Now it would be absolutely impossible for
us to return. It was too late to recall the telegram, and I refused to send a second
asking them to pay no attention to the first (as she suggested!). We decided to
stay in Algeciras until we heard something. The next day a cable from the
American Consul arrived. It said we might return whenever we wished. The
following day we came here, where Jane immediately became another person
entirely. She began to laugh and take pleasure in food, and become her old
normal self, moreso than she has been at any time since the stroke. So I'm
gratified, of course, and delighted that I managed to get her out of New York
in time. I think all will go well now for a while, perhaps for good, or until some
external situation changes everything. Of course that is all too likely to happen

in Morocco, it being what it is, but one might as well relax and enjoy the calm moment.

It seems Kazan wants someone else named Amram for Tennessee's new play. Audrey wrote me yesterday about it (Tenn's agent). It's an open question right now, but I imagine they'll decide to use the other composer. Kazan usually gets his way with Tennessee.

I was sorry to miss John Marshall by leaving New York when I did. I'd like to have talked with him about my project for Moroccan music. I did go to the Foundation with Peggy on the last day in New York. Events here now make the time element increasingly important, but they understand that, I'm sure.

Jane sends her love. She is about to get dinner.

I send mine.

TO JANE BOWLES

February 15, 1959
Philadelphia

I know you hate these air-letters, but they do save a lot of money, as well as making it possible to write without going all the way to a post-office to inquire how much postage has to be affixed to each letter. I only wish they had them in Tangier still, as they used to when the Tanger Socco was the British Post Office.

This is a quick note to thank you for your letter which arrived yesterday. I was very happy to have it, since it was the first one that told me at least a little something about yourself. Keep a list of postage spent on forwarding my mail, and naturally I'll reimburse you on my return, as I said I would. I am writing the Washington people after I get this off, to let them know I am back here. I don't think they know it yet. All I'm doing now is going to each performance to hang around watching it from the back, inasmuch as there is never a seat in the theatre for me to sit down in. Kazan wanders too, and occasionally says something like: "Watch the dialogue at the end of the next scene, and see what you think about some sound-effects." The music is extremely soft for my money—so much so that anyone sitting beyond the tenth row can't tell whether there is any or not, but no one seems to mind, and I can't get them to turn it up. We have not recorded it yet, and I am thinking of rewriting certain sequences tomorrow, sequences which precisely because they are so soft make no sense and have absolutely no dramatic impact as they are. I imagine that one of these days they will send me back to New York, because Cheryl Crawford will suddenly decide that the budget can't stand taking on my expenses. But when they do, I am not going to hang around New York with nowhere to live save in a hotel, and use up every cent of what I hope to make on the show; I still have no contract. I can't think what is wrong with Audrey Wood, except that she doesn't really care, since my earnings are so infinitesimal.

Did I tell you that Walter Wanger is willing to settle for a short story, from which he can have a film script made? What he is willing to pay I don't know. He still wants me to go out to Beverly Hills and "spend some time discussing the story and seeing some films," as he wrote in his most recent letter. However, if I am willing to accept less money, he is willing to dispense with my presence in California. I suppose it depends on the difference in money, really. He says: "If he wants to submit a short story on some sort of a speculative deal where we pay him so much down for doing it and, if we use it, so much more." That's his sentence. But the paragraph begins: "If Paul Bowles absolutely refuses to come to the coast." I suppose he finds it impossible to understand why anyone shouldn't be pleased to have a free trip to Beverly Hills. Remember he wants to get a hit-tune as well as a lot of sexy Parisian scenes! Anyway, he has a great hit running here in the U.S. now, called "I Want to Live." Everyone tells me it's very fine, and I must get out and see it one day. I never go into movie houses because I usually catch cold in them. I caught Asian flu watching Charlie Chaplin's new picture "A King in New York" in London last winter, you know. If I'd stayed home I wouldn't have had it, and without that I wouldn't have had pneumonia afterward.

I hope you have had Angèle put my new big radio into my room, unless you use it regularly, which I somehow doubt. It's the sort of thing that eager hands make off with when one's back is turned, especially since it's worth 10,000 pesetas there.

I think when I return I'll have to offer Larbi Yacoubi money for the grey parrot; I can't believe that with sufficient inducement he would refuse to give him up, can you? Have you ever had the Potts for dinner? I wager not. Did Ahmed get off to Brazil? You didn't mention him at all. I'm very happy that you've cut down on the drugs. It ought to make you feel generally stronger after a few weeks, once some of the poison has gone out of your blood.

A lot of people have told me they think this music is the best incidental score they've ever heard in the theatre, so I'm pleased about it, even though it's badly played, and execrably amplified. They play in the basement and the music is piped up to backstage. Max Marlin is with us, of course. He's all excited about Castro in Cuba, and great discussions go on between the musicians and the stage-hands. Most are anti-Castro, so Max has a good time defending him.

I'm glad to hear you're drinking Vichy. It's wonderful stuff for the liver, I know. Virgil served me some the night I had dinner with him, and I ended up drinking the whole bottle. A friend of mine in New York, the boy who has been bringing me kif occasionally—I mean last autumn before we left for Tangier— suddenly had an epileptiform attack in the street, and Karl Bissinger happened to be looking out his window on 2nd Avenue at the moment—pure chance— and saw him fall. He was taken to the hospital because he hit his head badly. Since then he has had four more such attacks, and has been given Dilantin by the doctors. He had never had anything before in his life, being very healthy up until then. It seems to be a mysterious ailment going the rounds now, and no one knows just what causes it. I saw him the other day here in Philadelphia, and he was optimistic because since taking Dilantin, which he began three weeks ago, he hasn't had another attack. Of course he had no stroke or anything . . . just suddenly fell over. He had forgotten his Dilantin in New York, though. Much love,

Bupple

TO JANE BOWLES

◆

February 27, 1959
Philadelphia

I'm glad the cat arrived; I thought you'd love its face. The tongue looks like a rose-petal. Your letter and some forwarded mail arrived day before yesterday. I've been so extremely busy since then that I haven't had a moment, literally, to answer. We taped all the music yesterday, and today I've been at the recording studio directing mixes and fades, etc. Also I've been having long daily sessions at the dentist's, and must continue with them when I get to New York. There's a lot of work to be done, as usual, but perhaps more than usual this time, because I haven't been going to any dentist for the past three years. Maybe you ought to have the work done that was to have been done at the hospital. I don't know what it is, but it ought not to be neglected, or it gets more and more complicated and expensive when eventually you do go. You remember the name of the dentist I suggested? Dr. Nils Bolling? You might look him up in the telephone directory.

When I was on my way back from Gibraltar to New York, I wired Libby to find out how to get into the house in Sixty-First Street, and was a bit shaken to get back a wire saying that she was sorry she couldn't have me there. After her letter sent to Tangier saying that I could always go there when I wanted, it was a surprise. In New York I went to the Chelsea, and called her at Stamford, and she went into a long unconvincing story about having so many dates in town every day that it wouldn't be possible to have me staying there, since she would be going in and out all day. However, it wasn't up to me to ask questions. A few days ago she phoned to say that the house was being redecorated, but that I could stay if I didn't mind the noise and inconvenience. Since I'll be out most of the time anyway, in the theatre, and not working at the piano or at anything in the house, it obviously doesn't matter to me, so I said I was delighted, and would stay. So I'll be there from tomorrow night on, until I sail back.

I was amused by your apologies at having opened the letter from the bank. It doesn't matter, naturally. In any case, I was pleased to see that I had so much money all at once, and I haven't been spending much (of my own) since I got here, so I ought to be well fixed by the time I leave, save for the dentists, who are hellishly high here. But I suppose their work is better, if that's any consolation.

I heard from Oliver—a ten-page letter from the Ritz in Boston where he's producing another sure-fire flop, at least according to everybody's gossip. Marc Blitzstein is doing the music . . . a musical version of O'Casey's *Juno and the Paycock*. It sounds like a mad idea. I have no news, really. Heard from Ahmed finally in Rio, and he sounds as if he liked it. He refers to the girl as "my wife," so maybe they really are married.

One day soon I must go down to Washington and fix up everything about the expedition. They have already bought most of the equipment, according to their most recent letter. I'm very eager to get started. I've had two lunches with the editors of *Holiday*, and drinks with a third man who has a special department on the mag for which he wants some short pieces, humorous, of all things. He thinks I can write funny pieces. I told him it was ridiculous, that I was serious. But he insisted that I should make an attempt to do humorous articles for him. He thinks there isn't enough humor in the magazine.

Did I tell you I saw Natica Waterbury? She has become a photographer and has a studio in New York with another girl. They are successful commercial photographers. She has a sort of boy-friend too, who lives here in Philadelphia. He has just bought her a Jaguar convertible. I had dinner with him alone last night, and he talked constantly about her, and insisted on buying me exactly what he always ordered for her. Oysters, consommé, duck and chocolate soufflé. The soufflé was good, I must say. It was a strange idea, I thought.

This must be cut short. I just wanted to let you have a few words from me so you'd know I was still thinking about you. And as I say, I haven't anything important to say except that I miss you. Much love,

Bupple

TO JANE BOWLES

March 18, 1959
New York City

This will be very short. I just don't seem to have time in New York to write a decent letter (or any at all, for that matter, it would seem, except now and then to you, and I have been quite a while without writing even you). Your two letters came, and I am going see Polikoff about it—I mean the special account business. I spoke to both him and Clareman last week when they were here one afternoon, but they said I would have to go into the office and look the thing up with a secretary, and I haven't yet found the day when I could get down there. My teeth have been taking up most of the time, what with an extraction and a capping job on a front tooth, and about a dozen fillings of various sizes and seriousness, and a large inlay to be made. However, I'm about finished now, and have only the fitting and installation of the cap job to be done.

I wanted to let you know I was still here and getting ready to move. Next week I'll be going to Washington to pick up the recording equipment, and after that there's really nothing more to do as far as I can see. I've seen Gian Carlo [Menotti] and Sam [Barber], and Sam is due to arrive in Tangier somewhere around the first of April. Gian Carlo will be down in July. He has taken the Brandolinis' house on the mountain for a month with Tommy Schippers. Virgil also intends to come over during the summer. So there will be a nucleus, which is always nice. I saw Allen Ginsberg and Jack Kerouac last night and am seeing them again tonight. Of course they never talk about anything but Bill Burroughs. He, incidentally, ought to be in Tangier very soon, according to his most recent letter to me from Paris. Allen was still worried about his conversation with you two years ago, but I calmed him down.

I've got to go and see about my income tax. Polikoff has charged me with all the expenses on Yerma last summer . . . $2,750, which is terrible, since it will raise my tax tremendously. I would never have come back if I'd known he was going to tag me with that. It's too much. Libby knows nothing about it and obviously doesn't want to discuss it. She did get your letter, by the way, and was very happy with it.

I'll close now, and send love,

Bupple

P.S. The boy we met on the ship wants to go to Tangier and make a movie along with me on my expedition. Virgil also wants to go along. Your mother has called twice from Miami late at night; she is "beside herself" because you haven't written. Send her a few lines, for God's sake.

TO ALLEN GINSBERG, PETER ORLOVSKY,
GREGORY CORSO, AND JACK KEROUAC

April 27, 1959
Funchal, Madeira

Dear Allen, Peter, Gregory and Jack (if present),

Night after last, after being led down dark, deep lanes with high walls on either side, sweet-smelling vegetation trailing high over our heads, after descending into ravines and climbing thousands of cobbled steps that were slippery with little flowers that grew out of their cracks, we came to a bar (I don't know how or when, but, anyway, it was still night, and now and then you could see the moon and its path in the ocean, but miles out, the horizon, and so we knew it was not yet time for dawn), one of those fine Madeira bars with more space in its private rooms than out front. And it was full of what Carroll insists are Rock-and-Roll boys from the beaches and mountains, wearing a mixture of city and country clothes, but all of them out of the year 1840, I should say, with that sort of daguerrotype character (character in the sense that the Y.M.C.A. would understand the word) all carved into their excellent faces. (They did all wear shoes, but many had not yet discovered socks.) In spite of the crowding, one of the private rooms was unoccupied, and we pressed through and took it over. There were four of us, and we ordered ginja, peanuts and beer and everything was going along nicely with smiles and confidences, and Carroll was regretting that we hadn't brought along, as he said, "exactly three time as much" pot as

we did. However, he was happy, and they were speaking what silly words of
English they knew and I was rattling along in Spanish to them, of which they
must have captured about a half, and they were replying in Portuguese of which
I got about a third. So, as I say, there was a pleasant amount of understanding
floating in the air above the table and collecting up in the darker corners of the
private room where the cobwebs waved in the shadows, and more drinks were
ordered and drunk, and what misunderstandings developed were quickly explained away, and Carroll kept saying: "Oh, how I'd like to turn them on!" and
shaking his head, and I think perhaps that was misunderstood, or perhaps not,
but they said "Boogie boogie!" and laughed delightedly, and Carroll whooped,
and at that moment a fifth one walked in and leaned over the table at Carroll
and said he liked to walk at night, and would Carroll walk? Carroll is lazy, but
very lazy, and he didn't feel like walking, so he invited the fifth one to sit down,
and this was not appreciated by the other two, who made unpleasant faces about
it to me and to each other. I wasn't pleased either, because since it was I who
was going to have to pay for the whole thing, I wanted first of all to be sure that
I was going to have enough money to get out without difficulties, and secondly,
I thought four was a better number than five. However, Carroll is impulsive,
and the harm was done. He sat down, and during the two hours which followed,
through a barrage of grimaces and overt remarks, eventually, on the part of the
original two, he and Carroll engaged in a conversation about Jack Kerouac, with
whom Carroll finally confused this fifth one, so that in the end he was calling
him Jack, and the fifth one, a sort of suave gorilla, very wide in the shoulders
and chest, was obediently answering to the name. (They are out together tonight.
I am sitting in the hotel writing this and listening to Moroccan (Chleuh) music,
and smoking a little of the pot that Libby gave us as a going-away present.)
(Carroll doesn't yet know about it, because we haven't quite finished the lot we
(he) brought from Johnny's.) I'll let him know of its existence when we get back
to Lisbon, when we'll need it more. We were walking in the garden this afternoon
on the way back from the market to buy papayas and chirimoyas, and Carroll
spied a photographer, one of those with a tripod and a pail of water and a big
black box into which they put their heads, and when the picture is ready it
comes out dripping wet from the pail of water. And he wanted to have his picture
taken. I didn't want it: but then I never want to do anything. So we took the
picture because he said it would be for you. At that moment Jack Kerouac
ambled up and said: "Oh, hello are you?" and Carroll immediately grabbed him
and made him sit in the middle. A moment after the man snapped the picture
a policeman came by and made us get off the bench, along with several other

youths who had gathered to watch the whole business. So here is your picture. And love from Funchal.

August 18, 1959
Tangier

Enclosed you will find my report on the first period of a little over a month. As you can see, I got infinitely less music recorded than I had counted on when Mr. Spivacke and I discussed the possibilities. A bit more than half the period of time was spent in Rabat trying to get in touch with Moroccan government authorities; once I had the permission in my pocket I was able to start work, but not until then. Another condition which has reduced the quantity of possible recordings is the wide discrepancy between the projected amount of recompense due performers and the actual sums required in order to get them to perform. As I said in my previous letter, the only course open to me has been to go ahead and record whatever I can get (assuming, naturally, that the material is of musicological importance); the result is simply that quantity has to be sacrificed to quality. Personally, I am delighted with the quality of everything I have recorded so far, even if I am disappointed not to have more of it. I confess that I had not expected to find anything so good as I got from the Haha tribe, for instance, or from the Guedra group of Goulimine.

I talked two nights ago with Mrs. Bowles on the telephone, and she told me that the second check had arrived. Tomorrow I expect to return to Tangier, cash it, and start out again to another region. It will not be in this direction: living and traveling conditions in this part of Morocco (I mean south of the Grand Atlas) are extremely difficult during the summer, with the thermometer at 140 degrees and everyone asleep during the day, and with a resulting reluctance on the part of the populace to bestir themselves to make music (which means automatically to engage in strenuous dancing, since the music and the dancing are one thing). In each place it is necessary to get on the good side of the local chief first, so that he will send out the order to the surrounding countryside, requiring that the people present themselves to the military post with their musical instruments; the money one pays afterwards is used to buy a sheep and other food in order to hold a festival in which everyone participates. If the governmental order does not go out, there is no music. All this is almost impossible in times of great heat. The night we recorded at Tafraout we began at ten o'clock, and it was still 108 outside the military post, with the walls giving forth heat like a burning oven. The electricity problem has been serious, too, with towns possessing only small generators which give either 220 volts, or direct current. This caused one small catastrophe, when we had to go out into the wilds at seventy kilometres south of Essaouira in order to record, and slept on the floor of the barracks, only to find that all the electrical information given us by the governmental people was wrong, and that there was no usable current in the region. We had to go back to Essaouira and have the Caïd transport all the musicians there, so that we were three days doing what should have taken one. However, I think I wrote you about that earlier. On the whole, the authorities have been most helpful and cooperative, and it is certainly true that I should have got nowhere without their goodwill and assistance.

I assume that when I get to Tangier I shall have an answer from you regarding the sending of the tapes, as well as instructions as to when you would like the accompanying descriptive sheets which Mr. Spivacke asked me to prepare for each tape. Please let me know whether the report I am sending herewith is satisfactory in its ensemble, or whether you want it done in some other fashion.

I am not certain what region I shall tackle next; I shall try to make it one where the heat is less intense than it has been down in the Anti-Atlas. We had a very unpleasant experience on the trail between Tafraout and Taroudant. There was a three-day sandstorm which clogged the motor of the car, so that it stopped in a part of the desert where there was nothing. We waited all day, but no car came by, and we had only two litres of water with us. The temperature remained above 135 in the shade during the entire day, and the wind was like a sheet of flame. Eventually we found a peasant who fetched us a skin of water—completely filthy water, naturally, but fortunately I had purifying tablets with me, so apart from the foul taste there were no consequences. In the evening a truck came by, and we were able to get word to Taroudant asking for a car to come and tow us there, later that night. I'm afraid this sort of thing is common down there in the summer months, and that is why I'd prefer to go back south when the edge has worn off the summer.

I shall keep you informed of my activities, and am hoping to hear from you in the very near future.

TO HAROLD SPIVACKE,
MUSIC DIVISION, THE LIBRARY OF CONGRESS

October 20, 1959
Khenifra

Enclosed you will find my report for the period September 17th to October 20th. It can scarcely be counted as a typical monthly report, inasmuch as it includes three weeks of work and two weeks of waiting in Tangier. Also, one of the weeks of work includes the time wasted accomplishing next to nothing in Fez. However, I am beginning to grow accustomed to such setbacks, and they do no more than infuriate me, whereas before they discouraged me. All in all, the government has not been too unpleasant about the project. Last week in Khemisset I ran into another intransigent official. I had wanted to get the music of the Zemmour Tribe. He insisted there was none. Of course, I knew there was. So I did some gentle insisting. Finally he showed his hand by saying: "The music of the Zemmour is completely without interest to anyone. Why should it be sent abroad as an example of our culture?" So there was no way of going further. When you meet up with that sort of man, it's useless to attempt to circumvent him, as he has complete power in his region. The best thing is to hurry on somewhere else. Here in Khenifra yesterday I met the Super-Caïd, to whom the katib in Meknès had telephoned two days earlier advising him of my imminent arrival. He was polite but not helpful at the outset. Finally he agreed to contact some cheikhats here. I met them this morning after he had conferred with them. They wanted 70,000 francs for a two-hour session. As a result of haggling and cutting out two singers, I got them down to 27,000 (for four singers and an accompanist). But that is still far too expensive, and God knows how good they will be. I am eager to get out of the Middle Atlas region, and go south where the music is better, more plentiful and far cheaper. But as you can see, tonight I'll have to pay more at one fell swoop than I did for the entire five weeks just past. Naturally I suspect dirty work at the crossroads, between the official and the cheikhats, but there is never any way of proving that sort of thing. You can take the music or leave it, and I decided to take it and go on tomorrow to Beni Mellal. I give you all these details, not because I think they can really be of interest to you or anyone else, but because I want to try and round out the picture of the conditions which apply generally to the project at this time. But as I have said before, technically it wouldn't have been possible to get the music before 1953, from then on until the present year political conditions would have made even this complete a coverage impossible, and from now on there will be increasing resistance to the carrying-out of such projects, as well as more governmental interference where it is allowed, not to mention the fact that the music itself will be disappearing rapidly (particularly the tribal music). So, looked at from the historical point of view, I am really operating under the most propitious conditions possible. That cheers me up! If only the country remains quiet until the end of the year, I think we can count ourselves extremely fortunate in the timing of the project. (There have been no uprisings at all this year, as you no doubt know, nor any war with outsiders.) (Last year there was the rebellion in the Rif as well as the Ifni war with Spain. The extreme south as well as the Rif have been accessible only since the early part of this year.) I also enclose a complete list of all recordings minus one. More anon.

TO WILLIAM BURROUGHS

November 15, 1959
Tangier

Back in Tangier again for a few days, notably the three glorious ones, as our Moslem press enjoys calling them. The Feast of the Throne and the two days which bolster it up, one on each side of it. It's cold, or so it seems to me. Perhaps after Marrakech, where I spent the greater part of the past month—there and in the Middle and Grand Atlas, although God knows it's colder in the Atlas, with snow lying all around. I now have to go to Rabat and see about an injunction the Moroccans just put on my recording project. Perhaps the American Embassy will be able to make itself heard, perhaps not. In any case, I have only another month to go to complete the project. Music from every corner of the kingdom, and very beautiful it is.

Of course I never have seen a shadow of *Naked Lunch*. But I'll look in the Librairie des Colonnes and see if they have it, before asking you to bother finding me a copy in Paris. How long do you intend to be remaining on there? And is it true that you're going to America?

A new antikif law makes it a crime to buy it or be found with it on one's person. I wonder why they bother to pass it without having ruled off at least a third of Moroccan territory for concentration camps. How otherwise can they accommodate the seven or eight million who will have to be incarcerated? As Cherifa says: "Just wind."

Brion has never written me, and I can't write him as I have no address for him. Out of sight, out of mind, perhaps, when one is living in the ville lumière. Me, I try to keep up with my correspondence, although it's difficult to find the time en voyage, since the paper work connected with the project takes literally every minute. No time for any fun, no time for anything but eating and sleeping and arranging recording sessions in government offices and getting across fords and condemned bridges to lost villages where a caid or khalifa waits with a troop of dancers and drummers. I try to answer all letters once a month when I'm back here in benighted Tangier (everyone now belongs to one of two groups: those who are leaving when the charter expires and those who have decided to stay) to cash my Rockefeller check which brings just about 50,000 francs more each month here than it would elsewhere in Morocco.

I hear Paul Lund is often seen with the guy who wrote the song "Show Me the Way to Go Home." Party gossip in the American set. Personally I know nothing, see nobody. I hear Ahmed is in Paris with the Marquis de L'Angle, whoever that is. His baby isn't yet born, although his common-law mother-in-law has arrived from Chicago or wherever in order to be in on the birthpangs. Jay Haselwood has been in New York for the first time since the war, and is due back this Friday. Apart from such tidbits I can't think of any local news capable of awakening any interest at your end. I have no plans, although it's possible that sometime during the winter I might go to Cairo and points south. The Assuan Dam is to be blessed in twelve weeks or so, isn't it?

And so now, touched by the last rays of the setting sun, we reluctantly say goodbye to lovely Aïn Hayani, leaving her enchanted purlieus to the tender mercies of the African dusk. Mysterious Aïn Hayani will be there waiting for us when next we turn our footsteps toward her fragrant alleys, her magic welcome ever fresh, ever delightful, like some inscrutable houri beckoning across her scented veils from her languorous corner of paradise. Adieu, Aïn Hayani!

Two ladies have moved in upstairs, live directly over us in Christopher's apartment. They hope to drive to Mombasa, but the thing is obviously impossible from here. "But it's not a real war in Algeria. It's just a few small areas of disaffection. That's what the French told us. They did say we'd have to wait several months for the visa, but once we get that we're all fixed up." So they wait.

If you get this, let me hear.

TO HAROLD SPIVACKE,

MUSIC DIVISION, THE LIBRARY OF CONGRESS

December 7, 1959
Hotel Transatlantique
Meknès

I have some interesting if unpleasant news to communicate to you (save that coming as it does at this late date, it can't really affect the project very profoundly). The Moroccan government has finally put the heat on: day before yesterday I was told in no uncertain terms by the Secretary General of the Province of Ksar-es-Souk that my document from the Présidence du Conseil at Rabat was worthless and that I could make no recordings without special permission from the Ministère de l'Intérieur. The new ruling amounts to a prohibition to make any recordings at all in Morocco.

From Tinerhir I went down into the desert to Erfoud, called on the Super-Caïd there as usual, and attempted to set up a recording session. He hedged, said he would have to get in touch with Ksar-es-Souk, then kept me on tenter-hooks for three days while I cooled my heels standing around outside his office. I decided I was wasting time, especially when he finally refused to receive me any more, even to tell me he had heard nothing further from Ksar-es-Souk— packed up and went myself to Ksar-es-Souk to see the authorities there. And there I was treated like a suspected spy on whom they hadn't really quite "got the goods," but who would soon be proven guilty and dealt with. So I travelled about a thousand kilometres out of my way for nothing, and am back here in Meknès as of last night, because I had already arranged (as I think I told you) to return here to record more Andaluz music. I'm hoping against hope that the people (semi-official) with whom I've made the arrangements will not have heard of my difficulties, and will allow the thing to go through. It will obviously not be possible to make any further tapes of folk-music, since the authorities are necessary in order to find and assemble the performers in such cases, but I'm counting on the government's not being quite efficient and swift enough to prevent my getting the material I've already arranged beforehand to get: the Andaluz and the Jewish songs.

I'm flabbergasted by the childishness of the government's procedure, which can only be the result of internal political squabbles, and I keep reminding myself of how lucky it is that the thing happened only after almost all the desired material was already recorded and safe in the offices of the American Embassy. There would have been no remedy had it happened earlier in the project. These people are unobliging and adamant. When the Secretary General informed me that my governmental document was useless, I asked him if he would mind writing as much on the document. He refused in an access of anger, saying that the sound of his own voice was enough for him, and that he would put nothing in writing. I said then that if I wanted something in writing to show my own government I supposed I should have to go to Rabat to get it, since naturally I had to show cause for not fulfilling the obligations of my project. He replied with a sneer, saying that if I did so, I would get more than I expected in the way of an answer. I thanked him and left the office, taking my worthless document with me.

I have spoken with the man who was to help me arrange the Andaluz session here in Meknès; he appears to have had no counter-orders regarding the affair and is willing to go ahead with the business; I'm counting heavily on that, and shall be bitterly disappointed if something occurs to prevent it. Actually, if that and the Jewish music can be secured, I shan't be too unhappy about the whole thing, as the only material which will have been lost as a result will be the folk music of the Tafilalt, the extreme south-eastern Morocco, although I naturally deplore not having it in order to round out the collection of tribal material. What I am angry about is their behavior with me, their lack of candor, their hypocrisy and the conspiratorial fashion in which they carry out their secret directives. There seems to be no way of getting a direct answer out of them. I could have waited indefinitely there at Erfoud for the musicians to be called, and would never have extracted even so much as a flat: "no." The absurd details of their behavior are too numerous and involved to recount in a letter, but it is enough to say that they are the opposite of what one would expect from government officials in any country. They have their ridiculous side, too, but I'm afraid that it will be only in recollection that I shall be able to find them amusing. Needless to say, I shan't go near another governmental office; that would be asking for trouble. What I manage to get (if anything) will have to be done quietly.

I'm sorry to have this sob-story to relate, but there's nothing to do about it, and I thought you ought to be kept *au courant* of all things relating to the project. I shall continue to keep you informed as to my success with the two sessions (or three, possibly) in prospect.

Until soon, then.

TO HAROLD SPIVACKE,
MUSIC DIVISION, THE LIBRARY OF CONGRESS

December 23, 1959
Tangier

I arrived back in Tangier last night, and found your letter of November twenty-third waiting for me. I hope you received my most recent missive sent from Erfoud or wherever it was, telling about the refusal of the secretary of the Governor of the Province of Ksar-es-Souk to accept my document from the central government at Rabat. I went on up to Meknès and discovered that the Andaluz musicians had already refused to record unless I paid them 50,000 francs an hour, which actually meant 100,000 francs an hour, since the secretary of the local musicians' union, or what corresponds to such an organization here, told me that I should also have to pay the same sum to the group of Melhoun (qsida) musicians who had recorded for me three months earlier without charge. (Why they did that I have never understood, but it was very kind of them. However, the secretary felt that he could not allow them to donate their services if the Andaluz men were paid, so that whatever sum the latter collected would have also to be given the Melhoun men.) Such sums were entirely outside my possibilities at that point, and would have been at any point, so I did not accept the Andaluz group's offer. For any sort of session it would have cost me $400, which was almost as bad as the Fez people's demand. However, I found a gold-mine right there in Meknès in the Jewish music, so I stayed on there and made three recordings, including one evening in the largest synagogue, where I got the entire service. They were charming and helpful in every way, and I am delighted that chance made me return to Meknès just then. I also recorded a program of modern popular music, which is a genre I had completely neglected until then. I got the muezzins of Fez, and then returned to Marrakech where I captured an excellent ensemble of Soussi music. That was the lot, and made exactly sixty tapes. I returned to Rabat with these and left them at the Embassy (which was in a tizzy because of Eisenhower's arrival the following day at Casablanca, and also because of the local political developments, which are disturbing indeed), left the equipment at the Embassy Annex, and came on to Tangier, being stopped on the road four times by soldiers who searched the car for hidden guns. I add that last phrase because the country is ostensibly on the brink of civil war at the moment, and consequently I can't help feeling even more lucky than I did last week that my project just happened to fall during the one calm year Morocco has known this decade. Now the whole round of murders and riots has started again, and nobody knows just what is going to happen. What is sure is that it would not be possible now to circulate freely everywhere as I have been doing since July, and get the government to help me find musicians. So the whole thing has been a piece of incredible good fortune. (Although until you have the tapes in your possession I shan't feel completely at ease about them.)

In this envelope I enclose a rough map I drew, to show the geographical coverage of the country. The red route in the southeast part with no towns indicated is my fruitless trek to Ksar-es-Souk province and the oases of Tafilalt. I've shown only the places where recordings were made.

With the sixty tapes I have also included five more in which all the important genres are represented. I thought these might be useful to whoever was going to study the music, in that they would enable him to identify the various (and widely divergent) kinds of music quickly, without having to consult the actual body of tapes. The quality of these copies is very bad, but that is unimportant for identification purposes. I did not choose necessarily what I thought were the best examples of each genre—merely representative ones. I hope this condensing of sixty tapes into five may prove useful to someone. At the close of Tape I, I included a pronouncing list of place-names and recordings groups.

At the Embassy Annex I collected my remaining tapes (unrecorded) and left one hundred thirty-five new tapes there with the equipment: the difference between sixty-five and two hundred. I hope that was the correct procedure. Naturally, no one at the Embassy had any idea of what was supposed to be done, either with the equipment or the tapes.

Now that the project is completed, I feel very much encouraged about its results. The collection, while not exhaustive, is certainly complete in that it contains good examples of every major variety of music which is to be found in Morocco, both in the city and the country. I think you will agree that the music is very much worthwhile recording, apart from any consideration of its being about to disappear.

Do you want me to prepare the regular monthly report of expenditures and send it to you, or is that not necessary for the final month? I hope to hear from you soon.

Whatever happens here within the Moroccan government, I am assuming that the Embassy in Rabat will be able to get the tapes safely out of the country and to Washington. I know there are people in high places in Rabat who are intent on preventing the tapes from reaching their destination, for the simple reason that they are so stupid that they imagine that the diffusion of such music abroad will hamper their efforts to persuade the world at large that Morocco is a modern, "civilized" country, and might thus indirectly reduce foreign investment. These men are a tiny minority but a powerful one; they are all city-bred and have never even heard Moroccan tribal music. They hate to admit that such a thing still exists in spite of their "deculturizing" programs, and the last thing they want is for the world outside (and particularly the United States) to possess evidence of what they consider to be their great shame—i.e.: the fact that Morocco is in general an unusually primitive region the vast majority of whose inhabitants have not been imbued with Arab culture, in spite of some eleven centuries of effort on the part of the Arab conquerors. This is an important part of their policy, both internally and externally, and by flouting it I have made even more enemies among that particular group of men. Eventually I shall probably be expelled from the country in any case, and this will just be one more count against me, so I am not unduly worried about it!

Let's say that if the tapes reach you in good condition I shall be more than satisfied.

THE 1960S

January 9, 1960
Tangier

Your letter of December fifteenth arrived a day or so after I got back from my last trip in the south. The holidays brought with them such a lot of ordinary daily activity that I haven't gotten around to answer it, or about two dozen other letters, until now. Nothing special happened, except that we went out a good deal more than we usually do, and people came in in quantities. The English of course go on giving parties through Twelfth Night, and since Tangier seems to have more English in it than ever, everything was very busy. I did manage to get some work done during the holiday period, which was surprising, but it was at the expense of my correspondence. The weather has been magnificent until yesterday. Now it is dark and rainy—typical bad Tangier winter weather. (I am running my paragraphs together in order to have more room.) Your new house sounds wonderful. What astonishes me is the speed with which it seems to be being constructed. I'm so used to the idea of its taking a year or so to build a house that when you speak in terms of weeks it seems impossible. Keep me posted as to its progress, and when you can, send some snaps. From all the things you've both always said, I never thought you'd be settling in Florida, but it does seem to be a very good idea from every point of view, and I'm sure you'll be happy there. The next time I go back to New York to do a show, I'll have to take a longer trip to see you than the "F" train to Union Turnpike provides! But I am eager to see your new set-up, of course. Your enclosed Christmas present arrived with your letter, and although I thank you for thinking of me, I don't think you should have sent anything at such a time, when you were putting everything into one big project like a house. I haven't used it yet, but I'll do as you suggest, and take Janie out somewhere to a delayed celebration one of these nights. Incidentally, she is very well and happy. Since I got back here last May fifteenth she has had only two attacks, and they have both been very short-lived and light. Both came in the wake of a period when she had been overdoing or getting overexcited. She has put on weight, and looks very healthy and well, and everyone remarks on it. There's no particular news. Negotiations are hanging fire for me to do a piece for *Life* on Fez; I'm waiting to hear from my agent. Then I have three articles to do for *Holiday*. All that will take a very long time, particularly as one of the pieces involves going to

Egypt (as you know) and scouring the Nile Valley. That will come last, and may of course at any point be decided against by them, or made impossible by outside developments. Apart from those writing plans, I have no projects. As you may have read, we are losing our charter in Tangier in April, which will mean that money can no longer move in and out of Tangier; once it enters it will be frozen, and the rate will be fixed by Rabat. I suppose it means inevitably that prices will soar sky-high, but we'll have to wait and see just how high before we make any decisions. Christopher Wanklyn is giving up his apartment and going to Portugal, but he intends to return eventually, so he says. In general the Americans and English are staying on, while the French and Spanish are leaving in droves. Which is all right, since the Moroccans like the Anglo-Saxons better than the Latins anyway. Perhaps the latter have been here long enough! We had a postcard yesterday from Donald Angus, whom we went to have drinks with one day when you were here. He is in Nairobi in Kenya, expects to be back sometime in March. Anne Harbach has been away all autumn in Italy and London, is due here next week. Yacoubi has a baby girl. Temsamany is in high society now. Dubbs is dead. He was living with Anne Harbach, as you know, and her Siamese contracted distemper, which poor Dubbs caught and never got over. When she went away she left him with Temsamany, and it was there that he died. I was very sad about it, as you can imagine. The grey parrot is brilliant in his conversation now. The green one still has nothing to say, but he sings a good deal. We still have three servants: Mina, Miriam and Angèle. Please give my love to everyone, and let me hear from you. And a delayed Happy New Year from me!

TO CHARLES-HENRI FORD

January 10, 1960
Tangier

Your Roman postcard has been in my pile of unanswered correspondence for many weeks, but because I was moving around constantly the pile merely augmented its height as the weeks went by. I was working on a project of recording Moroccan music for the Rockefeller Foundation; the project came to an end on the thirty-first of December, since when I've been a good deal more free.

I'm curious to know why you left Paris and whether you intend going back there when you've finished (if you do finish) with Rome. I seem never to get to any large cities any more except New York and London, and of those two New York makes me nervous and London has such foul air that it makes me literally ill. (The last time I was there I had both Asian flu and pneumonia complicated by pleurisy.) I did go to San Francisco last winter for a fortnight, and I spent a few months in Lisbon, neither of which is really a metropolis, naturally. What good are big cities? Has Paris still a life as it had thirty years ago? I wouldn't know because I haven't lived there in that long. Rome doubtless has, but is it a life one wants to be a part of? These are straight questions, not rhetorical ones. Because you're painting now, perhaps the answer to both is in the affirmative. Otherwise it might not be; I don't know, but I ask for information.

News—I don't know, either, about that. Have I any? I saw Ruth and Zachary in New York last spring. They were entertaining Karen Blixen and there was a terrific crush. I got the impression that everybody was there at once. Maurice Grosser was painting around Morocco this past summer; I saw him often in Rabat while I was there trying to get documents from the government. He went to New York and has never written. Brion Gysin no longer lives here, as you certainly know. In fact, most people have left Tangier, and more are leaving each week. Shops are closing, there is a bad economic crisis, the Moroccans have no work and are becoming criminally inclined as a result. Since Moroccans are not supposed any longer to know Europeans personally, no one has any Moroccan friends; the old pattern of mixed gatherings is gone, and the next step is to get rid of all non-Moroccans en masse. For that to happen, however, there has to be a change of government first, and that doesn't seem at the moment to be imminent. The only reason for being here now is the fact that one is here and it takes energy to find a new place to settle. After April it will be impossible to take anything out, in any case. Bank accounts will be frozen. (This obviously is the reason why so many people are rushing out now while they can take their money with them.)

Jane, who had a cerebral haemorrhage three years ago, is gradually recovering; she still can't read or write, which makes time pass slowly for her. Tangier is the best place for her; with a maid she can get around the streets. In New York she had to be in a hospital.

So this is my news; what's yours, besides the fact of being in Rome? Later in the year I'll probably go to Egypt for a few weeks, and then to Ceylon. This will doubtless involve my going to Genoa or Naples in order to make ship connections. (I won't fly.) Perhaps you'll be there.

TO JAMES PURDY

January 15, 1960
Tangier

Now that my Rockefeller journeying is over and I am here in Tangier, I have
a little leisure in which to write things like letters, stories and articles. Whatever
time there was during the work on the project (and there was extremely little,
since I passed most of it driving, waiting in government offices and doing the
actual recording) I had to spend compiling documentation on the material
recorded. That went on seemingly forever. The whole five-and-a-half-month
period was like one of these exceedingly strenuous vacations that people (not I)
go on, and from which they return more exhausted than when they started out.
Malcolm is the first complete book that Jane has read—and the only one—since
her illness three years ago. It took her three and a half months, exactly, to
complete the reading, but the fact that she was actually able to do it is a miracle.
The other day I noticed that she was depressed, but said nothing; a little later
she said sadly: "Malcolm's dead." She lived in the book during the time she was
reading it; she says it is one of the great books of this century. Now that she has
finished it (as of today) I can reread it. Forgive my long silence. All my best.

TO WILLIAM BURROUGHS

March 24, 1960
Marrakech

Today is Thursday and I was expected to go to the camel market, but since
I've been in the past as often as there are bicycles in Marrakech, I let it slide.
Naked Lunch is on sale here at the Mamounia, along with Churchill's Memoirs
and Pearl Buck. Two tourists looking at it: "It's rather expensive. I don't know
as I want to pay a pound for it." "Oh, is it a pound? I didn't realize." "Anyway,
I've got the Tropic of Capricorn book. That's quite enough." (Turning to the
proprietor:) "I say, have you got today's *Times* and last Sunday's *Observer*?" A
wild-haired halfwit in the Djemaa el Fna rushes up to me, does a double shuffle
and bump, says: "Good morning, sir. I represent the authentic original Moroccan
automatic comic." He does another bump and adds: "May I entertain you? It's
elegant, magnificent." This all in French. I say in Arabic: "We don't want

anything, thank you." He is disappointed, says sadly: "O.K., boy. How bout what nother day you like?" There are so many Germans around that most of the Djemaa el Fna characters go into that language at some point, although this one didn't. Down in the desert we had locusts and a sandstorm, but no earthquake, thank God. I dreamed of Brion last night; met him in the street and he didn't want to speak to me. I couldn't tell why, although I asked him outright. He smiled mysteriously. That's the trouble with friends who are bad correspondents: they gnaw at one's dreams. I wonder why he refuses to write. Jane was fine when I left her on March seventh. What are your plans? Has anyone ever sung the praises of the Seychelles in your presence? I keep hearing about what a paradise the place is. But it's hard to get to; ordinarily you have to go to Bombay first and take a ship from there. I'll be back in Tangier by the end of the month. No news.

TO RENA AND CLAUDE BOWLES
———————◆———————
September 4, 1960
Tangier

We are in the middle of more festivities; you know how they cramp one's style in this town, shutting off the streets, which are full of marching soldiers and parades. This time, with the Sultan here, they divide the town into two parts, like Berlin, and you can't get from one sector into the other. I don't know what the idea is, but it makes for great inconvenience. Yesterday Jane and I were just about to leave to go up onto the Mountain to a house where we were invited, when the doorbell rang, and it was Anne Harbach in a state because she had been trying to drive home and couldn't, so she wanted to sit somewhere for an hour or so. We told her she could stay here, but she didn't want to be alone, and it being a holiday, we had no servants at all. Today I haven't been out, but the whole town is crammed with Moroccans from other parts of the country, come to see the Mouloud being observed under the auspices of the Sultan. The people still seem to believe he can do something to bring back prosperity to Tangier, but nothing is going to bring back all the Europeans who have taken their capital elsewhere; every fourth or fifth shop or bank or office is empty, with "To Let" signs on it. Both the English and French-language newspapers were suppressed this week, and there is great indignation about that. The only non-Arabic paper left is the Spanish one, which they say will be shut down soon. I can't believe they will forbid the importation of papers from London and Paris, but of course they may; who knows? I get the news on the radio from the Voice of America rebroadcast from Tangier, which is very hard to understand, since it comes halfway around the world to get here. I am writing all this without paragraphs because it leaves more room for words; if I use more than two of these sheets of paper I shall have to wait in line forever to get the letter weighed. With two sheets I know I can put on seventy-five francs and have done with it. We have been right here all the time since I last wrote. Maurice Grosser has left to meet Virgil in Portugal, and Christopher Wanklyn has returned from his six month's tour around Europe. Gordon Sager went to Lisbon, didn't like it, went to London expecting to settle, didn't like it, and finally went to Athens, where I assume he does like it since he is staying on there. Peggy Bate is there, too, having decided to live in Greece indefinitely. I sent off my piece to *Life* and they liked it, so that's off my mind. Now I have two more pieces for *Holiday* to write before going to Egypt, so I don't imagine I'll get off before January. I've also completed the song-cycle I was writing, must have it photostated and take it to Gibraltar along with other things I want to mail from there. (I took a chance and mailed the article to *Life* from here, and it got through all right. A short story I posted to London doesn't seem to have had the same luck.) We had a gala affair here last Monday night. Barbara Hutton gave a big party for some two hundred guests, many of whom had come down from London and Paris. The entire Casbah was full of cars and police detailed to help the guests through the streets; one had the feeling that all Tangier had been put on the payroll for that night. Since we had received an invitation, we went, and Jane was busy for a week beforehand trying to arrange her clothes. You can imagine the excitement! Anne was busy having a new evening dress made for the occasion. Every hour there were telephonic consultations, and Jane changed her mind at least twenty times about going and not going. We did finally go, and everything came off all right. It was the most visually attractive party I've ever seen. Every detail had been planned, and the house looked like a palace ready to receive a Sultan in the Thousand and One Nights. There was even a throne room, with a throne from India (insured for $1,000,000) encrusted with literally thousands of pearls, rubies, sapphires and emeralds; the cushions one sat on were embroidered with real gems, big ones, so that they were not even very comfortable, but still, no one cared! There was a jazz orchestra on the top terrace, a group of gypsies dancing in one patio, a Moroccan orchestra with dancers in another room, and a concert pianist performing on an inner balcony in another part of the house. I've never seen so many glamorous evening dresses. And no one got drunk—at least, not by three, when we left. Since the party went on until nine the next morning, I can't vouch for those who stayed on. I noticed members of the secret police circulating among the guests; each guest had been insured for a million francs, in case of accident or loss. At one point an English woman I was sitting with exclaimed to her husband: "It's gone!" She was feeling of her wrist and referring to a bracelet. There was no point in searching for it in that crowd of guests and servants, and I never heard whether she got it back. It was the biggest party to be given here since the war, and it set Tangier agog. You can imagine the Moslems in the street lined up along the roofs above, looking down at the excitement going on in the Hutton house. Rumor had got around that invitations were being resold for 20,000 francs each, and they had a special squad at the door to check each arrival's name. They turned away more than thirty people who were trying to crash the affair with invitations they had purchased from scalpers. One woman arrived saying: "But my husband owns all the Mecca dance-halls in England." (Some chain of cheap entertainment palaces.) Another woman, the wife of a banker here, went into hysterics when she was refused admission, and had to be carried away weeping and threatening. Richard Rumbold and Hilda Young were not invited, and took it so hard that they decided to leave the next day by plane for London, thus cutting their stay here by a week. "Why should one stay where one isn't wanted?" they demanded. I was astonished to see that people still feel so strongly about such things, especially fairly bright people like them. Of course the British have a great sense of protocol and class, but still, a party is only a party, after all. I am wondering if your hot weather is calming down somewhat, now that it's September, and how your blood pressure is. You must send me a picture of the house so I can imagine you in it. It must be very pleasant there. And it will be nice when Autumn comes and you read of cold waves in the north, to know that you don't have to worry about it. Janie and I are alone today, because of the holiday, and she is upstairs at the moment at Christopher's, waiting for me to finish this letter so we can have lunch, so I suppose I should stop before she starves. I did want to get a note off to you, however, before we start another week of activity, with letters being put off from day to day. These days of festival are very difficult because of food. There is no way of buying any and no one to prepare it, and if one needs this or that one can't send out for it or go and get it oneself because everything is closed day after day, and there are no taxis. One has to stock up and trust that one has thought of everything beforehand. The two parrots are fine and Berred (Jane's cat, if you remember) is extremely lively because of some new vitamine she found for her. She eats two of those and begins to gallop around the apartment like a maniac, attacking everyone's legs and the furniture as well. I miss Dubbs. I think I told you Temsamany had gone to Germany to live. Hamburg, I believe. I hope he enjoys it, although I don't see how he could after Tangier. Yacoubi is living with the daughter of Will Rogers, who has taken up residence here.

I must stop. Jane has just come downstairs. Much love.

TO BARBARA TURNER,

CONTACT EDITIONS, SAUSALITO, CALIFORNIA
——————————————◆——————————————
December 14, 1960
Rock Hotel
Gibraltar

Thank you for your letter of November twenty-eighth. I can see that the collecting of the sort of recipes I should like to send you is going to take a good deal more work than I had imagined. Since you have a deadline of February first, it would perhaps be more practical if I renounced the project and sent you the one recipe I have been able to get for you. The Moroccans don't want to divulge their secret formulas for managing one another. They merely smile when I ask them, and say: "There is food for every purpose, if you know how to prepare it." One Marrakechi was kind enough to give me the following information (which can scarcely be considered a recipe for anything), and I give it to you merely to show you the sort of thing they are willing to give. It's called BEID EL BEITA F'KERR EL HMAR,* and requires three nights to prepare. "Buy an egg. Find a dead donkey, and the first night lodge the egg in its anus. The second night the egg must be put into a mousehole on top of a Moslem tomb. The third night it must be wrapped in a handkerchief and tied around the chest of the person desiring to perform the magic. The following day it must be given for breakfast, prepared in any fashion, to the other individual, who immediately upon eating it discovers that the bestower is necessary for his happiness." (Or her happiness; the sex of the two people seems to have nothing to do with the charm's efficacy.) But this is not a serious recipe, obviously, and I keep running into this sort of thing, rather than bonafide cookery secrets. (There are, of course, ordinary Moroccan dishes, not designed to produce any particular effect, and

---

* A white egg in a donkey's anus.

they are easy enough to get, but since I promised to send you the other sort, you wouldn't be likely to be interested in the formulas for Mrozeyia or Bastela.) Thus, regretfully I send the one enclosed true recipe, for Majoun. It comes from Fez, and has nothing to do with the one Alice Toklas included in her book, which was from Ksar el Kebhir. I'm sorry to let you down this way, but I haven't the time to undertake a gastronomical tour of the land.

TO CHARLES-HENRI FORD

February 7, 1961
Tangier

This needn't count as my annual missive. (I hadn't been aware there was such an institution, but if there is, this can be overlooked, as it's going to be very brief.)

If you go to Marrakech will you be passing through Tangier? Or will you avoid it? Marrakech is still the best city for folk-art, which you aren't looking for, obviously. Apart from that, the climate ought to be good there in March. I haven't been there since shortly before Christmas, when it was glacial. I took two heaters with me to use in my bedroom, and still had to wear a heavy woollen djellaba. By next month it ought to be as warm as, or even warmer than, Tangier. Last March I was there at the Mamounia for nine days, and it rained every day but one, and on that day there was a violent dust-storm, so that the sky was darker than on the rainy days. Unfortunately I know no one in Morocco—not in Marrakech, nor in Fez, nor in Rabat, nor in Tangier. Neither Europeans nor Moslems. Most of those I used to know before the war have died—the Moroccans, I mean. The Europeans have left, of course. I haven't bothered to make any new acquaintances since the war. (They are far less sympathetic than they used to be, but you needn't quote me because we would like to go on living here if possible, simply because it's too much trouble to pull up stakes and move.) On the other hand, you may easily find them pleasant; I don't know. They now all wear European clothing and behave the same as Europeans, which naturally deprives them of exotic interest, and since that is the only sort they ever had for me, they are now no more amusing than anyone living in Jersey City or Brooklyn—if that much. However, their manners are generally pleasant, particularly with non-residents. Let me hear more definitely if and when you intend to be in Tangier.

TO CHARLES-HENRI FORD

February 18, 1961
Tangier

How could my letter of information about Morocco be encouraging? Or are you being ironic? In any case, I'm glad you intend to come, and I hope you manage to pass through Tangier. I've heard various things about the *Sodom and Gomorrah* company and their location in the mountains near Ouarzazate. It seems they have found a particularly good casbah, but are building something wholly factitious beside it, so they can mix the false with the true. But obviously they couldn't have the décor for Sodom look recognizably Moroccan.

You ask me what my "chosen form of transportation" would be between Paris and Tangier. I suppose I should do as I used to do: take a train to Marseille and either the *Djenné* or the *Koutoubia* on here. But obviously if you don't mind flying, the plane is infinitely easier . . . something like four hours does the whole thing, which is otherwise three days of moving. I haven't done Paris–Tangier for twelve years, simply because I haven't gone to Paris. I take a ship to London ordinarily, and don't cross over to France at all. (I'm waiting for it to have a new government, but I think I may wait the rest of my life. Franco and Salazar are all right, but not de Gaulle. And not the ones who preceded him, like Mollet and Schmollet and Follet.)

I'd suggest the Hermitage for you if and when you come. It's a small, quiet hotel removed from the center of town, and has good food, if you are interested. There are, of course, many more central hotels. I don't dare ask you to stay here, because I think you would be too uncomfortable. It is far from town, and in the apartment where you would be there is no telephone to call a cab with, nor at the moment of writing any hot water. A part ça, c'est possible. Anyway, write and let me know your plans when they become definite.

TO NED ROREM

February 25, 1961
Tangier

GUESS WHO COMES NEXT WEEK: CHARLES-HENRI FORD
       "   "   "   "   MONTH: JOHN GOODWIN

Mail now takes roughly double the time it used to take, to get from the United States to Morocco. Whether this is due to the extra time necessitated by the censors at this end, who have to pass on each piece of mail, or not, is a moot question. Some say yes; some say no. Buffalo University? Who could have come here to Tangier recently who told me you were there? I can't recall. But an awful lot of people pass through here during any given season, and hand out scraps of news. Who they all are, God knows. The telephone rings. "Hello. Is this Paul Bowles?" "Speaking." "Well, this is Don Runcible. Elaine Schreiberman told me to look you up." "Who? I mean, who told you?" "Elaine Schreigerman, or is it Schiffelman?" "I don't know, I'm afraid." "Well, she's a friend of Muriel Rukeyser's." "Oh, really?" "She told me to be sure and look you up if I went to Morocco." "I see." Then there's generally a very long silence, while I try to think of reasons why I can't see anybody for the next three days. I did write a song-cycle last summer for Alice Esty, since you ask if occasionally I write tunes. I think she's doing it this winter. I don't know why Lilla should tell you I expect to be in Paris at any time in the future. Perhaps a gypsy told her. But I hope the gypsy's wrong. I expect to stay not only in Morocco, but in Tangier. That's about all I know of my future, except that at one point I'll go to Ceylon for a while. I wish you were intending to come here to Tangier instead of Rabat. However, perhaps you would be able to make a side trip up here. Rabat has become very modern. One-act plays? For Gian Carlo?

TO RICHARD SEAVER,
GROVE PRESS, NEW YORK

May 8, 1961
Tangier

Bill Burroughs tells me he has already sent off a letter to you about the enclosed typescripts, and so I want to get them into the mail as soon as I can.

For the past decade or so I have been collecting legends and tales, both on tape and directly in writing, provided for me by Moroccans adept in the art of story-telling. The literary tradition here is a strictly oral one, and it is not surprising that the most successful results should come, even at this late date, from illiterates. Story-telling has always been a national pastime here in Morocco; Yacoubi tells me that as a child he used to go daily to the cemetery outside the walls of Fez and sit for hours listening to the professional tale-spinners who made their living like minstrels wandering from town to town entertaining the populace. He remembers the stories, but when he comes to tell his own, he improvises. The enclosed text was recorded in October 1956, and I did not play it back until March of this year, when, since Yacoubi was not available, Mohammed Larbi Djilali helped me to prepare an exact translation of it. Nothing has been deleted or added or altered; the English version is a literal translation.

When I showed it to Burroughs, he was enthusiastic, and I suggested that he might want to furnish some comments. This he agreed to do. I enclose both texts. If you want further information of any sort, please don't hesitate to write and ask me.

TO RUTH FAINLIGHT AND ALAN SILLITOE
_____◆_____

July 26, 1961
Marrakech-Medina

Shortly before your letter arrived, another postal notice came, which I threw away. I imagine you haven't yet received the magazines. And then I came down here with Christopher [Wanklyn] and Allen Ginsberg, and we lived in and out of the new house which Christopher and I jointly rented last month when we were on our way to Essaouira. Or perhaps I've already written you about all that. The house is massive, hideously uncomfortable and primitive the way a machine-made chromolithograph of Mecca is primitive. That is to say it's a new Moslem-style house instead of an old óne. All the disadvantages of European contact and none of the advantages of being Moroccan. Quite the opposite of what the Japanese have accomplished. But anyway, it's a challenge, and the roof is magnificent by midnight when the temperature of the air drops from 115 shade to around 100. Then we lie on grass mats in sarongs, listen to music, smoke kif, drink mint tea, talk and look at the stars. At two-thirty a ring of lights around the house, about a half-mile distant, goes on, and the concert of muezzins commences. Each light is at the top of a minaret, and they are tall, and there are twenty or more of them. Unfortunately the mosque nearest to our house doesn't see fit to hire a muezzin with a good voice, so a good many of the finer points from the more distant muezzins are necessarily lost, while the bellower nearby goes into his frenzies screaming: Allah Akbar! The concert, which lasts until nearly five each morning, is almost identical every night. (I've recorded it several times.) There is a big ensemble of calls, then a long trio, always among the same three men, which lasts well over a half hour. One of these three does a Swiss yodel very well, which he artistically spaces throughout his text. I like the effect, but the bellower despises it and always covers it up, even though it means he has to shout himself hoarse. (There is supposed to be a rest of more or less equal length to the strophe after each cadence.) Eventually this aesthetic battle between the black towers on the horizon builds up too much tension, and there is another ensemble number, with thin obbligati of whining song like the sound of beggars, which is the most beautiful of all, I think. The calls subside, and then in leisurely fashion they all begin to sing. This goes on for a good hour, and only subsides with the dawn. Our house is a gigantic bird-cage; the birds who were living in it while it was empty, before we came, have no intention of moving out. They fly in and out all day, and perch at night in dark corners, without having any nests. It seems that the oasis here is an ornithologist's paradise: some four thousand varieties live here, and many of them live *only* here and aren't found elsewhere. The heat is pretty bad. It does something to one to live always in the midst of air that is hotter than one's blood. One becomes permanently giddy, and nothing seems particularly real. Only late at night when there is a breeze and the sun's heat has finally gone from the walls does one come alive. The rest is various stages of sleep. The appetite suffers, of course, and there isn't enough water, ever. It's traditionally a city of epidemics, so I don't touch the tap-water. I keep telling myself I'll buy a case of Vichy, for the shops open and shut on whim, and I never seem to have any to drink. Christopher will drink anything, so I am alone in my precautious predicament. Last week the final gem of Morocco went up in smoke. It was the Semmarine Souk here just outside our house, the great dramatic entrance into the medina of Marrakech, the reason why we took the house. More than five hundred shops burned with all their merchandise, and the whole quarter has got to be rebuilt. But it will no longer be of carved wood with ceilings of reed lattices over the streets. The whole medina smelled of charred wood and wetted down smoke for four days after the fire. On the roofs below us there are thousands of bolts of cloth, partially burned, spread out over a space a quarter of a mile square. Brocades and lamés—a great deal of gold thread is used—and out of the corner of one's eye one might say there was a huge troupe of Berber dancing girls down there on the terraces. The whole assortment glistens in the moonlight; guards are on duty all night, and call to each other in the dark. An enormous amount of money was lost; insurance covered only about a fifth of the merchandise. Everyone is feeling very poor around town these days, for the catastrophe will ruin the tourist business. Practically every bazaar of interest was destroyed, together with a treasury of ancient Moroccan objects. Perhaps the Medina will be pleasanter without tourists. I don't know. But it's a disaster for Marrakech, and for Morocco.

I hadn't realised that your projected return would be put off quite so far as you now say it is. I'm sorry it will be so late. I'm always intending to go to Ceylon, but I don't seem to go. This means that I'm thinking of it again for this winter. But the house here in Marrakech is obviously going to exert some pull in this direction, so it's a moot question as to which way I'll go.

Allen G. stayed with us exactly a week; we saw him off into the hot-looking wooden train for Casablanca day before yesterday. You ought to know him; I think you'd like him. Very easy to get on with, even in the most difficult circumstances, and full of a wonderful sweetness which is absolutely real, and integrated with his intellect. Being with him makes me aware of how very rare the quality is, particularly in intellectuals! Which Allen, practically alone among the Beats, certainly is.

We'll be going to Tangier in a day or two. Jane was well and working when I left her ten days ago. Keep us posted. Love to you both.

TO RENA AND CLAUDE BOWLES

September 12, 1961
Tangier

Here I am, writing without any news to give you. So little happens here that practically anything can be construed as news, but precisely because of that one is inclined to discount everything as uninteresting. Right now we are following news of two separate hurricanes which seem to be stirring up trouble in the States. Neither one is in your region, as far as I can make out from the report. Our own weather goes on being the same as always—clear and cool. I suppose your hot spell is over by now. You were telling me of the extreme heat in August. I expect to go back to Marrakech next month, when the south is cooler. Still waiting to hear whether my article reached *Holiday* or not, and if it did, whether they want changes.

Don't complain about your postage going up. Ours went up some time ago. This letter costs the equivalent of twenty-one cents, as do all my letters to the U.S. The rates on manuscripts are much higher. What costs two dollars to send eastward costs about five to send westward. I don't know why there is such a discrepancy as soon as the initial basic postage is topped by weight. Except that the postal system is considered a luxury, and is used primarily by Europeans still. (The authorities exercise their right to examine mail, of course, so that many letters come already torn open, which is a nuisance.) Which reminds me that we can no longer get the Voice of America on the radio, nor, most of the time, the BBC either, both being covered by jamming. What we get now is Peking (very strong), Moscow and Havana, all broadcasting in English, French and Spanish, and all over all the wave bands. There isn't much point in having a radio any more. We also get illegal stations in Algeria, also spouting political news, but they are more interesting because they at least include native music sometimes. It surprises me that Havana should be so present so far away, but the programs are beamed directly here (for Spain, of course) and emphasize that liberation is not far away, thanks to Fidel Castro. (He also intends to "liberate" Portugal and all the Portuguese colonies in Africa, incidentally!) All the newsstands in Tangier sell Cuban magazines now, and Morocco is very friendly with Cuba officially. So one can see clearly which way the wind is blowing around here. In one Cuban magazine there was an article promising the "liberation" of the state of Florida in the near future. Are you interested in being liberated? I imagine, somehow, that you're not too eager!

What Julian is trying now is to get Jane to agree to leave whatever she receives as a legacy to her mother in case of her death before Claire, but she is not going to do it, she says. I received Daddy's answer to my last letter, and am glad to hear everything is satisfactory financially. However, if there should be unexpected expenses suddenly, please remember that I am able to help. I must close and go into town with this and see if there is any mail. We are well, and Jane works every day on her new play. (Two pages of it blew out the window the other day. No copy. That always seems to happen to her. In Mexico a whole novel blew out of the hotel window once, and she enlisted a dozen Mexicans to look for the loose pages!)

TO JAMES PURDY

October 3, 1961
Tangier

Thanks so much for sending a letter in exchange for a postcard. I'm really ignorant of who owed whom; if it was I who owed, I see you've let it pass . . . I'm busy writing a novel to which I shan't sign my name. At least, I'm writing it, which is all I want. Do you never go years without working, the way I do? I started my last novel in 1953, finished it in '55. Better if I could write one to which I wanted to sign my name, but not all that much better. Did you like "A Friend of the World"? I'm delighted. Three short stories are all I've managed (plus another long story which isn't published) in the past four years; that seems shocking. The pieces I take on for *Holiday* and *Life* and *The Nation* take as much energy and time as novels, and don't exist once they're printed. Eager to see your rape-novel, or anything else you write. We had a hectic summer this year here in Tangier, with the Beat nucleus throbbing in our midst. They've scattered now—Burroughs to Harvard, Ginsberg to Greece, Corso to London and Orlovsky to Istanbul. Where they are at the moment is anyone's guess, however. I hear Burroughs couldn't stick it at Harvard, and is already back in London, although that may be false, since it came from Jane via a chain of most unreliable British beats. I did get a querulous letter from Burroughs sent from Massachusetts, in which he swore he'd lose his reason if he stayed long in the United States. Religious, yes; I know what you mean. (You applied it to the group.) There were about two dozen beats in town at once at one point in the season, and the manner in which they attacked the native cafés and the native kif convinced the Moslems that they were members of an American religious sect. I suppose the beards helped, and the long hair of their women, and their symbolic uniform, in praise of universal poverty. Whenever I was told about them by a Moroccan, I confirmed the theory of the religious cult, saying: "Oh, yes. It's well-known in America. They are often put in jail for their views." Many of them spent time in prison here, as well, for various offences, so it was not difficult for the Moroccans to believe that part of it, either. "They like Kennedy?" I said no. "They like Khrushchev?" No, I said. "Who do they like?" "Only God. But they say that's the same as themselves." The Moroccans were generally scornful. "Maybe they think God likes them, but if they do, they're crazy," was one café-man's reply. If Andrewski gets in touch with Jane, she'll surely answer. She is very busy writing. I'm not sure what, because she doesn't like to discuss it. Perhaps the reason why I never answered your question about [Charles Montagu] Doughty is that I've never read *Arabia Deserta*. Someone asked me the same question yesterday. Obviously many people have done so before, and my answer always has to be the same one. Is it particularly good? I've asked that before, too, and got various opinions, most of them favorable, naturally. But why do *you* ask? Do you think I ought to read Doughty? That is to say: do you think I'd enjoy it? Is it his style one remembers, or his content? Or the two? As the bomb comes nearer, one thinks of various ways of cheating it, of slipping out so as not to have to meet it. That could add a certain flavor of recklessness to living, I suppose. The revolt of the masses: an illicit mass death-wish. Cheat the Bomb! Any occupation which could be considered dangerous would be a forbidden activity. Driving a car would be listed as a subversive act. Leaning out the window could get one twenty years. I see the paper now, and must stop.

TO RUTH FAINLIGHT

━━━━━━━━━━━━━━━━━━━━━━◆━━━━━━━━━━━━━━━━━━━━━━

October 10, 1961
Tangier

It was good to get a long letter from you; I haven't replied because I've been hearing vague reports via Christopher (from Anne Harbach) that you would, wouldn't, might be coming here very soon. At one point you were taking her flat, then you weren't because you were in the hospital. Now, I'm not sure how things stand. I only hope you are not ill; that would seem to be the hauptsache. And do you really think you all will be coming down shortly?

Everything is about the same here: quite good, considering that the improved standard of living automatically brings its own discontent by making possible invidious comparisons which only two or three years ago were inconceivable. The Moroccans live more expensively than they did; they all have radios and bicycles, and many have motorcycles and even cars, but they eat less well and are far more dissatisfied with their lot than before because they see Europeans living better than they. However, there's no immediate prospect of trouble. It's a corner of paradise compared to the rest of the world, I suspect.

Jane is busy writing a play—possibly the same one she was intending to write when you were here, although I don't think she had yet begun to work at that time. I'm rewriting a piece for *Holiday* which was about seven thousand words too long. I do make things hard for myself, don't I? I'm about fifty pages into a novel to which I'll probably sign a pseudonym when it's finished. How is Carson McCullers's new novel, *Clock without Hands*? Or haven't you seen it? We have been receiving all the criticism of it from friends in the States, but of course there is no way of seeing the book itself here this year.

Still waiting to see Alan's new book, which hasn't arrived. How lucky he is to be able to write so frequently! How does it happen, do you suppose, that he isn't paralyzed by the feeling that life is just about over? I suspect it has something to do with Ban the Bomb marches, but that isn't really a satisfactory explanation;

it would have to be elaborated on considerably, and very likely only he could do it.

I haven't waited quite so long to answer this as you did, but on the other hand, my reply is less comprehensive, because I've got to get to lunch at this moment. Do write again and let me know how you are, and whether you will be coming down this autumn or only next spring, which seems a long way off at this point.

TO RENA AND CLAUDE BOWLES
———————————◆———————————
October 18, 1961
Tangier

Your letter thanking me for the telegram came ten days ago, I think. My last note crossed it en route. I had been counting on going down to Marrakech with Christopher Wanklyn this week, but he suddenly announced he was going to take Bob Faulkner along, and since the latter is an alcoholic who at any moment goes off the track, I thought the trip might turn out to be more trouble than it was worth, and declined at the last minute to go. Which is too bad, as it would be beautiful down there right now. October is the best month of the year. The worst part is that Christopher also drinks a good deal more when he is with Bob, and it gets boring. Even though we wouldn't have been staying in the same place, I should have had to eat most meals with them or it would have looked strange. So I thought I'd remain here this time. However, it's likely he'll be going down again in early November. The weather won't be as good then, but there's no help for that.

I found this old stationery for sale in a Moroccan shop down the street; it must be left over from the war. I hope it doesn't weigh too much per sheet. It looks a bit heavy for airmail. Did I tell you the green parrot died last month? We were afraid it might be psittacosis, and took it to the Institut Pasteur to have an autopsy performed, but they told us there was no way of discovering whether or not it had been. The grey one seems fine, so I assume it was something he ate. He was always loose, as you remember, and might easily have picked up something poisonous, like DDT or lead. Very sad, since I had had him for fourteen years and was very fond of him. Cherifa came down one evening at nine o'clock and merely announced that he was dead. And so he was, in rigor mortis, on the bathroom shelf.

We are having a difficult time getting foodstuffs now in the shops. All the canned goods are from Iron Curtain countries: Bulgarian jam, Czechoslovakian beans, Hungarian spices; even the matches (which don't light half the time) are from Poland. The Russians themselves have arrived to take over the Tangier port, which they intend to build and manage when it is finished. I don't know where they get all their power (inside the Moroccan government) from. The other day the biggest French-language daily in Casablanca was censured for reporting that the Russians were exploding nuclear weapons in Siberia and Nova Zembla. They called it imperialist propaganda. Only the Americans were testing harmful weapons. The Russians were doing nothing at all. Yet over the radio anyone can hear about the Russian tests, from outside Morocco. One mustn't print it, that's all. Their excuse is that they don't want to do anything to annoy friendly countries. When the U.S. hands them fifty million now and then it doesn't even make the newspapers. Yet the great democratic republic of China is here with its "technicians," examining all the tillable land to tell them what to plant and how to distribute it when (and if) it produces anything. Oh, well! One can't expect logic where it doesn't grow, and it certainly doesn't grow in the heads of the people around here. They think that when Castro takes over the U.S. government they are going to get bigger handouts from Washington! Yet no communist government has ever given them a penny, so far. Anyway, we have no more American products—not even medicines. All forbidden. Janie found two cans of corn the other day in a shop, and it was like finding a treasure. We're saving them for a feast! Even British goods are on the forbidden list. Incidentally, the new American Consulate, right opposite us on the other side of the street, is finally open. Very fancy, and, according to the Vice-Consul, about three times too big for their needs. It was planned long before Independence, when Tangier was international and the Americans maintained a Legation. But in spite of the fact that ten years have elapsed since the plans were drawn up, not a single modification was made. So this unnecessary palace is there, lighted up like a fair all night, and to no purpose. So goes the world.

It sounds as though Daddy's fracture were much better, for which I am thankful. It was a long pull, I'm sure, from the sound of it. You asked whether Claire had any money left directly to her. Yes, she did, exactly the same amount as Jane, whatever that amount was. I know it was divided equally among Claire, Jane, an aunt and Jane's cousin. I believe they are going to sell all the securities immediately, out of distrust of the stock market and what it might do during the next year. Although if there is a crash the estate tax will be lower than it would be if values remained high. However, it doesn't look as though there would be a crash, does it? Claire seems to fear inflation, instead. I have nothing to do with the whole thing, and I'll believe in the legacy when I see it. It seems the most realistic attitude! Julian obviously thinks there is a possibility that Claire will outlive Jane. He wrote Jane what she said was a rather nasty letter; for the first time I saw that she doesn't like him, at all. I must close. Much love to you both.

TO ALLEN GINSBERG

November 1, 1961
Tangier

Got back today from three days in Gibraltar, spent in the bank and in shops, as always. Rough passage in the Strait this morning, but Dramamine saved the day. I suppose this will be forwarded from Athens to wherever you are; I hope so, at least. Delighted to get your missive enclosing other missives and messages. I've been talking to Ahmed about trying to get down some more legends and tales; he's meshugah, of course, and never makes much sense, so I can't tell whether he will eventually do it or not. He's now got a German girl on the string, intends to go with her to Berlin and live with her family for four years until she is of age and can marry him. Few people alive could have less sense of reality; is intelligence the ability to learn from experience? If so, he's stupid. But I don't think he is, really, which means only that almost everything he says is a lie. For when he translates projects into action, there's very little semblance between the said and the done. But of course, he's always told me his concept of intelligence was the ability to blend truth and falsehood so expertly that no one could possibly distinguish them, one from the other. Thus, whether I dare write to Ferlinghetti suggesting a volume by him remains a moot point. I wish I had something myself to send him—a tome of kif stories, for instance. But there are only three. Ahmed seems not too interested in doing the sort of thing he has done so far; he wants to do one long thing, autobiographical. Perhaps his fantasy has played itself out in the past five years; it was 1956 when he did the last stories. I wish we had news of interest from here. None. Pam has moved into Inmeuble Itesa, or perhaps she had already done that before you left. We see her almost continuously. Michael Portman is back as of ten days ago; Jane is sure something ghastly is going to happen to everyone who says even hello to him. I had a letter from Bill on Monday. He feels he ought to be here to take care of Michael. Perhaps he ought. Christopher has been down in Marrakech for the past fortnight; he returned yesterday and is living at Anne Harbach's because he's rented out his flat to someone from Tunis until Christmas. I've almost decided to go to Ceylon later on in the season. I'd intended to get a reservation while I was in Gibraltar, but other business, such as errands for unlikely people, prevented me from remembering to go to the steamship agency until I was already on the ferry coming back this morning. (Sonia Kamalakar wanted a pound of orange lentils from Lipton's; Jane wanted pappadum for curry; Boulaich wanted corduroy trousers, socks and briefs and shampoo cream; Vera Jane Bodden wanted men's size Kleenex—the list was long and idiotic. My own list even longer and equally trivial, like everything else here.) And so I actually forgot to buy my ticket to Colombo, I was so occupied going up and down the hill to the Rock Hotel, from the Rock Hotel, and trying to get dirhams for dollars at various Indian shops, since Barclay's Bank now gives only 520 francs to the dollar. "Dollar not valuable these days. Business is at a standstill," says Mr. Sitaldas. Today is Remember Algeria Day, so everything is shut, including all the cafés; the taxis don't run, nor the buses. Martial tunes come over the radio, and each hour they announce new casualty figures. I suppose you're already in Israel. And do you still plan an eastward push from there? Very likely, I should think. At least I have permission to bring out whatever of the Rockefeller Collection I want on discs. Now, having got that from the government of the U.S., all I need is to find a company who might conceivably be interested in issuing such items. Surely such people exist, but who the hell are they? Didn't you mention one possibility to me—something called Atlantic, perhaps? Or am I mistaken? I listen to the Voice of America. The word they enjoy most using this month is "fight." Someone should inaugurate a Cheat-the-Bomb program; it would be worldwide, and its action would consist in the mass suicide of strategic workers. They could also demand cyanide capsules for every human being, with the contention that every man has the right to choose his own death. It wouldn't take more than half a million volunteers around the world to make an impression, I should think. Unfortunately it would probably be feasible only after the first nuclear war, when the unlucky survivors have made an inventory of what's left in the way of reasons for going ahead with existence. Mark Grotrian has also turned up here; both he and Michael Portman are living at the Armor. Michael's sister is en route from Paris in a car, to take him on a tour of Morocco. He seems rather more chipper than he did during the summer. The weather is still crystalline. My trip to Ceylon will probably take place soon after Christmas; return any time before the monsoons, which start end of May. If you get this and have the opportunity, let me know where you are going and more or less when.

TO JANE BOWLES

TO JANE BOWLES

November 1961
Marrakech

I just came from the Maison d'Amérique, where I got your letter. Glad to hear from you that all was well—at least when you wrote the missive. I wasn't sure how much you knew about the évènements, and for that reason couldn't decide what to say in the wire. For two days before I sent it I was trying to get to a post office, but it was impossible. Now that we are back here, we still can't find out how much was open knowledge and how much was completely hidden from the general public. Anyway, we were finally bouclés in Bou Izakarn, and couldn't move in any direction. They wouldn't even let us use the car to drive as far as the government office; we simply had to leave it in front of the café and walk everywhere. No circulation of any kind permitted. We soon discovered why, when convoys of troops came thundering through, several thousand of them, on their way God knows where. However, we still have no idea why all traffic was stopped for three whole days. The French down there said it was nation-wide, but I suspect it was more local in nature, and that in Tangier no one knew anything about it. Naturally I wanted to let you know we were all right, but there was absolutely no way of doing it, and as soon as they allowed traffic to rouler again we got out and kept moving northward. We slept in Essaouira night before last, and got in here last night at sunset. Then the first thing this morning I went around to the Maison d'Amérique. I was really afraid you would be in a state of hysteria, or near it, because obviously it must (or so it seemed to us) be a very serious situation for all movement to be prohibited, all over Morocco. At the same time it seemed possible that everyone was badly informed down there, and that any reference to the thing in a wire might upset you if you had been unaware of it. We are still in a state of mystification about the whole thing, as there has never been any reference to it on the radio or in the papers, and the people we ask don't seem to know about it. But in the Sahara where we were they had rocks across the streets and one couldn't move without the military demanding papers and telling us to stay out of the car. (We thought they were all just slightly crazy, and laughed about it for one entire day, getting out and unbuilding the blockades they had put across the trails and streets inside the ksour, and going merrily on our way.) Anyway, we had a wonderful trip which lasted from a week ago Monday until last night, or eight days. We stayed two nights in Taroudant at the house of Dr. Vitias (now married to a lady with a boil on the end of her nose), one night in Irherm (so cold we almost froze, although we had plenty of blankets for sleeping), two nights in Tata, which was magnificent, and where Christopher got the best recordings yet . . . absolutely fantastic music, one night in Tarhjijt, one night in Bou Izakarn, and one night in Essaouira. Needless to say, we listened fanatically to the radio, trying to get something relevant to the situation here, and did get a few references which merely made us more determined to get the actual facts, which needless to say we did not get. A French broadcast mentioned the "situation au Maroc," and referred to the general strike there. A Portuguese news program announced fighting here and there, which considerably upset us, because we couldn't make out where the trouble was, not knowing enough Portuguese, although we heard "duros combates" and references to Moulay Hassan, the O.A.S. and Bourguiba. The médecin-chef of the hospital (French) at Bou Izakarn insisted it had to do with Ben Barka and leftist demonstrations which had taken place in Casa, demanding his transference to some other prison, but that seemed scarcely a reason to stop all movement for three days. So perhaps you know something about all of it, because we don't. Anyway, everything seems normal enough now, so it was probably just hysteria connected with the Sultan's appearance in Marrakech for the parade last Saturday.

The mynah bird says: Hello Christophostophistopher, all the time now. They are rebuilding the souks fast, but of course the new ones are hideous, in concrete with metal stores in front—absolutely no style at all, and no cover over the street, so instead of the beautiful tunnels it is merely open streets like the Mellah, only uglier. However, there are plenty of fine souks left, so one needn't wail too much. We stopped at Chichaoua yesterday on the way here, and I got a pink rug I think you'll approve of. Don't worry about Helen Strauss. She can't sign contracts for me in the first place, and she's completely against the whole van Saher project anyway. I doubt that anything will ever come of the whole thing, since there's no money anywhere within reach at present. I'm glad you wrote Libby. I sent her a postcard by ordinary mail which probably won't arrive before Christmas. Boujemâa said Bobby Lester had been here; we missed him of course, but he saw him and arranged "things" for him, so everything went off well. I

think we'll be returning in a week. Christopher has to get back for money by
the first, he says. He suggested I stay here and wait for him as he intends to
return immediately, but I'll come back with him. Much love and until soon,

                                                                    Bupple

TO LAWRENCE FERLINGHETTI

CITY LIGHTS BOOKS, SAN FRANCISCO

December 11, 1961
Tangier

First I'd do well to explain why I'm writing: I've had three letters from Allen
Ginsberg recently (one from Athens and two from Tel Aviv) directing me to do
it. Perhaps he suspected I wouldn't take him seriously the first time, and for
that reason repeated his suggestion in each missive. In today's letter he managed
to persuade me that I should. The reason I had hesitated before was that I
believed I had nothing precise to offer; now he thinks I should suggest a group
of three short stories about kif in Morocco. It seems rather a small item, but
perhaps that's what you want. I shouldn't think it would contain more than forty
pages at the outside, but I don't know the format or type.

Previously Allen had made an alternate suggestion: a collection of legends by
Yacoubi, or perhaps a new work by him. The idea of getting him to do something
new seems impractical, because he is arranging an exhibit of new work, and
you know how painters are at such moments: they have no time for anything
but the business at hand, which always includes a good deal of cooking and
entertaining sandwiched in between painting and framing and pricing and making lists. As far as I know he has only four legends ready. (Two appeared in
issues of the old *Zero*, one in *Contact*, and one in *Evergreen*.)

I, on the other hand, could be relied upon to furnish an extra story to add to
my three, if you felt that said three were insufficient to constitute a tome. (The
three I can offer have been published in *Encounter*, *The London Magazine* and
Big Table.) Whatever you say is fine with me; I'd be delighted to appear under
your aegis. It would be good to have a few lines from you on the subject.

Aaron Copland working on a score in the 1930s

"I'm always pleased to have lots of blue around me," wrote Jane Bowles, shortly
after her arrival in Tangier in 1948, as quoted in Millicent Dillon's *A Little
Original Sin*

Moroccan acrobats at Tanger
Beach, 1956

Paul and Mohammed Larbi Djilali
during a trip through the countryside
taping Moroccan music, ca. 1959

Opposite
Gregory Corso, Paul Bowles, and
William Burroughs pose in Burroughs's
garden, Villa Mouneria, for what
became an infamous photo shoot. Ian
Sommerville and Michael Portman
crouch in the background, 1961

Cherifa in Tangier, 1960

Paul overlooks the bustling Djemaa-el-Fna, Marrakech, 1961

Casting a shadow in Tafilalt, near Erfoud, southeast Morocco, 1963

TO ALLEN GINSBERG

December 12, 1961
Tangier

Both yours from Tel Aviv, where I can't write you directly. However, this way will find you eventually, I suppose. Your exodus from Israel looks problematical, to judge from the most recent bulletin. I'm wondering whether you'll like Ceylon, because you'll see Colombo first, and Colombo is the Casablanca of Ceylon. You might easily be discouraged, and besides, Ceylon isn't in it with India as far as exoticism goes, obviously. But what it has is natural beauty and some pleasant people and a good climate. Also Kataragama, the crazy all-religion shrine, and the wonderful East Coast. But people—you might look up Justin Daraniyagala, whose address is: Nugegoda, Pasyala. A painter and mystic, a good friend. You might also try and contact Shaun Mandy (Taprobane, Weligama, Southern Province, Ceylon), the Irish writer and editor (for years, of the *Illustrated Weekly of India*). He purchased my island and paid out the rupees I can't collect. (It doesn't look as though I'd be out there this winter, since I haven't gone to Gib to try and get passage, and that has to be done months in advance, if one wants a good cabin.) But you know how Tangier does that little paralysing act on one. Kif-weeks fly by, seasons change, the sun shines, one works and writes letters, people come and go, and one remains in just the same position that one was in a good while ago. Life is pleasant like that; there seems no reason to alter conditions. Mandy might ask you down to the island, and you could smell my early-morning ghost there on the lower path; I was always there collecting champak blossoms that had fallen during the night, and sat on the south rock to watch the sunrise. If he invites, accept; he's a conversationalist, especially about literary figures. Daraniyagala's sister lives in Colombo and is atremble with distracted charm—a nice woman whom you might call. Mrs. Miriam de Saram * * *. If you want more varied suggestions, write me precisions: I know quite a few people on the island. If you meet a man named Herbert Kennerman (a Burgher) (the cousin of Peter Kennerman, a Communist leader of Ceylon), talk with him about me. I don't know his address or what he is doing. But he can present you to everyone, including Mr. Padmanabhe, whom I think you'd also like. He was the first man I knew in Ceylon, and he took me to his family, who invited me to live with them on a delightful tea-plantation in the hills near Ginigathena, and later at Gintota. I wish I were going to be there with you; if I knew for a fact that you were going to be there for a decent length of time and at a definite date, I'd make a determined effort to go out. But as it stands, it all looks fairly unsure. You may end up in Sikkim or Nepal for all you know, no? Thanks for the information about Hanover Records. For the moment, Jane has removed your letter (and Peter's) from its envelope and lost both, and before I had the chance to note down the address of Hanover. I've spent at least forty minutes this afternoon searching everywhere for it. And she'll never be able to tell me—will doubtless disclaim all knowledge of the letter's existence. That also is Tangier, or, at least, Jane. Harold Norse has been here for the past five weeks, with a car, hoping to be able to start for the south. All that keeps him is Tangier. I got off to Marrakech with Christopher last month; then we went on, way down, to the Sahara, to Tata and Aqqa and Icht and Tarhjijt. All magnificent, magnificent. Recorded drum orchestras at a nocturnal festival of black-robed people outside Tata. Were gone a month. C. now back in Marrakech until next week. He likes the house, which I admit is more gemütlich in the cooler season, although I still stayed at the Central because of Boujemâa and the short-wave. Ahmed down there at same time, as well as Ira Yeager. Ahmed with some American girl, pretending to be broke, and ordering burnouses and djellabas made to order. Having big show next week here. Write.

TO LAWRENCE FERLINGHETTI
CITY LIGHTS BOOKS, SAN FRANCISCO

———————————◆———————————

January 12, 1962
Tangier

Between yours of December nineteenth and yours of January sixth, I got busy and typed out two of the tales. (I had a carbon copy of the third.) It's just as well, I think. There were a few errors, as well as a few changes I wanted to make. Also, while the type used in *Big Table* is all right, that of *London Magazine* is much smaller, and that of *Encounter* useless anyway, since they print two columns to a page. Besides that, I'm adding a new one, in order to make four, so the tome won't be too thin. The stories aren't very long; the one in *Big Table* is the longest by far.

The title business has kept me thinking, but not with any great degree of productivity. The difficulty with finding a word that has some reference, even oblique, to kif, is that the word will necessarily be a Moghrebi word, and thus will have no reference at all save to the few who know the region. (*Moghrebi* itself could be used, I suppose: *Four Moghrebi Tales*, for instance. But of course no kif is suggested there.) Do you like *A Hundred Camels in the Court-yard . . .* ? On the title page we could have the whole quote:

> "A pipe of kif before breakfast gives a man the strength
> of a hundred camels in the courtyard."
> . . . MOGHREBI PROVERB

That would more or less capsulize the meaning, since the theme of all the stories is specifically the power of kif, rather than the subjective effects of it. I can think further if I have to; at least, I hope so. The last story is not completed. Will you let me have your ideas on all this? I want to go south next week, and the story has got to be finished before I leave—finished and mailed off. However, I'd appreciate a few words before you get the typescripts (which I'll send air-registered, in the hope they don't get censored at this end).

TO ALLEN GINSBERG
◆
January 17, 1962
Tangier

Never expected to be writing to you in Mombasa; I liked it a lot better than Nairobi, although Ahmed and I were there just before the monsoons, and it was hot. Are the Hadramaut men there, squatting with their poignards in Old Town, watching the dhows in the harbor? Or is it too early in the season? Sometimes they invite you out onto the anchored dhows; at least, they do if one of you is a Moslem. Mombasa to Bombay? Never did it. We did Colombo to Mombasa direct. Nine days in the *Issipingo* in '57. Hellish heat all the way, day and night. But once in Bombay you'll be staying in India a long time, I imagine, rather than fleeing once more by ship. Of course Jane got sick, and using that as an excuse, I remained where I was. She seemed so disinclined to smile at the idea of my departure for anywhere—even Marrakech. Thus, I'm here, wishing I were in Weligama or Kandy. Are you still expecting to meet Gary Snyder in Colombo? Are you still intending to go to Colombo at all? It's just as well I didn't start out in November hoping to meet you in early December out there, or I'd have been disappointed. But let me know definite plans, because Jane is better now, and up and around. She got into her bed about four days before Christmas and has been there ever since, more or less. It took three doctors to find out what was the matter with her, and they were treating her for other maladies before they eventually decided it was *herpes zoster*. The entry of the virus had her pulse going at double its normal speed; we all thought she was going to be extremely ill, but it turned out to be more pain than danger, although she can't see people yet, because her face is a mass of scabs and scars. Wrote Ferlinghetti, and he wants to do a small book of kif stories, so I am writing a further one to go with the other three. Wrote Shulman, but perhaps he is no longer at the Présidente, or perhaps postal delivery there is akin to ours here. Tangier has been overrun with Americans recently. They opened a *cave* down in the Medina, where they played trumpet, sax and guitar (with Moroccan drums to embroider) nights after eleven. Police took a dim view of the kif, so after ten days or so they closed it again by themselves, rather than waiting for it to be closed for them. A guy named Ted Joans has taken the apartment next to Ahmed's and set up housekeeping. He claims to be on his way to Tombouctou, but will keep the place here while he's gone. Ahmed delighted, as he has an enormous collection of jazz records. A. has been selling a lot of paintings, and ought to be happy. Bill writes from Paris, but not often. I don't know what he's doing there. I went to Nairobi to see Tom Mboya, who was fine with Ahmed and me and introduced us to everyone. Now, nearly five years later, he is important, and possibly has less time to converse. Tell me how he is if you see him. Did you ever get my Wilentz-directed letters? Trying to communicate is full of hazards. I'm taping *Howl* tomorrow from Joans's disc; it's a beautiful recording. Gerodias's monthly *Olympia* not extraordinary in its first number . . . a house organ, I should say. Still, they promise to pay a thousand dollars every month for a story. Gosh, says Ahmed, I send them lot stories fast. Michael Portman living with sister in the palmeraie outside Marrakech. I finally got out of the arrangement with Christopher, so I don't pay any more on the house there. Never stayed there again, after those two lousy nights I spent in it during the heat, although continued to pay half of all costs until first of January. For what? He's now got Bu Faulkner living with him, as well as Boujemâa, Farid and Hamid, and I think that suits him better. But write and give plans. And tell Peter, too. And love.

TO ALLEN GINSBERG

May 17, 1962
Tangier

Once I got a postcard from Gertrude Stein. How nice, she said, that Tangier is like George Sand remembered it and not like Madame Simon de l'Opéra remembered it! About India all I can say is that I'm glad it's the way it is rather than as I said it was. Also, ten years can be a long time in the life of a very young nation. When I was last there (1952) there were several million refugees sleeping in the streets of Bombay, and every nook and cranny was filled every night with rows of sleepers. Perhaps that emergency no longer exists, and perhaps they have built a good many hotels in the past decade. Furthermore, the very obvious gap between "English" hotels and Indian hotels has doubtless narrowed considerably. I wonder even how many "English" hotels remain in the country, where the servants go barefoot for fear of disturbing memsahib, and prostrate themselves when they come in the door. It was that way in all the hotels I saw in India. There seemed to be nothing between that and what amounted then to flophouses. And my distinct memory of these hotels is that while they were quite worth what they cost, staying in them did not constitute a cheap holiday. So Thank God a new era has come. It would be nice to look in on you there and see you sitting listening to Chatur Lal. I must make Ceylon next winter. Shaun Mandy claims it is scarcely habitable now, and that I must hurry. He also says he saw you in Bombay, with (he thought) Gregory. ". . . in the street in Bombay—sensational! Missed them in the coterie environment of Delhi." Jane is out to dinner. I sit here typing letters. Now I stop, and resume later.

Ferlinghetti is using the snap you took of me one morning in the house at Marrakech, on the back cover of the little book which he says will be out next month. He had an astonishing enthusiasm for the picture and insisted on using it, even though it is underexposed. I've been translating Moroccan material all spring. Eight stories completed now, plus a new one from Ahmed on which I'm working at the moment. Nothing more interesting to report. This past weekend Harold Norse and I visited Jejouka, where they still dress up as Pan and dance. It was worth all the difficulties of getting there, including the inevitable breakdown of the car and the climbs up muddy arroyos and the fleas and lice that bit all night. H. claimed to have been made ill by the expedition, and I haven't seen him since he dropped me off, the night we returned. (I forgot to mention that *Second Coming* had taken one of the longer Moroccan stories.)

Narayan and Sonia read and reread your letter; Narayan hopes some day to see the Marathi volume you mentioned, since it's his language. Tamara returned from Rome and Paris . . . somewhat more sure of herself and just as pleasant. Now in Madrid. Medina now stuffed with Eighthstreetniks who have rented houses. Bill was right: it's a real invasion, like nothing that has come before. I hope to hear a word from you occasionally. I'd like to be in India, but I'm pleased that you're there at least, and certainly no one could extract more from it per hour spent there than you, so all's well. And if Ceylon is enterable next winter I'll be there. Mandy has sold the island. But there are rest-houses. Love to Peter. Love to you.

TO RENA AND CLAUDE BOWLES
————————————————•————————————————

June 11, 1962
Tangier

My letter-writing hasn't been very good this spring. Each time I write you I have to apologize for not having written earlier. This time there was the unsureness about plans for our trip to the States; I wanted to have an approximate idea about the time we would be making it, and now I do have that. We will probably take the *Independence* leaving Algeciras on the sixth of September and arriving in New York on the twelfth. Eugenia Bankhead, Tallulah's sister, is a good friend of some official, and was able to book the passage for us in spite of everything's being filled. I haven't paid yet; for that reason I use the word *probably*. Until you have the ticket in your hands you can never be really certain, and nowadays even with the ticket you can't be sure of not finding someone in your cabin when you board the ship. It happened to me coming from Genoa once, and I had to sit around with my luggage until the ship got to Cannes before I could have the cabin. Anyway, I'll keep you informed, naturally. The reason we put off the trip until September is that Tennessee suddenly did arrive without letting us know, and has taken a house for four months. He's been here for about ten days already. Jane as usual feels very responsible for his welfare, and has been helping him get settled in. I got him a servant with whom he is satisfied, and so all is well on that score. He's got to go to Italy for a production of one of his plays at the end of this month, but he'll be back afterward. Having finished arranging Tennessee's problems, Jane is now busy doing the same for the Sillitoes, who were here a year and a half ago, and have just returned, this time with a ten-weeks-old baby. They, however, want to stay a year, so they must have a bigger house, and a garden. Great difficulties there, because practically every house within striking distance of Tangier is taken. They say this summer is going to be the busiest tourist season in history here in Tangier. All the hotels are booked solid until October. The U.S. Government has opened a school down in the Medina, where classes in Moghrebi are given to members of the State Department, so there are a good many new Americans here studying, and they also help fill the hotel rooms. It was about time somebody in the Consular service here learned a little of the language of the country. No one has ever bothered to learn a word so far. A letter from Libby a while ago told us that the insurance company had stipulated that she could no longer hand keys to her Sixty-First Street house out to friends, so we won't be able to use that as a base any more. We can, however, stay up in Greenwich with her if we want. It always meant a terrific saving, naturally, to be able to stay there in Sixty-First St., instead of in a hotel. Jane's mother will be at the Meurice where she used to live twenty years ago, and has offered to put Jane up with her when she wants to be in town. There won't be room for me there, of course. So I'll probably stay out in Connecticut and "commute" when I have something that requires my presence in Manhattan. I don't look forward to all that with any pleasure, I can tell you. However, since Claire isn't going to be in Florida there is no point in our going directly there from this side, especially as it's so difficult to get a ship. This is just a bulletin to keep you abreast of our decisions and plans. There is no important news—not even much unimportant news! Can't you get your systole down below 180? That seems awfully high, somehow. I suppose as long as you feel all right there's no cause for alarm. We're wondering whether Jane's financial adviser sold all the stocks before the crash. At least we know he got rid of most of them several months ago, but there were others that he had decided to hang on to, despite her pleas that he sell, as far back as February.

TO ALLEN GINSBERG AND PETER ORLOVSKY

August 2, 1962
Tangier

Impossible to vie with you for sending news. Tangier full of people because the King is living on the mountain in his palace. Large American cars rush

through the streets and there are police at every corner. Members of the Royal
Guard walk hand in hand along the boulevard, and a group of Reguibat now
wanders about, looking lost, trailing their long blue garments behind them. They
have been imported by Miss Hutton, whose guests they will entertain day after
tomorrow at the annual ball she gives. Jane has decided to go, but to stay away
from the room with the jewelled tapestry and sofa-cushions. Also not to go into
any part of the house directly under the terrace on the roof, for fear of being
crushed when the house caves in. Last year she worried about it for a few weeks,
until she discovered that our names had been crossed off the list anyway. But
this year she is buying a series of evening gowns and matching accessories, and
that of course augments her anguish, since she can't decide which to wear.
There was a similar difficulty for a fortnight before the amara of Sidi Kacem,
but we got through it and took John Crosby the columnist with us. The next
day she went into the hospital and was operated on. A week later she came out
and began the present megillah. However, there are only two more days to go,
and then she can settle down and go quietly mad planning the trip to New York,
which takes place on the sixth of September, God forbid. Alan Ansen has been
here a good month, living in the Muniriya. Gregory took his girlfriend away to
Italy, and I don't know where he is now. Tennessee also has left, giving up his
house for which he had paid four months' rent in advance, only to find that
there were all sorts of back utility bills due on it. And my house on the mountain
with the swimming pool is not very useful to me since the water company will
not turn on the water for it. However, it's quiet there at dusk, and more beautiful
than anywhere else. Ted Joans is still here, working at something with Ahmed,
whom I never even catch sight of anywhere anymore; I don't know where he
keeps himself. Ferlinghetti sent me a copy of my *Camels* book. I'm pleased with
the cover, and I don't think I would have been had I not got all involved in it
myself, so it was worth while. It was all your idea, so thanks. I've continued
translating long passages of texts recorded on tape in Moghrebi. *Evergreen* took
two, and are using one in the September issue, I think. It gives me a pleasant
satisfaction to work at them, even though I'm aware of it as a vicarious sort of
creativity. Have you recorded *Kaddish* yet? I played the record of *Howl* to
Tennessee, and he was thunderstruck, so he said, after pronouncing it "magnificent." I think he had been under the impression that it was "not about
anything"! A letter came for Tenn yesterday from Webb of *The Outsider*, asking
him for material. Ted Joans gave me number 2 of that review today; I haven't
read it, but the look of it reminds me of the more parochial organs in the Village
in the 'Twenties. Rather tatty, as Alan Sillitoe would say. He has a villa on the

mountain with a vast garden overlooking the sea. Nothing too magnificent for the proletariat, as Harold Clurman used to tell the comrades. I think the truth is that the India I liked is the India that no longer exists. My happiest memories are of the hotels and their impeccable service and the barefoot silent domestics who brought chhota mazri and pulled back the curtains on the gardens outside, and the crows that came down from the trees to rob strips of bacon and pieces of toast. So you see . . .

What plans? Ceylon? Time moves. Mail takes long.

TO ALLEN GINSBERG ET AL.

October 30, 1962
Gulfport, Florida

Your missive of September was forwarded, arrived. I've been moving fast in various directions, with scarcely ever more than three nights in the same bed. Awful. First at Libby's, then at Oliver Smith's, then at Libby's in Greenwich, then at John Goodwin's, again at Libby's, again at Oliver's, back and forth over and over. Finally down here to visit my parents who live facing a "yacht-basin" where scores of boats are moored in neat rows, and pelicans swoop above the palms on their way to dive for fish, and on the beach herons and cranes wade in proprietary fashion, eating as they go. It's better here than in New York, for a while, at least. Tennessee phoned me yesterday, from Key West, asking me to go down. When I refused, he said: Don't let the so-called Cuban crisis influence your decision. I hadn't thought of that. As to A Hundred Camels, I'm not aware of having anything "plotted out in detail"; I'm sure you can believe that. It plots itself without guidance, which provides the pleasure of putting it down. Anyway, the photo was good, I thought, with the bowl of corn flakes and all the kitchenware as if posed on the floor waiting for your shutter-click. Only Jane looked and said: You look as though you were eating something terrible. Or did I mention that to you earlier? She is out at the tip of Long Island now with Libby. We have passage on the *Constitution* to return to Casablanca on the thirteenth of November, but it will probably have to be postponed, our sailing, because it looks as though I were going to do the score for Tennessee's new show, opening tenth January on Broadway. Of course everyone excited over Mary McCarthy's espousing of Bill B. The bitchy ones say: A kiss from the Angel of Death, and so on. Harold Norse wrote angry letter to me, upbraiding me for allowing John Crosby to go with us to Sidi Kacem, and, as a matter of fact, for letting him into my apartment at all. I've been having two teeth extracted, and suffering from shards of bone impacted in jaw and gum, but everything connected with teeth is revolting. My plans for winter unstable because of Tenn's show, but certainly will be back in Tangier in January. Ceylon? I'd like it, but are you actually going to be there, or are you likely to get stuck in India? Of course, Ceylon will be fantastically dull after India, that's certain. But for natural beauty, if you like that, it's useful. Also for relaxation after the rigors of the mainland. Your note to Alan Ansen sent to American Express, Tangier, except that I have no idea whether he is still there or not; I should guess by now that he's fled the coop. I hear from practically nobody in Tangier . . . only Ahmed, who gave no news save that Irving Rosenthal and Marc Schleifer were there, Mohammed Larbi, Abdeslam Boulaich and Larbi Layachi, none of whom know Alan, so I can't ask them. Anyway, you'll find out eventually. I wish I were there with you, particularly if you're in Benares, which I don't know. And how can the land be now that everyone's getting belligerent about Mao Tse Tung, I wonder? I've seen Fred Jordan several times, as well as Rossett and Seaver, and they all seem friendly. I'll get in touch with Thiele as soon as I get back to New York, next week incha'Allah. Grove bringing out *Lunch* this month; Seaver worried about official reaction. What is this new novel by him called *The Ticket That Exploded?* He mentioned it in his last letter, but didn't elaborate, or categorize it stylistically. Said he might be going to Morocco this winter. Is sarod hard to master? How is Peter doing on it? Sorry I have no news of New York to give you. When I was there I saw no one but the dentist, the extractionist, and various doctors of Jane's. Enfin, keep in touch.

TO JANE BOWLES

November 20, 1962
New York City

I was so happy to get your letter, finally, although I knew already that you had arrived safely, through Libby at Louisa Carpenter's when "Billeh" telephoned Sister Bankhead, and she told him you had got to Tangier. Then your mother wrote me last week and confirmed the news. I merely decided you were busy, which is probably quite true. I'm very bored here, now that the music for the play is all written. However, I've been touching up the manuscript for my travel book, which Random House is going to bring out sometime next year. It will be called *Their Heads Are Green and Their Hands Are Blue*. They weren't very nice about their contract which I signed ten years ago with them; their position was that since I had not held to my side of it with regard to time of delivery of the three promised books, they were not bound to observe their side of it, which is purely financial. However, they are giving me half the advance they should have given me according to the terms. And since Helen Strauss had already insisted (in 1955) upon getting fifty percent of the original sum for me, I shall have been paid 75 percent of the promised advance before the book is published. I'm having lunch tomorrow again with Grove Press, about Larbi's book, and after that I ought to know a good deal more about the whole project than I do now. Thanks so much for seeing both him and Boulaich, and for making payments to them. Larbi wrote me the other day telling me he had seen you and that you had given him ten thousand francs. Naturally he was eager to know how much he was going to get, but I wrote him I'd tell him all about it when I saw him. One never knows who he is going to get to read him his mail, and the Moroccans being as envious as they are, it's better, obviously, not to go into any of it by letter. I've also heard from Boulaich, but not since you saw him. Yes, I *would* much prefer it if you could hand over the cash to Boulaich until I get there; it would be a thousand times easier than trying to send money orders. If you don't mind the nuisance. He certainly mustn't get more than a thousand francs a day, whatever happens. Which is why I hope you keep track of the dates and sums handed over.

We leave day after tomorrow morning, that is, the company, for New Haven. I am spending the night tomorrow at Libby's in town, as she is coming in for the two days beginning tomorrow, to work with Gerald, her accompanist. That will make it easier to get to the Grand Central (oser) the following morning. Of course I have no idea whether I'll have to go to Boston or not afterward. I'm hoping not, which will mean that all is going smoothly and they don't need me any further. I saw a run-through yesterday at the Morosco. Baddeley is going to be very good. I couldn't understand Millie's lines very well: she was still doing her Mrs. Constable drunk scene from *Summer House*. She is supposed to be progressively drunk throughout the play, which is fine, but her lines get sort of lost in the process. Tennessee seemed very depressed, and was wanting to cut everything drastically, but Audrey and Herbert were preventing him.

John Goodwin has given me his journal, asking me to cut and edit it for him. I ought to be able to do a lot of it on the ship en route, since I'll be all alone. What a shame it worked out this way, so that we each had to go alone! However,

I'm glad you're back home, and not here. Oliver has Henry Clifford staying in the house now, and the entire first floor is emptied out, with plasterers and paperhangers working all over the place. It's chaos. He very thoughtfully put it off until I had finished writing the music.

Cyril Connolly's ex-wife telephoned me today. Barbara. I think you know her, don't you? I couldn't accept her invitation. She's going to San Francisco to join, of all people, Ira Yeager.

I was riding down Park Avenue last week in a cab, and the radio was on beside the driver. Suddenly the announcer said: And now we have lovely Sandy Stewart singing "The Coloring Book," whereupon Sandy did sing, just like any other commercial pop queen. So now she's famous, singing on the Perry Como Show and all the juke boxes.

I can't wait to get out of New York and onto the ship. Let me know if there's anything you want, while I'm still here. I don't dare ask if you're working. But for God's sake, do. Oliver has every intention of coming to Tangier in the spring, and he seems to want you to come back with him, with a certain amount finished. Anyway, whether you do or don't come back, you really ought to go ahead on it now.

So let me hear from you, how you are and everything. Much love,

Bupple

TO JANE BOWLES

———————————◆———————————

December 5, 1962
New Haven, Connecticut

Your second letter came yesterday. I went over to William Morris to get it before taking the train up here. Characteristically, you say nothing about your work, except to detail possible reasons for interference. But really, no work depends on the ability to find the perfect adjectives while one is writing it. And any process or formula which will make it possible to get the skeleton constructed (I know you always object to my terminology, because you imagine I mean a preconceived outline, as in school composition, which I don't), any method or trick or manner, is valid, as long as the thing gets on paper. Then you can look for your precise words. Anyway, I'm glad that at least you feel like working.

Tennessee is in the depths of despair. I spent most of last night sitting in the Tap Room, first with Roger and Audrey and Lyn and Herbert and Tenn, and next with Lyn and Tenn, and finally only with him and he got more and more depressed, saying such things as: I should have known when to stop trying to write. And so on. This is principally because he feels Herbert has let him down, secondarily because the set is very unsatisfactory, makes everything look cluttered and detracts from the action, also gives practically no playing space in any scene, and makes an attempt at stylized vulgarity in order to reflect the principal character's innate bad taste. Which would have been all right if it had been asked for in the script, this last! But only now Tennessee says he meant the set to be beautiful, representative of Italy in general rather than of a villa built by an ex-chorus girl. And so on. I think that once he gets used to watching it with an audience he'll be less pessimistic and begin to see how to help everything. It seems to me it's a question of making each scene a more direct sequence from the one preceding, of keeping lights off the more salient and flamboyant details of the set throughout the play and concentrating on the actors. Of course the boy is weak and tentative, and that's the fault of whoever cast him. I never felt he was going to be right and I still don't. The music works all right, but Herbert's sound effects are impossible and are being omitted entirely for the performance tonight. I offered to take them over in the beginning, but he was evidently having fun playing around with them, and refused. So it's just too bad.

I see the paper is nearly exhausted. Boulaich should not get more than what I offered him, which is 1,000 francs a day until I return. Larbi should be kept down and not advanced large sums either. So far no contract has been drawn up because of haggling between Wm. Morris & Grove Press on account of the contingency of the prize. So he owes me money as things stand. Will write again very soon.

TO JANE BOWLES

December 11, 1962
New York City

Your third letter just received. I got back from New Haven last night, having spent night before last at Treetops, and having ridden into town with Libby and Louis afterward. Everything went well on the road, at least as far as I accompanied the show. The young man is still dreadful, but neither Tennessee nor Herbert wants to change him, so I suppose it will have to limp into town with things as they are. Hermione is magnificent, but that isn't enough. Millie too is brilliant, but of course her part is a tiny one and not crucial in any way. I'm going to try and reply to all your questions and remarks, since you claim I sometimes don't. I thought I generally did. First, however, I should tell you that I got a letter from your mother who seems to be in a state of awful nerves because she hasn't received any communication from you save the cable, since your arrival. She said she had been trying to get me on the phone, but they told her I was out of town. For God's sake, if you haven't written her, do. But I suppose you must have by the time you will receive this communication. Actually you can't reply to it, I imagine, so that I can get it before I leave. But anyway. I was sorry to hear that as you put it, everything has got to be a mess in Tangier and therefore you haven't worked. That was the very thing we were making great resolves about while you were still here . . . that you wouldn't *allow* the mess-tendency to take over, because that has always been the pattern, and that has been exactly what has always got in your way. Of course everything's a mess, but *please* forget the mess now and then each day, because otherwise you won't ever work. The mess is just the decor in which we live, but we can't let decor take over, really. I know you agree in principle, but does that help you to leave the mess outside regularly for a while and get inside to work? Also I know it's easy to talk and hard to do, but pretend you really live here in New York instead of there, and it might help. I mean, that you're only over there for a short while, and not permanently. I'm glad you've seen Abdeslam and like him. Of course you've known him for nearly two years, but perhaps not well enough to form any definite opinion about him. Don't worry about Larbi. I mean, give him money if he really needs it, but not too much, because otherwise his credit will be used up, and you know how Moroccans are about money already spent. They never seem really to count it. What interests them is what is coming. I signed the contract for his book today, and he will be getting around three hundred dollars when I'm back in Tangier, and more when the final manuscript is delivered. But don't mention sums to him. Just keep track of it all, so I'll know what I owe you and what he owes me. Can you, without putting too great a stress on yourself? I know figures are the most difficult thing for you. Of course I'll call Wero tomorrow, and try and get some final sort of instructions out of them for cleaning the wig. I'm sorry Cherifa is being difficult again. Is there no remedy? I heard from Ahmed, and it seems you've already given him the records, inasmuch as he thanked me. So that's fine. As to the wig again, I'll follow your instructions about mentioning having an extra one in the future. I'll write you again, telling exactly what she says about all this, so you'll have the instructions long before I arrive. I'll be sailing a week from tomorrow. I wish it were sooner, of course. Random House has already paid me for the travel book, for which I'm thankful, as I don't have to worry about that phase any longer. It's been something of a struggle to get it all through quickly. I just hope that the Larbi contract goes through all right, because even though I've signed it, William Morris still finds things in it to object to, and of course, Grove Press hasn't signed it or sent a check for advance royalties. However, I know they're completely sold on it, and have nothing but lavish praise for the whole thing, for which I'm also grateful. I noticed in Larbi's most recent letter that he has stopped working for Stuart, for which he remarks: Thank God. And I wonder if it isn't because he feels he can now live without working. I hope he isn't that stupid. But whatever it is, I'll be there so soon that there's nothing much to worry about. I'll set him straight on everything. If he's really in need . . . if his wife is giving birth to the baby or they need food, naturally he should get whatever you feel is right. Five thousand a week is all right, I suppose. He'll just get a bit less when I get back. But don't worry that I'm going to have a fit if he gets too much. What he must have particularly is a promise of more on my return, so he won't disappear. It would be tragic if he did that at this point. It's so crazy to see these impressive contracts with film rights, television, foreign rights etc., all with this name of his that he has invented, on the same page. You can imagine! And then to go to Grove Press and see their advance publicity on the book, and recall him and his taguia. It's all very funny.

Tomorrow I'm recording some of my stories on records for the company called Spoken Arts. It's going to take all day, God forbid. I think I've answered all your questions. The rest of the time before I sail I'm trying to feel fairly free, so I can shop and get my things together. I still have a lot of stuff at Libby's on Sixty-First Street. Much love. I can't wait to see you.

Bupple

TO JANE BOWLES

December 13, 1962
New York City

This is going to be very short, because I've got a million things to do. I just talked with Mr. Wero, and he told me that any fluid which is used by dry-cleaners anywhere in the world is perfectly good for cleaning the wig. He mentioned specifically benzine, ether, naphtha, carbon tetrachloride and something called renusit (which I take it is a trade-name meaning: "renews-it.") He also said not to buy the fluid at a drugstore, to buy it wherever dry-cleaners bought theirs, by the gallon. Only no water ever under any circumstances. I told him I was sure you knew that. He stressed the fact that there was no preference for one fluid over the others as far as their action on the wig went—only in the safety of the person cleaning it. So that ether, for instance, was more dangerous, naturally, than the others. Carbon tetrachloride of course is not inflammable, whereas the others are. But they all give off toxic fumes, as everyone knows, so it should be done in an open space rather than in a closed room. That's all. Perhaps at Stop-Pressing or Amaya they could tell you where to buy the stuff economically and what exactly they use. I hope this information is sufficient, because I couldn't get any more. Mrs. Wero was not in the place today. (However, I feel certain that he knows as much about it as she, and he was very polite and helpful, and not in a hurry to shut me off.)

Tennessee's play got enthusiastic reviews in all the Boston papers, and is entirely sold out for the two-week run there. Maybe it will be a hit. I had a call from A. J. Meyer last night from Boston about the book for Harvard Press, and he mentioned having tried to get seats. Another call came this morning from Cambridge, from the head of the Harvard University Press, Mark Carroll, and he wanted to confirm their interest. He also gave me a message for Charles, saying that he hoped he was making haste on his manuscript for them. So please give him that information, as I promised I'd get it to him quickly. In other words, he says: Hurry and finish it, please.

I read my two stories yesterday for Spoken Arts, to be brought out on a record next spring. God knows how they will sound. John Goodwin called last night; he's leaving for his plantation in the Dutch West Indies today, sent his love particularly to you, and said to tell you he thought he'd be passing through Tangier later on this season, probably in April. I'm bringing his journal with me, to correct and edit for publication. Rather a job, but there's no hurry on it, and it will give me something to do on the ship besides worry about my Arab café piece for *Holiday* and wonder whether Larbi and I will be able to finish the book in time for Grove Press. Everything is settled with Random House and the travel book will be out in the autumn. I wrote your mother last night; incha'Allah you've already communicated with her. So now I close.

Much love. Work a little. See you soon.

Bupple

P.S. Have you met the two beats you were so terrified of? I think one has gone to Algeria. Love again.

TO RICHARD SEAVER,

GROVE PRESS, NEW YORK

February 25, 1963

Tangier

Thank you for your bulletin stating that "Znagui" had arrived safely; in another week I ought to hear that you have the whole thing.

If the title doesn't seem right, let me know. I'm not very good at titles. It took me six weeks and many pages full of attempts, to get *No Exit* out of *Huis Clos*. The Bible was open at every book; Dante was spread out on the desk too, as you can imagine. At the end it was the Independent Subway which provided the two words, but that didn't stop Blanche Knopf from using it when her edition came out.

Tonight the cannon was fired ten times from the fortress in the Casbah. Charhadi, although he knew it was for the Aid es Seghir, preferred to think it a salute to the birth of his daughter, since he had just come from the hospital after the event. He is transfigured; I've never seen him look so alive.

Enclosed are the changes in the text I spoke of in my most recent note. I assume you'd rather have them immediately, before any copying or setting up of type is initiated. It looks like a mountain, the list. But they're all necessary. I had to standardize the place-names, and the hero can't very well be called by the supposedly real name of the author—not if the book is to be entered as fiction in the Formentor affair, can he? However, there won't be any more alterations or additions. (The description of the market in Aïn Moumen would spoil the rhythm of "The Wire," I've decided. Charhadi told me about it subsequent to the telling of the story, and I liked it so much I automatically wanted to include it, but I was mistaken, as I have been almost every time I've wanted to add extra material. The tale is more hermetic than I had imagined.)

This is all for the present. Let me know everything.

April 17, 1963
Tangier

I've been reading a great deal about you lately; people send me articles from
here and there. Then I enjoyed the piece by Ann Morrissette in *Evergreen*.
Someone from California wrote me that Francesca Pivano Sotsass or however
she spells her name changed publishers when hers refused to do *Naked Lunch*.
Then you were having an affair with someone's child; I couldn't make it out,
quite, whose child it was. Bits of international gossip that get around. I'm not
going to Corfu to the International Publishers' Conference. Grove Press could
get me only a cabin on the "Zion" of the Zim Line to Israel, with four in the
cabin. I decided to stay in Tangier. A letter yesterday hopefully suggested I go
by train. Via Albania, I assume, since it's opposite that coast. No sign of Pepe
el Culito. Wouldn't you like to go next winter to Ceylon and visit Arthur Clarke?
He spends most of his time under the water anyway, and is nice when he comes
up. I'm negotiating for a house in Asilah at the moment. The only inhabitant
I know there is Hamri, besides an Englishman who seems to come and go, and
has a house in the sea-wall just south of Raisuli's palace. Anyway, it will be a
magnificent place to spend the summer, with the waves breaking under the
windows on the sand. I hope you do come down and can come out. I'm taking
for granted the fact that I'll get it. Every night I was in New York I recorded
Symphony Sid, so I returned with a great stack of tapes of jazz, which I now
play so that there is always something new. Galleys just corrected for Random
and pages for Peter Owen. I'm always worried they won't receive them, for I
have to send them open. The postal prices here are insane now. The identical
parcel which Random sent me for $3.85 was going to cost $36 to send back. It
was in a big double envelope. I removed the outer envelope and tried to send
it then. At that point it was going to cost $19 and something. Then I suggested
sending it open, and it cost just under $6. It had come sealed, of course. God
knows. Brion writes Mohammed Larbi is staying with him in Paris. And George
Andrews is there. Libby Holman here with her husband and maid. The last
named is colored, and won't go out of the Hotel Minzah because she claims
everyone stares at her, and she thinks it's because she's colored. Actually they
think she's Moroccan and attractive. But she's sure everyone is making fun of
her. The only place she'll go is the Marhaba Palace because we always sit in the
hidden corner of the empty back room and Djilali flirts with her. You remember

Brion's head-waiter at 1001? To get back to the recipient of the Prix Formentor, which is what I was going for (except that obviously nobody knew what I intended to vote for), but maybe it will get the prize anyway. I inquired if it were possible to vote by proxy or in absentia, and they replied that it was not. It's on the American list of candidates, also on the German. Grove sent me their edition. I like it better than the Gerodias edition. (Or is it spelled like that?) (I speak of the Prix Formentor, above, and I mean the International Publishers' Prize, called this year suddenly the International Literary Prize. I have nothing to do with the Prix Formentor.) Went to Sister Bankhead's tonight. Bu Faulkner there, and Anne Harbach. Probably Paul Lund later. Libby had to get back to the hotel to take her maid out to dinner. Worse than traveling with a baby. But a girl of great charm. Charhadi, who wrote the book Grove is publishing, often asks about you. He remembers you from Sidi Ali and other sin spots. Ira [Cohen] has a little money. His mother was just here. I have no idea what he's going to do with the money, however. You'll remember that last year his grandfather sent him a thousand dollars for the magazine, and he suddenly began to travel compulsively. I don't think it will necessarily be due to lack of money if the magazine fails to appear. It will be for lack of sustained and concentrated interest. However, that's a private suspicion, and not for quoting. I like and respect Ira because he's brilliant and serious. I wish he weren't so nervous. Short and long range. I'll contribute something.

TO JOSEPH FOX,

RANDOM HOUSE, NEW YORK

●

April 29, 1963

Tangier

I have your letter of the twelfth of April, to which this purports to be an answer. Miss Ennis had already given me a copy of the questionnaire to bring back with me and fill in at my leisure. When I saw the questions, however, I reacted adversely. Of course, I've always complained that the writer is not accorded a place within the framework of American society, so I ought not to object to a document which does its best to make him feel he "belongs." Therefore, it's probable that I'm all wrong about the writer being persecuted and forced to remain outside; in that case, I hadn't understood what life in the United States is about. Whatever the truth there may be, I still feel irremediably alienated, as they like to say, and more at home if I'm physically outside as well. I suppose it's just that I don't want to play.

For the jacket, I'll list geographical facts chronologically, and you ought to be able to get sufficient material from the mess to fashion a blurb. I was born in 1911 in New York City. My first publication was in the old *transition* in 1928. I entered the University of Virginia in 1929, which I quit for the Left Bank. Two years later I made my first visit to North Africa, a tentative trip which lasted for four years. I should have been back here to live earlier if it had not been for the War. As it was, there was a five-year stay in Latin America. After the War I returned to Morocco and bought a small house in the Medina of Tangier; this became my base of operations for travel southward and eastward. In 1949 I first saw Ceylon and India. I began to go regularly in that direction, and ended by buying an island off the south coast of Ceylon, which served as a winter headquarters until 1959. Now once again I live all year 'round in Morocco.

These seem to be the pertinent facts for this particular book. I had some new pictures taken earlier in the week, but I'm not satisfied with them, and intend to continue trying. I'll send the least objectionable when I've finished. It should be next week—I mean during the week of May 5th to May 12th. I hope this isn't too late. I've got nothing recent to send you; that's the difficulty.

I'm moving down the coast this week, to a house I've discovered in the sea-wall of Asilah. That's going to complicate life. It will not interfere with receiving mail.

If you want more information, I'll be glad to send it to you; just tell me what you want to know. I imagine my paragraph here will be enough.

TO ALLEN GINSBERG

June 1, 1963
Asilah

Dear Allen,

And of course Dear Peter. Yours very welcome. Delighted to see you doing everything I should have done, but would have done had I hit it when I was eighteen and had the energy. Instead, I was happy with Europe. Isabelle Gerofi showed me the City Lights thing with all the photos in it: Howrah Bridge and so on. Ted Joans says Ferlinghetti is en route to Tangier for the summer. May be an unfounded rumor. Bill [Burroughs] writes he will be down this month, and will stay all summer. I have a house in the sea-wall of Asilah. The waves breaking below induce relaxation successfully. The house is Indian. Owner used to be stationed in Bombay, brought back doors, cabinets and much furniture, around which he built a Moroccan house. Result completely successful. The Moroccan puritanism and simplicity sets off the baroque Indian perfectly. Not even noticeably hybrid. Grove submitted my translation from Moghrebi (A *Life Full of Holes*) to the Formentor Prize Committee, but it did not win. Which presumably means that it will be published this August. Banaras must be magnificent, even though one is officially there on an intellectual level. I suppose a spiritual level would be a subheading of that. Yeah, namastutti indeed! I hope this catches you in Banaras before you leave for Canada. And if you can't get through the Iron Curtain will you be coming via the Mediterranean? That would be good for Bill and me. Although I now notice you are spending several months in the U.S. before returning to India. So probably Bill won't still be here anyway by then. Can't think of any news about Tangier that would appeal to you. Many tourists in large groups being herded around the Medina. *Gentlemen's Quarterly* recently had nineteen models (male) and one mannequin (female) living in York Castle, being photographed interminably in the alleys of the Casbah. Sometimes took two hours to get the creases right in the trousers, the legend runs. It's to be a Tangier issue. *Look* also doing a spread. No apparent reason. NBC News came looking for a beat story, but I suspect didn't get a very satisfactory one. Sonia and Narayan involved in a court case dealing with the geyser in their bathroom. Sonia's telling of the story quite good. It's the Aachor here. Pandemonium of drums within the walls. (The Portuguese managed to get them all inside one wall with only one entrance, and then they put a moat around the wall which comes out on both sides into the sea. Administrative tactics. But with a still-existing visible result, in that directly outside the walls are fields of canebrake and groves of olives and figs.) So, no more news and much love.

TO IRA COHEN

Summer 1963
Asilah

Good. Good. Everything's understood. If I'm free to do what I want, all is well. And you can see that a think-piece could conceivably take a very long time. The more think, the more time. Whereas fiction takes no thought at all, of course. In any case, now I'm making notes of ideas that occur to me, as they come. Eventually I'll have to write such a piece, I can see. But it might easily not be in time for *Genauer*. (I knew an art-critic named Emily Genauer; when I see your spelling, I can't keep from thinking of her. She came to see me in Tangier in 1955 or 1956 with her husband, and then she went away again.) The Tangier Guennaoua are here in Asilah at the moment; I witnessed them last night around one thirty, met two of them again this morning in the street at the Parada, whereupon they asked me if I could employ them in my house. After my negative reply, they suggested I return to the house where they were playing. I intend to, tonight at some point. What sort of beetles did you bring back from Marrakech? Cantharides? Glad you have fasoukh at hand; it's useful for so many things, including a slight but subtle consciousness alteration. I've told you about it, probably . . . I refer to my experiments in New York in 1933. (I used to be a maniac on the subject of fasoukh, of course.) (Carried it everywhere with me . . . to the Andes, the West Indies, Beverly Hills and San Francisco, testing its effects, which are definite if limited.) And what is the use of the poppies, and what is their color? Are your "kaaba l'ouzel," as you call them, crescent-shaped, with confectioner's sugar outside? I strongly suspect they are *cabrhozels*—"gazelle-horns," and never yet have I seen one containing kif. However, perhaps you had some made specially for you. There's a page about djaoui in my new book, received Wednesday from London. But I thought you were au courant on the subject; I thought you were present the day Mohammed Larbi held forth on the subject at Itesa. Its properties are pretty much purely associational, subjective: the olfactory crystal ball.

TO JOSEPH FOX,
RANDOM HOUSE, NEW YORK

July 22, 1963
Asilah

The advance copy of *Heads* arrived; I duly remarked the cost of postage and was correspondingly grateful to you for having bothered to send the book by air.

The format is good, the type is excellent, the jacket is attractive, and I'm very much taken with the cover with its use of the same emblem as *Let It Come Down*.

The information in the caption under the photograph of Taprobane is at variance with that on the back flap of the dust jacket: the former gives 1959–1962, and the latter gives 1952–1959. I suppose one may take one's choice. Then there is a completely inexplicable error (which was not in the proofs) putting the Parador of Ketama in Bab Berret. (I always wondered why you were so preoccupied with that generator!) Apart from those two blunders I like to assume the book is readable, although I'm aware that only cranks really read these days, and that the day of the book is almost forgotten. So I have no reason to assume anything, in reality.

I'm happy to have the book, and delighted that no photos of my face appeared in connection with it, although I can't go so far as to suggest that anyone would be likely to purchase it because of having read the two paragraphs reproduced on the back of the jacket . . . or, indeed, any other paragraph contained in the collection. However, it's all very flattering, and one looks better smiling than wincing; there's no doubt about that.

I can't think of anyone anywhere who would be interested in seeing the book, which is why I haven't replied to Miss Ennis's inquiring letter. Each decade I know fewer people. By 1980 life will be perfect.

TO NED ROREM
◆
August 27, 1963
Asilah

Not that it's germane to anything but the writing of this letter. But since the only other time I've taken mescaline was your fly-horror evening in the Poconos, it seems important to say that I'm writing from somewhere down there. Eight hours have gone past and I've felt nothing more than the sensation of being a tiny human rowboat with a huge motor attached to it. Much energy, inability to sit still, to eat or drink. Capable of talking at length, but inclined to be polemical, and, probably, unpleasant, although I haven't asked the opinion of anyone. I imagined that forcing myself to write you a letter would focus my energies sufficiently to keep me in one place. It seems to be doing that, at least. Yes, it's unpleasant, I suppose. A supremely unpleasant experience, naturally. And, I shouldn't think, of any use to anyone, save in retrospect. And even then! Is it really of interest to make up one's mind about a segment of reality? Today the whole summer has opened up, like an enormous abscess, and spewed out its essence. How did it happen? A breathless day, thick with fog from dawn on. Not fog. It came up out of the water, and with an enveloping stench that caught one's breath; everyone was saying: The air smells of shit. I walked two miles up the beach, and it was just as thick and hot and cloying as back here by the house where the waves are stiff with the black crust of rotten seaweed, and only now and then lick into the pools in the rocks where the sewage has lain these several months. Just as bad everywhere. Instead of coming with its water to clean away our filth, the ocean has decided to cover us with its own corruption. So the sweat runs down the chest inside the shirt, and the fog collects on the hairs of the jacket, and drips, and one doesn't know whether one is hot or cold. One shivers. It got to be quite awful at seven o'clock. The fog had turned black, and was moving around the rooftops in tatters, and the smell of excrement was vast and sweet all around. What is it? I asked the Moslems. Kharra, they said calmly. ¿No reconoces la mierda cuando la hueles?* I knew there would come a bad day eventually, and so I'm not astonished to be examining it. Perhaps the interesting thing about mescaline is the fact that it enables one to look closely and calmly at pure horror without feeling anything at all, save perhaps a vague desire to repair to another world as quietly as one can. But it makes me cantankerous. In all my conversations I find myself leading the inquisition. Oh? Yes? When? Aha, and how? I see. But why? Oh, you think so. And what makes you think so? I went to see Alfred Chester and quizzed him for a while. When I came out into the street it was as though the play had been finished for a good half hour, and only a work light was burning, and the play was over forever, and the sets had been struck, and the doors were open onto the street. Probably Fifty-Third Street. Whatever mescaline does, it doesn't make me coherent. But neither does it supply any feeling of there being an interior, unreachable cosmos. It says: See where you are? Look around. This is what it's like. Can you stand seeing it? Touching it, smelling it? Fortunately one draws no conclusions, since everything is far too real to be able to mean anything. As I say, you examine horror very closely, without even any interest. Disgust is what one would feel if one were alive. Instead of that, one knows that it's all artificial, the structure of reality itself. Disgust is something that ought to be felt *for* one by someone. But of course, there is not even anyone to experience the disgust, so it remains there, unfelt, but all around one—unregistered loathing, unattainable nausea, as wide as the smile of the sea while it belches up its corruption. So then I tried to eat dinner. Not possible. Yes, salad and soup and melon and Coca-Cola and

---

* Shit, they said calmly. Don't you know shit when you smell it?

Vichy, but not beef! And we agreed that this is the season of polio and meningitis and uncharted fevers, because it always is when the shit gets too thick for lack of rain, and the cherqi blows it all up into dust towers and scatters it over the land. And Larbi complained of his liver, and wailed: If I smoke kif it gets worse, but I have to smoke it or I'll burst. But what's going to happen anyway? And I said: What do you mean? And he said: We're all dying in any case. Which doesn't sound like a Moslem talking. And then he said: How many times have I taken hold of a rifle butt and pushed it away so that they hurt someone else instead of me? Who? I said, forgetting. The police, the soldiers, the guards. Whoever has command and whoever we're fighting. How does it happen you've never become a Communist? I asked him. He smiled one of those subtle, wise, very dramatic smiles, but innocently. I know all about them, he said. And do you think they're wrong? I went on. No. They're right. But what difference does it make? Nobody can do right. The world doesn't want that. The world has to be wrong, and the soldiers have to point guns at us and kill us, and that's the world. But perhaps some day it won't be like that, I said. You're still a Communist, he said. Only Communists think the world can be good. The world can't ever be good, and life can't ever be any different. Don't you know that? I said I did know it and did believe it, but he looked sceptical. I see it's half past one now. The room is full of insects, borne in by the stench of the ocean. I should think that if I stopped typing I might be able to go to sleep, but I doubt that whoever is seeing to such things for me is going to bother trying. Probably I should only lie awake, in any case. I've been through several changes of clothing. Everything is soaked in sweat as soon as I get it on my body. At least, I remember that you asked me to write and tell you whether I could send any of the notes I'd made on the libretto. And of course I am not able to now. If only it would rain for an hour and wash out the sweet smell of urine that fills the alleys. Each day since the first of May, when I came to Asilah, the smell has got a little stronger, the stains on the cement have grown blacker and thicker as layer dries on layer. The fishheads crawl with maggots and bristle with flies. Sometimes I take out a litre of gasoline and pour it over a particularly lively pile of garbage beside the front door. When I light it, the neighbors stick their heads out of the windows above and watch. They think it has something to do with my religion, and very likely it has. Yes, yes, of course. Don't we all want to be cremated? We who no longer have any connection with the earth. I took a lot of wild walks at top speed around the Medina, trying to lose the motor that was inside, or at least to run it down for a while. Nothing changed. I came back and lay down and read Robbe-Grillet for an hour, running with sweat and sometimes shivering with what I thought was cold. At twilight the fog lifted itself right off the sea and rose into the air several hundred metres up, and there was the moon, and all the rest of the spots in the sky the same as always. But the heat was worse than ever, and the stench strong because the tide had risen further. The waves were having difficulty breaking against the side of the house, they were so laden with the putrefaction they had found inside. Although the slaughter-house is outside the ramparts, it is not more than two hundred feet from here, and the blood runs down among mountains of garbage, because the town dump is also right here at the same spot. Four months of living here, and being aware of it, and amused by the fact, and it took the mescaline to convince me of its existence, to make me be able to say: But of course. You knew that all the time. And you knew the people were all as loathsome as the sea and the air. They smooth the lapels of your jacket while they tell you their lies . . . *Entina ketsfhem hsin menn hnaya.* (*Entina!* What a word, when they could say *enta,* like other people. But no: *entina*). *Entina ouahad rajel hsin.** A large grasshopper just sprang into my face. How it got into the Medina at all, I don't understand. Give my best to you, if you see you.

TO NED ROREM

September 16, 1963
Asilah

Yes. The memory of that evening when I wrote the letter is like a rather low cobweb hanging over me. I remember the fact of writing it, and I think it took forever, but I don't really recall what it felt like to be writing it, except that I connect the act with an attempt to get rid of a basic nausea. You ask if I'll ever take it again. I feel it would be rash to say no. But certainly not in Asilah!

Alfred Chester has been living two houses down the sea-wall from me for the past two and a half months. He arrived in late June with two wild dogs from Salamis. Perhaps you can paint yourself a picture of the complications occasioned by the two fanged monsters . . . down to lawsuits by irate parents. A small civil war broke out a fortnight after he had taken up residence, set off by one of the regular attacks by the dogs upon a small child. The parents went to complain to Alfred, and not being able to make themselves understood by him, grew bored

* You understand better than we do . . . You are a fine man.

and went to raise hell with the Moslem landlord who had rented him his flat. Others took up the complaint: What did he mean by letting Nazarenes into the quarter? (Overlooking the fact that Alfred is militantly Jewish and the further fact that I, a real Nazarene, had been living in the quarter since the first of May.) Still others came to the defense of the landlord. The clamor was startling, and it went on for hours, men shouting, women screaming, fists shaking, doors slamming, children crying. And Alfred grinning out of his shut windows up above the street. All day I took a back way through the Medina, so as not to have to push my way through the throng in my street.

And to think Purdy promised me I should do the music for *Color of Darkness* four years ago! How is it going to be? Have you seen any rehearsals? Although, with a broken ankle in Saratoga it doesn't seem likely, somehow. I suppose you'll go down before opening. I'd consider it a great favor if you'd let me know how it's received. You're aware that one can know next to nothing here. Now that I reconsider, it was then a question of making a film, and it was the soundtrack he swore I should have.

To return to the "evening." You ask if I was alone, and I was. Completely. My sleep-in servant had gone to Tangier for the first time during the whole summer, because I had never given him permission before. (He always had a day a week with his wife while I was in Tangier, so don't imagine mistreatment. I merely reread the sentence, and saw how colonial it looked!) So there was no one in the house, and I suppose I thought it was a propitious time, noting the absence of the cat, for me to play. Mescaline, l'extase des souris . . . Or more likely I felt intuitively that it was time to create an arbitrary milestone that might, in retrospect at least, serve the purpose of seeming to have cleared the atmosphere at the breaking up of summer. One can conjecture.

Please give my greeting to Mrs. Ames. I remember our evenings of talking, and it was thirty-three years ago this month. Let me hear what happens with plays, opera, ankle, plans for Morocco, everything. More than that I can't say. As you note, collaboration is not a transoceanic thing. I'll probably be in Asilah during October.

TO RENA AND CLAUDE BOWLES
_____◆_____

November 28, 1963
Tangier

Since I last wrote you Jane and I have been on a long trip through the south of Morocco. We started out two weeks ago with Christopher, went to Casablanca, then Marrakech, then over the Grand Atlas to Taroudant, then on to Agadir and Tiznit, and then up into the Anti Atlas, which is the desert. The weather was perfect the entire time, and we managed to get in on a great native ceremony, an ahouache, in Tafraout, which made the trip as far as we were concerned. Jane loved every minute of it, and we got back two nights ago.

Today is Thanksgiving and we are having dinner at the Macdonalds', along with other Americans, most of whom, like the Macdonalds, are with the State Department here in Tangier. The State Department nowadays doesn't necessarily mean the diplomatic service, since they have opened an official school for the teaching of Arabic to future diplomats who will be holding posts in Arabic-speaking countries hereabouts—a very good idea, it seems to me, since until now the Americans come over without knowing a word, and thus can't communicate with the people of the country. (I don't think most of them can manage yet, but it's at least a beginning.)

What a mess the Kennedy murder is! Very much like a gangster film so far. It hasn't been possible to buy an American paper since the news broke, so we have to be content with French and Spanish news, and they, of course, see a gigantic sinister plot behind the whole affair. (And of course they may be right.) Whatever the truth may be, it's certainly a scandal, the way the thing was handled in Dallas, and enough to make one suspect that the police were in on the arrangements of the higher-ups, and wanted to help by allowing the assassin to be removed, to insure silence. The Moroccans were very emotional about it, and actually wept when they talked about it. The entire country was shut down on Monday . . . no schools, banks, movies, bars, shops, or music on the radio. If their own king had died they couldn't have observed a more complete day of mourning. They all believe that when Jacqueline was here in Marrakech last month staying at the Sultan's palace, arrangements were made to help Morocco with military material, but secretly, so Nasser wouldn't exploit the information, and that now there is danger of the promises not being implemented. If such promises were made, which is likely, it is also possible that they will now fall through, which will be tragic in the event of an attack. However, only time will tell.

I can't make this very long, because we are on our way out to the Macdonalds' now. But I wanted you to know I had received your most recent letter, and to tell you of our journey to the desert. You just have enjoyed Franklin Robbin's visit to Gulfport. Not having seen him since 1942, I can't imagine what he looks like now, or what he is like. Perhaps some day I'll meet him there in Gulfport when he's visiting you.

It's chilly here in Tangier; one notices it more coming up from the south, naturally. But they haven't given us any heat yet, and we are wondering if and when they are going to start the furnace. However, we have fireplaces and heaters, so we don't mind too much. It merely costs more! So I'll close, sending much love.

TO JOHN GOODWIN

November 29, 1963
Tangier

Thanks for the pages from [Anthony] Carson, although I can't say anything good about the writing, can you? Occasionally a felicitous metaphor, and then back to the self-indulgent hyperbole. Christopher Wanklyn, who knows him, and who is the "other" in the Gibraltar anecdote, says it is all "humorous" prose, which hadn't occurred to me when I read it. Christopher also says Carson was constantly drunk while he was here. The pieces are from *The New Statesman* and *Punch*. His information only serves to identify the material as far as I'm concerned, without making it any more palatable. As reporting it's totally irresponsible, so I suppose it must be meant to be amusing. The fact that you eviscerated the book shows, I imagine, in what esteem you held it!

Jane and I just got back from a long trip in the deep south: Marrakech, Tizi n'Test, Taroudant, Agadir, Tiznit, Tafraout, Essaouira. All wonderful as always, with bits of good luck thrown in, such as an ahouache in Tafraout and perfect weather the whole time. Jane was very much set up by the voyage, first because she finally managed for the first time to get across the Grand Atlas without flipping, and then because she hadn't been in the desert since 1949, and was very much excited to find that it still exists as she remembered it, and that therefore her memories of it are accurate and not a subjective sentimental mishmash that had accreted over the years. So now of course she is full of projects involving further southern travel, which is fine. The new hotel in Tafraout is catégorie luxe, and the packs of jackals come baying out of the wilderness right up to the windows in the small hours of the night. The best corner of Morocco, certainly, that region. Saisissant, the Saharan sky, every time one makes contact with it again.

What news of Marion Dorn? Louis left for New York just before we went south, and no further information since. Arrivals in Tangier continue thick and fast, with four new ones telephoning yesterday alone; Jane tries to distinguish the beats by their voices, deciding, I'm afraid, that if they have what she calls "Jewish" accents, they must be beat. Perhaps it's a way; I don't know. I'm given strict instructions not to see any of them.

I assume we won't be seeing you this season. Are you still planning on Egypt? Let me hear when you can. (Of course, the man described as a strange idiot with an owl who is ruining his poor employees is Brion; that bringue was one of his refrains when he had the Mil y Una. "I'm betraying my little brown brothers . . ." But no one can be identified as me, since I never met Carson, and I guess it's just as well, seeing what he did with the others.)

TO ALAN ROSS,
THE LONDON MAGAZINE
———————————————◆———————————————
December 15, 1963
Tangier

With this note is the typescript of "Zohra" by Driss ben Hamed Charhadi. I don't know, of course, whether you will find that it has a place in the magazine or not, but I hope you will, because it seems, like everything Charhadi has done, an example of good storytelling: simple but not unsubtle. My translation is literal, sentence by sentence. I may have bent over backwards in trying to keep the language as stark as it is in Moghrebi; however, I believed that to lend it any style whatever would be to destylize it in effect.

This is a segment of a novel called A *Life Full of Holes* which Grove Press in New York will publish early in 1964. You may already have seen other parts in numbers of *Evergreen Review*, in 1962 and 1963. I shall be most eager to have your reaction to the piece, whether or not you think it suitable for *The London Magazine*.

What is the title of the volume to be published by Eyre and Spottiswoode (spelling?) in which you are including my story *The Time of Friendship*? And when do you expect it to appear? Forgive my questions, but here I am thoroughly out of touch with all worlds save this particular corner of the Moslem world, and that is being very much isolated indeed!

TO OLIVER EVANS

January 13, 1964
Tangier

Three days ago we said good-bye to Bill Gray and three of his friends who had been spending the week with him in the Hotel Atlas, here in Tangier. They all talked of you; the unfortunate thing is that I can't recall their names, although they live in New Orleans, so you doubtless will be able to figure out their identity. They had a large Mercedes with them which they left on the other side of the Strait, but they resolved to return later this year bringing it along with them.

The Carson [McCullers] saga sounds difficult, but as you say, she is really extremely ill, so it isn't surprising. There were a lot of "permanent" occupants of the house in question in Brooklyn Heights. Jane and I were among them during the winter of 1940–41, and we left in April for Mexico. Carson had already moved out, as it was into her two rooms (originally Gypsy Rose Lee's) that we moved. Oliver Smith was also there on the same floor; he had been there during Carson's occupancy as well, and did have some magnificent stories to tell about her drunkenness, but I don't think they belong in your work! The address of the house was Seven Middagh Street, which is what everyone called it. Richard Wright eventually moved into the basement with his wife and child, with Auden and Chester Kallman on the top floor, after Britten and Pears had gone elsewhere. I remember visiting them one morning in what had been our community dining-room. Sometimes Carson came with Reeves, who was in uniform at the time, being in the army. (Peers or Pears—I've forgotten the spelling—is a tenor, has lived for years with Benjamin B., and sung his works innumerable times.) Obviously, many people came and went—practically everyone I knew came at one time or another, including Virgil Thomson and Aaron Copland, yes. And Denis de Rougemont, Tchelitchew, Dalí, and Genia Berman, Bernstein, Kirstein and Blitzstein. . . . (It begins to sound like Santa's address to his reindeer in "The Night before Christmas.") Anyway, it was full of people always, and Auden ran it and paid for the servants and food, and we all paid him regularly on a cooperative basis, and it worked very well except for a few terrible rows, which were inevitable. Since Jane and I did not live there while Carson was an inhabitant, I really couldn't say whether she had a "surly" character, but as I remember her, she was friendly and rather shy in those days. It was several years later that I got to know her better—when she had moved to Nyack, precisely. Later in Paris she was getting ready for her illness; she seemed in a ghastly state.

You ask about Christopher Isherwood: I first met him in Berlin in the spring of 1931, when he was living on the Nollendorfplatz, if I remember correctly. We used to meet for lunch every day at one thirty at the Café des Westens on the Kurfürstendamm. Over the years in between I've seen him in New York and Tangier, as well as in Santa Monica at his home. And yes, I do like him very much. I wonder why you've had a difficult time, unless he shuts you out, which is conceivable.

I must write Tennessee. Not that I expect him to reply. (And it is difficult to carry on a monologue correspondence. One never believes one's letters have really reached and been read by one's correspondent.)

Did I tell you I've sold the Moroccan novel to five foreign publishers before publication? Very much pleased.

TO NED ROREM

◆

February 5, 1964
Tangier

One way of keeping partially à la page is to receive a letter from you from time to time, written on the back of a photocopy of a piece of yours in the *Voice*. Your most recent arrived yesterday; I beg to accuse reception. Glad to hear of your visit to Ahmed, and to be able to assume that the girl he is with is the same one who lived here with him; one never knows what changes of partners will come about. It sounds like Laurel; we'll say it was she. I don't quite understand what he thinks he's doing in New York without having ever bothered to arrange an exhibit beforehand; perhaps he was just tired of Tangier. What happened to Marc Blitzstein? I saw the notice in *Time*, but am unable, naturally, to get any further details on the murder here. Tell me what you hear. I'm sorry to lose Marc. Ça va continuer de plus en plus vite, the snuffing out of one's friends. Not to mention oneself, but that's in another category, of course! Jane leaves tomorrow for Marrakech early in the morning, motoring with the president of Air Liquide and Oxyton, Ltd., whatever they are. Sir Michael Duff and the Comtesse de Breteuil and Nina Mdvani, and David Herbert, will go down, so she won't be alone. I refused to go, on dental grounds. Every rose has its thorn and every cloud its silver lining. My broken-off-at-the-gumline bicuspid at least has made it possible for me to have five days of solitude here, which will come in mighty handy for the novel I'm getting into. In any case, I'm counting on that. The weather has been astonishing—the finest winter I remember seeing here. No winter, liquid light and strong sun and no wind and great flowering of plants. I suppose God will send the rain and wind later and kill everything. Janie went into Italica this morning to get some money, and Monsieur Pomanarov said she owed him for a large tin of dusting powder by Yardley and that it was nine hundred francs. She said she had never bought dusting powder in her life, as if he had accused her of being an habitué of a blue movie den in the Zoco. He lost control of himself and screamed at her: "I give you credit and then you don't want to pay!" Aicha tried to calm him in Arabic, but since that is one of the few languages he doesn't speak (he's a Shanghai Russian) it was to no avail, and Jane retired to the street to cry. Her greatest indignation came during the next eight hours at home, however. She went to visit Charles Gallagher and told him about it, referring furiously to Monsieur Pomanarov as a "shopkeeper" and a "fishmonger." Charles took a stand and said that one of the "points" of Tangier was precisely that one *did* get to know the shopkeepers and invite them to one's house and play bridge with them. He cited Jay Haselwood as an example. "But Jay's a bartender!" Jane cried. "That's a whole other category!" Charles then hazarded the guess that Monsieur Pomanarov was just another poor Jewish businessman living under tension, and had happened to take it out on her. "Is he Jewish?" she demanded after some thought, and in a completely reasonable manner. A querschnitt of what life these days is like in Tangier. Your sang-froid in "starting," as you italicise, an opera less than twelve months before a scheduled performance, is admirable, the moreso in that I assume it's justified. Buen trabajo. I know all about being forty, but the feeling doesn't last. One simply becomes a little more respectable. Are you considering going to Alger? It must be pretty horrible. And when you ask about housing here, do you mean hotel rooms or apartments or houses? So anyway, until soon.

May 21, 1964
Tangier

Fortunately there is no way of my finding out the date of my last letter to you. I feel that if I should discover the truth I should be so ashamed I'd be unable to write to you at all. Tonight I had dinner with Lawrence Stewart and Lee Gershwin, and received messages from you. It seemed imperative that I let you know I had received them. Jane is going with them tomorrow to Tetuan or Xauen, and I imagine we'll be dining together again tomorrow night.

One of the awkward things about writing a friend after a considerable time-lapse is that one feels one should have something important to say. Something ought to have happened in the interim—things should have changed enough to warrant comment on them. But you have lived in Morocco, and although the country has changed enormously, the business of living in it is still pretty much the same, and that means that very little happens beyond the things that one makes happen all by oneself. News also remains outside the place: I did not know until this evening, for instance, that your book had already been published. I suppose it's a shameful admission to make, merely because it shows how insulated one can be as a result of living on in this country. And yet I have no desire to live anywhere else—a fact which is borne in upon me each time I visit the United States or Europe. I haven't been in Paris in fourteen years, or in London in seven. Jane and I did go two years ago to New York, and we intend to go again in December to visit our respective parents. (I shall also try my hand at giving classes for three months at the University of South Florida; I've never done it before, although I've been asked. It seemed to me an absurdity, and it still does, but I'm willing to try it once.) One reason why I don't move around any more is that travel of any kind has become so difficult, unless one is willing to use the air, which I'm not. There seem to be people everywhere, and they all seem to be more like one another than I am used to having them be, and while I realize that this is the state of the planet and that each year it is going to be more like this, I don't want to be reminded of it any more often than is necessary. Thus Morocco is in fact a refuge more than anything else, and I am quite willing to recognize it as that.

I saw Brion Gysin one day last summer when he came to visit me in Asilah. He appears to find it absolutely essential to be in Paris all the time; otherwise he'll die of hunger, he says. He complains bitterly about the city's decline, but

I feel it must have certain compensations which he doesn't mention during his tirades. Lawrence Stewart will carry this note to you when he leaves Morocco. Jane and I both send much love.

TO RENA AND CLAUDE BOWLES

June 12 [*1964*]
Tangier

I have had this envelope addressed to you for several days, with the intention of writing you while on the beach, where we go each day. But there always seems to be someone there to talk with, so that each day ends with no letter written. This will be short, as the post office closes at six thirty, and it is now twenty to six and I must walk in to mail it. Christopher took us to Merkala Beach today—at the foot of the Old Mountain. I don't remember whether we ever went there when you were here; I doubt it. But now it is equipped with a café where you can get cold drinks, so Janie likes it.

You ask about my finger. It is much better, although the doctor says it will not be straight again. It has a crook at the end—that is, the last joint will not straighten out. It is a damaged tendon, and the doctor says he can operate, grafting a new tendon of plastic, but he won't guarantee that the joint will bend, whereas now I can type with it, and have almost as much strength in it as I had before hitting it. I feel it's better to leave it as it is, rather than go in for dubious surgery.

Jane had two operations last year, the first one leaving her with a hernia which the second failed to correct, although the doctor put in a large piece of plastic screen. She is naturally very much upset, but actually the hernia is not too noticeable. And it doesn't seem sensible to undergo a third operation on purely aesthetic grounds.

Tennessee was here for about ten days a while ago; he seemed to enjoy it more than last time. He felt that the "atmosphere" had cleared considerably since his other visit. It probably has, but living here we don't notice it one way or the other. The Beatniks have invaded Tangier at last. Every day one sees more beards and filthy bluejeans, and the girls look like escapees from lunatic asylums, with white lipstick and black smeared around their eyes, and matted hair hanging around their shoulders. The leaders of the "movement" have moved their headquarters here, and direct the activities from here. Allen Ginsberg,

Gregory Corso and Burroughs are all established in Tangier now, sending out their publications from here. The residents have been outdoing themselves giving parties for them.

No particular news from us. All goes on as ever. I have two new editions which will appear: a book of short stories in Spanish, from Barcelona, and *Let It Come Down* in a British pocket edition. How is Daddy after his sunstroke? The sun can be treacherous at that latitude, I know. I got a terrible burn in Cuba in 1945 when I was there with Oliver. In bed two days, lying on my stomach, with the doctor coming to cut the skin off my back and pour on sulfathiazole powder. They doubtless have something better now. Gordon Sager has taken Bob Faulkner's apartment for the summer while Bob visits his mother in New Hampshire. The only place I have been since early December is Gibraltar.

TO JAMES LEO HERLIHY

December 1, 1964
Tangier

When I was living on my island off Ceylon a friend named Hugh Gibb came to spend a fortnight with me; he had just returned from a sojourn in the Maldives, and was the only European to have gone and stayed with the people there. According to him they were all Moslems, and lived a fine windswept sort of life, eating fish and fruit, and plying among the hundreds of islands. The same year my ship, the *Issipingo*, took a course en route to Mombasa that brought it within a mile or two of certain of the outer Maldives, and I must say it looked incredibly pristine. I sat all morning on deck watching the strips of sand and palms slip by. I remember it moved me to start a novel at the moment, so that while I looked at the islands I invented the opening pages of the book. Perhaps if the Maldives had been more numerous, or more widely scattered, I should have got far enough into it to be able to hang on to it. As it was, once the stimulus had become invisible (after lunch, that is), I purposely forgot about it. By the time I got to Kenya I wondered why I'd thought of starting that particular story, and threw the pages out. But it always happens that way. *Sky* I started in order to make the hotel room at the Belvedere in Fez more real than it was. It began with the hotel room and extended itself beyond, fortunately. *Let It Come Down* I started while sailing past Tangier on the M.S. *Gen. Walter* one foggy winter night; I was going from Antwerp to Colombo, but Tangier was outside in the dark, so I had to be there, too. *The Spider's House* began on the *Andrea Doria* on the way to New York. Unthinkable situation; I had to be back somehow in Fez from where I'd come. I don't expect further difficulties when *LWAFH* appears in French, since it's already unequivocally banned now—in any form. I told you, I think, how one police chief said to me: "There are truths which are too bitter to be told," à propos of the book? (I translate literally, of course.) On another day, still regarding the same subject, another police-sergeant remarked: "A good writer doesn't just write about life as it is. He writes about it the way it should be, and then he does good to humanity." Every book-seller in Morocco was sent a form letter announcing that possession of the book was an offence. The proprietor of my neighborhood stationery store showed it to me, being a Russian (Soviet) citizen and interested in such matters. (Up until three years ago he sold mags and papers published in Peking; then he stopped.) Braziller will issue *LWAFH* in N.Y. The resistance is important, but one can't consider it anything less than a second front. Thus the danger of premature action (probably inevitable).

TO RENA AND CLAUDE BOWLES
◆

December 12, 1964
Tangier

Since I last wrote you I have retyped and rewritten my new book, gone to Spain and visited up and down the Costa del Sol taking hundreds of notes, returned and got into the middle of the *Holiday* article, and generally let my correspondence go to the dogs. I have quite a pile of letters to answer. One letter I found on my return from across the Strait was an invitation from the Cuban Government to visit Havana for the months of January and February, all expenses paid. They are evidently trying to get writers and artists there, so they will return home and announce to all and sundry how magnificent it is there under the new regime. From what I've heard, hotel accommodations are pretty awful there anyway. I don't see how many people would accept their invitations at the moment, even if they were not prevented from it by law, as is the case with Americans. Obviously I wouldn't have accepted in any case. Havana was no great shakes under Batista, and it must be unbearable under Castro. And Cuba isn't an interesting country in any case, no matter what sort of political regime it may have. Jane was horrified that such a communication should have arrived, and thought I ought to take it to the American Consul, but I assured her it was routine, which it is.

For a long time Jane was trying to decide whether or not to go to London with David Herbert for Christmas. I probably wrote you about it two months ago. She has been discussing the pros and cons of it for at least three months. Finally she decided against going, a definite decision, only to try two days before the ship was due in Gibraltar (coming from Australia) to get passage again. This involved cables to Naples and Marseille and Gibraltar, and proved fruitless. Then after David had left she thought of flying up, and although he has been gone ten days, she still thinks of taking a plane to London. (She hates planes.) She seems to imagine that if she saw certain people it might do some good for her with regard to the novel, which is being published, it appears, in February. She was invited to stay with the publisher and his wife, and had a ten-day invitation to Veynal Castle in North Wales—the very beautiful place where Sir Michael Duff had us, back in 1949. But nothing seemed to influence her in either direction. The more attractive it was made there, the more she determined to stay here; conversely, the more difficult it became to get there, and the less reason there was for going, the more often she talked about the necessity of getting there. And who knows, she may go yet, as she reminds me every day. And I answer: "I wouldn't put it past you." But of course, I'm pretty sure she's not going to budge; she feels she's more interesting if she's about to disappear to London. It's that simple. It's a game she obliges everyone to play with her.

People seem to be leaving Tangier at present. Last week Brion Gysin, Bill Burroughs, and the Moroccan who wrote the book I translated into English last year, all went to New York. Brion thinks he may make a fortune with an invention of his called the Dream Machine. He has signed a contract with a manufacturing firm which will produce them en masse. It's like the nineteenth-century "whirligig" that you looked into, although the principle is different, his machine benefitting by modern science. It turns electrically and produces what neurologists call the "alpha wave," which corresponds to nineteen flashes per second and hits the optic nerve in such a way that it induces hallucinations (not to mention frequent epileptic seizures)! Anyway, it promises a new kick to the juvenile delinquents. So far there is no law against such a contraption. If people want to knock themselves out with the alpha wave, they're at liberty to do it, I suppose.

I imagine we'll be right here for Christmas. We've already been invited to Marguerite McBey's for Christmas Eve dinner . . . one of our old friends here who has a fine house on the Mountain overlooking the sea. After New Year's she is leaving for Peru for the winter. Nothing much happens. I am tied up in my article, and hope to meet the deadline. Love to you both.

TO ANGUS STEWART

April 3, 1965
New York City

Here in this tough town: a blizzard as we arrived yesterday. Today cold, with a knifelike wind blowing around the knifelike edges of the buildings. Steel, chromium, glass, concrete, faceless people. No wonder a man can be murdered in a subway car while a score of them watch impassively: "Just sit still. It's none of our business." A couple last night in the restaurant, while I ate Chinese food: "For Christ's sake!" "What's Christ got to do with it?" "Huh? Who are you? I thought you was Christ, maybe." "Ah, go fuck yaself." "So sell the property, see what good it does ya." "Ah, shut up!" "Ya want some more chow mein?" "Whadda you care if I want some more chow mein? Just shut up." "Yeah, you're right. You're always right." "Ah, shut up, ya stupid sonofabitch." It went on during the whole meal, a fitting introduction to arrival in town. Bill Burroughs has disappeared for the nonce; no one knows where he is, including Grove Press. Spoke with Tennessee last night on the phone. His first words: "They're fucking you in New Jersey, Baby." (Seems a new production of *Glass Menagerie* is running, without my name on the boards. However, I'll collect, at least.) My manuscript delivered, being re-thermofaxed. Visited *Holiday* offices, saw Ronald Searle's comic illustrations to my as yet unwritten Casablanca piece, which will not be comic. Persuaded them to suppress certain drawings which were particularly inapropos. Jane spending the weekend in Bucks County. Everything fantastically cheap here save food and lodgings, which last fantastically expensive. A filthy room for sixteen dollars a night, and I have to clean the bathroom myself.

Don't let the cat climb up the chimney; get Manuel to block it if you don't want to make a fire. The beast is crazy, I believe.

Nothing but Selma and Martin Luther King on the radio, every fifteen minutes, no matter where I tune. America is a degenerate adolescent giant on a rampage. One has to take it seriously, if only to keep out of its way. Hard to imagine what will be happening here in a few years. Hard enough to believe

what is happening now. Got a room full of varicolored orchids—dozens—
presented to Jane in Madeira. What about Casablanca? Write me, for God's
sake!

TO JANE BOWLES

April 12, 1965
Gulfport, Florida

I may have a letter from you today, once the postman on his motorcycle
comes past, but again I may not, so I am writing anyway. I hope everything is
going well where you are, and that you are enjoying your visit with Libby and
Louis. My father seems a bit better than when I arrived, but of course he cannot
walk at all, or even move from his bed or chair without assistance, nor will he
be able to at any time again. Each night after he is put to sleep, my mother
and I discuss possible procedures to follow with regard to him. She is completely
against putting him into a home, but she isn't strong enough to cope with him
by herself. Her brother Paul had been helping her until my arrival, but when
I got here he delivered an ultimatum announcing that he could not go on. In
the light of all this, there seems to be nothing to do but find a nurse who can
come in each day and get him irrigated and from his bed to his chair. The great
difficulty is that he has no idea where he is or what is going on. What actually
happened is that while he was in the hospital he was given drugs which caused
a minor cerebral haemorrhage . . . this according to the doctors. Naturally my
mother ought not to keep him here with her all alone, for he is a bit like Dr.
Roux's husband, and has little fits of rage when he insists on getting up by
himself—or at least on making a desperate attempt to do that—and of course
that makes it doubly difficult for whoever is taking care of him. He doesn't realize
that he is not mobile, that he is attached by a tube to a bottle which is on the
floor near him (since his bladder no longer functions at all). Once he did that
and had to be rushed to the hospital again. He would have been dead in an
hour if they had delayed. The only sensible thing would be for him to be in a
home where he could have constant medical care, but she won't consider that,
so some sort of stop-gap has to be found.

I am wondering if you really intend to go to New Orleans or not. Could you
let me know? I might go there for a few days by myself, just to get a rest from
here, and then return to see how the schedule we devise is working out. Obviously

I am as worried about my mother as about him, since she isn't up to doing all she is insisting on doing, and might easily collapse if she tried to continue this way. I'd like to see how a routine with a nurse functions, before I leave definitively. If you still want to do the New Orleans stint, I'll wait, but obviously you'd have to do it before you went to see your mother, as by the time you leave Miami it will be at least mid-May, and I'll be back in New York long before that. It's difficult to be here under these circumstances. There is no way I can get to any store in any town. The only car available seems to belong to Pauline's daughter, a teen-ager who needs it every minute for her social engagements. And as you know, the United States belongs completely to the teen-agers now. No one would think of asking one to forgo anything for five minutes; it's inconceivable. By the time one is twenty-five one has lost most of one's civic rights and is only fit to dodder around in the background. What a delightful civilization it is! However, I'll spare you my remarks. But do let me know how you feel about New Orleans. I had a letter, forwarded by Helen Strauss's office, from them down there, saying to come along. I confess I'm not particularly eager to go. It would merely be an interlude between now and the time when some sort of routine here in the house would have been inaugurated. If I don't go soon I shall simply stay on here and then go directly back to New York, and hope for the best. It gets hotter and hotter here . . . in the nineties every day now. I imagine Miami is cooler, being on the Atlantic. I had a letter from John Hopkins, saying Tangier had remained absolutely calm, and that the only news they had about the Moroccan situation came from *The New York Times* and *Herald Tribune*. But I know that doesn't particularly interest you in any case, and you undoubtedly know much more than I by now. Neither the papers nor the radio ever mention the world at large down here. One would think that the United States was the only country in the world. There's no way of finding out anything. I suppose it's rather like being a Moroccan in Morocco—rather worse, in fact, for they do give international news there in Standard Arabic every night for those who can understand it, at least. Here, absolutely nothing. The papers are full of bathing beauties and real estate reports, and the radio never mentions anything outside of local events, excepting occasionally a short report on Viet Nam. Let me hear from you, even if it's two or three lines telling me when you plan to be in Miami.

May 17, 1965
New York City

This is not going to be a verbose letter. After two nights on the train, I feel like getting to bed, and it's ten thirty. I slept pretty well both nights, but being tossed from side to side isn't like lying in a still bed, and the roar of the train isn't quite as restful as silence, or even relative quiet. New Mexico was wonderful for sleep. Nothing but the sound of the wind in the piñon trees outside the window. Haven't "heard" such silence in years. In Morocco there's always a dog barking somewhere, or roosters crowing, or distant traffic on a road. Out there, there wasn't a sound, and the forest backed right up into the snow-covered peaks behind the house. And such pure air! Naturally it makes one feel drunk, being 7000 feet high. In any case, it seems to be good for the health, as everyone says I look very well. I noticed that the little pains I had in my finger-joints disappeared immediately, so it must be indicated for people like me. However, here I am back in the filthy city, where you can scarcely breathe the air, it's so full of fumes. Jane and I both got back today, and she is already busy rushing around. I suppose she feels like it after sitting so long doing nothing in Miami.

I'm glad you received the vitamins; of course in themselves they won't put weight on you, but they may inspire you to eat a bit more, which *would* help. 93 pounds, indeed! You should put on at least ten as soon as possible. I hope now and then you'll send me a little bulletin of your weight, so I can keep track. Also delighted to hear that Daddy is coming along well and has a little more energy than he had before. If I'd only had access to a car while I was there, I could have gone and bought the TV set myself, so he could have had it several weeks earlier. I was afraid, after I left, that you were not going to buy it, and I'm very happy to hear you have. It ought to help fill in little corners of empty time in a satisfactory manner. If there was anything to look at over in Tangier, even I might have one, but as it is, there is no point at all. I do very well with my short-wave radio, which has eight bands and can get about half the world. Mostly I listen to the news in various languages and from various countries with various kinds of governments, and compare notes; it's instructive if you're interested in the psychology of politics. Today I received the page-proofs in French of a book of mine which is being published in Paris, so I have a big job ahead of me. I did quite a bit of rewriting (after reflection) on the new book while I was in Santa Fe, and now have got to collate the new sections into what I'd thought was the definitive draft of the manuscript. I still hope to have some sort of decision on it before I leave. "The Glass Menagerie" got good reviews, so I imagine it will run a bit; so far it's only a limited engagement, until June 26th.

I looked at several places in Santa Fe, not with any idea of choosing those particular ones, since by the time we were wanting anything, there would be a whole different selection, but just to get a general idea. Prices are high out there if one thinks of buying; it seems everyone wants to live there—particularly people with money. However, rents are a good deal less than in New York City. (And who wants to live here at *any* price?) I must close. Much love to both of you.

TO ANGUS STEWART

August 2, 1965
Tangier

Hadn't realized that you were upset by Tangier this time, save perhaps physically, since you wrote you might be undergoing medical treatment on arriving back home. I hope nothing's amiss now. Shame about Blond, although he didn't make too good an impression here in Tangier when he visited. However, I can't believe finding another publisher will prove so difficult. Since Random House found my new book too "nihilistic," it turns out that Simon & Schuster will be doing it instead. Never had dealings with them before. Just made a trip into southern places: Safi, Essaouira, Tiznit, Taroudant, and then up to Marrakech and finally to Fez. I'd thought to do a similar stint with you; another time, incha'Allah. The Sight Savers await whoever comes to take them away. Never noticed the magnetic pot-holders weren't present until you mentioned them. Aicha obviously invented Minnie on the spur of the moment, which is why when I returned from America she began an intensive campaign to get everyone to call the beast by that name; she insisted you had bestowed the name on it. In any case, it's still nameless, thank God. We expect Bill Burroughs to arrive soon; he's finishing a book for Grove Press and will then set sail. Sometimes wind, sometimes calm, but always sun. I wish I had a car, to get into the country every day. Did I tell you *Holiday* is sending me to Iran, Pakistan and Afghanistan? And I know nothing about any of them. Also Little, Brown offers $15,000 to do a book on Cairo. I'd have to live there for at least a year in order to manage it. Why can't they make it Fez or Marrakech instead? My experience of Cairo is limited to one day at this point. I suppose they figure that if I know Tangier

I must know Cairo too, since they're only twenty miles apart. Hundreds of hotel reservations are said to have been cancelled here because of Boumédienne's jailing of Ben Bella. Algiers, Tangier, all same. Now the papers run articles headed: LA CRISE TOURISTIQUE A TANGER. Anyway, all best.

TO RENA BOWLES

November 23, 1965
Marrakech

A note from Marrakech. I thought I'd get some good weather here, at least, but this is the third day, and still no clear skies. The whole country seems to be shrouded in clouds and rain, month after month, this year. It's the first time anyone has ever seen it this way, and of course everyone blames it on nuclear experimentation; perhaps it's true. Who knows? In any case, tomorrow I'm going back to Tangier. There's no point in being here in bad weather. Am having dinner tonight at Christopher's house, which he has finally made into a really beautiful place. Of course, now that he's got it finished, he's leaving (December 8th) for Japan, Siam, Peking, Persia and various other exotic spots. I think he has enjoyed building, designing and furnishing the house more than he enjoys just living in it, and that I can understand, since he is all alone. What good is a big house for one lone man? He'd really be happier in a room or two, except that he does enjoy having guests, and playing host. This city is shabbier and poorer than I've ever seen it, and there are soldiers with machine-guns and bayonets every few feet, hundreds of them, all over the town, night and day, just standing at attention. The government obviously is taking no chances! I don't know what's going to happen in Morocco. Things seem to go from bad to worse. Did I tell you *Holiday* finally changed my assignment from Pakistan to Istanbul? Why they want another piece on Istanbul when I wrote them one only eleven years ago, I don't know, but they do. I can't believe it's changed that much. I'm glad you had Aunt Ulla and Uncle Harold for a while; even though you didn't get to see very much of them it was better than nothing. And glad, of course, that everything goes along smoothly at home. (Smoothly, I realize, is not exactly the word, but everything is relative.) You ask the title of my new book, to appear, supposedly, in February. *Up above the World*. It's a murder mystery about beatniks, decidedly light, and probably will get awful notices. However, I was tired of writing about North Africa. The rumor about

Temsamany seems to have been unfounded. No sign of him. Jane is well and happy. I spoke on the phone with her night before last. Must close, but wanted you to have this. Much love to you both.

TO VIRGIL THOMSON

November 29, 1965
Tangier

Your letter with its request made me feel forlorn: I don't possess a single photo or snapshot of Harry or Touche, nor one of any of the Little Friends. It's as though they'd never existed. Even Jane might as well not have been around before 1945 or later; the earliest snap I have of her dates from the mid-forties. The earliest of me from around 1939. Obviously I arranged it that way, what with my passion for total consumption of everything, including memory. (Whatever is left over in the mind has not been put to use.) In any case, it makes it well-nigh impossible for me to oblige with snaps, save for the two I am going to send you: one taken by you or Harry or Victor Kraft down in a burlesque on the Bowery when Rudy Burckhardt was making a film in which we were supposed to eat popcorn and applaud the show—perhaps you remember the occasion (1939?)—and the other taken at New Canaan by Touche when he and Teddy had that house out there one summer (early '40s). These are the earliest I have, and I regret it very much, since it makes it impossible for me to be of help to you. The two snaps I do have I'll send as soon as I get them copied, which will be in two or three days, but whether you'll find either of them usable is another matter. I hope so.

When will the book be out? I'm most eager to see it completed. Mine is due in February. For no sensible reason I expect it to be a complete critical flop. If it isn't put down unmercifully I'll be delighted. Gallimard has bought *Two Serious Ladies*; I wonder how it will come out in translation. Not too brilliant, I imagine.

You'll be hearing from me again in a few days.

TO RENA AND CLAUDE BOWLES
——————————◆——————————

December 27, 1965
Tangier

I should have written several days ago—that is, before Christmas rather than after it, but everything else managed to creep in first, including Christmas itself, which we passed quietly enough, although the day was marred by news that Jay Haselwood, the proprietor of the Parade Bar, had dropped dead at two o'clock in the afternoon. This upset Jane considerably, as we had known him since 1948. The holiday activities haven't really got under way yet. I know Jane has accepted invitations for every day this week. More and more I dislike going out in Tangier. The people are dull, and they drink far too much, which makes them duller, and it's always problematical whether one's going to be able to get a taxi or not, since the taxi system has partially broken down. All in all, it's easier and pleasanter to stay home, and if one must see people, have them come here. At least you don't have to worry about getting home. I'm busy translating another book from the Arabic. I published one two years ago, as you know, and it has gone on and been done into French, Italian and Dutch, with great success, particularly the French edition, which unfortunately had such a big success in France that the Moroccans got wind of it and divided themselves into two camps—those in favor and those against. The againsts won, there was a government meeting about it in Rabat, and the Moroccan police seized all copies in the country and forbade the future entry of the book into Morocco. Of course they gave no reasons at all for the ban, but it's obvious that it's because the book presents the country as it really is, and not the way the government would like it to be. The new one will probably not be so controversial. I hope not, in any case! My own novel is scheduled for March now, so Simon & Schuster write me. We have been having a tremendous amount of rain, and still it goes on. The flowers that should be coming out now came out two months ago; there's nothing left. I hope to hear from you soon.

TO WEBSTER SCHOTT

February 2, 1966
Tangier

Forgive my tardy reply: I have been in the hinterlands.

Naturally enough, I was taken aback by your letter, never before having received a request for elucidation (save for the rhetorical questions put by disgruntled or suspicious readers, and those fall into a different category). The wording of your key phrase inevitably suggests that I am to take a defensive attitude with regard to *Up above the World*, and it goes without saying that I can't do that. (In case you haven't a copy of your own missive at hand, I'll quote from it: " . . . would appreciate very much hearing from you what you were trying to do in the novel.") The meaning here is that whatever I was attempting to do, or imagined I was doing, I did not do, and as a result, one reader—but a pivotal reader—is left in doubt as to my intentions. I am the first to agree that these intentions ought to be crystal-clear, but I can't very well argue that they are, since you have already stated that they are not.

I was telling a story whose line is necessarily presented as a puzzle because the course of the plot is determined by the material. The "meaning" of the book is certainly not this convoluted and improbable tale of brainwashing as applied by the hero to his victims, however; nor is the book a *roman à thèse* any more than was *The Sheltering Sky*. (On the other hand, it has very little in common with that book save in the (probably obsessive) use of certain external situations.) But writing all this to you is farcical, because you are already aware of it. A sentence from Borges should have been included in the front of the book: "Each moment as it is being lived exists, but not the imaginary total." I've said nothing, but I have answered your letter.

TO JAMES LEO HERLIHY

April 8, 1966
Tangier

You've been moving around; I've been sitting still. I'd thought my last letter to you was more recent than November, but apparently it wasn't. Since then I've reread *Cowboy* and discovered *All Fall Down*, which I hadn't read at all.

The sequence of events was that I'd kept talking with Bill Burroughs about *Cowboy*, so that finally he asked to read it. He came out of it ecstatic, and immediately ordered a copy for himself. Then he happened to be in Gibraltar, and saw a copy of the Penguin I, which he grabbed and brought back to me here. I read it once, and I think liked it even more than *Cowboy*, if one has to make comparisons, which one doesn't. I found it totally right. What I admire beyond the style is the easy way in which both books capture the United States and its particular essence, without, however expressing any opinion extrinsic to the story, without even a hint of disaffection. Wonderful! I suppose that strikes me because I've always been afraid to tackle America; I know quite well that my hatred would show through all defences. For years I've thought of a thousand points of view which would aid me in masking my feelings and thus make it possible to use the place as a locale for a book, but there seems to be no way. It may be you don't even have the murderous emotions about the U.S., but whether you do or don't the miracle remains. You've either hit on the right way of looking at it (from the beginning) or found a way of hiding your hatred. In the latter case, it would be literary skill; in the former, you could consider yourself blessed by fortune first of all. It doesn't matter, either way. Chester found this place too much for him, and fled some weeks before Christmas. His epistles from New York have been full of sadness—nostalgia for Morocco; the last I heard, he was about to return here. Your mention of a journal echoes what Bill Burroughs has been telling me for years. "Keep a journal," he says. "It's the most useful thing you can do."

I've always thought it would be like making faces at oneself in the mirror. Who is one writing for in a journal? If it's oneself, it's obviously a farce. If it's for publication, then it's immediately censored, while one is writing it, and is no longer strictly speaking a journal. Is there another way of looking at it? A letter, I suppose. I understand diaries and notebooks, but I don't think I understand the journal. A daily newsletter to the public? Will you come to Tangier? Will I be here? Has Lilla van Saher really given birth? I'm glad you got the copy of *Up above the World* and read it and had reactions to it. Let's hope for a meeting here in summer, although I may be in Thailand.

April 30, 1966
Tangier

I'm glad you went on about the journal business, and in the end we agree: that whatever words one puts down under whatever circumstances are always meant for other eyes and other minds. Your mention of "witnesses" is a good way of illustrating the existential dilemma of consciousness (the impossibility of being the thing in itself for itself). In *Huis Clos* Sartre makes Inez say to Estelle: "Wouldn't you like me to be your mirror?" And later: "Suppose the mirror should begin to lie?" A good enough reason why Hell should be other people, if we need them in order to credit the validity of our own experience! It still seems to me that the formalized life of primitives must be emotionally satisfying, if only because so many of the acts of daily life are performed in the manner of a ritual, and before witnesses. (Then I worry: Could it be that my nostalgia for that lost childhood is merely a disinclination to assume the responsibilities that becoming civilized demands? Then I answer: No. We're still primitives. We don't really want to be civilized. In another ten thousand years, perhaps.) But the journal: you say it was therapeutic. "Instead of committing murder, I committed my feelings to paper." But to me writing fiction is the same sort of therapy. When life is unbearable, I apply the principle of the counterirritant: I invent something still worse, beside which the actuality seems fairly benign. I suppose the necessity is to persuade the reader of the impossibility, or even of the undesirability, of happiness. Once I've found the pattern that makes it possible to get it off my chest, I feel better. And about the hatred of America: naturally I mask it, because I mask everything. Too much importance is given the writer and not enough to his work. What difference does it make who he is and what he feels, since he's merely a machine for transmission of ideas? In reality he doesn't exist—he's a cipher, a blank. A spy sent into life by the forces of death. His main objective is to get the information across the border, back into death. Then he can be given a mythical personality: "He spent his time among us, betrayed us, and took the material across the border." I don't think a writer ever participates in anything; his pretences at it are mimetic. All he can do is keep the machine functioning and learn to manage it with decreasing (we hope) clumsiness. A spy *is* devious and, as much as is possible, anonymous. His personal convictions and emotions are automatically "masked." This all sounds far too serious. But you got me started. It would be fine to see you here in June,

IF I'm to be here, and at the moment everything connected with Bangkok is still hanging fire. However, now that I know there's a possibility of your coming I'll keep in close touch with you. I'll be going probably by freighter, and they're few. And so a lot of time may go by before I leave.

TO IRA COHEN

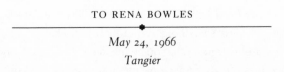

May 9, 1966
Tangier

I have begun to get letters and broadsides from the Timothy Leary Defense Fund. I don't know how you feel about him personally (Bill of course is thoroughly disenchanted) but as a blatant infringement of civil liberties the case bears watching and even defending. It occurred to me that it could be an idea to issue the Hypnotic Music record in connection with the defense, announcing that all profits would go to the Fund. (Obviously costs would be deducted, unless someone is very flush.) It seemed worth writing you about, in any case. I could make up a new tape that could be used as matrix. What are you doing with your Jilala tape, by the way? Is it coming out as a record? Still no one has seen Alfred.

TO RENA BOWLES

May 24, 1966
Tangier

Yes, it does seem a long time since I'd heard from you, until your letter arrived yesterday (and also a long time since I've written you). I've been busy going to rehearsals of the chorus which is performing the music I've written for the production by the American School here of *Oedipus* (to have its first performance here Friday night). Now a pianist who is a friend of the American Consul-General has arrived, and he is giving a recital tomorrow. The Consul had Jane and me to hear him do a private performance at the Residence, because he wanted me to write an article on his technique to be translated into French and Spanish for the newspapers. I protested that I hadn't done anything like that in twenty years, but he wouldn't let me off, so I had to spend all day Sunday racking my brains for something to say! Awful! More than anything I am trying to find some sort of ship to take me to Bangkok. The money has been deposited to my account in New York, so I must bestir myself and get out there, or the first thing I know I shan't have time to write the book for the deadline. Our weather is getting slowly warmer, so that soon I won't have to wear a topcoat when I go out in the evening. So far, however, it is a necessity. I'm glad to hear that Gulfport was not in the path of the storms that hit Saint Petersburg and Tampa. It seems Morocco and Algeria have once again opened hostilities on the border. As usual it was triggered by Nasser, who is determined to get all of North Africa under his thumb. The biggest stumbling-block for him is Morocco, because it is not socialist (and has, of all terrible things, a king). Algeria long ago fell to him, and refugees arriving here tell of terror and torture everywhere. There doesn't seem to be any way of his getting Morocco save by fomenting a civil war, and so far he has been completely unsuccessful in his attempts to start one. You speak of seeing Truman Capote on TV. It's nineteen years since I've seen him, I think. He is deformed, as you know—something glandular . . . a huge misshapen head and a peculiarly shaped stunted body. However, he always was as bright as a whip, and out for nobody but himself. We always knew he'd be successful. Twenty percent of his energy goes on writing, and eighty percent on buttering up the right people. Did I ever send you a copy of the book I tape-recorded (and did into English from Arabic)? Called A *Life Full of Holes*. I suspect somehow that I didn't. I think you'd like it. Wish I were there to take Daddy out for his morning walk. It seems too bad that he can't get out. But I suppose afternoon is all right. Give him my love, and also everyone else, saving plenty for yourself!

TO JAMES LEO HERLIHY

June 11, 1966
Tangier

Your letter has been here several days, but I've written no letters—only cables, the past few days. My mother died Wednesday, and my life has been vague during this time. I'll have to go back to the States sometime soon, but not before you would be coming, and even not before you would have been here a while. So it seems fine, your arrival. It will be wonderful to see you. The reason why I shan't be going to the U.S. immediately is that I intend to go from there on to Thailand, and shall have to arrange ships from here before sailing, because I don't under any conditions want to be caught in New York for a long time, trying to get out and not being able to. You speak of nausea in connection with attempts to work. It's the real thing, that kind of nausea, too, and I think it comes from a sensation of having been there before—that is, from a not very well defined feeling of doing again what one has already done. And of course one always hopes to be covering new ground, at least for oneself. There are certainly all kinds of games one can invent, but without going necessarily as far as Roussel (*Comment J'ai Écrit Certaines de Mes Œuvres* or whatever it's called) or even going as far as Roussel if one has to (since subject matter is so unimportant finally) it's possible to invent a viable method, and a different one for getting through each work. (Method having to do, of course, only with working, and not with one's idea of the finished product.) (Finished product always turning out to be what it wants to be.) (I've never had even a remote insight into what was going to happen in any of my short stories, and I've always gone into them fully conscious of that fact, full of curiosity as to what it was going to be about.) (The old surrealist technique, I suppose, but none the less practical.) Give my love to Lilla when you see her. Have you found out yet if the baby is hers? I shut this off and take it out to post, or you won't hear from me before leaving New York. I hope you do come; let me know.

TO JANE BOWLES

◆

September 21, 1966
Bangkok

They have air-letter forms in this country, but I know how much you hate them, and so I'm writing on ordinary paper. Thank God I finally got a letter from you; I hadn't had anything in well over a month. A month and a half it was, actually, since you wrote the last, from Miami, and which I received in Los Angeles. Anyway, I now know you're back in Tangier, which is a comfort, as I had no idea what you were going to do in the United States as long as you were there. You might have extended your stay and gone to see Libby, or

something else. And I see now that you rather wish you had. But at least you
have the trip behind you, which I should think would be something.

Did the ship go directly to Tangier? I gather so, from your letter. That must
have been wonderful, not having to land in Algeciras and get across by ferry. I
wish they all did that. I won't go into what goes on in Tangier because you
don't sound too enthusiastic about it, but at least I feel better knowing you're
at home, rather than wandering around New York.

We finally got ashore two days ago—somewhat earlier than we had been led
to expect when the ship was anchored some fifteen miles away in the Bight of
Bangkok, along with about twenty other freighters which hadn't been able to
get space at the docks here in the city. As far as I know, the ship is still waiting
out there, although I must telephone and find out, as I wasn't able to give any
tips, the chief steward not having any money to exchange for traveler's checks.
Bangkok is a big surprise to me, because I had expected something smaller—
perhaps the size of Casablanca. But it turns out to be almost as big as Paris, and
twice as noisy. In the aggregate it looks terribly dull, but if one can bear to
wander on foot, all the details are fascinating. It's a question of heat and reserve
energy, really. A little like Colombo in certain respects, but more varied eth-
nically, and far more interesting. I don't know whether they are going to allow
me to remain or not. If they don't, as you know I shan't be too disappointed,
since I can go elsewhere. Also, in a short stay here I can gather enough material
for a piece for *Holiday*, so that the visit won't even be that much wasted. They
particularly asked me to agree on a Bangkok piece, which I refused to make
definite because I felt I couldn't do both a book and an article on the same
material. It would have made me nervous, trying to plan two separate entities.

This won't be an extensive letter because I've got too many things to do, and
distances are so great that it takes half the day to get from one place to another.
I mean one spends just about half one's day in taxis, covering miles of no-man's
land, getting from one "center" to another. I've never seen such an aimless and
haphazard city. I suppose it's really a collection of towns. Everything is fine;
Oliver Evans is here, teaching, but I haven't seen him yet. I hope you feel better
and can work on something. Let me know about everything. Did you put the
plant in my flat or yours? Pauvre Berred; I'm sad.

TO HERBERT MACHIZ

September 29, 1966
Bangkok

Just came upstairs from curry two feet from the Menam Chao Phraya. A little like Venice with three-inch cockroaches clattering about. The populace paddles by in sampans to see what the farangs are up to in their neon-flooded hotels where electric organs whine and bump.

It seems to me that everybody went to Tangier this summer, and before going wrote me saying they'd see me there. And there was I for eight weeks on a Norwegian freighter going down to Panama, up to Los Angeles and San Francisco, across to Manila, up again to Hong Kong, and on to this place. I'm sorry I missed you, but perhaps under your own steam you found something for next year in our town. Or perhaps it so repelled you that you'll never think of it again. It's hard to tell what anyone's reaction is going to be. And then no place is ever as one had imagined it before going, and certainly not like what others say it is. Bangkok, for instance, people said: It's the brothel of the world. It's a honky-tonk strip. You'll be devoured by mosquitoes. And others: It's quaint, it's so delicate and beautiful. I don't find any of those assessments exact. In the first place, it's vast, huge, endless. Like Los Angeles with the boulevards intersected by canals. And behind the boulevards it swarms with strange life: people, costumes, smells, sounds and signs. The traffic is the worst I've ever seen, and next to nobody knows how to drive. There seem to be no traffic laws, and surely there is no law of causality in the minds of the people, with the consequence that the accidents occur every few minutes and are ghastly. But no one loses face by dying, and since accidents are considered providential and not connected with the way one handles the vehicle, no face is lost in killing either. So everyone's happy, except timid souls like me. One can't walk because there's no way of crossing the streets. A city utterly unprepared for contemporary life, but throwing itself into that life with great zest; everything is fun. The boxers come into the ring and pray for five minutes; then they dance a while; then the music changes and the fight rhythm begins (oboes, drums and cymbals that sound more like triangles) and they go to it, kicking and punching every part of each others' anatomy, all in strict rhythm. When they finish, the winner often prostrates himself before the loser, if he's conscious.

TO ANGUS STEWART

September 30, 1966
Menam Chao Phraya, Thailand

A note. I see yours was written on the final day of July, and today is the final day of September. So the service wasn't rapid, but that may be a result of forwarding. I'm told one is lucky to get any mail at all here. So I am lucky, inasmuch as I got an enormous amount early this week, and have written at least twenty letters since then without having come to the bottom of the pile. Let's see. How can the publisher's contract be dragged into a divorce suit . . . a new wrinkle. Extreme cruelty: book not published as he'd promised her it would be. Humiliation in public: no reviews in TLS. Yes, one would like to buy up a litter of Thais and transship them, only one wonders if they could live without their habitual diet of orchid corollas. Surely half would arrive dead, and there would have to be special heating installations in their quarters, if any arrived in good condition. The habitat is so confusing that it's impossible to write about it. All paradoxical. As someone told me yesterday: India's still Europe. A circle is a circle. In Burma it's already an ellipse, but by the time it gets to Siam it has become a triangle. (How would one know that Phraya is pronounced: fijaa, with the accent on the final syllable? The transliteration is merely a feeble symbol of the inner and outer life.) I don't know whether I can do anything with such a country, nor do I know whether they're going to allow me to try. As of now, I can't remain here later than October eighteenth. Some sort of miracle will have to be worked before that if I'm to stay on. They have a quota for Americans, for which I surely don't blame them. (The place swarms with G.I.'s wearing mean faces.) Yesterday a cabdriver asked me: Please, where you home? I said: New York. He said: Ah, British gentlemen, like Christopher Columbus and Captain Cook. All millionaire. Not like Merican, rough, bang, you, boy, quick. English gentleman all sirs. If I born English gentleman always have sun my land . . . The conversation got quite out of hand after that, but I could see he objected to the Americans' manner. (Last night at dinner I spoke to a boy waiting on table: Would you call the waiter? *You want cold water?* No, no. I just want my waiter. *Ah, warm water?* The waiter! The boy! Where is he? Then his face changed: *You want boy? Eleven o'clock in lane. All working now.* When my own waiter finally appeared, he said: I not leaving yet. Misunderstandings proliferate like the vegetation.) I don't know what will become of this country. So, I'll wait for your letter.

TO JOHN GOODWIN

October 5, 1966
Bangkok

Your letter here and appreciated. Am having such a difficult time trying to get permission to remain; it doesn't look as though it were going to be possible, for which drat! However, what can't be managed can't be regretted. The great suspicion here is that everyone is either a beatnik or a night club entertainer, and either category is bad from their point of view. Easy enough to convince individuals, but not members of the bureaucracy; the system grinds away like any other. Have been up to Ayutthaya, and that is the extent of my para-Bangkok activities, save for a beautiful afternoon in sampans somewhere south of Thonburi in the jungle, to visit a temple called Oparsi, quite disconnected and unvisited. It was some novices and monks who suggested the trip. It's terribly difficult to give oneself over to those people sufficiently; one's true nature, or at least what one has got used to thinking is one's true nature, keeps wanting to assert itself in gestures like looking at one's watch, or suggesting that we sit there rather than here, so as not to have the mosquitoes or to be out of the sun . . . hard to insist on not existing for an extended period. And of course, one sharp inflection in one's voice is fatal, even though it be used to an annoying small child or a dog; they are always watching and weighing. Do they expect us to be perfect? Not knowing Thai is of course the heaviest burden to have to carry around. I haven't even tried to learn to count; I made a decision to learn nothing; if the machine should suddenly allow me to stay, I suppose I'll learn in spite of myself, but I have no burning desire to start a new tongue at this date. Got my proofs of *Love with a Few Hairs* the other day, and it took me two days to list all the typos therein; the British are almost as bad as the French these days for sloppiness. Yes, my ship, the M/V "Tarantel," went from New York down the coast to Charleston, Panama, and other less interesting places, and then up the coast to L.A. (Long Beach, actually) and San Francisco, then across to Manila and Hong Kong, and finally here. We were holed up in the Manila harbor for a full week by a typhoon outside, and then went to an American base called Subic, around the Bataan Peninsula. Depressing place, Philippines, and above all Manila with its garbage. You ask about *Up above the World*. Critical reception very satisfying; it seemed the emperor had on very fine garments for once. I thought *Life's* piece the most intelligent, but I think I've written you about all that, haven't I? Financially it did very well, because of the film sale, plus, of course, the paperback rights. Jane's book is a tome called *The Collected Works of Jane Bowles*. I can't make her write more. I think she feels she's done her stint, which is criminal to my way of thinking, but I suppose not to yours, since you announce the same state of mind in yourself. Just as criminal. But of course I'm a Puritan, and can't justify life any other way. If I could, I should, of course. And then, I'm obliged to earn a living, which is a better excuse than the Puritan deal, although they're both operative. Bangkok is like Houston, Texas, swarming with G.I.'s and their floozies, all of whom wear magenta slacks, with very high-heeled gold shoes.

TO ANGUS STEWART

October 7, 1966
Bangkok

This unexpectedly rapid postal service is such a novelty that I feel I must take constant advantage of it; how did they ever arrange such a thing, I wonder? It takes a week to ten days for a letter to go by air from Rome to Tangier, which must be about a twentieth of the distance. And so, two and a half days from here to London. I tell you, these here G.I.'s of ours have really put the place on the map. You gotta hand it to 'em. You should have seen a mass arrival for R and R yesterday, here at the hotel! (Rest and Recreation, straight from Viet Nam.) It was terrifying. Even quite proper-looking Thai citizens crowded around on the periphery, thinking that, after all, if the hundred-baht notes were going to be literally tossed into the air, they might as well collect a few themselves. (A soldier here gets exactly fifty baht a month as wages.) (The G.I.'s were handing out twice that amount as tips to porters and taxi drivers downstairs at noon.) Naturally, the entire hotel has disintegrated 100% overnight. No service at all, not even on the telephone. The room boys have become pimps and are not even on duty, and the maids have come over all peculiar-like, and do nothing but giggle and back away when you ask them a question. It took me 55 minutes to get my breakfast this morning, and then there was no butter or marmalade on the tray. Every other day everything has been normal—even when a party of fifty or more excited Italians descended en masse for two days. Nothing, but nothing, can destroy all the patterns as swiftly as the arrival of a few G.I.'s, contemptuously emptying their pockets of what they think of as fake money. Like: "How the hell much is that in *real* money, Bud?" Of course, I've always known all this, but I'd never seen it happen before my eyes, and I hadn't realized the impact could be quite so shatteringly dramatic. It's a mass hysteria which sweeps over everyone. When in desperation I finally asked to speak on the phone to the head receptionist, who I'd imagined would remain impervious to the general madness, she said: Yes, Mr. Bobbles, what can I do for you this morning? I said: Can you put me in touch with someone who can take my order for breakfast? She said: What would you like? Knowing that she had no menu there at reception, I said in surprise: Are you taking the order yourself? She said: I see, just milk for you this morning. Very well, Mr. Bobbles. And why was that? Because all the G.I.'s take only milk for breakfast, because they think it's good for a hangover. She had already hung up, and I had to begin all over again. I thought I'd told you all about *Love with a Few Hairs* when I saw you in Tangier earlier in the year; didn't I? Surely there's nothing secret involved! The Moroccan police will probably ban this one as well, if only because it's by a Moroccan. Bangkok goes on being exciting and exhausting, and I still haven't got permission to stay here. What you mean—I'm going to make a lot of Thailand? Make in which sense, please? I doubt there'll be a book in any case. I ran into a rich Thai who wants a sentimental companion, as he puts it rather chillingly. I corrected the proofs of *Love* the other day. Your typesetters are almost as sloppy as the ones employed by Gallimard. Opium is most unpleasant. Bikkhus make the best ciceroni for visiting the wats and ruins, I've found. * They can get one entry into all sorts of otherwise forbidden places, and then they provide a beautiful tranquility. What temples one finds in every street! So, I'm going to order up some papaya to settle my stomach; as I said above, most unpleasant.

---

* Buddhist monks make the best tour guides . . .

TO JANE BOWLES

October 9, 1966
Bangkok

I've just had my dinner downstairs, and since there's nothing to do at night in Bangkok except go to bed, I thought I'd write you. (It's the least amusing city from the point of view of amusement. No place to walk or sit. Like America: either movies or night clubs and bars. None of the agréments of Europe, and certainly none of Morocco!) My days have been spent half trying to get permission to stay, and half seeing what I could see. I should have concentrated completely on seeing the sights, since the effort that has gone into prolonging my visit seems to have been wasted. I still have to leave on the 18th or before, unless I leave for a neighboring country and come in again, in which case I can stay another 15 days. Tomorrow I'm going to a travel agency and inquire about Laos; it's the nearest border. A distant cousin and great friend of Villiers David had me to lunch today and suggested it, in case I was interested in getting a bit more time here, and it seems a good idea, if feasible. That way, at least I could get a better ship out of Thailand, whereas if I set sail this week I have to take what I can get, which is a non-air-conditioned freighter of 3,000 tons. So far not one of the connections or interviews or letters has borne fruit; thus my project for doing a book on Bangkok is doomed. However, as I say, I can get an article for *Holiday* out of it, I'm certain. I want to get certain statistics from the USIS about the present boom, since it's by far the most salient feature of the present anatomy of the land. The old residents think of nothing but getting out, not permanently, but for vacations as long as they can make them. They say they don't go out any more, such as to the films or restaurants, only because of the G.I.'s and their behavior. It's depressing. Thanks for sending the names and addresses Charles gave you for Japan. I may be needing them, after all. Except that there were no addresses—only names and identifying cities. I had dinner with Oliver Evans last night, and he is giving up his house with the lotus pool. Too many robberies. He's lost nearly everything he had in the house, including rings one day, watch another, camera another, his valises broken open another, and so on. The servants, he thinks, must have had the extra key to his bedroom where he kept everything. It wasn't that he took unknown people home, either, which one might suspect. He had a ghastly landlady, for one thing, like Señora Rebollar in Mexico, who claimed that his houseboy had seduced one of his maids . . . she lives next door . . . and was asking 2,000 baht recompense. To be given to her, the landlady, not to the girl! Oliver had signed a lease, and she has let him out of it in return for a new Frigidaire (huge) and an air-conditioner and a floor fan. He thinks it's a lucky break, but I'd say he's being had in a big way. But obviously he's very eager to escape and get into a hotel. It seems the city is swarming with burglars. At least, that's what the residents claim, and newspaper stories would seem to back them up in their anecdotes. So I'm rather glad to have been, and to be, in a hotel quietly, without domestic worries. Servants are as in Ceylon. One has to have four or five in order to get any work done. The employer is also legally responsible for their health, and it seems they are always getting ill, and asking for cures for one thing and another. Gordon wrote me he was thinking of taking a flat somewhere in the Boulevard section. I assume he can't take the Castle any longer because of the restrictions it places on his privacy. I'm astonished he's stayed as long as he has done. I'd imagined he'd be fed up long before this. Which children are making orchestras? Surely not the Jewish ones who live in Itesa. Must be the Moslem ones from Aïn Hayani. But they used to do that several years ago, when I had the front flat down on the first floor. They drove me mad with their racket, sitting right under the balcony there for hours on end, banging and yelling. I had a letter from Jane Wilson at William Morris saying that Holt, Rinehart would like the book of stories, but would not pay what they had originally offered. However, I showed the letter to Oliver Evans, and he was astounded at the price they offered, which was a third less than the initial suggested advance: 5 instead of 7½. He insists it's phenomenal for short stories, and thinks that no one but Tennessee or Truman would get it. Novels up to any figure, but stories are a drag on the market, and the publisher can't ever get back his investment. I wrote I'd accept if they would publish in the Spring. I thought I ought to have some sort of face-saving device, and not simply accede quietly! The name of my accountant is Kaufman, Levy and Goldstein. I thought the money for your book automatically was to be paid in dollars in America. That's what Owen told me originally. Now not? I don't have to pay the English taxes on it, however. They are simply deducted before you ever see a penny, if it's subject to British income tax. But if so, it's dishonest of Owen to have assured me it would be otherwise. I corrected the galleys on Mrabet's little book last week and sent them off to Owen. It makes quite a sizeable volume after all: 176 pages. I'd been afraid it would be too slight. I'm not in love with Bangkok. The country around is lovely, and the temples and canals and all that are very beautiful, but the difficulties involved in just living are too much.

TO JANE BOWLES

October 31, 1966
Bangkok

I have your letter about the lost check from last spring, and can't quite make out whether it has been traced or not. You (or Carla [Grissman]) mention that I might have been paid on last June 15th. But of course they never told us that afterward, nor did they then have any record of it. It was certainly never credited to our account before we left for America. However, since I don't know any more than that, there is nothing I can say from here.

I shall answer the Swedish publisher and say that as far as I know, only Peter Owen has pictures of you, and that they had better write and ask him for one. He can certainly supply it if he wants to—that is, if he is willing to spend five or six shillings, which is probably not the case. I still think it's up to him, as the agent for the sale of the book. I don't hear from him at the moment as he's in New York. Jane Wilson sent me a whole page of review from the Virginia Kirkus Service, of your Farrar, Straus book. They're obviously impressed and full of respect, and not knowing which way to turn, after calling you a "neglected genius," turn to "the early Purdy" as comparison, adding Carson and the "unexpected lunacy and wit of Ivy Compton-Burnett." None of which you'd read when you wrote *Two Serious Ladies*. For *In the Summer House* they bring in "the influence of the author's friend Tennessee Williams, though even here, through the creation of the wounded and tipsy Mrs. Constable, we have something of a Bowles original." You'll undoubtedly have seen it; in any case I'll save it with my papers and show it to you. It's completely favorable in every statement, but leaves me with the feeling that the critic was totally bewildered by having read the book, had enjoyed it but was disturbed for not being able to analyze his reactions, because it was even more different than he thought from anything else he had ever read. Each time he finds a possible influence or comparison he invalidates it by an expression like: "but her achievement in the end is pretty much *sui generis*." ("But even here she is very much herself; it is always Jane Bowles's voice speaking.") Since the review is meant for booksellers it will be successful in the sense that they will all be aware of the book. Whether it will make them order more copies or not is hard to tell, but I should think definitely it would with a good many of them. I know you claim never to be interested in such things, but with a reprint like this you really haven't anything else to be very much interested in. It should sell as many copies as possible, since that is the most accurate way of gauging how well it has fulfilled its purpose, which was to consolidate your name in the field of current letters. Therefore you should be interested, etc. But I'm sure you are in any case, and also in whether Penguin and Peter Owen send for me to have me go to London. I naturally am waiting to hear from Owen one way or the other, but I feel it will drag on forever (since it's a question of money each one would be willing to pay . . . oy!). Not that I would be haggling, but between them it would be hard to decide how much each was to pay and for what. You should be reading Marta's saga of Set right now, in order to feel empathy for me, who am studying the history of Siam. Dragons, earthquakes, pink elephants, kingdoms being dissolved by spies leaving urns of magic powder buried in strategic parts of a city, all with dates and statistics. Mine however is not theoretical but factual, the dragons being cobras, the pink elephants being the steeds of the kings in battle, and naturally the magic is still used, just as in you know where. I try to write a page a day, and I'll be delighted when I'm over this part. (I had to have something to constitute le corps d'une œuvre, so I thought I might as well try the hardest part first, and make that the body onto which to add from either end.) Anyway, it's a bore. I literally only sleep, work and eat. (About three times a week I eat with Oliver Evans, but see nobody else.) Thank God I didn't decide to go to Kyoto. So much lost time.

TO JOSEPH MCPHILLIPS
◆————————————————————◆
December 27, 1966
Chiang Mai, Thailand

As I was getting into the lift this afternoon here at the hotel, they called out to me from the desk, saying I was wanted on the telephone. I went and answered it; the American Consulate was calling, saying I must come immediately to pick up a very important document. I went back out and took a ricksha to the Consulate, where they handed me your letter, first making me sign for it. I read it walking through the street, and thought about it the rest of the afternoon.

As you know, I have never written a play, and since I haven't I am inclined to suspect that it is because I have no facility in that direction. Naturally I am most pleased that not only you but the students like "The Garden" well enough to be willing to be involved in a play taken from it; otherwise I should merely

reply that the thing was impossible. I don't feel that it's impossible, although a
very short story almost devoid of dialogue does not easily become a full-length
play, as you're well aware. In its present state, "The Garden" would seem to
lend itself more to opera or ballet than straight drama. I think any dramatic
version of it would need to be highly stylized (in the manner of your production
of *Oedipus*), with principal emphasis on staging and presentation rather than
interpretation of roles and projection of dialogue. Unfortunately I haven't got a
copy of the text with me, so I can't get the whole thing firmly in my mind in
order to deal with it as an entity. (It will be in the collection Holt, Rinehart are
publishing next spring.) I realize that time is most important, of course, and
that you would like a definite reply now, but you can see my position, without
even a copy of the story to go over in my mind. It's one thing to have written
a thing three and a half years ago, and another to have it in one's hands, in
written form. Can we leave it at the point of my saying that I'm not hostile to
the idea of doing something with "The Garden" for you? I expect to be in
Tangier at the end of February; I haven't been successful in getting earlier passage.
As things stand now, I'll leave Bangkok on the 20th or thereabouts of January,
bound for Genoa, when I'll catch an American Export liner for Algeciras. The
trip from Bangkok takes about thirty days, so that I should be in Genoa around
a month after I embark. I should say: expect me in Tangier the first of March,
or a few days before, depending on how long I am obliged to wait in Genoa.
Any idea I get in the interim I'll send you. (For instance, if you did decide you
wanted to do it, even under the circumstances—without a text—it would be
possible to stage all the purely choreographed scenes in advance (assuming, of
course, that I sent you a breakdown of scenes). The dialogue could thus be
written last. You could be well into rehearsal of your big scenes before I ever
got back to Tangier, if it proved necessary.) (When I speak of big scenes, I mean
scenes of mass participation.) The townspeople appear only about halfway
through, in any case. Early scenes are husband, wife and witch. I'd follow the
story exactly in a series of short scenes which would be played first on one side
of the stage and then the other. Nothing onstage but a palm trunk, a few palm
branches, and palm hasiras. (Or anything made of palm.) A curved backdrop
of light grey, representing the sky. Do you agree on the kind of approach? The
scenes would be short and in basic colloquial English, nothing more. The
essentially choreographed scenes would be done, in one way or another, to
music; the dialogue scenes might or might not. Night dialogue scenes particularly
might be enhanced by use of offstage music. And so on. I'll be making notes
on the project. You can still write me in Bangkok and I'll get it before I sail.

TO ANDREAS BROWN,

GOTHAM BOOK MART, NEW YORK
◆

January 18, 1967
Bangkok

I have your letter generously enclosing the two clippings about Jane's book. Many thanks for parting with them. I'll take them back to Tangier with me. Jane may easily not have seen *The Saturday Review*, even though the magazine is still arriving, I'm sure. She never reads, as you know, and therefore doesn't look inside a magazine from one year's end to the next. I had another letter from her doctor (you know who) yesterday, saying she was not well, that she seemed to have fallen into an excessively depressed state in which she only eats, sleeps and sits silently all day waiting for night. It seems she does not even telephone anyone any more. All this would account for the fact that I have not had a letter from her since September. Whenever I disappear Cherifa takes over with her potions, and Jane goes into a tailspin.

It is true that Larbi and I discussed the letters when he came aboard the "Tarantel" to see me last summer. I think you should see them first, however, because their subject-matter is of the most banal kind. They're far from having any literary implications, apart from the fact that he is in a situation directly caused by having done the book. (If I had imagined the Moroccan government was going to react in the way it has, I'd never have encouraged him to produce the story, and he would have gone on living the way he was living, unmarried and with no responsibilities. Yet, strangely enough, I think he is happier for having done it, and would not want to be back in the pre-book situation. Certainly he has learned a lot about the world. But does he say what he intends to do? I ask because Ira Yeager wrote me last week that Larbi was going to have to leave the U.S. This seems awful.) I'll hope to hear more about it from you when you've spoken with him. Incidentally, you can write me (I don't say you should!) to Port Said. (*Passenger aboard M.S. SIMBA, arriving at Port Said Feb.* 15, *c/o Damanhour Shipping Agency, P.O. Box #126, Port Said, Egypt.*) All that would be the address. I sail on Monday the 23rd from Bangkok. The ship calls at three ports in Malaysia, which is nice, and then goes straight to the Canal. I disembark at Genoa and take the *Constitution* from there to Algeciras.

I dramatized "The Garden," the story which was in *Art and Literature*, for the American School to present this year. They're already working on it. Being certain that no one would see it gave me the courage, since obviously I haven't any notion of how to do such a thing, never having written a play. If the kids enjoy doing it, it will have served its purpose. I suddenly realize I've told you this.

Jane hasn't a single story which hasn't been published. The material in the note-books all had to do with novels-in-progress, but not completed. I've read the Rorem book and corrected the ms. of the Thomson.

TO CHARLES-HENRI FORD

March 18, 1967
Tangier

Tangier again, after visiting Malaysia and finding it as pleasant as it was twelve years ago when I was last there. Far better to be in Singapore or Kuala Lumpur or Penang than Bangkok. Have six months in which to write my book, God forbid. Arrived to find Jane very ill. Soon I shall take her to Spain to the hospital for a month's observation. Her medication begins to tell . . . ten years of constant sedation can't help anyone into superior health. Haven't read any Kerouac since *On the Road*. Brion is in Marrakech with The Rolling Stones. They were here last week. Very much rolling (in money) and very stoned. Supposedly they're on a musical tour of Morocco; that is, they are looking for Moroccan music. But I think the jduq and the raita (datura) will get them before the Gnaoua or the Jilala do. Or perhaps LSD immunizes them to such simple substances. Is Ruth's Moroccan doctor named Josué Corco? He's the only one I can think of in New York. That may not be accurate, the surname, but it's similar to the correct one. Did I promise you a copy of *A Hundred Camels in the Courtyard?* If so, I'll keep the promise, but first you must let me know where you want it sent. I'll write City Lights and order a copy for you, having them post it directly to you. Went to a wonderful lunch today at Louise de Meuron's. From one thirty to seven, it lasted, without benefit of entertainment or kif, both of which aid her night parties considerably. (A Swiss baroness who loves to spend money for her guests.) Anyway, everything is the same as always.

March 25, 1967
Tangier

Yes, here I am, back under bright skies. (Thailand never had such a sky as we have here.) A little more than three weeks . . . long enough to have meshed again with the cogs of Tangier habits. Only Jane is very ill, having been for the past six months or so in a really bad depression. (They claim she's better now, though to me she seems fairly far gone, not being able to dress or wash, and resisting all helpful suggestions, naturally.) I am going to have to take her to Spain and leave her in a hospital, I'm afraid. But she should be having medication in any case. A clinical depression is not generally something one can climb out of by oneself. They say a month or so ought to do. Anyway, that's my present difficulty.

Their Heads Are Green. About half of each piece, I think, was written in the place with which it deals; the rest was out of memory later. As I'm doing (or shall be doing) with the Bangkok book that looms ahead of me menacingly . . . deadline October first, God forbid . . . About journeying, which you don't seem to enjoy too much, it would be good to do it in peace if it were possible, but the act itself militates against it. The only peace is that of being cut off from the outside world, and perhaps that is very important, although always one yearns to reestablish the connection, panting to get at mail, going miles to find a copy of "Time," and dreaming of what it will be like when the test is over. If it ever is. (Since I often believe I won't return, what with microbes and other local hazards, I was convinced I wouldn't get back here from Southeast Asia. No anguish, just the dry conviction that this time would be the time.) Years ago in *Rien Que la Terre*, that unpleasant man Paul Morand wrote that it isn't important to be going somewhere, but that one simply feels better being en route, being, that is, nowhere for the moment.

I'll ask Holt, Rinehart to send you a copy of *The Time of Friendship* when it's ready, which ought to be in June. I imagine next month I'll get galleys. At the instant I'm taping a novel in Arabic, for lack of something better to do. Imagine you haven't seen *Love with a Few Hairs*, which came out in London in January. Would you be interested in having it? I have three copies, and can send you one if you like.

I hear Alfred Chester is back here after having gone wild for a while and ended up in a London loony-bin. I haven't seen him in a year and a half. The Moslem grapevine has him living in a fisherman's house right on the beach, and fighting with the natives continually. But you probably don't know him, so my remarks mean nothing. As Susan Sontag insisted: You have to remember at all times that Alfred is crazy, but really crazy. I know he's adept at making you forget it, but remember it.

Malaysia, where I spent ten days after leaving Siam, is a better tourist land. Penang Island hasn't changed: one of the most propitious places for living. Singapore has far more traffic than the last time I was there, but is still pleasant. Kuala Lumpur, which I'd never before seen, is overcrowded but very fine. Even Port Swettenham was a relief after Bangkok.

Let me hear.

TO BILL GRAY

April 19, 1967
Tangier

Sorry to be so late in answering your letter, but I've had to go twice across to Spain, first to look for a hospital for Jane, and then to accompany her and install her there. She is now in the Sanatorio of the Sacred Heart. The sisters seem to be of the sweet variety rather than the sour. (I've been in hospitals where the nurses were nuns of the latter sort, and they're not ideal. But these all appear to be goodness itself.) Naturally Jane won't be happy there, but happiness is a side issue in crises, and she could scarcely have been more miserable than she was here, where nothing whatever was being done for her.

I see you are still preoccupied with "happiness" as a concept! It seems to me that if during any given day one doesn't have an appointment with the dentist or with someone whose presence makes one suffer, one can call the day a happy one. Sufficient unto the day is the lack of evil thereof, no? Obviously, when life comes to be only one horror after another, it's time to call it quits. But generally there is some little moment that can be savored, between the ghastly ones, a moment when one can collect oneself and say: Yes, I can continue another day. (You are looking forward to "days in wine and roses and nights of love and laughter." Can such a program actually be made real? Even youth was never like that, at least for me, and I should think middle age would make it all even less realizable. But everyone has his own star and his own means of locomotion for getting to it. All I want is an old age without too much pain inside and derision outside (although the whole thing will undoubtedly be well-nigh unbearable) and I hope I shan't be totally alone.)

Tennessee ought to be contented. But we always imagine others should find it easy to accept their lives, whereas our own lives have built-in troubles that others couldn't have. And since no one can be anyone but himself, no one can really know anything about anyone else, much less make suggestions or criticisms . . . Every consciousness is an isolated entity, and life consists of the continually frustrated attempt to make contact. But is there anything objectionable about that state of affairs?

I'm busy with rehearsals of the play for the American School. It opens next Friday. I'm glad to have something to keep me active during this period of being alone.

TO JANE BOWLES
———————————◆———————————
April 29, 1967
Tangier

Tangier again, and everything is the same as always. I was glad to see that you didn't look ill, but it made me terribly sad to realize how desperately unhappy you were there. Above all I hope that when I return you will be a little more agile and able to walk about more easily. I hate to see you moving so slowly and with such difficulty. I wish you'd write me, even a line or two, about how the fruit and vegetable situation has been solved, if it has. You really need more exercise and fresh fruit. Also I think vitamins would be indicated. I suppose they're unknown in Málaga, and I'll have to get them in Gibraltar, incha'Allah.

Fatoma says you took your good wig with you in a suitcase. The old one is here in the hatbox with the egghead Sonia made a face on. If you look I'm sure you'll find the new one there in your luggage or in a drawer or in the closet.

I wish you would get well and come back. You don't know how depressing it is with the flat completely empty. And I keep remembering how unhappy you were the day I saw you, and I feel miserable. I saw Isabelle today, and she gave me the address of the sanatorium in Belgium. I must write them tonight. I accepted the teaching job for one semester (five months) rather than the entire year.

Don't lose your copy of *Dos Señoras de Aupa*. We have no other copy, and there are none in Tangier. Please send me a few words.

TO JAMES LEO HERLIHY

May 5, 1967
Tangier

Today I'm posting you a copy of *Love with a Few Hairs*, before it becomes impossible to send it through the mails. (It's under consideration now at police headquarters; there's always that whiff of apprehension in the atmosphere. One can never relax and know that everything's all right in this place; Big Brother is so prone to misunderstand and decide that one really meant to insult the country.) For this reason Mrabet grows glum from time to time, being certain they will throw him into jail for having dared to write a book. I can scarcely reassure him successfully, remembering some of their past eccentricities. In any case, let me know when it arrives. I look forward to seeing the STORY next month, and you can look forward to seeing my own collection, probably in June also. How lucky you are to be able to do libretti and screen treatments; why do you even think of being writer-in-residence? A California college offered me $18,000 last week for being that there, six hours a week and so on. Two reasons for knowing that it won't happen. First, I haven't a clue as to how to go about teaching, never having been taught. Second, they wouldn't be able to clear me even if I wanted to accept. It's happened five times to me, this sort of offer, and it's always from a state-controlled institution, which means no ex-members. Only a privately financed institution can have me. Jane now in hospital in Málaga. For how long, I don't know. I am here, having teeth repaired, champing at the bit the whole time. (Unfortunate metaphor, considering the dental work.) Yes, as you say, the danger of contagion in cases of depressive irrationality is considerable. After a few hours of wrangling and attempts at calming, I often felt that my own mind was none too reliable in its behavior. Found also that a constant lurking thought consisted of immediate suicide, merely to escape the whole nightmare. Ridiculous, but real. A Venezuelan Indian? Moving in? Still extant? I'd like to make a trip down to the desert. Everyone's down at a place called Tam Tam, where there's an amara going on. But I'm here, as I say. And hope to hear from you.

TO JAMES PURDY

June 1, 1967
Tangier

Eustace Chisholm arrived. Thank you. I found it exciting to read; it seemed to go back to the world of *Dream Palace*, which I've always loved. And the subliminal pornography is deft. And as always, I'm delighted with the way you tell a story, a way which can come only from inhabiting the invented cosmos, knowing one's way around in it, as it were, with one's eyes shut. It's the thing I admire in Jane's work, too. (She's in Málaga in the hospital; I went to see her last week and she was a bit stronger, but not yet well enough to come home.) The weather is beautiful and windy, with a very hot sun. I'm going to ask Peter Owen to send you a copy of *Love with a Few Hairs* direct from London. I can't do it from here because of the police ban on it in Morocco. (Why, I don't know.) But doubtless I've already complained about that to you. Sorry you're not here. Bill Burroughs was through a fortnight ago on his way to Marrakech, where he is now, living in the Medina and working. I was down there a while back, and found it too full of tourists to be altogether pleasant. But there was a folk festival on, which probably accounted for some of them. So anyway, I'm glad your address is still the same, although I must go and look it up in the front of *Eustace Chisholm*, where I pasted your letter in lieu of an inscription.

TO JAMES LEO HERLIHY

June 1967
Tangier

The other evening I was posting a letter at the only box in the quarter; otherwise one has to go to the Boulevard de Paris on the corner. I lifted up the iron flap, and was about to drop in my missive, when a Jewish boy, yarmulke and all, tapped my arm. "Oh, monsieur, don't put your letters into this box. The Moslems put kerosene and matches in every day. The letters all get burned." I made a few incredulous noises, did not put my letter into the box, thanked him, and came home. The same evening I told Mrabet of the incident. "The little son-of-a-bitch!" he growled when I'd finished. "You see how the Jews are? Making even the Christians unhappy. What sort of thing is that to tell an American in the street?" "But is it true?" I wanted to know. "Do they make fires inside the mailbox or not?" "Of course they do! I could have told you that two years ago." I was indignant. "But you've seen me post my letters there plenty of times. Why didn't you tell me?" He looked very dour. "I don't like informers," he said darkly. "That's for the Jews." Now I take my letters into the city to mail. On the same subject more or less, a bit of amusing side-information. It is, of course, permitted, even recommended, to kill Jews, whereas the same permissiveness doesn't apply to Christians. On the other hand (this I didn't know) it is forbidden to steal from Jews, whereas it is all right to steal from Christians. Reason: because the Christians forgive and the Jews don't! I imagine that *Love with a Few Hairs* will be arriving more or less at the same time as this letter; it ought to. I sent it by seamail because the air rates from here are wondrously high. I took the *Ibn Batuta* last week to Málaga to see Jane. She didn't seem much better; she merely had more energy to expend in repeating the details in the progress of her illness. From being a fish-stinking provincial port Málaga has become a sort of national monument of tourism; everything is floodlighted and shipshape for the Swedes and Germans, and even the poor look like middle-class. In other words, it's like Madrid fifteen years ago. Bill Burroughs rang my bell one afternoon a few weeks back, on his way south from London to Marrakech. I think he plans to come north when the weather down there gets too strong, and spend the summer in Tangier. Jimmy Baldwin is expected in another fortnight or so, from Istanbul; he wants to visit the Amara of Moulay Abdelkader, which is said to be extraordinary. I think we'll all go together. Brion Gysin, Geoffroy de Thoisy and I took a long walk this afternoon, out past the Moujahiddin to a ruined Spanish military tower that stands atop a hill there. The goats surrounded us, friendly and curious, nibbling dried yellow asters and leaving everything else. We smoked some kif in the shelter of the tower, for the wind was very rough. I had my Grundig Elektronisches Notizbuch with me, and on the way back when a dog began to bark behind an iron-grilled gate, I walked over and held the loudspeaker to his muzzle so he could hear the voice that came out of it. Several more dogs rushed out. Brion suggested I record rather than playback. At that point a very fey and very drunk middle-aged English lady, strung with long necklaces, staggered through the garden and turned her bleary but enraged eyes on us to ask, in incredible French: "Vous cherchez *moi*? Vous voulez *moi*?" (The *moi*, with the facial contortions that accompanied it, was sheer Bernhardt; the thin arms came up and waved in the air.) Geoffroy said, "Non. On regardait vos chiens." We walked on while she raved behind the gate. *Playboy* asked for a piece on going to pieces in the tropics. I have no ideas. Wrote them from Thailand asking if it was a forgone conclusion that hot climates cause disintegration; they replied that if I could show to their satisfaction that such is not the case, they would be happy. But I haven't written the article. Hope WEDDING doesn't drive you mad. Let me hear.

TO ANDREAS BROWN,
GOTHAM BOOK MART, NEW YORK

June 9, 1967
Tangier

I was waiting, have been waiting for a long time, to receive the parcel you mentioned having sent, but now, since there has been no sign of it for so long, I'm writing anyhow. I hate to think it's lost, the soap and the copy of *The Delicate Prey*. The police are being very difficult this year, and have banned my new book (with Mrabet), *Love with a Few Hairs*. Went to the Librairie des Colonnes and removed their copies, notified all bookstores in Morocco that the book was illegal. Perhaps they are examining other packages that arrive for me. What can one do? We are now prisoners in the country, in the sense that if an American leaves Morocco he can't get back in, as it has been declared off-limits for U.S. citizens. As long as Americans stay where they are, everything is all right. I heard from Larbi today, saying he thought he would be leaving the United States within the month. I can see he will come here, being drawn by the prospect of seeing his two children, but what will happen after that I don't know. Besides, everyone says he will be tossed into jail the day he shows his face here. That's only street gossip, of course, but still, it sounds sinister. I'm wondering if you have seen Oliver Evans since his return from Bangkok. Yes, I remember something about the Prokofiev letter; I had several, some of which I gave Aaron Copland, and some of which were stolen out of Libby Holman's house. The edition of *Yallah!* you ask about was published in London circa 1957, shortly after the Obolensky edition in New York, I think. I have a review and a photograph from *The Observer*. There were three editions: the first in German by Conzett & Huber, Zurich, then the N.Y., then the London. Jane is getting along in the hospital in Málaga; I saw her a fortnight ago. Look forward to your Tenn book, and to seeing you when you come. If you see Marian Cummings, give her my love, please. She has enormous charm. Esoteric information: It is meritorious to kill Jews, but it is forbidden to steal from them. It is not rec-ommended to kill Christians, but it is perfectly all right to steal from them. And the reason one cannot steal from a Jew is that the Jew does not forgive. Words of a new song: Our love started out so fine. And then it grew Christian. (*Nesrani* is a slang synonym for *bessel*, which means unattractive or undesirable.) What the poor Christian has to put up with in heathen lands! I'm waiting for an advance copy of *The Time of Friendship* from Holt, Rinehart, but so far nothing. I asked for white linen with crimson lettering; I wonder if they have complied.

TO NED ROREM

June 22, 1967
Tangier

Braziller sent xeroxes, as you no doubt know. The only statement I disagree with is the one on page 197: "Paul and I were taken with jitters, chills, fear." Jitters and chills, but not fear. I was confident that the expedition would never get to the bad places I'd been to with majoun. So for accuracy's sake you ought not to state that I experienced fear with mescaline. With Prestonia (given me by Bill Burroughs) yes. But not with mescaline that time at John's. The only other time I took it was at Asilah, when I experienced disgust. The Pennsylvania week-end I've always remembered with wonder and pleasure; the only drawback was John's insistence that I accept mescaline phenomena as truth. (I never reached a point where I ceased rejecting them, whence his frantic admonitions to "let yourself go!") I didn't quite understand the reference (on page 201) to sin and darkness; there is apparently some unexpressed connection between me and sin in the sentence, but it's not clear to me what it is. And wait a minute—on page 192, what was the hashish "orgy" with Shirley Gabis? If there was an orgy, I went out before it came in. Or perhaps, this being Part Two, reference is being made to an earlier passage, in Part One or Part Two. Anyway, I look forward to seeing the finished product. * * *

Do you think of appearing here? I hope so. I'm told the State Department ruling has been rescinded, so that Morocco is no longer off-limits. Presumably now I can go to Málaga to see Jane.

I'll hope to hear.

August 31, 1967
Tangier

You probably will refuse to believe me when I tell you I can't write the Bangkok book. I don't mean that I'm unable to meet the deadline: I mean that I find it an impossible book to write. My struggle with it has been going on since I returned to Morocco in March. Until recently I had imagined that somehow I should find a way of doing it. This was only because I was too much involved in the writing of it to be able to realize that my material was not going to make a good book.

One thing which went wrong was that in the middle of my stay in Thailand I began to receive letters from our doctor here in Tangier telling me that Mrs. Bowles was ill. The unspecified illness was soon identified as a nervous depression, and I was told that my presence here was required, as she needed to be placed in a sanatorium in Europe, and no one else but me could do it. I cut short my stay in Bangkok and returned here, to find that I had a full-time job cut out for me, shuttling back and forth between Tangier and Málaga, trying to correlate the instructions of the two doctors here with those of the doctor in Spain. This went on until a little over three weeks ago, when I brought Mrs. Bowles back to Morocco. (Within a week after her arrival she had to undergo another operation, from which she is still slowly recovering.)

However, even such hindrances (which can be almost overwhelming) would not stand in the way of doing a work about which I had a strong positive feeling, and I've finally been forced to recognize a fact which I should have known much earlier, before I did so much work on the project—and that is that it is very difficult to write an entire book about a city toward which one feels no warmth. It's not the working conditions which have finally put me off—it's my reaction to Bangkok itself.

Naturally I am unhappy about my failure, and shall return the advance Little, Brown made me. (Unfortunately Helen Strauss is no longer at William Morris, nor Jane Wilson either. There is nobody I know left there, and I'd have liked to confer with somebody in the agency about the mechanics of returning the money.)

Please let me hear from you.

TO JAMES LEO HERLIHY

September 4, 1967
Tangier

The regular evening spectacle of brilliance and evolving colors in the sky above The Mountain and the sea, very visible from the window behind my back, is taking place, and Princess Ruspoli is downstairs drinking whiskey with Jane. I am announced for nine, and have the obligation of putting in a half hour with them and with someone I haven't met, named Madeleine de la Grandière. (Jane insists on referring to her as Madeleine Goldberg, because she can't remember her real name. After we'd been several weeks at a place in Massachusetts near Ipswich Beach, Jane still believed it was called Lipschitz Beach, and was very much surprised when she finally saw the word written out. Like Nina Mdvani's new husband's name is Anthony Harwood, but to Jane he's Anthony Horowitz.) A letter today from James Purdy makes me feel he is not in a very good way. He feels *Eustace Chisholm* was a failure. And he adds that the reason is that he is not Jewish or a Negro or a "taker of LSD." What can you gather from all that? The next sentence reads: "This whole country is a dried pool of shit." Is it a non-sequitur, or something graver? Strange man. Thanks for the *New Republic* tear-sheet. Flattering words do massage secret places; the trick is not to allow them to touch the mind. Went to Larache today, about sixty miles down the coast. Magnificent light-effects over rolling hills, salt marshes stacked with long rows of salt pyramids, sand dunes, estuaries and sea. We had a bit of a time finding the city jail, which was far outside the town atop a cliff overlooking the ocean. It was a big, brand-new bordj—just four high walls painted orange, and a mediaeval-looking gate. Mrabet rang a bell, the moqaddem opened the gate, and he went in to visit a friend who had decided to kill a policeman. I sat in the sun, alone in the landscape save for a small boy reclining on top of a wall a hundred feet away. Soon he asked me in French what time it was. This didn't keep me from replying automatically in Spanish, which he failed to understand. I then told him in Arabic, reflecting that times have changed and that a whole new generation has appeared, for which the only non-Arabic language is French. Only the fathers in Northern Morocco now speak Spanish. I meant to thank you for the kif poster with the text taken from "He of the Assembly." Yes, any review you can cull would be welcome. I still haven't seen the Times. Holt, Rinehart are unusually remiss. I was sad to hear about Carson. Her life has been even worse than Jane's. What did you have to do with the

Zoo Story in Paris? I'm looking for an Amer. publisher for *Love with a Few Hairs*. Not yet.

TO LIBBY HOLMAN
◆

September 9, 1967
Tangier

This is going to be a short note because just as I sat down to write it Jane sent Angèle upstairs to say that there was a beatnik girl with her, and she wanted me to help her. Some college graduate who liked Jane's book; she was here last week, too, and it's only Jane who insists on calling her a beatnik. (I think the reason is that the girl hints she would like to be invited to dinner, and Jane thus has as much as made a vow not to invite her, ever.) (As Jane recovers, she gets onto a higher and higher horse, I find. And the reason for that is that she has suddenly cut out all medication, for the first time in ten years; as a result of "being on her own," as it were, she is extremely energetic, and the energy releases heretofore unsuspected reserves of aggression. So she has her own way or else.)

At last I have been sent a review of my recent book, and it was good (*The New Republic*). I'm annoyed with Holt, Rinehart for not even sending me one review; I should think they could have cut out the *Times Book Review* piece.

Jane has, to answer your question, Aicha to look after her, as well as another maid named Habiba, and Angèle, who comes in irregularly. There is also the other Spanish woman, Maruja, who fills in at crucial moments. Jane may have to go soon for another operation, but it's not certain. The stitches ripped out of the first, and she nearly died of pain for ten days, all without having the surgeon look at her because, as she claimed, he was "indifferent" to her suffering. When she finally went with Dr. Roux, they were horrified to see what had happened. I don't know all the details, so I can't expatiate further on it.

Gerald's songs look beautiful, but I have no piano on which to try them out, and so I can't really know what they sound like, naturally, not being Nadia Boulanger or Lenny Bernstein. Thanks so much for sending them to me. I've put them away with my own music, until the time when I'm in a place where there's a piano.

I imagine the September third concert in East Hampton was a great success. I'd love to have been there to hear it if I could have come right back.

[letterhead] Oriental Hotel
Bangkok, Thailand
November 1, 1967
Tangier

A certain amount of confusion around here makes it easier to use this paper than to look for better, since a block of it was right here in front of me by the typewriter. So forgive.

I suppose one reason I didn't write earlier is that I didn't want to have to give explanations why I wasn't sending a sentence or two for Braziller to use for your book. Because of my appearance in the cast of characters, above all in such a favorable light, I couldn't bring myself to make public comments on the volume. It would have been much simpler if I hadn't been referred to at all in its pages. Mutual admiration always looks so yenty, as Jane would say, having made an adjective out of it. She came home from the hospital today, incidentally. At the moment I'm being secretary for her, taking dictated letters and dialing her phone numbers. She has three Moslem servants and one Spanish dame de compagnie who also markets and prepares meals. (The Moslems make her nervous, she claims.) But of course those people are incapable of making her calls for her and writing her letters. I hope this time she is going to be all right; it's about sixteen months that she has been too ill to leave the apartment by herself: she falls down unless she is held up. All this began in the summer of 1966 when she was in New York with me. I don't quite know what happened. I set sail for Bangkok and she began to dose herself with strong medicines (and doubtless to take more alcohol), so that the inevitable happened, and she slid quickly down into a clinical depression. Anyway, now she is infinitely better—certainly much better than when you saw her in New York.

I'm about to set out on a motor trip into the Rif, and perhaps other places. While Jane recuperates it's easier on everybody if I'm out of the way. Mrabet drives expertly; we'll probably make for Alhucemas first because everyone says it's a lot warmer there than here on the Atlantic coast. But who knows?

Alfred Chester is back in Tangier after a two-year absence in Asilah and America. Brion is also here. Bill Burroughs has gone back to London. I hope to get a reply from you.

TO JAMES LEO HERLIHY

November 6, 1967
Tangier

Returned today from a stirring voyage through the Rif; I wanted to make sure that the untouched world was still here. It is. Xauen, Ketama, Targuist, Al Hoceima (ex-Villa Sanjurho, more recently Alhucemas), Talamagait, Tizi Ouzli, Aknoul, and then to Taza, Fez, Meknès and back home. The only new section was between Talamagait and Taza, which for a very good reason I had never before seen, the reason being that it was a dissident sector up until five or six years ago, and I last went to the Rif in 1959 when I did my recordings there. It's a country in itself, the Rif, and although it lost its independence in 1925 when the French helped the Spanish win it, and was handed over to Rabat when the Spanish gave up their protectorate, the Riffians still expect to be free one day. Ask a Riffian if he's Moroccan and hear his reply. Anyway, Jane had another operation last week, and is in bed now once again. Better-humored, if a little fractious at night; but then, she's in considerable pain all the time. I just came up from downstairs. The practicante was there to give her an injection so she could sleep. I hope you are gaining control of your liver. Perhaps you shouldn't drink any alcohol at all, like me since 1941. Or eat eggs or drink milk. Still haven't worked out the contract business for *Love with a Few Hairs* in New York. And I take it you won't be showing it to Dutton, in any case. I still have hopes that your friends may find a way of tackling the film. It would be fun. Mrabet has four friends eating dinner with him in the next room, and he is entertaining them with tales told him in Al Hoceima by an old fisherman who was sitting on a deserted beach we drove out to. Naturally Farid el Atrache is wailing on a tape-recorder, and the kif fumes are strong. They're waiting for me to sit and watch them eat, so I'll stop. Let me hear you're better.

TO OLIVER EVANS

November 13, 1967
Tangier

Your letter of October nineteenth has been lying here for a while; in the meantime there arrived one from Mr. Finestone which I haven't yet answered. Jane had another operation two weeks ago today, and her pain seems to be increasing each day. She lies screaming all night, and there doesn't seem to be anything the doctors can do for her. No injection calms the pain. This preoccupation has kept me from doing much of anything, as I'm always on the alert for poundings on the ceiling by one of the maids, summoning me; it happens at any hour of the day or night. The trouble is that she sometimes tries to get out of bed by herself, and falls, and that always makes everything worse. Both the surgeon and her regular doctor are coming this afternoon. Not that they will be able to make a prognosis between them. I doubt that any doctor could.

I shall write Mr. Finestone today, and try to reply to the few questions in his letter. There is one difficulty, beyond the problem of former adherence to "totalitarian" politics, and that is Jane. I don't know whether it would be possible for me to be in the college if she were with me, as I'd have no time for anything but caring for her. Here at least there are four servants working night and day on stagger systems, but there we'd have nobody, and it would be terrible, as she can't even light herself a cigarette, and has become used to being served by others. That of course is no one's concern but my own, and I mention it to you *en passant*. But the idea of going there does interest me. And you have always said you believed I'd be capable of doing what is required of me, even though I never have before.

The Bangkok book I have abandoned wholly, and am returning Little, Brown's advance. It's impossible for me to work, no matter how hard I try, and it has been that way since I returned from Thailand. I'm sorry, after the wonderful résumé you wrote at my behest. I hope it will prove to have been of some use to you yourself. As you know, I never give up on writing projects. But this one was one that didn't interest me in the beginning; I accepted it out of greed, and I hope I've learned better, so that I shan't get myself into that sort of thing again.

I'd like to hear from you.

November 16, 1967
Tangier

Your letter the only one in the box today. The rainy times have begun; last night we had our first radiator heat, which meant that Manuel was in the basement making the furnace go. Extraordinary for these days in Morocco. Practically no apartment houses supply heat of any sort any more. That was for colonial days, when things were good, and Nazarenes ran them, and Moroccans got what was left over. Now things are terrible, Moroccans run them, and obviously there's nothing left over, so that nobody gets anything except the government and the families of those working in it. Dissatisfaction, turning to disaffection. Trouble expected in March, and don't ask me why it should be March. Ramadan begins in eighteen days, so they say. Still haven't sold *LWAFH* in New York—waiting for abridged contracts. Did sign with Gallimard on it, so that we can have further difficulties with the local police. (One policeman, upbraiding me for having translated the book, said: "One does not write about bitter truths—only sweet truths.") I was back in 1917, being lectured by my grandmother on the subject-matter of the stories I wrote each day (yes, I was six years old). "Why don't you write about pretty things instead of horrid things?" Or my father, who wrote me a letter after reading *The Delicate Prey*, saying: "What gutters have you lain in? Why don't you try sitting on the curb for a while? The world might look better from there." Thanks for letting me into the secret structure of the film project! They're asking me to teach in California— San Fernando Valley State College. I wonder what that would be like. This particular time they think they can clear me, although the other seven institutions weren't able to. I can't believe it. California? UCLA wasn't able to a few years ago, and now with Reagan . . . ? I've never been to the Seychelles. Years ago Alec Waugh told me they had been delightful, but that they have fallen into a kind of paralysis. Twice in London I tried to book passage, but found that one had to go first to Bombay and get a ship from there. Nice and warm, yes, and a special local vegetation, and a populace that speaks a French patois mixed with English. Must be vaguely like the Antilles fifty years ago. The Maldives sound pleasant, too.

January 22, 1968
Tangier

Have six weeks passed since my last note? They may easily have; I've been busy trying to take care of Jane, who entered an unexpected manic phase suddenly, and brought the house tumbling down on our heads. After giving away her money and clothes, she issued checks for which there was insufficient provision, and that's considered a crime in Morocco. The account was in my name, with a joint provision, so the blame accrued to me. I've been paying off the debts, which are considerable so far and continue to pop up, although I've already taken her to Spain to the hospital. But in less than a month of living at the Hotel Atlas she threw out several thousand dollars. As usual, whiskey was the culprit; the blend of heavy sedation and White Horse is particularly noxious, as you know. At least, she can't get any more liquor where she is; I know that. The place is guarded by nuns.

A young Moroccan cinéaste got in touch with me shortly after Christmas, with a project of filming *LWAFH* under a French aegis. He has now returned to Paris; seemed intelligent, and had generally healthy and fresh ideas on how to do it. Of course he saw the Moroccan police ban on it as merely an extra and welcome hazard; he thinks it should be done right in Tangier. They love to put one over on the authorities . . . that is, if they live outside the country! Anyway, I'll tell you if and when anything concrete rears its head. Naturally I'd prefer Americans to do it, and the idea of Israel seems genial. The last place I'd have thought of! But why not? I heard today that the American edition is scheduled for March. I hope it's better-looking than the English. Our new book is well on its way to completion, and Mrabet is already planning one about his experiences in the USA, which ought to be amusing. Was my remark on resistance cloudy? I meant that forces of resistance must beware of allowing their hand to be forced too soon. Disaffection must be far greater than it is at present. Not sure what you want me to elucidate. I'm a believer in conspiracy rather than political candor. One says yes until one has a good chance to strike and win. One doesn't go around screaming no. One does not announce one's beliefs; one is a hypocrite of necessity. One plans, organizes, studies, and eventually strikes. No?

P.S. The news about Jane is not for circulation. Please. She's in the hospital. That's enough to say, if you say anything.

February 9, 1968
Tangier

Sorry your cat disappeared. Mine lives with the Princess Ruspoli and hunts all day in the gardens on the Mountain. No question of my getting him back. Jane in Spain again in hospital. No end to her troubles. Or mine. This time she ran up enormous bills all over town, and I am still paying them off. Have sent for three thousand dollars so far with which to do it (as she emptied the bank account) and still haven't got them all. She went to the American Consulate and staged a lie-in strike on the floor, saying: When you give me the money I want, I'll get up. She finally settled for a glass of whiskey and went on her way, only to return there the following day and every day thereafter, in order to try and work the same strategy. But they got in touch with me. (I knew nothing about any of it, as she was living at the Atlas Hotel in town all those weeks.) And with an interne from the Beni Makada Hospital I took her across to Algeciras, and then in a cab to Málaga. Calm here now. Not even Alfred disturbs it. He has been holed up on the Mountain for several weeks with some Zailachi he knows. I called one day and Alfred answered in falsetto, a ridiculous voice, saying: No tá quí, Señor Alfréd. So I gave up. Why does he never go for a rest in a hospital like Jane, I wonder? I'm going to send you a tape of my own electronic pieces, and you can tell me what you think. Apparently somebody in Los Angeles saw *The Great Society*, for I got a letter asking if they could print the poems, along with others, in a small volume. I agreed. It ought to be out soon. Probably I told you earlier. Tatiana Andrews has been here with a vengeance, borrowing money from everyone. I think she found her amphetamine and methedrine in Marrakech, where everybody seems to have congregated recently. I don't open the door when she rings. Too expensive. We've had a month of clear weather, and now it's turned cloudy. But springlike, with flowers all over the fields. I suppose the bad weather will come in March and April. Nothing more now. New Mrabet book nearly finished. Called *Lemon*.

TO JAMES LEO HERLIHY

March 22, 1968
Tangier

I wonder where you are: Florida, California, Mexico, Caribbean? Or Manhattan? The wondering is natural, since it's a long time that I haven't heard from you.

Nothing new, save that I finished the new Mrabet book and sent it off to the agents, so I don't need to worry about that for the time being. *Love with a Few Hairs* was finally published in New York, but I haven't seen any reviews yet, if indeed any have appeared.

Popular wisdom elicited from Mrabet in conversation: The only way to make a woman shut up is to screw her. Better not beat her, though, or she'll think you're in love with her.

Spring came in beautifully, on schedule yesterday; before that we'd had a long session of clouds, rain and gale. (Our wind generally lasts a week or ten days without stopping, as you know.) A man lived on the top floor of a four-story empty building in Emsallah. He was leaning out the window looking down into the street, when another man gestured to him. Come down. He went down to the door to see what the other wanted. Have you got a piece of bread? said the passer-by. Wait here, said the tenant, and went back upstairs. After a while he called out the window: Come on up. The passer-by went in and climbed to the top. I'm sorry. I haven't any bread, said the tenant, and shut the door. These things really happen here. A boy named Abdeslam is here cutting, Mrabet is recording Oum Kalsoum's recent concert in Casablanca, from one tape-recorder to another, and a very noisy wedding, complete with beribboned bull, oboes and drums, just made its way past the window on its way down to Aïn Hayani. The drums go on being audible, although the whole crowd has now slipped into one of the alleys of the village and can no longer be seen—only the bright green hill and the fences of cactus and the acacia trees covered with yellow flowers. We got through the Aid el Kebir safely. It got to be traumatic when I lived in the Medina . . . the morass of blood and guts and hoofs and horns was unsettling . . .

I'll hope for a word one day soon.

TO OLIVER EVANS

May 15, 1968
Tangier

I was going to write this to Dr. Finestone, but at the last minute I decided to write it to you instead. It is to say that still I don't understand of what my work is to consist. In his most recent note to me he asks me to let him know as soon as possible what books I shall be using in my course. He also sent me my schedule: one meeting a week to consider creative writing (7 p.m. to 10 p.m.) and two a week to consider the Existential novel (3 to 4:30). When I showed this to my Princeton friends, they immediately said: But you're going to have to prepare a series of lectures, write them out beforehand, and then read them to a public of several hundred people; do you realize that? This, of course, paralyzed me. I replied that no one had told me such a thing. They said that doubtless it was assumed that I was aware of it without being told. Can you tell me: would I be giving a lecture course (a term which they tell me does not mean the same thing as a "class") or what would I be giving? I know it won't be possible for me to write a series of articles beforehand; there simply isn't time. It would require a good many months. I take several months to write one piece for *Holiday*. A lecture—even one—would take me at least as long, if not longer. I don't think anyone at San Fernando understands: I have no conception of what goes on in a college classroom, or how classes are conducted. It might almost as well be a chemical refinery, as far as my being able to imagine the procedure which fills the duration of a given "class." You all assume I have a familiarity with the formalities of the educational process, and I have none at all. But I must know soon what is going to be expected of me, and try to prepare for the work. If it involves the writing of a series of lectures on any subject, I shall have to decline. We are already only two weeks' distant from the beginning of June. Each day I feel more desperate. I must have some sort of expository material from you, listing in detail exactly what I must do, here in Tangier now (if there is still time), in order to be able to function in September there in the United States. The only thing I know is that I must read a dozen or so books (this means rereading them, but it's the same thing in the end). But would it not be preferable if I were to read them in English translation, since it is with the English versions that we shall be dealing? How am I to read them in English in Morocco? Or should I order them from Paris in French and study them in the original? (I've never read any of the material in translation.) I shan't continue in this vein or you'll decide I'm paranoid. But really, I'm stumped, because I don't know what is expected of me. Try to envisage my ignorance and explain to me what goes on in a classroom. What is a course? a lecture course? a seminar? a class? Who does the talking in each? What is the teaching process? Does one tell students one's own reactions to books, or does one remain wholly objective in approach? Does one interpret? Above all, *what is the preliminary work?* Until soon, I hope.

TO JANE BOWLES

July 1968
Tangier

I've got letters from the doctor and from the Madre Superiora, but none from you. Also John Hopkins wrote me a long letter about his visit to you. I wish I knew whether you like this place any better than the other, or the same, or less well. Doctor Ortiz writes me that he is giving you some medication, but he doesn't specify what sort. I've got to go over and see for myself what's happening and how you are.

When Jesus García returns next week I'll get your glasses prescription from him in order to bring it to you in Málaga. I don't know whether it's still valid or not. We shall have to go together to an oculist and optometrist. But is there a decent one there in the city? I wonder.

I get a great many letters from your mother, who somehow doesn't believe me when I say you're not well enough to go to New York and Miami. In each letter she says: Promise me you won't leave Jane in Europe when you go to the United States. She says she can take care of you there in her apartment. I have written her once again today, saying that if she wants to see you this year she and Julian will have to visit you in Málaga. I know it will be much more expensive, but what can I do? I'll be back at the end of January, which is not very far off. If she and Julian can visit you in October or thereabouts, it would be the best solution. I hope eventually you can write her to that effect, so she won't imagine I'm trying to keep you from her or anything like that.

I've been listening to the Republican Convention in Miami Beach. Such excitement over whether they're going to run Nixon, Reagan or Rockefeller. Bill Burroughs is here for a few days, on his way to Chicago to cover the Democratic Convention for *Esquire Magazine*! I suppose the point was to find the most apolitical person they could.

I'm still seeing Buffard every three or four days. He is now trying to rebase my appliances, which have worn down like a pair of old shoes, on the sides. I'm having dinner Monday night at Mme. Roux's, or with her, I don't know which. Apart from her and the Gerofis I haven't seen anyone. It seems Christopher is back from Tokyo already. Something wrong. I haven't seen him; he's having dinner tonight at Brion's apartment, but I haven't been asked. I send all my love, and wish you could write.

TO HAROLD NORSE

July 30, 1968
Tangier

Gracias por tu carta. Studio Sunbeam, indeed! Operation Euphoria. Bill is here; had dinner with him and Brion last night. A man named Sherbill was there who said he knew you. Used to have a magazine called the East Side Review. He has been around for the past several months, staying with the Menebbhis, although recently he's been in a hotel, and at the moment he's gone to Spain to see his mother and father. Jobs on West Coast or anywhere: I don't know how to look for or find them. This is the eighth that has come my way, and the first out of four that I've accepted that has actually come through (or I think it'll come through, at least) because of the impossibility up to now of clearing me politically. The others discovered later, weeks after I'd accepted the tentative appointment, that due to circumstances beyond their control it would not after all be possible to employ me. How this institution has managed, I shudder to think, particularly with Reagan there watching. It would be wonderful if I were to get all the way out there only to discover that again "after all" it was not going to be possible. But I can't believe they'll let that happen. Jane is still in Spain, in a clínica de reposo near Málaga. So it's Krishnamurti who's at Gstaad; I wondered why you were there. Incidentally, Bill is very happy to have been cleared; he claims he owes as much to scientology as to apomorphine. I asked what the scientology had cured him of. Old thought patterns, he said. Anyway, he seemed in excellent form. And you. I hope you are, too. Andreas Brown is arriving shortly in Tangier. Wish we all could see you.

TO NORMAN GLASS

December 16, 1968
San Fernando Valley State College
Northridge, California

Your letter, instead of being delivered by special delivery to me, was placed in my box at the college here, so that it very likely remained there several days until I took it out this morning. I come up here to Northridge on Mondays and Wednesdays. Today is Monday, so that even if it got here quickly, I did not receive it quickly.

It is very thoughtful of you to suggest looking after Jane in order to let me stay on here and make some money, and actually nothing would please me more. But knowing her, I also know that what she wants is to see me and have me remove her from her prison, and as a matter of fact, when her mother tried to take her out of the clinic and whisk her off to Miami with her, the authorities there at the institution refused, saying that since her husband has placed her there, only he had the right to get her out. (I assume that in the event of my death, poor Jane would find it rather difficult to get them to release her, so let's hope I get back safely to do what has to be done. She's all right, actually, but I was afraid to leave her alone in Tangier after my experience of doing just that two years ago when I went to Bangkok. Alone, she seems to find no reason to go on living. Anyway, that is my responsibility, little as I may like carrying it. Who needs responsibilities?) As to the money business, I should like to be carefree and say that three hundred dollars are of no ultimate importance, and send them off to you light-heartedly and feel that I was helping thereby. But in view of the constant hospital, medical and doctor bills (every fifteen days I have to send off a bank draft to Spain) I need to hold on to everything I can amass in order to be able to continue paying, not only now but, I'm afraid, later, when I return to Tangier. It's not the kind of illness that presents a hopeful prognosis at any point. And it has been going on for so long that I'm a bit despondent about it. I should like to be able to say: Yes, I'll help Norman. But it would be an irresponsible act on my part. First things first. And I hope you don't consider me a monster for saying such a thing. In any case, I can only write you my decision and hope that you don't take it amiss. I have friendship to give, but not money. Others have more money than friendship, some have both, some have neither. But anyway.

Solutions are generally unexpected. I hope one has appeared. I don't think

suicide solves anything except the suffering of an incurable disease or the waiting
for a death sentence to be carried out. But I shan't write any more, because I
feel I have no right to.

February 23, 1969
Tangier

On the ship I put my memory to work and came up with a list—nothing
more—of events and people which would serve as nuclei from which to work
in recapturing the material for each year.

The book would start off with a section dealing with the things that happened
before memory begins, and go on through the recall of early childhood into late
childhood, stressing the opposing pressures of the paternal and maternal family
groups, and the resulting need for developing secrecy.

The anguish of adolescence is somewhat alleviated by my discovery of automatic writing (1927) and by subsequent publication in *transition* in 1928.
From high school to art school; from there to University of Virginia, chosen
because Edgar Allan Poe had gone there.

The tossing of a coin decides that I shall run away from college. Paris (Tristan
Tzara), the Paris *Herald* where I work, hikes to Switzerland and the Riviera. In
Paris Prokofiev agrees to take me as a pupil in composition, but I go to Germany
instead. Return to New York (1929). Henry Cowell sends me to Aaron Copland,
who teaches me music. Return to the University of Virginia, completing first
year, then more study with Copland (1930).

In March 1931 I go to Paris, meet Gertrude Stein, Cocteau, Tchelitchew,
Pound, Gide. To Berlin. First meetings with Spender and Isherwood. To Han-
nover to see Kurt Schwitters and his Merzbau. To Holland, to stay in Kastel
Eerde with Krishnamurti. During the Summer Gertrude Stein suggests I go to
Tangier. Copland and I go. The following Winter I return to Paris to study with
Nadia Boulanger. After a few lessons I have enough and go to Italy. Later to
Granada to see Manuel de Falla, and back to Morocco (Spring 1932) where I
catch typhoid. Convalescence in Monte Carlo with my mother.

In December 1932 to Algiers and down to the Sahara. By camel across the

Great Eastern Erg into South Tunisia, arriving in Tunis in the Spring of 1933. Thence to Tangier. I take a house there and rent it to Djuna Barnes, who is writing *Nightwood*. Then from Cádiz to Puerto Rico (Barranquitas). Next to New York, where I study harmony with Roger Sessions.

In the Spring of 1934 I return to Morocco and settle in Fez. In Autumn of the same year I sail to Barranquilla, Colombia. Amoebic dysentery in the Andes. To Los Angeles, then to San Francisco, arriving in the Spring of 1935 in New York to stay and write music. Meet Balanchine and Kirstein. Eugene Berman devises a ballet for him and me to do, and I begin work on it.

In 1936 Kirstein, not wanting the Berman subject, commissions me to write the score of the ballet *Yankee Clipper*. I compose my first theatre score for Orson Welles. Later in the year I write a second, also for Welles. Meet E. E. Cummings for first time.

1937. Miguel Covarrubias suggests I go to Tehuantepec, which I do. Visit Guatemala. First performance *Yankee Clipper* by Philadelphia Orchestra. In February 1938 I marry Jane Auer. Panama, Costa Rica, Guatemala, then France, where we settle at Eze-Village. In Autumn Orson Welles asks me to return to write a theatre score. We go back to New York. Meet Dalí for first time. In December we join Communist Party. Saroyan arrives in New York and asks me to write score for *My Heart's in the Highlands*. Clifford Odets gives me his apartment in which to work at it. Jane and I take a house on Staten Island. Leonard Bernstein spends week-ends there with us (Summer and Autumn of 1939). Meet Auden for first time.

Early 1940 I provide score for another Saroyan play (*Love's Old Sweet Song*) (Theatre Guild). Am given commission to write score for film for the U.S. Department of Agriculture, in Albuquerque. After completing this work I leave for Mexico. In Acapulco Tennessee Williams comes to the house and introduces himself. I return to New York to write the score for the Maurice Evans–Helen Hayes *Twelfth Night*, then for Philip Barry's *Liberty Jones* and Lillian Hellman's *Watch on the Rhine*. Jane and I go to live at a rooming-house in Brooklyn Heights run by Auden. Benjamin Britten has his piano in the living room, and I put mine into the cellar where I work at a ballet commissioned by Kirstein (*Pastorelas*). I meet Carson McCullers for the first time. Receive Guggenheim Fellowship. We return to Mexico (Spring 1941) and spend remainder of the year there. I complete *Pastorelas* and begin work on *The Wind Remains* (opera). In the Summer of 1942 we return to New York to live at Holden Hall, my aunt's house in the country, where we are visited by the F.B.I. I complete the opera. It is performed in the Spring of 1943 at the Museum of Modern Art, Leonard Bernstein conducting, with staging by Merce Cunningham. Jane's novel, *Two Serious Ladies*, is published by Knopf.

Virgil Thomson suggests I join staff of the *Herald Tribune* to write musical criticism, which I do. I am asked by the Belgian Government-in-Exile to do the score for a documentary film called *Congo*. (Paul Robeson is narrator.) The Marquis de Cuevas commissions me to do the ballet *Colloque Sentimentale* with Dalí. I spend the Summer of 1944 in Mexico. Peggy Guggenheim issues records of my Sonata for Flute to sell in her gallery. Tennessee Williams comes to see me with the script of a play which needs music (*The Glass Menagerie*). I hear that Jean-Paul Sartre is in the U.S. and suggest to Oliver Smith that we obtain the rights to *Huis Clos*, which we do, meeting him in Washington. I begin to translate the play. I meet Elia Kazan and provide him with a score for *Jacobowsky and the Colonel*. Meet José Ferrer and furnish the score for *Cyrano de Bergerac*. Spend the Summer of 1945 in Cuba and Salvador. I am writing a series of short stories, most of which are being published in *Harper's Bazaar* and *Mademoiselle*. I resign from the *Herald Tribune*, but continue to write Sunday articles for the paper. I spend 1946 writing stories and doing more theatre scores, also a *Concerto for Two Pianos, Winds and Percussion*. In December I am asked to translate Giraudoux's *La Folle de Chaillot*, and go to the West Indies to do it.

On the strength of the short stories, Doubleday gives me (Spring 1947) an advance on a novel, and I go back to Morocco and write it (*The Sheltering Sky*). When I send it to the publishers, they tell me it is not a novel, and reject it. Libby Holman comes to Morocco and asks me to make an opera out of García Lorca's *Yerma*. I begin to translate it. New Directions accepts *The Sheltering Sky*. I return to New York to write the score for Tennessee Williams's *Summer and Smoke*. When the show is open, he and I go back to Morocco to stay at El Farhar. Afterward he goes to Rome, and Jane and I to the Algerian Sahara, and then to Paris, returning to El Farhar in the Spring. Truman Capote spends the Summer at El Farhar with us. Gore Vidal arrives.

In the Autumn Jane and I go to London. *The Sheltering Sky* is published there. Meetings with Maugham, Angus Wilson, Cyril Connolly, etc. I leave for Ceylon to spend the Winter, returning to London and Paris in the late Spring. Libby Holman returns to Morocco in the Summer, and we spend a month in Andalusia. Back to the Sahara in the Winter, Spain in the Spring (1951), where I pick up Jane, and to Tangier. I complete *Let It Come Down* and set out for Bombay. I stay in India and Ceylon until June, then go to the Italian Alps. Peggy Guggenheim invites me to stay with her in Venice. In the

Autumn I go to Tangier and Madrid. While in Madrid I buy the island of Taprobane off the south coast of Ceylon. In January 1953 I go to New York to spend the Winter at Libby Holman's. Spring I spend in Tangier writing A *Picnic Cantata*. Tennessee Williams suggests my name to Luchino Visconti, to work on the scenario of a film (*Senso*), and I spend the Summer in Rome, working on it. Then I go to Istanbul, returning to Tangier with Williams in the late Autumn. I go back to New York in December to write the score for Jane's play *In the Summer House*. When that is done I return to Tangier. I meet William Burroughs for the first time. In the Autumn Jane and I set out for Ceylon. I begin *The Spider's House*. We spend the Winter on Taprobane. Peggy Guggenheim comes to visit us there. I complete *The Spider's House*. Jane returns to Tangier and I go to Japan. By mid-summer I am back in Tangier. In the Autumn Christopher Isherwood visits. The following Spring my parents come to Tangier (1956). Later in the year I go to London, thence to Cape Town, and Ceylon, spending the Winter there. In the Spring to East Africa (Kenya, Zanzibar) and back to Tangier. Allen Ginsberg arrives in Tangier for the first time. Jane being ill, I take her to England twice during the Summer, the second time remaining there until the Winter, when we return to Tangier. In February 1958 we leave for Madeira, where Jane's passport expires. In Lisbon the American Embassy refuses to issue another (on orders from the F.B.I.) and Jane is obliged to go immediately to New York. I remain in Portugal until after the elections in June, and then go to Denver to try out *Yerma*. From there we take the opera to Ithaca, New York. Jane enters New York Hospital for three months. I go to Hollywood to work with José Ferrer. At the end of the year Jane and I go back to Tangier. I receive a wire asking me to return to New York to do the score of *Sweet Bird of Youth*. I go. Afterward I go to Madeira for *Holiday* magazine, then to Tangier. Tennessee Williams is there. I receive a Rockefeller Grant to record Moroccan music for the archives of the Library of Congress. The last six months of 1959 I spend making field trips in the interior of Morocco. In 1960 I continue recording, in various regions not previously covered.

In 1961 I rent a house in Marrakech. Tennessee Williams comes. Allen Ginsberg returns to Morocco and I take him to Marrakech. I pass a quiet year, writing short stories. In 1962 I begin the translation from the Arabic of *A Life Full of Holes*. Jane and I go to New York, where I write the score for *The Milk Train Doesn't Stop Here Any More* (Williams). We return to Tangier at Christmas time. I continue translating. Random House publishes *Their Heads Are Green and Their Hands Are Blue*. I take a house in Asilah for six months, afterward going to the Sahara.

The following year (1964) Tennessee Williams again comes to Tangier. I am writing *Up above the World*. I go to Spain. In March 1965 Jane and I go to New York. I continue to Santa Fe. In the Summer we return to Tangier. I translate *Love with a Few Hairs*. In June 1966 Jane and I go again to New York, she to see Farrar, Straus about her collected works, and I take a ship to Bangkok. In December I hear from Jane's doctor in Tangier that she is ill, and return to Tangier, abandoning the book I am writing for Little, Brown. (In Tangier I suggest to Alec Waugh that he take over the project, which he does.) I begin the translation of *The Lemon*. *The Time of Friendship* is published. I translate ten short stories from the Arabic under the title of *M'Hashish*, and leave for Los Angeles. This brings us up to the present.

If this sequential listing serves no other purpose, at least it is useful to me as a basic memorandum; I have no notes with which to document the account. It is a chronological skeleton, nothing more, as you can see. I'll hope to hear your reaction soon.

TO NORMAN GLASS
———————————◆———————————

June 5, 1969
Tangier

I can see that your life is somewhat chaotic, or you'd recall that you wrote me not too long ago, and from Paris, well after your latest suicide. I wonder who and what I represent to you, that I should have appeared in dreams. In any case, I'm happy that it should have been useful on that one occasion in the lorry. Obviously if I did not remember you with affection I should not have continued writing to you these past few years. That makes sense, I should think; no? However, I consistently scourged you for your vanity, which I confused with khutzpah. So much so that Harold Norse still refers to you by the epithet I used in my letters to him in 1964: the khutzpah kid. Now I've decided it was merely youthful vanity. But it was a bit psychopathic, even so! You ask if I know Japan. Unfortunately I don't; I was there for only four days in 1955. It gave me a taste for the place, although I doubt I'd want to live there. It would be like exiling oneself among insects. Fascinating, but not psychically nourishing. California on the other hand is by no means an exile. Not enough of one, perhaps, for doing quote creative unquote work, but still, better, I should think, for constant living. The climate, too, is infinitely superior to that of Japan, which is pretty terrible. Yes, I can see you in California, and I can see you being very successful if you feel like it. The reason is that it's very much a center of today's life and thought, horrible though its freeways be. But life is easy there and any work one does pays so beautifully that one can scarcely gripe about the cars and smog. Anyway, you ought to go there sometime, just to have the experience. My reactions were very different from what I'd expected they'd be. I hated what I knew beforehand I'd hate, but there were a lot of things I rather loved, and they were all surprises for me. Tangier is pleasant now, with the odor of flowers and plants in the air. For a long time it has smelled only of the sea, because the cherqi was blowing without respite. Now that it's stopped, one savors the air. No news. I signed a contract with Putnam, finally. All best to you.

TO DANIEL HALPERN

June 16, 1969
Tangier

Nothing interesting has happened. I got back yesterday from Spain, where I'd gone to take Jane back to the clinic. The weather is now traditional summertime. It was just a month late in arriving; I hope it stays on for the extra month at the end, but I wonder.

While I was in Spain John Hopkins took Brion for a ride on his motorcycle to the Caves; returning they were clipped head-on by a car, and Brion's foot was badly gashed. He had one toe amputated yesterday, and is now waiting to see if gangrene is coming. The doctor assures him it isn't. But he must be in bed for two months. I went to see him at the Hospital Español and he was in fine spirits.

Your suggestion that I write a story involving Antaeus started the wheels moving inside, and I suddenly set to work and did write it. (Antaeus is shown as a Moroccan explaining the fight with Heracles to a visitor who comes to Tangier twenty years after the occasion. He remembers Heracles as an inept fighter who was also a little crazy according to him, since he kept trying to lift him off the ground, a mystifying procedure to Antaeus. Antaeus won, and is still the champion in his part of Africa. He takes the visitor for a walk into the country, feeds him a stupefying drug, and robs him.)

I hope everything is fine in København, and that I'll see you when you say I will. Apparently you had a rewarding voyage.

TO NED ROREM

July 2, 1969
Tangier

Let the Levins and Plauts look me up; why not? Maybe I'd enjoy seeing them, although why they'd want to see me on a vacation trip is more than I know. The other day, brring, hello, is this Paul Bowles? Speaking. You don't know me. My name is Blossom Tarweight. I'm with educational teevee and I'd just like to know one thing. Where would I get the most camels, and that wouldn't involve too much travelling (I suggested M'hamid). Also, would Ksar es Souk be a good headquarters, I means lots of sheiks and camels? (I told her it was all neon-lighted and full of American construction workers, which it is this year.) Not Ksar es *Souk!* she cried. (I said yes.) Well, excuse me for bothering you. End of telephone conversation. Apparently now I'm an information service. It's happened several times. An old Moroccan hand. California was instructive, yes. I decided Americans were not so much criminal as hopelessly lost. It doesn't change the prognosis, I agree. But it changes my outlook a bit, which matters to me. I'm on the verge of writing my "autobiography" for Putnam. I heard today quite by accident that Oliver Evans had sold all the letters I ever wrote him to the University of Texas. I have nothing against that; I sold Stein's and Toklas's and Tenn's. But it does make me wary in a way I haven't been before, when I sit down to write a letter. Will they be dancing on the moon this month? Will they bring us back lunar viruses to play with? Brion has a new penthouse with lots of view and even more glare. Nobody else is here, save Alec Waugh, the sweet older brother of Evelyn. I'll probably have to take Jane back to the clinic soon. ¿Qué pasa allí? hasta la tuya.

TO OLIVER EVANS

July 5, 1969
Tangier

Your Friday-the-thirteenth missive arrived, and I have been a rather long time answering it. No particular reason, save that I have Jane on my hands, always, in the adjacent room, lying on the floor. She doesn't ask for much, but often she cries out as though she were in sudden pain, and I have to rush to see what's the matter. Usually it's because she's trying to reach for a cigarette or a match or an ashtray, or her pet hate Aqaya has just gone through the room. Every night she vows she'll kill her before dawn, but so far she hasn't.

Your account of David's extravagant adventures didn't astonish me at all, although I found myself wondering how anybody could have such khutzpah. But obviously he does have it. What struck me as the most incredible detail in the story is the fact that the administration granted him another full year in which to bring his activities to a head, which, being compulsive, he undoubtedly will strive to do.

I managed to write a six-page short story a fortnight ago. How, I don't know. Perhaps it was a side-effect of desperation. It's the only work I've done this year. And time goes on and my deadline for Putnam draws nearer. I'm trying to steel myself to take Jane back to the hospital for a while, so I can get started. The doctors all think it necessary, but the difficult part is broaching it to her. She's asked a good many Moroccans to kill her, promising them I'd pay them subsequently; not a good situation, to have them all saying I'll put out money for her death. (Another reason for sequestering her for a bit.)

Your traffic saga is incredible—as much so as the behavior of the two goons who stopped us. Mrabet never tires of telling the tale; you are a cross between an archbishop and a dean.

TO NED ROREM

August 20, 1969
Tangier

The wind howls and the countryside is the color of a lion. For a week the cicadas have been screaming; I think by now most of them have burst, for there are far fewer. The end of summer is in some ways like the end of Ramadan: tempers are short and the fuzz runs riot. Rabat sent up a mobile unit to keep Tangier in line. They are encamped between Vasco da Gama and Jews' River, where hundreds of eucalyptus trees have been felled (the last pleasant woods nearby), and from there they prowl, attacking when they see fit. A hundred or so Europeans were forcibly shaven and deported last week, their chains and beads ripped from around their necks and their clothing slashed with the admonition that when they buy new garments they see to it that they are regulation. Presumably they will be allowed back in when they've bought proper garb. The

Moroccan youths have fared much worse, of course, as they are beaten, hand-cuffed, dragged any old way through the street to the police van, and then detained in underground rooms at an abandoned school indefinitely, living under pretty unpleasant conditions. So far no news of specific tortures, save that the whole campaign seems in itself a form of unnecessary agony. Jack was very eager to get out; he left while he still had a temperature, because the ticket agent told Maurice and me that all flights for the coming fortnight were booked solid. Jack took this news very hard, and insisted on bolting. He did right, I'm sure. Since he left I've been sick in bed three days with the same complaint exactly. It's a late-summer epidemic which has swept over the town in the past ten days or so. The dust gets so germ-laden after so many months without any rain that one marvels the disease is so benign. You speak about the end. Yes, but of what? Something is always ending. But now it seems to be a case of "life as we know it." Then it will be life as we don't know it. A test for man's much-touted adaptability. Personally I don't think it's going to work; I think it will break "man as we know him." Genocide will result, also the emergence of an already adapted type of human being which will function acceptably under the new conditions. The new book goes along haltingly; I wonder which are going to be more difficult, the early parts or the later. At this point I can't imagine it. A long letter from Peggy [Guggenheim] yesterday; she debates at length on whether or not she is ready to die. Her operation came out perfectly, but she's a horoscope-worshipper as you know, and there's a very dark spot looming, to hit within the next four or five months. Thanks for classing me still as a composer. I'm not composing, as you must know, since I never compose any more unless someone needs music immediately. Your friends will have to contact me by post. The telephone is dead once again, and they won't be able to notify me of their presence. I expect to go and see Jane in September. Mrabet wants to go to Italy, probably because he likes Italian shoes. Maurice paints every day, of course. He tries to use Ahmed, his houseboy, as a model, but each time as soon as the pose is set, Ahmed very slowly falls asleep, in spite of Maurice's coughing, shuffling of feet, and banging of ashtray on table, so that there is nothing to do but work on the still life, since the big canvas of olive trees at Sidi Kacem has forcibly been abandoned for the past several days because of the violent wind that showers hot sand. He arrives and grins in his annoyed fashion, saying: Oh, I'm out of sorts. I can't paint. Sidi Kacem's impossible, Abderrahman won't let his brother come so I can finish that portrait, Ahmed invariably falls asleep, so I can't use him, and now he's cooked my still-life that I set up. No, of course I can't make it again with new vegetables. It was nice to hear from you. A bientôt et tendresses.

TO PETER RAND

September 28, 1969
Tangier

It was good you came around the last night, or perhaps I should never have read the book. Reviews, favorable or not, can destroy the desire to read a book. I suppose it's the feeling that one hasn't done one's own discovering. In any case, I've seen no reviews (for the simple reason, I suppose, that the novel isn't yet published), and I have read the book. The fact that I'm rereading it after a fortnight means nothing special, since I might be doing that even though I'd only liked it somewhat. I think it's one of the best first novels I've ever read. The writing is generally superb; it's the style that impresses me. Casual and with pinpoint precision. Beautiful dialogue and great sense of place. What more can one ask for? On the debit side (which you don't want to hear, but since I'm saying everything I might as well say that too), I regretted the excessively melodramatic finale, for which the rest of the book had not prepared me, save perhaps the narrator's precipitate exit on page 145. Up until then, it was not that kind of book (that punishes incest with death all around), nor, I'd imagined, was the narrator the kind of individual who cracks up at contact with incest. I'd like to hear what you have to say on the subject. The book is so incredibly well done that I can't help holding it against you for not keeping it purer. Has all this anything to do with what you said about Doubleday's interference? If so, it's truly criminal of them. But what writing!

I think Dan mentioned getting a story out of you if you have one to spare. Can you drop me a line about it? Jean Genet is here, staying at the Minzah, but I haven't seen him. At the moment I'm in bed with a cough. Probably all sorts of things are happening, but I wouldn't know about them. All I know is what I hear out the window.

So when you can, let me hear from you.

TO JOYCE ROCHAT
———————————————•———————————————
October 30, 1969
Tangier

Thank you for your letter. You don't really ask any specific questions that I can answer, save the rather general one about influences of which I might be aware. I can't think of a satisfactory reply to that, save that in 1946 I translated and adapted Sartre's *Huis Clos* for Broadway. Prior to that, of course, I had read *La Nausée*, *L'Imaginaire* and *Le Mur* with enormous admiration. (I am not such an admirer of post-war Sartre.)

As to Camus, I first read *La Peste* in 1947, more or less at the halfway point in writing *The Sheltering Sky*. *L'Étranger* I didn't read until considerably later, well after I'd read *Le Mythe de Sisyphe*. My personal opinion is that Camus had no influence whatever on my writing. People have pointed out to me the parallel between his *Le Renégat* and my *A Distant Episode*. But since my tale was published in 1946 in *Partisan Review*, and his didn't see the light of day until 1957, there obviously can be no question of influence.

Lautréamont, Gide and Proust were great favorites of mine when I was in my teens and early twenties; those years are always important for their formative effect. But I can't think of anyone I wanted to emulate.

I'm sure many questions will occur to you as you go along, and I shall be pleased to make the attempt, at least, to provide suitable answers to them.

TO PETER RAND
———————————————•———————————————
November 8, 1969
Tangier

A note because I'm going up to Sidi Amar in a few minutes. However, I'll single-space this in case I think of something I want to say while writing.

It was good to have your letter and to know you'd received mine. And above all to hear that soon you'll be sending me something for *Antaeus*. I'm really very happy about that, and await the arrival of the ms. eagerly.

Your letter throws light on the book. From what I can see, the difficulty was an inner one rather than a technical one. For a part of the time you wrote illumined by the truth of your own cosmos; then you came back, as it were, and thought of what you were writing as a book rather than merely living it as you had been doing. Obviously, as soon as one can detach oneself from the inner world sufficiently to consider that the thing one is doing is "writing a book," one has shifted position radically, and is in danger of losing contact with certain aspects of the original closed cosmos. I was vaguely aware of this problem when I started *The Sheltering Sky*; that is to say, I suspected that there would come a point in it where my inventive powers would be inadequate to pull the weight of what I consciously had constructed with them. (This does not come up at all in a short story, of course, and that was all I'd written until then.) And I decided that if and when I reached that point, I would not give it a thought (not think about it, not reread, not shift my position for an instant, but keep the cosmos hermetic). Clearly, the only way I would be able to continue to write under such conditions, would be to switch from conscious to unconscious. (That's why surrealist discipline is so useful.) It would be like switching from manual to automatic. And the moment did come, of course, when I was down in the Sahara, and I knew that the point had been reached. (The Kafka quote for the third part suggested itself then.) So I shifted to automatic and went ahead full speed. It's the only way I can write a novel, not being a born novelist. You probably are a born one, but even so, it would have been a way of handling the making of the work, a way of observing nothing but the laws of the closed cosmos. Don't let the air in: it kills the fetus!

So anyway, thanks for the ad; I was pleased to be considered a possibility in the paternity case. If you have a copy of the *Times* review I'd enjoy seeing it, but don't put yourself out. My cough is gone. I went to Spain last week to see Jane; she's better. I quote from a letter sent me by the Head of the English Department at Randolph-Macon College in Virginia . . . "I wish you would recommend another book like *Firestorm*. I have the whole Department reading it."

TO JOHN GOODWIN

◆

November 10, 1969
Tangier

I thought you knew me well enough by now to realize that I'm never piqued, miffed, or froissé. I'd been waiting for a reply to the letter I wrote you last spring when I got back here and was caring for Jane. Apparently it never reached you;

no matter. What happened at Christmas time was that I caught Hong Kong flu and stayed in bed for the entire holidays, both before Christmas and after New Year's. I lost the acting job Gadge Kazan had given me in *The Arrangement*, after going through Costume and all at Warner's. Very sad. Perhaps God didn't want it, my sentencing Kirk Douglas to the insane asylum and commiserating with Faye Dunaway. Anyway, I'm busy working on my autobiography for Putnam, and it goes very slowly, perhaps because I have a difficult time remembering what happened so many years ago. After five months I've grown only from the age of four to the age of eleven, and that's not nearly fast enough to meet the deadline. I took care of Jane for four and a half months, buying food and preparing it, and serving it and often putting it into her mouth. But she seemed to get worse rather than better, and in mid-July I took her back to the clinic. Was over there week before last, and found her looking much healthier, and in slightly better spirits. *The Lemon* is finally out, in London; *M'Hashish* still hasn't appeared, although Ferlinghetti said its publication was imminent. Both are translations from Mrabet's Moghrebi. I heard from Gold and Fizdale this afternoon that they plan to visit Tangier next month, directly after Ramadan (which begins this evening, God forbid). Charles Gallagher was here last month, and told me you had given up your house in Santa Fe and moved somewhere thirty or forty miles away. What's the basis of this report? I hope you get this, at least.

THE 1970S

January 7, 1970
Tangier

Your last word was a note accompanying the tear-sheets of articles by and about Gore, plus that horrendous piece on Tennessee, for all of which many thanks. It came in handy, as one might say, in that within forty-eight hours after I'd finished reading the *Esquire* documents on the Vidal–Buckley feud, Gore himself sat here talking to me. He spent three nights in Tangier, en route to stay at the Gettys' in Marrakech, so we ate together each night. He also gave an interview to Dan Halpern, a Valley State alumnus who lives here and works at the American School, and who, egged on by me, is going to start a magazine in Tangier shortly. The interview, obviously, is for that. Gore rids himself of a certain amount of spleen therein, which is fun. I continue on my autobiography, but it goes slowly. Taking three weeks off last month to travel in the desert did not advance it, save that perhaps I've worked better since I returned. I went because some people who had been writing me since I was in Northridge, saying they wanted to make a film of me showing the relationship of my work to Morocco or some such thing, suddenly appeared on the scene, ready to start shooting. They've now been shooting for nearly four months; the southern voyage came after many sessions here in the apartment and in cafés roundabout. Now they want me to make another trip, this time to the end of the Oued Drâa and over the Djebel Bani. If they paid my expenses it would be pleasanter! The last trip cost me about eight hundred dollars. Hotels in Morocco are expensive now, and no better than they ever were. More gadgets and less comfort. More noise, fewer pleasing views from the windows. City Lights has brought out Mrabet's *M'Hashish*. I hope people find it engrossing. He's at a name-giving ceremony tonight.

March 17, 1970
Tangier

Strange, your feeling hostile towards me in Tunisia. Whether you are aware
of it or not, I must be a father figure somewhere in one of the grottoes of your
mind, otherwise you could not have such a violent reaction to my being unable
to have you living here with me. I should have made the same reply to anyone
else who asked me, but I doubt that anyone else would find me "hostile and
pernicious" because of my reply. (And what else could I have answered? You
couldn't very well have slept on the divan in the living-room.) So, anyway . . .

The works (anent your Nerval translation, which I should very much like to
see when it appears) which I have translated from Maghrebi are as follows: *A
Life Full of Holes*, novel; *Love with a Few Hairs*, novel; *The Lemon*, novel;
M'Hashish, collection of short stories. These are the only books. There are also
a good many stories and hekayas, which have appeared in magazines. *The Spider's
House* takes place in Fez and environs. *M'Hashish* is published in the same
series as *A Hundred Camels in the Courtyard* and the Burroughs–Ginsberg *Yage
Letters*: City Lights Books.

I've spent half the Winter in the Sahara, and must have travelled ten thousand
miles back and forth and up and down. It effectively kept me from making any
headway on my autobiography. So I can blame the lack of progress on voyages
instead of writer's block. Nothing happens in Tangier. Today is Aachor . . .
darboukas and toys, tambourines and walnuts. No word from Alfred. No word
from Harold Norse since I left Los Angeles. Jane still in the hospital in Málaga.
Try sending your story to Gordon Lish, *Esquire Magazine*, and see. And let me
hear.

April 24, 1970
Tangier

More notes. Thanks for yours of the fifteenth; they take eight days to pass
from here to there or from there to here. I had a letter from Oliver Evans

yesterday; he is in the hospital in Rome, and has been for several weeks. However, he expects to be out by the end of June. He's been seeing a good deal of Gore, he says. Not sure exactly what the trouble is, although it has to do with his heart and blood pressure. They don't want him to drink at all. Difficult for him. * * *

The subject of Tennessee's *Antaeus* poem suddenly arrived in Tangier: "the poet," whom I'd not seen for eight years. Staying at the Velasquez with a Moroccan Jewish girl with whom he lives in New York. They thought they'd like to see Tangier again. He's a good poet, incidentally. New Directions published a volume a few years ago. I'll ask him to give me something to send you to look at for the next issue.

I wrote you about receiving the Fowles book. Many, many thanks. But I'd like his address, in order to be able to write him and thank him. Incidentally, it's a brilliant work, isn't it? I should think Forster's mantle falls right on his shoulders. At page 178.

TO DANIEL HALPERN,
ANTAEUS, NEW YORK

◆

November 17, 1970
Tangier

Your most recent letter sanguine relative to *Antaeus*. Apparently you have some sort of certainty that a number two is possible, or you wouldn't be arranging with Villiers. Wonderful! But didn't you take the Charhadi story with you? I can't find it anywhere. Although I'll continue to search for it until I'm convinced it's no longer here among the typescripts lying around. Is *Mediterranean Review* using the Mrabet interview you sent them? They wrote asking for more information on him. I take it the copies hadn't yet arrived when you wrote, or you'd have mentioned general reaction to the mag. I liked Djuna's letter to Peggy, and the fact that Peggy sent it to you. Maurice broke up over it when I regaled him with the story. I'll wager you don't write D's biography! [(Charles) Frederick] Nicklaus sent me his New Directions volume of poems. Beautifully printed; I haven't read a line so far. You never mention Columbia; I assume you're not there after all. However, it sounds as though life were a good deal more interesting without it. What about the Gary Conklin film project? I suppose he can't furnish you with a copy. It costs money, and according to him he hasn't managed to get hold of any so far. Where did you ever see *The New Left*? While I was in the Party I was called on the carpet about that letter. Of course it dates from 1931; I wrote it after having lunch with Pound in Montparnasse, being angry at the editors, and immediately forgot all about it. In 1939 a comrade showed it to me with a long face, demanding an explanation. Incidentally, if you keep my name in the magazine as Consulting Editor, you ought always to send me proofs so I can correct them. No? So I'm delighted it goes on, and I will go on looking for Charhadi.

Keep me abreast.

TO DANIEL HALPERN,

ANTAEUS, NEW YORK

February 17, 1971

Tangier

Your letter yesterday. Thanks for letting me know the Kay Boyle poem reached you. As for mine, I wrote it around Christmastime, perhaps two months ago. Circumstances: kif-cutting was going on at the moment. But why is it *weird*?

I see they're giving Gary's film again tonight next door to the Museum of Modern Art. Andreas wrote me he did not particularly like the film; he thought there was too much tourism in it. You didn't express yourself on that. Some day I hope to see it and judge for myself.

There is a poet here on an Amy Lowell fellowship. (I never heard of the institution.) He has sent poems which I shall have to forward to you. Perhaps you know him; his name is Mike Wolfe. Seems to have been living here for eight months, but I never came in touch with him until last week. Young, face not visible because of beard, so I have no idea what he looks like. Only God can see the faces of today's young poets.

You know how much I hope to see *The Delicate Prey* available again. Obviously I should be more than delighted to have it in either paperback or hardcover, although I should think paperback would be more practical. It seems to me that Don Gold should not object to such a project. After all, the book has been out of print for a good sixteen years, including the two paperback editions. Carol and I went up to see Amber de Gramont day before yesterday. It's astonishing to hear how well she speaks Arabic. She and I played a game called *Ha hiya* there in the garden. My book has reached the year 1967 . . . comes on apace, but no problems solved as yet regarding the end. *Vertumnus* (what the hell does that mean?) has nothing of mine . . . only a piece of Mrabet's on kif.

Perhaps he considered my translation as a contribution from me. I think I told you I had looked everywhere for the Thailand material without success. Good, good. Keep me informed as to all.

TO WILLIAM TARG,
G. P. PUTNAM'S SONS, NEW YORK

February 23, 1971
Tangier

Thank you for your three simultaneous communications. I'm not overly preoccupied about the title. I'm sure I can find something apposite sooner or later. But I am a bit worried about my ability to "flesh out" the people and make characters of them, as you suggested. Naturally I shall do what I can, but the truth is that I don't remember people very well—either what they wear or look like. For years critics have objected to the facelessness of my fictional people, although that is deliberate on my part. And at the time I was writing about in the section you mean, I did not have reactions to people as people, but only as forces to propel me, as a glider uses air-currents. For that reason any attempt now to describe them or my reactions to them risks being false; what one doesn't remember one ends by inventing, and I have been very careful to keep hazy recall and invention out of the chronicle. But as I say, I'll do what I can to suggest reactions on my part. I have a feeling that this can become a cause of friction between us at one point or another; if it does do so, I want you to know beforehand that I shall make every effort to provide the qualities you would like to find in the manuscript. If in spite of that I am unable to, I hope you will know that such is the case, and that I am not being difficult! I am sending you more of the manuscript in a few days, as soon as I have finished correcting it.

TO WILLIAM TARG,
G. P. PUTNAM'S SONS, NEW YORK

June 13, 1971
Tangier

Thank you for your helpful letters of June second and fourth respectively; I found them awaiting me on my return from Spain. I shall make a big effort to

supplement the text with additional material, as you suggest. Naturally I have
no idea as to how successful I shall be. Generally when the doors of the mind
swing shut at a certain moment in recall, there are cogent reasons for the action,
and not much is accomplished by resisting the force. However, I agree that
memory is not entirely automatic, and can in some instances be cajoled. (Obviously I have tried to avoid writing anything which could conceivably offend
anyone, regardless of whether the anyone still lives or not; this in itself is fairly
constricting.) You ask what I *really* thought and felt about Alice Toklas. I should
think it would be clear that I thought of her as a hostess, and not much more.
This ties up with your remark that the book seems to be more "travel narrative"
than "subjective, personal commentary." Places have always been more important to me than people. That is to say, people give the landscape scale; the
landscape is not a backdrop for them. My dreams are seldom of people; they
are almost always of places, directions, relative positions of objects around me.
The human beings in them are faceless, anonymous. I accept this as a basic
condition of existence. If in the book I seem "always on the move—nomadic
—and not often enough in a relaxed and cerebral mood," it is not because of
failure to transform adequately the memory into words, but because I always
have been on the move, and very seldom in a relaxed state. Is there any reason
to invent a fictitious tranquillity? And if the mention of the people whom I have
glimpsed on my way past them lacks precision in describing them, it is only
because I never really *saw* them or thought about them, since for me they were
manipulable objects to be used or somehow got around, in order to continue
my trajectory. It's a bit late now for me to try and give them personalities. This
is the problem of which I was aware before I decided to try and make the book,
and which kept me from wanting to undertake the project in the first place.
However, there's no point in my spending my time insisting upon all this, when
I could be spending it in trying to remedy it. I'll do what I can to pad the passages
on Williams, Vidal, Barnes, Guggenheim, Cohen, Herbert, Hutton and others,
but obviously I guarantee no results! At the moment I can't envisage a foreword
or a dedication—OR a title.

Your letter of June fourth suggested further remarks on William Burroughs;
I shall also try and furnish something more than I recalled while writing about
him. I enclose an alphabetical list of the principal people who appear in the
book. Doubtless you will want to add many others, since I suppose if one indexes
the characters, one must include everyone mentioned. I've also appended the
list of my published books. Among the xeroxed pages Putnam has sent me there

are thirteen pages missing (351 through 363); I really need them at some point, and should appreciate having them sent.

I'll hope to hear from you.

TO WILLIAM TARG,

G. P. PUTNAM'S SONS, NEW YORK

June 29, 1971

Tangier

Yesterday I posted you some auxiliary material, and at the same time received the missing xeroxes, for which I am grateful. They must simply never have arrived with the others, earlier.

The matter of the title worries me, inasmuch as I still like *Without Stopping*, and can't seem to find another phrase or word which suits. Of course, I realize that the very elements in the text which make that title an apposite one are the ones you want to minimize, and yet what I have given is as accurate a picture of my life as I was able to draw. I can't help going back to your letter of June second, where you express a wish that I had been a different person and lived a life unlike the life I actually lived. " . . . you seem always on the move—*nomadic*—and not often enough in a relaxed and cerebral mood . . ." I doubt that I have ever been in a "relaxed," not to say "cerebral" state for more than two or three minutes, without feeling the ever-present doubt, disbelief and vague *angst* that has kept me going. Only in action is there a possibility of relief, but what action can a writer engage in save writing—that is, what meaningful action? Moving from one place to another at least gives the illusion of engaging in a further, complementary kind of action. Perhaps I have not made this clear in the text, but to make it clearer than it is would give the book a pathological cast which I should like to avoid, since I doubt that it would make anything more understandable, and might easily falsify the material. More later, and forgive my divagations.

TO DANIEL HALPERN,
ANTAEUS, NEW YORK

June 30, 1971
Tangier

We have an editorial crisis in the offices of *Antaeus*. The page-proofs arrived yesterday, and everything looked fine until I came to the Zavidowsky piece. First of all, it's not a "document"; it's a critical article, which is precisely what we have scrupulously avoided until now. (The cornerstone of the magazine's policy, we agreed, was to avoid all critical material.) Second, even if *Antaeus* did publish criticism, the Zavidowsky article would not pass muster, at least with me, because it bristles with lengthy quotations and reads like a master's thesis. It is exactly the sort of piece that infuriates me when I see it in a so-called "intellectual" magazine.

Didn't you have any interview ready? I'm curious to know what happened that induced you to change policy. But above all, how can the Zavidowksy possibly be considered a document? (That is, any more than anything else included in the issue.) A document could conceivably be letters, pages from a journal, a reprint of something originally printed some time ago, and which in being presented in a contemporary context has a meaning in some way different from its first intention—it could be any one of many things, but it can't by any stretch of the imagination be a straight essay like the Zavidowsky. What can be done about it? Have you an interview to substitute? Please get in touch with me so that we can straighten out the situation. If the Z. appears in the pages of *Antaeus*, there is no editorial policy left to the magazine. It might as well be any one of the pretentious "reviews" that proliferate on campuses. Anyway, I'll hope to hear from you.

TO DAVID DIAMOND

[April 29, 1972]
At sea

This will bear an Italian stamp, I imagine, since I'm going to post it aboard, and we arrive in Genova tomorrow morning. I'm en route to Lausanne for a week or two.

I was surprised to hear you ask all those whys (with regard to my recent book). One might as well ask: why does one have a daily life? Why do the things that happen to one happen? The Moslems of course don't ask why, since they assume that everything was decided at the beginning of time. We of course assume that we know better, and so we analyze motives. If any one feels like attributing motivations to the actions listed in the book, he's at liberty to do so. Wherever I myself had even an inkling of my reasons I gave them, or tried to. Certainly you wouldn't want invented motivations long after the fact. I had certain experiences; did I bring them about, or did they come about accidentally? How could I know now if I didn't know at the time? Are one's experiences the cause or the effect of one's personality, or both, or neither? When I wrote the book I was not preoccupied by such considerations, or obviously I could never have finished it. What happened happened; whether it should or shouldn't have I don't know, nor do I even know whether or not it's of any interest. (I shouldn't think it could be, finally. On the other hand, it does explain my fiction, even though no one seems to think so!) How could you remember all that about Cummings? What I recall I couldn't write: his violent anti-Semitism, for instance. When will your book be out?

TO DAVID DIAMOND

June 5, 1972
Tangier

You musn't think I'm engaging in a criticism-bee with you. I said what I said about the ponderous tone of the manuscript you sent me only because you had been frank about your reservations about my book, and although it went against the grain—for it always goes against the grain to bring oneself to disagree with someone—I gave you my first reaction to the material in question. But certainly not in order to criticize. (I mention all this because of your expression "contra rays" at the end of your letter. Why do you think in those terms?)

I'd say you learn a technique for survival by trial and error, by making deductions, by using your intuition and wit. It could include asking questions (but not of other people—only of oneself) if the answers to the questions happened to be necessary for planning tactics. Why formulate questions if action gives the result more quickly? I always assumed that other people's answers were for other people's lives, and that only my own decisions would be useful in my life. Basic mistrust, surely.

Do you remember the night when you made a great point of kissing a dog? Helvetia went home and had hysterics, after which Jane cut her wrists. It didn't all happen the same night, but led fairly swiftly up into tragedy. As I recall, it was Virgil's suggestion to you, rather than your kissing the dog, that sent Helvetia off. It was a bad week.

You should get this before you leave for the United States. Have a good trip, and let me hear when you can, and see more of the manuscript when you feel like sending it.

TO NORMAN GLASS
◆

July 15, 1972
Tangier

Merci de ta lettre. Peter Owen is here, getting sunburned. His wife, too, and one of his daughters, aged twelve. Tonight is Louise de Meuron's annual Gnaoua party; she gives out cards which have to be presented to the police before one can get onto the property. Good idea, as there are always hordes of gate-crashers. I do know *L'Herne*; in fact, I have the Burroughs number. But I have few ideas on suicide. I can imagine it only as a last resort, when the alternative would be much worse. Thus I couldn't say much about it in writing. Suicide is the ultimate masturbatory act, l'onanisme par excellence.

Daniel Halpern appears to have gone to Panama on holiday. However, I'll mention your chapters the first time I write. Chapters of what, I wonder. Do you really think of buying a house? Prices are high. Besides, there are no houses such as you describe; they all have more rooms, that is, if they're European houses, and native houses don't have bathrooms, or even running water, generally. It sounds to me as if you wanted a flat rather than a house. Hideous little shacks bring four and five million francs now. That is, forty or fifty thousand French francs. Ridiculous, but I wonder if prices will drop soon. Abdelouahaid my driver read me your Arabic exercise. Bravo! You see, I don't read Arabic. My acquaintance is phonetic. I have to lecture a group of schoolteachers next week on Moroccan music. Oy! Then I hope to get off to Marrakech. Ah!

TO JAMES LEO HERLIHY

October 4, 1972
Lausanne

Forgive me for the late reply. I don't really know why I don't get around to answering letters quickly. That is to say, I have no really legitimate excuse, since I'm not writing a novel. What I'm doing here is sitting in a dentist's chair three or four hours a day while they torture me. I was planning on setting out for Tangier on Sunday, but today they told me I should stay an extra week. And nothing to do here, or at least I don't find anything, save a film in English now and then, like A *Clockwork Orange*, which I thought beautifully prophetic— much moreso than *2001*. Abdelouahaid drove me up from Genoa, so at least I have him to eat with, which is something. But Schweiz is expensive, unfortunately, and the only pleasant pastime is buying things that are unavailable in Morocco. And that means just about everything. Our shops, as you know, are stocked with fourth-rate merchandise from Poland, Czechoslovakia and the People's Republic of China. (And cheesy Moroccan souvenirs for tourists.) With regard to your mention of searching for ideas in technique in Barth and Vonnegut and Burroughs, how about Borges and Raymond Roussel? Your open invitation to Hop Bottom is highly appreciated. But somehow I can't imagine getting myself across the Atlantic. At least, not unless I'm forced out of Morocco. (I don't really like the U.S., but don't tell anyone.) Perhaps before I get to the Western Hemisphere again you'll appear in Tangier. Did Tennessee go to Thailand? I wonder why he likes it. Apparently he came across something I didn't. Anyway, I hope this reaches you somewhere eventually.

TO CAROL ARDMAN

December 19, 1972
Tangier

The green canary is singing praises of lettuce just behind me; I haven't yet had breakfast. Jock has gone back to the States, so that Fatoma has the whole flat to herself. Dan arrived night before last, thus detonating Mrabet's long smouldering fury. However, they're on speaking terms, and I think all will be well. But perhaps only because Dan promised to pay him half of what *Trans-atlantic Review* paid him for the interview. (I believe it will come to seventeen dollars and a half.) Mrabet now says it's the principle of the thing. *Aunque sea solamente un dólar, quiero mi parte.** Peggy Guggenheim arrives tonight at the airport. Will she want to stay downstairs in number nine? God knows. It would be more fitting if she were to go straight to the Minzah. The measuring cup is wonderful, and I thank you. I'll deliver the cups of poison to the Gerofis the first time I'm in town with Abdelouahaid after five in the afternoon. Still I have no tape of the Stravinsky ballets. At least I have my passport back. As to the permis de résidence, they tell me it will take several months. And I had no procès-verbal like last year. The Elijah Purdy piece from Warhol's review arrived. He really has paranoia there. Why does he expect to be more famous than he is, I wonder. Choukri comes every day. He and Mrabet have a new custom, which is to eat together in the Zoco Chico every night. What this presages, I can't imagine at present. But I imagine that if anyone is going to influence anyone (literarily), it will be M. influencing C. Dan and Peter Rand are eating with Noel Mostert tonight; how they get in touch with people so swiftly I don't know. Perhaps they use a telephone. Paula Paley not coming. Charlie Munroe just went back to Marrakech; seems *Love Hairs* is still being planned, with Peter Powell coming next week. Maybe we'll have the two films done at once. On verra. Your flat sounds fine.

TO DANIEL HALPERN,
ANTAEUS, NEW YORK

April 3, 1973
Tangier

Ever since receiving the Purdy manuscript I've been busy on it. The difference between it and the Burgess interview is that once one has rewritten the sentences one can understand it. There was no way of making sense out of the Burgess. But what's the matter with Purdy? Why do his sentences start out and never finish? Why does he start out with one construction and alter it within the sentence (or even phrase) to a different construction? Did you intend to use the entire section you sent me, or a part? I'll continue with the work, and when it's

---

* *Even if it's only a dollar, I want my share.*

completed I'll send it to Sankey for Number Eleven. (Talented children striking adult attitudes, inexplicably having observed the adults of several generations previous. That's what his characters make me think of.) I meant to cross out three paragraphs, incidentally, in the George Staples story, if you've received it. The three follow one another, and have to do with the boy's curriculum and classes, all this unnecessary to the tale. You can find them easily enough, I should think. There was a good deal of rewriting needed in that one, too. Let me know what you think of it. I hope that envelope containing a miscellany reaches you. It cost $9.60 to send. Too much for my dwindling resources! The design enclosed, if reduced by half, ought to make a very pretty cover, don't you think? I've written Burroughs again. If he never answers, we shouldn't be surprised. It will simply mean he doesn't want to do the introduction. Thus I shouldn't hold up the book for him in the event of no reply. Police and gendarmes are swarming over the countryside these days, making it difficult to go anywhere by car. Now the government claims it has caught the principal rebels, which one can take cum grano salis.

TO DANIEL HALPERN,
ANTAEUS, NEW YORK

◆────────────────────────────────

April 11, 1973
Tangier

I had your letter and the envelope containing the material yesterday afternoon. Haven't yet read any of it, although I sniffed of the story and didn't like the smell. Besides, the first nine pages are typed in italics, after which there is a complete break, in the middle of a sentence, and on page ten we have something quite different, in another kind of type. Is this meant? One can't believe it, for it's wholly out of style with the rest of the manuscript. I'll give my opinion when I've read it.

I suspect that the Arguedas is untranslatable here in Tangier. The existing dictionaries don't have the dialectal vocabulary in them. One would need a Latin-American lexicon, or the translator would have to have lived in the countries in question. Barbara Howe sent me one of those uncrackable nuts, and I had to send it back to her. It was stuffed with words from no dictionary, at whose meaning one could only guess.

Why is it so hard to get good fiction? I know the obvious answers, but I still suspect that fewer young writers practise writing fiction than write poetry. Thus there are fewer good young fiction writers than there are good young poets. But the demand for poetry hasn't grown proportionately. Anyway, as for the Purdy excerpt, I think you could use it, but seriously truncated. I've gone through it carefully, made several hundred corrections, and it seems to me that pages 18 through 34 would make a good unit. After that it becomes redundant for our purposes (although doubtless not in its novelistic context). Have you a copy and do you agree? I ask because you told me to send it directly to Sankey when I had finished editing it. More anon.

P.S. Let me know if you received the Gerst book and the other material.

TO CAROL ARDMAN

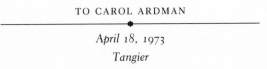

April 18, 1973
Tangier

Things seem better here for the nonce, although there are still roadblocks everywhere. According to the government several hundred people have been caught and executed, which accounts for the present calm. Those who are left are not happy, however. The weather now is chilly and clear, with a sharp little east wind as usual. It's difficult to give any sort of compte-rendu of events, because there are no events to speak of, beyond things like Maurice has gone to Marrakech and Tom Wright writes from Ecuador where he's living with a group of head-shrinkers, the Jivaro tribe. Each letter is full of the bloodiest sort of reports about what the Indians did to somebody else recently, as though he were waiting for them to do the same thing to him. If they like you they make friends with you; if they don't, they kill you, he says with relish. It seems he has hired an old German Nazi to pilot him up the streams. So now I can say that Carol is working in the Body Donation Division! I didn't realize you'd never met Andreas Brown; somehow I imagined you'd seen him many times with Dan. Leslie and Leonardo are in Spain now. At the end of the month Leslie goes to England and Leonardo returns here. I think they meet again here later. I'm waiting to hear from Dan about the Purdy business. I want to use only half of the excerpt; it seems quite enough for *Antaeus*. Mrabet is finishing his Riffian Cook Book. A call went out last week from the Algerian radio asking Moslems to kill all Americans on sight. You probably saw it in the paper. I doubt that the Moroccans will take it seriously, though. A short story about a tomato? New idea! Choukri and Mrabet fast friends, because C. allows M. to take girls to his apartment. I wondered how it could last!

TO DANIEL HALPERN,

ANTAEUS, NEW YORK

———————————————•———————————————

May 9, 1973
Tangier

If I haven't written, it's because I've been in Spain. Jane died last Friday; I was with her up to within an hour, went back to the hotel, and received a telephone call from the hospital, saying that it had just happened. You could do me a favor if you'd tell some of her friends. Eventually I can write them all, but at the moment I have neither the energy nor the time to write a series of letters. I doubt that any notice of it has appeared in the press. The burial was completely private, in the chapel of the Sagrado Corazón cemetery in Málaga.

As I told you, Black Sparrow recently asked me to put together what I could find of Jane's unpublished works. I was doing that when I was summoned to Spain. An interview with her was brought me last week on a cassette; it will be good for the book, even though it was made back in 1962. And I shall add a few pages from her journal, and some letters, and the three things that appeared in *Antæus*. I haven't told Sparrow that I could get together such a book as yet, so if you know of a New York publisher who might be interested, let me know. I didn't have the interview when I last wrote Martin of Sparrow, nor had I thought of letters. It was Marguerite [McBey] who thought of that angle.

Andreas Brown would be a good man to get in touch with for the purpose of telling Jane's friends of her death, I should think. He keeps lists of names and addresses, which I don't seem to be very good at, since I haven't the address of even one of Jane's relatives, for instance. I'll write again when I'm a bit more tranquil.

TO CAROL ARDMAN

May 11, 1973
Tangier

A week ago yesterday I received a telegram from the doctor in Málaga, asking me to go there as quickly as possible, because Jane was gravely ill. I got the seven o'clock ferry to Algeciras, with Abdelouahaid, and we were in Málaga in time for lunch. At the clinic I found Jane unconscious. She had had another stroke on Monday night. I stayed until seven and went back to the hotel. At nine I had a call from the Mother Superior, saying that Jane had just died. The following day from dawn to dark I was busy with the funeral and burial. So at last, after sixteen years of anguish, it is over.

Elizabeth Segal arrived, bringing the cassette of interviews from Tom Lopez, which you gave her for me. Thanks. She seemed an exceptionally nice girl. (Both Mrabet and Abdelouahaid went overboard in her favor, which means something, since they never agree on anything.) I feel that I should give you news of Tangier, but I've been more or less out of it for the past week, and don't know much. Leonardo and Leslie are back from Seville after a month and a half. Tom writes he's returning immediately from South America. Apparently he's been having what's laughingly called the time of his life, there in the Amazon forest. Targuisti sold all the paintings Brion had left in his care, to Ouakrim for 100,000 francs, gave the money to a puta, and is now very depressed because Brion has cut off his allowance. Maurice returned night before last from a month in Marrakech; he leaves in three days for Turkey. I'm having Pam's mother to tea tomorrow. She seems all right, but what a lonely existence! The police are now confiscating even the Michelin road maps of Morocco. It's forbidden to have any map of any sort. Guide books are not yet illegal. I wanted to let you know about Jane principally, so love for now.

TO AUDREY WOOD

May 11, 1973
Tangier

Just a note, to let you know that Jane died a week ago today in Málaga. She had a further stroke on the night of April 30th, and never recovered consciousness. Fortunately I arrived in time to spend the afternoon of Friday at her bedside. She died that evening without coming out of the coma. More than sixteen years of suffering, since the first stroke destroyed her eyesight.

There is nothing to keep me here now, save habit, but I shall probably stay on until outer circumstances force me to leave, since each time I've gone back to the States I've found it less like a place where I want to live.

I wish I had some way of writing Tennessee, but I know your ways have parted, and besides, who ever knows where he is these days? If you do have an address, I'd be grateful if you could send it to me. Forgive the short note, and much love.

TO DANIEL HALPERN,
ANTAEUS, NEW YORK

◆

May 14, 1973
Tangier

I had an awful dream night before last, in which you had sent that Anthony Burgess interview to Sankey to be run in the magazine, and the magazine arrived with it. Then you were suddenly here, and I was ranting wildly, and Drue walked in and held up her hand. "It was all Stanley Kubrick's fault!" she cried. "He was going to sue us for $140,000 unless we ran the piece." "But why?" I asked. "Guilt," she said. "But you know those people." "I don't know anything!" I shouted. "Good-bye!" And I rushed out and slammed the door so that part of Itesa collapsed. I hope it's not prophetic!

I'm sending back the Dowell story today by air registered. Let me know if it arrives. The galleys of number ten haven't yet come. Is it going to hold up things? I'm sending off the Purdy piece to Sankey at the same time. I was glad to hear you have a new piece by Rand.

You're going to Kashmir? So is John Goodwin, in August. He may have Peggy Guggenheim with him, according to his latest letter of last week. Undoubtedly you'll run into them somewhere out there. I could make it, but only by leaving now. Or it might even be too late for this year. Tangier to London to Cape Town to Bombay. Difficult, what with the Canal shut and so few ships running. One would think that people liked planes.

TO DANIEL HALPERN,

ANTAEUS, NEW YORK

May 22, 1973
Tangier

Thanks for your letters, and for letting Andreas Brown know about Jane; perhaps it was through him that Virgil heard. Or perhaps Maurice wrote him before he left for Turkey. I have written to the William Morris Agency asking them to send you a story by Choukri called "Bachir Alive and Dead." I hope you received the one by Dowell which I returned to you airmail about ten days ago. There are so many things I ought to be doing, such as translating the Berber stories for you and looking through Jane's notebooks (although I don't really believe that anything more can be squeezed out of them besides what I've copied, and a page or two here and there. Of course there are the three pieces published in *Antaeus*). But for no good reason I don't seem to be doing anything at all but write innumerable letters. I owe them, it's true, and then I keep thinking of people whom I must notify of Jane's death, people who will resent it unless I myself write them and tell them. I suppose that eventually I'll get through all this and establish a normal work routine. I had a wire yesterday from Tennessee asking me to phone him in London. But of course I have no phone. So I wired the Hotel Barclay to tell him that. The wire was from New York giving the London address for yesterday. I don't know where he's on his way to, if anywhere. Carol wrote yesterday that she intended to leave New York on the sixth of June, coming here via Valencia. Maybe you'll see her before she leaves. I hope number 10 is all right. The galleys never arrived. (Personally, I don't believe Sankey ever sent them.) However, the page proofs seem all right.

TO VIRGIL THOMSON

May 25, 1973
Tangier

I know Maurice has written you about Jane, but I wanted to write you myself. She had been growing noticeably weaker over the past six months or so, and the Mother Superior had warned me that I should be prepared for any eventuality.

The evening of April 30th, she suddenly collapsed, immediately after being fed her supper. It was another cerebral lesion; she became unconscious, and remained so. For some reason, the doctor did not notify me until two days later. I arrived in Málaga the fourth and spent the afternoon with her. She was still in a coma, and seemed to be breathing with difficulty. I left the hospital to go and have dinner. At nine I received a call saying she had just died.

Back in Tangier I saw Maurice, who had arrived during my absence. He was here only a few days, having painted several pictures in Marrakech, and then, as you know, left by car for Barcelona to pick up Ramón Senabre. I imagine he is in Istanbul by now, or about to arrive there. Wisely he has left the flat unoccupied. Summer renters in Tangier are better done without.

That's about all. I'm here indefinitely.

TO ALEC FRANCE
◆
June 13, 1973
Tangier

Your letter arrived yesterday, and I hasten to answer in the event that time is of the essence and you want to make plans.

Unless Morocco becomes uninhabitable between now and the time you intend to visit it, I shall be here, and should be pleased to talk with you. I agree that not very much can be accomplished by mail. A few hours of conversation are usually more satisfactory than even an extended correspondence.

As to influences: they exist, obviously; but I'm not the one to indicate them because I'm not aware of them as such. I've admired Sartre and Borges since the early 'forties, and Camus since the late 'forties. And before that in the 'thirties I admired Kafka, and in the 'twenties Gide. To assign influences, however, is another matter, and not one in which I could be of much help. The autobiography is nowhere meant to be "cryptic." Personalities: Malcolm McConnell was here a year or so ago for a week; he'd just published a thick book on East Africa. Bill Eagleton and his wife were here this winter and I had dinner with them. I had thought of accepting his invitation to visit them in Algiers, but my wife's death came between plan and execution.

If you come to Tangier I shall be delighted to see you.

TO VIRGIL THOMSON

June 26, 1973
Tangier

I was glad to have your letter, and I thank you for it. You may be sure that for a good many years I've reflected on the possibility of being left alone by Jane, and now that it has happened, I think of it a great deal more. The principal difference between then and now is that my degree of interest in everything has been diminished almost to the point of non-existence. That makes a great difference, since there is no compelling reason to do anything whatever.

I haven't heard from Maurice since his departure, but in some roundabout fashion I can't recall at the moment, I did hear that his illness had persisted and that he was still in Greece. I hope he can clear it all up, but gastronomically he's something of a hedonist, I'm afraid, and will eat things he knows perfectly well are going to hurt him. Then he says he oughtn't to have done it. However, apart from the liver he seems always to be in very good condition. I hope he manages to get to Turkey and paint there.

Dan Halpern wants to publish a small volume of notes and letters of Jane's. I had only three letters to contribute; perhaps you have one or two somewhere, but I doubt it. She was not a very active correspondent; letters were as hard for her to write as her own work.

I'm looking forward to a quiet summer, but I suppose that depends on the Moroccans. I hope all is well with you.

TO HOWARD GRIFFIN

August 29, 1973
Tangier

The book arrived yesterday. My driver was certain it was a letter-bomb, and would not let me open it in the car. Instead, he himself took it into the courtyard of the market and slit open its backside very carefully with a wire. I think he was annoyed to discover that it wasn't what he had thought. Of course, the Moroccans can't wait for the bombs to begin arriving here.

Anyway, it is a charming little book, and I am delighted to have it. Thank you for sending it to me.

The summer so far has been relatively uneventful. Tennessee arrived in mid-July and stayed until mid-August, and there were some good parties in gardens, where there was room to have Jilala or Aissaoua or Gnaoua musicians and dancers.

Tom Wright returned from Amazonia in the spring, and has been here ever since. I think he found the place very exciting, as when he came back he spoke of having made friends with cannibals. His address is the same as before, since he is in the same apartment.

With the dollar where it is, I feel it incumbent upon me to remain where I am. Thus I haven't travelled at all this year. You have to run as fast as you can to stay in one place, let alone try to get to another.

Perhaps we'll see you here again in the near future?

TO JAMES LEO HERLIHY

November 26, 1973
Tangier

God knows where you are, but I'm sending this to Key West, as it seems more likely you'd be there than in Hop Bottom, although there is no particular reason why you should be. I ran across your letter of July 31st a while ago, and suspect that I never answered it. It must have arrived while Tennessee was here in Tangier, and since I must have written you about that, *perhaps* I replied during August. Everything before the Mideast War seems very long ago; there has been such excitement here ever since that started, that the era before it is dim in memory. Recruiting continues at a great rate; the country intends to send all its soldiers to Syria, and indeed, has been continuing to send them after the cease-fire, which is qualified as only a break to let everyone catch his breath. Moroccans all believe the war has barely begun. As long as there is a Jew left in Palestine it won't be over. They seem to attach no importance whatever to "borders" and withdrawals from occupied territories. There are no borders because there is no country called Israel. In other words, they believe Arafat should control it all. Sadat and Hussein must go. At this point there seem to be only two possible solutions: either we (the U.S. & Europe) must attack the Arab nations and force them to capitulate oilwise, or we must oblige Israel to retire to the pre-1967 frontiers and wait to see whether that will make any difference to the Moslems, or whether, as I suspect, they will find pretexts to continue the oil squeeze anyway. In the meantime the American Consuls in Morocco have appointed local gauleiters to assist in evacuation of citizens should it become necessary. They tell you to keep a bag packed, ready to leave at a few hours' notice. But nobody takes it seriously, as far as I know. Mrabet's book *The Boy Who Set the Fire* is due out next week, says the publisher. Carol left on the 15th for New York. Let me hear if you get this.

TO DANIEL HALPERN,
ANTAEUS, NEW YORK

January 29, 1974
Tangier

I sent off the galleys yesterday; it took from four ten to six fifteen. First they claimed it was forbidden to send papers in an envelope; they had to be rolled and wrapped in paper, and it had to be special paper. We set out in search of a shop that would sell paper. After trying three, we went to Emsallah to a store where Abdelouahaid knew the proprietor. He finally consented to sell one sheet of paper rather than a huge roll. We took that back to the customs office. Then they said we must have medium thick twine to tie the papers up with; no glue or masking tape or Scotch tape allowed. We came back to Itesa and got scissors, twine (I had one small length, otherwise we would have had to go to the Zoco de Fuera to look for that) and marking pens, and took everything to the customs office. The envelope I had been going to send the galleys in was there. Why don't you put it in this? they said, holding up the envelope. Because you said it was forbidden, I told them. Yes, they said. Probably it's better to wrap the parcel. At the end when I tried to pay the postage, they had no change at all. Where can I get change? I asked them. They didn't know, but they said they had been doing me a great favor allowing me to send all those papers, and did I expect them to go out and rustle up change for me as well? Anyway, you asked for definitions of moqaddem, chaouch and amghar. Moqaddem is either gauleiter of a quarter or the head of a branch of a religious brotherhood. Chaouch is office-boy, messenger, or doorman. Amghar is the Tachelhait word for man. No one here ever heard it used as a delineating term. Where did you hear it used? Roditi has sent me *An Early View of Algiers* (1852) by Eugène Fromentin (relevant in 1974, and ideal for the translation issue), with an introductory note by Norman Glass. Shall I send it on to you? Fromentin is good. Let me hear.

P.S. (And to answer your question, you agreed to $200 for a short story. But I'm waiting to hear from my agent that Viking has paid the royalties on *Prey*.)

TO CAROL ARDMAN

March 20, 1974
Tangier

The weather is more wintry now than it was in January and February—but that's March in Tangier. The cold wind blows through the flat as if the windows were open. We took Francis (whom nobody calls that) up to Marta's day before yesterday. He was quite wonderful in the car, merely sitting calmly in the back window without anyone's touching him, looking out at the countryside, exactly like a dog. The only thing he wouldn't stand for was being shut into the basket. Being fantastically strong, he naturally gave a spring, and forced his way out, every time anyone managed to get him in. With six dogs and a cat on the property I don't know how he'll fare, but I made an appointment to go up tomorrow to see Seudiya and find out if he's eating or not. (Marta's in Rome.) Thank God there was at least that place to take him to; without it Jeffrey Miller would have no hands left. "I'll probably miss the little bastard," he remarked, once we'd left Francis behind. So it wasn't all that bad. Fatoma claims he clawed the haïti mercilessly, so she took it down. So you've met Edwin Denby. Tom writes from Bogota, saying it's all just what he wanted. I wrote you perhaps two months ago, telling you Mrabet had received your letter; maybe the letter went astray. Incredible that your article has been rejected. Gasoline went up again last week; it's now 1.62 a liter, which makes it about $1.48 a gallon at the consular rate of exchange, which is 4.40 to the dollar. And it's due to rise to 2 dirhams shortly, so they say. Food likewise is rising each week, and so are riots and arrests. Nothing but trouble, naturally. And one can't get money. A new racket has been discovered by the Casablanca people: if you send for dollars, they invest the sum right there for a month at ten percent. Then two weeks or so later you receive your money. Six weeks of waiting, while they rob you. Harriet stays in bed. Angus about to return. Forgive this smattering of news.

TO CAROL ARDMAN

March 23, 1974
Tangier

I had been going to go up to Marta's on Thursday afternoon to take Francis some Amichat and see how he was acclimatizing himself to the new situation, but Abdelouahaid's father died on Wednesday, and that shattered all such plans. In the meantime Mrabet dreamed that Marta had run over Francis in the road in front of the house and killed him. Of course I'm used to his dreams. Yesterday I finally got up to Marta's, to be met by the grim-faced Seudiya. "That cat is dead," she said. The story seemed to be that one of the dogs had bitten Francis's throat, and Dr. Preston was unable to save him. Then she said uncomfortably: "He's buried where we bury the black cats, next to that tree down there." And remembering that I was in Morocco, I had a vision of midnight sacrifices (only black cats used) and was consoled by the thought that Marta was in Italy, so that at least she was innocent. But then Mrabet, when I told him of the accident, shook his head, saying: "The Princesa did it. She told me so in her dream, two nights ago. She said she ran over him, but what really happened was that she bit his throat with her eye-teeth." Rome or no Rome; that didn't matter; she did it from there. Why not? And so on. A perfect story for Brion Gysin, who as you know insists that Marta spends most of her time engaging in magic practises. Anyway, I was shocked and sad, because he was such a beautiful cat, and after all, he was yours. I can't understand it at all, and am somehow inclined to doubt the whole thing—except, of course, his death. What a shame I ever took him up there! I left the Amichat for the resident cat, and came home, disgusted. And particularly annoyed by Mrabet's having dreamed of the death before it happened. That's all I have to report.

TO CAROL ARDMAN

April 26, 1974
Tangier

How can you go to a Turkish bath disguised as a man? Seems difficult to me. Dan Halpern finally did what he'd been threatening to do: get Columbia U. to wire me offering me a job. I sent a wire day before yesterday which said: awaiting letter. The letter came yesterday, along with another wire asking me to telephone. How can I do that? There's no way. I'd have to stand all day in the baqqal waiting for the operator to ring back, and then, do you believe I'd actually get Columbia University, and the man (Frank MacShane) I'm supposed to talk to? Ridiculous! So now I've got to send another wire, explaining why I can't telephone. By that time they won't want me anyway. There are two big reasons why I don't want such a job. It's in New York City (1), and the pay ($7,500) is not enough for me to be able to save anything out of it, once I've paid my fare by ship round-trip, and paid four months of hotel. To put myself out to that extent, I've got to be able to have something to show at the end of the work. (2) Perhaps they'll give me a raincheck for 1975, by which time I might conceivably be able to arrange living quarters. But I hate the idea of being in New York! I've tried for three years to discourage Dan from getting me involved. But of course he means well and is trying to "help" me, although I've given no sign of wanting such help. Roditi came by yesterday; he's here for two days and leaves tomorrow for Paris. Marguerite is coming tonight to do Mrabet's portrait. I wonder why. She got back from Bali a fortnight ago. David tells everyone that Choukri's book is "too crude." ¿Qué quiere decir eso?* Tom writes delightedly about Bogotá. Angus is coming this afternoon. Jeffrey Miller still doing his bibliography. The Yogi is leaving for London, and that's good; he tried to borrow $200 from me last night. When I said no, he asked Mrabet for it! All for now.

TO JOHN SANKEY,
VILLIERS PUBLICATIONS, LONDON

June 17, 1974
Tangier

Thank you for sending the copies of *Antaeus* #13/14; they arrived last week.

As you may know, the restrictions on material leaving Morocco have become much more stringent in the past months. (Having several thousand soldiers still in Syria, the government considers itself to be still officially at war with Israel, and this fact justifies its precautionary examination of all correspondence being sent out of the country.) Inasmuch as there are several Jewish writers in translations from the Yiddish represented in the materials set up in the galleys plus

* Now what is that supposed to mean?

Ionesco's remark that Israel deserves to exist more than any other country, I am not going to take the chance of being involved in sending seditious texts through the mails. I am thus reduced to taking a step which I know from past experience is highly objectionable to you, that of listing the corrections (with the exception of the list of contributors, which I enclose) and sending you this extra work, being convinced that were I to send you the galleys, not only would they stand a poor chance of reaching you, but my own security as a still tolerated resident of Morocco would be seriously threatened. If I were able to take the packet to Gibraltar and post it, I think I could probably get it through customs, but unfortunately the police have my passport and I can't leave the country until they provide it with a new visa.

Thus my apologies.

TO CAROL ARDMAN
—◆—
August 10, 1974
Tangier

I've thought of something else, although it may not be practical to get hold of, and that's the Ced-o-Flora you brought last year for the leaves of the plants on the terrace. I know you got it more or less by accident last year, from friends who kept a florist shop, so if it involves a trip to some distant part of town, for God's sake don't think of it. Noel came around last night. His tanker book was run in *The New Yorker*, but I never managed to see it because they no longer allow me to receive the magazine. My subscription lasts until the end of the year, but they stopped delivering it in March and I haven't seen an issue since. They're getting worse and worse here; I don't know what it is. The streets are torn up and as full of people as the streets in India. Everything looks poverty-stricken and yet prices are constantly going higher and higher. Of course great preparations are going ahead for war, which the grapevine claims will start during Ramadan. I don't believe it because I can't see Spain fighting with Morocco somehow. It seems insanity for us to continue provocations, with Spain's much larger army and superior technique, but of course the Moroccans expect an immediate victory, including invasion of Andalucia and getting back Granada and Sevilla at last. My own suspicion is that this country needs a diversion, and that's the only one they can hit on at the moment. But I should imagine the serious trouble would be with Algeria, not Spain. They're also calling up soldiers

to send again to Syria for resumption of that war there. Plus ça change . . .
Anyway, the weather is fine and the dollar is at 4.25 and may go up, now that
King Nixon has abdicated, although I doubt that Rabat will allow much of a
rise. Very few tourists this year, the hotels next to empty. Only groups of Germans
in buses. I'll look for you at the airport.

TO ALEC FRANCE
———————————◆———————————
November 28, 1974
Tangier

Having just received your long letter, and considering it something in the
nature of a plea for a swift reply, I'm sitting here after dinner writing you. Mrabet
has tolba performing at his house, so he isn't here, otherwise we would doubtless
be translating his new book of stories. (I finally sent off the final version of his
autobiographical volume, and hope it arrives safely at the publisher's.)

To get to the material in your letter. First, for out-of-catalogue records: If you
write Maurice Grosser at * * * and ask him about a shop called Greenspan's,
run by a friend of his, I'm certain you'll be able to find copies of other records
of my music. Greenspan himself, who was here in Tangier, assured me he had
a good many of my records, and offered to send me some. But since I had no
record-player, I thought it useless. Your first numbered question: (1) Yes. The
city is certainly Constantine; the bath is imaginary, but inspired by Sidi Harazem
as it was in 1931. Lazrag was the name of a man who accepted my seventeen
jackal skins in Laghouat and agreed to make me a coat. It never got made,
however. The deformity comes from a character who used to frequent a café in
the Quartier Réservé Moulay Abdallah in Fez. (2) No. (3) No; it was inspired
by a walking trip I took to a place called Landa, in the State of Guerrero, in
Mexico. (An extraordinary spot it was.)

I follow you in your concern with exactly what purpose I put language to,
naturally. But not in your assumption that one necessarily uses words in only
one of two possible ways. Does the using of words to clarify one's innate sense
of a situation rule out using them also to assuage nostalgia, for instance? To
create the illusion, that is, of a place one is not in, or of a situation that formerly
existed, or perhaps never existed? The latter use, I assume, is what you mean
by "escape." I suppose in the invoking of that which is not, one temporarily
"escapes" from that which is. But my feeling is that it is the desire to create the

non-existent which takes precedence over whatever desire to "escape" may be present. But in a sense all art is an escape from reality for the artist while he is busy making it, if by reality is meant daily social intercourse. In that sense, using words would always be a kind of "escape" from the world outside, the same as the practice of any other art. I think what you want to know is my attitude in the matter, no? The observable phenomena of existence are all a writer has to work with, but what he does with them depends on him. My own design has been to recreate reality in such a way that it becomes unreal, impossible wouldn't you say? But there is no way of doing that unless unreality can be made to seem as "real" as the original reality. Then it isn't fantasy, but although converse, still a recognizable kind of reality. At least, that's hoped for, and sometimes attained. You'd know in which works. But I do reject the idea that one must be going either away from, or toward, the attainment of reality. Isn't it more a concentration (static) upon the aspects of reality capable of being worked upon and transmuted, that is, made into a personal statement by the alteration? You speak of your dilemma, but is it really that? I mean, for the structural purposes of the dissertation are you obliged to assume this centripetal-centrifugal concept? I wish I could be of real help in a thing like this, but even in conversation it's difficult.

TO NED ROREM

November 30, 1974
Tangier

Once again thanks for your faithfulness in seeing that I was sent a copy of the new book. Only you and Purdy manage to get each new work to me, and I consider it a double miracle, first that you should think of it, and even more that you should actually get it done (the sending, I mean). Probably I think of myself rather as a convict does, and am constantly surprised when people who are out in the world remember me by according me such favors.

This "final" diary doesn't necessarily preclude eventual memoirs or journals, I hope. Because even though the first two contained much material that was completely over my head (that is, unbecoming to my image of you) the third seems much more like what I think the others should have been, right down to the soundness of the opinions stated. So I needn't expatiate on the pleasure it has given me. Even the obit motif, already fairly strong in the New York book, and much more pronounced in this one, didn't rub me the wrong way, perhaps because you seem to accept the idea of death (other people's, that is) with more equanimity. Probably by the time you're my age you'll be astonished afresh each day by the fact that you're still drawing breath, that so far you've been "spared."

Two details having to do with me. Whoever remarked that your arrival in Taxco with your father has a connection with *Cold Point* is quite mistaken. Whatever others may have imagined, I believed implicitly that you were your father's son, and that was that. The diving-board there was a Colonel Ramsdell and his adopted son. Also, to this day I've never tried LSD. The substance I wrote you about from Asilah in 1963 was mescaline. Insignificant, but a matter of pride with me, like Virgil's boast in 1932 that he had never been inside the Louvre. Hasta luego.

TO ALEC FRANCE

———————————◆———————————

February 12, 1975
Tangier

An immediate if short reply to your letter of 5/ii. First, it wasn't my idea that Mrs. Rochat send me a copy of her dissertation. I've seen it—your copy—and even if I possessed a copy I doubt that I'd look at it. To me it's utter drivel. Don't quote. I suppose one should be flattered to have nonsense written about one, but it's difficult to feel that way. De Quincey: I've read, naturally, the *Confessions* and *The Fine Art of Murder*, but nothing more. (I'm not certain of the second title, as I read both books in French, back in the 'forties.) That was number one on your list. (2): I'd say 1950 is nearer to the date. But even before that, between 1947 and 1950, I smoked fairly often, and for the effect. Majoun, however, was my favorite companion at that time. (3): No, the record isn't straight here. *Up above the World* was written entirely under kif, if one may use the word "under." Perhaps "over" would be more accurate. And if I recall, "The Hyena" and "The Garden." This doesn't mean that I wasn't smoking at all when I wrote some of the other stories. Perhaps [Lawrence] Stewart confuses the direct effect of kif on the writing with its general action on the personality over the years, which is a dimming one. That is, the ego doesn't feel the need to assert itself. Very likely Stewart finds this regrettable. (4): Never felt I knew the place well enough to write about it. (5): The stones seemed appropriate, even inevitable. Subsequently I discovered that it was indeed a practice in certain societies.

However, it's not a surprising thing to have occur to one's subconscious—not if one subscribes in any measure to Jung's idea. (6): Castration as punishment for onanism strikes me as too explicit, like a lot of Freud. Castration or impotence would be enough. I doubt very much that onanism is a necessary adjunct. I had read a few books by Freud; the only ones I remember are *Totem and Taboo* and *Wit and the Unconscious,* if that's the correct title. (7): Without thinking about it I've always placed Indian philosophy at the top, as a kind of ultimate attainment, the goal of all religions. Carol well, all well here. Bonjour to Ruth & Brandle.

TO CAROL ARDMAN
———————————◆———————————
February 17, 1975
Tangier

The weather is very clear and windy, and since yesterday millions of small flowers have appeared, growing close to the ground. I suppose they were waiting for the extra bit of rain that fell night before last, and were ready to open. Each day new people arrive and announce themselves. I can't keep them straight any longer. Some go, some stay on for a few days. Some are Mount Hermon students on the exchange program. One is George Staples's stand-in at the American School, another his girlfriend, a history teacher there. Another someone sent by a new Italian publisher who is bringing out *M'Hashish* and *100 Camels* next month in Italian. (Three days and nights we had him, and Mrabet had to take him to his hotel after midnight each time.) And our famous Carlos Lacerda, from Rio, who seemed to be conducting an in-depth study of the household. He was, as you may remember, going to take Mrabet to Brazil for reasons of publicity. But after seeing him he changed his mind. Now he writes from Paris, referring to "the ineffable Mrabet." Lesley Blanch is still in Marrakech. If you watched *Watch on the Rhine* you must have heard my music, which Paul Lukas fusses around with at one point. They screwed me on that, but my lawyer got an injunction against further showing of the film during the year 1942. (By screwed, I mean, they paid me and didn't give screen credit, giving it instead to Alfred Newman.) I was glad to hear you'd been paid, at least, by *Ms.* and *Ingenue.* Mama Pussycat is about to have a family, and has become insistent about getting into number twenty. Terrible yowling when I won't let her in. Jock and Mustapha are in Erfoud. Roy Lathrop lives in number five; I imagine you know. The book of Jane's things will be out in September, the Eberhardt I don't know when. A writers' conference! You must tell me all about it when it happens. Had dinner at Claudio's with Paula and Christopher.

TO ALEC FRANCE

March 2, 1975
Tangier

You do come up with the damnedest questions! Today being the Aid el Arche, I ought to have the time to answer them with attention. You can see I've single-spaced the paper to make room. The difficulty, I can see, is going to be memory. Such as the stone-in-the mouth business. As I said, I simply wrote it. Not more than a year subsequent to that, I came across an account of death-ritual in either a present-day primitive society or an antique one in which the identical practice existed. Who's to say whether I had already seen a reference to such a custom, long before "You Are Not I," or whether I invented it there and saw the corroboration later? Neither supposition would be surprising. Your question no. 1: Do you see a similarity between wanting to bring back something from the realm of sleep and seeing an image in sleep which turns out to correspond with a physical fact? They seem to me two entirely different phenomena. The first comes from a natural desire to extend the advantages of dream to real life; the second is purely a matter of ESP. "A Thousand Days for Mokhtar" was recounted to me by Smail Abdelkader in 1947, and I made a tale out of it because it created a resonance in me. (Although this is really a third kind of phenomenon, connected intimately with the subconscious of the protagonist, who, although he believed he had paid the butcher, recalled eventually that he hadn't.) I'm inclined to believe Smail's story. If it was a tall tale, it's the only one he ever told me. As to "Baraka," I'd say it was Mrabet's variation on Moroccan tradition. (Moroccans are obsessed with dreams, as you know, although they have a feeble system for interpreting them, I think.) One of the reasons I'm here is surely that on arriving I found a people admirably attuned to my own fantasies. Remember page 4 of "At Paso Rojo": "He loves it here because everything is his," she thought. And then of course there is the inevitable corollary, which she adds: "and some of the things could never have been his if he had not purposely changed to fit them." I think it's a question of that: the fit was already so close that I labored to make it a perfect fit. 2) Stewart is not in the groove with regard to my "belief" in magic. The Moroccans make minimal distinction between tseuheur and tsoukil, both being considered forms of magic-making. Obviously tsoukil works very well on anyone. I naturally reserve judgment on tseuheur as far as they're concerned; for the uninitiated I should think it useless. Now, to get to the business of kif and the ego. *Without Stopping* of course has no "revelation." On the contrary, everything is covered, but there are clues everywhere which can be used to uncover, if anyone wants to bother doing it. I have several which I thought showed the presence of excessive compulsiveness and overriding anguish. They were signs of serious illness, and thus I didn't discuss them. But at the same time they were the basis of my behavior for many years; my return to writing fiction was an effort to get rid of them as we've seen. We know how my early adolescence was plagued by this chronic angst that was capable of generating great nervous tension. One might have thought that the angst would diminish as time went on, but instead of that, it increased to the point of being well-nigh unbearable. The writing of music, which engaged only certain functions of the mind, was useless for helping to reduce the tension. But then I discovered that fiction-writing, by fanning the angst until it was at "white-heat," produced a sort of immunity from the abiding worry. This might sound like a solution to my problem, but it wasn't, because my problem was not that of producing fiction, but of continuing to live from one day to the next without exploding, without finding myself in a catastrophic situation. My state didn't improve merely because I was writing stories that helped solve inner troubles. Nerves still ragged, still had nightmares, still had to walk ten miles as fast as possible every day, and that kind of nonsense. Then I discovered that kif was a brake on the reaching of the white-heat. I could write using it, but I need never fear I'd get burned, as it were. As soon as I realized that, all the compulsiveness, all the angst and nightmares vanished. It was only after they'd been gone for some time that I realized how life had changed, how safe I was from the horrors that had gnawed inside. Naturally I don't like to remember all this, as it makes my life seem completely outside my control, and introduces a pathological note which is annoying to have to reflect on, particularly at my age. However, I can see that since writing is a kind of efflorescence of my private writhings, it would have been helpful to dwell a bit more on it with you, if not in *Without Stopping*. But I confess that it wouldn't have occurred to me to say all this unless you had written your recent letter. My putting it out of mind is symptomatic. In any case, it all comes down to saying that it was absolutely necessary to throw out the baby along with the bath-water. An analyst probably would have done it differently; it doesn't matter to me. I solved my day-to-day problem, and found living enjoyable at last, or perhaps I should say bearable, which is all anyone should ask for. I'm sure all this leaves various boxes open and their contents unexamined, but it constitutes an attempt to give a satisfactory answer to your question. As to feeling that one has another novel in one, I can only say that I always feel the possibility latent, now, the same as after writing *The Spider's House*. Incentive is something else. It would be far too easy to attribute its lack to kif. There is an important economic factor: I now live on an income from capital invested. Age has a bit to do with it, as does Jane's death. (I no longer have to make something to show her, which I did as long as she lived.) Whatever part, quantitatively or qualitatively, kif may have played in my literary decrescendo over the past two decades or so, I am only grateful to it for its action. I think you can understand how one feels after having been trapped in a cave, to come out into the reassuring light of day. Perhaps I should have found my way out eventually in any case, kif or no kif, but the fact remains that I did it with kif. (Perhaps the place where we get stuck in trying to work out the theory— with its paradox or its anomaly—is at the point where we confidently ascribe certain effects to cannabis, adducing as proof only the user's purely subjective impression, necessarily a distorted one. Isn't that quite possible? I'm not at all sure that kif has ever "liberated my subconscious," although I've often believed it could be of great help to other people in relaxing them. But what's needed is precise information about the action of cannabis on the chemistry of the brain. Then one could talk about its relation to the workings of the ego and the id. But now all we know is what the person who has the cannabis in him says he feels. Which is next to nothing, as far as elaborating a viable theory goes.) I think you're right, too, in suggesting that there may be considerably more ego-relaxation and id-assertion in the elaborative phase than you might have supposed. In case I haven't made it clear enough, your compulsion theory is accurate. I can't go on from there, but perhaps you can. Is any of this of any use? I think I'd better stop. The copy of Henderson did arrive two days ago, and I thank you for sending it. I know you said it would be the best introduction to Bellow. On verra. All this talk about compulsion makes me want to quote a line of my own: compulsiveness is doom. And any wind in contrast smells of God.

My best to all three. Let me have your reactions.

TO ALEC FRANCE
———————————————•———————————————

March 27, 1975
Tangier

I doubt that this letter will advance matters much, as I have the feeling that I've more or less exhausted the expressible facets of self-knowledge! But let me go through your questions and objections, and try to make something out of them. The Mokhtar story is one of subconscious guilt, I suppose. (I mentioned that the people here couldn't be psychoanalyzed using Freudian concepts as regards sexual matters. Guilt about money is perfectly common.) The two kinds of "magic" used here could be called "words" and "poison," if one wanted to make *tseuheur* and *tsoukil* clear to rational minds. Since they're often used together, it's hard to separate their effects. *Tsoukil* works ("obviously") because it's purely physical. Perhaps that makes it clear. As far as I'm concerned, nothing can suspend the laws of science; when things look peculiar, it's lack of sufficient knowledge of the laws, nothing more. They say *kif* does mean delight, but one would have to go further east to find the word being used in that sense. Here it's purely of the vegetable kingdom. To get to kif versus angst. I'd say I used it as one uses an anaesthetic ointment to keep down irritation of a skin disease. Then one ceases to scratch, and that brings about healing. Why was the kif anaesthetic? That I can't answer, for with some people it isn't, at all. (I suspect it stopped me from simultaneous thinking and feeling, which was unbearable.) (One at a time is enough!) Re "the kif-influenced mind" and its "relations to its former worries": the worries, instead of being inside one, are next door, as it were. At arm's length, if you like, rather than inside. And that keeping them at arm's length is the anaesthetic ointment; the longer they can be kept away, the less likelihood there is of recurrence. One would need to know brain anatomy to discover what happens. I suspect that certain passages are blocked, and new ones form eventually. About your regression theory, I don't really understand it, so can't discuss it. Kif relaxes me only after stretching the nerves so taut that they seem to break and fall limp. To answer another question: my mother always listened when I read aloud my early-age writings, yes. But I was always looking for others, who showed more astonishment than she on hearing them. Some, indeed showed dismay, declaring that I should not be allowed to sit writing the entire time. These were the true enemies. My father, whom I never allowed to see or hear any of my literary efforts, was merely a vast encumbrance that had to be got around or destroyed somehow, even for me to meet my enemies. I'm not going to continue on another sheet, and so my replies are brief. I can see that you considered me something less than a fully cooperative interviewee, perhaps less than candid. I regret it, and yet I don't know where I was devious or secretive. I think that having spent my life trying to hide everything from everyone, I've ended up by no longer being able to find many things myself. Seriously.

TO ALEC FRANCE

April 16, 1975
Tangier

A word before I set out for Marrakech (in the morning). A great book, the Orwell, and I'm enjoying every page. By now I've read all the critical pieces, and am going through the letters I didn't read as I skipped through it at first. A shame he died at such an early age, for he was one of the really good ones. And thank you; it goes with me to Marrakech.

In various ways I suppose you could draw a parallel between Henry Miller's and my political attitude, at least as it comes out in the writing. I doubt that I'm as apolitical as he in my reactions to the daily news. But probably we both accept the process of decay in much the same way. It becomes decor, finally.

I expect to be back in Tangier in about ten days, incha'Allah.

Thanks again for Eric Blair.

TO CAROL ARDMAN

May 21, 1975
Tangier

Your voluminous missive arrived yesterday. Your news is always so lively that I'm hard put to tell you anything of equal interest. But then, you know how it is here. You ask how I am. Fine. And what I am "doing." Working as always. Hallman is bringing out a tiny volume containing three stories; it ought to be ready next month. I just finished typing and xeroxing Mrabet's new book for 1976: the one he insists on calling *Harmless Poisons*. (I don't think it's particularly apt for the book, but he does.) He hasn't finished the drawings for it, but probably will soon. At the moment he's concentrating on preparations for another big Jilala party at Tessa's, before she leaves her house to some French people and goes to England for the summer. Gavin is in Marrakech at John's house, along with Peggy Heubrecht. I think he'll be back in a day or so. Maurice complains about the weather, which is consistently grey and dirty so that he can't work. Our winter is still in full swing, with rain on and off all day every day. Camus's *The Renegade* was written several years after "A Distant Episode," as you know. I doubt that he ever saw "Episode"; the material probably came, as in my case, directly from the place. Have you read Gide's *Vatican Swindle*, or as it is sometimes called: *Lafcadio's Adventures? (Les Caves du Vatican.)* My favorite. Marta Ruspoli has been after me to help her in her struggle to get free of the lawyers who are swindling her in the U.S. That is, she thinks I know journalists who could publicize it in the press, but I've assured her I don't. I finally got the name of someone in Cleveland (from the editor of *The Nation* in New York). People are so illogical! If you see Ellen Ann give her my love. Mrabet received your letter, claiming that he didn't understand it when I translated it for him. There are soldiers once again in the post office. Brion in Paris.

TO JEFFREY MILLER

June 1, 1975
Tangier

This week I came across what is probably the earliest letter from me. It was in a valise among photos and papers; how it got there I don't know. In any case, it was mailed on January 4, 1915, five days after my fourth birthday, and is printed in pencil. It reads:

DEAR MISS ANNA.

THANK YOU FOR THE ERECTOR. I HAVE BEEN MAKING LETTERS WITH IT. MONDAY THE 3RD I WAS PLAYING WITH A LITTLE YELLOW SPIDER, BUT HE WAS SO TINY THAT I LOST IT. DO YOU NOTICE MY RED CROSS STICKER, AND MY OTHER LITTLE SANTA CLAUS? LOVE FROM PAUL.

If you want, I can send you a xerox of it, although it may be too early to be of interest to you.

Nothing much happens here. Now and then a Jilala party, and occasionally a flurry of news about an attack in the Sahara, or rumors of a skirmish on the border between Ceuta and Castillejos. I can't take the Saharan business very seriously, although once Spain gets out it could become another matter, with Algeria and Morocco both trying to grab the phosphate.

I spent about two weeks at John Hopkins's house in the palmeraie outside Marrakech. It was quiet, and I got Mrabet's new book finished. My own little tome, with three stories in it, ought to be appearing soon; I corrected galleys last month. Joe McPhillips came by yesterday bringing a crowd of people and a large chocolate cake from the Memorial Day Fair being held at the American School. Cake better than the people, I thought.

I hope all is well by you. By me it gives fine.

TO CAROL ARDMAN

December 14, 1975
Tangier

You ask about Thanksgiving; there was none. I didn't think of it until the day after. Alec and Virginia are in the States. Paula and Bill are busy packing up their furniture preparatory to leaving definitively. They're going to live on Martha's Vineyard in a house bought by Bill's father years ago from James Cagney. That's all I know. Joe McPhillips got back night before last from West Africa via Paris, and we had dinner at Gavin's, along with Peggy Heubrecht and Ann Lambston, if that's the way she spells it. (An English writer who just published a fictional book on Jacqueline Onassis and Lee Radziwill.) Strange Singer should ask you to review the Eberhardt. It certainly wouldn't have looked good to anyone with a nose for literary scandal.

All Libby's papers and letters are collected by Temple University, I seem to remember. Boston? What about that Swedish gentleman who was so eager to get blues records? Has he disappeared? Is Louis Schanker back from Easthampton at last? The Katzenjammer Kids return to Europe day after tomorrow. But as they warned: Oh, we'll be back! Yesterday was the Aid el Kebir; better it should be yesterday than tomorrow. This year the government has made a four-day holiday out of it. I still haven't finished the examinations for the life-insurance policy which the new buyers of the film-rights to *Sky* insist on taking out for me (with them as beneficiaries). They indicated either Dr. Little or Dr. Anderson. As Little's dead, it was Anderson. But he couldn't make a cardiogram, and so

I've had to do it piecemeal, and it isn't finished yet. And in the end there'll be a fight over who's going to pay for it all. Not a penny in it for me, thus not a penny from me. The Film Funding Corporation claims it can't afford to start production without a guarantee, in the event I die before Oct. 16, 1976 (copyright expiration). I don't know.

TO CAROL ARDMAN

February 11, 1976
Tangier

In reference to your remark at the beginning of your letter, Clareman isn't doing anything at all for me any more. I've switched completely. That is to say, I no longer have a lawyer, period. What I had to pay him I now pay the bank. I think the bearer of the astonishing news about the $450,000 got things crooked. There was a sum set aside years ago which would provide $280 a month for about fifty years, in case Jane happened to live that long. But it was strictly understood that if and when Jane died, the monthly sum would cease to arrive. Obviously very little of the money was disbursed—perhaps $25,000 in all, if that. When Jane died, the money went back into Libby's estate, or so I assume, since that's what both she and Clareman told me would happen. Although why the sum should have been so large I don't know, since Jane would have had to live 150 years to use it up. A nice review of Mrabet's book. I wrote Singer asking him whether fiction for his mag must necessarily treat of drugs, but he hasn't had time to reply. There are some new people here in Tangier, although they're leaving the day after tomorrow for Paris, Los Angeles and the Caribbean. They say they'll be back maybe in May. A jetset girl and her cronies, who seem to be legion. Did I tell you Noel Mostert finally bought the house Aaron Copland and I had in 1931? Probably I did. Now Tennessee writes that he'd like to have a house here and use Tangier as a base, and can I find him one. Gavin ought to know more about it than I do. Maurice arrived today, but I haven't yet talked to him. I got my proofs from *High Times* this afternoon. The new *Antaeus* looked good. Over 300 pages. Mrabet's sitting opposite me, cutting, and from time to time speaks to me. This helps account for the lack of any rhythm in the letter's writing. But never mind. Steve Reich and Elizabeth Taylor! So religious so suddenly. Gordon Sager is in Venice, staying with Peggy Guggenheim. The BBC said yesterday that the USSR had sent an envoy to Algeria asking them to play down the war with Morocco, because Russia needs the phosphate that only Morocco can supply. Except that judging by the wheat shortage there the phosphate doesn't seem to have benefited them all that much. We still don't know whether they're going to make the film of *The Lemon*. They asked for an extension of their option, but that's all. Nor do I know whether the film of *Sky* is going ahead or backwards. At least now my life is insured for the cost of production, however much that may be. Prices of imported food continue to rise drastically, and the dollar is still at four dirhams. My electric bill this month was $42, which is a 600% rise in rates from last month. Insane! Anyway, much love. I hope Olsson turns up. Forgive this long ramble.

TO JOHN MARTIN,
BLACK SPARROW PRESS, SANTA BARBARA, CALIF.

March 24, 1976
Tangier

It's not the rendering of the oral Arabic texts into written English that makes collaborating with Mrabet difficult, but trying to help him maintain some sort of diplomatic relationship with the outside world, which to him is obviously not a part of total reality. Long ago I learned that when he dictates a letter he uses me purely as a machine. "I asked you to write a letter, not to make suggestions." He knows enough English to be aware of any alteration in the text, as I've discovered when he has crumpled a slightly changed missive and tossed it into the fireplace. This is all relative to the letter he dictated night before last, in which he refused (in rather graceless terms, or so I thought) to comply with your suggestion that he make the drawings you had envisaged including in twenty-six copies of *Harmless Poisons*. Agreeing or not agreeing to do the thing is of course his affair, but the manner in which he rejected the idea was peculiarly Moroccan and even more peculiarly Mrabetlike. It would have been enough for him to explain that such an endeavor would take him a long time to accomplish (mainly because each time he gives up drawing for a few months, things don't turn out well for a long time, and he has to discard everything he draws until he hits the vein). I suppose it's that way for most people who rely solely on the subconscious, with no control whatever over their activity. Instead of that, he was so convinced that had he done what you asked he would have been being exploited by you, that he was truculent about the whole thing. When the letter was finished, I remarked that it wasn't a very friendly letter to send his publisher. "What do you mean?" he cried. "Did I insult him? Did I say anything wrong? I told the truth." So, as I say, it's these things that make my translating life complicated. I'll do my best to see that a cover drawing gets off to you soon.

TO ALEC FRANCE

◆

June 3, 1976
Tangier

Yes, I went to Marrakech and saw a lot of fancy houses being built by the jetset (somewhat belatedly, it seems to me) and waited for sun. It rained eleven days out of fourteen, so much so that the water was dripping all over my bed, and wet it so that it never really dried out again while I was there. The cold I came down with wasn't intense, but it lingered. Here it isn't raining, nor does it seem to feel like doing so. And the moral of that is: never count on the weather's doing otherwise than you might expect it to do from having observed what it has been used to doing in other years. (Last year I went down there at exactly the same time in May, and it rained *every* day.) The Bowleswork seems to be increasing in volume. What a job! But one day, if I go on existing long enough, I shall be able to read it. I don't get the *New York Review of Books*, nor can I imagine their being interested in anything that has to do with me—not even my carefully considered and perfectly structured social and political attitudes. If they take the essay I'll make a tajine out of an old pair of belgha.* It hasn't occurred to me that kif was a form of regression. But why not? Tennessee's *Memoirs* gave me an epidermal affliction. My skin crawled for the entire time it took me to get through it. Simple embarrassment at the striptease of the soul, and a soul that should have remained covered. And then the added discomfort of the writing. Or was it written? Dictated, recorded, transcribed, perhaps, and never reread. Nothing else could account for the sloppiness of the writing. Agony. Hachouma. Haram. Anyway, *Feminine Wiles* is not yet published, and it is the only volume that is under way. It contains a few letters and a few other things. Scraps from old valises. I can't imagine who the man who lived on the hill might have been. (*Enderby*, which I've not seen.) 25 volumes of autobiography? Could it have been Jim Ede, of ninety-odd other books. Sad

---

* I'll make a stew out of an old pair of slippers.

about Borges. Tennessee has just been judge at the Cannes Festival; seems they could never get him to go and see the films. Anyway, my best to Ruth and Brandle. Sorry you're not here this summer.

TO DANIEL HALPERN,
ANTAEUS, NEW YORK

November 18, 1976
Tangier

I received a batch of galleys today from Wickersham, all marked *Antaeus* 24. Six weeks or two months ago I corrected the galleys for 24, and they were completely different. I assume Wickersham has made an error in numbering, as on the invoice accompanying the galleys the words "Spring Issue" appeared. In any case, I'll go ahead and correct them, taking for granted they're the proofs of no. 25. Is it the pulp number? I haven't looked into the texts yet.

I hope you received the paragraph I sent about Bishop Middleton; I may have addressed it to Gail, thinking she was still there. A new explanation of the English. * * *

I went today to Msoura, a megalithic tomb in the middle of the wilderness. A perfect circle of huge slabs. The entrance has lost one of its pillars and its lintel; the remaining stone is a bit over twenty feet high, looks like a huge lingam, and is an object of great veneration to the people roundabout. A beautiful, very old man with a staff appeared, and told us a long story in Moghrebi of how the Spanish had come, about fifty years ago, and dug and dug, and finally lifted out a big stone that lay in the center of the circle. They had shipped it away to Spain, but before leaving they'd given a big feast for everyone in the region, and they'd all eaten mechoui and listened to music and danced. Yes, my son, he told Abdelouahaid. They carried it away. The Christians wanted it for themselves. So anyway, all best.

April 4, 1977
Tangier

The second cassette arrived safely. Thanks very much. I have no way of getting any music here, which is all right for a few years, but eventually one feels that one has to know what's going on in the world (musically, I mean). Thus my pleasure in receiving your two cassettes. You'll be interested to know that one Moroccan on hearing the first tape of Lou Harrison's music couldn't rest until he'd copied it. He came by yesterday to report the reactions of various friends: Senegalese, Iraqis and Nigerians, all of whom expressed more or less the same thought—that it was music which described Paradise of one kind or another. (I wonder what Lou would make of that.) The Moroccan himself speaks of it as *"música escrita por un diós."* I'm delighted, if astonished, by these reactions. Astonished because I've always ridiculed the bromide: Music is a universal language, simply in that I've found it to be so patently untrue. People have to accustom themselves to an unfamiliar musical idiom much in the same way they have to learn and live with a language in order to understand it. Harmony in particular seems to get in the way for non-Europeans; harmonic progressions set up no psychological tension. They complain that European music is static and clogged with extraneous sounds.

I'm interested to know what you're doing in place of editing *Soundings*, and if there's anyone else to pick up where you've left off. Obviously there should be such an organ, always functioning, but is there anyone to take it in hand? I know the answer is that such things happen, and stop when they stop, and so on. Still, I can't help wishing that someone may make it happen again.

Anyway, again thanks, and I'll bring this to a stop.

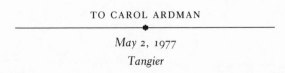

May 2, 1977
Tangier

From what people tell me, an enormous percentage of mail is going astray this year, and not all the trouble is here in Tangier. I got a letter day before yesterday that had been sent to Johannesburg by mistake and taken to the post office there, so that it arrived here with a South African frank on it. And Delhi and Osaka and Manila, as you know. Perhaps the postal services of the world need employees who can read. Millicent Dillon, who is writing Jane's biography, left ten days ago, and said she'd look you up in New York. I hope she does, for I think you'd like her. The day she left, Lenny Bernstein arrived, and we spent three days talking, something we hadn't done since thirty-five years ago. Strangely enough he's exactly the same as he was then: I can't see any difference except in appearance. It was fine to see him. He told me Victor Kraft had died some time ago, and Aaron is sending the son to school somewhere in New England. How were the extractions? I hope you had some whiskey ready: I always got into bed afterward and drank myself into a stupor. About Tangier, not much. Leonardo and Leslie are back, having tried Lisbon and found it wanting. John Hopkins is in Paris. Brion in Turkey. Big Cynthia has been here all year, living at the Velasquez. Now and then her boyfriend, Max de Ford, visits her from Amsterdam, and then she sees no one. Otherwise she's everywhere you go. Dan is rehearsing for the Tangier Players once again. He also tutors a Persian girl who is behind in her classes at the American School. Both Mrabet and I have new books coming out this month. His is *The Big Mirror* and mine a collection of stories. I have a feeling I shan't be very happy about the presentation of mine: when I saw the galleys I didn't like the type face. I dream about Libby Holman. Let me hear.

TO CHARLES-HENRI FORD

●

June 7, 1977
Tangier

With you I always have a feeling that by the time my missive crosses the sea you'll have changed addresses. There's already a warning note in your most recent: ". . . but I'm not sure it's a set-up for the future." (Loft-living.) So I shan't be surprised if you're in Xania or Xanadu when this gets to Greene Street.

I *was* surprised, however, to hear you'd been seeing Oliver Smith. Is he still critical of my wanting to live here, I wonder? Naturally he wouldn't live here, nor would most people, but I don't know why that would make him feel that I shouldn't.

John Goodwin, who was coming, has put off his trip until October, which may mean October 1979 for all I know. Sometimes he comes and sometimes he doesn't.

Is television watchable now? I've seen very little in my life except at Libby's in 1952, and I must say it wasn't worth the time it took to look at. One can catch glimpses of it here in cafés today as one goes by, and it still looks terrible, like a snowstorm. And if the snow abates, what one sees is someone playing a lute, or a politician perspiring. I haven't even seen a film since 1968 when I was in Los Angeles. (You can't go here: there's no air inside the hangar, and you bring home several dozen fleas on you.) And since I'm virtually a prisoner because the government won't send permission for me to continue living here, thus making it impossible for me to get an exit visa, I can't go to Gibraltar to see a film either.

Life in third-world countries!

The camels are out at Sidi Amar, waiting for tourists to come and mount them to be photographed. And the thousands who work in Belgium are here drunk, hitting people with their Mercedes sedans.

TO CAROL ARDMAN
—————————————◆—————————————

August 30, 1977
Tangier

Yours of the 23rd just to hand. I'd say Trika weighted you down. But apparently it didn't matter too much. You see, Miami Beach can come in handy; I always knew it. Sorry about your mother; I hope she's on the mend. And you? The interior disturbance didn't prolong itself, did it? In any case, there are so many different kinds of medicine in New York. Quelle richesse! And for sending on the two books to Black Sparrow, how many thanks! I expect to hear from him sometime this week. Or am I being optimistic with regard to the U.S. postal system? It would seem that between New York and Los Angeles there should be no problem, but I suppose that's only the way it would seem. Hannetta keeps writing six- and eight-page letters, but never mentions the tapes she took for Jeffrey Miller. She now has five Spaniards visiting her, none of whom speaks a word of English, and one of whom is in a wheel-chair. She has a passion for wheel-chairs, as you know. "Oh, I have lots of friends in wheel-chairs. Floyd collected 'em." John and Ellen Ann came over night before last; they still propagandize for my visit to the States, although with less assurance. Today I got a Cartier-engraved invitation to a cocktail party in Far Hills to be held in their honor on the 24th of September. It's only a week after the Aid es Seghir; I think I'll have to send regrets. (Explainable on religious grounds.) I don't know how one "understands" a poem, really (with reference to your remarks on *Next to Nothing*). A lyric poem, a song in which the words are both sounds and image-makers, is more of an object than an argument. If it's good, it reveals more of the writer's interior self than any prose he could construct. The only way you can understand a rock is to accept a priori the fact that it's a rock, which automatically precludes the necessity of trying to "understand" it. Poem is a poem is a poem . . . (This obviously doesn't apply to didactic poetry.) May the spider thrive.

TO PETER GARLAND

September 10, 1977
Tangier

Your letter, having been put with my electricity bills, has remained there until ten minutes ago, when I discovered it. A letter which I haven't answered is like a time-bomb. The only way to defuse it is to reply. Summer is always the busiest season by far. More visitors turn up, both European and American, and have to be entertained in one way or another, so that correspondence often suffers. Now, whether you are still in the United States or not, I don't know, but perhaps this can be forwarded successfully if you're not.

I've always felt that Lenny B. would be all right if one could kidnap him and hold him prisoner, far from everything that could remind him of the concept of being successful. I'll look him up in Heaven or Hell when I get there and see how he's doing.

Yes, if you do see Lou Harrison, naturally I'd be more than delighted to have a tape of his music. What he himself likes best, rather than what he thinks I might like. Or perhaps there's no difference, which would be flattering to me! I can't think of anything that would please me more. (Perhaps you should mention that you have already provided me with sections of *Pacifica Rondo*, plus the four pieces for harp solo and harp with percussion and/or celesta.) I've never asked anyone for such a thing until now, and wouldn't now were it not for the fact that it was you who suggested it.

Can anything "get better" now? Or are there people who still believe amelioration is a possibility, and that life is not on its way out? I don't know, being shut up here away from the world. (The Moslems don't live in the world; they live in the Moslem world, the unacceptable parts of which probably have more to do with the future than I like to think.) In any case, let me know what happens, and whether this reaches you.

TO CAROL ARDMAN

◆

December 3, 1977

Tangier

I hope the editor at *Signature* didn't want the entire rewrite because you included Amelia Perrier's name. I read the Carré *Small Town in Germany* and enjoyed it, but it's the sort of book you read and immediately forget . . . or at least, I did. Why don't you want to fall in love with A.'s writing or B.'s writing? It makes reading so much more fun. Or I should think it would, for anyone. Or perhaps I don't know what you mean by "fall in love with," although it seems simple enough as a concept.

It's cold and clear now, and the ground is soaked with all the rain we've had, and the buttercups are up everywhere. Naturally from your letters I have no idea of whether you'll be coming for the holidays or not. I do know that Hannetta arrives on the 16th, and that the same night Tessa Codrington is giving a party, which seems terrible timing.

The American School gave a performance of two plays by Israel Horowitz last night at the Palais de Moulay Hafid. I stayed home and had my dinner quietly. I've been three times to see their presentations in that depressing ballroom, and last year I vowed to go no more. It's "arena" theatre, with the floodlights in your eyes the entire time. The kids burble and mumble in a variety of accents, and their voices bounce off the tile walls like marbles. The air is mausoleum-temperature, and everybody is afflicted with either head colds or bronchitis.

I'll be eager to hear the scandals Peggy Lewis recounts to you; I hope you don't forget them all.

TO CAROL ARDMAN

February 26, 1978
Tangier

I'm still spending most of my time doing the sound score for *Orestes*. Joe McPhillips returned night before last from the States. He hasn't been around yet, but John and Ellen Ann came by last night to tell me he was in a state of euphoria. What about, they couldn't grasp, but anyway, he was manic. He said everyone in America was so happy that each one had tears in his eyes. Tears of what? I asked John. Tears of gratitude for being American, he said. What's going on over there that could have given him such an impression? Has Nadia left Princeton for good? I hope not. What good will her presence in Tangier do her father? Apparently she's not sufficiently emancipated to disregard the old family pull. Here it's warmer, but very rainy and windy. Dan had a great time over Mouloud in Fez and Meknès, and thinks of returning during the Feast of the Throne next week. Mrabet is sick again with his liver; I haven't seen him all this week. You probably saw the big review in the Sunday *Times* Book Section, of Jane's book, by Francine du Plessix Gray. (That middle name I'm not sure about, but it's near enough to be recognizable.) In any case, it more than made up for the Broyard kharra that came out earlier. I hear there was a very good one in the *New Republic*, but I haven't seen it. Dan Halpern's secretary will send it. Did I tell you Jeffrey Miller now runs Cadmus Editions? He's going to publish Choukri's *Tennessee Williams in Tangier*. James Purdy writes he'll soon have a new novel out: *Narrow Rooms*. I don't know if I told you about Gavin's accident. Nearly two weeks ago he was hit by a motorcycle (out of control—no brakes) on the Old Mountain Road. He's still in bed, and has had to postpone his trip to Los Angeles. The Moroccan who hit him was, as he says, kiffed to the gills, and waved to him, leaving him lying flat on the road, as he went on down the hill. I see my time is up. I'll get back to *Orestes*. (I hope I don't have to rehearse the singers in the chorus. In fact, I won't!) Most of the time is taken getting background sounds on tape. When it accompanies singing, it has to have definite tonality. I enjoy doing it, no matter how hard it may be. And it generally is, because of lack of equipment.

TO BRION GYSIN
◆

March 17, 1978
Tangier

I intended to answer your letter when the announced cassette had arrived, but I notice yours is dated the 28th of February, and no cassette has yet appeared, so I write anyway. Besides, I'm in bed with grippe, a state which has gone on all week. The cassette may or may not put in an appearance; it's not the only item promised recently which is late in coming, naturally. The mail service gets constantly spottier.

I heard yesterday from Mister Burroughs; apparently he likes Boulder, even in winter. (I was there once in summer, and the climate seemed fine.)

The building boom here continues, with everything permanently torn up. Clearly it will never stop. Like the Costa del Sol, which is as chaotic and disembowelled today as it was in 1960 when the bulldozing began. The rich Moroccans get richer by the day, and the rest watch with a certain cynicism. Their attitude would seem to be: It won't last forever. The machine will break some day, and that will be nice.

Mrabet has been for three weeks in the Spanish Hospital after the removal of half his stomach. (I saw it subsequently, with a black Vesuvius rising up out of the slab of meat.) I hope he recovers. The remark sounds asinine; what I mean is that it has got infected, and the present abscess has affected his lungs, so he's not in good shape. When they go to pieces, they really explode.

No particular news. Tangier is visually monstrous, as of course are all the other cities here. But then, who expects anything else from this shopworn planet? Or from a race that has outlived its viability.

TO JOHN MARTIN,
BLACK SPARROW PRESS, SANTA BARBARA, CALIF.
◆

July 12, 1978
Tangier

On reading over Gore's foreword to my short stories, I came across another misstatement that I hadn't noticed before, for some strange reason. That is the listing of the Marquis de Sade as an "influence" on my writing. It heads the list of four French writers, one of whom I deleted months ago when you sent me the piece: Huysmans. I remember telling you that "to this day I still have never read any Huysmans." And now I must add Sade to the Huysmans deletion, for I also still have not read a book by him. (Although in 1950 I attempted *Les Cent Vingt Jours de Sodome*. Of course it's well-nigh unreadable.) So it would be nonsense to list either Huysmans or Sade. In his place one could put Lautréamont. (Gore's list is wholly arbitrary, invented by him . . . what he imagines my literary influences would have been—perhaps ought to have been, but weren't. I know his point is that the influences were "exotic" rather than American, but it would be better to name the right "exotics.") This could have been taken care of in proof-correcting, but why even set up the names in type?

Tennessee arrived night before last. We had dinner last night, and he'll be around this afternoon. One has to catch him while he's still in a place, or he's gone before one knows it. He appears and disappears without warning, and seldom does he say where he's going, or if he does, he goes somewhere else. Motivations?

I hope *The Voice* has reached you by now.

TO JOHN MARTIN,
BLACK SPARROW PRESS, SANTA BARBARA, CALIF.

August 11, 1978
Tangier

Fine; I'll bend my efforts to extracting a design of some sort for what Mrabet wants to call *The Beach Café and The Voice*. He seems to be under the impression that a photograph of himself at the café in question would make a cover. I reminded him that whatever picture of the author was to be used appeared inside the book at the back. "This time it will be on the front," he replied firmly. Knowing that at such moments there's nothing to be gained by further argument, I let the subject drop. I'll bring it up again in the hope that the instant I choose will find him in a more malleable state. I'll get something out of him eventually.

As to the timing of publication of the two books, I think the Mrabet book ought to appear first, inasmuch as the collected short stories and *Five Eyes* are both "my" books in a sense, and it seems logical to separate them by the Mrabet work. It remains to get a good cover design, which I'll do as soon as it seems practical. (At the moment we're in Ramadan, when absolutely nothing gets done. Mrabet spends all his time at his café preparing food for the clients to order once the sun has set and the cannon has been fired; consequently I see him seldom and for very short periods.)

Did I thank you for the J. C. Oates *Triumph of the Spider Monkey*? I read it twice. She has incredible versatility, and, I imagine, total faith in the power of her imagination. I hope she never succumbs to the contemporary mania for destroying the frontiers between fiction and fact. Anyway, thanks. I enclose the hand medallion of Mrabet. It might look less crude made smaller.

TO BRION GYSIN

September 7, 1978
Tangier

That cassette has not arrived. I'm assuming it hasn't been sent, but if it has, it must be lost by now. So summer is over and most visitors have left here to go back where they came from. The town now has traffic problems like any other, and the streets were never meant for long lines of cars. Better now to leave the car in one central spot and do everything on foot.

The mystery surrounding Gilles Dehon condenses. Who is he? What does he do? How does it happen that I keep receiving postcards from Egypt, Greece and other fairly far-flung places, interspersed with other messages from Paris? Now he says you're having an exhibit at the Beaubourg and have nothing to complain about.

Everyone says the picture Marguerite brought back and presented to the American School looks fine in its frame and setting. I haven't seen it since its framing and presentation.

No news. Tennessee was here in July for ten days. I saw him only twice, as he was busy with the friend he brought with him. A letter from Gore says someone called Ssecnirp Teregram (You know how he likes to spell everything backwards) was in Ravello complaining about Ynot. Here people come and go, including Beckett and Genet as usual. I don't know either of the two personnages. Mrabet's incision closed up finally (more than four months after having been made) and he's now back into heavy smoking. At least he didn't observe Ramadan, or he'd be back in the Hospital Español. Tangier grows bigger and uglier by the week: a city under construction, rather like the whole Costa del Sol fifteen years ago. (A typical modern mess.) The Mountain is going over to the Kuwaitis and Saudis—another way of becoming exclusively Moslem. I was cursed as a Jew and pelted with pebbles for clandestinely nibbling a galleta on the beach at Merkala during Ramadan. Not on the sand among the people—by myself sitting on a rock higher up. Chouf had l'yehoudi!* And so on. I think they've forgotten there are any Nazarenes left in Tangier. Maurice saw George Greaves coming toward him on the Boulevard Pasteur. As he came opposite him, he said: Hello. The man scarcely glanced at him, replied: Shalom, and continued. It wasn't George, but the rabbi en route to the synagogue there on the corner. Anyway, hasta luego.

TO WILLIAM BURROUGHS

November 31, 1978
Tangier

The muezzin has called a good many times since your letter from Boulder came. Apart from that, nothing much else has happened here. (They now have loudspeakers at the tops of the minarets so that the calls will be sure to awaken everyone sleeping within two miles; the call used to last two minutes or so. Now it lasts twenty-five minutes. The fejr is a regular signal for me to get up and shut my window and turn on the fan. Then I go back to sleep for another six hours.)

The news that interests most people the most is that gasoline has gone up to 2.53 Dh. a liter. With the dollar at 3.86 you can see how many dollars it costs to buy a gallon. In spite of the sinking dollar, many bazaars now have price-tags in dollars on their goods. They're willing to accept 200 dollars instead of 200 dirhams for that brass teapot.

Several people sent me clippings about the Nova Convention. Was it fun? I couldn't agree with what I read in the *Times*: that you are the Dickens of the Twentieth Century. (Anne Waldman, more or less.) If she'd said Lautréamont, or even Rimbaud, I could have seen my way to understanding. Dickens? With all his stuffy sentimentality? She says your readings remind her of his reading. How many times did she hear Dickens read, I wonder? I don't imagine you argued with her about it.

* Look at that Jew!

Gavin Lambert tells me he saw you recently in L.A., and that you seemed dubious about the wisdom of his living here. I have the feeling he won't be staying on much longer. He can come and go as he likes. I, on the other hand, can't even go to Gibraltar because Rabat doesn't recognize my existence. Peculiar.

TO HENRY MILLER
━━━━━━━━━━━━━━━━━━◆━━━━━━━━━━━━━━━━━━

January 21, 1979
Tangier

The letter you wrote Mohammed Mrabet produced more of an effect on me than it did on him. He brought it in the other day asking me to read it to him (that is, translate it for him). Of course he was pleased, particularly with the concept of writing with the guts, which made him reiterate: He's right, that man! He understands!

I showed him some pictures of you taken at various periods of your life, and tried to explain, more or less, who you are. Naturally he was very pleased, and appreciated your writing to him. Although he's published seven books, he's never read one, save for part of the Qoran when he was a boy at the mcid.

But I was the one who could fully appreciate your letter. It gave me the feeling that the years I'd spent gathering and translating Mrabet texts had paid off, that I'd been justified in keeping the style straight and devoid of decoration. There's no collaboration between us; I simply translate what comes up on the tape. And the tapes always advance the argument, as you say, "Simply and tellingly." My principal concern has been to avoid making it affectedly simple—*faux-naif*, if it doesn't sound natural, it doesn't exist. Thus your letter made me happy.

We shook hands and spoke for thirty seconds once in Northridge in 1968. I wish it had been longer, mais enfin and so forth. (The first thing of yours I read was "Dream of Mobile" in *View*. I remember the stir it caused in the little office there.)

Once again thank you for writing the letter.

TO JOHN MARTIN,
BLACK SPARROW PRESS, SANTA BARBARA, CALIF.

February 14, 1979
Tangier

I neglected to answer a question in your last letter; it had to do with the possibility of having William Morris send you the novella I mentioned (*Here to Learn*). I haven't even heard yet that it has arrived safely in New York. You suggested that after magazine publication (hypothetical) you'd like to see it. Yes, of course. Only it may be somewhat short for a volume, containing 57 pages of typescript. An advantage is that, like *The Big Mirror*, it's divided into twenty-two chapters.

Someone sent me, as I may have told you, a copy of *Always Merry and Bright*, the life of Henry Miller. In spite of being spattered with typos and sloppy writing it's good reading, largely because of the presentation of Miller's personality. Perhaps you've read it. I found it so interesting that I was constantly enraged by the misuse of words, misspellings and syntactical mutations, in such quantity that would have stopped me from reading most books. Yet I'm up to page 487. Miller must be an amazing man.

I await proofs, which I suppose will be along one day soon.

TO ROBERT KIRSCH,
LOS ANGELES TIMES

February 15, 1979
Tangier

I am in receipt of your letter of the third of February. I think I can answer it in a few brief sentences.

In the past few decades the reviewing of books (along with the writing, editing and publishing of them) has undergone a process of degeneration. In the light of the general cultural bankruptcy, this is an expected phenomenon. At present, newspaper criticism of books is a private matter between publisher and reviewer. The author who is seriously concerned about the reviews of his work is primarily interested in sales, not in writing. This is natural, and harmless enough for the

author, as long as he is clear in his own mind about it, and admits that his eye
is on money rather than the perfecting of his art.

TO WILLIAM BURROUGHS

April 11, 1979
Tangier

Your letter came during my six-week period of worrying about proofs for two
books which didn't arrive. One was Choukri's book *Tennessee Williams in Tangier* and the other my collected stories. Both were mailed in Santa Barbara,
although by different publishers. Then the editor of Black Sparrow wrote me,
"unnerved," "stunned" by a visit to his office by two detectives looking for me.
There it sounded like the beginning of a Ross McDonald mystery. A woman in
Santa Barbara had got rid of her husband by putting eight bullets into him;
among her papers was an unmailed letter to Peter Bowles, Black Sparrow Press,
etc. The detectives decided that Peter must be Paul, but refused to give the
woman's name or suggest what might be in the letter. So could it be that the
proofs were interfered with in Santa Barbara? I'd assumed that the trouble lay
right here, naturally.

Last week I received in the mail a copy of your Scientology-Ali's Smile book
in German, together with a letter asking for a volume of stories. I assume you've
dealt with these people, or rather, this woman, Sylvia Pogorzalek of Bonn.
Anything special to tell me about her?

John Hopkins and Ellen Ann are in the States, waiting for a child to be born.
Kuwaitis have bought Louise de Meuron's property. They and the Saudis are
buying the Mountain piece by piece, too. True believers will now sit in rooms
where infidels drank cocktails and discussed improper subjects.

No, I don't read Dickens either. I like *Huckleberry Finn* (at least, the first
three quarters of it) better.

I hope all's well.

TO HENRY MILLER

September 7, 1979
Tangier

I agree with you about doing things slowly; now that I think of it, it's one of the reasons why I'm still here. One can set one's life metronome at the speed that seems convenient for living. In the States, the constant reminder that time is passing, that one must be quick, removes all the savor of being in the midst of living.

You ask about New Directions. Laughlin did not handle my first book very professionally, and since his principal editor was leaving for Random House, I went along with him for the next three books. It's dangerous to have a publisher who has no interest in making money. (He'd already had his accountants complete his 1949 income tax in December, so he couldn't afford to make anything on *The Sheltering Sky* until after December 31st. Thus he printed only 3,500 copies in 1949. But it's not interesting, that long saga. At one point he decided to sue my agent.)

Probably the Moroccans would have made good Zoroastrians, but they weren't given the opportunity. The Moslems arrived here, finding groups of Jews and Christians scattered here and there. It was a question of: Islam or else. The city-dwellers are still trying to get rid of the animistic sub-stratum that prevails in the countryside.

The work involved in writing a letter for Mrabet is minimal, being both easier and quicker than writing a letter in which I have to think of what I'm saying. It counts as nothing weighed against the excitement and pleasure Mrabet gets when he receives a letter from you. Anyway, he's glad to know that you received his last letter and his drawing. At the moment he's writing a book about his wife.

It's possible that the stories of my collection recommended by Vidal aren't the ones you would find the most interesting. I'm glad you're reading the book.

TO JEFFREY MILLER

November 1, 1979
Tangier

I'm glad to be able to report that the moment of sacrifice is over, has been over for three hours. Nothing is left but the heavy smoke that hangs over the city and the nauseating odor it carries, penetrating the house with everything shut against it. About thirty thousand sheep were killed in Tangier this morning, in spite of the very high prices they fetched this year, averaging $200 each, which makes about six million dollars the people in town paid out, simply for their sheep, and another million at least for the special food that has to go with the mutton. The high price is partially accounted for by the government's taking about $30 on each sheep as a war-tax. A useful system whereby piety pays for bombs.

I had a note from Susan Dwyer of *Antaeus* yesterday, saying that she'd sent a manuscript to you. I'd asked her to, without having any idea as to whether it might interest you. It evokes a period of American life which seems terribly distant now, when everything appeared to be running smoothly, and pleasures were direct and simple. I don't know whether I ever showed you the diary itself when you were here; probably not. It was among the papers I took from my parents' house ten years ago. Fortunately I had it with me, so that Andreas Brown did not have a chance to send it with almost everything else to Austin.

I offered *Next to Nothing* to John Martin; I don't know whether he'll want it. I thought it was time it had another edition, since the present one is now listed at $150, according to a rare-book catalogue I received a fortnight ago. Let me hear.

THE 1980S

(To Those Interested in Surviving the Coming Decade)
[Published in *Le Journal de Tanger*, Tangier, Morocco,
Saturday, January 12, 1980]

[January 1980]
Tangier

We are aware that this message is addressed to a tiny minority of people who, for one reason or another, prefer to continue their existence during the Nineteen Eighties. The democratic ideal, upon which the civilization of the Twentieth Century is widely believed to rest, demands that any minority, however small, must be taken into consideration. The following suggestions are proffered with the aim of preventing unnecessary suffering.

For those who have already applied to Humanity International for their VQ Tabs (personal cyanide pellets) there is no problem, save perhaps for some who live in rural areas of the more remote countries. Deliveries are being speeded up, however, and by April it is predicted that every citizen of every country which recognizes our organization can be provided with his own tablet, to be used at his discretion.

A word of warning (which is by no means a digression) is in order at this point. Recently the market has been flooded with a spate of inferior and dangerous brands of cyanide (Zoffo, Suremort, Hallelujah, Adios and others). These products are definitely not approved by Humanity International, and we cannot advise too strongly against their use. Death has been known to take a full half-hour in the case of Adios, according to a report issued by the research laboratories of the Attu Branch of Humanity International in November 1979. Those interested in the ideal escape will not find a product equal to our approved VQ Tabs; they are buffered, with added salidehydro-cyanuro-desoxycholic acid. The only safe pellet, the only one guaranteeing instant relief. No coma, no pain. Our service is absolutely gratis, as we constantly attempt to make clear in our thousands of broadcasts carried out in sixty-three languages. Unfortunately, human nature being what it is, suspicion is always aroused by the distribution of gifts; people feel that something paid for must be superior to something handed out free of charge, and this suspicion has been exploited by several unscrupulous pharmaceutical companies eager to profit by the present popularity of cyanide.

Humanity International does not, as has been charged, "recommend" the use of its VQ Tabs; it simply supplies them to those who ask for them. The worldwide response to our offers speaks for itself. In order partially to offset the accusations that have been levelled at the organization, we seize this occasion to address ourselves to the minority, to those hardy individuals who have decided to make the attempt to get through the entire decade without medical assistance.

First let us consider sustenance. It goes without saying that luxuries such as meat, fish, poultry, milk, eggs, butter, sugar, fruit and vegetables will soon be unobtainable. The recently developed protein substitutes such as Protoproxy should be used in quantity. An entirely new attitude toward food must be adopted. The concepts of "edible" and "inedible" must be abandoned. Both are preconceived ideas which are no longer applicable to reality. It has been proven, for instance, that cats, dogs and rats will not only sustain life indefinitely if eaten in sufficient quantity, but that truly excellent dishes can be prepared with them by the efficient housewife. With an eye to preserving the gourmet tradition during the coming years, Humanity International has issued three useful handbooks: *Fifty Tasty Kitty Recipes, Man's Best Friend and How to Cook Him* (which lists breeds and culinary treatment appropriate to each breed), and *The Rat Comes into His Own* (with a special chapter on the preparation of mice). For the first time in history these readily available sources of food, formerly used only in extreme situations and totally without scientific supervision, have been studied assiduously by top-flight dieticians and chefs, whose expertise is now within the reach of anyone who wishes to profit by it.

The kind of foodstuffs we enjoy today will be in increasingly short supply, due largely to lack of fuel for delivery. We must learn the science of harvesting and preserving all edible plants. Each year billions of tons of weeds go to waste and disintegrate into the soil, only to produce more unused weeds. This great natural resource must be exploited. It is true that citizens of tropical countries will be likely to have greater access to food, but this advantage will be outweighed by the incidence of disease.

Money will not be a problem, since it will be entirely without purchasing power. In addition, the list of purchasable commodities will rapidly shrink to zero.

Living space, on the other hand, will present intolerable difficulties to those accustomed to personal privacy. Because of the geometric progression in population increase and the impossibility of constructing new dwellings or even repairing old ones, requisitioning of floor-space will shortly be instituted. The target of fifteen cubic meters minimum to be allocated to each adult is admittedly utopian, at least during the coming decade. For the foreseeable future the figure will remain in the vicinity of ten cubic meters. Since people who previously enjoyed the use of an entire house or apartment will now be restricted to one corner of one room, a certain amount of dissatisfaction, even of confusion, may result. A few practical hints here may be useful.

There are always ways of making your corner comfortable, even attractive. Cut out a large triangle of thick foam rubber (if you are unable to find any, bags of straw or shavings will do) and fit it into the corner on the floor. On top of that you can pile attractive rags and stuffed sacks. The walls behind can be covered with artistically chosen magazine covers or tasteful advertisements, varnished over. If you have time, you can cut them up first and make personalized collages. A screen to provide a modicum of privacy can be constructed out of old crates, and perhaps covered with wrapping paper to give it that soigné look demanded by today's housewife.

The idea that fresh air is essential for healthy sleep was discarded by medical experts fifty years ago. It has been proven that, on the contrary, the instinct of the human species is to burrow deep into a relatively airless spot when sleep is desired. Apart from the possibility of contagious diseases, it is just as healthy to sleep shut into a room with several others as it was to sleep in your own room with the window open. Actually this enforced communal living can prove to be a blessing. It serves as a deterrent to mass attacks on living quarters by bands of starving teen-agers.

Survival in the Eighties will require enormous adaptability to adverse physical circumstances. A new, functional life-style is waiting to be created, one which will take into account the future as well as the present rapid deterioration of the situation. This requires a high order of talent, but there will be those who will rise to the occasion. Reduced circumstances need not, and indeed, must not be allowed to result in shabbiness, which comes from a morbid clinging to concepts of style no longer realizable. We must learn that the only consideration of any importance in the matter of clothing is that it should provide the warmth essential to normal human functioning. As the seasons change, the number of garments will vary, and from this simple phenomenon we can evolve a style that will be the very essence of sartorial elegance. Instead of the three sweaters, blanket and mittens of winter, we find that when spring comes, we may have only two sweaters and no blanket at all. It is from such small things that we create the poetry of a truly functional life-style. The greatest pleasure comes from the close inspection of ordinary objects, we are told. Those who have chosen to brave it out can reap spiritual profit, if they will, from this unique opportunity.

Your corner need not be in total darkness every night. You can make your own lamps out of rags soaked in vegetable oil, squeezed into interesting shapes and placed in oil-filled saucers. They give a dull, romantic glow. A welcome addition to gala affairs is a set of small alcohol burners to be used as hand-warmers. (Stock all the burning alcohol you can now; during a cold spell it has been known to make the difference between life and death.) The ideal garment for winter corner-sitting is a large woolen blanket with a slit in the center for the head. Your corner can be made cozy, and you can be comfortable in it. It is up to you to decide whether you want to make the effort.

We at Humanity International believe firmly that if it is worthwhile living at all (and a few of those who read this will be of the opinion that it is) then it is also worthwhile to spend the effort necessary to transform what could otherwise be a humdrum existence into a meaningful life, a life of joy created, not in spite of hardships, but thanks to them. This is Humanity International's New Year message to the courageous.

Remember, VQ Tabs are always yours for the asking.

Paul Bowles
Director of Public Relations
Humanity International

TO HANS BERTENS

◆

January 25, 1980
Tangier

I was pleased to have your letter of January twenty-second. Re: *Up above the World*, yes, I think your assumption of assessment and condemnation by the author was unjustified, and probably got in the way of your understanding what the book was about. It's interesting, too, that you mention the same assumption regarding Port Moresby. (Yes, I knew it was in New Guinea.) But clearly you're taking for granted a prejudice on the part of the author against one of his characters where absolutely none was either felt or shown in the text. The voice of the narrator in dealing with Amar is necessarily different from the voice of the narrator telling about Soto, but they are both noncommittal, neutral, content to describe and not judge. I'd say if the writer shows any feeling with regard to Norton, Moresby and Soto, it's one of sympathy—at least, sufficient sympathy to observe them in a tolerant fashion.

"The Hours after Noon" is a tale about how a woman's subconscious fastens together bits of information about a man in such a way that in ridding herself of his presence she also has him murdered; she becomes aware of what the hidden part of her mind has done only after the death of her victim. I didn't think it presented any problems. (With regard to Mr. Van Siclen; the surname is what we think of in the States as an "old American name." There is a Van Siclen Avenue in Brooklyn. Also a De Kalb Avenue! It didn't occur to me that the name was specifically Dutch when I used it, I assure you. It's as American as Roosevelt or Vanderbilt. Very likely the spelling was altered three centuries ago. Perhaps I should have said Mr. Van Siclen was American; I suppose I thought it would be apparent from his dialogue. I certainly never meant him to be mistaken for Dutch.)

There was a point you brought up in your previous letter, when you said you had a Calvinist upbringing, and that you suspected I had as well. I don't know; to me a Calvinist background sounds vaguely religious, as though behavior were based on some fixed set of religious principles. This was not at all the case with me. None of my grandparents and neither of my parents was affiliated with any church; they did not believe in attending church. Being New Englanders, they were Puritans by tradition, but they were also agnostics. (I admit that the agnosticism would not necessarily cancel out the puritanism, but it might make it a little less codified in its application to behavior.)

To get back to Dutch names: it's not surprising that Kristians Tonny's name doesn't sound Dutch. His father's name was Antonius Johannes Kristians, and Tonny was Tony Kristians.

"Doña Faustina": the important consideration here is not the number of babies killed, but the number of their hearts devoured by Doña Faustina. She believed she could transmit the power of thirty-seven to her offspring. And although he knew nothing about the hearts, he suddenly was given the power of life and death over thirty-seven men. He exercised it and was thereby made happy, thus bringing good out of evil. I think it's made clear that the writer is sympathetic to the idea of freeing the bandits.

It was very conscientious of you to reread *Up above the World*; I'm glad you came around somewhat to my viewpoint about it. Day Slade is not presented as any more admirable than Soto—just more ordinary. It would be confusing to let her views on Soto influence one. She is a completely uninteresting woman whose stock reactions to what the reader suspects are extreme situations help to set off Vero's eccentric personality. I think this is enough for one letter!

TO JOHN HOPKINS

February 1, 1980
Tangier

I haven't had an answer to my last letter, so I assume it never reached you. This year postal disappearance is more common than last, I've noticed; many items fail to arrive instead of a few. It seems we've both been engaged in sending letters to the paper, the difference being that yours was a real letter to a real paper, while mine is a fake letter sent to *Le Journal de Tanger* (enclosed). Roditi has a reply to it (in French) appearing in tomorrow's edition. He claims to have a company named Avatar which converts human corpses into cat food, dog food, and rat food, and for no extra charge will print the portrait of the deceased on the label of the tin. I wish Gavin hadn't gone to Guatemala, or you to England, so that we could have a whole series of such letters, objecting, agreeing, suggesting, accusing. It would be rather like Roditi's *Vampires of Istanbul*, the story made up of nothing but newspaper letters and editorials.

Dan Halpern was here for three days, or perhaps I told you earlier. A reception tomorrow at Forbes's for the new ambassador in Rabat. I hope it's not seized by the guerrilleros of Asilah.

Nothing to report. Today is exactly like a very clear day in June. Hot, with a few cool veins in the air now and then. One such day makes ten thousand cases of grippe two days later among the Moroccans. They're all out lying on the ground as though it were actually summer. Una cosa fatal.

I hear the new landlord of your house won't allow people into your flat unless they pay extra. Isn't that a bit thick?

All best, and hi to Ellen Ann.

TO PETER GARLAND

March 11, 1980
Tangier

Yours of the twenty-first of February reached me yesterday, and I'm glad to see that I can still reach you in Patzcuaro. Or can I? This may not get there before the first of April, since the trajectory seems to take roughly three weeks.

The University of Texas is at Austin. I'm looking forward to the appearance of Mr. Buckner later this month, realizing it's suppositious and not at all certain.

It's difficult for me to know exactly how many instruments each piece is written for, since I haven't access to the scores. *The Wind Remains* has about ten, as I recall, all woodwind, brass and percussion, with one electric violin and two singers. (The MGM recording is execrable; Carlos Surinach, who conducted, had his own ideas about tempi, some of which were exactly twice as slow as they should have been, others being speeded up into nonsense. He didn't like the idea of an American setting García Lorca, anyway. Bernstein, on the other hand, whatever you may think of him, did a fine job, possibly because I was present all the time at rehearsals, but principally because he understood and liked the music.) I'll look up the *Herald Tribune* reviews and send them along when you have a fixed residence. I did write a few pieces on jazz and popular music for *View*. I have more or less a complete run of the magazine, and can find them if you're interested.

I just thought of a work that might be considered: *Music for a Farce* (1938). Clarinet, trumpet, piano and percussion. On the other hand, it's probably my best-known work simply because it's been recorded three times. (Not that any of my works is what could be called "well-known"; but relatively.)

I didn't know you were interested in Isabelle Eberhardt. In 1931, when I lived at 17 Quai Voltaire, a little elderly woman who lived in the same building used to regale me with stories about Eberhardt. The raconteuse was Lucie Delarue-Mardrus, a novelist whose husband had translated *Les Mille et Une Nuits* into French, and I was more interested in her than in this woman of whom I'd never heard, who had lived in the desert and died there. Cocteau mentions her in glowing terms, but I became interested only in the 'fifties when I read Blanch's piece on her. Then I found the Mackworth.

TO GARY CONKLIN

———————————◆———————————

March 28, 1980

Tangier

The Greene film book is a delight. It illumes a whole new (to me) facet of his talent. I'd read only his literary criticism, and was completely unaware he'd done film criticism. First I read the reviews of films I'd seen, and agreed wholeheartedly with his opinions; then I read the reviews of films I'd heard of but never seen, and finally those of films that were unknown to me. What's extraordinary about the reviews is that one gets just as much out of those concerning material about which one knew nothing beforehand. That's surely a sign of good critical functioning!

I love his assessment of W. C. Fields and Garbo; no one has encapsulated their essence as he has. And I was happy to find a review of one of my favorite films, *Son of Mongolia*, and to be reminded of certain details which hadn't crossed my mind in forty-two years, and to find that he liked the same details. (Nobody seems to have seen that picture, and I suppose it's not surprising. The only Russian films that seem to be revived regularly are Eisenstein's.) Anyway, many thanks for sending the book; I'll enjoy it for a long time to come.

Nothing much happens here. Yesterday I received copies of *The Beach Café and The Voice*, Mrabet's new book from Black Sparrow. And someone wrote me from L.A. expressing interest in making a film out of "The Eye," a new story which the man saw in the 1979 *Best American Short Stories*. If you've read it, you'll wonder, as I do, why he'd think it a good one to use, when there are plenty of better ones for that purpose.

Hasta luego, ojalá, and all best.

TO PETER GARLAND

September 11, 1980
Tangier

I should have written you earlier, when the cassette of Madagascar items arrived, but I wanted at the same time to send you the promised Concerto and Cantata. Whatever I made turned out to be so objectionable that I waited and used borrowed equipment. I hope you have the tape by the time you receive this; it was sent about ten days ago, I should think. In any case, the Malgache music is delightful, varied, and performed with finesse. I was astonished to hear European harmony and harmonic sequences. My driver listened, and remarked: Ah, they've gone to the Conservatory. Shortly, when another genre came up (without harmonizing), he remarked: These haven't gone to the Conservatory. And I suppose it's a fairly accurate observation, if one lets "conservatory" imply a contact of some sort with urban culture. Certainly the French made an all-out effort to "civilize" the Malgaches during their occupation, and found them exceptionally amenable to foreign influences. (I notice that the music seems to please everyone who hears it, which is surely of importance if one is evaluating it.) Thank you for adding it to my collection, such as it is.

I received the *Soundings* announcement today. I'm happy to know you haven't abandoned its publication; there's an enormous need for it.

I spent today out in the Anjra. Beautiful country: valleys and peaks on one side and on the other the entire strait spread out below, and the mountains of Spain beyond. I sat on the limb of an old fig tree that kept letting fall very sweet black figs, and listened for a sound of some sort. It came only as the whirring of partridges now and then. There was an American along who had never been scorpion-catching, and was perhaps a bit incredulous about it. Naturally a scorpion had to be produced for him, to show him how easy it was once one learned to recognize their doorways (which are everywhere). A spear of palmetto coated with saliva is bait; once they seize it you pull slowly; when you see their pincers you jerk them out into the open. Today's was garnet red and very combative. I decreed that it should not be killed. But they sting people! Abdelouahaid objected; according to his way of thinking it was evil and should be destroyed.

Any word from Buckner? Thanks again for the tape.

TO WENDY LESSER,
THE THREEPENNY REVIEW,
BERKELEY, CALIF.

————————————◆————————————

October 25, 1980
Tangier

Yes, I recovered quickly from whatever malady the students forgot in my flat. My recipe for swift reinstatement of health is to sleep twelve hours a night. But try that in the United States!

I wonder what your beautifully candid student had in mind when she claimed she had a hard time *thinking*. I suppose we've arrived at a point where no shame attaches to such an admission. Amusing, but ominous, I'd say.

I hope Gore comes across with the promised piece; if he agreed, then I believe he will. It seems to me an excellent idea for a regular feature, if you can find an articulate writer every three months. (God knows Gore is nothing if not articulate! More than that, his criticism is a pleasure to read.)

I shouldn't want to have to exchange the freedom to publish whatever one wants with the possible heightening of quality resulting from censorship. We won't produce the equivalent of *samizdat* writing until we need to, will we? I suppose that will come, but I hope not for a while.

I can understand your feeling about the back-room at the Gotham Book Mart, but it seems to me that *The Threepenny Review* has already differentiated itself sufficiently to be free of "identity" problems. I agree that this doesn't guarantee success, but it's a sine qua non for achieving the only kind of success you want.

Your mother is probably right: a review isn't a book, and needs the sort of hustling she suggests. (Although it seems that these days even books have to be hustled. My first intimation of this new sort of literary world came long ago: in 1949 Truman Capote sat over lunch at the Farhar here and expounded Bennett Cerf's opinion that a writer had to help sell his own works, had to be a tout, a barker, a town crier (an idiot, I thought to myself) if he expected to have success. Subsequently Truman told me that at least fifty percent of his time was taken up with this sort of salemanship; this confidence came in the 'fifties.)

With regard to Reagan, unfortunately I don't feel "well away from it all." It's one world, no matter where you are.

TO MILLICENT DILLON

November 21, 1980
Tangier

I can imagine how disturbing those optical phenomena must have been, because I've had the identical trouble from time to time since I was about twenty. The first time the fluorescent zigzags began to flash across my field of vision I was sure I had syphilis or leprosy or some dire disease that would finish me off. I went to a doctor in Paris, who took the whole thing very lightly, calling it "migraine ophthalmique." Since then there have been whole periods involving years when I thought they'd gone forever. Then, if I'm fatigued, something can begin flashing and blinking somewhere behind my eyes, and I know it's going to spread and curl and cover the whole field of vision. "So it's back again," I think, and if I can, I lie down for the length of time it takes the whole little TV show to disappear, which it generally does in about a half hour or even less. Usually there's no pain with it, but occasionally there is, in the region of a temple. The main trouble with all that is that one can't see while it's going on . . . or at least, see well. If you can remain in perfect health, I don't believe the symptoms return to bother you. But try that! Because by "perfect health" I mean never being in the least nervous about anything, and always taking one's time, and sleeping nine hours every night, and so on! No one ever gave me an electroencephalograph, or I should probably have worried about the condition all these years. My doctor told me it was a question of eating and sleeping correctly. So I think you can relax, at least insofar as its dangers go. But can anyone like you or me remain always in a state of relaxation?

I haven't yet completed that roll of film, so I have no pictures of the house at Farsioua. I'm working on something new which I call *Points in Time* (non-fiction). I look forward to seeing proofs of the biography. Mrabet has arrived, so good-bye.

TO WENDY LESSER,
THE THREEPENNY REVIEW,
BERKELEY, CALIF.

January 14, 1981
Tangier

Since the galleys of your mother's Jane Bowles book arrived yesterday, I've done nothing but read them. (It's a nasty experience for me seeing myself in it: a kind of idiot looking on approvingly, even collaborating, while Jane forged ahead with her self-destruction. Of course, only hindsight makes that apparent.)

I'm delighted that you want to use "Rumor and a Ladder." Certainly I'm free to let you have it. As to the copyright, however, I'm not certain whether John Martin of Black Sparrow has already copyrighted the materials for *Midnight Mass* or not. Somehow I doubt it. In any case, you can inquire, and proceed accordingly, copyrighting it in my name if it isn't already protected. I put in the numbers purposely, but I don't suppose they're essential, if for any reason you'd like to suppress them. I do think the big spaces between "chapters" are needed, in the event you decide to do away with the numerals. For my part, I like the numbers, which further separate one part from the next.

I think J. C. Oates is wildly uneven. Probably that's a natural concomitant of prolificity and virtuosity. And she does write a great deal. Some of her stories are absolutely first-rate, some very good, some unnecessary.

Thanks for offering to send proofs; I always appreciate it.

I'll hope to be hearing from you.

TO STEVE MILLER,
RED OZIER PRESS, NEW YORK

TO STEVE MILLER,
RED OZIER PRESS, NEW YORK

February 8, 1981
Tangier

Many thanks for the books, which arrived day before yesterday. Those who have seen them have admired them.

You told me that you intended to include artwork in the Rey Rosa book. This set me thinking. It would be ideal if the artist you choose to supply this were to do proto-Mayan designs, like those in the codices. Don't you agree that European-looking illustrations or decorations would detract from the basic ambience of the text, which is an evocation of both the past and the present Central American scene?

Do you ever see Rey Rosa? I have no idea where he is, but I suppose he's still in New York at the School of Visual Arts.

This year everyone is going to be very sad in Morocco. There has been no rain since last May, and as a result there will be no crops this summer. The earth is as hard as rock, and to make sure that everything would be killed God provided the coldest winter in fifty-four years, so that whatever life was left in the ground was frozen solid for a month. All this is particularly bad for a nation at war (and a defensive war, in the bargain). It would be nice if the United States could understand this, and come across with a bit of aid for Morocco. (After all, she's trying to keep the Soviets from getting an Atlantic port, which Libya and Algeria are doing their best to get for the U.S.S.R.) But the game of politics must be played otherwise.

TO RODRIGO REY ROSA

May 9, 1981
Tangier

Gracias por las páginas de la obra nueva. Tienen el mismo encanto, el mismo misterio, de las que se van a publicar por Red Ozier. Comprendo su deseo de expandir su trabajo; es normal y necesario, ese deseo, y espero que siempre lo tendrá.

El único peligro en tales momentos, me parece, consiste en querer cambiarlo (su manera natural de escribir) en lugar de dejarlo como está ahora, guiandolo mientras que se extiende de su propia manera, sin forzarlo! Por ejemplo, si escoje en el principio una materia que exige tal ensanche, todo vendrá naturalmente. Y sin miedo de emplear diálogo, lo que emplearía solamente cuando una frase hablada parece imprescindible, y aun en esos momentos con el mínimo de palabras—tres o cuatro, punto. Idealmente el diálogo debería puntuar la prosa como tiros de fusil puntuan el silencio. Entre menos, más fuerte en su efecto. Así lo veo yo. Como digo, hay que encontrar un "argumento" antes, uno que va a necesitar un tratamiento más amplio, y aplicar la misma técnica. Poco a poco el terreno se extendera más con cada obra, si así lo quiere Ud.

Sobre las formas teatrales no puedo hablar. No las recomiendo para uno que no tiene una gran facilidad en inventar diálogo.

Espero que esta carte illegará antes de su salida de New York. Y la dirección en Guatemala que me dió, aun sirve? * * * Espero recibir de sus noticias antes que viaje.*

TO PHIL NURENBERG

June 11, 1981
Tangier

To answer your postcard, I do remember my meeting with Anaïs Nin in New York; that is, I remember one particular meeting on Eighth Street in the snow.

---

* Thanks for the pages from the new work. They have the same charm, the same mystery as those Red Ozier is going to publish. I understand your desire to expand your work; such a desire is normal and necessary, and I hope you'll always have it.

The only danger in such moments, it seems to me, is wanting to change it (your natural way of writing) instead of allowing it to remain as it is now, guiding it while it extends in its own way, without forcing it. For example, if you choose at the outset a subject that requires this kind of expansion, then it will all come naturally. And you won't be afraid of using dialogue, which you'll use only when a spoken sentence seems absolutely necessary, and even in those moments with a minimum of words—three or four, period. Ideally, dialogue should punctuate prose the way rifle shots punctuate silence. The less it's used, the stronger its effect. That's how I see it. As I say, you've got to find a "story" first, one that will need a fuller treatment, and apply the same technique. Little by little, with each work, the terrain will grow larger and larger, if that's the way you want it.

I can't speak about dramatic forms. I don't recommend them to anyone who doesn't have great facility in inventing dialogue.

I hope this letter arrives before you leave New York. Is the address in Guatemala you gave me still good? * * * I hope to receive news from you before you travel.

(I probably had already met her indoors previously . . . it seems to me I had, years, before, and Noguchi and Tamayo were there. Or perhaps I'm hallucinating.) In any case, the snow scene remains. Jane and I had just left a grocery store in Eighth Street, and I was carrying a very voluminous paper bag. The idea was to get home to Tenth Street as fast as possible. But Nin appeared, and engaged Jane in the longest conversation on record while I stood trying to keep the melting snow from dissolving the bag. After forty minutes Nin went on her way; she had been telling Jane how much she disliked Jane's novel. So obviously I never forgot the meeting. Perhaps ten years ago she wrote to me, a honeyed letter, which I couldn't bring myself to answer. Then she died. What interested me about her was the fact that she was a bigamist for years, with one husband in New York and one on the Pacific Coast, and (so they say) neither one knew of the other's existence. Apparently she removed the dust jackets of her books when she was with her Pacific husband, because there was mention of Hugo somewhere in the blurbs. The only true bigamist I've ever known. (I might add that Jane subsequently received an eight-page letter from Nin, detailing the faults in the novel. We had great fun with that.)

I never knew Leary very well, although I saw him many times here on his several visits to Tangier, the first having been in 1961. We always got on perfectly together.

TO MILLICENT DILLON

July 1, 1981
Tangier

I've read and reread the book so often that it's made me dream of Jane. The scene I remember most vividly is one where she and I were sitting with others around a table talking. Suddenly she becomes fractious and began to upbraid me. I was angry, so I rose and walked toward the door. I heard her call out: Good bye. And then I heard myself saying: There is no good bye from me to you. As I walked through the doorway I woke up. (The first dream I ever had of Jane where we weren't on good terms.)

I envy you if you're able to sustain a uniform degree of interest throughout *Ulysses*. People are always saying they do. People also claim to be clairvoyant and to levitate.

I found the story of the Franciscan monk in a volume of The Royal Geographical Society's Supplementary Papers. I had the book when you were here; perhaps I showed it to you.

I was interested in your tale about the transsexual. Did he give any understandable reasons why he wanted to undergo such trouble and pain?

My students will appear any day now. ¡Qué lástima!

TO WENDY LESSER,
THE THREEPENNY REVIEW,
BERKELEY, CALIF.

October 25, 1981
Tangier

Having heard from my agent that Peter Owen in London wants to publish *Points in Time* as soon as possible, I thought I ought to communicate the information to you in the event that you prefer to print the three excerpts from it you've selected before they appear in book form. Not that the book would have widespread distribution in the States, I'm sure. I just thought I'd notify you so you could use the pieces in the Winter Issue if you preferred.

Even though I'm not a partisan of the heroic present for use in fiction save for special effects (rather like cut-ups) I enjoyed Kate Wheeler's story about the mythomaniacs. The tense didn't bother me after the first few paragraphs. I suppose the reason writers like to use it is that they imagine it brings the action closer, making everything more immediate. A fallacy! Because of its artificiality (recounting a past action in the present tense in conversation works only in the most colloquial sort of dialogue, and generally, when used in writing, for humorous purposes) the heroic present places the action one step farther away by hanging this literary scrim between the reader and the recounting of the action. I think it's a device which should be used sparingly.

We slid through the Aid el Kebir with a minimum number of sheep sacrificed. (The king had recommended not slaughtering millions of sheep this year because of the drought; with his sanction as spiritual ruler people were free to abstain. A great help.)

◆

March 6, 1982

Tangier

I have yours of 26/ii. and thanks. Also for your brief exposition of contemporary American tendencies. Is there an organization known as the Moral Majority? You mentioned it, but what is it? I've never heard of it. (Like the League of Decency which used to exist, and maybe still does, for all I know, or the Blue Laws of certain states?) I assume all such groups are organized primarily to fight pornography, or is that not their principal aim? But printed pornography is one thing, and being preoccupied with other people's lives is something very different. Other people's lives are an abstraction like good, evil, truth, justice, and so on; how can one spend energy worrying about such things? As soon as one does, one is functioning in a vacuum. Good-bye, rationality. Farewell, intellect. Sexuality is personal; that of others has no meaning, and certainly no interest, any more than the accounts of surgical interventions a person has undergone. Your description of what people are like nowadays there is enough to keep me from ever returning, and from caring what further ravages they make on their culture. How can such a society remain viable for long? But I suppose it will outlast me!

Have you ever read *El Periquillo Sarniente*, the great Mexican picaresque novel? Katherine Anne Porter made a fine translation of it. I recommend it if you're vacationing in Mexico. (I believe the author is Lizardi, but it's several decades since I read the book.) How about *The Plumed Serpent*, for all its "power-of-the-blood" nonsense? No one has ever described Jalisco as beautifully as Lawrence. Flandrau's *Viva México* is another delight. Anyway, I hope you find some good places down there.

I look forward to seeing the new *Threepenny Review*.

◆

November 19, 1982

Tangier

Your letter of the ninth reached me this afternoon, recounting your relaxation of schedule in London. I was interested to hear you'd met Ruth Fainlight then for the first time. I haven't seen her in nearly twenty years, although we correspond occasionally, and she sends me her books. When I first met her and Alan Sillitoe they were living in the same building where I live.

About *Up above the World* I think you could say that Part One is a prologue which supplies enough circumstantial evidence to make one pretty certain that Vero has killed his mother. This establishes him as the evil hero of the book. Then the action begins. I think the first "hint," as you called it, that something could be amiss is: "If only my son had been able to meet me. So unnecessary . . ." One wonders fleetingly, I should think, what sort of son this is who can't manage to meet his mother who has come from England to see him? But then the "hints" or subliminal suggestions come fast and furious.

Going back to *Up above the World* (I'm rereading your letter), I suppose Part Four (Thorny's recapitulation) qualifies as a flashback. At the same time it repeats the events narrated in Part Two (Chap. 15), adding motivational detail completely lacking in the prior recounting. In a film I'd show the same trip twice, the first time briefly, as though Vero and Thorny were making a jaunt down to the coast to seabathe, and then again in the context of Thorny's recap. I'd use the same shots, to emphasize the message: We've made this trip before, but it's different now.

Anyway, I was glad to hear from you.

TO STEPHEN DAVIS
<hr />

December 11, 1982
Tangier

Thanks for yours of the twenty-second November, with enclosures. I do have the King Crimson cassette * * *

Ordinarily I don't like rock. But there seems to have been discovered a way out, which it's clear could lead to something important. (John Hassel, David Byrne, etc. are making contact with Steve Reich, which is a healthy sign. King Crimson in The Sheltering Sky is sniffing the way out.) Someone who seems to have mastered the new idiom is Richard Horowitz. Extreme subtlety, the general lack of which has always been shown in rock.

I'm not sure whether I wrote to thank you for sending the Charhadi book; I have a feeling I did, but that's not enough. I appreciate it, and have added it to the various editions of *A Life Full of Holes*.

No news. It's chilly here.

January 18, 1983
Tangier

Your letter of the second of January is with me; thank you.

I was interested in your comparison of *Points in Time* to *In the American Grain*, of which I'm particularly fond. Yet, not having that kind of mind, I hadn't previously put them together in my head. If I'm aware of any sort of similarity between what I'm doing and what has already been done, I can't go on. Later I may see resemblances, but that's after the fact. WCW was very far from my mind when I was working on PIT. I meant it to be a journey across time, with stops here and there along the way; naturally I chose stops which interested me.

It's too bad that Black Sparrow let *Harmless Poisons* go out of print. Mrabet became disillusioned about Black Sparrow some time ago, and found a new publisher, also in California, who is bringing out a new collection of his tales this spring. I've never heard *Harmless Poisons* read aloud—only spoken, and in Arabic, at the time of recording.

It's a good many years since I read *Manhattan Transfer*, or any Dos Passos, for that matter. I remember liking that and *The 42nd Parallel* at the time. Then Sartre and the War arrived, and I felt I knew Dos Passos, and went on to explore new territory, as one always does. (I never stopped to dally with Faulkner, though; I read the books, but didn't believe them, which meant never going back to them.)

This note is meant primarily to say that I hope you and the Fulbright come together, even though you say you think it would be foolish of their people to accord you the grant. That doesn't make sense.

January 26, 1983
Tangier

Many thanks for sending me the essay(s) by Metcalf. It/They contain interesting observations. Like most critics, however, he stresses the importance of the subject-matter. This presupposes that the writer has a preconceived idea of what he is going to do, and that this determines the writing used in order to accomplish the bringing forth of his idea. I think he would have reached other conclusions, perhaps not so complimentary, in any case quite distinct from those he expressed, if he had considered the possibility that the act of writing itself creates the subject-matter, and that the latter is merely a form, like a dressmaker's dummy, upon which to arrange the writing. Most of my fiction came into being in this manner, with the result that I'm always surprised to see what I've written, and at a loss to know why it's what it is. Therefore, since the material is not consciously controlled, it's difficult for me to consider it a phenomenon as interesting or meaningful as the writing which has engendered it. I doubt that Metcalf ever questions his basic assumption that a writer does not write unless he knows what he intends to write about. But this is by no means a foregone conclusion. After all, we settle down each night to dream without knowing what we're going to dream. The images and impressions arrange themselves automatically in such a way as to seem to have meaning—at least, during the duration of the dream, and occasionally even in retrospect.

So thanks again for your thoughtfulness.

TO GENA DAGEL

February 2, 1983
Tangier

Thank you for your letter of January twenty-seventh; it came unusually quickly.

I was surprised to hear you characterize my music as "cynical in tone," and am rather hard put to know what you mean. Perhaps you mean that certain pieces seem to be pastiches of past styles. It's hard to see how any music can be cynical.

The volume which Peter Garland is publishing is composed solely of songs. At the moment it's a long way from completion, there being many permissions still needed.

I was pleased to hear that Austin had an "underground" of Bowles enthusiasts. I shall probably be dead before it reaches any impressive proportions!

When I began to write *Let It Come Down* I planned it all in detail, save for the last section, which I left to take care of itself as the writing went ahead. Very likely I suspected, without thinking about it (which in that final part I scrupu-lously refrained from doing; deciding anything beforehand would have ruined the flow), that Dyar would have to do away with Thami. I just kept writing and let it happen the way it had to happen. I wonder where you saw the letter to my publisher saying that my characters had made a mess of the last part. I don't recall writing it, of course, but I see what I meant. The mess was resolved by Daisy's visit to the cabin.

I hope you're no longer curious about that matter. Thank you for keeping in touch with me.

TO RICHARD PEABODY

February 6, 1983
Tangier

I've reread the material by Paul Metcalf which you sent me, and as a result feel impelled to say to him: I'm over here, not over there where you're looking. Hide and seek, only the mystification is mutual. From various conjectures of his, I'm led to think that his mystification comes from a feeling of not having been successful in reaching what he might call the essence of the person beneath the writing. But what need is there of that? The writer is what he has written, and nothing more. I can see that Metcalf went through the books expecting to find elements which are not there. That's a common enough occurrence. What strikes me as inexplicable is that at no time does he pinpoint the qualities which he believes to be absent. Thence my own mystification. Let me take *Without Stopping*: he found it hard to understand why I wrote it, and suspected that it was undertaken for money. It was, indeed, and solely for that reason, although he seems to be disposed not to believe this, remarking that I never seemed to be "poor." My income always has been what I'd call minimal, and this is the best reason for never touching the capital which produces it. But if Metcalf read the autobiography he must have noted that Mrs. Bowles was constantly moving between hospitals in England, the United States and Spain. Even at that time this cost money. I decided that Putnam's offer of $15,000 would be of use, and undertook the writing of something I had every wish and reason not to write. (And since I hope that you will communicate some of these explanations to him, say that I was specifically requested by my editor to put in as many names as I could recall!) I'm fully aware that there is no acceptable pretext for writing a bad book. I knew this one would be bad before I started it, but I wrote it anyway, for money. Every minute of the writing went against the grain, because I found it a terrible bore and entirely devoid of interest.

On the other hand, Metcalf suspects that *Up above the World* also had a mercenary motive behind it, and in this he is quite mistaken. I simply wanted to see if I could write a "suspense" novel that would be unlike others of its genre. I wasn't so ingenuous as to imagine that it would be a commercial success, nor was it one, by any means. But I was happy to have published it, knowing that it was the best written of the four novels.

On page 41 Metcalf makes an odd remark: "this book, *and the life it represents, are* (is) *particularly flat."* (Italics mine) Then he adds: "He seems to *admit* this . . ." There is the implication here that writers generally lead exciting lives, and also, I think, the tacit assumption that the work is a by-product of the life, rather than the other way around. (Both are equally conceivable, as is the failure to see any connection between the two phenomena.) I suppose the idea is that if one has led a dull life one shouldn't write an autobiography, and with that I'd agree wholeheartedly. Most people, writers included, lead humdrum lives, but they can scarcely be faulted for that—only for recording them. So clearly whether the life is "flat" or not is beside the point. Back to the $15,000.

A few minor points; Metcalf draws a distinction between "The Frozen Fields" and "He of the Assembly" (page 34). The first he finds written with "persuasive clarity"; the second he calls a "fantasy." Both stories are wholly realistic, Donald imagining a wolf and He of the Assembly imagining a soup kettle and a boat. If the first is "thoroughly American," the second is thoroughly Moroccan, both being grounded firmly in life as it is.

The first paragraph of page 38 is perspicacious of Metcalf, although I don't think it applies after a certain number of years, when both the pleasant and the unpleasant are no longer noticed.

On page 39, writing about *Midnight Mass*, he says: "These stories add little to his stature." I gather from this that he takes it as axiomatic that each book written by a good writer will be superior to the one preceding it. Onward and upward, as it were. Is a writer on his way somewhere?

If you do communicate with Metcalf, you might say that I agree entirely with his final paragraph. What can one expect of a synthetic nation coming at the end of the time of man? Given time, it might have attained maturity, in spite of misapplied democracy. But there is no time now.

I hope you'll forgive me for unloading all this on you. Metcalf comes so near at times that I wanted to help him make contact, if possible.

TO CHARLES-HENRI FORD

March 13, 1983
Tangier

I've written to Red Ozier suggesting they send me *O.K. III*, as well as some copies of my translation of Rodrigo Rey Rosa's book. They gave me only two, after promising a dozen. (Of course the promise was made when I waived payment on royalties two years ago.)

I shouldn't think our correspondence could equal that of Fowlie and Miller; there, at least, I'm sure you had two letter-writers. I'm not a letter-writer; my correspondence lacks a *fond sérieux*. As Gore V. wrote somewhere (I'm forced to paraphrase) "If you get a letter from Paul, it's about what he had for breakfast." Hyperbole, but poetically true. I can't believe I ever wrote an "interesting" letter. It seems to me a good letter has to have the smell of the personality of the one who writes it. And I think my eagerness to avoid leaving any such smell is the same, whether it's a letter or a novel or whatever. Don't risk giving offense with halitosis or B.O.!

Anyway, your travel schedule is formidable. You ask why I no longer travel. The reason is so obvious: there are no more ships. The pleasure of travel consisted largely in having first-class accommodations on good ships, preferably for long periods of time. There were the ports-of-call, which were very important, and there were also comfortable trains in Europe, Asia and North America, which one could take on leaving the last port. Now it's all flying Greyhound buses, and there are no porters anywhere, and a hundred times the people going from one place to another. I think all these constitute a valid reason for staying at home. Who is San Antonio? Don't know him.

TO GAVIN LAMBERT

March 15, 1983
Tangier

Yours of the first here as of yesterday. Yes, now our weather is more usual: bright sun and 17 degrees C. The wisteria is abloom as is the mimosa.

I found it difficult to believe Tennessee's death. Being sick in bed and feverish at the time I heard the news on BBC, I was convinced for a whole day that it was a false report, and that we'd soon hear that he'd been resuscitated! Like you, I'd always considered his hypochondria merely a facet of his temperament, and consequently assumed that he was in excellent health and would probably outlive me. And given the details of his death, I still feel the same way. It could as easily have been an automobile accident.

[Moumen] Smihi's satisfaction with the title *Qaftan d'Amour Constellé de Passion* gave me my first glimpse of his Moroccan side; it seems incredible that after so many years of living in Paris he shouldn't sense the absurdity of such a title, for any film. He was here briefly before he went to Casablanca; I imagine he'll be back soon.

Someone told me several years ago that Patrick O'Higgins had died. Is this true, or only a Tangier fantasy? How in God's name can Bette Davis make herself look remotely like Madame? Perhaps a reverse nose-job to begin with, which might set a fashion. And HR's voice was so deep, and she had no nervous tics. Ah well, I hope I get to see this phenomenon.

Joe doesn't seem to be back here yet. I say "seem" because I don't know; no one has mentioned his arrival.

Tenn's obituary in *The London Times* was very long, and, I thought, snide. It kept stressing the elements which prevented him from being a good playwright. The prevailing tense was "would have."

TO GAVIN LAMBERT

April 17, 1983
Tangier

Too bad! Your return will coincide with the beginning of my busy season. Having to give the classes seems more onerous than usual this year, in anticipation, at least.

Bette Davis must be nearly eighty now; am I correct? I remember she came to a terrible dinner in 1953, at the Ritz-Carlton in Boston during the try-out of Jane's play. Unfortunately she was seated at the head of a long table, and felt compelled to address her remarks to the entire ensemble. It wasn't difficult for her; she had what's called a carrying voice, and one particularly suited to express venom. I was thunderstruck. (I always thought she was fun on the screen, though.)

Smihi is back in Paris: I haven't heard from him. I suspect he's having trouble with his last film, completed but not distributed.

I'm going to Douggie Harbach's tonight for dinner, and I'm wondering if Joe will be there. It seems to me he's been gone this time for longer than usual, so he may possibly be back.

Magic Hotel sounds like one of the places that used to exist in the back alleys of the Medina here: there were Casa Delirio and Hotel Satan. I'd always coveted the glass enseigne that hung outside the latter, but Geoffroy de Thoisy kept an eye on it, and when the place ceased to function and was dismantled, he was right there to grab it. In his apartment it looked bigger than it had in the street, but Satan was beautifully painted, complete with pitchfork.

TO WENDY LESSER,
THE THREEPENNY REVIEW,
BERKELEY, CALIF.

————————————◆————————————

April 22, 1983
Tangier

In answer to yours of the third asking if I'd be interested in writing about Tennessee W., I can only say that elegies are not my forte; my mind would lock in stasis if I were to try to express myself in that genre. There's much to say, but it will remain unsaid. Although I didn't see Tennessee very often, I thought of him as one of my closest friends, and of course I still do think of him in that way. Whether people die or remain alive, it's the same: if we were friends, we are friends. Someone always has to die first, and most of my friends have died before me. It seems there's a Tennessee Williams Review at Harvard; they asked me to send something immediately after he died. Last week something called the *Dictionary of Literary Biography* wrote saying it was preparing a 350-page volume on T. W., and also requested a few words. If I were to write anything, I'd do it for you, but I'm not going to write anything.

I finally received the third copy of the *Review of Contemporary Fiction* sent me by the editor; the other two disappeared en route.

Your experience with the history professor would make good material for a story, it seems to me. I couldn't handle it, because I don't know the milieu, but your mother could do it beautifully.

TO JOEL REDON

April 23, 1983
Tangier

There are many questions in your letter of the seventh of April. Let's see: yes, I shall be teaching again this summer. I've been doing it for the past three years. Satisfying? Not terribly. No, it doesn't pay very well. It makes me feel a little less isolated.

No, I'd had no word from Tennessee since he left Tangier last autumn. He was here for less than a week then. I don't understand what you mean by the expression "lost his will." Do you mean will-power? Or the desire to live, or what? In any case, I wasn't aware that he'd lost anything.

I've heard of Anna Kavan, and read only one thing by her, years ago. She was well-known in England as a junkie. I'd never heard of her habit of sitting in front of a mirror. It would certainly put me off if I did it.

When I put a date at the end of a story, it's when I've written the last line. The first draft is the final draft; I almost never change anything. I write the story in longhand, copy it on the typewriter, go through it carefully, making any necessary cuts or additions, then retype it, and date it. It's really all one operation. In the case of certain stories, it has all taken place during the same day, from the beginning to the end. One story, "Reminders of Bouselham," was written synthetically, and rewritten and rewritten and cut up and pasted together. That was an experiment, and I repeated it in the case of "The Eye." But these are exceptions.

I've been corresponding with Irving Stettner for several years. Everyone tells me he's a delightful man. Mrabet does write him letters. I don't "ghostwrite" them; I merely translate them as he dictates. Jeffrey Miller has prepared a bibliography of my works—a 522-page manuscript! I've never read *The Wrong People*. Robin Maugham used to live here. Have you read his *Search for Nirvana*? It's a bit like the excerpt you sent me.

P.S. A *souk* is a market. *Medina* is a city—generally the part built by the Moslems. A *casbah* is a fort, usually inside the medina. A *muezzin* is the man who cries the calls to prayer from a minaret. Women henna their hands for cosmetic reasons as well as magic ones. Bridegrooms have their hands hennaed before the wedding. *Harira* is composed of (you said *comprised of*, which is impossible) a meat stock, chick peas, noodles & vegetables. It is generally eaten immediately after the cannon is fired at sunset, often with a plate of dates.

May 15, 1983
Tangier

It was kind of you to give me such a clear exposition of how you edited the current issue of *TPR*. I can see that keeping the review going involves a lot of activity on your part. In general the manuscripts don't fall like manna from heaven; they have to be hunted out, considered, discussed, perhaps altered.

Thank you for your kind words about *The Spider's House*. This is the one piece of writing that the publishers wanted changed. I've always regretted having had to accede. But Random House insisted that I insert a section in which Stenham and Lee have sex in the open air at the festival. It didn't fit into my conception, but I wrote the extra part and it was inserted. I still marvel at their khutzpah. I suppose I should instead marvel at my acquiescence, but it seemed to be a question of publish or not publish. It was Bennett Cerf, if I recall, who wanted so much to have a sex scene.

I'm happy for you about the fellowship to take you underground. A nice subject; will Patricia Hearst figure in it?

I had a letter the other day from your mother; she said she'd be leaving for China in less than three weeks. She said that Janet Lewis had remarked to her that Jane Bowles sounded like Jane Austen. Your mother agreed, as do I.

I just finished writing a ten-thousand-word autobiography for a literary encyclopaedia of some sort. (The Gale Research Corp.) I thought I'd finished raking over the coals of my life, but I was wrong.

August 7, 1983
Tangier

I appreciate your courteous reply to my note, which I thought of as being a purely defensive document. If the present letter is brief, it is only because I'm still in the midst of giving my summer classes to students from the New York School of Visual Arts. (There are many manuscripts to read, correct, ameliorate if possible.)

I am still moved to wonder why you find it of interest to "discover" the author, to see him "reveal himself." Has he not already revealed himself in his work? Of what interest can it be to know about his personality and his life apart from his work? I should say that an author has no interest either in revealing or concealing "himself," since that "himself" is non-existent, save as an individual to those who know him.

It may be that my denial that a writer is anything more than a transmitting machine has something to do with my not conceiving of life as a "journey." Yes, one assumes that one is en route to gradual disintegration and death, but those things can be waited for in stasis. There's no reason to suppose that everyone thinks of life in terms of a voyage. And I still can't fathom why the author himself should loom so large in your appreciation of his work.

This is about it, and thanks again.

TO STEPHEN DAVIS

September 6, 1983
Tangier

No rain in many months; everything dried up. Water comes on in the morning and goes off a few hours later, still in the morning, after which no more water until the following day. The ants are thirsty and have invaded the apartment, falling into the stored water and having to be fished out before one can boil it. Flour and powdered milk are full of weevils. All very difficult.

The teaching is over until next year, if there is a next year. It's a six-week season beginning the first of July.

I was delighted to have the clipping of the Police show. Someone had sent me the tape of *Synchronicity*, and someone else the text of the songs. So I have a little collection. I thought *Tea in the Sahara* one of the weaker numbers of the album from the point of view of both lyrics and music. But some of the material is really good, such as *Wrapped around Your Finger* and *Miss Gradenko*. I thought King Crimson's *The Sheltering Sky* (in last year's album *Discipline*) more interesting musically than *Tea in the Sahara*; whether it's rock music or not I don't know. It didn't sound like the rest of the material in the album.

Apparently you think of coming here toward the end of the year. Great drug scandal here at present; more than eighty in jail here in Tangier, all to do with hard products. I look forward to seeing you.

TO JOEL REDON

September 7, 1983
Tangier

Thank you for your letter and the envelope of pages from the Williams–Windham correspondence. This note will consist of answers to your various questions and comments on your remarks. First, no play of Tennessee's is set specifically in Morocco. *Camino Real* used the Zoco Chico as its visual setting, no mention being made of Tangier or Morocco. Some people imagine that *Suddenly Last Summer* was meant to be North Africa, but again it was set in a no-man's land which could have been Mediterranean or Latin American. It certainly wasn't Morocco. (Of course the stage action took place in New Orleans, with the unnamed country figuring only in the tale told by the girl.)

I can't imagine what you mean when you say you never keep anything you write. It doesn't seem to be a serious attitude for a writer! * * *

Not having the context of the sentence you quoted, I can only suppose that Ishmael should be taken in its usual sense: that of an outcast or wanderer. You recall the opening sentence of *Moby Dick*: "Call me Ishmael."

A letter from Gore Vidal yesterday, largely about Tennessee. I quote: "How curious that The Bird (Gore has always called T. The Bird) who most feared suffocation suffocated to death: a good seven minutes of ghastly awareness. There is a Bowlesian principle at work: what is most feared fearfully happens." This seems germane to the xeroxed page you sent in which T. recounts his hospital experiences.

Buffie Johnson will be in New York in another fortnight. Then the summer will be really over. I hope you can cope with New York!

TO REGINA WEINREICH

November 8, 1983
Tangier

I've no further word from Leo Lerman or from Mary Ellen Mark. Was it Lerman who told you the photographs were wonderful? It's hard to know what's being planned, if anything. Since I don't receive all mail that's sent to me, it's possible that there has been a communication which has so far failed to reach me. No way of knowing.

I can't believe you're serious when you say that I "state many things about Jane's adventures plainly without really indicating what" I was doing at the time. Are you sure that, knowing what's in the Dillon book, you aren't reading more into the Autobiography than is actually in it? My impression is that I gave the same amount of information about myself that I gave about Jane. As to my sex life, it has always been largely imaginary; what few "relationships and intimacies" there were are all recounted in the Autobiography. I think what people really want to know is: With whom have you been to bed? To answer that, it would be necessary to have known their names. The Sins of Omission charge doesn't hold water, it seems to me, in reference to the Autobiography.

The Burroughs film sounds interesting; someone sent me the *Times* review of it.

The rainy season has finally arrived, and things are wet, to the great joy of the Moroccans, who had begun to fear another drought.

At the moment I'm translating (from the Spanish) although I expect to do something else shortly. How's your jazz program? Does it continue?

TO PHIL NURENBERG

November 17, 1984
Tangier

I have yours of November sixth. I was amused by your description of New Directions's direction with regard to the Stettner book. It tallies with my own experience when ND published *The Sheltering Sky* in early December 1949. Advance reviews indicated a first printing of ten thousand, but ND published only thirty-five hundred, which were exhausted immediately, with the result that the two weeks before Christmas saw no copies on bookseller's shelves. The reason for all this was grotesque: Laughlin's accountants had already made out his taxes for the year and as always New Directions was entered as a loss. Thus he couldn't afford to print ten thousand copies during 1949 for fear that his tax returns would have to be redone if he showed a profit. In January, when no holiday shopping was being done, he printed more, and continued to print more. But the book suffered by being unavailable during December while the reviews were coming in. His principal reader, David McDowell, left at the end of December and went to Random House, where I published the next four books. Laughlin wrote me, when he heard that Random House was publishing *The Deli-*

cate Prey, that he was considering a lawsuit against my agent for having abrogated a telephonic agreement giving the book to him, but nothing was in writing, so that evaporated. I remember that he upbraided me in letters for some time afterward. He didn't want to pay an advance; he wanted to send me $75 a month for a year. I thanked him for his generosity, but regretted that I was unable to accept it, having signed with Random House. All water under the bridge.

Since then we've met and resumed friendship.

Forgive this letter. Yours set it off.

TO SANCHE DE GRAMONT [TED MORGAN]

December 19, 1984
Tangier

Since everyone here, when you're mentioned, always refers to you by the name you had when you were here, I feel justified in using it myself (at the risk of annoying you, since obviously you prefer the new one).

I'm glad for Bill Burroughs's sake that you're doing his biography. Its existence ought to preclude the writing of a lot of half-baked ones by his admirers.

I'm not in close touch with Burroughs, although occasionally I get a postcard from him which I don't answer because I never know his address.

I expect to be here all through January, so that the thirteenth is as feasible a day for me as any other. (Although I see now that this is the date for your arrival in Tangier, and not necessarily the date when you will come to Inmueble Itesa.) I still have no telephone; in fact, everything is exactly the same as it was fifteen years ago.

So I'll look forward to seeing you.

TO BENNETT LERNER

April 23, 1985
Tangier

Thank you once again for your care in preparing the Sonatina for performance. Your suggestions of course are valid. The one I'm not completely in accord with is on page 5, line 2, measures 5, 6, and 7. You suggest tying the B's between measures 5 and 6. But in measure 5 there's a fermata, and over measure 6 Lento. By the time one reaches measure 7 there will be no B sounding. (No D either, for that matter, but that is unimportant.) So I think it's better to repeat the B in measure 7. One could eliminate the D in measures 7 and 8, if you think it would look better. Page 6, line 2, measure 6 is certainly wrong. The grace note (for such it was meant to be) should be cut, and the sixteenth note altered to an eighth. With the fermata in the left hand an appoggiatura is meaningless in any case. I'm glad you found that, although it's a bit late to incorporate the change into the published version: forty years or so! On page 22, line 3, measure 2, I found an error myself. (If I can do that, there must be many of them.) It's enclosed, on a bit of your music paper. Page 11, line 4, measure 3, you're correct there, too. The note should be A instead of B, so that it's a 6/4 chord like the others.

When John Kirkpatrick played the piece at a League of Composers concert in 1935 (I think) he marked fingerings on the manuscript, and these were retained in publication. Incidentally, when Marc Blitzstein reviewed the concert for *Modern Music*, he said of the piece: ". . . what is called damned clever," and "whiter even than the White Russians dispense it." (I can't imagine which "White Russians" he was thinking of.) To me personally Marc said: I didn't know you had it in you. At the time my feeling was that since the piece made no attempt to be anything but unabashedly "white," it amused him and he could afford to admire it as a kind of working model of "whiteness."

I began writing the Sonatina in Monte Carlo in November 1932. When it was half finished, I went to the Sahara. There I worked on a different piece, which I began and finished there. Later in Algiers I returned to the Sonatina, and completed it before going on to Morocco.

As to the Dance, it's taken, as I've said, from *The Wind Remains*. Carlos Surinach didn't include it when he recorded the piece, but it's a part of the score. When Lenny conducted it at the Museum of Modern Art, Merce Cunningham was the dancer. I wrote this particular piece outside Cuernavaca in the autumn of 1941. I can't think of anything more to say about either of these items, and I don't know whether you can make literate program notes of what I've written. ¡Ojalá!

As you must know, your decision to reanimate my music means a great deal to me. I hope you won't find too many more errors.

TO SANCHE DE GRAMONT [TED MORGAN]

May 1, 1985
Tangier

Brion's remark about me (that if one sent me a twenty-seven word letter one would get back a reply with the same number of words in it) seems to be of a piece with his long-time opinion of me as an ungenerous character. When he was doing some work for me here in Tangier in 1950 and I was paying him by the page, he once asked me to advance him a few dollars. I said that was not part of our agreement, and refused. When I have the pages I'll pay for them, I told him, adding that I knew I was difficult, but that I had to function in that manner. As he shut the door after letting me out, he said: No, You're not difficult; you're simply mean. I've thought about it for some years, and have decided that he was probably right. The meanness, however, is not personal; it's just New England parsimony, and I've never questioned its correctness. * * *

Today is May Day, which means an endless parade of marchers and floats, God forbid.

TO WAYNE POUNDS

August 30, 1985
Tangier

Your letter is dated May twentieth; I received it August twelfth, which is fairly quick service for surface mail.

Reading the Jameson essay was like reading (for once) a good science-fiction story, where things to come are presented as things already here. (Who was it, Jaspers or Heidegger, who said that the great catastrophe had happened, that we needn't expect anything more awful?) From the Jameson one gets the impression that the planet has been sprayed with a depersonalizing gas which makes it impossible for a human being to know who or where he is. To me no "periodization" is persuasive: the results are too inexact. If you've lived through several so-called periods, you conceive of each one as a continuation of the preceding one, which indeed it is. I notice you remark that Jameson "diagnoses" American life perfectly. Does that mean you consider his piece an accurate description of present-day conditions in the U.S.? If so, there must have been tremendous changes in the past seventeen years, when I last saw the place. One gets the feeling that both landscape and inhabitants are dead, not to be renewed or revived. Oracular! The shadow cast before the coming event (nuclear), which these desensitized people will eventually find themselves longing to experience. Mektoub. A fascinating, very depressing essay, I call it. (As a layman, I find many of its references meaningless: texts by Althusser, Derrida, Adorno, Lefebvre, Debord, Lacan and Foucault mean nothing to me because I'm wholly ignorant of them. But I doubt that having read all of these authors I'd find the Jameson piece any less gruesome.)

Thanks very much for *The Inner Geography*; I was glad to see a consideration of *Midnight Mass*, which I thought showed your usual perspicacity. The poems I'll have to report on later. I had two deadlines to meet this summer, met at the expense of other occupations. Saludos y abrazos.

TO ALLEN HIBBARD

December 7, 1985
Tangier

You were right: my classes through July and August made all correspondence impossible. I still haven't exhausted the list of unanswered letters which accumulated during the summer.

I'm surprised to hear that you thought the ending of "A Distant Episode" ambiguous. He had to be made conscious once more before he could cross over into insanity. He goes mad while looking at the calendar. We can only assume that he will be dead within a day or two when he has run far enough into the desert. It certainly is not a question of being "primitive" or "civilized."

You ask whether I "follow" new music. It's a bit difficult here to sample everything that is being done, even though certain friends do send me cassettes of things they think I'd enjoy. Others send rock and jazz occasionally. Rock has never been one of my enthusiasms; it seems to be metamorphosing somewhat, and is distinctly more interesting at times. I think of David Byrne, The Talking Heads, the Police. Even King Crimson's The Sheltering Sky was more integrated than rock was ten years ago. I suppose that's a hopeful sign; eventually the two idioms of rock and jazz may fuse to make a viable popular music.

Thanks for your monologue. Since it's really a portrait rather than an anecdote,

I'd have appreciated a sentence or two helping to situate the woman. Or is it a girl? How does one explain her having been in Mexico for three years? Is she perhaps a student? Not that any of these things is important, but if one knew them all she would have more solidity as speaker. As I say, a sentence or two establishing her (more firmly would be good). I hope you don't mind my offering my opinion.

TO REGINA WEINREICH

December 7, 1985
Tangier

You write me about PEN. What exactly is it? What does it do? I assume it has a purpose beyond holding meetings at which writers appear. Why does it need funds for a Writers' Congress? What in God's name *is* a Writers' Congress? What is done at such conventions? Literature is discussed, I suppose. But why is that necessary or interesting? What is accomplished by such gatherings? Books are written, published, and read, and logically that should be the entire cycle. If they're discussed in public, something has been added, and I suspect the publishers of being guilty. Or is it even more abject? Is it the writers who are discussed, rather than the books?

I received three Burroughs books in the mail the other day: *Queer, Junky* and *Exterminator!* Not to be compared with *Naked Lunch*, it goes without saying. Now that Perelman is dead, Bill is our foremost humorist. Not that he's not many other things besides.

You ask me if I correspond with Gore; he was here for a few days in October, and in great form. Yes, I liked the Tennessee Williams piece and the account of Calvino's burial. Whenever Gore publishes something in the *NYRB* that he thinks I should see, he asks Barbara Epstein to send it to me. I consider that friendly.

Yes, Chester and Glass were the other Americans living in Asilah in the summer of 1963. With me, that made three in the town. Far too many Americans for such a small town, but it's people like that who teach one patience.

The Dutch TV script was "all about" me. They claimed to like it, shot me only for two days, paid me, and went to the desert to shoot background scenes. I hear no more about Ahmed Yacoubi. We're having cold weather.

TO RICHARD PEABODY
◆

January 22, 1986
Tangier

Thanks for sending the new *Gargoyle*. And more particularly for your own *Echt and Ersatz* and *Morton's Salt Girl*. (I imagine the image of the Salt Girl has replaced that of the Shaker in native costume, which one automatically associated with table salt sixty years ago—the era I best remember.)

I liked most "An Audience with Angels," "The Black Velvet Girl," "Retreat," in *E. & E.*, and "Hitching" in *Salt Girl*. (I realize that a non-poet's reactions can scarcely be of interest to you; I'm merely expressing my preferences.)

It's slight comfort to hear that you preferred *The Wind Remains* to *Einstein on the Beach*! The phraseology suggests that neither piece rates, or that may be because I assume you, like me, consider Glass the Emperor in his new clothes, not wearing a shred of musical talent. (Although I'm told he has a theatre sense. That I can't check on from Tangier.) He must have something, even if it's only a facility for writing scales, arpeggios and Czerny finger exercises, and I suppose it's his poker-faced way of presenting absurdities that pleases his public. I can do without his particular variety of minimalism.

Unfortunate, all Reagan's indignant rhetoric on Qaddhafi, where he characterized the men considered here to be Palestinian patriots as "criminals." After all, "terrorist" means "patriot." (It results in a heavier guard around the American Consulate across the street from me.) The two viewpoints are drifting farther apart; I doubt they can be reconciled.

TO RUTH FAINLIGHT
◆

April 10, 1986
Tangier

Fifteen to Infinity got here safely; thank you.

The poems are good, as you well know. Even when they are passionate they remain simple and straight. Of course, I have no right to express myself on the merits of poetry, since I read so little of it. And I was about to say: since I myself am not a poet; but obviously it's not necessary to write poetry oneself to appreciate what others write!

I was curious to know the meaning of the volume's title until I found the one about David and his camera. (To me David is an infant-in-arms still; it's hard to imagine that bit of baby-flesh grown into a man.) The deaths of my friends don't impress me as unbelievable phenomena; I take them for granted. But the metamorphosis achieved by passing from infancy to adulthood always astonishes me.

And you, have you changed so much in the intervening years? I wonder why you imagine you'd like that silver metal crab now, when it disgusted you twenty-five years ago. In any case, it's still here, and if you ever return to Tangier you can test yourself with it.

Our spring, as always, is very late. In spite of the flowering trees and the greenness everywhere, the air says that it's winter.

I've been doing radio, TV and magazine interviews, and they all (the French, Dutch and Spanish) want to hear about the same thing: what Tangier was like in the International days. It's strange, this sudden surge of interest in day before yesterday. Nostalgia for simpler times?

I have no news. My best to you and Alan.

TO JOHN HOPKINS

June 11, 1986
Tangier

Travel books about Tangier and the Sahara in the 'thirties? The only one I can think of is Wyndham Lewis's *Journey into Barbary* (1931). But I don't know how heavily one can rely on his accuracy. Undoubtedly there are French ones, but I can't even think of them offhand. It ought not to be difficult to imagine the landscape and life then, remembering what things were like when you first arrived, and erasing whatever gadgets came between the 30's and 60's (like radios and gas stations). Everything has changed much faster during the years you've been here than it did between the 'thirties and the 'fifties, I should say.

Tessa came by the other day with Gavin Young. (Have you read his two books: *Slow Boats to China* and *Slow Boats Home*? I liked both very much. I read them in Penguin editions.)

Surprising that you're taking the family to the States. Are they old enough to appreciate the difference? I imagine one at least is.

(The French were still "cleaning up" the Tafilalt in 1934, when I was there, and the Saghro went on until 1936, didn't it?)

No news; things are quiet.

TO JOEL REDON

June 24, 1986
Tangier

I'm glad to know that you have a fixed address (if indeed that turns out to be true!) so that I can write you and thank you for the various gifts you've sent recently. The newest one is the piece on Cecil Beaton. Only three days ago someone who was here from New York asked me if I considered Beaton a snob, and I replied that I didn't. Obviously the visitor had just read the review you sent, only he didn't mention it. I went on to explain that a portrait photographer naturally had to cultivate either wealthy or famous friends, since his livelihood depended upon precisely that. But I'd never thought of Beaton as a snob. He seemed much too simple and wasn't a name-dropper. I can see how one could make out a case for snobbery if one hadn't known him, since he was always with celebrities. But that was his work, so it was all quite natural.

The [Dotson] Rader book on Tennessee came. Thanks. Rader was cashing in on a superficial and relatively short-lived acquaintanceship with T. W., and he made it as sensational as possible. His exaggerations are painful, and his style is scarcely a pleasure to see.

I hope all goes well with you and that Manhattan isn't too muggy.

TO CAROL ARDMAN

July 19, 1986
Tangier

A certain amount of water would have passed under the bridge since I received your letter, if it hadn't dried up first, this being summer.

If you went away for the fourth of July, you've probably returned by now, or gone away again.

As usual there's no news from Tangier. People keep coming, from obscure magazines (to me obscure, at any rate) in France and Germany, wanting to have the eternal interview. If I were more conversant with contemporary European culture I'd know which ones to accept and which to refuse. My impulse is to refuse them all, since I dislike having to answer questions as though I were in court. (The one who came yesterday was a friend of Claude Thomas, so I gave her my afternoon.) I always feel afterwards that it's been a terrible waste of time and energy.

I saw Marguerite McBey night before last at Patrick de Laurière's annual dinner-concert; she'd just returned from London and had the news that Brion Gysin had died, which I was sorry to hear, even though I'd known for some time that he was very ill. (It wasn't cancer, however.)

I've been writing short stories and correcting French translations of a volume of stories to come out later this year. Gavin has still not returned from California, although he was due in time for Thanksgiving 1985. Claude Thomas is here. Her excellent translation of Jane's book *Plain Pleasures* is out, and now she's translating a collection of my short stories. (It's a different collection from the one I mentioned at the beginning of the paragraph, of which Claude is not the translator.)

Abdelouahaid sends his greeting to you. He's about to go on vacation to Sidi Harazem. I hope Mrabet doesn't want a vacation, too.

Un abrazo fuerte.

TO BRION GYSIN
[Published in *Cover/Arts New York*, Summer 1987]
◆

August 6, 1986
Tangier

I was planning to write you last month because I hadn't heard from you recently, and was wondering how you were. Then I went to a concert at Patrick de Laurière's and saw Marguerite. As I walked in front of her to get to my seat she looked up with her enormous eyes and said: "You've heard about Brion's death?" For a split second I didn't believe she was serious. That's always my reaction when I'm unprepared for bad news. During the music I thought about it, and began to feel bereft and annoyed with myself for not having written the letter I'd meant to write. Clearly it would have changed nothing, and this is certainly not that letter.

I don't know how you and Jane met, but one evening she told me: "Tomorrow night we're eating with some new people. I told them we were going to the Stravinsky concert and they want to go too." We ate somewhere on the Left Bank, and you and Denham Fouts and Jane and I went on to the Salle Pleyel. Six years went by before we met again, in New York, and then another six before you came here to Morocco. It was only then that I got to know you and discover that you were an ideal traveling companion, more observant and articulate than I, with an awareness that was always present in full force. I admired your intelligence because it was something adamant, not subject to outside influences.

And so we had the nights when we wandered through Moulay Abdallah, the weeks in the Algerian Sahara, and the year when Mil y Una was running beautifully, with the Djebala musicians you had the genius to bring into Tangier from their last rural hideouts. What a shame that the place was doomed to fall into the hands of Mary Cook! But nothing seemed to depress you; you always went on to something else. Even much later, after the three operations, you kept going, and gave every sign of being unconcerned. I ought to have told you then how very much that impressed me. But it is precisely such simple reactions which are the most difficult to express, so I pretended to take it all for granted, and kept silent.

Now the line has been cut, and you exist only in the minds of us who remember you. And when our lines have been cut as well, we shall all be a part of the same grand néant. Even that consoling thought isn't of much help; I'm still sad to think that you're no longer here. Enough for now.

TO CAROL ARDMAN

◆

October 19, 1986
Tangier

I've put off writing practically everybody in the hope of being able to refer to my illness in the past tense. But I now see that I can't go on forever that way, because exactly a month after the operation I'm still in bed and able only to scribble with my knees up. Briefly, an aneurism in my knee had to be got around so the blood could get to the lower leg and foot, which had become numb and very cold. So the surgeon in Rabat had to make a large incision in my abdomen and cut the sympathetic nerve. It feels as though he had cut everything else as well. That's that, and I'm not working, except to correct the translation into

French of *The Spider's House*. So you can believe I'm not giving interviews, even though some people have had the khutzpah to try and get them even though I'm lying here defenseless! But journalists are insane, as we know.

Your life sounds full and reasonably happy. Forgive me if I don't write more. It's uncomfortable.

TO JOHN HOPKINS

May 16, 1987
Tangier

Everything goes so slowly this spring. Most of the time each day I spend taking therapeutic walks and doing exercises given me by the masseur. There remains little time for writing letters, and what there should be for that seems to be taken up by people who come from foreign parts for various reasons. Ten days ago a film maker, Bernardo Bertolucci, was here for three days with his scenarist, and we talked about nothing but *The Sheltering Sky*. Last week two men from the German magazine *Stern* came and asked innumerable questions. At the moment Daniel Halpern of *Antaeus* is here. Drue Heinz was to have come with him, but she phoned from London saying she couldn't get a seat on a plane and in any case wasn't feeling too well.

I don't understand your present agent's about-face on your new book. It sounds either neurotic or highly insecure intellectually. I should have written you earlier asking you to send the ms., but as usual I owe several dozen letters, and have managed to answer only those demanding an immediate reply: agent, accountant, publishers of translations of Jane's and my own books. Jane seems to have more success each year. The play, too, was a great success in Munich this spring. A shame she couldn't have known about it all.

I was very happy about Claude's translation of *Midnight Mass*. It helped to compensate for my chagrin on seeing the shambles of *The Delicate Prey* when it came out. But French reviewers clearly don't notice the difference; they don't really review books, anyway, but go on endlessly about the author. Thank you for your invitation, but here I am as always.

TO RUTH FAINLIGHT

April 1, 1988
Tangier

It seems to me that I can never, shall never catch up on my correspondence; there are always a score or so of letters that must be answered, so that when I answer them I'm obliged to apologize for being so dilatory.

Michelle Green has long since left Tangier and gone back to *People Magazine*. I believe she intends to return here at some point before completing her book. I don't quite understand what that book is going to be. Apparently she subscribes to that myth which has Tangier being a cultural center during the ten or fifteen years after the Second World War, and is working very hard to prove it. I think it was Fleur Cowles who started the rumor in her magazine *Flair*. Since you wrote your letter various things will have happened: your trip to Egypt, the publication of your Selecteds, and possibly the acquisition of a house.

It was you who first made me acquainted with Sholem Aleichem and his wonderful stories. Possibly you haven't seen *The New Yorker* of March 28th, in which there's a very long piece by Cynthia Ozick called *Sholem Aleichem's Revolution*. It made me want to reread the stories, which I can't do, no longer having them.

A concert of my music is taking place day after tomorrow in Nice. Too bad it's so far and that I'm so averse to present-day travel, or I'd go and hear it. But it will be broadcast by France-Musique and France-Culture, so I'll have tapes eventually and can listen at home.

Give my best to Alan. Love to you.

TO DANIEL HALPERN,
ECCO PRESS, NEW YORK

April 22, 1988
Tangier

You tell me that if I want to add to that diary I may. But the deadline was April 15th, which is why I stopped writing it and sent it off to you. I can easily continue with it, but I'd like to know when the final deadline is.

For the literary influences you want to send to *The New York Times Book*

Review, I'll list Borges, pre-war Sartre and Lewis Carroll. (I don't know whether "pre-war" is allowable, but post-war Sartre was not an influence.)

About a month ago I met David Herbert in the street; he told me that Drue Heinz had sent me a small jar of caviar. I suppose it was sent via him, but he didn't explain how I was to get hold of it, and I don't want to bother him by going to his house to ask for it. If you see Drue, will you ask her if she really sent it, or if David was pulling my leg?

Spring is here, but it's no different from December.

TO ALLEN HIBBARD

───────────────◆───────────────

May 8, 1988
Tangier

Yours has been here for a week, but as you know, it's Ramadan. And as you don't know, I've been suffering with a pinched nerve in my leg, and it produced the sort of pain that makes one think he's nauseated, although he's not.

My rights to my novels (filmwise) belong to Universal, Twentieth Century Fox and Aldridge, and there's nothing to be done about that. Bertolucci may still do *Sky*, but since I haven't heard from him since he was here a year ago, I wonder. Myself, I don't see how a successful film could be made of that one. But perhaps I haven't enough faith in the director.

Will you accept the Twayne offer? And if you do, will you be allowed to write what you please?

The card I sent was Cézanne, as I remember.

Phillip Ramey counts on arriving in Tangier before the end of May. He thought he had a fine flat all arranged for, but at the last minute the mad lady who was to let it to him decided she wouldn't, so he's got to stay once again at a hotel.

Mrabet's youngest (4 years) keeps coming to the typewriter and pushing her fingers between mine, and causing a certain amount of havoc in the typing of this missive. Fortunately the paper is of the sort that allows erasure.

A concert of my chamber music was given last month in Nice. The tape was sent me some time ago by the director, but the Moroccans confiscated it because its presence was not explicitly marked on the envelope it came in. Abdelouahaid worked magic, paid 2,000 francs, and brought it to me. These two days I've been listening, smiling and grinding my teeth. Some of the performances made me wonder why I'd ever been a composer. The meaning of the music is often completely effaced by the performer's insistence upon exhibiting his technique.

Let me know whether you'll be coming or not. It will be great to see you again, in the event you do come.

TO ROBERT BRIATTE

August 5, 1988
Tangier

Quel dommage que vous n'ayez pas pu aller au Mexique. (Je n'ai pas moyen d'être sûr si "ayez" devrait être "ayiez" ou pas. Je n'ai même pas un dictionnaire anglais-français.) Mais ce n'est pas la bonne saison là-bas, de toute façon: il pleut tous les jours. Quand-même j'aurais aimé avoir vos réactions à ce pays insensé. J'espère que votre jambe est en train de s'améliorer. Les jambes sont des choses ennuyeuses, mais, comme m'a dit mon chirurgien, elles sont préférables aux chaises roulantes.

Merci pour votre aide chez *France Culture*. Ils ne m'ont pas envoyé une cassette du concert, mais peut-être ça viendra.

La censure n'a pas bloqué *Delteil*, dont je vous remercie. Il a dû avoir une vie d'une grande variété. Si je ne vous ai pas écrit pendant le mois de juillet, c'est parce que j'étais convaincu que vous étiez au Mexique.

Il a fait très chaud ici dernièrement, mais en ce moment les matinées sont assez fraiches. Au moment de votre visite, on aura sans doute ces brouillards qui arrivent chaque année vers la fin d'août.*

---

* It is too bad that you were not able to go to Mexico. (I have no way of telling whether "ayez" should be "ayiez" or not. I have not even got a French-English dictionary.) But it is not the right season over there, in any case: it rains every day. Still, I would have liked to know your reactions to that insane country. I hope your leg is getting better. Legs are annoying things, but, as my surgeon said, they are better than wheelchairs.

Thank you for your help with *France Culture*. I have not received a tape of the concert from them, but perhaps it will arrive.

The censors did not confiscate *Delteil*, for which I thank you. He must have led quite a varied life. If I did not write you during July, it is because I was certain you were in Mexico.

It has been quite hot here lately, but the mornings are presently rather cool. When you visit, we will probably have those mists that arrive each year toward the end of August.

May 31, 1989
Tangier

You did write me not long ago, and I failed to reply. My stack of unanswered mail grows larger by the week, and I never seem to find the time to answer everything. Certain letters must be answered, but they are not the ones from people I know. They are from the bank, accountant, agents in various countries, publishers and that sort of thing.

The biography you mention can't even be discussed. It's so full of errors that one can't begin to list them all. Even the photographs are wrong. One supposed to be me is my cousin, another purporting to be me is of my father, taken around 1888. The so-called "self-portrait" is a drawing made in Fez in 1948, by Ahmed Yacoubi. Obviously the author holds it against me that I refused to give him any information at any point. He was forced to invent. Of course Gore told me that if I agreed to cooperate, half the material would be wrong, but if I failed to do so, everything would be wrong. A man has been here for the past several days, busy writing a biography of Gore. I warned him I'd be unable to help him, but he came anyway, and went away pretending not to be disappointed.

I have no idea where Roditi is; I believe somewhere in the U.S. The address I have for him is * * * A more practical address might be: c/o Bard College, Annandale-on-Hudson, New York. He's probably at neither place, but a letter sent to Bard might be forwarded.

Was Marianne Wiggins in your 1982 class here, before she became Mrs. Salman Rushdie? You probably don't remember whether she was or not.

June 3, 1989
Tangier

Your letter of May 23rd came yesterday. I have seen the Lauçanno biography, although I haven't read it from cover to cover. I knew I'd be angry when I saw it, so I spared myself a certain amount of indignation by skipping through it.

Lauçanno has not been pleased with me since he first suggested writing the book and I refused to have anything to do with it. This was after begging him not to undertake the project. When he announced that he was under contract with Weidenfeld and Nicolson I realized that I could not stop him legally or otherwise, short of murdering him, and wrote the publishers that they must present the work as an unauthorized biography. I also told him that I would answer no questions, and tell him nothing. He should have known that this would be my reaction, but clearly he resented it. There are a good many details in the text which would not have been included had I agreed to cooperate a bit with him.

Last year when he visited Tangier, he spoke for hours every day with Mrabet, and I did not interrupt their conversation. Having refused to have anything to do with the biography, I could not very well involve myself in whatever they were discussing. I heard Mrabet inveighing against Black Sparrow, but it didn't occur to me that the biographer would be so irresponsible as to credit me with Mrabet's wanderings. Knowing that whatever I said would go directly into the text, I refrained from being so stupid as to make such an indefensible statement as the one you quote—namely that I never received a dime from Black Sparrow! The book is so full of faults that one can't begin to list them. Gore Vidal warned me that if I collaborated, half the material would be wrong, and if I didn't, everything would be wrong. In the course of events this was beautifully borne out. I'm glad you gave the quote the benefit of the doubt by presuming it "inaccurate" as a report.

TO REGINA WEINREICH

August 2, 1989
Tangier

I've received only one letter from you that has gone unanswered; it was the one in which you spoke of the unusually attractive Marianne Wiggins, who clearly has gone on to better things. A lady of my acquaintance who should have known better hastened to mail me a copy of Ms. Wiggins's husband's book as soon as the Khomeiniacs of Iran had sentenced him to death. This resulted in the arrival of the police at the post office and the sending of my dossier along with the offending book to the government in Rabat. Since then books which are said to have been sent me have failed to be delivered. It's difficult to live as a non-Moslem in a Moslem land.

My response to Sawyer-Lauçanno's biography was one letter of recrimination and accusation. I regret not having arranged for his poisoning on his first visit to Tangier; it would have been so simple. It's too late now; murder for vengeance is senseless. For practical purposes it's another story. I've always suspected he'd already received an advance from Weidenfeld, so that my entreaties to leave me alone necessarily fell upon deaf ears. "You know I'd never write anything that would hurt you," he would murmur. (He even included a photograph of my father taken in 1888, saying that it was I; and an early drawing by Ahmed Yacoubi was presented as a self-portrait by me.) There's no doubt that he was annoyed by my steadfast refusal to assist him in any way, although I had told him in the beginning that if he insisted on writing the book I'd have nothing to do with it. I think he constantly hoped that I'd relent and cooperate with him. Thus he's the one who murdered for revenge, and I'm left with no recourse but to regret the day he first presented himself here.

I finished my piece for Aperture at the beginning of the year. Rodrigo is here, and has been here for many months.

All goes well. I had dinner with Bertolucci in June.

TO EDOUARD RODITI

September 9, 1989
Tangier

Summer is over and autumn hasn't arrived. Bertolucci has, and will shortly begin shooting *The Sheltering Sky* with two actors of whom I've never heard, playing the two leads. He'll take them to Djanet, near the Libyan border of Algeria, and to Agadez in Niger. They'll both probably fall ill with hepatitis.

What a wicked man Sawyer-Lauçanno is! You undoubtedly know that, having talked with him. He gleefully reported your shadowy memories of nigh on to sixty years ago, imagining they'd amuse readers of today. I doubt that the book amused anyone. The writing of it must have been a compulsive act; he felt it necessary to express his resentment that I refused to have anything to do with it. But since I begged him in the beginning not to undertake it, I don't see how he could have expected me to change my mind once he'd accepted his advance and started to write it. Fortunately Tangier is relatively isolated, so that I don't have to see too many people who've read the book.

I didn't know the commentator at radio station Medi-Un, who killed his wife.

I did, however, attend the Forbes dinner. The best part of that very fancy bash was a fringe benefit: he brought several hundred musicians and dancers from the Moroccan deep south, and they were housed for a week at the school opposite where I live. Thus I was able to go every night and watch their rehearsals until the final night when they lined the street leading to the Palais Mendoub. (Security was so tight that guests had to wait in a queue for half an hour, moving forward very slowly toward the entrance.)

André Ostier did not photograph Mrabet, I didn't even know he was in Tangier. The one that all the photographers were shooting was Mick Jagger, who caused a sensation standing in the doorway of the Minzah.

Anyway, this is this, and best.

TO REGINA WEINREICH

October 9, 1989
Tangier

Your first paragraph deals with the Bertolucci film. Your fantasy is a little out of kilter. I like all three of the leads, and particularly Debra Winger, whom I go to visit often at her house on the Mountain. Bertolucci wrote in a part for me in the script; I've already put in five days of work, and expect to have to work next week again.

What makes you think I missed Malcolm Forbes's birthday party? I certainly did not miss it, and can't understand what Forbes meant by saying I wasn't present. He himself introduced me to Elizabeth Taylor, who was at his side throughout. I sat at the next table to his, where he had installed his family and Miss Taylor, while the Crown Prince sat at his right. So I was able to watch them carefully during the four hours it took to eat dinner. The Crown Prince scarcely opened his mouth, and looked unutterably bored. For him it was just another of those state occasions he is forced to attend, and I got the impression that he doesn't understand much English, and of course all the conversation at the table was in that language, and not in French.

I thought the *Times* review showed only hostility and contempt for my work. It got quite a bit wrong, exposing Broyard's ignorance, such as calling *The Time of Friendship* a novel. It seems to me that even if the reviewer hasn't read the material, he should at least check on titles before launching into the review. Clearly Broyard didn't think the work warranted such basic care. The whole idea of Bowles bores him stiff, he makes clear. But why then, I wonder, did he ask to write about it?

The weather is still in the throes of Indian Summer. Some day soon it will turn cold all at once. Then the hospitals will be full of pneumonia patients.

TO ROBERT BRIATTE

October 25, 1989
Tangier

Vous avez raison. Tout le temps que j'aurais pu employer en écrivant des lettres a été gaspillé devant la caméra. Depuis un mois je travaille pour The Sahara Company, Ltd. Mon dernier jour payé était hier. Aujourd'hui l'équipe et les acteurs sont parti à Erfoud, où ils vont rester quelque temps. Ensuite ils vont à Zagora, et puis à Ouarzazate. De là ils volent jusqu'à Beni Abbès en Algérie, et puis à Djanet. Après une quinzaine de jours à Noël ils continueront jusqu'à Agadez en Niger. (Ma correspondance a beaucoup souffert, mais on me payait si bien que je n'ai pas pu refuser.) Il est possible que Bertolucci coupera les séquences où je parais. Lui, il n'a pas dit cela, mais je me demande si ma présence ne va pas nuire au film.

Les deux livres de chez Plon sont arrivés. J'ai lu la biographie et je la trouve excellent. Merci d'avoir écrit un livre dans lequel le lecteur peut avoir confiance. Quand vous aurez des critiques, faites-moi savoir. Je regrette que mon petit journal ne soit pas plus long. Mais c'est bien comme ça, et Matthieussent a fait un bon travail.*

---

* You are right. All the time I might have spent writing letters was wasted in front of the camera. For the past month I have been working for The Sahara Company, Ltd. My last payday was yesterday. Today the actors and crew left for Erfoud, where they will be staying for a while. Afterward they are going to Zagora, and then on to Ouarzazate. From there they will be flying to Beni Abbès in Algeria, and then to Djanet. After about two weeks at Christmas they will go on to Agadez in Niger. (My correspondence has suffered greatly, but they paid me so well I could not refuse.) It is possible that Bertolucci will cut the sequences in which I appear. He did not say that, but I wonder if my presence might not hurt the film.

The two books from Plon arrived. I have read the biography and find it excellent. Thank you for writing a book the reader can trust. When you receive some reviews, let me know. I am sorry my little diary is not any longer. But it is fine like that, and Matthieussent has done a good job.

LATER
LETTERS

May 10, 1990
Tangier

I had fifty of these slips xeroxed last month, and am still sending them out, because once again I've been attacked by sciatica, which makes just about everything next to impossible. The pain makes it difficult to concentrate on anything else.

I send this to Seattle because I have the impression that you're not in Cairo now. (I wonder if you wish you were, or if you're relieved to have left it.)

In the Bertolucci film I was what he called "The Visible Spectator." It's hard to imagine what the result will be, with me wearing clothing from 1947. At least, I wasn't asked to act. I merely stared into the camera and watched the actors play their parts. Anyway, all my best. Phillip Ramey came on Sunday.

TO THE EDITOR,
BOSTON GLOBE MAGAZINE
[Published in the *Boston Globe Magazine*,
Sunday, July 15, 1990]

June 5, 1990
Tangier

I regret to bring up a subject which at this late date can interest no one. In a letter published in the *Globe*, Mr. Christopher Sawyer-Lauçanno seems to be under the impression that I approve of his biography of me. Certainly he remembers that he and his editor at Weidenfeld and Nicolson assured me that the title-page of that unfortunate volume would bear the legend "An unauthorized biography," which it does not. A book whose author sees fit to alter facts so that they conform to his preconceived notions can hardly claim to have been authorized. The biography is willfully inaccurate, and in many instances defamatory.

November 25, 1990
Tangier

I'm in bed writing this, with Habiba sitting at my feet, sewing new pockets into my trousers. (I wonder if you'll be able to decipher this letter.)

At last I've finished that book for Jancovici, the novella that takes place in Mali. Having completed it, I feel much freer. People continue to come, so that I don't feel completely free. A Spaniard just came while I was having lunch. Another will come at three. This one is a journalist, according to his business card, which he left at the door yesterday. The other day I had a TV crew from Sydney, Australia, and the following day a French woman who laughed between each sentence. Rodrigo comes every afternoon at tea time. How he manages to walk all that way from the Charf in the pouring rain, I don't know. He has typed the entire book on Mali, for which I'm most grateful. At the moment I'm searching for a suitable title for the book. In the beginning Jancovici thought it should be called *Miquel Barceló*, but when he's read it, it's likely he'll want to give it a different title.

It's now cold and rainy every day—typical nasty winter weather. But at least I have the fireplace, which makes the flat inhabitable.

Mrabet now wants to sell the house at Mraierh, buy land on the road and build another house, combined with restaurant, bar and hotel rooms upstairs. I have a feeling that will occupy many years. And if he does it, it will probably be a failure. It seems completely improbable. Habiba has finished sewing the pockets. G. will be here in December.

January 29, 1991
Tangier

I can't find any other stationery, and apologize for this. My new maid, although otherwise excellent, has a mania for neatness, and consequently messes up all my papers each day, arranging everything according to size. My own disorder makes it much easier to function, but what can I say?

We've been going through other kinds of disorder here. Yesterday there was a third riot. This time the police shot no one, keeping the maniacs back with tear gas, not allowing them to leave Beni Makada, although they tried all afternoon, until dark. Even so, every shop was shut, as were cafés and restaurants. The idea was to force everyone to fast. The Ramadan was in support of Saddam's jihad. Americans are really objects of hatred at the moment, but then, so are Europeans. One professor explained to me: Saddam will do away with Europe and America, because this is a war to the finish against Christians and Jews. The world will all be Islam when we complete it. I asked him how he could be so sure that Saddam would win. "He has already won," he replied. "America no longer exists. It is just a stain on the map, like Israel. When the stains are rubbed out, the world will be clean, and Morocco will help to rub out the stains."

£600 seems extremely high for air fare to London–Tangier. I'm sorry, however, that you weren't here for my birthday. We had Jilala and very good food. The winter is being unusually cold, but beautifully clear, at least. Love to E. A.

Bon travail.

TO DANIEL HALPERN,

ECCO PRESS, NEW YORK

———————————•———————————

April 10, 1991

Tangier

Days arrived. Thanks. It looks splendid. I like the type it's set in. Will anyone pay such a high price for such a small object? Apparently yes.

The only detail which ruffled me is the substitution of the word "gotten" for "got" (page 100, paragraph 1, line 2). Your copy editor must have decided that my English was not up to the mark. In my books the past participle of the verb "get" is "got," and certainly not "gotten." The same copy editor changed "Hôpital" to "Hôspital" (page 39). Otherwise I could find nothing to carp about. The cover is great.

Tangier is still empty of tourists. People seem to think the Moroccans are Iraqis, and will resent the intrusion of the U.S. in the Iraq–Kuwait affair. The amusing part is that the Moroccans are convinced that Saddam won the war, and that Bush is very angry about it. Better they should think that than the opposite.

Anyway, I've never received a copy of *Antaeus* 62/63. Thank you for the book. ¿Cuando nos vemos?*

---

* When will we see each other?

ARABIC GLOSSARY

Aachor. Anniversary of the death of al-Husayn, the Prophet Muhammad's grand-son. In Morocco, a sort of "children's day," on which the children are given toy drums and tambourines.

ahouache. A Berber ceremony of the Anti-Atlas mountains that involves groups of dancers, singers, and percussionists, with the dancers forming a large circle.

Aid el Arche. The Feast of the Throne, which celebrates the King of Morocco's coronation.

Aid el Kebir. Festival commemorating the culmination of the month of the pilgrimage to Mecca, the Hajj.

Aid es Seghir. Festival celebrating the end of Ramadan, the month of Muslim fasting.

Aissaoua. A Sufi religious brotherhood based in the city of Meknès. Named after its founder, the sixteenth-century saint Sidi Muhammad ben Aissa.

amara. Festival in commemoration of a Muslim saint. Also called a *moussem.*

baqqal. Grocer. By extension, his shop.

baraka. Blessing, good fortune, luck.

bastela. A Moroccan lozenge-shaped meat pie, covered in fillo dough.

bled. The land, the country, countryside.

bordj. Fort, guard-post. Anglicized plural, *bordjes.*

caïd. Chief. A term also used for an administrator or government official. Now usually transliterated *qa'id.*

cheikhat. Singing-girls and dancers from itinerant musical troupes.

cherqi. The "eastern" wind that blows north from the Sahara. It brings hot, dry temperatures.

Chleuh. The generic Moroccan term for Berbers. Specifically, it refers to the Sousis, or Berbers from the Anti-Atlas mountains and the Sous river valley.

Dar el Beida. Arabic name for the city of Casablanca.

darbouka. Medium-sized, hourglass-shaped drum with membrane of skin and pottery body.

djaoui. A resin incense, of a hard and rock-like appearance.

djellaba. Traditional Moroccan long-sleeved burnous with hood.

eheud. Incense associated with Moroccan Jews.

fejr. Islamic dawn prayer.

fasoukh. Incense, of gummy texture, used to drive away sorcerers and malevolent spirits.

flouss. Generic term for money; small change.

Gnaoua or **Guennaoua**. (*see* Aissaoua, Jilala) Quasi-mystical brotherhood of blacks, known for dancing and sorcery. From the Tuareg *agnaw*—"black."

hachouma. Shame.

haïti. Traditional Moroccan wall-covering.

Hamdou'llah. "Praise be to God."

hammam. Bath, especially public steam bath. Moroccan version of ancient Roman *thermum*.

hanout. Store, shop.

haram. Forbidden.

hasaluban. Gum incense. Frankincense.

hasira. Woven-grass mat, used to cover floors in place of carpets.

hekaya. Story; tale.

incha'Allah. "God willing."

Istiqlal. Independence; refers to Moroccan independence from French/Spanish colonialism in 1956. Also Moroccan Independence Party (Hizb al-Istiqlal).

jduq jmel. Literally, "camel's cud." A hallucinogenic plant.

Jilala. (*see* Aissaoua) Religious brotherhood. Name refers to "glory" of God, as well as to the twelfth-century saint of Baghdad, Moulay 'Abd el-Qadir el-Jilani or "Jilali."

katib. Secretary.

khalifa. Government official; assistant to a *caïd*.

kharra. Shit. Moroccan vulgarity.

kif. The fine leaves at the base of the flowers of the common hemp plant, Cannabis sativa, chopped fine and usually mixed (in a ratio of seven to four) with tobacco grown in the same soil.

ksour. Fortified villages, usually in southern Morocco.

m'ska. Gum arabic for incense.

majoun. Jam. Here, made of figs and powdered cannabis; sometimes mixed with hashish oil.

mcid. Tangier pronunciation of *msjid*, primary school attached to a mosque.

mechoui. Barbeque, usually of an entire sheep.

meharistes. Native troops; auxiliary troops of the French colonial administration.

Mektoub. It is written.

melhoun (qsida). The language in which *qsidas*, poetic odes, are usually sung.

mezziane. Delightful; very good.

moqaddem. Gauleiter of quarter or village; local head of religious brotherhood.

mouddin. Muezzin, prayer-caller. Used in one of the letters here for the actual call to prayer, or *adan*.

Moul. Master; owner.

Moulay. Master, Lord; a title of respect, often reserved for one who is a cherif, or descendant of the Prophet Muhammad.

Mouloud. Prophet's birthday celebration (Aid al-Mouloud); also used for a saint's birthday celebration.

mrozeyia. Meat baked with honey.

na'als. Sandals.

oued. Stream bed or watercourse, usually dry.

Ouled Naïl. Berber singing-girls and courtesans from the Aurès mountains of Algeria.

raita (datura). Hallucinogenic plant, similar to Jimson weed.

Reguibat. Nomadic tribespeople from the western Sahara.

Saghro. Mountainous region in southern Morocco.

seroual. Trousers; often, the wide "Turkish trousers" worn beneath traditional clothing, such as a *djellaba*.

Sidi Kacem. Town in northwest Morocco near Tangier. Named after a Muslim saint who is buried there.

souk. Market.

taguia. Small Muslim skull-cap.

Tanja. Arabic word for Tangier.

tolba. "Students"; usually refers to professional Qur'an reciters.

tseuheur. Generic term for magic; specifically, it is word- and sympathetic-magic.

tsoukil. Euphemism for poison.

BIOGRAPHICAL GLOSSARY

Abdekader. See Abdelkader Cadour.

Álvarez, Antonio. A young Mexican painter whom Bowles met in Taxco in late 1941.

Ames, Elizabeth. The Executive Director of Yaddo, the endowed retreat for artists at Saratoga Springs, New York; Bowles was invited to Yaddo in 1930.

Antheil, Böske. George Antheil's Hungarian wife; Bowles met the Antheils in Cagnes-sur-Mer on the French Riviera in late 1932 when he lived there briefly.

Antheil, George. 1900–1959. American pianist and composer; studied at the Philadelphia Conservatory and under Ernest Bloch. His major work was "Ballet mécanique," which was performed in New York in April 1926, and then in Paris later that year. Antheil's early works are massive, dissonant, truly symphonic in scale, and are closer in idiom to the Russians than to the Americans of that time.

Ardman, Carol. A young American writer from New York City who lived in Tangier in the early seventies and befriended Bowles there; she lived in the same building as Bowles.

Arno, Peter. 1904–1968. Cartoonist whose work was regularly featured on the covers of *The New Yorker*, beginning in the 1920s. Bowles admired his work.

Auer, Claire Stajer. 1891–1971. Jane Bowles's mother.

Baldwin, Dorothy. A friend of Bowles's paternal grandmother whom he met in Glenora, New York, while a child. She was married to Maurice Becker. Baldwin was responsible for Bowles being introduced to Henry Cowell, who in turn introduced him to Aaron Copland.

Barber, Samuel. 1910–1981. American composer; in 1935, he received the American Prix de Rome and his first Pulitzer Prize for music. He won another Pulitzer Prize in 1959 for his opera, *Vanessa*, which had a libretto by his friend Gian Carlo Menotti, and another in 1963 for his First Piano Concerto. Other works include *Dover Beach*, 1931, and the ballets *Medea*, 1946, and *Souvenirs*, 1955. Bowles knew him through Menotti.

Becker, Maurice. 1889–1975. American cartoonist, painter, and watercolorist, born in Russia. Married to Dorothy Baldwin. In the late 1920s, Bowles frequented their studio in Greenwich Village, where he met the painters John Marin and Stuart Davis.

Berman, Eugene (Genia). 1899–1972. Russian romantic painter whom Bowles met in Paris in the early 1930s, introduced by Virgil Thomson. Bowles later worked on a ballet with Berman while living in Baltimore, but the project was abandoned for want of a sponsor. Berman did the cover art for one of Bowles's Éditions de la Vipère music publications.

Bertens, Hans. Dutch scholar; lecturer in American Literature at the Royal University of Utrecht. Bertens corresponded with Bowles while writing his dissertation, *The Fiction of Paul Bowles: The Soul Is the Weariest Part of the Body,* 1979.

Bissinger, Karl. American photographer who photographed Jane Bowles on assignment from *Harper's Bazaar* in 1946; Bissinger and Jane Bowles became friends; Bissinger later photographed Paul Bowles.

Blitzstein, Marc. 1905–1964. American composer who studied with Nadia Boulanger in Paris and Arnold Schoenberg in Berlin; composed eight operas and many film scores, including the score for *Spanish Earth* with Virgil Thomson. Bowles met Blitzstein in 1933 through the Young Composers Group organized by Aaron Copland. He is best known for his adaptation of *The Threepenny Opera* (1952) and his *The Cradle Will Rock,* 1936.

Boulaïch, Abdelouhaid. Bowles's devoted Moroccan chauffeur and friend of twenty-five years.

von Braun, Sigismund. A minor government official and sculptor; Bowles met him in 1931 in Berlin.

Briatte, Robert. French scholar and biographer of Paul Bowles; author of *Paul Bowles, 2117 Tanger Socco,* Paris, 1989.

Brown, Andreas. b. 1934. Owner of the Gotham Book Mart in New York City.

Burns, Daniel. b. circa 1901. A French teacher in New York City who lived near the Bowleses on Long Island; Paul Bowles first met him while still in high school in Flushing. Burns introduced him to French literature more advanced than that in the curriculum and also encouraged Bowles's interest in music.

Cadour, Abdelkader. An ingenuous Moroccan chamber boy at the hotel in

Marrakech where Bowles and Harry Dunham stayed in 1931. Harry Dunham decided to employ him as a valet, then left for Paris. The boy went to Paris with Bowles.

Charhadi, Driss ben Hamed. Pseudonym for Larbi Layachi, a young Moroccan storyteller whose tales Bowles began recording and translating in 1962; Layachi dictated autobiographical episodes in Moghrebi Arabic, which Bowles recorded and translated into English. This work was published by Grove Press as A *Life Full of Holes* in 1964.

Chavez, Carlos. 1899–1978. One of Mexico's two most important twentieth-century composers, along with Silvestre Revueltas. Chavez was director of the National Conservatory and conductor of the Orquesta Sinfonica de Mexico from 1928 to 1952.

Cherifa. b. circa 1928. Moroccan woman from Mraier, a village near Tangier. She was the daughter of a cherif, one who claims direct descendancy from the prophet Mohammed. Cherifa worked in the grain market selling wheat, and Paul introduced her to Jane Bowles in 1948. Jane was involved with Cherifa until her illness, which some have suggested was caused by Cherifa administering "magic" substances to her in her food. Paul Bowles's house in the Casbah of Tangier was given to Cherifa at Jane Bowles's request.

Chester, Alfred. 1928–1971. American novelist, short-story writer, and literary critic. Author of *Here Be Dragons, Jamie Is My Heart's Desire, Behold Goliath,* and other works. He lived in Morocco in the 1960s and had a troubled friendship with Bowles.

Choukri, Mohamed. b. circa 1935. Moroccan writer of Riffian parentage who was illiterate until age twenty. Author of *Jean Genet in Tangier, Tennessee Williams in Tangier,* and *For Bread Alone,* all non-fictional works translated by Bowles.

Cohen, Ira. American poet, editor, and photographer who lived in Tangier in the early 1960s. While in Tangier he edited and published the single issue of *Gnaoua.*

Conklin, Gary. American filmmaker who traveled to Morocco to make a documentary film about Paul Bowles, *Paul Bowles in the Land of the Jumblies,* 1969.

Cowell, Henry. 1897–1965. American pianist, composer, teacher, and publisher of *New Music Quarterly.* He taught at the New School, Stanford, Mills, and the University of California at Berkeley. Bowles played his music for

Cowell and he, in turn, introduced Bowles to Aaron Copland. Cowell published five of Bowles's compositions in the April 1935 issue of *New Music: A Quarterly of Modern Compositions*.

Cowen, Katherine. An American woman Bowles met in 1929 in Paris; she showed him photographs of Marrakech and introduced him to Tristan Tzara. Bowles later composed a musical portrait of her, "Portrait of KMC," which was performed in a concert at the Midtown Center in New York, January 26, 1936.

Crawford, Cheryl. 1902–1986. American theater producer and director associated with Lee Strasberg and Elia Kazan; produced several of Tennessee Williams's plays, including *Sweet Bird of Youth*, 1959, with Bowles's incidental music.

Crevel, René. 1901–1935. French surrealist poet. Committed suicide in Paris, aged thirty-four. He left a note: "Je suis dégoûlé de tout."

Crouch, Mary [Oliver]. b. circa 1907. A close friend of Bowles from childhood: He met her and her mother, a half-Cree Indian, through the Hoagland sisters, who owned a property near Bowles's paternal grandparents' home. Mary Crouch married Jock Oliver, an Englishman, in 1929, and is referred to variously as Mary Crouch and Mary Oliver in Bowles's letters.

Dagel, Gena. A young American scholar who wrote her doctoral dissertation on Bowles's music, "Paul Bowles: Manufactured Savage," University of Texas at Austin, 1984. Her *Conversations with Paul Bowles*, a collection of interviews, was published in 1993.

Davis, Stephen. A young American journalist whose interview with Bowles, "Paul Bowles in Tangier," was published in 1980; his profile of Bowles, "Mercury at 80," appeared in the *Boston Globe Magazine*.

Denby, Edwin. 1903–1983. American poet and dance critic born in Tientsin, China. He was the dance critic for *Modern Music*, 1929–30, and for the *New York Herald Tribune*, 1936–42. He worked on the Orson Welles production of *Horse Eats Hat*, 1936, at the Federal Theater. The score for this production was composed by Bowles with assistance from Virgil Thomson. Denby was a friend of the Bowleses in the early 1940s and visited them in Tangier in early 1948; they traveled together to Fez.

Desnos, Robert. 1900–1945. French radio writer, playwright, novelist, and poet, best known for his surrealist poetry. During World War II he lampooned Nazi occupying forces on French radio and was arrested and sent to Auschwitz, Buchenwald, and Terezen, where he contracted typhoid and died after the camp was liberated.

de Spirito, Romolo. A tenor who sang Bowles's music, both art songs and the zarzuela *The Wind Remains*, presented at the Museum of Modern Art on March 30, 1943. In 1946 he recorded eight of Bowles's songs, issued by Disc as "Night without Sleep."

Diamond, David. b. 1915. American composer who studied with Roger Sessions and Nadia Boulanger. In Paris he was encouraged in his work by Maurice Ravel and André Gide. Bowles met him in New York in the mid-thirties.

Dillon, Millicent. American fiction writer and biographer; author of a biography of Jane Bowles, *A Little Original Sin: The Life and Work of Jane Bowles*, 1981; and editor of *Out in the World*, a collection of Jane Bowles's letters.

Djilali, Mohammed Larbi. A young Moroccan who drove Bowles and Christopher Wanklyn on their trips throughout Morocco to record indigenous music for the Library of Congress in 1959. He assisted Bowles in making the arrangements with caïds and musicians.

Doughty, Charles Montagu. 1843–1926. English explorer and travel writer. After extensive explorations at Al-Hijr, the ancient caravan city of Arabia, he traveled with a tribe of bedouins to the legendary oasis city of Keybar, forbidden to unbelievers, and was expelled after four months of detention. The scientific and literary account of his explorations, *Travels in Arabia Deserta*, was published by the Cambridge University Press in 1888 and reissued with an introduction by T. E. Lawrence in 1921. In 1969 Doughty was honored by the government of Dubai with a postage stamp bearing his image.

Drissi, Abdallah. A young Fassi aristocrat whom Bowles met and became friends with in Fez in 1931; he and his brother were the only remaining direct descendants of Moulay Idriss, the founder of Morocco; they lived in medieval splendor in a palace located in the Nejjarine quarter of Fez. Bowles was later their houseguest for a number of weeks.

Dunham, Amelia. Harry Dunham's sister. After hearing Bowles's music performed in London in 1931, she suggested to Bowles that anyone who wrote such music ought to be hospitalized for treatment.

Dunham, Harry. circa 1910–1943. A student at Princeton in 1930 when Bowles met him, introduced by John Widdicombe. In 1933 Bowles composed music for a film edited by Dunham, *Bride of Samoa*, originally shown as *Siva*. Dunham became involved with the Nazi youth movement in Germany but after returning to New York was dissuaded by Bowles and his other friends from such politics; he then joined the Communist party and made movies for them. Dunham worked on the Orson Welles production of *Too Much Johnson*, shooting film sequences; Bowles composed music for this production, which was never presented. Bowles subsequently made a small suite out of the music he had composed, titled *Music for a Farce*.

Dunphy, Jack. b. 1914. Novelist and playwright; longtime friend and companion of Truman Capote.

Evans, Oliver. 1915–1981. American poet, translator, and biographer. Evans suggested that Bowles be invited to teach at San Fernando Valley State University in Northridge, California, where he was on the faculty. Bowles taught one semester there in 1968.

Fainlight, Ruth. b. 1931. American poet, writer, and translator. Married English novelist Alan Sillitoe in 1959. The Sillitoes befriended Bowles when they lived in Tangier for a year in the late 1960s.

el-Fassi, Allal. b. 1906. An early Moroccan nationalist who served as the head of the Istiqlal party. "For a quarter of a century Allal el-Fassi was acknowledged as the leader of native nationalism, and, after the King, was perhaps the chief architect of independence . . . In 1961 he was elected President of the *Conseil Constitutionnel* charged with drafting Morocco's new constitution." *Morocco Independent under Mohammed the Fifth* by Rom Landau, Allen & Unwin, London, 1961.

Faulkner, Bob. A friend of Jane Bowles who worked on *The New Yorker* in the 1930s; he accompanied the Bowleses to New Mexico in the fall of 1939, when Paul Bowles was commissioned to write music for *Roots in the Soil*, a documentary film produced under the auspices of the Department of Agriculture.

Faÿ, Bernard. 1893–1942. French historian, educator, and lecturer; he studied at the Sorbonne and Harvard universities and was appointed to the chair of American Civilization at the Collège de France in 1932. Bowles was introduced to him in Paris in 1931 by Gertrude Stein.

Ferrer, José. 1912–1992. American stage and film actor born in Puerto Rico; he studied at Princeton. Bowles was commissioned to write the incidental music for Ferrer's production of Rostand's *Cyrano de Bergerac*, which premiered at the Alvin Theater in New York City, October 8, 1946, and subsequently composed incidental music for Ferrer's production of *Edwin Booth* in 1958.

Finestone, Harold. Professor and chairman of the English Department at San Fernando Valley State University in Northridge, California. At his invitation, Bowles taught there for one semester in 1968.

Fizdale, Robert (Bobby). b. 1920. American concert and recording duo-pianist with Arthur Gold. Gold and Fizdale commissioned several compositions from Paul Bowles, including his *Concerto for Two Pianos, Winds and Percussion, Picnic Cantata*, and *Night Waltz*. Their first recording of Bowles's music was of two short piano pieces, included in the Art of This Century recording of Bowles's *Sonata for Flute and Piano*. *See* Arthur Gold.

Ford, Charles-Henri. b. 1913. American poet, editor, artist, and filmmaker; edited *Blues: A Magazine of New Rhythms*, 1929–30; founded and edited *View* (magazine) and View Editions, 1940–47; author of *The Young and Evil* with Parker Tyler, Obelisk Press, 1933, and numerous books of poetry. In 1933 Bowles shared his house in Tangier with Ford and Djuna Barnes, who was then writing *Nightwood*. Bowles and Ford collaborated on an opera in the early 1940s, *Denmark Vesey*, never completed because the score was lost.

Fordyce, Michael. A resident of Tangier in the 1950s. He and Bowles traveled to Portugal in 1956.

Fox, Joseph. Paul Bowles's editor at Random House for *Their Heads Are Green and Their Hands Are Blue*, 1963.

France, Alec. A young American scholar who visited Bowles in 1974; he was doing research for his dissertation on Bowles, which was cut short by his suicide.

Fuhs, Julian. Claire Auer's second husband and Jane Bowles's stepfather; a refugee from Germany and a musician. He married Claire Auer in 1938.

Gabo, Naum. 1890–1977. Russian-American sculptor and leading member of the Constructivist movement. Younger brother of Antoine Pevsner. Influenced by the Cubists, Aleksandr Archipenko, and Laszlo Moholy-Nagy. Author, with Pevsner, of *Realistic Manifesto*.

Garland, Peter. Young American composer, ethnomusicologist, and founding editor of Soundings Press; Garland edited and published Paul Bowles's *Selected Songs*, 1984, and his *Concerto for Two Pianos, Winds and Percussion*.

Gerofi, Isabelle and Yvonne. Belgian booksellers who ran the Librairie des Colonnes bookstore in Tangier, a Gallimard bookstore, from the late 1940s until the 1970s. Friends of both Jane and Paul Bowles.

Ghazi, Ahmed. Tangier friend from 1931.

Glanville-Hicks, Peggy. 1912–1990. Australian composer who studied with Vaughan Williams and Nadia Boulanger. She lived in America from 1942 to 1959. Bowles and Glanville-Hicks were extremely close friends. One of her compositions, *Letters from Morocco*, with texts from Bowles's letters to her, premiered at the Museum of Modern Art in New York conducted by Leopold Stokowski. Another earlier composition, "Ballade," consisted of three songs set to poems of Bowles. She also wrote music criticism, serving as music critic for the *New York Herald Tribune* from 1948 to 1950, a post Bowles had held earlier in the decade.

Glass, Norman. An English writer who lived in North Africa for some time. His translations from French into English include Gerard de Nerval's *Journey to the Orient*, Panther Books, New York, 1973. He lived in Tangier in the 1960s.

Gold, Arthur. 1919–1990. Canadian duo-pianist who played with Robert Fizdale. Gold and Fizdale met while students at the Juilliard School in New York City. Their debut was a recital at Town Hall in New York City, February 15, 1946; the program included music by Bowles. *See* Robert Fizdale.

Goodwin, John. A friend of the Bowleses and Tennessee Williams.

Gramont, Sanche de. See Ted Morgan.

Gray, William (Bill). born c. 1920–1992. Chairman of the English Department at Randolph-Macon College and acquaintance of Paul Bowles.

Green, Michelle. Senior writer at *People* magazine; author of *The Dream at the End of the World: Paul Bowles and the Literary Renegades in Tangier*, 1991.

Grissman, Carla. A teacher at the American School in Tangier in the mid-1960s; she befriended Jane Bowles, encouraging her to continue her writing, and then became her secretary.

Grosser, Maurice. American painter. Grosser first met Jane Bowles at Kirk and Constance Askew's salon in New York City in the 1930s and painted several portraits of Jane Bowles. He later became friends of the Bowleses, living in Tangier, sometimes residing in their building.

Gysin, Brion. 1916–1986. English painter, inventor, writer, recording artist, and restaurateur. He studied at the Sorbonne, the University of Bordeaux, and the Archives de India at the University of Seville, and was a Fulbright fellow from 1949 to 1952. Author of *The Exterminator*, with William Burroughs, 1960; and *The Process*, 1969. Bowles invited Gysin to Morocco, where they lived and traveled together for several months.

Halpern, Daniel. b. 1945. American poet, editor, and publisher. Founded *Antaeus* in 1970 with backing from Paul Bowles, who has served as a consulting editor to the magazine. Author of several works of poetry, including *Traveling on Credit*, 1972, and *Life among Others*, 1978. Founding editor of the Ecco Press, he published a Paul Bowles reader, *Too Far from Home*, in 1993.

Hamill, Katharine. A close friend of Jane Bowles, whom she met in New York City in the late 1940s. She worked for *Fortune* magazine as a writer.

Harbach, Anne. Ex-wife of the son of Otto Harbach, longtime resident of Tangier. Anne Harbach accompanied Jane Bowles from Tangier to London, and then to Oxford, in September 1957, where Jane was readmitted to the Radcliffe Infirmary.

Harbach, Douggie. Longtime resident of Tangier. Sister-in-law of Anne Harbach and friend of the Bowleses.

Haselwood, Jay. American expatriate and owner of the Parade Bar in Tangier; friend of the Bowleses.

Herbert, The Hon. David. Younger brother of the 15th Earl of Pembroke; longtime resident of Tangier. Friend of the Bowleses. Paul Bowles wrote the foreword to his autobiography, *Second Son*, 1972.

Herlihy, James Leo. 1927–1993. American novelist, playwright, and actor. Author of *All Fall Down*, 1959, *Midnight Cowboy*, 1965, and *The Season of the Witch*, 1971. Herlihy played the leading role in the Boston and Paris productions of Edward Albee's "The Zoo Story" and has appeared in motion pictures and television.

Hibbard, Allen. Young American scholar and writer; author of *Paul Bowles: A Study of the Short Fiction*, Twayne Publishers, 1993.

Hoagland, Anna. One of three spinster sisters, Miss Anna, Miss Sue, and Miss Jane, who lived in Brooklyn, New York; they had a summer house, Lasata, adjacent to Bowles's paternal grandparents in Glenora, New York. While still a child, Paul would visit the sisters in Brooklyn and they would take him to museums, concerts, and movies. It was one of the Hoagland sisters, Miss Sue, who, along with Mrs. Crouch, helped Bowles to secure a passport, unbeknownst to his parents, in 1929.

von Hoershelman, Natasha. A close friend of Jane Bowles, whom she met in New York City in the late 1940s; she worked at *Fortune* magazine as the head of the research department.

Holman, Libby. 1904–1971. American singer in musicals. Holman made such songs as "Body and Soul" and "Moanin' Low" famous. She married Zachary Smith Reynolds of the Reynolds Tobacco family in 1931; he died in 1932, either a suicide or murdered. Holman was charged with his murder but the case was never brought to trial. The Bowleses met Libby Holman in 1945 in Hartford, Connecticut, introduced by John Latouche. Holman commissioned Bowles to write an opera based on Federico García Lorca's play *Yerma* in 1950. Bowles translated the play, wrote the libretto, and composed the music, which he worked intermittently on for years. It was presented at Denver University on July 29, 1958.

Hopkins, Ellen-Ann. née *Ragsdale.* Wife of the novelist, John Hopkins. From Little Rock, Arkansas. She lived in Tangier in the early 1970s.

Hopkins, John. b. 1938. American novelist educated at Princeton University. Hopkins traveled widely in South America before settling in Tangier, where he wrote *The Attempt*, Viking, New York, 1967, and *Tangier Buzzless Flies*, Atheneum, New York, 1972. He was a teacher and headmaster at the American School of Tangier and now lives with his family in England.

Hoyningen-Huene, George. 1900–1968. A New York photographer known particularly for his portraits and his fashion work.

Joans, Ted. b. 1928. Black American poet, painter, and travel writer who lived briefly in Tangier in the 1960s while en route to Tombouctou. Author of *Black Pow Wow.*

Jordan, Fred. One of the three senior editors at Grove Press, along with Richard Seaver and founder Barney Rosset. Jordan was responsible for *Evergreen* magazine in the early 1960s.

Kamalakar, Narayan. An East Indian who, with his wife, Sonia, came to Morocco in the 1950s with a scientific expedition. Since funds were wanting, the Kamalakars stayed on in Tangier. The Kamalakars held salons devoted to esoteric religious interests.

Kamalakar, Sonia. A Georgian Russian who was a close friend of Jane Bowles.

Kirsch, Robert. Former editor of the *Los Angeles Times Book Review.*

Kraft (Kraftsov), Victor. Aaron Copland's longtime associate whom he described in a letter to Carlos Chavez as "a young violinist, who is a pupil, companion, secretary and friend."

Krishnamurti, Jiddu. 1895–1986. East Indian religious philosopher originally associated with the Theological Society. Author of more than forty books, he traveled around the world speaking to large audiences. Paul Bowles visited Krishnamurti at Kastel Eerde in the Netherlands in 1931; the visit was arranged by his friend Carlo Suarès, who edited *Carnets*, a magazine devoted to Krishnamurti's writings.

Lambert, Gavin. b. 1924. English film critic, novelist, biographer, and screenwriter. Editor of *Sight and Sound*, 1950–56; wrote the novel and screenplay for *Inside Daisy Clover*. Author of biographies of Vivian Leigh and Norma Shearer. Lambert lived in Tangier in the 1970s and is a close friend of Bowles.

Larbi, Mohammed. *See* Mohammed Larbi Djilali.

Latouche, John (a.k.a. Touche). 1917–56. American songwriter and poet from Virginia, and a close friend of the Bowleses in New York. Bruce Morrissette introduced Bowles to Latouche; Latouche introduced Paul to Jane Auer in the winter of 1937. Bowles composed music for a film, *Congo*, 1944, written by Latouche and narrated by Paul Robeson.

Laughlin, James. b. 1914. American publisher, poet, and editor; founder of New Directions, an important avant-garde publisher of both American and foreign authors. Published *The Sheltering Sky*, 1949.

Lavillatte, Comtesse de. A good friend of Paul's during his early years in Paris. Bowles had met her daughter Christine aboard ship on his first voyage to Europe in 1929; she was returning to Paris to have her first child. Paul stayed several times with the de Lavillatte family at their chateau in the Creuse.

Layachi, Larbi. *See* Driss ben Hamed Charhadi.

Lehmann, John. b. 1907. English publisher and editor. Worked for Leonard and Virginia Woolf's Hogarth Press in the 1940s; founded the publishing firm of John Lehmann Limited in 1946. Published the first editions of *The Sheltering Sky*, *A Little Stone* (*The Delicate Prey*, lacking two stories deemed unpublishable in England at the time), and *Let It Come Down*.

Lerman, Leo. b. 1914. Contributing editor to *Mademoiselle* in the 1940s, former editor of *Vogue* and *Vanity Fair*; friend of both Jane and Paul Bowles. He favorably reviewed Jane Bowles's novel, *Two Serious Ladies*, shortly after its publication in 1943.

Lerner, Bennett. Concert and recording pianist; he premiered two Bowles compositions: *Orosí*, in February 1983 at Carnegie Recital Hall, and *Iquitos* (retitled *Tierra Mojada*) at the Greenwich Music School in September 1983.

Lesser, Wendy. Founding editor of *The Threepenny Review* and daughter of Jane Bowles's biographer, Millicent Dillon. Paul Bowles has been a contributing editor to her review.

Lewis, Dione. A close friend of Jane Bowles, whom she met in New York City in the 1930s.

Lund, Paul. A friend of William Burroughs; he ran a bar in Tangier.

McBey, Marguerite. Longtime resident of Tangier; a painter. Close friend of both Jane and Paul Bowles.

McDowell, David. Editor at Random House who worked on *The Delicate Prey*, *Let It Come Down*, and *The Spider's House*.

Machiz, Herbert. New York theater director; he directed Tennessee Williams's *Garden District* (*Suddenly Last Summer* and *Something Unspoken*), which opened in January 1958. He also directed *The Milk Train Doesn't Stop Here Anymore*, with incidental music by Bowles, which opened in New York at the Morosco Theater in January 1963.

McKay, Claude. 1890–1948. Black American poet and novelist born in Jamaica; he came to the United States in 1912. Bowles met McKay in Tangier, where he was then living, 1931.

Macleod, Norman. 1906–1985. American poet, novelist, and editor; served as the American editor of *Front* and *Morada*, 1930–32. Bowles met Macleod sometime in the early 1930s and formed an unfavorable opinion of him.

McPhee, Colin. 1900–1964. American composer and ethnomusicologist. He lived in Bali for a number of years and composed *Tabuh-tabuhan* for two pianos and orchestra and *Balinese Ceremonial Music* for two pianos. He later taught in Los Angeles and wrote *Music in Bali*, 1966. McPhee knew the Bowleses in New York in the 1940s and would visit them on Long Island on weekends.

McPhillips, Joseph, III. Headmaster of the American School of Tangier; he came to Morocco in the early 1960s with John Hopkins, after studying at Princeton University. Longtime friend of both the Bowleses, he has commissioned numerous theater scores from Paul Bowles for the American School, including productions of "The Bacchae," "Oedipus the King," and "Caligula."

Mannheim, Anne Miracle. French artist whom Bowles met in Paris in 1932, while she was estranged from her husband, who lived in Germany. She and Bowles traveled to Clavières, in the Italian Alps, to ski, but Bowles fell

ill. She later did the artwork on one of the covers of Bowles's music publications under the imprint Éditions de la Vipère.

Marlowe, Sylvia. 1908–1981. Harpsichordist and friend of Jane Bowles; they
met in the late 1930s in New York City.

Marshall, John. Official at The Rockefeller Foundation in New York City responsible for overseeing Paul Bowles's grant to record indigenous music in
Morocco in 1959.

Martin, John. Founding publisher and editor of Black Sparrow Press, which
reissued most of Bowles's works in the 1960s and 1970s; he published *The
Collected Stories* of Paul Bowles and most of Mrabet's works translated from
the spoken Moghrebi by Paul Bowles.

Massenbach, Baronin von. Paul Bowles's landlady in Berlin when he lived in
that city in 1931. English by birth, married to a German nobleman, and
violently pro-German.

Mboya, Tom. 1930–1969. Kenyan nationalist leader in movement for self-
government by blacks. President of the Nairobi People's Convention party,
he preferred nonviolent means to achieve black rule in Kenya. Bowles met
and interviewed Mboya when he was in East Africa in 1957.

Menotti, Gian Carlo. b.1911. American composer of Italian birth; has written
operas, including *Amalia Goes to the Ball*, 1935; *The Consul*, 1950; and
The Saint of Bleecker Street, 1955. Founder in 1958 and director of the
Spoleto Festival of Two Worlds. Bowles knew Menotti and Samuel Barber
in New York in the 1940s.

Merlo, Frank. Tennessee Williams's friend and companion for fifteen years. He
died in 1963. Bowles knew him through his friendship with Tennessee
Williams. Bowles traveled with Williams and Merlo from New York to
Tangier in 1948; they then traveled in Morocco.

Metcalf, Paul. b. 1917. American poet, writer, and teacher. Bowles had a brief
three-way correspondence with Metcalf and Richard Peabody, editor of
Gargoyle magazine. Metcalf wrote an essay on Bowles, "A Journey in Search
of Bowles," which appeared in the Paul Bowles/Coleman Dowell issue of
The Review of Contemporary Fiction.

Meuron, Louise de. A Swiss baroness and longtime resident of Tangier; friend
of the Bowleses.

Michie, James. Paul Bowles's editor at William Heinemann, Ltd., London, for
The Hours after Noon, 1959. Sonia Orwell had arranged an appointment
for Bowles at Hamish Hamilton Ltd., but Bowles mistakenly went to Hei-

nemann; the editors at Heinemann signed up the book immediately, not knowing that Bowles had intended to go to another publisher.

Miller, Steve. Cofounder with Ken Botnick of The Red Ozier Press in New York City; Red Ozier published Bowles's translation of Rodrigo Rey Rosa's *The Path Doubles Back* in a limited edition, 1982.

Moore, Anne Carroll. Former head of the Children's Section of the Fifth Avenue Branch of the New York Public Library; she was a friend of Bowles's family. She first suggested the idea of study at the University of Virginia at Charlottesville.

Morgan, Ted (Sanche de Gramont). b. 1932. Prolific Franco-American non-fiction writer, journalist, biographer, and novelist. A count and member of one of France's oldest families, he changed his citizenship because the American Embassy gave him aid when he was wounded in Katanga, in the Congo, where he was serving as a journalist. He lived with his wife and children in Tangier in the late 1960s. Amber de Gramont is his daughter.

Morrissette, Bruce. Emeritus professor of Romance Languages at the University of Chicago. A close friend of Paul Bowles; they met in Virginia in 1928 where they were both students, Bowles at the University of Virginia at Charlottesville and Morrissette at the University of Richmond. Morrissette edited his university's literary magazine, *The Messenger.* Bowles was invited to solicit material for an issue and it was in his capacity as editorial adviser to Morrissette that he first made contact with Gertrude Stein and other established writers.

Mrabet, Mohammed. b. circa 1935. Moroccan storyteller of Riffian parentage; Paul Bowles has been translating his stories since 1965, most of which have been published by Black Sparrow Press.

Nabokov, Nicolas. 1903–1978. Russian-born composer who came to the United States in 1933. He composed scores for *Ode,* Diaghilev's Ballets Russes, 1928; George Balanchine's *Don Quixote,* 1969; and W. H. Auden's *Love's Labor Lost,* 1971. Cousin of novelist Vladimir Nabokov.

Nicklaus, (Charles) Frederick. b. 1936. American editor and poet whose work has appeared in *Antaeus.*

Norman, Dorothy. b. 1905. Editor, photographer, writer, and publisher. She edited and published *Twice a Year,* a semi-annual journal of literature, the arts, and civil liberties, from 1937 to 1948. Bowles met Norman in the 1930s; it was at her apartment in New York City that he had a contretemps with Alfred Stieglitz over the issue of American versus expatriate arts.

Norse, Harold. b. 1916. American poet, translator, and editor. Norse lived in Tangier in the early 1960s and became friends with Bowles.

Nurenberg, Phil. An admirer of Bowles's writings who initiated a brief correspondence.

Nutting, Cherie. A young American photographer who has lived intermittently in Tangier since the early 1980s. Married to Bachir Attar, hereditary leader of the Master Musicians of Jajouka. Friend of Paul Bowles.

Oliver, Mary Crouch. See Mary [Oliver] Crouch.

Orlovsky, Peter. Longtime companion of Allen Ginsberg; he accompanied Ginsberg to Tangier in the 1960s.

Owen, Peter. English publisher; founder of Peter Owen, Ltd. Owen has published Bowles's works in the United Kingdom since shortly after the demise of John Lehmann Ltd. Owen visited the Bowleses in 1962 soliciting work from them. Owen also publishes Jane Bowles's works in the U.K.

Peabody, Richard. Novelist and editor of *Gargoyle* magazine.

Portman, Michael. An English artist and protégé of William Burroughs who visited Burroughs frequently in Tangier.

Pounds, Wayne. A young American scholar and author of a study of Bowles's work, *Paul Bowles: The Inner Geography*, 1985.

Putnam, Samuel. 1892–1950. American editor, journalist, translator, and author of *Paris Was Our Mistress: Memoirs of a Lost and Found Generation*, 1947. He edited the *New Review* of Paris in the early 1930s.

Ramani, Hassan. A young Algerian Bowles met on the train from Tunis to Algiers in 1933; Bowles was without funds because of the bank moratorium in America, and Hassan Ramani kindly offered his hospitality. Bowles stayed for a time with Ramani's family in Constantine. Bowles later used the Ramani name in one of his most famous stories, "A Distant Episode."

Rand, Peter. b. 1942. American novelist; worked as advisory fiction editor at *Antaeus* in New York City, 1970–72; author of *Firestorm*, 1969, and *The Time of the Emergency*, 1977; both novels are admired by Bowles.

Redon, Joel. b. 1961. American "primitive" novelist; author of *Bloodstream*. A former student of Bowles's creative writing class, taught in Tangier under the auspices of the New York School of Visual Arts.

Reis, Mrs. Director of the League of Composers concerts in New York City in the 1930s.

Revueltas, Silvestre. 1899–1940. One of Mexico's two leading composers. Revueltas taught at the Conservatorio Nacional de Mexico. Upon meeting Revueltas in Mexico City in April 1937, Bowles was invited to the conservatory where Revueltas conducted an impromptu performance of his *Homenaje a García Lorca*; Bowles was deeply impressed by both Revueltas's person and music. Bowles wrote a beautiful obituary for Revueltas, published in *Modern Music* in 1941.

Rey Rosa, Rodrigo. b. 1958. Guatemalan writer and close friend of Bowles, he studied with Bowles in 1982. Rey Rosa wrote in Spanish; Bowles translated it into English and proposed publication of a collection of his short fictions to City Lights, which accepted and published *The Beggar's Knife*, 1985.

Rivière, Jacques. 1886–1925. French literary critic. Editor of the *Nouvelle Revue Française*, he was associated and identified with the journal from its founding in 1909.

Robbins, Franklin. Cousin of Paul Bowles.

Rochat, Joyce. American scholar who wrote her dissertation, "The Naturalistic–Existential Rapprochement in Albert Camus' *L'Étranger* and Paul Bowles's *Let It Come Down*: A Comparative Study in Absurdism," for the University of Michigan, 1971.

Roditi, Edouard. 1910–1992. American poet, translator, critic, and journalist; born in Paris. Attended Balliol College, Oxford, 1927–28, took his degree at the University of Chicago in 1939, and did graduate work at the University of California at Berkeley. In the 1930s he produced the first and best English translations of André Breton's works, which marked the start of a long career as a translator of many languages, including French, Spanish, German, and Turkish. Lifelong friend of Paul Bowles.

Romany, Marie. Well-known character in Greenwich Village in the 1920s and 1930s. She ran a restaurant and told fortunes.

Ross, Alan. b. 1922. English editor, poet, and nonfiction writer. On the staff of *The Observer*, 1950–71, and editor of *The London Magazine* from 1961.

Ross, Jean. An Englishwoman who grew up in Alexandria, Egypt; she lived in Berlin in the early 1930s and was introduced to Bowles by Christopher Isherwood, who has immortalized her as Sally Bowles in *The Berlin Stories*.

Ruggles, Carl. 1876–1971. American composer and painter; ceased composing entirely after the 1930s.

Ruspoli, Princess Marta. An American woman from Cincinnati married to an Italian nobleman, from whom she was estranged. A longtime resident of

Tangier. She and Jane Bowles were close friends during the mid-1960s. Also a friend of Paul Bowles.

Sager, Gordon. American novelist and friend of the Bowleses. Characters in his novel, *Run, Sheep, Run*, a roman à clef, were partially based on the Bowleses, whom he knew in Mexico in 1940. He lived in Tangier in the mid-1950s.

Saher, Lilla von. Hungarian actress and friend of Tennessee Williams and Jane Bowles; she traveled with Williams, Frank Merlo, John Goodwin, and Jane Bowles to Europe on the *Queen Frederica* in June 1956. Paul Bowles corresponded with her briefly in the early 1960s.

Saint-Simon, Duc de. Brother of the Comtesse de Lavillatte. *See* Comtesse de Lavillatte.

Salemson, Harold. b. 1910. American novelist, critic, editor, and publisher. Educated in France. Founded *Tambour* in Paris, a magazine which published articles and literature in both French and English; it ran for eight issues in 1929–30. Bowles contributed poems to *Tambour*, issues 4, 6, and 8.

Sankey, John. English printer of *Antaeus* magazine.

Schanker, Louis. Abstract painter; third husband of Libby Holman.

Schott, Webster. Kansas City book reviewer; he reviewed Bowles's *Up above the World* favorably. Bowles wrote three letters to him in response.

Seaver, Richard. Former editor at Grove Press. Seaver edited Driss ben Hamed Charhadi's *A Life Full of Holes*, translated from the spoken Moghrebi by Paul Bowles.

Sessions, Roger. 1896–1985. American composer, theorist, teacher, and author. He has had an enormous influence on 20th-century American music. While at Yaddo in 1930 Aaron Copland visited Sessions with Bowles; Copland showed Sessions a Bowles composition which Sessions played but found of little interest. Bowles briefly studied harmony with him in 1940.

Sintenis, Renée. 1888–1965. German sculptor known largely for her bronze castings of animals. Bowles became acquainted with her in Berlin in 1931.

Sions, Harry. Former editor at Little, Brown and Company. Sions was Bowles's editor for a book on Bangkok that he did not complete because of Jane Bowles's illness and because Bowles found the subject intractable; he returned Little, Brown's advance.

Slonimsky, Nicolas. b. 1894. American composer, conductor, and musicologist.

Born in St. Petersburg, Russia. He conducted the Boston Chamber Orchestra from 1927 to 1934. Slonimsky has been responsible for some of the major reference works on music in English, e.g., *Thesaurus of Scales & Melodic Patterns* and *Baker's Biographical Dictionary of Musicians*.

Smith, Oliver. b. 1918. Bowles's second cousin. He was the outstanding Broadway set designer during the 1950s, 1960s, and 1970s. Smith purchased a house with Bowles in Amrah, the Casbah of Tangier, in 1948.

Spivacke, Harold. Chief, Music Division of the Library of Congress while Bowles was recording Moroccan music for the Library in 1959.

Stettner, Irving. b. 1922. American poet, painter, editor and publisher of *Stroker* magazine. Stettner published numerous Mohammed Mrabet letters in *Stroker*, all of which were dictated and translated by Bowles. His book, *Thumbing Down to the Riviera*, was published by Writers Unlimited in 1986.

Stewart, Angus. b. 1936. English novelist and poet born in Australia. Author of two novels, a book of epitaphs (with a foreword by W. H. Auden), and a nonfiction work, *Tangier: A Writer's Notebook*, 1977. Stewart lived intermittently in Tangier during the late 1960s and early 1970s.

Strauss, Helen. Paul Bowles's literary agent at the William Morris Agency in New York City from 1947 until the early 1970s.

Suarès, Carlo. An Alexandrian banker who lived in Paris with his wife and children; editor of *Carnets*, a magazine devoted to the writings of Krishnamurti. Friend of Edouard Roditi and Paul Bowles; Bowles frequently stayed at Suarès's apartment in Paris in 1931–32.

Targ, William. Former editor in chief of G. P. Putnam's Sons. Bowles's editor for *Without Stopping*, Targ proposed this work to Bowles in 1968 while Bowles was on his way to California to teach.

Temsamany, Abdelmjid. A friend of Paul Bowles's in Agadir, Morocco, in the early 1930s.

Temsamany, Mohammed. Bowles's Moroccan chauffeur from 1950 until the mid-1960s.

Thoma, Richard. b. 1902. American poet and editor who lived in Paris in the 1920s and early 1930s. Associate editor of Samuel Putnam's *New Review*, 1931–32. Author of three books of poems published in Paris in the 1930s. Bowles set to music three of Thoma's poems, entitled "Green Songs."

Thomas, Claude. French translator and friend of Paul Bowles; she lives in Paris and Tangier. Thomas is one of the very few French translators of whose work Bowles approves. She has translated work by both Jane and Paul Bowles.

Thompson, Anita. Kristians Tonny's American girlfriend in the early 1930s. Bowles met her and Tonny when he first visited Tangier with Aaron Copland in 1931.

Titus, Edward. 1870–1952. Polish-born American publisher. Married to Helena Rubinstein, whose profits from her cosmetics empire financed the Black Manikin Press, 1926–32. In 1929 Titus took over *This Quarter* and published it through 1932.

Tonny, Kristians. 1907–77. Dutch surrealist artist. Bowles met Tonny in Tangier in 1931 at Gertrude Stein's suggestion. Tonny and his wife, Marie-Claire Ivanoff, came to New York in 1937, then traveled with Jane Auer and Paul Bowles to Mexico. Tonny did the cover art for one of Bowles's Éditions de la Vipère music publications.

Trimmer, Mr. and Mrs. The parents of an Anglican clergyman whom Bowles met in Colombo, Ceylon, in 1951. The Trimmers kindly invited Bowles to be a guest at their upland tea plantation, where Bowles stayed for several weeks.

Turner, Barbara. Editor of Contact Editions, which published *The Artist's and Writer's Cookbook,* 1961; it included Bowles's recipe for Majoun Kedanne.

Turner, George. A young American from Evanston, Illinois, who met Bowles in Ghardaïa, Algeria, in 1933. Bowles and Turner traveled together in Algeria and took a camel trip across the tip of the Great Eastern Erg to El-Oued. The character of Tunner in *The Sheltering Sky* is partially based on Turner.

Tyler, Parker. 1907–1974. American author, film critic, and editor. Co-author with Charles-Henri Ford of *The Young and Evil,* Obelisk Press, Paris, 1933. Associate editor of *Blues,* 1929–30, and of *View,* 1940–47. Bowles was a frequent contributor to *View* and was the music critic for the magazine for a short while.

Upton, William Treat. 1870–1961. American musicologist interested in the art song.

Villiers, David. English poet and friend of Bowles. Bowles set one of Villiers's poems, "The Heart Grows Old," to music.

Wanklyn, Christopher. A Canadian painter and journalist who has lived in

Morocco since 1954. A close friend of Bowles, he accompanied him on his travels around Morocco recording music in 1959. Bowles and Wanklyn shared a house in Marrakech for a time in the 1960s.

Weinreich, Regina. A writer and filmmaker from New York who taught with Paul Bowles at the School of Visual Arts in Tangier in 1983 and finished a documentary about him, Paul Bowles: The Complete Outsider, in 1993.

Widdicombe, John. A close friend of Bowles whom he met while they were both students at the University of Virginia in 1929; it was through Widdicombe that Bowles met Harry Dunham at Princeton. Widdicombe looked Bowles up in Tangier in the summer of 1934 and they traveled together in Morocco.

Williams, Colonel Charles. The director of The American Foundouk, a foundation established to care for maimed animals. Bowles worked for Col. Williams briefly, in the summer of 1934, as his secretary in Fez, Morocco.

Wood, Audrey. Theatrical agent who represented Tennessee Williams, William Inge, Carson McCullers, Jane Bowles, and others. A friend of both Jane and Paul Bowles.

el-Yacoubi, Ahmed ben Driss. 1931–198?. Moroccan painter born in Fez. Bowles met Yacoubi in the summer of 1947 while living in Fez and writing The Sheltering Sky. Yacoubi became a close friend and traveled with Bowles to India, Japan, Ceylon, Rome, and New York. He exhibited widely. In the mid-1950s Bowles introduced Yacoubi to the English painter Francis Bacon, who tutored Yacoubi in technique and brought him oil paints from England.

Yeager, Ira. A young American painter and jeweler who lived in Tangier in the early 1960s and befriended both Jane and Paul Bowles.

NOTES

3. *The City without Jews*: Opera based upon a novel by the same title, by Hugo Bettauer, 1926.

3. *Fools*: Alfred A. Knopf, New York, published *Children and Fools*, a collection of nine short stories by Thomas Mann, in 1928.

9. "This Quarter": Parisian literary magazine, 1925–32, edited at first by Ethel Moorhead and Ernest Walsh and later by Edward Titus and Samuel Putnam.

10. *Tambour*: Literary periodical, in French and in English, published in Paris by Harold Salemson. There were eight issues, which appeared irregularly between February 1929 and June 1930.

11. little book of verse in French: *Flute de Jade*, by Tsao Chang-Ling. Collected, edited, and translated by Franz Toussaint, 1920. Published in France.

12. *El Amor Brujo (Wedded by Witchcraft)*: Ballet, music composed by Manuel de Falla (1876–1946). *El Retablo de Maese Pedro (Master Peter's Puppet Show)*: Opera, music composed by de Falla to a libretto by the composer, based on an incident in *Don Quixote*, 1923. *Nights in the Gardens of Spain (Noches en los Jardines de España)*: Orchestral work composed by de Falla, 1909–15. *The Three Cornered Hat (El Sombrero de Tres Picos)*: Ballet, music composed by de Falla, based on Alarcón's story, 1919. "La Fille aux cheveux de lin": Piano solo by Claude Debussy; it is number 8 of the *Douze Préludes*, book I, 1910. "Beau Soir": Song composed by Debussy c. 1876, with words by Paul Bourget. *La Vida Breve (Life Is Short)*: Opera, with music composed by de Falla to a libretto by Carlos Fernandez Shaw, 1913.

13. "The Wild Party": Narrative erotic poem by Josef Moncure March with illustrations by Reginald Marsh. First edition consisted of 750 numbered copies sold to subscribers only by Pascal Covici, Chicago, 1928.

13. Frank Harris's autobiography: *My Life and Loves*, an erotic autobiography published privately in three volumes, 1923–27. Considered to be largely fictional, it nevertheless created a scandal upon its publication.

14. *Blues: Blues: A Magazine of New Rhythms*, edited by Charles-Henri Ford and Parker Tyler, 1929–30. It was published first in Columbus, Mississippi, and then in New York City after Ford and Tyler moved there.

15. Roerich Musée: Manhattan museum that houses paintings by Nicholas Roerich; the paintings are of Indian, Tibetan, and Russian subjects.

17. *transition*: Literary magazine edited by Eugene Jolas in Paris which published early poems by Bowles, including "Spire Song" in number 12, March 1928, and "Entity" in number 13, Summer 1928.

17. the Mercury: *The American Mercury*, a monthly magazine founded by H. L. Mencken and George Jean Nathan in 1924 and edited by Mencken until 1934.

23. Victor has some Fushiwara records: RCA, the Radio Corporation of America, issued phonograph records under the name "Victor."

23. The novel is growing slowly: The novel, based upon Bowles's travels in France, Switzerland, and Germany, was to be called *Without Stopping*. It was never published, except for the chapter referred to, "A White Goat's Shadow," which appeared in *Argo: An Individual Review* (Princeton, New Jersey), December 1930.

29. Wheels . . . the Nocturne Névritique: The manuscripts for these and the other early compositions that Bowles refers to in his letters of 1930 to Morrissette have not survived.

37. *Bifur*: French literary magazine edited by Ribemont Dessaignes in Paris. *Bifur* ran for eight issues, from May 1929 to June 1931.

38. Sonata in *blues* 7: "Sonata and Three Poems" (1. Sonata; 2. Along brighter lines; 3. Promenade des Anglais; 4. Poem). *Blues* 7, Fall 1929.

38. the Fountains and the Pines: The symphonic poems *Fountains of Rome*, 1917, and *Pines of Rome*, 1924, by Ottorino Respighi (1879–1936).

41. L'Ersatz d'Amour: The author of *L'Ersatz d'Amour*, 1923, was "Willy" (Henri Gauthier-Villars), first husband of the French writer Colette.

41. *South Wind*: Novel by the English writer Norman Douglas (1868–1952), published in 1917. A witty philosophical fantasy set on the island of Nepenthe, an idealized Capri, the novel was received as a masterpiece.

51. The Capriccio: Composition by Igor Stravinsky (1882–1971) for piano and orchestra, 1929.

52. L'Histoire: Stravinsky's ballet score *L'Histoire du Soldat*, 1918, was more classical and stringent than his earlier *The Firebird* and *Petrouchka*.

52. Schaeffner says of Stravinsky: Paul Bowles recalls that the material came from *Modern Music*. Bowles seems to be paraphrasing an article by André Schaeffner entitled "Stravinsky's 'Capriccio,' " which appeared in *Modern Music*, vol. 7, Feb.–March, 1930.

52. *Mavra*: An opéra bouffe by Stravinsky, *Mavra* was first performed in Paris in 1923; it was based on a story by Pushkin.

53. *Le Canard Enchaîné*: Satirical weekly published in Paris since 1915.

53. *Ondt & the Gracehoper*: Appeared as a part of "Work in Progress," the name given to the portions of James Joyce's *Finnegans Wake* that appeared in *transition* magazine.

54. handh: *The Hound and Horn*.

55. *new masses*: Radical journal of art and social criticism, affiliated with the Communist Party, published in the U.S. from 1926 to 1948. It began as *The Masses*, a socialist periodical later called *The Liberator*, that appeared from 1911 to 1924.

57. Theremin: An electrical musical instrument invented by the Russian scientist Lev Theremin. It somewhat resembles a radio receiver, appearing to draw musical sounds from the air by means of electric oscillations that vary in pitch as the hand approaches or recedes from the apparatus.

57. *Portrait of a Man with Red Hair*: Novel by the English writer Hugh Walpole (1884–1941), published in 1925.

58. some of Poe's poems: The quotations are from poems written when Edgar Allan Poe (1808–49) was in his teens: "The Lake: To ____," "Dream-Land," "Spirits of the Dead," and "Fairy-Land."

60. La Symphonie des Psaumes . . . Pulcinella: *La Symphonie des Psaumes (Symphony of Psalms)*, 1930, a work for chorus and orchestra by Stravinsky. *Pulcinella*, a ballet

composed by Stravinsky, based on Giovanni Battista Pergolesi's music, that was first performed in Paris in 1920.

60. concerto for flute & piano: *Sonata No. 1 for Flute and Piano*, by Paul Bowles, completed in Grenoble, France, in 1932. Issued in 1943 on Art of This Century, Recording No. 1., Vol. 1.

63. *Modern Editions*: The Modern Editions Press published two series of pamphlets under the editorship of Kathleen Tankersley Young in New York City. Paul Bowles's first separate publication was *Two Poems* ("Watervariation" and "Message"), which appeared in the second series in late 1933.

68. the duc writes asking me to the chateau: The Duc de Saint-Simon, brother of the Comtesse de Lavillatte, who was the mother of Bowles's friend Christine de Lavillatte.

70. stieglitz's is a good place: From 1929 until his death Alfred Stieglitz (1864–1946), the American photographer and art dealer, had a gallery in New York City called An American Place.

75. an acquaintance with description . . . : Two of the works of Gertrude Stein that Bowles refers to were published as *An Acquaintance with Description* (Seizin Press, 1929) and *Lucy Church Amiably* (Plain Editions, Paris, 1931; first American edition, Something Else Press, New York, 1961). "Madame Récamier" was included in *Operas and Plays* (Plain Editions, Paris, 1932).

75. the george hugney one: *Dix Portraits, Texte Accompagné de la Traduction de G. Hugnet et de V. Thomson* by Gertrude Stein, Éditions de la Montagne, Librairie Gallimard, Paris, 1930.

89. presenting Haroun-al-Raschid: A performance based on the life of Hārūn al-Raschīd (763 or 766–809), who ruled Islam at the zenith of its empire. The legendary splendor of his reign is celebrated in *The Thousand and One Nights*.

91. the Arab, who is pretending to stay with the Countess: The Arab is young Abdelkader Cadour. The Countess is the Comtesse de Lavillatte, at whose address Bowles used to receive mail.

92. the Arab's finding Gide: On his first afternoon in Paris, the Moroccan boy Abdel-kader Cadour had gone for a walk on his own and encountered a generous old French gentleman who spoke Arabic and asked him up to his apartment for tea. A few days later, Bowles took Abdelkader to the vernissage of an exhibition of photographs. "All Paris was there," Bowles writes in *Without Stopping*. Bowles met people he knew, got separated from the boy, and suddenly "heard his excited voice shouting above the several hundred other voices, saying: '*Monsieur Paul! Monsieur Paul! Viens vite!*' I hurried toward the sound and met him rushing toward me, still crying: '*Viens! Regarde!* There's the nice old man who gave me the fifty francs! Look!' Occupying a place of honor at the end of the hall was a huge photograph of André Gide, wearing a beret. It became the joke of the month around Paris."

97. when in hell my money is coming: In February 1932 Bowles received an inheritance of $800 from his Aunt Adelaide, which had fallen to him on his twenty-first birthday a few weeks before.

97. fifth group of songs: *See below*, 100.

98. La Création du Monde: Ballet by Darius Milhaud (1892–1974), first performed in Paris in 1923.

98. flute sonata: Probably *Sonata for Flute and Piano*, 1932, issued on Art of This

Century Recording, Album No. 1 (1943?), featuring Rene Le Roy, flute, and George Reeves, piano.

100. my songs and my flute: For the flute composition, see above, 60. The songs: "It Was a Long Trip Back," "Here I Am," "Will You Allow Me to Lie in the Grass," "In the Platinum Forest," "Things Shall Go On," and "Today, More than Ever." All were sung by Ada MacLeish at the Yaddo concert in 1932, with Aaron Copland playing piano accompaniment.

110. Anabase: *Scènes d'Anabase*, music for tenor, oboe, and piano by Paul Bowles with text by St.-Jean Perse. Two sections were published, "Ainsi Parfois Nos Seuils," in the *Cos Cob Song Volume: Ten Songs by American Composers*, New York, 1935, and "Part III," in *New Music: A Quarterly of Modern Compositions*, San Francisco, 1935.

110. Piano Sonatina: *Sonatina for Piano Solo*, by Paul Bowles. Elkan-Vogel, Philadelphia, 1947.

110. Cantata: *Cantata for Soprano, Four Male Voices, and Harmonium*, by Paul Bowles, 1933. Subtitled *Par le Détroit*. Datelined on manuscript: "Laghouat [Algeria] Jan 1933."

113. *Malaisie*: A novel by Henri Fauconnier, Paris, 1931.

118. the League: League of Composers, New York City. Founded in 1923, the league concerns itself with the interests of living composers and the acquaintance of the public with their works. It gives several concerts each season, sponsors occasional broadcasts and stage performances, holds receptions in honor of musicians, and, from 1927 to 1947, published a quarterly, *Modern Music*, edited by Minna Lederman.

119. The Tokalon: A brand of skin cream.

124. the girl of three years ago: Bowles wrote of her to Bruce Morrissette in the fall of 1929. She was English, her name was Peggy, and he'd met her when they were both in art school the year before.

129. two short things from Useful Knowledge: Bowles composed music for "Scenes from the Door" and "April Fool Baby."

131. *Bride of Samoa*: Film edited by Harry Dunham with score by Paul Bowles, 1933.

131. a new Piano Sonatina: *Sonatina for Piano Solo*, by Paul Bowles. Elkan-Vogel, Philadelphia, 1947.

140. p*axUx1x e*nzr@o*uxtXe: The solution is "Paul en route."

143. Danger de Mort: Six songs for voice and piano, by Paul Bowles with text by Georges Linze. Parts IV and VI were published in *New Music: A Quarterly of Modern Compositions*, San Francisco, 1935.

151. *Grammaire Historique de la Langue Française*, by Auguste Branchet, Paris, J. Hetzel, 1867?; *El Genio del Séptimo Arte: Apología de Charlot*, by Santiago Aguilar, Madrid, Compañía Ibero-Americana de Publicaciones, 1930 (Series title: Biblioteca Popular de Cinema).

154. "Scenes from the Door": Bowles wrote two songs with texts by Gertrude Stein for voice and piano accompaniment, "Red Faces" and "The Ford," that were published by his Éditions de la Vipère with the title *Scenes from the Door* in 1933.

155. letter of Gertrude's: Bowles wrote a song for voice and piano accompaniment using as text excerpts from a letter to him from Gertrude Stein; titled "Letter to Freddy," it was published in *New Music: A Quarterly of Modern Compositions* in 1935, and reprinted separately by G. Schirmer in 1947.

155. Set one of Cocteau's: Bowles composed *Memnon* in 1935, a suite for voice and piano with texts by Jean Cocteau; the songs are "Les Statues," "Memnon," "Athena," "Recette," and "Le Sourire." It was first performed at Town Hall, New York, in January of 1944.

157. First the Vipères would publish Virgil: Éditions de la Vipère was Bowles's musical imprint. He published a few works of his own in editions of 100, including *Scenes from the Door, Two Portraits for Piano,* and *Green Songs* (with text by Richard Thoma).

157. portrait of Virgil: Bowles composed a number of musical portraits of friends for the piano. *Two Portraits for Piano* contains "Portrait of K.M.C." (Katherine Cowen) and "Portrait of B.A.M." (Bruce Archer Morrissette). His portrait of Virgil Thomson has never been published and the manuscript has been lost.

157. until I broke his glasses: Paul Bowles would like the reader to know that the person he struck put his glasses on only after being cornered.

158. Reminiscent Piano Pieces: "Café Sin Nombre" was published in *New Music: A Quarterly of Modern Compositions,* 1935; it was also recorded by Bowles, on piano, and issued on a phonodisc by New Music Quarterly Recording in 1938. "Guayanilla" and "La Femme de Dakar" were premiered at Midtown Center, New York, in January 1936.

158. ¿¿¿toz sen vait???: When asked by the editors about the meaning of this phrase, Paul Bowles replied, "I can't break the code."

159. the Portrait. *See* 157.

162. our venus and adonis film: A film by Harry Dunham, 1935; Bowles composed the incidental music.

163. vesey: *Denmark Vesey,* an opera with libretto by Charles-Henri Ford and music by Paul Bowles. The opera was never produced but a portion of it was performed in oratorio form by the Juanita Hall Choir in a benefit performance for *New Masses* magazine. It tells the story of an unsuccessful slave uprising led by Denmark Vesey, a slave who purchased his freedom with the proceeds of a lottery he had won.

164. the Fair's Dream of Venus: A pavilion that Salvador Dalí designed for the New York World's Fair of 1939–40. "In front of the spectator is a long animated panorama that includes a thirty-foot glass-and-steel tank filled with water, at the bottom of which is a room from a Dream House. Lovely girls plunge into the tank and by their actions seem to reveal the secrets of some dreams. The representation includes Dalí's famous 'Soft Watches,' 'Piano Women,' 'Anthropomorphic Seaweed,' 'Exploding Giraffes,' a cow at the bottom of the sea, a couch in the shape of Garbo's lips, and of course 'Living liquid ladies'. . . ." from the official Guide Book, as quoted in *Dawn of a New Day: The New York World's Fair, 1939/40,* by Helen A. Harrison, New York, New York University Press, 1980.

165. *Foyers d'Incendie*: By Nicolas Calas, Éditions de Noël, Paris, 1938.

166. recent pact: The Molotov-Ribbentrop nonaggression pact between the Soviet Union and the Third Reich, signed on August 23, 1939, was followed on September 3 by the German attack on Poland and the outbreak of the Second World War. Word of the pact sharply divided the American left; some who had joined the Communist Party quit it in dismay at seeing the leading antifascist power join hands with the common enemy. There were others, Bowles among them, who for a time took what seemed to them a more coolheaded view.

171. have you read virgil's book?: *The State of Music*, by Virgil Thomson, William Morrow, New York, 1939.

173. one-act opera: *The Wind Remains*, zarzuela for piano and orchestra. Based on *Así Que Pasen Cinco Años* by Federico García Lorca. First produced on March 30, 1943, at the Museum of Modern Art with Schuyler Watts as producer and theater director; Leonard Bernstein, conductor; Merce Cunningham, choreographer and dancer; and Oliver Smith, set designer. Sung by Romolo de Spirito and Jeanne Stephens. Sponsored by Yvonne de Casa Fuerte for the *Sérénade* concert series.

173. two-piano sonata: *Sonata for Two Pianos, Four Hands*, by Paul Bowles, G. Schirmer, Inc., New York, 1949.

173. five scores for the theatre [1945–46]: During this period Bowles completed scores for *Ondine*, play by Jean Giraudoux, translated by Schuyler Watt, never produced; *Cyrano de Bergerac*, Rostand's play adapted by Brian Hooker; *The Dancer*, play by Julian Funt; *Land's End*, play by Thomas Job, adapted from *Dawn in Lyonesse* by Mary Ellen Chase; *Twilight Bar*, play by Arthur Koestler, produced and directed by George Abbott in 1946; and *On Whitman Avenue*, play by Maxine Wood, directed by Dorothy Heyward, which premiered at the Cort Theatre, New York, May 8, 1947.

173. a lot of songs: In 1946, a productive year, the songs Bowles composed included "Baby, Baby," with words by Paul Bowles, Mercury Music Corp., New York, 1946; "Song of an Old Woman," with words by Jane Bowles; "Once a Lady Was Here," with words by Paul Bowles; "Lonesome Man, Ballads," "Sugar in the Cane," "Heavenly Grass," and "Cabin," all with words by Tennessee Williams. Except for the first song, these were published by G. Schirmer, New York, in 1946.

175. The advance came through: The advance was from Doubleday. When the editors at Doubleday read the manuscript they rejected it; the work then went to New Directions in New York and John Lehmann in London, who became its publishers. The English edition appeared in September 1949, a few weeks before the American.

175. the new two-piano concerto: *Concerto for Two Pianos, Winds and Percussion*, 1946. Commissioned by Arthur Gold and Robert Fizdale. First performed at Town Hall, New York, November 14, 1948, with Lukas Foss conducting.

176. So send V*iew*: Magazine edited by Charles-Henri Ford and Parker Tyler, New York City, 1940–47. Bowles contributed translations and stories, and guest-edited the "Tropical Americana" issue, May 1945; all contributions to this issue were either written by or translated by Bowles.

187. Romolo never returned the score of *Denmark Vesey*: The score, lost by Romolo de Spirito's accompanist, has not been found.

188. Palinurus: Cyril Connolly (1903–74), author of *The Unquiet Grave: A Word Cycle by Palinurus*, London, 1944, and editor of the British literary magazine *Horizon*, which was published from 1940 to 1950.

195. *Summer and Smoke*: Play by Tennessee Williams, with incidental music by Paul Bowles. Bowles's score was written to accompany the New York production, which opened in Manhattan at the Music Box Theatre on October 6, 1948.

197. She has almost decided to be tattooed like a friend of hers: The friend was Cherifa. *See* the biographical note.

198. She has just completed a long story: "It was also in Fez, with Paul's help and advice, that Jane finished her long short story, 'Camp Cataract' " (Millicent Dillon, A *Little Original Sin*, 159).

198. the novel she started years ago: The novel, *Out in the World*, was never completed.
203. *One Arm: One Arm, and Other Stories*, by Tennessee Williams, New Directions, New York, 1948.
214. Jane's play: *In the Summer House. See below*, 515.
215. Gordon Sager's book: *Run, Sheep, Run*, by Gordon Sager, Vanguard Press, New York, 1950. A novel set in Mexico in the forties and partially based upon Paul and Jane Bowles.
217. a house on its own small island: Taprobane, a tiny island off the coast of Ceylon which Bowles bought and lived on periodically for a number of years in the fifties. Bowles eventually sold the island.
222. The title Let It Come Down is tentative: The book appeared as *Let It Come Down*, Random House, New York, 1952; John Lehmann, London, 1952.
223. García Lorca opera: *Yerma*, an opera based on Federico García Lorca's play of the same title with music and libretto by Paul Bowles, was first performed at Denver University on July 28, 1958, directed by Angna Enters, with Libby Holman singing. The opera was commissioned by Holman.
223. a recording of my Concerto: The recording, on Columbia Masterworks, appeared at about the same time as the concerto's first performance at Town Hall in November 1948.
224. the little friends: Paul and Jane Bowles's group of friends in New York, including John Latouche, Teddy Griffis, Harry Dunham, and Marian Dunham. Virgil Thomson gave them this name.
225. The new book is about Tangier: *Let It Come Down*.
225. the other thing is there in black and white, dated 1938: Bowles joined the Communist Party in 1939 and quit it in 1940.
227. If Chalia moves her bed out: A character in Bowles's story "At Paso Rojo."
227. If Van says . . . . : In the story "How Many Midnights."
227. Mokhtar's dream: In "A Thousand Days for Mokhtar."
227. the employee on the river boat . . . . : In "Call at Corazón."
229. "Doña Faustina": The story was published in *New Directions* 12, New York, 1950, in the collection *The Hours after Noon*, Heinemann, London, 1959, and in *Collected Stories*, 1939–1976, Black Sparrow Press, Santa Barbara, 1979.
229. *Two Serious Ladies*: Jane Bowles's novel was originally published by Alfred A. Knopf, New York, in 1943. New Directions did not reprint it.
230. *Cyrano de Bergerac*: The play by Edmond Rostand, adapted by Brian Hooker with incidental music by Paul Bowles, opened at the Alvin Theater, New York, on October 8, 1946, with José Ferrer directing and playing the leading role.
230. ten sets of the Concerto: Bowles's *Concerto for Two Pianos, Winds and Percussion*, performed by Arthur Gold and Robert Fizdale, duo-pianists, with a group conducted by Daniel Saidenberg, was released on Columbia Masterworks phonodiscs in 1948.
234. Music for a Farce: Bowles's piece for clarinet, trumpet, percussion, and piano was published by the Weintraub Music Company, New York, in 1953.
234. Three Songs from the Sierra: "Que Te Falta," "Ya Llegó," and "El Carbonero," with texts from the old Spanish, composed by Bowles in 1944. "Ya Llegó" is included in *Selected Songs*, published in 1984 by Soundings Press, Santa Fe, New Mexico. Its title has been changed to "Mes de Mayo."
240. the translation of a very bad novel in French: *The Lost Trail of the Sahara*, by R. Frison-Roche. Prentice-Hall, New York, 1951.

242. the score exists: The score of Bowles's incidental theater music for José Ferrer's *Cyrano de Bergerac*.

245. If you send a dubbing of the Cantata: The cantata was Bowles's *Par le Détroit*. Margot Rebeil and Peggy Glanville-Hicks performed it and made records of it.

246. Concerto Bobby and Arthur are playing: Bowles's full orchestral version, 1949, of the *Concerto for Two Pianos, Winds and Percussion*, now the *Concerto for Two Pianos and Orchestra*, which Arthur Gold and Robert Fizdale were performing.

247. the Vincent Sheean book: *Rage of Soul*, Random House, New York, 1952, which deals with the impact of East Indian mysticism upon a sophisticated American couple. It was described by F. H. Bullock in the *New York Herald Tribune* as an "effort to present esoteric ideas in an attractive fashion with not altogether successful results."

248. *dein' Liebe*: The change from *deine* to *dein'* that Bowles requested has not been made in later printings or editions.

254. finished my Cantata: A *Picnic Cantata for Four Women's Voices, Two Pianos and Percussion*. Music by Paul Bowles, text by James Schuyler. First performance at Town Hall, New York, March 23, 1954, with duo-pianists Gold and Fizdale. As Paul Bowles describes it, "the text by James Schuyler consists of a series of conversations carried on by four girls who drive out to the country for a picnic on Sunday."

261. that accursed opera: *Yerma. See above*, 223.

261. *The Transposed Heads* arrived: Peggy Glanville-Hicks's first major opera, 1954. Based on a novella by Thomas Mann, *The Transposed Heads, A Legend of India*, translated by H. T. Lowe-Porter, Knopf, New York, 1941.

262. book on Africa: *Yallah!*, text by Paul Bowles, photographs by Peter W. Haeberlin, 1957. Haeberlin took photographs throughout his travels in North Africa but died without leaving notes as to the precise settings of these photographs. The publishers, Manesse in Switzerland, and McDowell, Oblensky in New York, commissioned Bowles to reconstruct Haeberlin's itinerary and write commentary on the photographs.

266. writing the article for *Holiday*: Either "Parrots I Have Known," *Holiday*, November, 1956, or "The Incredible Arab," August, 1956.

267. Cotorrito hates it with poison in his heart: Cotorrito was the Bowleses' green parrot from the Amazon.

269. the news about Touche: Latouche died of a massive heart attack in 1956.

271. I sold both the pieces: "Worlds of Tangier," *Holiday*, March 1958, and "The Frozen Fields," *Harper's Bazaar*, July 1957.

275. Douglas Moore . . . and Otto Luening: Moore and Luening were composers on the grants committee of The American Academy and Institute of Arts, which awarded Bowles money from its fund for medical emergencies.

279. they are still furious about the last book: *The Spider's House*, published by Random House, New York, in 1955 and MacDonald, London, in 1957. Set in Fez in 1954, the novel sympathetically portrays a young Moroccan who is in conflict with the Istiqlal, which by 1958 had become the ruling party.

281. What a shame they didn't get around to my project: Bowles's project was to record indigenous Moroccan music in the field. He carried it out the following year for the Library of Congress under the auspices of the Rockefeller Foundation.

289. *Sweet Bird of Youth*: The play by Tennessee Williams, with incidental music by

Paul Bowles, opened at the Martin Beck Theater in New York on March 10, 1959. It was directed by Elia Kazan, produced by Cheryl Crawford, and starred Paul Newman.

310. Dubbs is dead: Dubbs was the Bowleses' housecat.

312. *Malcolm* is the first complete book that Jane has read . . . since her illness: James Purdy's novel was published by Farrar, Straus & Giroux in 1959.

318. the *Sodom and Gomorrah* company: The film *Sodom and Gomorrah*, 1961, a U.S./Italian/French coproduction directed by Robert Aldrich and Sergio Leone, starred Stewart Granger, Pier Angeli, Anouk Aimée, and Rossanna Podestà.

323. Jane works every day on her new play: The play, set in Camp Cataract, was never completed. Joseph McPhillips fashioned a script based on the story, which was produced in Vienna under the title *Camp Cataract*.

324. "A Friend of the World": Bowles's story appeared in *Encounter*, London, in March 1961.

328. Inmeuble Itesa: The name of the building in which Paul Bowles lived.

332. an extra story to add to my three: Bowles added his unpublished story "The Wind at Beni Midar" to "A Friend of the World," "Merkala Beach" (retitled "The Story of Lahcen and Idir"), and "He of the Assembly" to make *A Hundred Camels in the Courtyard*, published by City Lights Books, San Francisco, in 1962.

341. the score for Tennessee's new show: *The Milk Train Doesn't Stop Here Anymore*, by Tennessee Williams, with incidental music by Paul Bowles, had tryouts in New Haven and opened in New York at the Morosco Theater on January 16, 1963. It was directed by Herbert Machiz.

343. the Grand Central (oser): *oser*, a word which Jane used frequently, meant "having hope but no confidence." She thought it was Yiddish, but it appears to be French.

346. I signed the contract for his book: *A Life Full of Holes: A Novel Tape-recorded in Moghrebi and Translated into English by Paul Bowles*, by Driss ben Hamed Charhadi, pseudonym of Larbi Layachi. Grove Press, New York, 1964.

347. I'm recording some of my stories: The recording, *Paul Bowles Reads The Delicate Prey and A Distant Episode*, was released by Spoken Arts in 1963.

349. "Znagui" had arrived safely: A chapter of *A Life Full of Holes*.

349. to get *No Exit* out of *Huis Clos*: Bowles translated Sartre's play for a stage production, directed by John Huston, that opened in New York on November 26, 1946. *No Exit* was a great success. When Knopf later published the play in another translation Bowles's title, which bore no copyright, was naturally retained.

353. Formentor Prize Committee: Bowles's slip of the pen, which he's made before; he corrected himself in his letter to Burroughs of April 17, 1963. It was the International Literary Prize, not the Formentor Prize.

358. when they should say *Enta*, like other people: Bowles's objection is to a usage peculiar to the North of Morocco in which a feminine personal pronoun replaces a masculine one.

369. LWAFH: *Love with a Few Hairs*, by Mohammed Mrabet, taped and translated from the Moghrebi by Paul Bowles, Peter Owen, London, 1967; George Braziller, New York, 1968.

374. page-proofs in French of a book of mine: *Une Vie Pleine de Trous (A Life Full of Holes)*, Gallimard, Paris, 1965.

374. rewriting . . . on the new book: *Up above the World*, Simon & Schuster, New York, 1966.

377. Little Friends: *See above,* 224.
378. busy translating another book from the Arabic: *Love with a Few Hairs. See above,* 369.
382. Timothy Leary Defense Fund: Timothy Leary was arrested in Millbrook, New York, in 1965 and in Laredo, Texas, in 1966 for possession of small amounts of marijuana. In 1966, a small group informally created by Diane di Prima and Allen Ginsberg, the Timothy Leary Defense Fund, began to send letters arguing that Leary was being prosecuted not for his actions but for his ideas.
382. the Hypnotic Music record: A phonodisc with recordings of trance music played by the various religious brotherhoods—the Hamatcha, Jilala, Gnaoua, and Aissaoua—was eventually issued under Ira Cohen's auspices. Separate tape recordings made by Paul Bowles, Brion Gysin, and Ira Cohen were used to make the matrix for the phonodiscs.
384. without going necessarily as far as Roussel: The title of Raymond Roussel's book is *Comment J'ai Écrit Certains de Mes Livres,* A. Lemerre, Paris, 1935.
392. Mrabet's little book: *Love with a Few Hairs.*
394. Marta's saga of Set: Princess Ruspoli's book, *L'Épervier Divin.*
394. not only you but the students like "The Garden": Bowles wrote "The Garden" in Asilah in 1963; it appeared in the Autumn–Winter 1964 issue of *Art & Literature* (Lausanne) and is included in the *Collected Stories.* Bowles's dramatization was performed at the American School in Tangier in April 1968.
397. corrected the ms. of the Thomson: *Virgil Thomson by Virgil Thomson,* Knopf, New York, 1947.
398. I'm taping a novel in Arabic: *The Lemon,* by Mohammed Mrabet, taped and translated from the Moghrebi by Paul Bowles, Peter Owen, London, 1969; McGraw-Hill, New York, 1972.
401. *Dos Señoras de Aupa:* The Spanish translation of Jane Bowles's *Two Serious Ladies.*
404. The edition of *Yallah!* you ask about: *See above,* 262.
412. LWAFH: *Love with a Few Hairs. See above,* 369.
414. a small volume: *Scenes,* by Paul Bowles, Black Sparrow Press, Los Angeles, 1968.
414. Called *Lemon: See above,* 398.
421. *Pastorelas:* Ballet music by Paul Bowles for two voices and orchestra. First American performance at Hunter College, New York, in January 1947, by the American Ballet Caravan, directed by George Balanchine; Leon Barzin conducted the orchestra. Bowles writes in *Without Stopping* that "the esthetic of the ballet was based on the pre-Christmas *posadas* as celebrated by the Indians of Mexico; vocal sequences using the actual words and melodies were interspersed throughout the score."
422. *Jacobowsky and the Colonel.* Franz Werfel's play, adapted by S. N. Behrman, directed by Elia Kazan, and presented by The Theatre Guild. Incidental music composed by Paul Bowles. It opened at the Martin Beck Theatre, New York, March 14, 1944.
422. *La Folle de Chaillot (The Madwoman of Chaillot):* play by Jean Giraudoux.
422. El Farhar: A hotel on the Old Mountain in Tangier where the Bowleses occasionally stayed.
425. I signed a contract with Putnam: Contract with G. P. Putnam's Sons for Bowles's autobiography, published in 1972 as *Without Stopping.*

429. one of the best first novels: Peter Rand's *Firestorm*, published by Doubleday, New York, in 1969.

431. paternity case: Presumably Bowles was referred to as an influence on Rand's *Firestorm* in blurbs or advertisements.

444. I do know *L'Herne*: Important literary annual published in Paris since 1961.

461. The city is certainly Constantine: Here Bowles answers questions about his short story "By the Water."

474. *Feminine Wiles*: Jane Bowles's letters, edited by Millicent Dillon, Black Sparrow Press, Santa Barbara, 1976.

481. sound score for *Orestes*: Musique concrète score by Paul Bowles for the American School at Tangier theater production.

483. *The Beach Café & The Voice*: Two novellas by Mohammed Mrabet, taped and translated from the Moghrebi by Paul Bowles, Black Sparrow Press, Santa Barbara, 1980.

483. *Five Eyes, Stories by Abdeslam Boulaïch, Mohamed Choukri, Larbi Layachi, Mohammed Mrabet, Ahmed Yacoubi*, edited and translated by Paul Bowles, Black Sparrow Press, Santa Barbara, 1979.

490. saying that she'd sent a manuscript to you: Transcription of a journal kept by Bowles's mother or grandmother; Cadmus Editions elected not to publish.

490. *Next to Nothing*: Bowles's poem was first published by Starstreams 5, Kathmandu, Nepal, 1976, and then in *Next to Nothing: Collected Poems, 1926–1977*, Black Sparrow Press, Santa Barbara, 1981.

497. "The Hours after Noon": The story first appeared in *Zero Anthology #8*, New York, 1956, and then in *The Hours after Noon*, a collection of Bowles's short stories, published by Heinemann, London, in 1959.

499. *The Wind Remains: See above*, 173.

499. Blanch's piece on her: Lesley Blanch writes on Isabelle Eberhardt in *The Wilder Shores of Love*. Lady Isabel Burton, Jane Elizabeth Digby Law, Lady Ellenborough, Aimee Duboc du Rivery, and Isabelle Eberhardt are treated in this work published by Simon & Schuster, New York, in 1954.

499. Then I found the Mackworth: *The Destiny of Isabelle Eberhardt*, by Cecily Mackworth, Routledge & Kegan Paul, London, 1951.

499. Greene film book: *Graham Greene on Film: Collected Film Criticism, 1935–1940*, Simon & Schuster, New York, 1972. Published in England as *The Pleasure Dome*, Secker & Warburg, 1972. From 1935 to 1939 Graham Greene was the film critic for *The Spectator*.

502. Your mother is probably right: Millicent Dillon, author of *A Little Original Sin: The Life and Work of Jane Bowles*, 1981.

503. *Points in Time*: Peter Owen, London, 1982; Ecco Press, New York, 1982.

503. *Midnight Mass*: A collection of twelve stories by Bowles that gathers those written subsequent to the publication of the *Collected Stories, 1939–1976*. Black Sparrow Press, Santa Barbara, 1981.

510. *In the American Grain*: Essays by William Carlos Williams published by New Directions, New York, in 1933.

510. the essay(s) by Metcalf: Paul Metcalf wrote an essay on Bowles, "A Journey in Search of Bowles," which appeared in the Paul Bowles/Coleman Dowell issue of *The Review of Contemporary Fiction*, Vol. 2:3, Fall 1982 (Elmwood Park, Illinois).

515. *Qaftan d'Amour Constellé de Passion*: The second film in a series by Smihi about

his native Tangier; written by Moumen Smihi and Gavin Lambert for an Imago Film/Cine Magma Moroccan-French co-production. It was screened at the 1988 Carthage Film Festival as *Kaftan el-Hob*.

515. try-out of Jane's play: *In the Summer House* by Jane Bowles with incidental theater music by Paul Bowles. The New York opening was at the Playhouse Theater on December 29, 1953, with Judith Anderson, Mildred Dunnock, Elizabeth Ross, and Jean Stapleton, directed by José Quintero.

517. *The Wrong People*: By Robin Maugham, Gay Modern Classics Series GMP Pubs., U.K. 1986.

518. TO PAUL METCALF: This letter was published in *The Review of Contemporary Fiction*, Fall 1984.

522. Sonatina: A composition for piano solo by Bowles, published by Elkan-Vogel, Philadelphia, in 1947.

525. *The Inner Geography*: A study of Bowles's fiction by Wayne Pounds. Peter Lang, New York, Berne, Frankfurt am Main, 1985. American University Studies, Series IV, English Language and Literature, Vol. 24.

527. *Fifteen to Infinity*: Poems by Ruth Fainlight, Hutchinson, London, 1983.

536. The biography you mention can't even be discussed: *An Invisible Spectator: A Biography of Paul Bowles* by Christopher Sawyer-Lauçanno, 1989.

536. Was Marianne Wiggins: Marianne Wiggins was a student of Bowles's at the School of Visual Arts in Tangier during the summer of 1983.

537. a copy of Ms. Wiggins's husband's book: Salman Rushdie's *The Satanic Verses*, 1989, condemned as heretical by the Islamic government of Iran.

538. my piece for Aperture: Paul Bowles wrote the introduction to William Betsch's *The Hakima: A Tragedy in Fez*, An Aperture Book, City of Paris/Kodak-Pathé Foundation, Aperture Foundation, Inc., 1991.

544. that book for Jancovici: *Too Far from Home* by Paul Bowles, Editions Bischofberger, Zurich, 1993. Originally the novella was to have been published by a Parisian press, but the terms of the contract were not honored and thus it went to Editions Bischofberger. It is included in *Too Far from Home: The Selected Writings of Paul Bowles*, Ecco Press, New York, 1993.

545. *Days* arrived: *Days, Tangier Journal: 1987–1989* by Paul Bowles, Ecco Press, New York, 1991; published in England by Peter Owen, London, 1990, under the title *Two Years beside the Strait: Tangier Journal 1987–1989*.

ACKNOWLEDGMENTS

Thanks are due many persons for kindnesses and many institutions for assistance. They have made available to me nearly seven thousand pages of Paul Bowles's letters, spanning more than six decades and addressed to 140 correspondents.

Almost all—recipients of letters, scholars, curators, special collections librarians, booksellers, literary executors, editors, publishers, collectors, and others —have been generous with their time and assistance.

I list in alphabetical order those persons and institutions that have assisted with letter copies, permissions, and information: John Ahouse, Curator, American Literature Collections, Doheny Library, University of Southern California; Gillian B. Anderson, Music Specialist, Music Division, Library of Congress; Carol Ardman; Bachir Attar; Don Bachardy; Hans Bertens, Lecturer in American Literature, Royal University of Utrecht; Bibliothèque Nationale, Paris; Simon Bischoff, Archiv Paul Bowles, Schweizerische Stiftung für die Photographie, Zürich; Michael Blechner, Associate Librarian, McFarlin Library, University of Tulsa; Robert Briatte, French biographer of Paul Bowles; Andreas Brown, Gotham Book Mart and Gallery; Edward Burns; William S. Burroughs; John Cage; Rebecca Campbell Cape, Assistant Curator of Manuscripts, Lilly Library, Indiana University; Jack Clareman, Esq.; Hannetta Clark; Ira Cohen; Clint Colby, Special Collections Librarian, University of Arizona; Suzanne Comer, editor, University of Texas Press, Austin; Gary Conklin; Aaron Copland and his assistant, Ronald Caltabiano; Mrs. Sidney Cowell; Joan St. C. Crane, Curator, American Literature Collection, Alderman Library, University of Virginia; Stephen Davis; Ines Delgado de Torres, Translation Center, PEN American Center, Columbia University; David Diamond; Stuart Dick, Special Collections, University of Delaware; Millicent Dillon; Ellen S. Dunlap, Research Librarian, Humanities Research Center, University of Texas; Ruth Fainlight; Dr. David Farmer, Assistant Director, Humanities Research Center, University of Texas; Lawrence Ferlinghetti, City Lights; Theodore M. Finney Memorial Library, Library of Congress; Dan Franklin, Peter Owen, Ltd.; Dr. Donald Gallup, Curator, Collection of American Literature, Beinecke Library, Yale University; Peter Garland, Soundings Press; Allen Ginsberg; Peggy Glanville-Hicks; John Goodwin; Howard B. Gottlieb, Director, Mugar Memorial Library, Boston University; Professor William S. Gray, Randolph-Macon College; Dr. Theodore Grieder, Librarian, Bobst and Fales Libraries, New York University; Dan Halpern, *Antaeus*/Ecco Press; Dr. Bonnie Hardwick, Curator of Manuscripts, Bancroft Library, University of California at Berkeley; Sir Rupert Hart-Davis; William Heinemann, Ltd.; Cathy Henderson, Research Librarian, Harry Ransom Humanities Research Center; James Leo Herlihy; Allen Hibbard; Ruth Hilton, Music Librarian, Bobst Library, New York University; Stephen Holgate, USIS, Rabat; John Hopkins; Michael Horowitz, John Howell Books; Warren Hovious, Archivist, Rockefeller Archive Center; Peter Howard, Serendipity Books; Ann Hyde, Manuscripts Librarian, Kenneth Spencer Research Library, University of Kansas; Richard Jackson, Head, Americana Collection, Library and Museum of the Performing Arts, Lincoln Center; Maria Jolas; Robert Kirsch, the *Los Angeles Times*; Donald S. Klopfer, Random House; Gavin Lambert; Jack Larsen; Christine Laude, Centre de Documentation Benjamin Franklin, Paris; James Laughlin, New Directions, and his Norfolk assistant, Liz Marraffino; Ned Leavitt, William Morris Agency, New York; Minna Lederman (Mrs. Mell Daniel); Bennett Lerner; Wendy Lesser, founding editor, *Threepenny Review*; Little, Brown & Co.; Kenneth H. Lohf, Librarian for Rare Books and Manuscripts, Butler Library, Columbia University; Joseph Losey and his assistant, Celia Parker; Edward Lyon and Kathleen Manwaring, George Arents Research Library, Syracuse University; Joseph McPhillips, Headmaster, American School of Tangier; Kamala Markandaya (Purnaiya-Taylor); John Martin, Black Sparrow Press; William Matheson, Chief, Rare Book and Special Collections Division, Library of Congress; Francis O. Matson, Curator, Berg Collection, New York Public Library; Gwyn Metz, Betty Parsons Gallery; Carol Moore, Special Collections, Arizona State University; Ted Morgan (Sanche de Gramont); Bruce A. Morrissette, with assistance from James Morrissette and Margaret Baughman; James Murdoch, Literary Executor for Peggy Glanville-Hicks; Timothy D. Murray, Associate Librarian, Special Collections, University of Delaware; New York Public Library; Dorothy Norman; Phil Nurenberg; Cherie Nutting; Gerald F. Parsons, Jr., Reference Librarian, Archive of Folk Song, Music Division, Library of Congress; Richard Patteson; John R. Payne, Associate Librarian, Humanities Research Center, University of Texas; Vivian Perlis, Director, School of Music, Yale University; Nancy J. Peters, City Lights; Wayne Pounds; James Purdy; Joel Redon; Rodrigo Rey Rosa; Hans Richter; Heddy A. Richter, Curator, American Literature Collection, Doheny Library, University of Southern California; Edouard Roditi; Michael Rogers, *Rolling Stone*; Clifford de Roode, Librarian, American Library in Paris; Ned Rorem; Christina Rosset, Grove Press; Webster

Schott; Richard Seaver, Richard Seaver Books; Robert Setrakian, President, William Saroyan Foundation; Wayne D. Shirley, Reference Librarian, Library of Congress; Alan Sillitoe; Ralph Sipper, Joseph the Provider Books; Irving Stettner, *Stroker*; Angus Stewart; John D. Stinson, Rare Books and Manuscripts Division, New York Public Library; William Targ, Editor in Chief, G. P. Putnam's Sons; Susan Tate, Special Collections Library, Ilih Dunlop Little Memorial Library, University of Georgia at Athens; Saundra Taylor, Curator of Manuscripts, Lilly Library, Indiana University; Virgil Thomson and his assistant, Christopher Cox; Howard Tilton Memorial Library, Tulane University; Gore Vidal; Brooke Whiting, Curator of Rare Books, Special Collections, University of California at Los Angeles; John Widdicombe; Robert Wilson, Phoenix Book Shop; State Historical Society of Wisconsin; Michael Wolfe, Tomboctou Books; Audrey Wood, International Creative Management; Marilyn Wurzberger, Librarian, Special Collections, Arizona State University at Tempe; David S. Zeidberg, Head, Special Collections, University Research Library, University of California at Los Angeles.

I am also grateful to Francis Bacon, Djuna Barnes, Eileen J. Hose, literary executor for Sir Cecil Beaton, Leonard Bernstein, Fleur Cowles, Peggy Guggenheim, Christopher Isherwood, Lincoln Kirstein, Angus Wilson, and others, all of whom graciously replied to my queries, informing me they had either looked through their papers without success in finding letters from Paul Bowles or hadn't, they thought, corresponded with him; Fleur Cowles regretfully reported her correspondence with Paul Bowles had been disposed of by a negligent secretary when she was in hospital; Peggy Guggenheim told me she never kept letters after replying to them. I should also like to acknowledge the kind assistance of Comte Raymond de Lavillatte who wrote to inform me there are two de Lavillatte families in France, giving genealogical details—as I was searching for letters to Christine de Lavillatte, Comtesse de Guendulaine, and her mother, the Comtesse de Lavillatte. The search, I am sorry to say, was in vain.

I should also like to express my gratitude to the following persons for assistance: Robert Hemenway, for his help in arranging and editing the letters; Leslie Gardner, director, Artellus, Ltd., London, who dealt with both Christina Rosset and Audrey Wood on my behalf, searched files, photocopied letters, made telephone calls, answered letters, and kindly allowed me the use of her offices as depot for correspondence and letter copies from France and England; Patti Lewis, librarian, for searching for information on short notice; Kathleen Miller, for organizing the mass of papers into a proper and legible manuscript; Mark Miller and Dr. Sue von Bayer, for translating my queries into literate French;

and Margaret Randall, who visited the office of the Casa de las Americas in Havana, Cuba, on my behalf, in order to access a brief correspondence in their files. Communication was conducted via a publisher in Toronto, Canada, who forwarded letters in two directions, as letters mailed to Haydee Santamaria at the Casa de las Americas failed to arrive there for whatever reasons. (After this considerable expenditure of effort it turned out Paul Bowles had written a two-line note declining to be a panelist for a literary award.)

Inevitably with a project such as this involving the cooperation of so many people there were a few who withheld theirs, but I am confident the minor lacunae that resulted haven't interfered with the breadth of this collection.

Above all, I wish to thank Paul Bowles, who (undoubtedly with some trepidation) agreed to my assembling his letters for publication; his unfailing courtesy and impeccable politesse have been at my disposal at all junctures of this long endeavor, and he has assisted in whatever way I have requested at all times.

Lastly, I wish to thank Farrar, Straus and Giroux: my editor, John Glusman, for his quick intelligence, alacrity, and crisp insistence on excellence in all matters; his assistant, Jori Finkel, for her help in preparing the endnotes and photo insert; and my publisher, Roger Straus, who welcomed this book to his house with enthusiasm.

—J.M.

INDEX